中英文对照
Chinese / English

（京）新登字 041 号

图书在版编目（CIP）数据

西安统计年鉴.2013 / 西安市统计局，国家统计局西安调查队 编.
—北京：中国统计出版社，2013.9
ISBN 978-7-5037-6948-1

Ⅰ.①西…
Ⅱ.①西… ②国…
Ⅲ.①统计资料-西安市-2013-年鉴
Ⅳ.①C832.411-54

中国版本图书馆CIP数据核字(2013)第212458号

西安统计年鉴—2013

作　　者/ 西安市统计局　国家统计局西安调查队
责任编辑/ 陈越月
装帧设计/ 西安力天世纪品牌策划设计有限公司
出版发行/ 中国统计出版社
地　　址/ 北京市丰台区西三环南路甲6号　邮政编码/100073
办公地址/ 北京市丰台区西三环南路甲6号
电　　话/ 邮购（010）63376909　书店（010）68783171
网　　址/ http://csp.stats.gov.cn
印　　刷/ 西安一印制板有限责任公司
经　　销/ 新华书店
开　　本/ 890×1240毫米 1/16
字　　数/ 1360千字
印　　张/ 43
版　　别/ 2013年9月第1版
版　　次/ 2013年9月第1次印刷
定　　价/ 260.00元

本书附同版本光盘一张，光盘内容以书面文字为准。
如有印装差错，由本社发行部调换。

《西安统计年鉴—2013》编辑部

XI'AN STATISTICAL YEARBOOK-2013
EDITORLAL STAFF

编者说明

一、《西安统计年鉴—2013》系统收录了全市、区县及开发区2012年经济、社会各方面统计数据，以及重要历史年份主要统计数据，是一部全面记载西安市国民经济和社会发展情况的大型连续性统计文献资料和重要工具书。

二、本年鉴正文内容分为二十一个篇章：（一）综合；（二）基本单位；（三）国民经济核算；（四）人口、从业人员与职工工资；（五）固定资产投资；（六）财政；（七）物价指数；（八）人民生活；（九）城市公用事业；（十）环境保护；（十一）农业；（十二）工业；（十三）能源；（十四）建筑业；（十五）运输和邮电；（十六）国内贸易；（十七）对外经济贸易和旅游；（十八）金融业；（十九）教育和科技；（二十）文化、体育、卫生、社会福利和其他；（二十一）企业调查。同时，为方便读者使用，各篇章前设有简要说明和2012年主要统计指标，对本篇章的主要内容、资料来源、以及历史变动情况予以简要概述，篇末附有主要统计指标解释。

三、本年鉴统计资料的统计标准，按当时国家统计制度执行，有关指标的涵义、口径、范围、计算方法等，在不同时期可能有所不同，使用时请注意。国民经济行业分类按GB/T4754—2011标准执行。为了便于新旧行业标准对比，对部分主要指标按GB/T4754—2002标准编辑了分行业数据。

四、为便于国内外读者查阅，本年鉴全部内容均采用中英文对照编辑。

五、本年鉴各篇资料均为正式年报数，因此，凡与本年鉴有出入的均以本年鉴为准。

六、本年鉴中的部分指标合计数或相对数由于单位取舍不同产生的计算误差均未作机械调整。

七、本年鉴所使用的计量单位均依据2012年统计报表制度。

八、本年鉴使用的符号说明："空白"表示该项统计指标无数据或数据不详；"#"表示其中项；"*"表示另有注解。

感谢社会各界长期以来对《西安统计年鉴》的广泛关注和大力支持。为进一步做好工作，更好地为广大读者服务，希望社会各界提出宝贵意见。

PREFACE

I. Xi'an Statistical Yearbook 2013 is a periodical statistic yearbook which record economic and social development of Xi'an all-around in 2012 and some selected data series in historical important years. With its features of comprehensive and intensive information, this practically provides data covering the situation of social and economic developments in Xi'an.

II. The book contains twenty-one parts, 1.General Survey; 2.Basic Unit; 3.National Economic Account; 4.Population, Employment and Wages; 5.Investment in Fixed Assets; 6.Government Finance; 7.Price Indices; 8.People's Livelihood; 9.Urban Public Utilities; 10.Environmental Protection; 11.Agriculture; 12.Industry; 13. energy;14.Construction; 15Transportation, Post and Telecommunication Service; 16Domestic Trade; 17.Foreign Trade; 18.Banking and Insurance; 19.Education, Science and Technology; 20.Culture, Sports, Public Health, Social Welfare Institutions and Other Social Activities; 21.Enterprises Investigation. Meanwhile, in order to facilitate the reader to use, each chapter provides a brief description and key statistical indicators in 2012, gives a brief overview of this chapter about main contents, data sources and historical data. After each chapter attached with "Main Statistical Indicators"

III. The data of various years in conformity to the statistical standards prescribed by national statistical system of the time. The meaning, scope and calculating method of indicators may have some difference in different periods, which readers must pay attention to national industries classification is carried out according to standard GB/T4754 -2011. For the sake of comparison of the old and new industry standards, we edit the division' s data in some major indicators according to standard GB/T4754 -2011.

IV. For the convenience of being consulted by foreigners, the book is Chinese-English bilingual edition.

V. All the data in this yearbook are from formal annual report. If there are some differences between the historic information and the data of this yearbook, we should take the data in this book as the standard.

VI. Statistical discrepancies due to rounding are not adjusted automatically in this yearbook.

VII. Unit of measurement are used in this yearbook according to 2012 statistics system.

VIII. Explanations on symbols used in this yearbook:

(Blank) indicates the data not available;

# indicates the items of the total.

* indicates some other explanatory note.

Here we would like to express our sincere thanks to the people for their concerning and support to the Xi'an statistical yearbook. In order to do better and provide better service to readers, we hope that the whole society fields can propose constructive advices.

生产总值（亿元）

Gross Domestic Product (100 million yuan)

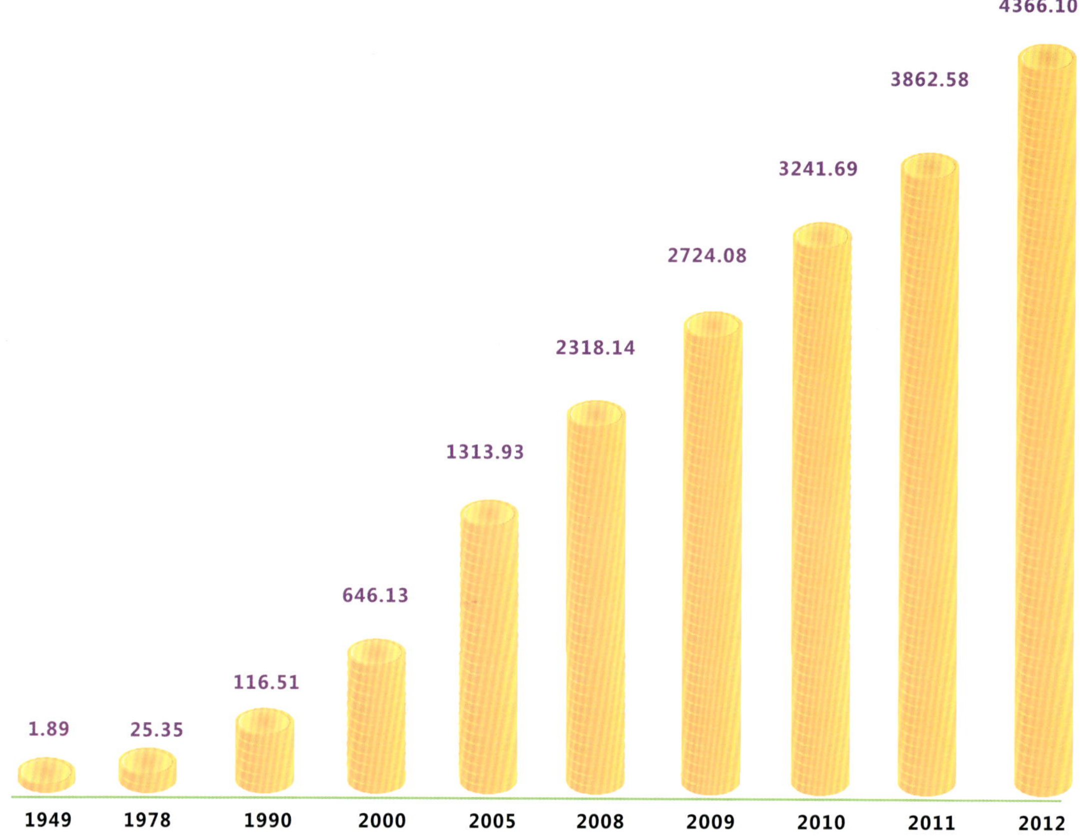

生产总值指数（以上年为100）

Indices of Gross Domestic Product (preceding year = 100)

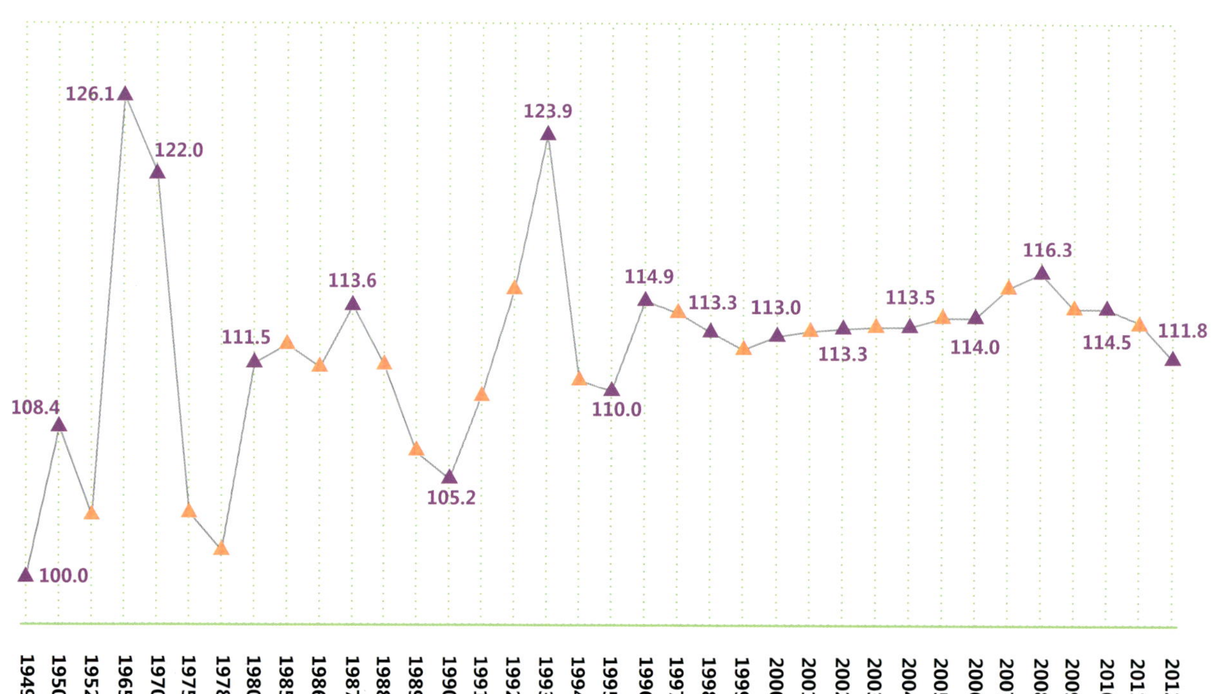

生产总值构成(%)

Composition of Gross Domestic Product (%)

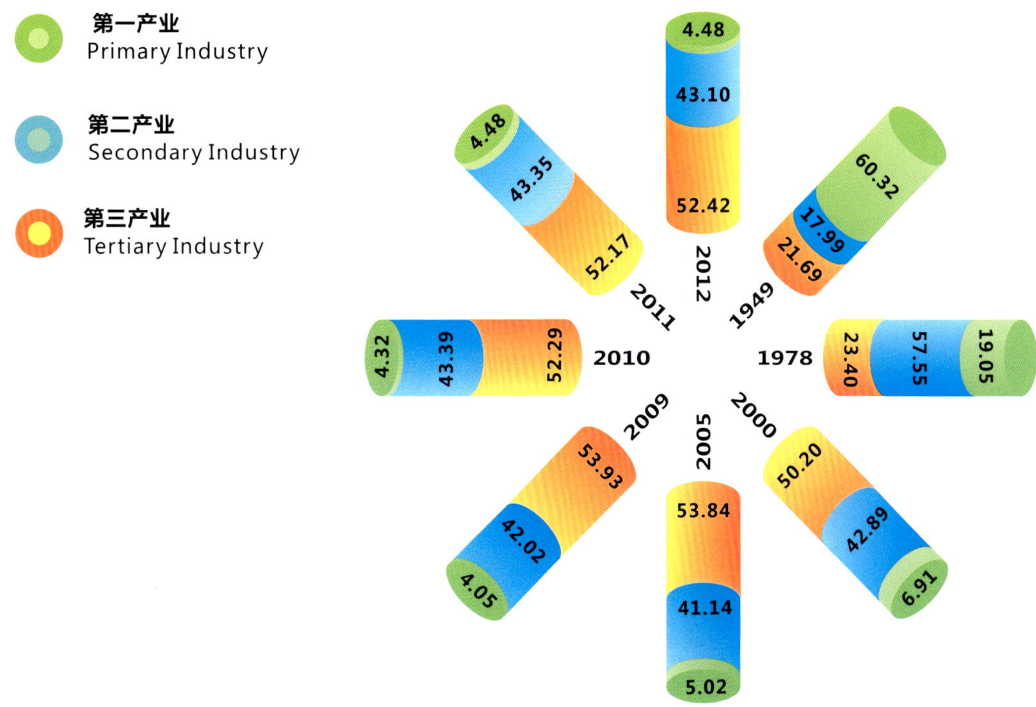

人均GDP(元/人)

Per Capita GDP(yuan/person)

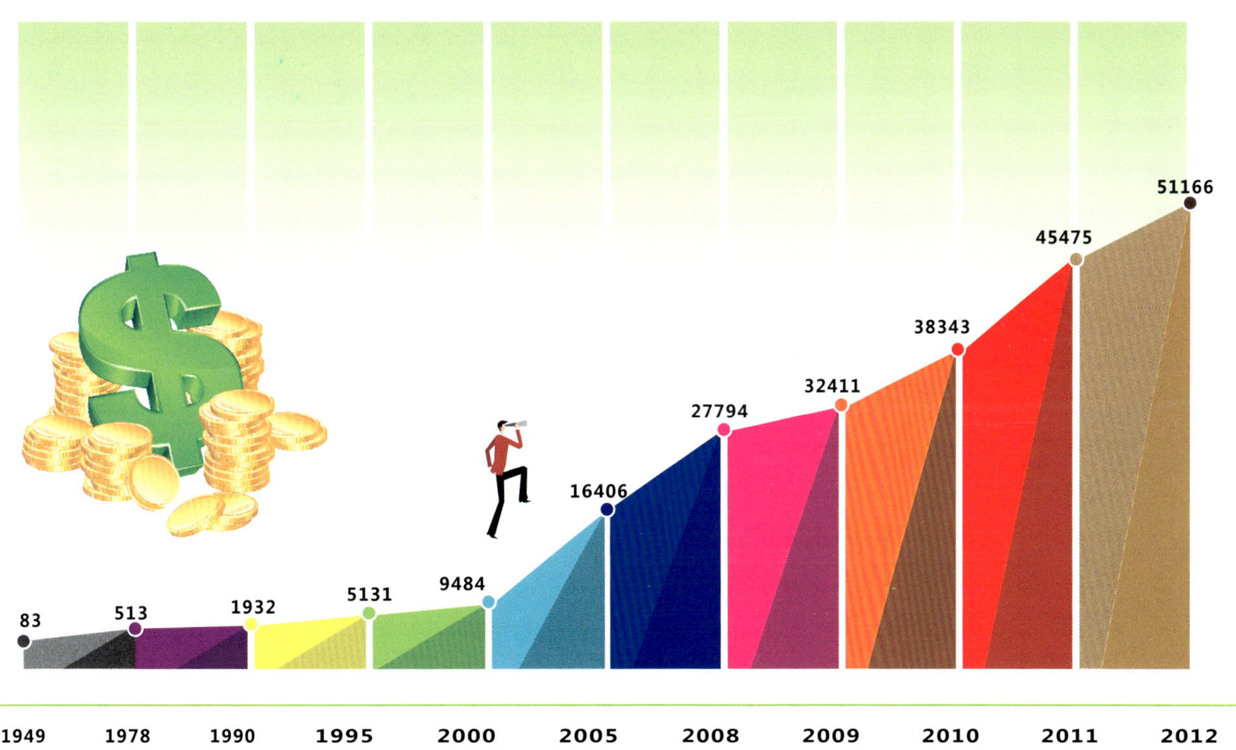

年末常住人口(万人)

Year-end Permanent population（10000 persons）

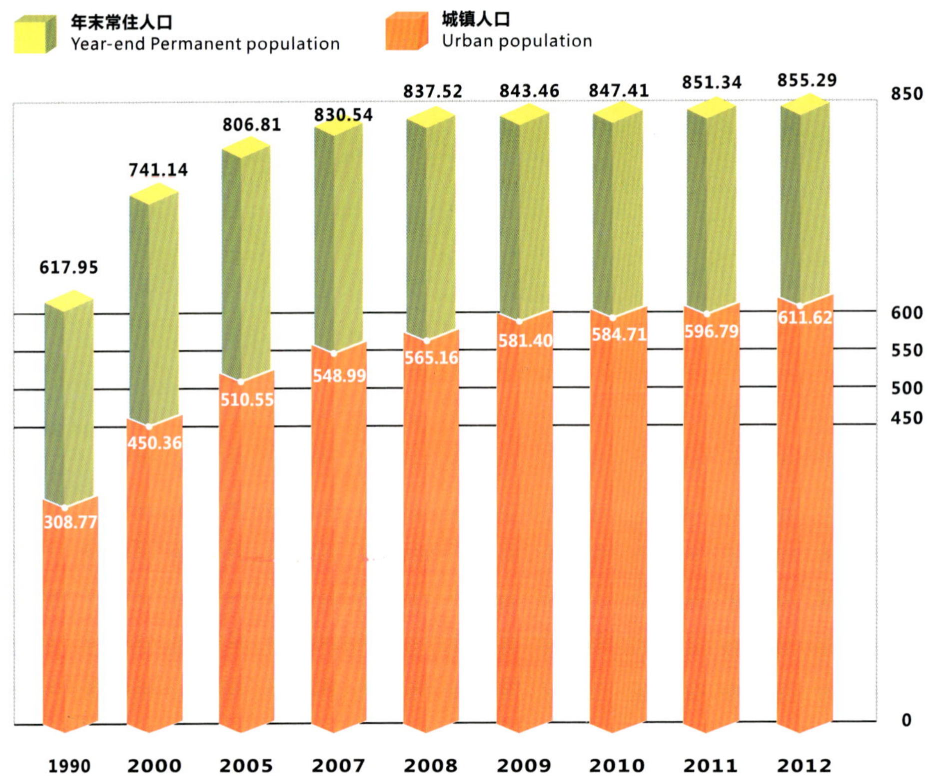

社会从业人数（万人）

Social Workers(10000 persons)

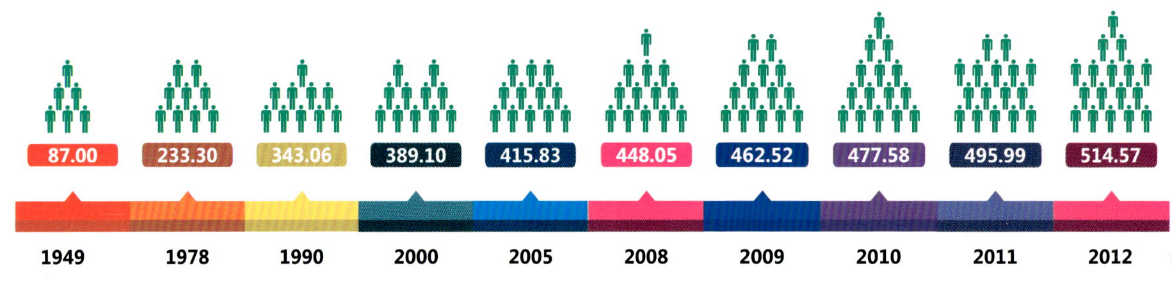

固定资产投资(亿元）

Investment in Fixed Assets(100 million yuan)

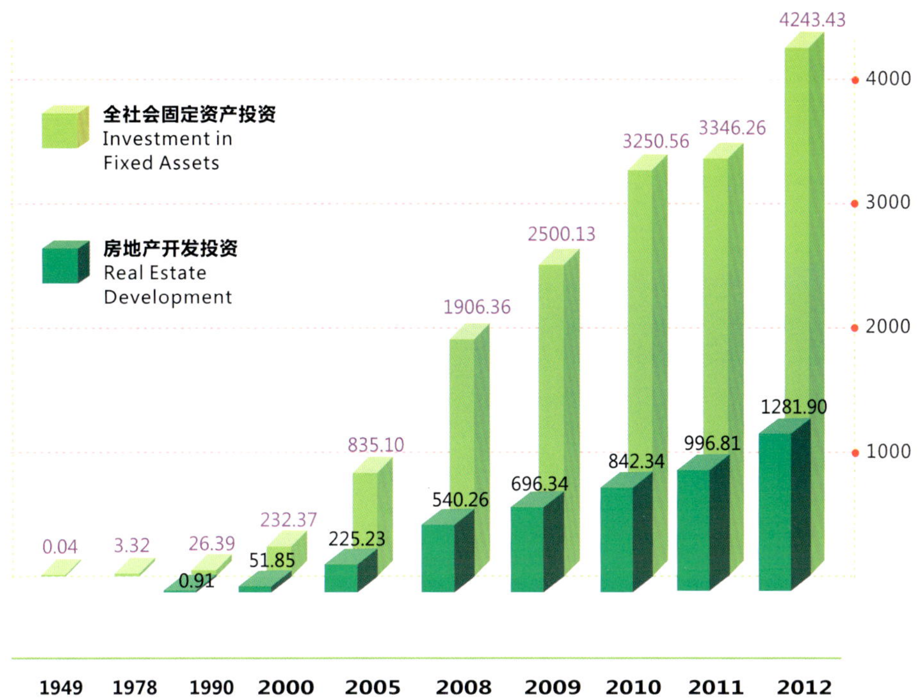

新增固定资产及住宅竣工面积

Newly Increased Fixed Assets and Residenctial Area of Completion

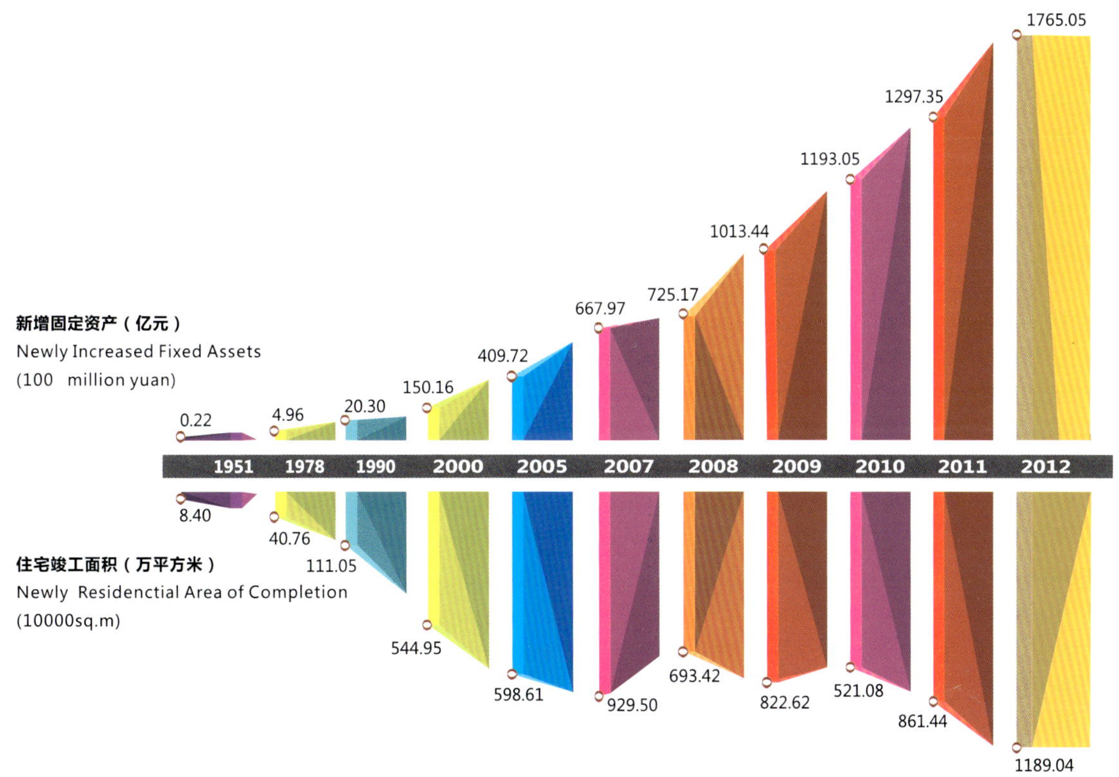

农林牧渔及服务业总产值(亿元)

Gross Output Value of Farming,Forestry, Animal Husbandry,Fishery and Service(100 million yuan)

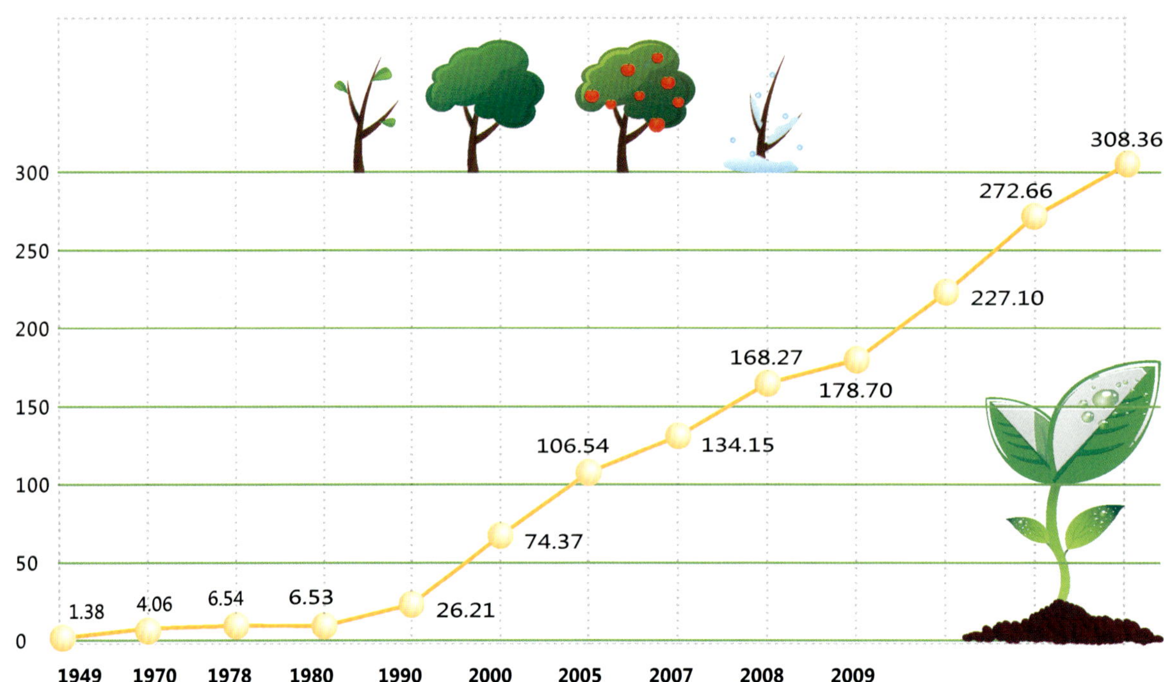

粮食、蔬菜产量(万吨)

Grain ,Vegetables Product(10000 ton)

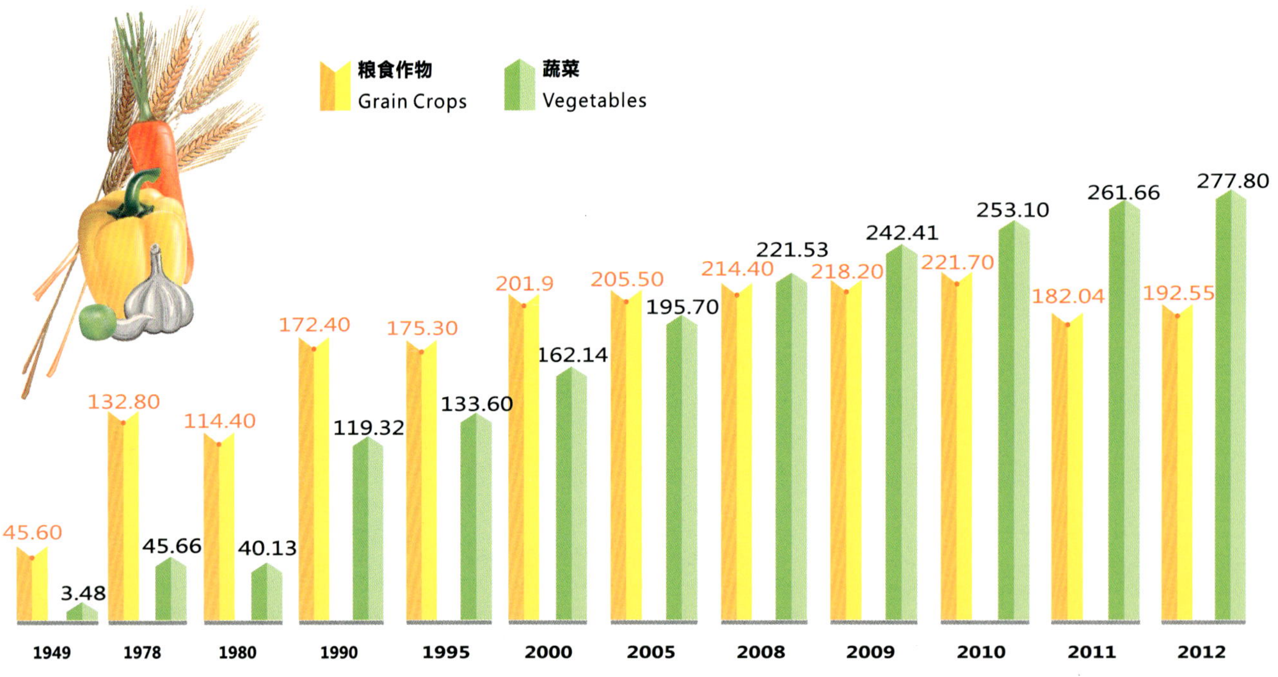

规模以上工业企业主要产品产量

Output Of Major Industrial Products Of Enterprises Above Designated Size

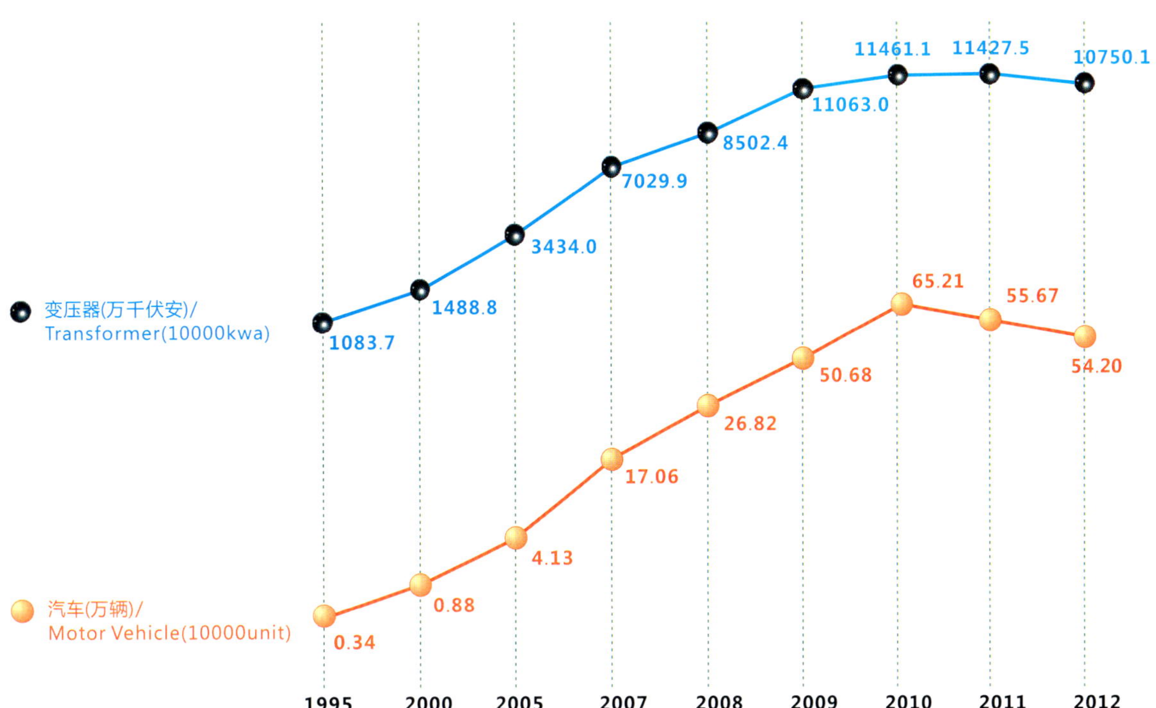

全部工业增加值及指数

Value-added of Industry and Index

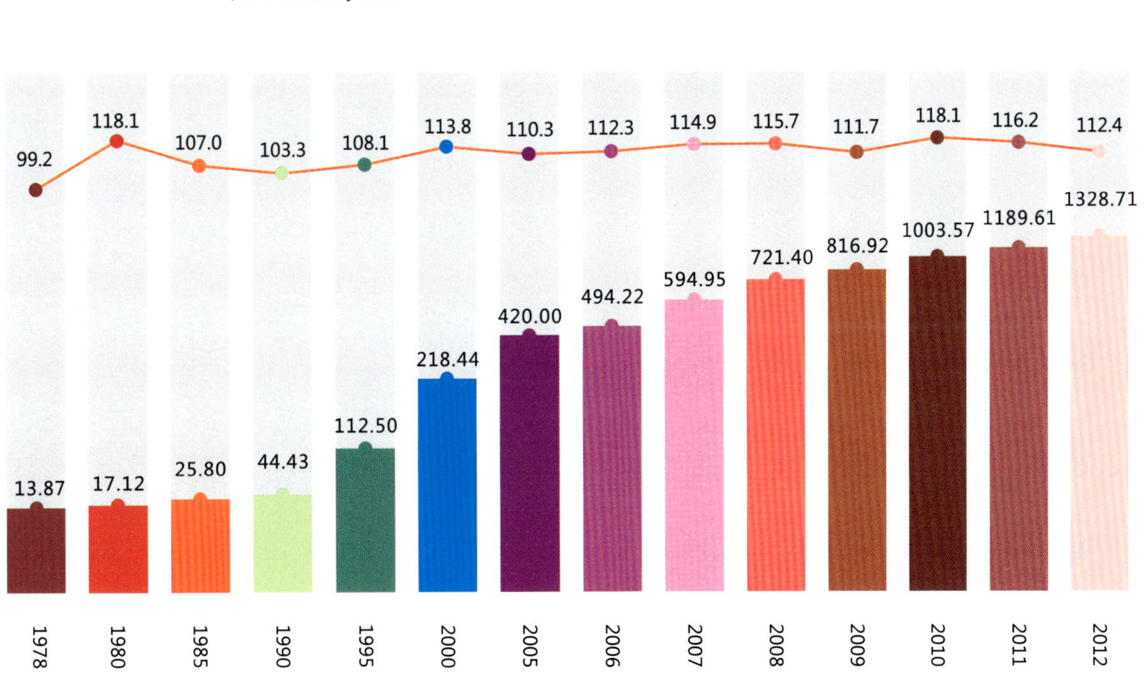

交通
Traffic

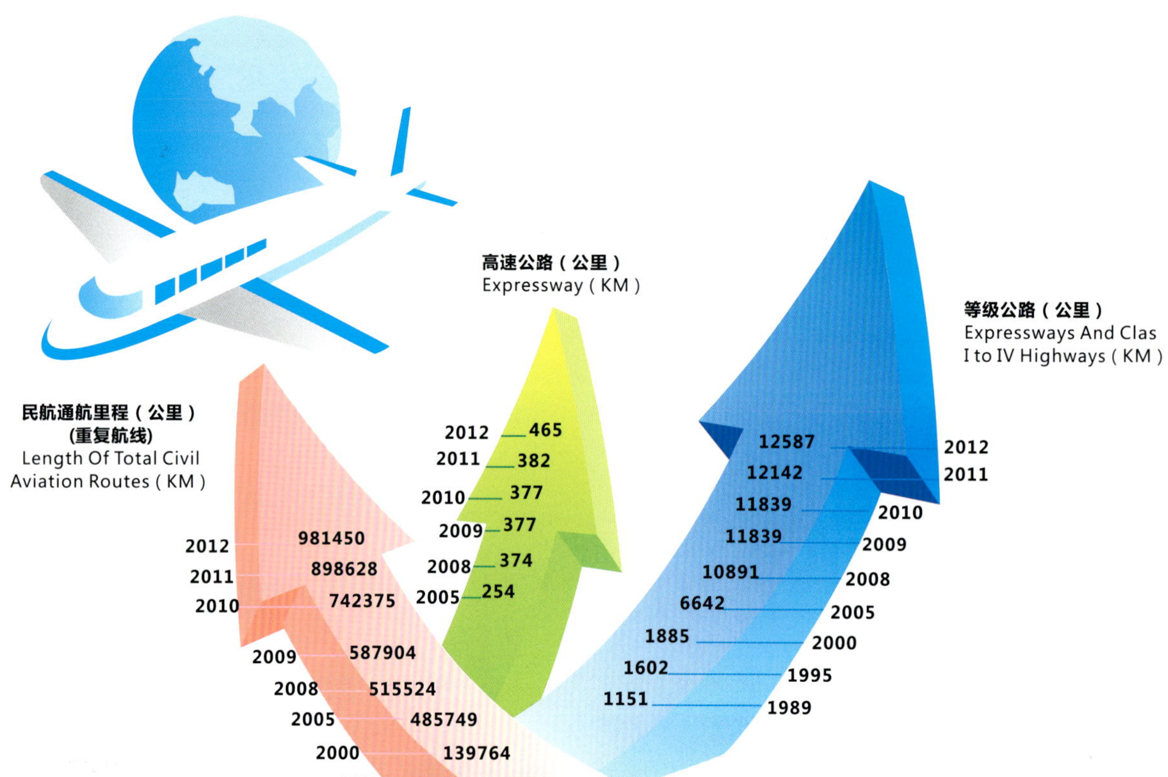

全社会车辆数（万辆）
Possession Of Civil Vehicles(10000 unit)

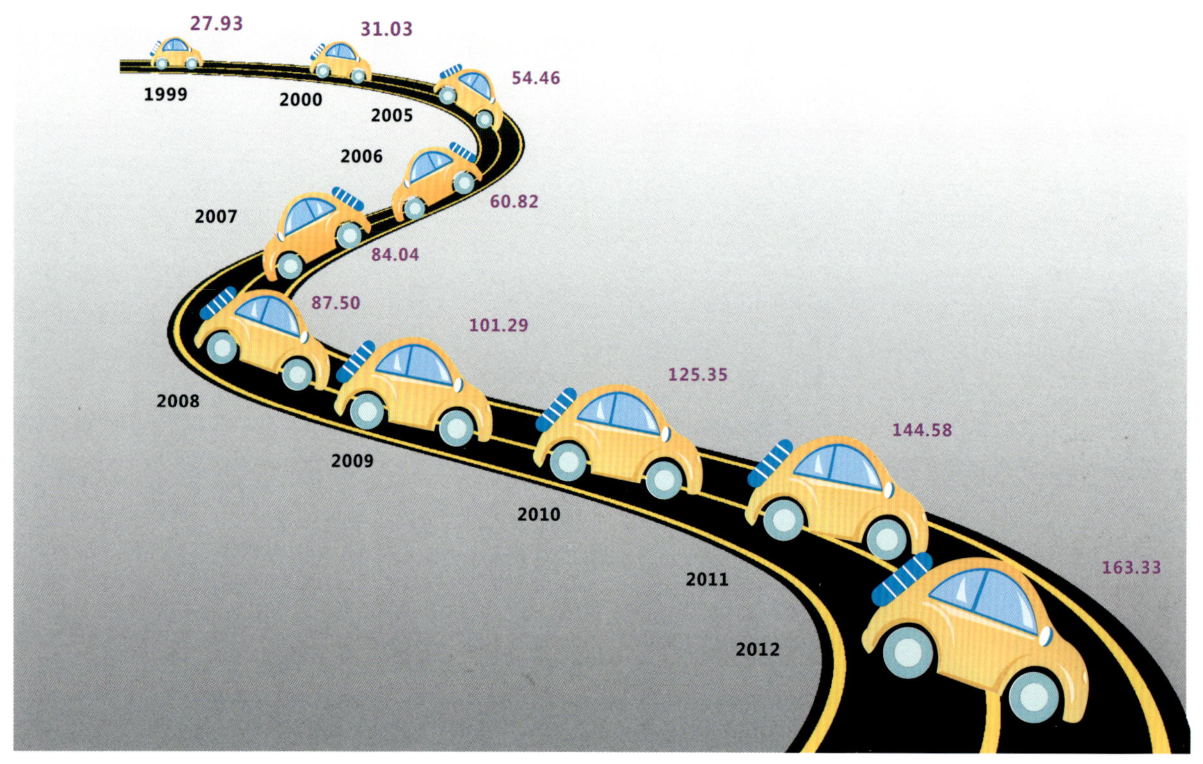

社会消费品零售总额(亿元)

Total Retail Sales of Consumer Goods(100 million yuan)

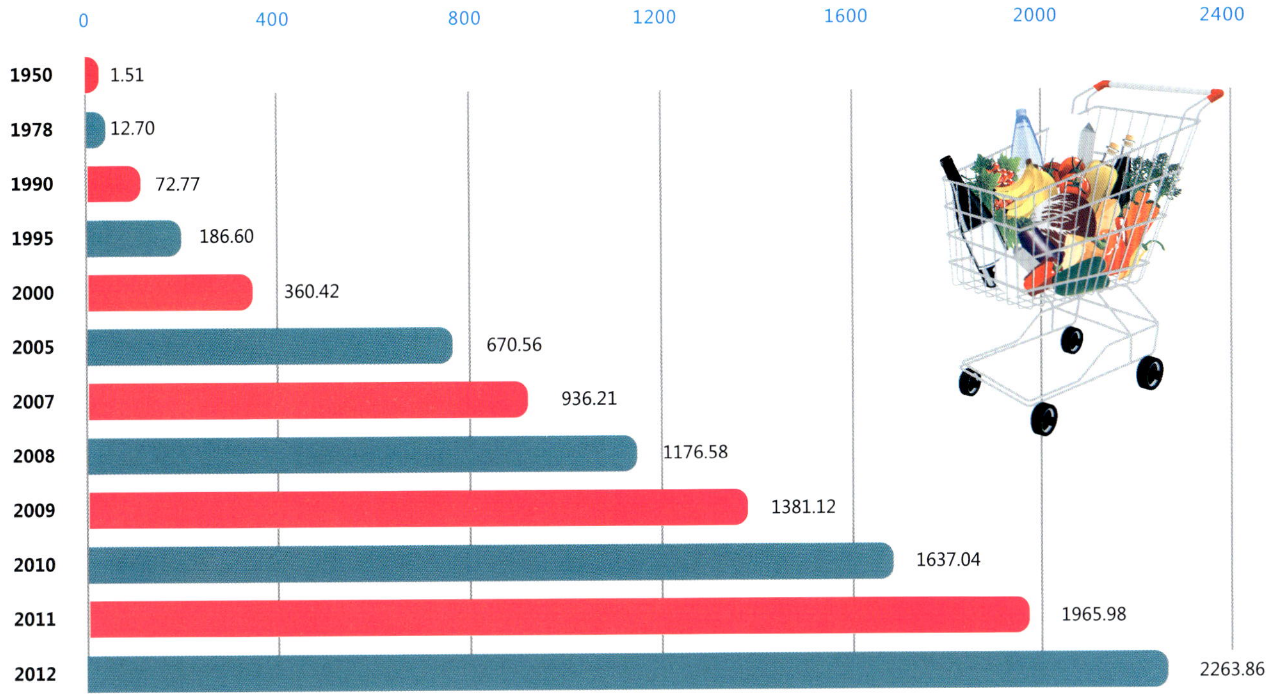

经营网点（个）

Bussiness Network (unit)

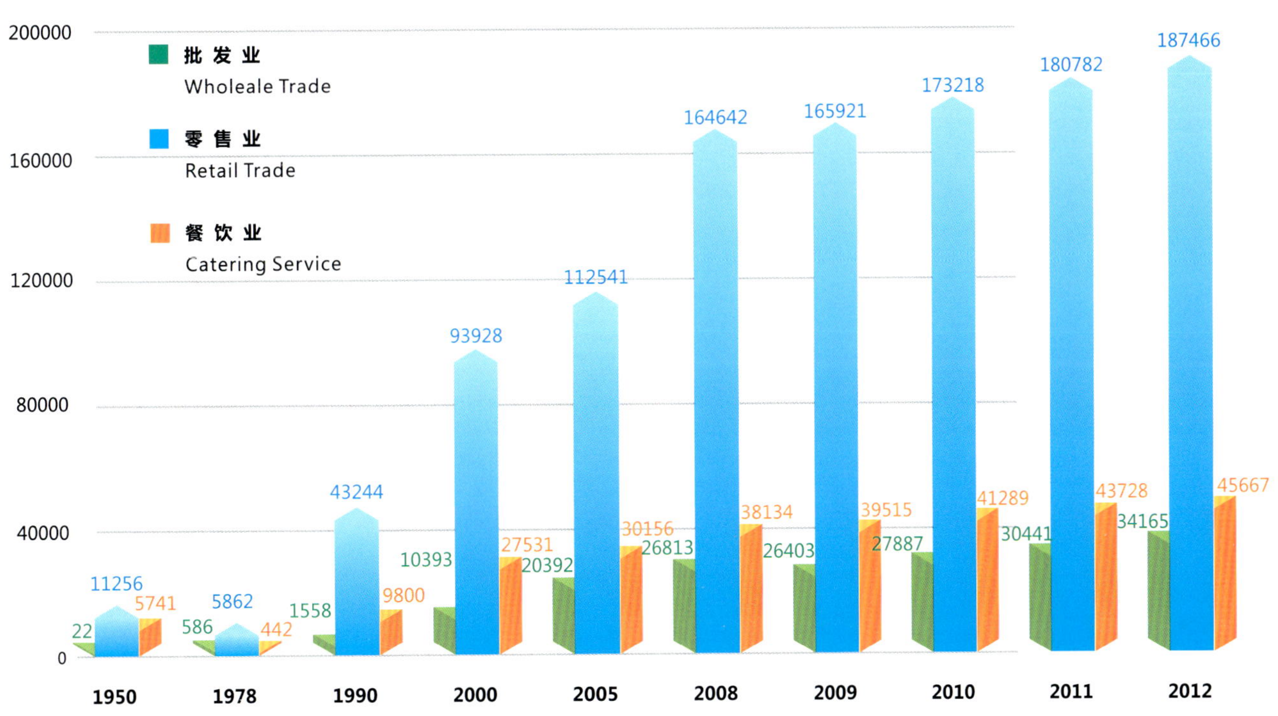

实际利用外商直接投资额（亿美元）
Foreign Direct Investment(USD 100million)

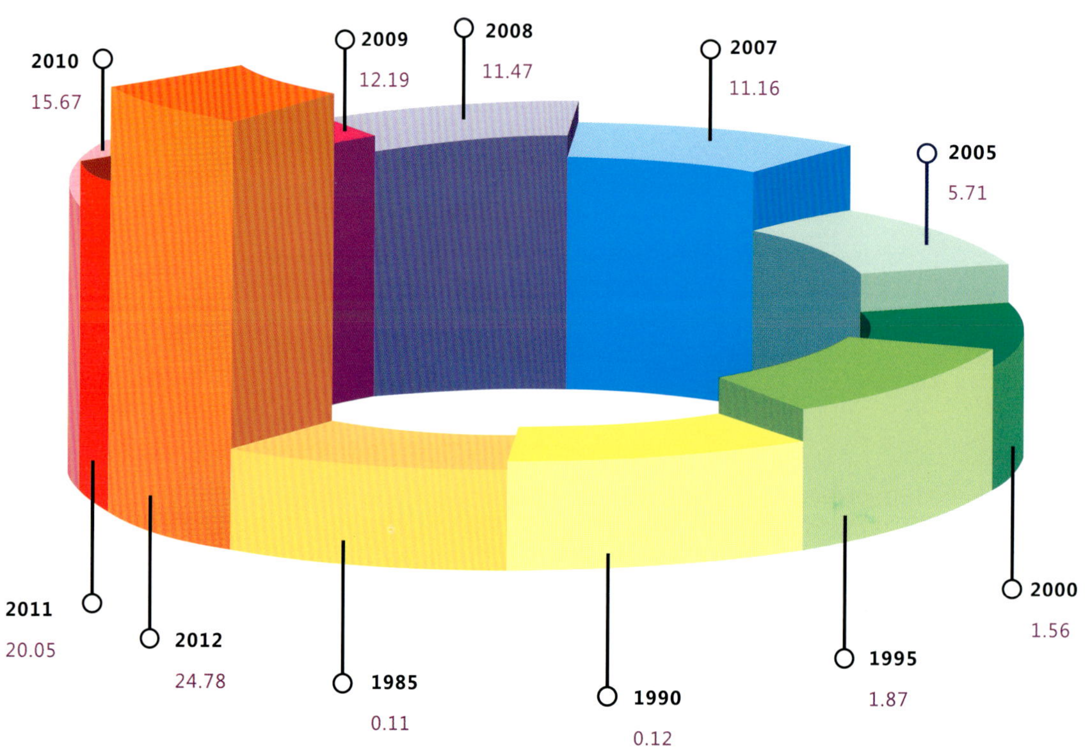

进出口总额（亿美元）
Total Value OF Imports And Exports(USD 100 million)

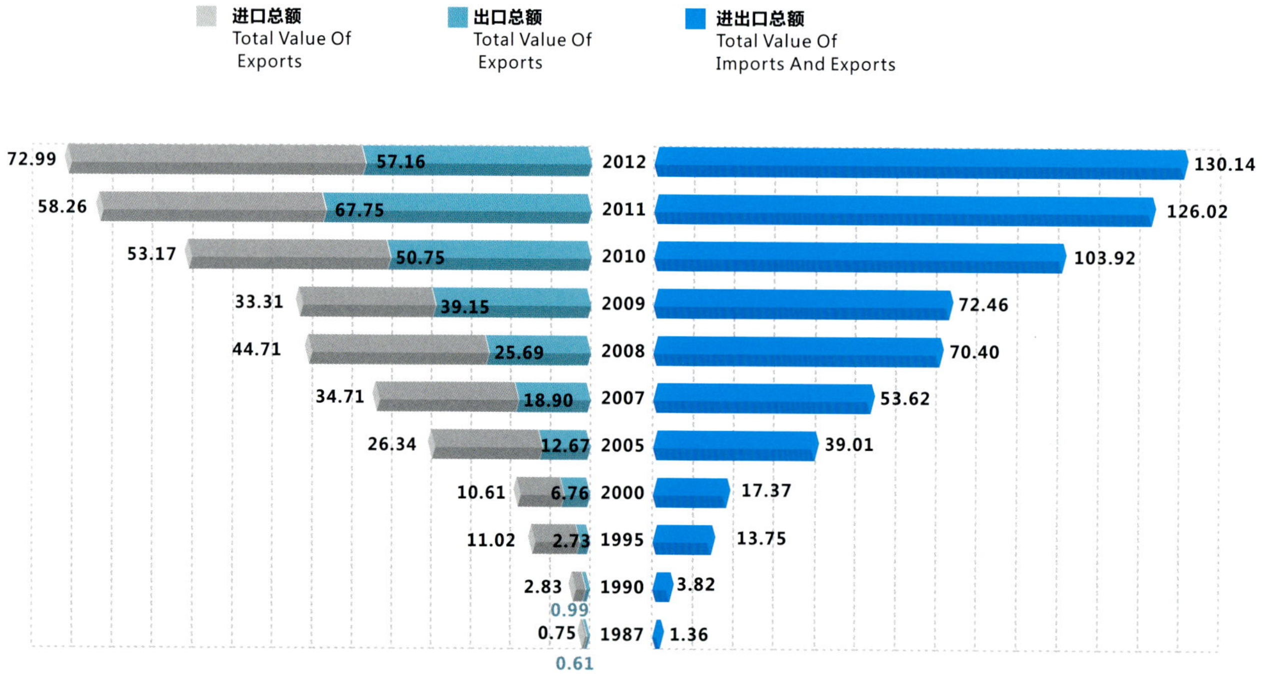

旅游人数及收入

Number of Tourists and Tourism Income

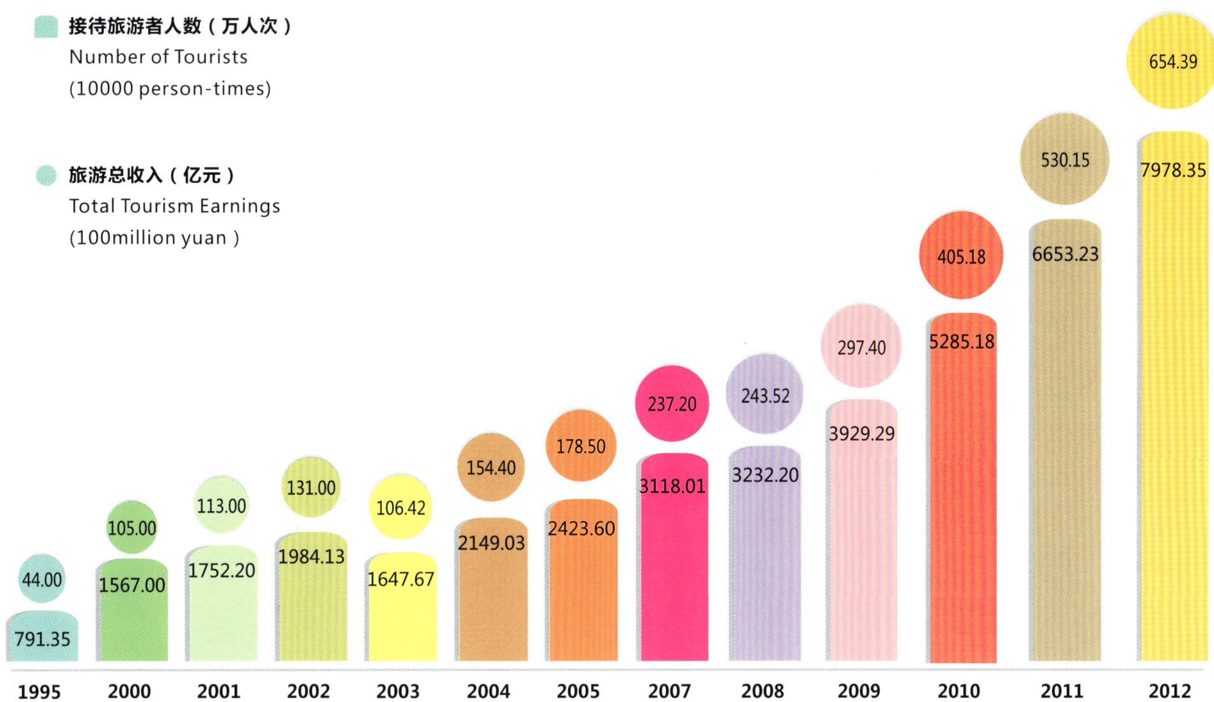

国际旅游人数及收入

Number of International Tourists and Tourism Income

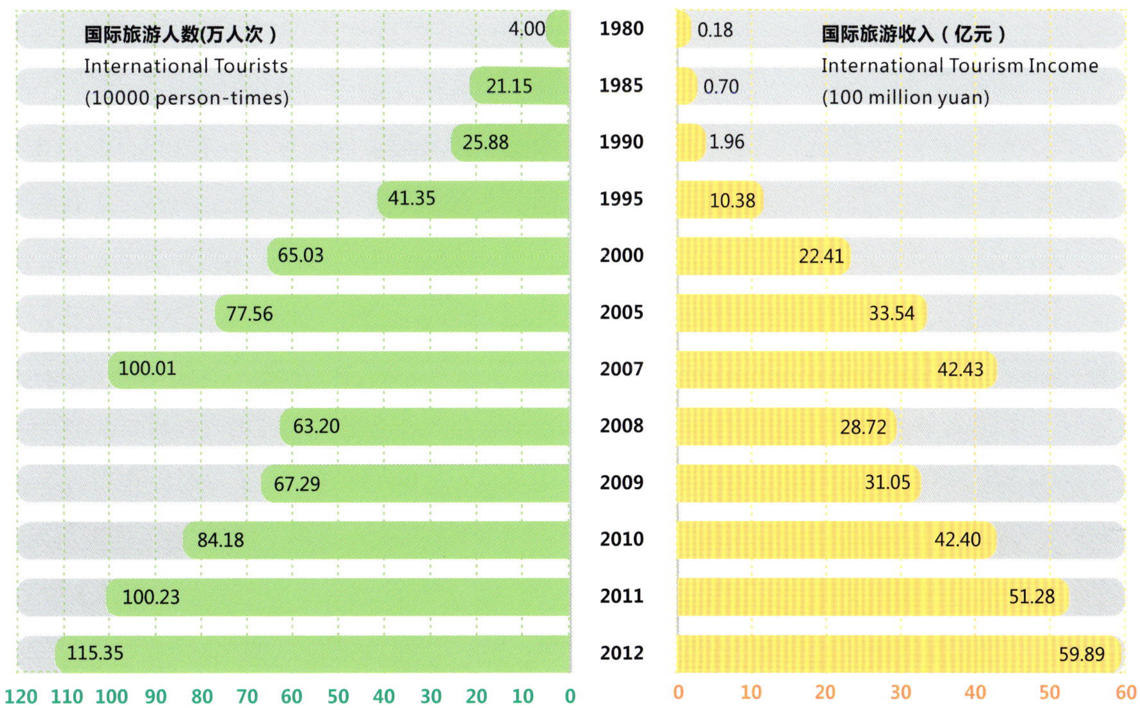

财政收支（亿元）

Govement Revenue and Expenditure (100 million yuan)

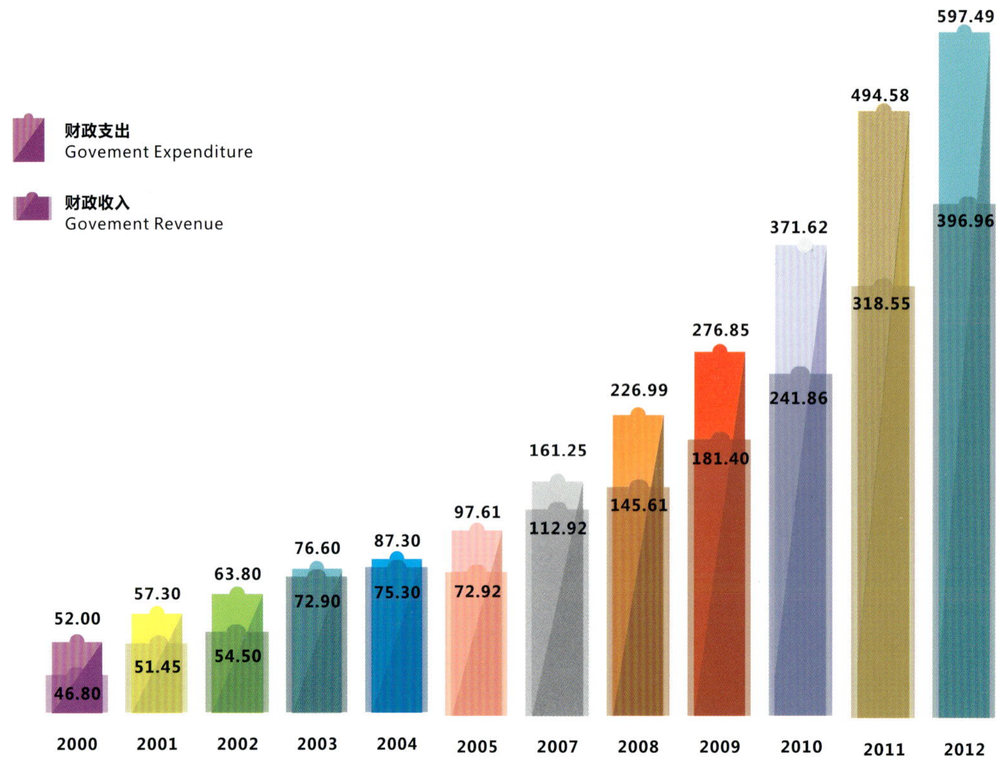

金融机构人民币存贷款年末余额（亿元）

Year-end Deposit and Loans in Financial Institutions (100 million yuan)

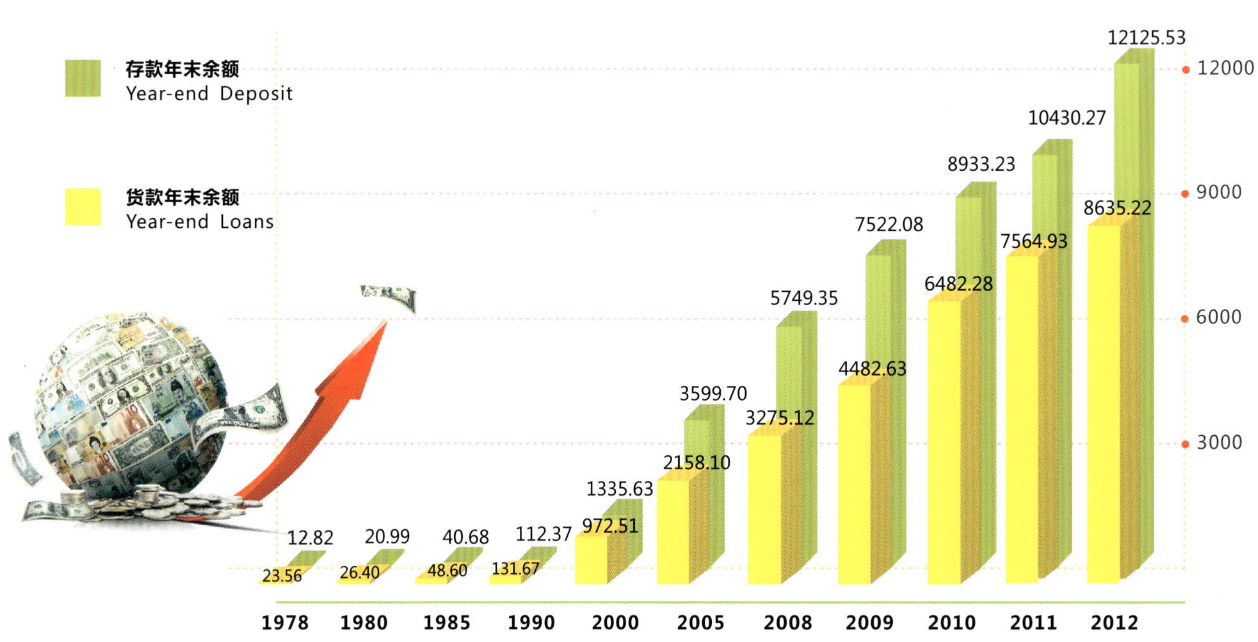

建成区面积(平方公里)
Area of Regions Built-up (sq.km)

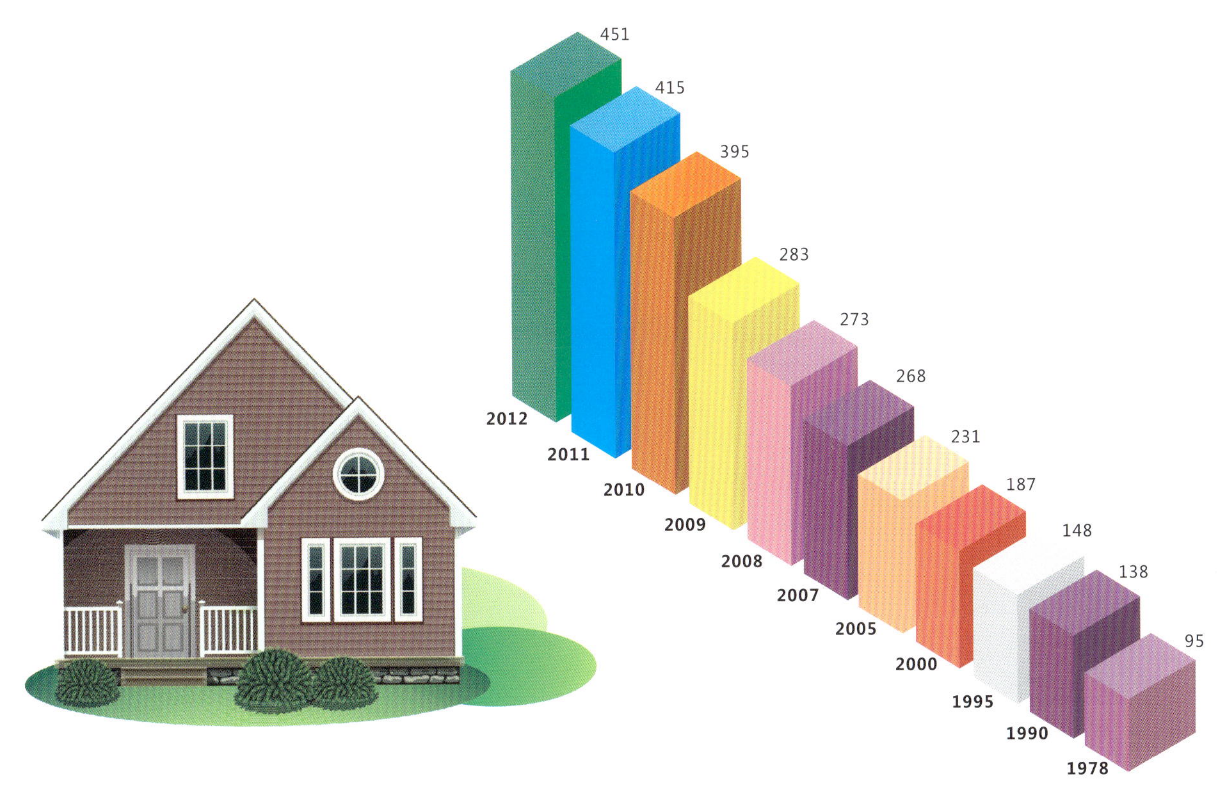

城市公共运营车辆（辆）
City Operating Vehicles (unit)

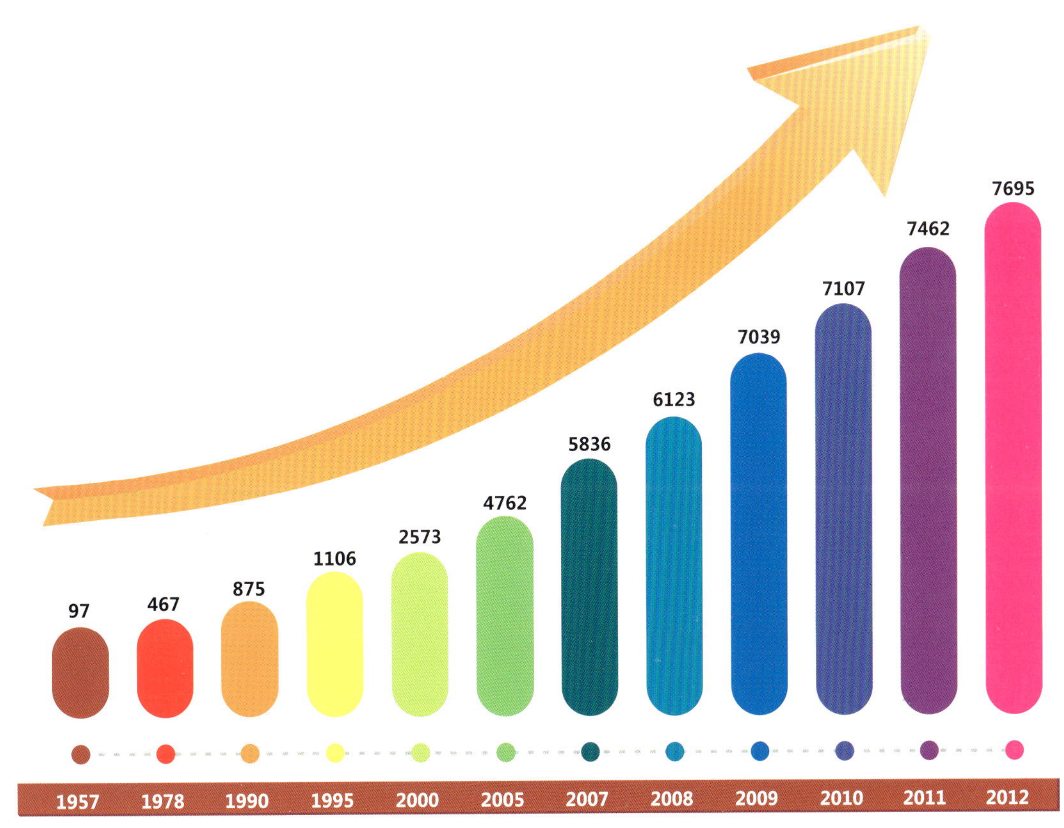

天然气供气总量(万立方米)

Total Natural Gas Supply (10000 cu.m)

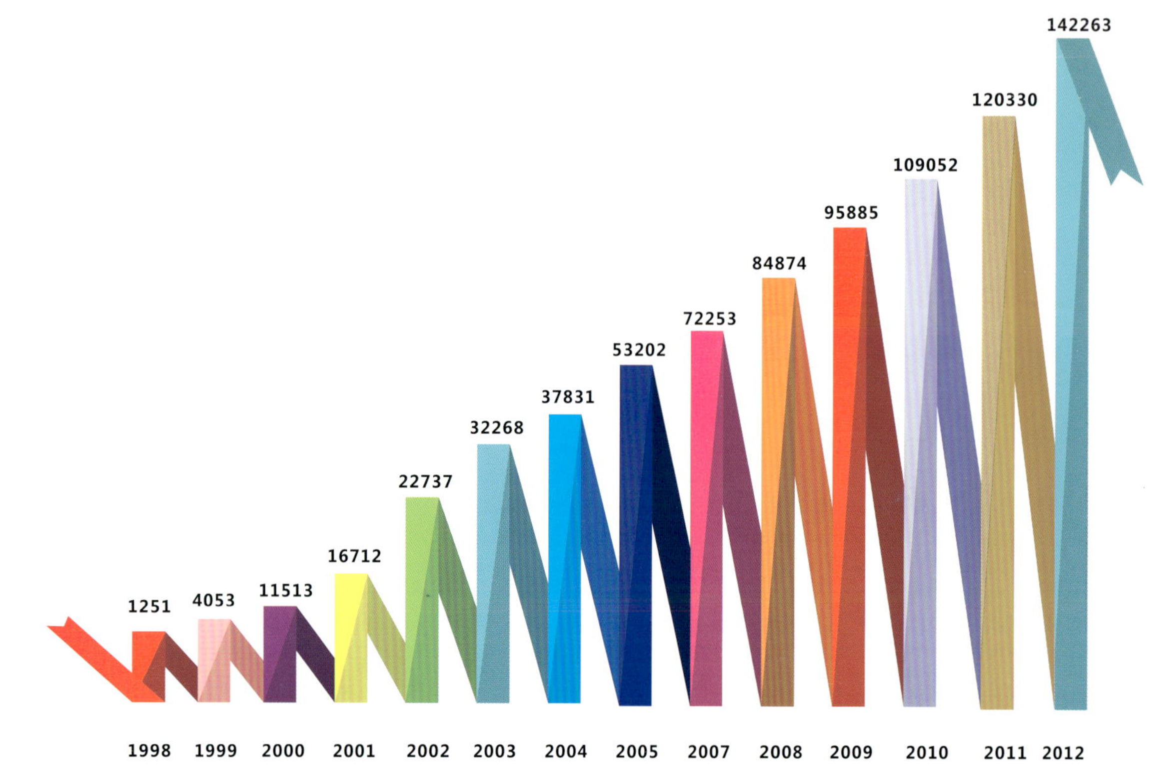

园林绿地总面积（公顷）

Total Area of Park,Gardens and Green Area (hectare)

普通教育在校学生（万人）

Total Enrollment of Regular Education (10000 persons)

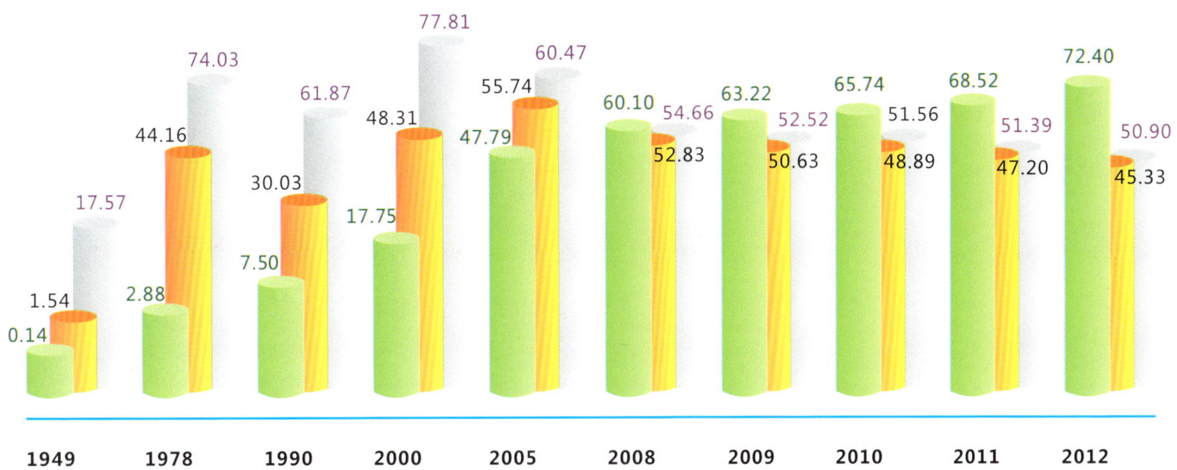

专任教师（万人）

Full-time Teachers (10000 persons)

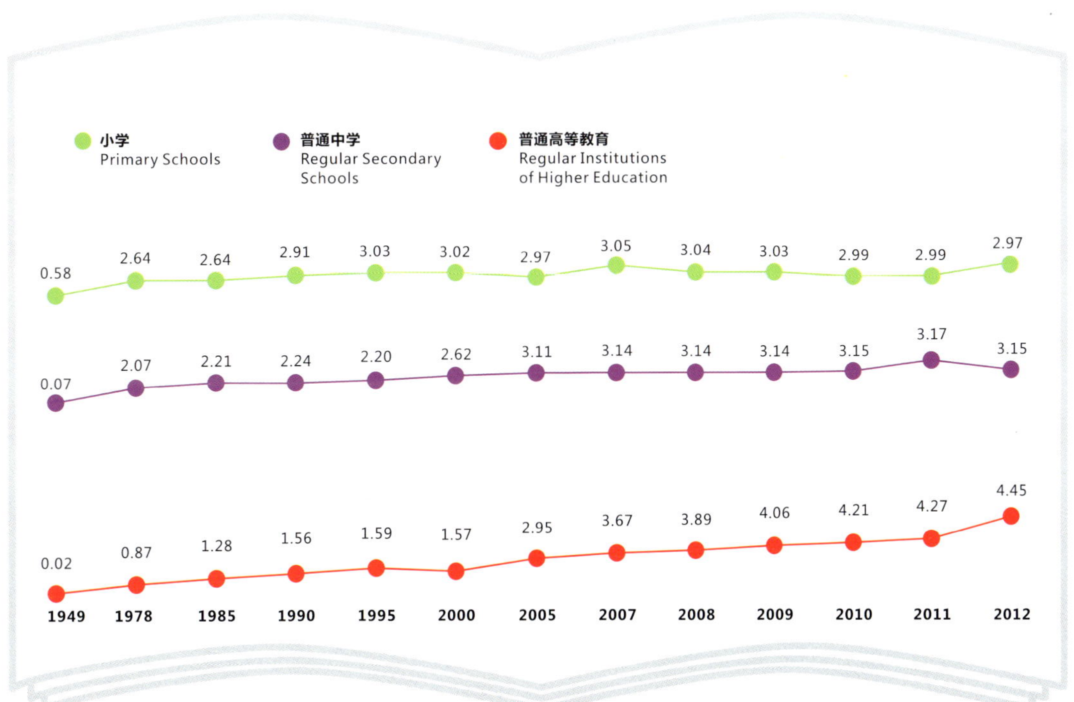

城乡居民收入(元)

The Income of Urban and Rural Residents (yuan)

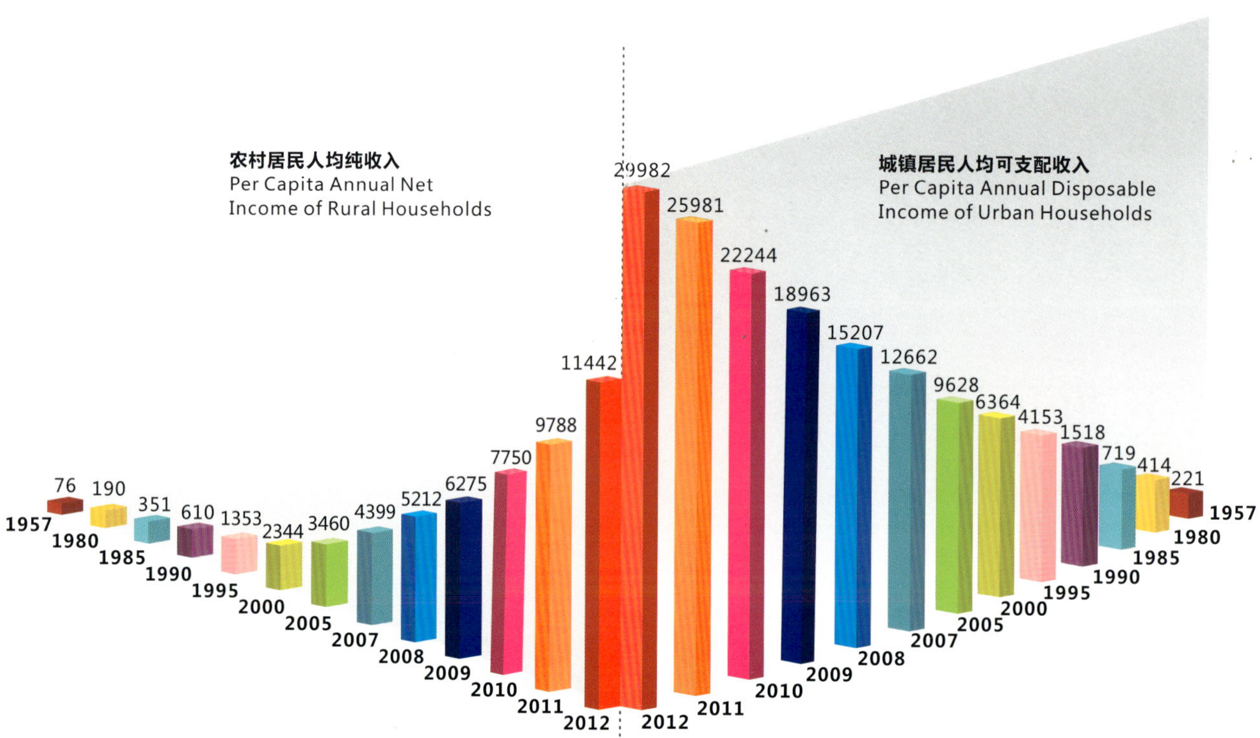

价格指数（以上年价格为100）

Price Indices (the price of preceding year=100)

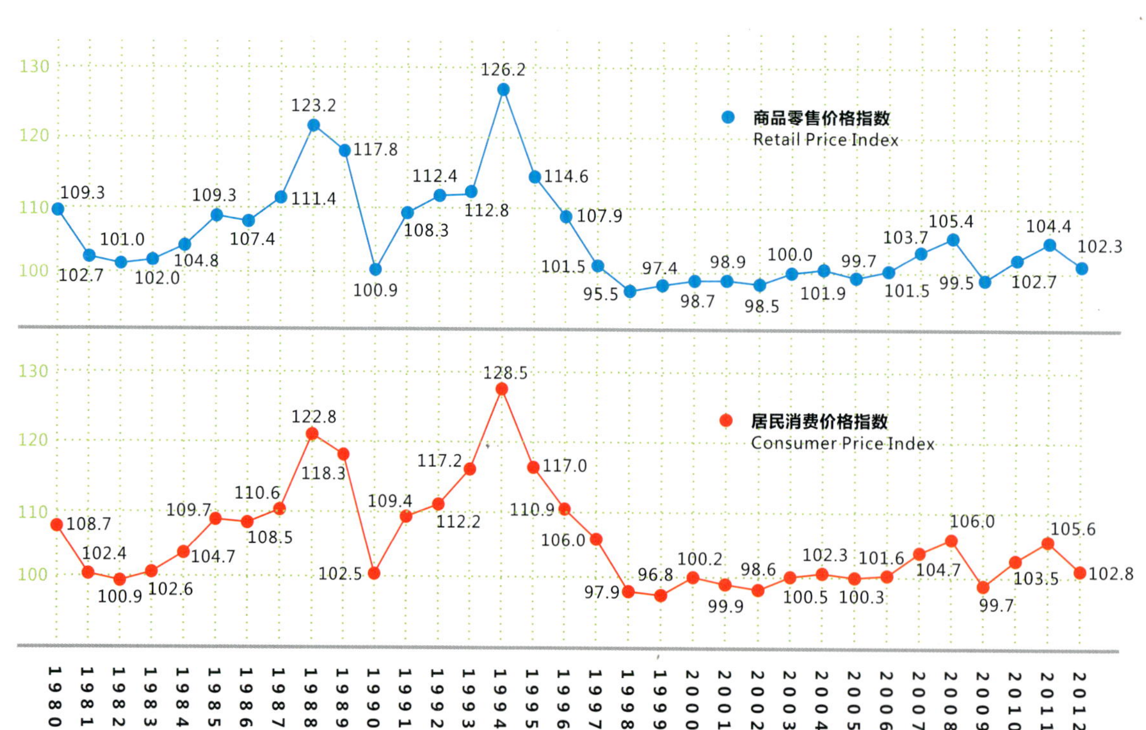

目　　录

一、综　　合

二、基本单位

三、国民经济核算

四、人口、从业人员与职工工资

五、固定资产投资

六、财　　政

七、物价指数

八、人民生活

九、城市公用事业

十、环境保护

十一、农　　业

十二、工　业

十三、能　源

十四、建筑业

十五、运输和邮电

十六、国内贸易

十七、对外经济贸易和旅游

十八、金融业

十九、教育和科技

二十、文化、体育、卫生、社会福利和其他

二十一、企业调查

CONTENTS

CHAPTER 1 GENERAL SURVEY

CHAPTER 2 BASIC UNIT

CHAPTER 3 NATIONAL ECONOMIC ACCOUNTS

CHAPTER 4 POPULATION,EMPLOYMENT AND WAGES

CHAPTER 5 INVESTMENT IN FIXED ASSETS

CHAPTER 6 GOVERNMENT FINANCE

CHAPTER 7 PRICE INDICES

CHAPTER 8 PEOPLE'S LIVELIHOOD

CHAPTER 9 URBAN PUBLIC UTLITIES

CHAPTER 10 ENVIRONMENT PROTECTION

CHAPTER 11 AGRICULTURE

CHAPTER 12 INDUSTRY

CHAPTER 13 ENERGY

CHAPTER 14 CONSTRUCTION

CHAPTER 15 TRANSPORT, POSTAL AND TELECOMMUNICATION SERVICES

CHAPTER 16 DOMESTIC TRADE

CHAPTER 17 FOREIGN TRADE AND ECONOMIC COOPERATION, TOURISM

CHAPTER 18 FINANCIAL LNTERMEDIATION

CHAPTER 19 EDUCATION, SCIENCE AND TECHNOLOGY

CHAPTER 20 CULTURES, SPORTS, SANITATION SOCIAL WELFARE INSTITUTIONS AND OTHER SOCIALACTIVITIES

CHAPTER 21 ENTERPRISES INVESTIGATION

西安市2012年国民经济和社会发展统计公报[1]

西安市统计局　国家统计局西安调查队

2013年2月28日

2012年，在国际经济环境复杂多变和国内经济下行压力加大的困难局面下，全市人民在市委、市政府的正确领导下，坚持以科学发展为主题，以加快转变经济发展方式为主线，按照稳中求进的工作总基调，认真贯彻落实中央、省各项决策部署，全力以赴稳增长，多措并举惠民生，真抓实干促和谐。全市经济保持平稳较快增长，各项社会事业取得新的进步。

一、综合

初步核算，全年实现生产总值[2]（GDP）4369.37亿元，比上年增长11.8%。其中，第一产业增加值195.59亿元，增长6.0%；第二产业增加值1893.79亿元，增长11.8%；第三产业增加值2279.99亿元，增长12.2%。第一产业增加值占生产总值的比重为4.5%，第二产业增加值比重为43.3%，第三产业增加值比重为52.2%。

全年非公有制经济增加值2245.75亿元，占生产总值比重为51.4%，比上年提高0.8个百分点。

图1 2008—2012年生产总值及其增长速度

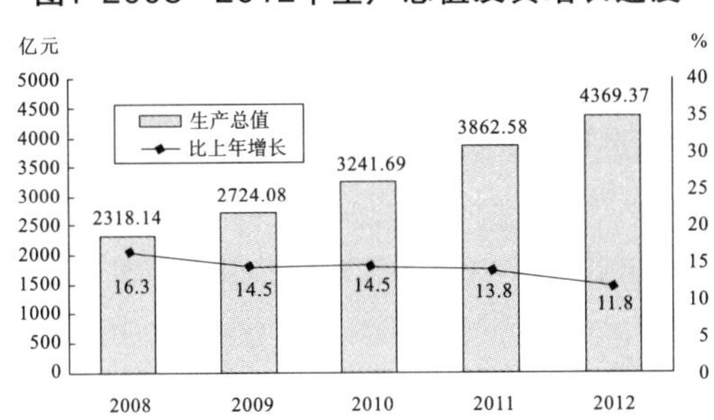

全年居民消费价格比上年上涨2.8%，其中，食品价格上涨5.2%。商品零售价格上涨2.3%，工业生产者出厂价格上涨0.5%，工业生产者购进价格下降2.8%，固定资产投资价格上涨1.9%，新建住宅销售价格上涨0.5%。

图2 2012年居民消费价格月度涨跌幅度

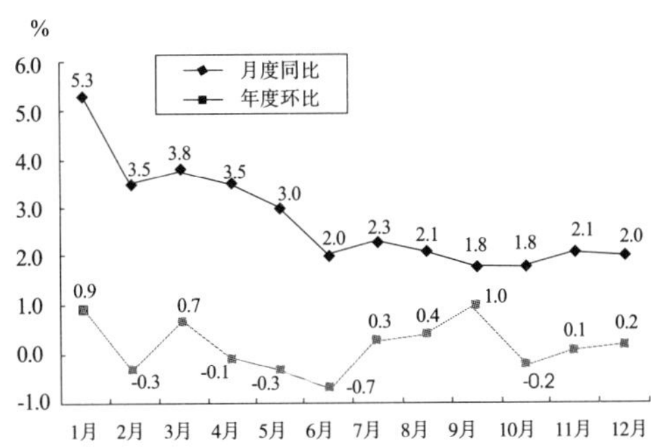

表1 2012年全市居民消费价格比上年涨跌幅度

指　标	涨跌幅度(%)
居民消费价格	2.8
食 品	5.2
其中：粮食	4.7
烟 酒	3.8
衣 着	2.1
家庭设备用品及维修服务	2.4
医疗保健和个人用品	4.2
交通和通信	-1.1
娱乐教育文化用品及服务	1.0
居 住	1.3

全年城镇新增就业人数12.42万人，下岗失业人员再就业5.02万人，就业困难人员实现再就业1.32万人。城镇登记失业率3.49%。

全年财政总收入753.07亿元，比上年增长15.9%。地方财政一般预算收入396.96亿元，增长24.6%，其中，营业税、增值税、企业所得税和个人所得税分别增长18.8%、0.3%、13.8%和-6.3%。全年地方财政一般预算支出597.49亿元，比上年增长20.8%，其中，医疗卫生支出增长23.1%，农林水事务支出增长16.2%，教育支出增长44.3%，社会保障和就业支出增长10.4%，一般公共服务支出增长25.8%，节能环保支出增长1.1倍。

二、农业

全年粮食播种面积572.50万亩，比上年下降0.1%；油料播种面积7.70万亩，下降12.8%；蔬菜播种面积97.82万亩，增长0.9%；棉花播种面积5.00万亩，下降16.3%。全年粮食产量192.54万吨，比上年增长5.8%，其中，夏粮95.73万吨，增长5.7%，秋粮96.81万吨，增长5.8%。

表2　2012年全市农业主要产品产量

产品名称	计量单位	产 量	比上年增长（%）
油 料	万吨	1.15	-1.7
蔬 菜	万吨	277.80	6.2
园林水果	万吨	93.21	2.3
肉 类	万吨	15.17	4.9
奶 类	万吨	66.64	2.8
禽 蛋	万吨	13.00	3.4
大牲畜年末存栏数	万头	21.19	-0.2
猪年末存栏数	万头	96.60	2.3
羊年末存栏数	万只	28.46	-3.9
家禽年末存栏数	万只	1176.73	2.0

全年农用机械总动力298.40万千瓦，比上年增长3.4%；农田有效灌溉面积267.84万亩，增长2.1%；农用化肥施用实物量80.79万吨，增长2.8%。

三、工业和建筑业

全年全部工业实现增加值1340.75亿元，比上年增长12.4%。规模以上工业增加值1144.29亿元，增长13.0%。其中，轻工业增加值247.15亿元，增长12.2%；重工业增加值897.14亿元，增长13.2%。

图3　2008—2012年全部工业增加值及其增长速度

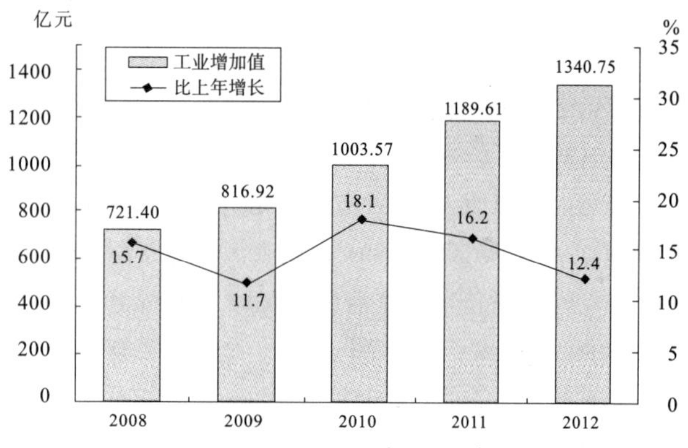

全年规模以上工业[3]中，农副食品加工业增加值比上年增长12.8%；通用设备制造业增长16.1%；专用设备制造业增长16.6%；汽车制造业增长12.5%；铁路、船舶、航空航天和其他运输设备制造业增长13.4%；六大高耗能行业[4]增长13.5%，其中，非金属矿物制品业增长20.3%，化学原料及化学制品制造业增长1.3%，有色金属冶炼及压延加工业增长23.0%，黑色金属冶炼及压延加工业增长3.6%，电力、热力的生产和供应业增长8.4%，石油加工、炼焦及核燃料加工业增长35.0%。

表3　2012年全市规模以上工业主要产品产量

产品名称	计量单位	产 量	比上年增长（%）
发电量	亿千瓦小时	99.48	4.7
原油加工量	万吨	217.47	42.0
乳制品	万吨	124.44	12.3
液体乳	万吨	115.80	12.0
商品混凝土	万立方米	2455.03	26.3
机制纸	万吨	27.61	-31.1
交流电动机	万千瓦	442.79	-21.6
饲料	万吨	81.42	24.2
合成洗涤剂	万吨	11.60	33.5
水泥	万吨	534.16	-8.7
风机	万台	0.13	8.3
汽车	万辆	54.17	-2.7
其中：轿车	万辆	36.62	-5.3
高压开关板	面	20643	85.7
变压器	万千伏安	10750.10	-5.9
电力电缆	万千米	1.17	56.0
气体压缩机	万台	594.51	-12.2
电子元件	亿只	9.90	-13.8

全市规模以上工业企业经济效益综合指数为229.6，比上年提高17.7个百分点。规模以上工业企业主营业务收入3529.20亿元，增长8.6%。实现利润总额132.80亿元，增长1.1%。

全年建筑业实现增加值553.04亿元，比上年增长10.3%。全年具有资质等级的总承包和专业承包建筑企业379家。

图4 2008—2012年建筑业增加值及其增长速度

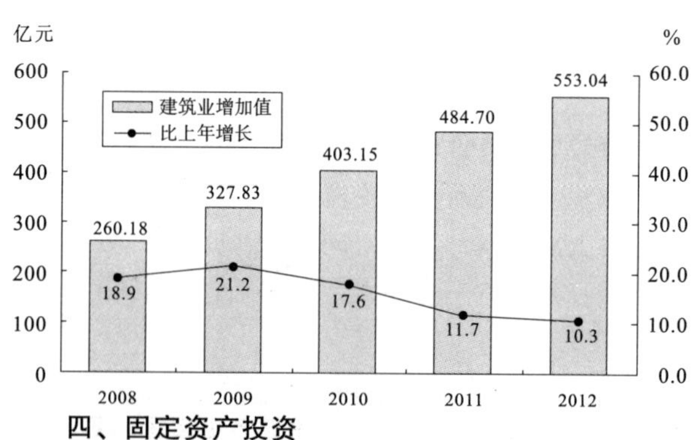

四、固定资产投资

全年全社会固定资产投资4243.43亿元，比上年增长26.6%，扣除价格因素，实际增长24.2%。其中，固定资产投资（不含农户）4165.99亿元，增长27.0%。

在固定资产投资（不含农户）中，第一产业投资99.34亿元，比上年增长37.5%；第二产业投资671.92亿元，增长38.9%，其中，工业投资578.17亿元，增长44.9%；第三产业投资3394.73亿元，增长24.6%。

表4　2012年重点行业固定资产投资及其增长速度

行业	投资额(亿元)	比上年增长(%)
农、林、牧、渔业	99.34	37.5
制造业	482.35	31.7
交通运输、仓储及邮政业	292.83	42.6
信息传输、软件和信息技术服务业	68.78	105.8
批发和零售业	121.05	8.6
住宿和餐饮业	49.57	-17.2
水利、环境和公共设施管理业	325.75	-33.6
教育	65.13	-13.7
卫生和社会工作	59.14	106.5
公共管理、社会保障和社会组织	109.90	-34.1

全年房地产开发投资1281.90亿元，比上年增长28.6%；商品房销售面积1538.91万平方米，下降13.4%。

表5　2012年房地产开发和销售主要指标

指标	计量单位	绝对量	比上年增长（%）
房地产开发投资	亿元	1281.90	28.6
#住宅	亿元	1011.67	21.3
房屋施工面积	万平方米	9947.89	20.6
#住宅	万平方米	8294.92	16.7
新开工面积	万平方米	2848.50	16.1
#住宅	万平方米	2313.67	7.9
房屋竣工面积	万平方米	1063.70	68.6
#住宅	万平方米	903.82	60.1
商品房销售面积	万平方米	1538.91	-13.4
#住宅	万平方米	1383.87	-17.4

全年新增固定资产1765.05亿元，固定资产交付使用率42.4%。各类房屋竣工面积1626.25万平方米，竣工率11.5%。共有1122个城镇建设项目建成投产，项目建成投产率53.8%。

五、国内贸易

全年社会消费品零售总额2236.06亿元，比上年增长15.5%，扣除价格因素，实际增长12.9%。按经营单位所在地统计，城镇消费品零售额2167.38亿元，增长15.4%；乡村消费品零售额68.68亿元，增长19.8%。按消费形态统计，商品零售额2013.74亿元，增长16.2%；餐饮收入额222.32亿元，增长9.7%。

图5　2008—2012年社会消费品零售总额及其增长速度

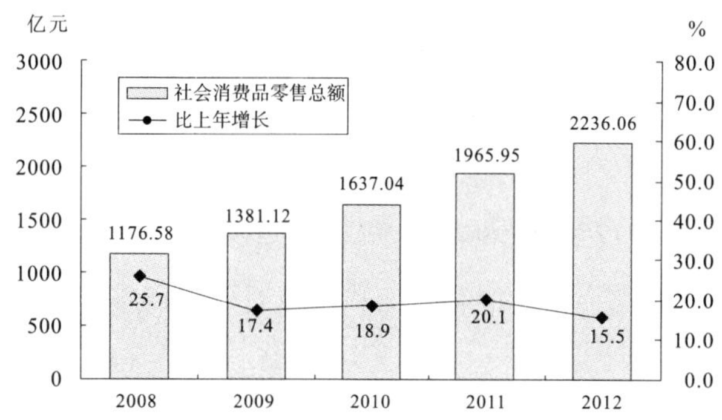

在限额以上企业商品零售额中，粮油、食品、饮料、烟酒类零售额比上年增长25.8%，服装、鞋帽、针、纺织品类增长23.0%，体育、娱乐用品类增长9.1%，书报杂志类增长13.2%，日用品类增长23.5%，家用电器和音像器材类增长5.5%，通讯器材类增长16.0%，家具类增长20.9%，金银珠宝类增长4.9%，汽车类增长6.4%。

六、对外经济

全年进出口总额130.14亿美元，比上年增长3.3%。其中，出口72.99亿美元，增长25.3%；进口57.15亿美元，下降15.6%。

图6　2008—2012年进出口总额及其增长速度

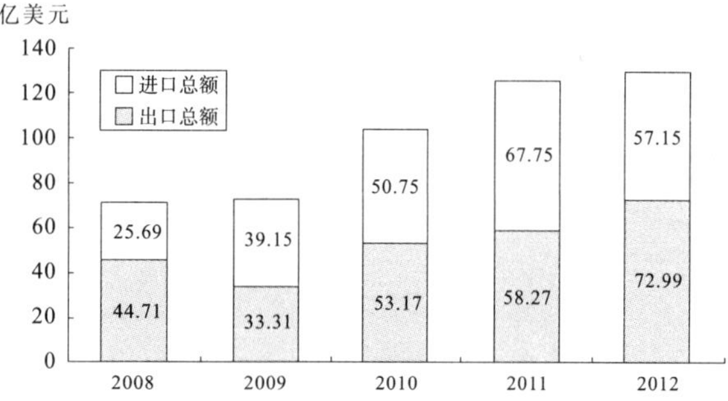

在进出口总额中，一般贸易进出口68.82亿美元，比上年下降8.6%，占进出口总额的52.9%；加工贸易进出口40.51亿美元，增长10.1%，占进出口总额的31.1%。

主要进出口商品中，机电产品出口49.32亿美元，比上年增长27.7%，进口42.29亿美元，增长0.6%；农产品出口5.36亿美元，增长11.3%，进口0.61亿美元，下降57.2%；矿产品出口2.45亿美元，下降31.5%，进口7.04亿美元，下降27.8%；纺织服装出口3.38亿美元，增长90.5%，进口484万美元，增长29.8%。

全年批准外商直接投资项目87个，合同利用外商直接投资36.03亿美元，比上年增长2倍；实际利用外商直接投资24.78亿美元，增长23.6%。

七、交通、邮电和旅游

全年货物运输总量4.49亿吨，比上年增长14.5%；货物运输周转量595.87亿吨公里，增长14.3%。旅客运输总量3.62亿人次，增长5.3%；旅客运输周转量338.74亿人公里，增长4.8%。

表6　2012年各种运输方式完成货物运输量及其增长速度

指　标	单位	绝对数	比上年增长（%）
货物运输总量	万吨	44924.33	14.5
公路	万吨	44082.00	14.8
铁路	万吨	824.85	0.2
民航（吞吐量）	万吨	17.48	1.3
货物运输周转量	亿吨公里	595.87	14.3
公路	亿吨公里	372.90	19.9
铁路	亿吨公里	221.99	6.2
民航	亿吨公里	0.98	-15.1

表7　2012年各种运输方式完成旅客运输量及其增长速度

指　标	单位	绝对数	比上年增长（%）
旅客运输总量	万人次	36153.79	5.3
公路	万人次	30893.00	5.2
铁路	万人次	2918.70	1.8
民航（吞吐量）	万人次	2342.09	10.7
旅客运输周转量	亿人公里	338.74	4.8
公路	亿人公里	170.87	6.6
铁路	亿人公里	60.93	0.8
民航	亿人公里	106.94	4.2

年末全市机动车保有量达到160.82万辆，比上年末增长13.2%，其中，私人汽车保有量139.96万辆，增长15.0%。

全年邮政业务总收入9.58亿元，比上年增长7.9%；电信业务总收入116.23亿元，增长12.8%。年末全市固定电话用户311.02万户；移动电话用户1803.54万户，其中，3G移动电话用户[5]394.97万户。

全年共接待国内游客7863万人次，比上年增长20.0%；境外游客115.35万人次，增长15.1%。全年实现旅游总收入654.39亿元，增长23.4%，其中，外汇收入7.49亿美元，增长16.8%。

八、金融

年末全市金融机构本外币各项存款余额12285.96亿元，比上年增长16.7%。人民币存款余额12125.53亿元，增长16.3%，其中，城乡居民储蓄存款余额4787.03亿元，增长15.2%。金融机构本外币贷款余额8808.04亿元，增长14.4%。人民币贷款余额8635.22亿元，增长14.1%，其中，短期贷款余额1917.51亿元，增长34.0%；中长期贷款余额6378.88亿元，增长10.4%。

全年证券市场各类证券交易总额8812.15亿元，比上年下降10.5%。年末全市拥有上市股份公司29家，上市总股本219.02亿股，总市值1780.31亿元。年末股票市场累计开户数171.75万户，比上年末增长4.1%。

年末全市共有保险公司48家，其中，财产险23家，人寿险25家。保险专业中介机构107家。全年保费收入176.78亿元，比上年增长6.8%，其中，财产险保费收入55.70亿元，增16.4%；人身险保费收入121.08亿元，增长2.9%。全年支付各类保险赔款给付49.61亿元，比上年增长29.5%，其中，财产险、人身险分别为29.94和19.67亿元，分别比上年增长39.2%和17.0%。

九、教育、科学技术和文化

全市普通高校62所，在校学生72.40万人，毕业生18.64万人，另有研究生培养单位44个，在学研究生8.47万人，毕业生2.30万人；成人高等学校15所，在校学生15.98万人，毕业生5.05万人；普通中学419所，在校学生45.33万人，毕业生15.64万人；小学1322所，在校学生50.85万人，毕业生8.88万人。小学、初中学龄人口入学率分别为99.96%和99.67%。

全年实施市级科技计划项目337项，其中，高新技术专项26项，科技创新和成果转化项目216项。重点扶持高新技术企业118家，支持建设农业科技示范园19家，实施区县工业科技引导项目10个。全年技术市场交易额303.75亿元。申请专利量15029件，专利授权量3475件。

全市博物馆94个，公共图书馆 15个，艺术表演团体13个[6]，文化馆15个，文化站181个。全年组织开展各类群众文化活动7846场次。全市拥有电视台1座、广播电台1座、广播电视台7座，电视人口覆盖率和广播人口覆盖率分别达98.83%和99.45%。

全年举办各类群众体育展示表演和竞赛活动共计260项次，体育社团举办和承办体育赛事305项次，其中，国际性和全国性赛事22项次。新建城市社区全民健身器材配送工程40个、乡镇农民体育健身工程7个、社区全民健身路径50个。全市已有社会体育指导员8600名，晨晚练点1600个，健身气功站点140个、在册练功人数6118人。

2012年，我市培养输送运动员参加国际、国内各项比赛获得8金3银，其中，在伦敦奥运会上，我市培养输送的运动员获得2金1银。

十、卫生和社会服务

年末全市共有各类卫生机构5576个，其中，医院、卫生院376个；各类卫生技术人员6.64万人，其中，执业（助理）医师2.31万人；卫生机构床位4.42万张。

全市社会福利收养类单位72个，共有床位1.11万张，年末在院人数7554人。年末城市低保对象5.5万户、10.93万人，发放低保金5.35亿元；农村低保对象5.69万户、17.41万人，发放低保金2.78亿元。4517人纳入农村五保供养[7]，发放供养金 2291万元。全年救助城市医疗困难群众1.24万人次；救助农村医疗困难群众28.37万人次。

十一、人口、人民生活和社会保障

年末常住人口855.29万人，其中，男性人口439.21万人，占51.4%；女性人口416.08万人，占48.6%，性别比为105.56（以女性为100，男性对女性的比例）。全年出生人口8.64万人，出生率为10.13‰；死亡人口4.75万人，死亡率为5.57‰。全年净增人口3.95万人，自然增长率为4.56‰。城镇人口611.62万人，占71.51%；乡村人口243.67万人，占28.49%。年末全市户籍总人口795.98万人，比上年增长0.5%。

全年城镇居民人均可支配收入29982元，扣除价格因素，比上年实际增长12.3%；农民人均纯收入11442元，实际增长13.7%。城镇居民人均消费性支出21434元，比上年增长11.0%；农村居民人均总支出10964元，增长17.0%。城镇居民人均现住房建筑面积32.98平方米，农村居民人均住房面积78平方米。

图7　2008—2012年城乡居民收入

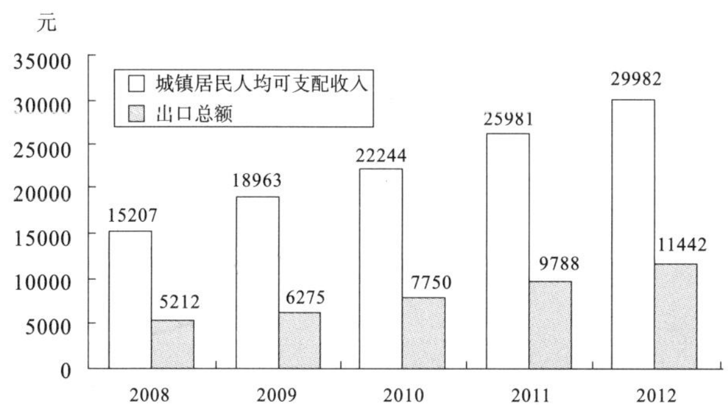

全市城镇基本医疗保险参保人数413.60万人；城镇职工养老保险参保人数241.63万人；失业保险参保人数139.84万人；工伤保险参保人数133.47万人，职工生育保险参保人数97.19万人。参加农村新型合作医疗的农民人数达397.53万人，实际参合率97.7%。

十二、城市建设、环境和安全生产

全年完成市政公用设施投资251.60亿元，新增人行天桥8座，建设公交港湾71处，新增城区集中供热面积1559万平方米，新建改造绿地广场122个，新建道路面积95万平方米。

全年城市环境空气质量好于国家二级标准（良好）以上的天数306天，比上年增加1天。二氧化硫年平均浓度为0.040毫克/标立方米，比上年下降4.8%；二氧化氮年平均浓度为0.042毫克/标立方米，上升2.4%；可吸入颗粒物年平均浓度为0.118毫克/标立方米，与上年持平。全市集中式饮用水源地的水质达标率为100%。区域环境噪声等效声级均值为55.3分贝，道路交通噪声等效声级均值为68.2分贝。

全年共发生各类安全生产事故5029起，比上年增加830起；死亡553人，比上年减少13人；受伤2492人，比上年增加221人；经济损失4524万元，比上年增加1743.47万元。

注释：

[1]本公报数据为初步统计数，部分数据因四舍五入的原因，存在着分项与合计不等的情况。

[2]地区生产总值、各产业增加值绝对数按现价计算，增长速度按不变价格计算。

[3]2012年起，国家统计局执行新的国民经济行业分类标准，工业行业大类由原来的39个调整为41个，固定资产投资（不含农户）行业分类也按新的标准进行了调整。

[4]六大高耗能行业分别为：化学原料和化学制品制造业、非金属矿物制品业、黑色金属冶炼和压延加工业、有色金属冶炼和压延加工业、石油加工炼焦和核燃料加工业、电力热力生产和供应业。

[5]3G是指第三代蜂窝移动通信系统（3rd-generation，简称3G），3G移动电话用户是指报告期末在计费系统拥有使用信息、占用3G网络资源的在网用户。

[6]全市艺术表演团体、文化馆、全年组织开展各类群众文化活动数据不含省直单位数据。

[7]农村五保供养是指老年、残疾和未满16周岁的村民，无劳动能力、无生活来源又无法定赡养、抚养、扶养义务人，或者其法定赡养、抚养、扶养义务人无赡养、抚养、扶养能力的村民，在吃、穿、住、医、葬方面得到的生活照顾和物质帮助。

资料来源：本公报中物价数据来自国家统计局西安调查队；城镇新增就业、登记失业率、社会保障数据来自西安市人力资源和社会保障局；财政数据来自

市财政局；进出口数据来自西安海关；利用外资数据来自市商务局；铁路运输数据来自西安铁路局；公路运输数据来自市交通运输局；民航运输数据来自西安咸阳国际机场；机动车数据来自市车管所；邮政业务数据来自市邮政局；电信数据来自中国移动西安分公司、中国电信西安分公司、中国联通西安分公司、陕西铁通西安分公司；旅游数据来自市旅游局；货币金融数据来自中国人民银行西安分行营业管理部；证券数据、保险业数据来自市金融办；教育数据来自市教育局；科技数据来自市科技局；艺术表演团体、公共图书馆、文化馆、广播、电视数据来自市文化广电新闻出版局；博物馆数据来自市文物局；体育数据来自市体育局；卫生、新农合数据来自市卫生局；社会服务、低保和五保供养数据来自市民政局；集中供热面积、建成区绿化面积来自市城乡建设委员会；环境监测数据来自市环境保护局；安全生产数据来自市安全生产监督管理局；其他数据均来自市统计局。

Statistical Communique of Xi'an City on the 2012 National Economic and Social Development

Xi'an Municipal Bureau of Statistics and NBS Survey Office in Xi' an

Feb.28th, 2013

In 2012, the municipal party committee and municipal government of Xi'an seized the theme of 'Scientific Outlook on Development', closely center on the main line of transformation of economic development way, implement various macro-control policies from Chinese Communist Party Central Committee, actively responded to the new domestic and international economic environment. Above of all, the economy of the whole city maintained steady and rapid development, the steady start opened a ' Twelfth Five-Year' new and bright age.

I. General Outlook

In 2012, the gross domestic product (GDP) preliminarily estimated was 436.937 billion Yuan, up by 11.8 percent against the previous year. Analyzed by different industries, the value added of the primary industry was 19.559 billion Yuan, up by 6.0 percent; the value added of the secondary industry was 189.3796 billion Yuan, a rise of 11.8 percent; and the value added of the tertiary industry was 227.999 billion Yuan, up by 12.2 percent. The value added of the primary industry accounted for 4.5 percent of the GDP, that of the secondary industry accounted for 43.3 percent, and that of the tertiary industry accounted for 52.2 percent.

The value added of non-public sectors of the economy is 224.575 billion, accounted for the proportion of GDP is 51.4, an increase of 0.8 percent over the previous year.

Table 1 The GDP and growth rate in 2008–2012

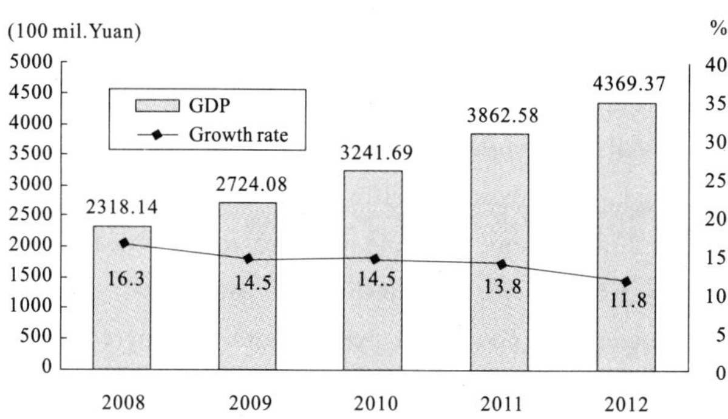

The general level of consumer prices in Xi'an was up by 2.8 percent against the previous year. Of this total, the prices for food went up by 5.2 percent; the retail prices for commodities up by 2.3 percent; the producer prices for manufactured goods were up by 0.5 percent; The purchasing prices for manufactured goods went down by 2.8 percent. The fixed asset investment price went up by 1.9 percent and the price of newly founded house increased by 0.5 percent.

Table 2 The rate of increase and decrease of CPI in 2012

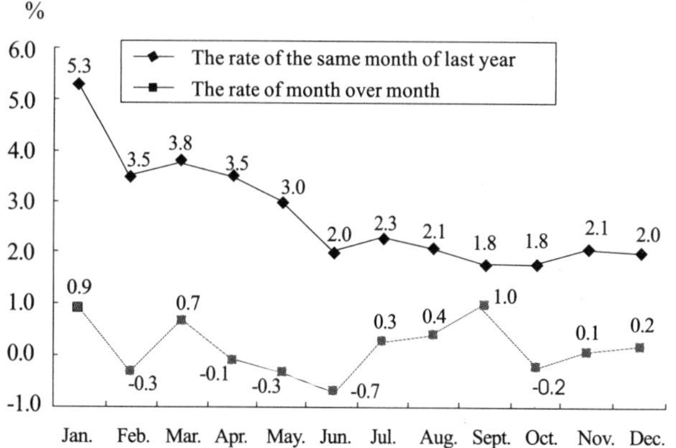

Sheet 1 Up and fall extent of Residents Consumer Price Indices with previous year (2012)

Item	2012(%)
Consumer Price Index	2.8
Food	5.2
#Grain	4.7
Tobacco and liquor	3.8
Clothing	2.1
Household facilities and maintaining services	2.4
Medical, Health and Personal Articles	4.2
Transportation and Communication	-1.1
Recreation, Education and Cultural articles and Services	1.0
Residence	1.3

In 2012, the newly increased employed people in urban areas in Xi'an numbered 124.2 thousand. The number of reemployment of laid-off workers was 50.2 thousand, and the number of reemployment of people who were difficult to find job was 13.2 thousand. The urban unemployment rate through unemployment registration was 3.49 percent at the end of 2012. The financial revenue totaled 75.307 billion Yuan, an increase of 15.9 percent as compared with the previous year. The General Budget Revenue of Regional Finance reached 39.696 billion Yuan, up by 24.6 percent. Of this, business tax, value added tax, income tax of enterprises and individual income tax were up by 18.8 percent, 0.3 percent, 13.8 percent and -6.3 percent respectively. The General Budget Expenditure of Regional Finance totaled 59.749 billion Yuan, up by 20.8 percent. Of this total expenditure, the expenditure on health care was up by 23.1 percent; that on agriculture, forestry and water affairs was up by 16.2 percent; that on education was up by 44.3 percent; that on social security and employment was up by 10.4 percent; that on general public service was up by 25.8 percent; that on environmental protection was up by 110 percent.

II. Agriculture

In 2012, the sown area of grain was 5725.0 thousand hectares, a decrease of 0.1 percent as compared with the previous year; the sown area of oil-bearing crops was 77.0 thousand hectares, a decrease of 12.8 percent; the sown area of vegetables was 978.2 thousand hectares, up by 0.9 percent; the sown area of cotton was 50.0 thousand hectares, a decrease of 16.3 percent. The total output of grain in 2012 was 1.9254 million tons, an increase of 5.8 percent. Of this, the output of summer crops was 0.9573 million tons, up by 5.7 percent, and that of the autumn grain was 0.9681 million tons, an increase of 5.8 percent.

Sheet 2 Mail Product of Agriculture Production in 2012

Name of Product	Units	Output	Increase over the last year (%)
Oil	10,000 tons	1.15	-1.7
Vegetable	10,000 tons	277.80	6.2
Fruit	10,000 tons	93.21	2.3
Meat	10,000 tons	15.17	4.9
Milk	10,000 tons	66.64	2.8
Poultry eggs	10,000 tons	13.00	3.4
Year-end Cattle on hand	10,000 head	21.19	-0.2
Year-end Pig on hand	10,000 head	96.60	2.3
Year-end Sheep on hand	10,000 head	28.46	-3.9
Year-end Fowl on hand	10,000 head	1176.73	2.0

The total power of agricultural machinery was 2.9840 million kilowatts, up by 3.4 percent against the previous year; over 2678.4 thousand hectares of farmland was with effective irrigation systems, an increase of 2.1 percent; the total of fertilizer utilized (physical quantity) was 807.9 thousand tons, up by 2.8 percent.

IIII. Industry and Construction

In 2012, the value added by the industrial sector was 134.075 billion Yuan, up by 12.4 percent over the previous year. The value added of industrial enterprises above the designated size was 114.429 billion Yuan, up by 13 percent. Of this, the value added of the light industry was 24.715 billion Yuan, up by 12.2 percent; that of the heavy industry was 89.714 billion Yuan, up by 13.2 percent.

Table 3 The whole value added of Industry and growth rate in 2008-2012

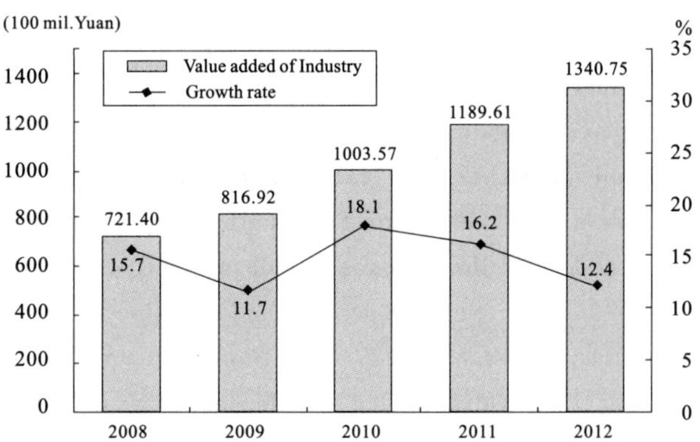

In 2012, of the industrial enterprises above designated size, the growth of value added for processing of food from agricultural products was up by 12.8 percent over the previous year; for manufacture of general machinery up by 16.1 percent; for manufacture of special purpose machinery up by 16.6 percent; for manufacture of car up by 12.5 percent; for manufacture of transport equipment up by 13.4 percent; The growth of the value added for the major six high energy consuming industries were 13.5 percent, of which, that of the manufacture of non-metallic mineral products was 20.3 percent, manufacture of raw chemical materials and chemical products 1.3 percent, smelting and pressing of ferrous metals 23.0 percent, smelting and pressing of non-ferrous metals 3.6 percent, production and supply of electric power and heat power 8.4 percent and 35.0 percent for processing of petroleum, coking, processing of nuclear fuel.

Sheet 3 Output of Major Industrial Products above designated size in Xi' an(2012)

Name of Product	Units	Output	Increase over the last year (%)
Electricity	100 million kilo watt-hour	99.48	4.7
Crude Oil Processing	10,000 tons	217.47	42.0
Dairy	10,000 tons	124.44	12.3
Liquid milk	10,000 tons	115.80	12.0
Commercial Concrete	10,000 cubic meter	2455.03	26.3
Machine-made paper and Cardboard	10,000 tons	27.61	-31.1
AC motors	10,000 Kilowatt	442.79	-21.6
Feed	10,000 tons	81.42	24.2
Synthetic detergent	10,000 tons	11.60	33.5
Cement	10,000 tons	534.16	-8.7
Draught fan	10,000 units	0.13	8.3
Motor vehicle	10,000 units	54.17	-2.7
#Car	10,000 units	36.62	-5.3
High voltage switch board	unit	20643	85.7
Transformer	10,000 kilovolt amperes	10750.10	-5.9
Electric cable	10,000 Km	1.17	56.0
Gas compressor	10,000 units	594.51	-12.2
Electronic component	100 million units	9.90	-13.8

The composite index on economic benefits of the industrial enterprises above the designated size in 2012 was 229.6, an increase of 17.7 percent over the previous year. The main business income of the industrial enterprises above designated size is 352.920 billion Yuan, up by 8.6 percent over the previous year. The profit was 13.280 billion Yuan, up by 1.1 percent. In 2012, the value added by the construction enterprises in Xi'an was 55.304 billion Yuan, up by 10.3 percent over the previous year, and 379 construction enterprises qualified for general contracts and specialized contracts.

Table 4 The value added of construction and growth rate in 2008-2012

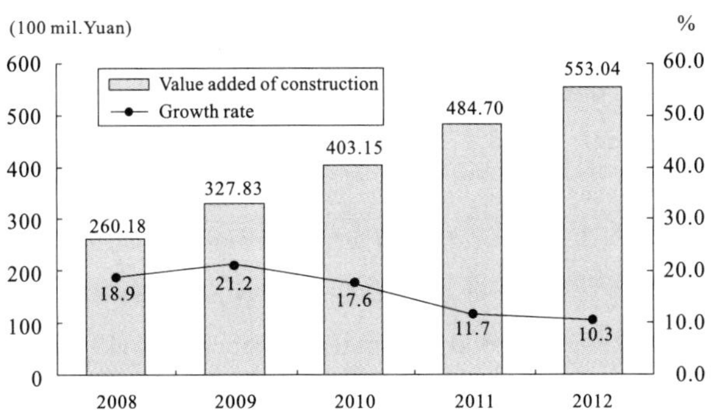

IV. Investment in Fixed Assets

The completed investment in fixed assets of the city in 2012 was 424.343 billion Yuan, up by 26.6 percent over the previous year. The real growth was 24.2 percent after deducting the price factors. Of the total investment in urban areas was 416.599 billion Yuan, up by 27.0 percent.

In whole investment, the investment in the primary industry was 9.934 billion Yuan, up by 37.5percent against the previous year; in the secondary industry, it was 67.192 billion Yuan, up by 38.9 percent, of which industrial investment was 57.817 billion Yuan, up by 44.9 percent; in the tertiary industry, it was 339.473billion Yuan, up by 24.6 percent.

Sheet 4 The investment in fixed assets and growth rate in Key industries in 2012

Industries	Investment (100 million Yuan)	Growth rate (%)
Agriculture, Forestry, Animal hus bandry and fishery	99.34	37.5
Manufacturing	482.35	31.7
Transportation, storage and postal services	292.83	42.6
Information transmission, computer services and software industry	68.78	105.8
Wholesale and retail trade	121.05	8.6
Accommodation and catering industry	49.57	-17.2
Water Conservancy, environment and public facilities administration industry	325.75	-33.6
Education	65.13	-13.7
Sanitations, social security and social welfare	59.14	106.5
Public administration and social organizations	109.90	-34.1

In 2012, the investment in real estate development was 128.190 billion Yuan, up by 28.6 percent; the sold area of commercial housing was 15.3891 million square meters, decreased by 13.4 percent.

Sheet 5 Mail Indicators of Real estate development and sales in 2012

Item	Units	Absolute Number	Increase over the last year (%)
Investment in Real Estate Development	100 million Yuan	1281.90	28.6
# Residential Building	100 million Yuan	1011.67	21.3
Floor Space of Commercial Houses Construction	10,000 sq.m	9947.89	20.6
# Residential Building	10,000 sq.m	8294.92	16.7
Floor Space of Newly Construction	10,000 sq.m	2848.50	16.1
# Residential Building	10,000 sq.m	1313.67	7.9
Floor Space of Commercial Houses Completed	10,000 sq.m	1063.70	68.6
# Residential Building	10,000 sq.m	903.82	60.1
Floor Space of Commercial Houses Sold	10,000 sq.m	1538.91	-13.4
# Residential Building	10,000 sq.m	1383.87	-17.4

The value of fixed assets increased in 2012, was 176.505 billion Yuan, and the rate of projects delivered of fixed assets was 42.4 percent. The completed area of various kinds of buildings was 16.2625 million square meters, and the rate of completed area was 11.5 percent. 1122 projects of urban construction were completed and put into use this year, and the rate of construction projects completed and put into use was 53.8 percent.

V. Domestic Trade

In 2012, the total retail sales of consumer goods reached 223.606 billion Yuan, a growth of 15.5 percent over the previous year or a real growth of 12.9 percent after deducting price factors. An analysis on different areas showed that the retail sales of consumer goods in urban areas stood at 216.738 billion Yuan, up by 15.4 percent, and that in rural areas reached 6.868 billion Yuan, up by 19.8 percent. Grouped by consumption patterns, the income of retail sales of commodities was 201.374 billion Yuan, up by 16.2 percent; that of catering industry was 22.232 billion Yuan, up by 9.7 percent.

Table 5 The total retail sales of social consumer goods and growth rate in 2008-2012

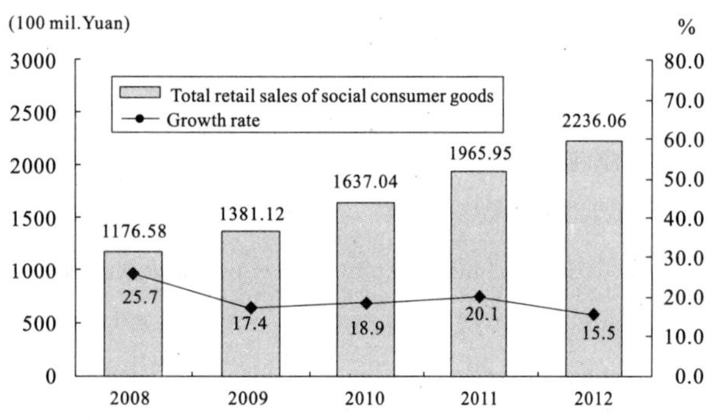

Of the total retail sales by wholesale and retail enterprises above designated size, the sales of food, beverage, wine and cigarette was up by 25.8 percent; clothing ,shoes, hats, and needle textiles up by 23.0 percent; sports-recreation up by 9.1 percent; books, newspapers and magazines up by 13.2 percent; daily necessities up by 23.5 percent; electric and electronic appliances for household use and audio-video equipment up by 5.5 percent; telecommunication equipment down by 16.0 percent; furniture increased by 20.9 percent; gold, silver and jewelry up by 4.9 percent and motor vehicles up by 6.4 percent.

VI. Foreign Economic Relations

In 2012, the total value of imports and exports reached 13.014 billion US Dollars, up by 3.3 percent over the previous year. Of this, the value of exports was 7.299 billion US Dollars, up by 25.3 percent, and that of imports was 5.715 billion US Dollars, decreased by 15.6 percent.

Table 6 The total imports and exports and growth rate in 2008-2012

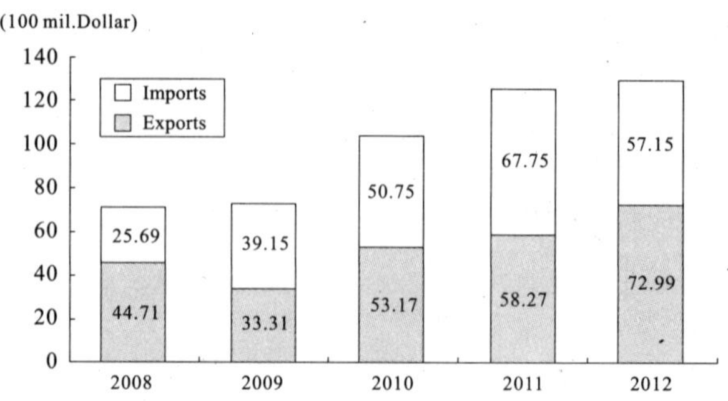

In total imports and exports, the value of imports and exports of general trade was 6.882 billion US Dollars, decreased by 8.6 percent, accounted for 52.9 percent of import and export whole value of Xi' an region. The value of processing trade was 4.051 billion US Dollars, up by 10.1percent, accounted for 31.1 percent of import and export whole value of Xi' an region.

Of the main import and export commodities, the value of exports of electromechanical products was 4.932 billion US Dollars, an increase of 27.7 percent; that of imports of electromechanical products was 4.229 billion US Dollars, up by 0.6 percent. The value of exports of agricultural product was 0.536 billion US Dollars, up by 11.3 percent; that of imports of agricultural products was 0.061 billion US Dollars, decreased by 57.2 percent. The value of exports of mineral products was 0.245 billion US Dollars, down by 31.5 percent; that of imports of mineral products was 0.704 billion US Dollars, decreased by 27.8 percent. The value of exports of textile products was 0.338 billion US Dollars, an increase of 90.5 percent; that of imports of textile products was 4.84 million US Dollars, up by 29.8 percent.

In 2012, there were 87 Foreign Direct Investment projects approved in Xi'an; the contracted Foreign Direct Investment was 3.603 billion US dollars, almost twice as large as the previous year; the realized Foreign Direct Investment was 2.478 billion US dollars, up by 23.6 percent.

VII. Transportation, Post, Telecommunications and Tourism

In 2012, the total freight traffic reached 0.449 billion ton, up by 14.5 percent over the previous year. The total goods transportation turnover reached 59.587 billion ton-kilometers, up by 14.3 percent over the previous year. The Total passenger transport reached 0.362 billion, up by 5.3 percent over the previous year. The passenger transport turnover reached 33.874 billion person-kilometers, up by 4.8 percent over the previous year.

Sheet 6 The Total Freight Traffic and growth rate created by Kinds of transport Mode in 2012

Index	Unit	Amount	Growth rate (%)
The Total Freight Traffic	10,000 tons	44924.33	14.5
Highway	10,000 tons	44082.00	14.8
Railway	10,000 tons	824.85	0.2
Airway	10,000 tons	17.48	1.3
Goods Transportation Turnover	100 million ton-kilometers	595.87	14.3
Highway	100 million ton-kilometers	372.90	19.9
Railway	100 million ton-kilometers	221.99	6.2
Airway	100 million ton-kilometers	0.98	-15.1

Sheet 7 The Total Passenger Traffic and growth rate created by Kinds of transport Mode in 2012

Index	Unit	Amount	Growth rate (%)
The Total Passenger Transport	10,000 person	36153.79	5.3
Highway	10,000 person	30893.00	5.2
Railway	10,000 person	2918.70	1.8
Airway	10,000 person	2342.09	10.7
The passenger Transportturnover	billion person-kilometers	33.874	4.8
Highway	billion person-kilometers	17.087	6.6
Railway	billion person-kilometers	6.093	0.8
Airway	billion person-kilometers	10.694	4.2

The total number of motor vehicles for civilian use reached 1608.2 thousand by the end of 2012, up by 13.2 percent, of which private-owned vehicles numbered 1399.6 thousand, up 15.0 percent. The revenue of post services totaled 0.958 billion Yuan, up by 7.9 percent over the previous year; that of telecommunication services was 11.623 billion Yuan, up by 12.8 percent. At the end of 2012, there were 3.1102 million fixed telephone users; there were 18.0354 million mobile phone users, of which the number of telecom and China Unicom 3G[5] mobile phone was 3949.7 thousand. The total of domestic tourists was 78.63 million person-times, up by 20.0 percent; that of oversea tourists was 1153.5 thousand person-times, up by 15.1 percent. The revenue from tourism totaled 65.439 billion Yuan, up by 23.4 percent. Of this, the revenue from foreign exchange was 0.749 billion US Dollars, up by 16.8 percent.

VIII. Financial Intermediation

Savings deposit in RMB and foreign currencies in all items of financial institutions totaled 1228.596 billion Yuan at the end of 2012, an increase of 16.7 percent as compared with the end of the previous year. The savings deposit in RMB stood at 1212.553 billion Yan, an increase of 16.3 percent, of which the savings deposit of urban and rural residents was 478.703 billion Yuan, up by 15.2 percent. Loans in all items of financial institutions in RMB and foreign currencies reached 880.804 billion Yuan, an increase of 14.4 percent as compared with the end of the previous year. The loans in RMB stood at 863.522 billion Yuan, an increase of 14.1 percent, of which the short-term loans totaled 191.751 billion Yuan, up by 34.0 percent, and medium -and- long term loans reached 637.888 billion Yuan, up by 10.4 percent. The trading volume of stock exchange market was 881.215 billion Yuan in 2012, a decrease of 10.5 percent as compared with the previous year. There were 29 listed companies in Xi'an at the end of 2012 of which the total capital stock was 21.902 billion Yuan, and the total market value was 178.031 billion Yuan. The were 1.7175 million accounts in stock market at the end of 2012, an increase of 4.1 percent as compared with the end of the previous year.

By the end of 2012, there were 48 insurance institutions, of which the number of property insurance was 23, and that of life insurance was 25. There were 107 intermediary organs of insurance. The received by the insurance companies totaled 17.678 billion Yuan in 2012, up by 6.8 percent. Of this, the revenue from property insurance was 5.570 billion Yuan, up by 16.4 percent; that from life insurance was 12.108 billion Yuan, up by 2.9 percent. In total, insurance companies paid an indemnity worth of 4.961 billion Yuan, up by 29.5 percent over the previous year, of which the worth of property insurance and life insurance were 2.994 billion Yuan and 1.967 billion Yuan respectively, up by 39.2 percent and 17.0 percent respectively.

IX. Education、Science & Technology and Culture

There were 62 general universities and colleges, with 724.0 thousand general tertiary education enrollments, including 186.4 thousand graduates; There were 44 post-graduate training units, with 84.7 thousand student in school and 23.0 thousand graduates. There were 15 adult training units, with 159.8 thousand student in school and 50.5 thousand graduates. there were 419 general middle schools and high schools, with 453.3 thousand junior high education enrollments and 156.4 thousand graduates; there were 1322 primary schools, with 508.5 thousand primary education enrollments and 88.8 thousand graduates. The enrollment rates for school-age population of primary school and junior high school were 99.96 percent and 99.67 percent respectively.

337 science and technology projects were carried out in 2012 (including 26 projects of high technology). Of this, there were 216 projects carried out for technology innovation and achievements transfer. There were 118 high-tech enterprises major supported, 19 technology demonstration towns and 10 important direction projects of industry science and technology in districts and counties implemented. The turnover in technology market reached 30.375 billion Yuan. 15029* patents were applied in 2012, including of 3475 patents accredited.

By the end of 2012, there were 94 museums, 15 public libraries, 13 art-performing groups[6], 15 Cultural center ,181 culture stations. 7846 various kinds of mass cultural activities were organized in 2012. There were 1 television stations, 1 radio broadcasting stations, and 7 radio broadcasting and television stations. The coverage rate of television broadcasting and radio broadcasting were 98.83 percent and 99.45 percent respectively.

260 mass sports performances and competition activities were organized in 2012, and 305 sports competition were organized and host by sports associations, including 22 international and national sports competition. In 2012, there were 40 fitness equipment delivery projects of urban communities, 7 fitness projects for township farmers, and 50 public national fitness paths of community built. There were 8600 social sport instructors, 1600 sites for morning and evening exercise and 140 sites for fitness Qigong, with 6118 taking part in fitness Qigong. In 2012, the delegation of Xi'an won 8 gold medals and 3 silver medals in the National and international Games, of which 2 gold medals and 1 silver medals were gained in London Olympic Games.

X. Health and Sanitation

At the end of 2012, there were 5,576 health institutions in Xi'an, including 376 general hospitals and health centers. There were all 66.4 thousand health care workers, including 23.1 thousand practicing (assistant) doctors. General health centers in Xi'an possessed 44.2 thousand beds. There were 72 social welfare adoption class units, with a total of 11.1thousand beds, and 7554 people were in them at the end of the year. There were 55 thousand of urban low-income households, with 109.3 thousand people, and 535 million Yuan were distributed to them. There were 56.9 thousand of village low-income households, with 174.1 thousand people, and 278 million Yuan were distributed to them. 4517 people were in the rural five guarantees[7] , and 22.91 million Yuan were distributed. 12.4 thousand urban residents and 283.7 thousand rural residents gained medical relief ; XI. Population, Living Conditions and Social Security

The resident population of Xi' an city at the end of 2012 was 8.5529 million, 4.3921 million male and 4.1608 million female, accounted for 51.4 percent and 48.6 percent respectively. The sex ratio was 105.56(granted the female was 100).The born population in the whole year was 86.4 thousand, and the birth rate was 10.13 ‰ .The death population in the whole year was 47.5 thousand, and the death rate was 5.57‰. The net growth of population was 39.5 thousand and the natural growth rate was 4.56‰ . The urban population was 6.1162 million, accounted for 71.51 percent; the rural population was 2.4367 million, accounted for 28.49 percent. The total household population was 7.9598 million, up by 0.5 percent by previous year.

In 2012, the annual per capita disposable income of urban households was 29982 Yuan, or a real increase of 12.3 percent over the previous year when the factors of price increase were deducted, and that of rural households was 11442 Yuan, or a real increase of 13.7 percent. the annual per capita consumer spending of rural households was 21434 Yuan, increased by 11.0 percent, and annual per capita total spending of rural households was 10964 Yuan, increased by 17.0 percent. The annual per capita building area of urban households was 32.98 square meters, and annual per capita living space of rural households was 78 square meters.

Table 7 Urban and rural resident's income in 2008-2012

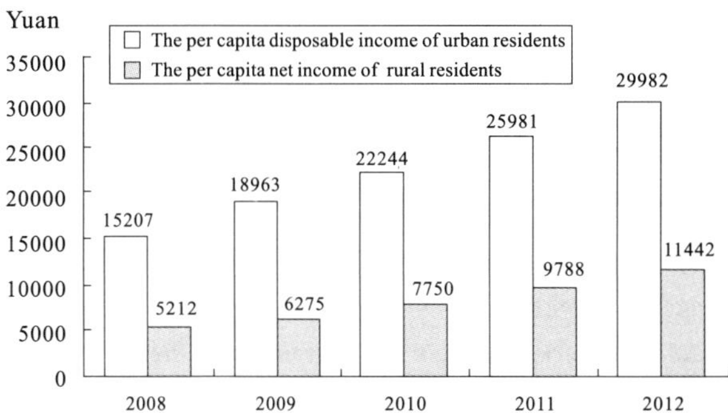

By the end of 2012, a total of 4.1360 million people participated in urban basic health insurance program; a total of 2.4163 million people participated in basic pension program for staff and workers of enterprises; a total of 1.3984 million people participated in unemployment insurance programs; a total of 1.3347 million people participated in work accident insurance; a total of 971.9 thousand people participated in maternity insurance programs for staff and workers. The number of farmers taking part in the new cooperative medical care system in rural areas reached 3.9753 million, with a participation rate of 97.7 percent, hundred percent covered.

XII. Urban Construction, Environment and Work Safety

The total investment of municipal utilities was 25.16 billion Yuan.8 pedestrian bridges and 71 bus harbors were newly built. 15.59 million Square meters area for centralized heating in urban areas was newly added 122 green squares were reformed and newly built. 0.95 million Square meters area for landscaping in urban was newly added.

In 2012, there were 306 days with air quality better than standard Grade II, 1 day more than last year. The annual mean concentration of Sulfur dioxide, Nitrogen dioxide and respirable particulate matter was 0.040 Mg / cu.m, 0.042 Mg / cu.m and 0.118 Mg / cu.m, a decrease by 4.8 percent, 2.4 percent and 0.0 percent. All of water quality of reference water source reached the state standard. The average value of sound level equivalent of regional environmental noises was 55.3 decibel, and the average value of sound level equivalent of transportation noises was 68.2 decibel.

In 2012, various kinds of work accidents amounted to 5029, an increase of 830 as compared with the previous year. Of this, there were 553 people dead, a decrease of 13 person; there were 2,492 people injured, a increase of 221; the property losses was 45.24 million Yuan, a decrease of 17.4347 million Yuan.

Notes:

1. All figures in this Communiqué are preliminary statistics.

2. Gross domestic product (GDP) and value added as quoted in this Communiqué are calculated at current prices, whereas their growth rates are at constant prices.

3.Since 2012, the national bureau of statistics to implement new classification standard of the national economy industry, industry groups changed from 39 to 41, investment in fixed assets (excluding farmers) industry classification also is adjusted according to the new standard.

4. Six highly energy-consuming industries are: manufacture of raw chemical materials and chemical products, manufacture of non-metallic mineral products, smelting and pressing of ferrous metals, smelting and pressing of non-ferrous metals, oil processing, coking and nuclear fuel processing, and production and supply of electricity and heat.

5. 3G refers to the third generation cellular mobile communication system (3rd - generation, referred to as \"3G\"), the 3G mobile phone users refers to those who own using information in the billing system of the final report, and take up the 3G network resources in the network.

6. The data of city's performing arts groups, cultural centers and year-round organize all kinds of activities do not contain that of directly under the units.

7. Rural five guarantees is refers to the elderly, disabled, and those under the age of 16 villagers, without labor ability, the source of life, and has no fixed support, raising, the obligation of maintenance, or its legal support, raising, the obligation of maintenance support, raising, the villagers of bring up ability, who gain help in the care of life and material such as eat, wear, live, medical, and buried.

Data Sources:

In this communiqué, data of price are from NBS Survey Office in Xi'an ;data of newly increased employed people, unemployment rate through unemployment registration and social security are from the Xi'an Municipal Bureau of Human Resources and Social Security; financial data are from the Xi'an Municipal Bureau of Finance; data of imports and exports are from the Xi'an Customs; data of utilizing foreign capital are from the Xi'an Municipal Bureau of Business; data of railway transportation are from the Xi'an Municipal Bureau of Railways; data of highway transportation are from the Xi'an Municipal Bureau of Transport; data of air transport are from the Xi'an-Xian yang International Airport; data of motor vehicles for civilian use are from the Xi'an vehicle administration; data of post services are from the Xi'an Municipal Bureau of post; data of telecommunications are from Xi'an branch of China Mobile、China Unicom、China Telecom, and Shaanxi CTT; data of tourism are from the Xi'an Tourism Administration; data of monetary and financial are from business management department for Xi'an branch of the People's Bank of China; data of listed companies and insurance are from Xi'an Municipal Finance Office; data of education are from the Xi'an Municipal Bureau of Education; data of technology are from Xi'an Municipal Bureau of Technology; data of art-performing groups, public libraries, culture centers, radio and television are from the Xi'an Municipal Bureau of Culture, Radio, Press and Publication; data of museum are from Xi'an Municipal Bureau of Heritage; data of sports are from the Xi'an Municipal Bureau of Sport; data of health and new cooperative medical care system in rural areas are from the Xi'an Municipal Bureau of Health; data of central heating area and green area are from Xi'an Municipal Urban and Rural Construction Committee; data of sewage treatment in urban and environment monitoring are from the Xi'an Municipal Bureau of Environmental Protection; data of work safety are from the State Administration of Work Safety; all the other data are from Xi'an Municipal Bureau of Statistics.

1 综合

GENERAL SURVEY

资料整理：张小文　刘　婷

Data management:Zhang Xiaowen　Liu Ting

第一部分　综合

一、简要说明

本章资料主要包括西安市行政区划、自然地理、自然资源、气象、国民经济和社会发展等综合资料，由西安市统计局综合处根据局内各专业处及有关部门统计资料进行整理和编辑。

二、主要指标

生产总值（亿元）	4366.10	比上年增长	11.8%
农林牧渔业总产值（亿元）	308.36	比上年增长	6.0%
工业增加值（亿元）	1328.71	比上年增长	12.4%
全社会固定资产投资额（亿元）	4243.43	比上年增长	26.8%
社会消费品零售总额（亿元）	2263.86	比上年增长	15.2%
地方财政一般预算收入（亿元）	396.96	比上年增长	24.6%
地方财政一般预算支出（亿元）	597.49	比上年增长	20.8%
出口总额（亿美元）	72.99	比上年增长	25.3%
城镇居民人均可支配收入（元）	29982	比上年增长	15.4%
农村居民人均纯收入（元）	11442	比上年增长	16.9%

1　GENERAL SURVEY

Ⅰ.Brief Introduction

This chapter consists of mainly unified data of administrative divisions, natural geography, natural resources, meteorology, national economy and social development of Xi'an city. It is compiled by Integration Division according to the reported data from other divisions of the Xi'an Bureau of Statistics and other departments of the municipal government.

Ⅱ.Major Indicators

		Increase over Preceding Year
Gross Domestic Product (100 mil. Yuan)	4366.10	11.8%
Gross Output Value of Farming, Forestry, Animal, Husbandry and Fishery (100 mil. Yuan)	308.36	6.0%
Gross Industrial Added Value (100 mil. Yuan)	1328.71	12.4%
Investment Fulfilled In Fixed Assets (100 mil. Yuan)	4243.43	26.8%
Total Retail Sales of Consumer Goods (100 mil. Yuan)	2263.86	15.2%
Local Government Revenue (100 mil. Yuan)	396.96	24.6%
Local Government Expenditures (100 mil. Yuan)	597.49	20.8%
Total Value of Exports (USD 100 mil.)	72.99	25.3%
Per Capita Annual Disposable Income of Urban Households (Yuan)	29982	15.4%
Per Capita Net Income of Rural Residents (Yuan)	11442	16.9%

1-1 行政区划（2012年末）

Administrative Division（End of 2012）

单位：个 (unit)

地　区	Region	乡镇及街道办 Township and Urban Subdistrict Office	镇数 Town	街道办事处 Urban Subdistrict Office	村民委员会 Villagers' Committee	社区居委会 Neighbourhood Committee
西安市	**Xi'an**	**176**	**67**	**109**	**3020**	**728**
（一）市辖区	**Urban Districts**	**108**	**2**	**106**	**1519**	**680**
新城区	Xincheng	9		9	1	104
碑林区	Beilin	8		8		103
莲湖区	Lianhu	9		9	3	129
灞桥区	Baqiao	9		9	223	37
未央区	Weiyang	8		8	103	78
雁塔区	Yanta	8		8	92	119
阎良区	Yanliang	7	2	5	80	23
临潼区	Lintong	23		23	284	37
长安区	Chang'an	22		22	600	33
沣东新城	Fengdongxincheng	5		5	133	17
（二）四县	**Four Counties**	**68**	**65**	**3**	**1501**	**48**
蓝田县	Lantian	22	22		519	9
周至县	Zhouzhi	22	22		376	14
户　县	Huxian	16	16		518	21
高陵县	Gaoling	8	5	3	88	4

注：本表数据来源市民政局。

1-2 土地面积和常住人口密度（2012年）

Statistics on Land Area and Density of Permanent Population（2012）

地 区	Region	土地面积 Area 绝对数（平方公里）Absolute Value (sq.km)	比重（%）Proportion (%)	常住人口（万人）Total of Permanent Population (10 000 persons)	常住人口密度（人/平方公里）Density of Permanent Population (person/sq.km)
西安市	**Xi 'an**	**10108**	**100**	**855.29**	**846**
(一)市区	**Urban Districts**	**3582**	**35.4**	**656.50**	**1833**
新城区	Xincheng	30	0.3	59.44	19813
碑林区	Beilin	24	0.2	62.08	25867
莲湖区	Lianhu	43	0.4	70.25	16337
灞桥区	Baqiao	325	3.2	60.16	1851
未央区	Weiyang	262	2.6	81.46	3109
雁塔区	Yanta	149	1.5	118.89	7979
阎良区	Yanliang	244	2.4	28.23	1157
临潼区	Lintong	915	9.1	66.45	726
长安区	Chang'an	1590	15.7	109.54	689
(二)四县	**Four Counties**	**6526**	**64.6**	**198.79**	**305**
蓝田县	Lantian	2008	19.9	51.88	258
周至县	Zhouzhi	2949	29.2	57.00	193
户 县	Huxian	1282	12.7	56.10	438
高陵县	Gaoling	287	2.8	33.81	1178

注：本表土地面积数据来源市国土资源局。

1-3 自然状况和资源（2012年）

Nature Conditions and Resources（2012）

指　标	Item	2012
一、自然状况	**Nature Conditions**	
土地总面积（平方公里）	Total Land Area (sq.km)	10108
#市区面积	Urban Area	3582
气候（市区）	Climate (Urban Area)	
年平均气温（℃）	Average Annual Temperature (℃)	14.6
年降水量（毫米）	Total Annual Precipitation (mm)	426.7
日照总时数（小时）	Total Sunshine Time (hour)	1546.6
平均风速（米/秒）	Average Wind-speed (m/sec.)	1.2
二、自然资源	**Natural Resources**	
年末实有耕地面积（万亩）	Cultivated Area Year-end (10 000 mu)	369.91
林业用地面积（千公顷）	Area of Forestry (1 000 hectare)	508.39
全市水面面积（万亩）	Whole Water Area (10 000 mu)	4. 58
水资源总量（亿立方米）	Total Water Resource (0.1 billion cu.m)	21. 11
#天然地表水资源总量	Total Savageness Surface Water Resource	17. 74
地下水资源总量（亿立方米）	Total Ground Water Resource (0.1 billion cu.m)	12. 88

注：本表数据来源市气象局、林业局、水务局等。
全市水面面积包括湖泊、水库、鱼塘、城市段河流面积等。

1-4 气象情况（2012年）

Climate Condition（2012）

地 区	Region	平均气温（℃）Average Temperature (℃)	日照时数（小时）Sunshine Time (hour)	降水天数（天）Raining days (day)	年降水量（毫米）Total Annual Precipitation (mm)	平均风速（米/秒）Average Wind-speed (m/second)
市 区	Urban Districts	14.6	1546.6	105	426.7	1.2
临潼区	Lintong	14.0	1819.7	183	484.9	1.6
长安区	Chang'an	13.2	1526.5	116	532.2	1.5
蓝田县	Lantian	13.1	2066.2	103	517.9	1.5
周至县	Zhouzhi	13.3	1534.9	109	211.2	1.0
户 县	Huxian	14.5	1817.0	115	511.4	0.8
高陵县	Gaoling	14.2	2011.2	72	442.4	1.4

注：本表数据来源市气象局（下同）。

1-5 市区及县各月平均气温（2012年）

Average Temperature of Xi'an and the Districts of each Month（2012)

单位：℃ (℃)

月 份	Month	市区 Urban	临潼 Lintong	长安 Chang'an	蓝田 Lantian	周至 Zhouzhi	户县 Huxian	高陵 Gaoling
一月	January	-0.4	-1.1	-1.5	-0.2	-1.4	-0.5	-1.1
二月	February	2.5	1.9	1.0	0.4	1.5	2.2	1.9
三月	March	8.6	8.3	7.5	7.3	7.6	8.4	8.4
四月	April	18.1	17.9	16.8	15.5	16.9	18.2	17.7
五月	May	22.2	21.6	20.7	20.0	20.5	21.8	21.5
六月	June	27.3	26.4	25.9	25.9	25.5	27.3	26.9
七月	July	27.9	27.4	26.3	27.2	26.4	27.6	27.9
八月	August	26.0	25. 0	24.4	24.8	24.5	25.7	25.8
九月	September	20.2	19.4	18.9	19.3	19.0	20.2	20.0
十月	October	15.3	14.5	13.7	13.9	13.8	15.2	14.8
十一月	November	6.8	6.3	5.5	5.1	5.5	6.7	6.4
十二月	December	1.2	0.5	0.0	-0.7	-0.3	0.9	0.6

1-6 市区及县各月日照时数（2012年）

Sunshine Duration of Xi'an and the Districts of each Month（2012）

单位：小时 (hour)

月 份	Month	市区 Urban	临潼 Lintong	长安 Chang'an	蓝田 Lantian	周至 Zhouzhi	户县 Huxian	高陵 Gaoling
一月	January	81.0	61.2	81.0	114.9	66.1	92.1	100.0
二月	February	76.0	78.0	75.1	104.0	65.5	97.8	138.6
三月	March	121.8	130.5	121.4	163.9	111.7	133.5	161.4
四月	April	187.3	243.8	199.9	241.9	207.9	217.6	231.4
五月	May	132.5	146.5	177.2	182.4	160.4	170.2	178.3
六月	June	171.5	254.0	204.5	255.9	200.7	226.5	239.5
七月	July	128.8	195.3	161.1	225.6	117.9	141.5	170.1
八月	August	127.4	167.2	119.0	152.6	75.7	108.5	188.5
九月	September	135.7	135.7	166.4	196.5	139.0	150.6	169.0
十月	October	117.2	111.8	142.5	150.9	118.8	143.9	144.9
十一月	November	148.4	159.3	154.3	143.3	148.3	170.7	130.0
十二月	December	119.0	136.4	124.1	134.3	122.9	164.1	159.5

1-7 市区及县各月降水天数（2012年）

Precipitation Days of Xi'an and the Districts of each Month（2012）

单位：天 (day)

月 份	Month	市区 Urban	临潼 Lintong	长安 Chang'an	蓝田 Lantian	周至 Zhouzhi	户县 Huxian	高陵 Gaoling
一月	January	5	5	5	6	7	6	2
二月	February	2	2	5	5	4	6	1
三月	March	8	15	10	9	10	10	7
四月	April	8	10	6	6	8	8	2
五月	May	13	23	15	14	18	16	10
六月	June	8	10	8	6	8	9	5
七月	July	14	34	15	13	14	15	11
八月	August	11	22	11	8	10	11	7
九月	September	13	31	14	13	12	12	12
十月	October	11	15	12	10	9	11	8
十一月	November	7	14	8	7	6	7	5
十二月	December	5	2	7	6	3	4	2

1-8 市区及县各月降水量（2012年）

Amount of Precipitation of Xi'an and the Districts of each Month（2012）

单位：毫米 (mm)

月 份	Month	市区 Urban	临潼 Lintong	长安 Chang'an	蓝田 Lantian	周至 Zhouzhi	户县 Huxian	高陵 Gaoling
一月	January	5.0	3.9	8.4	7.2	15.9	12.7	5.5
二月	February	0.3	0.7	1.5	1.5	1.4	1.1	0.2
三月	March	14.5	17.2	9.0	12.7	2.0	12.3	17.4
四月	April	21.0	27.0	29.2	16.7	1.3	17.1	16.8
五月	May	55.8	51.5	80.8	72.5	7.7	70.1	63.4
六月	June	22.6	29.3	28.7	22.4	28.1	35.0	20.8
七月	July	84.4	124.3	141.8	148.5	6.9	65.6	98.9
八月	August	102.9	92.9	89.6	80.8	30.4	158.7	88.8
九月	September	83.8	94.6	94.6	109.1	98.9	96.8	102.1
十月	October	17.1	20.0	36.1	22.1	13.5	23.3	16.1
十一月	November	18.0	22.6	20.3	21.4	4.3	18.3	11.1
十二月	December	1.3	0.9	1.2	3.0	0.8	0.4	1.3

1-9 市区及县各月平均风速（2012年）

Average Wind Velocity of Xi'an and the Districts of each Month（2012）

单位：米/秒 (m/s)

月 份	Month	市区 Urban Districts	临潼 Lintong	长安 Chang'an	蓝田 Lantian	周至 Zhouzhi	户县 Huxian	高陵 Gaoling
一月	January	0.9	1.2	1.3	0.8	0.8	0.5	0.8
二月	February	1.1	1.6	1.6	1.2	1.0	0.7	1.1
三月	March	1.3	2.0	1.6	1.7	1.3	0.9	1.7
四月	April	1.3	1.8	1.8	1.9	1.3	1.1	1.5
五月	May	1.3	1.6	1.5	1.7	1.1	1.0	1.3
六月	June	1.4	1.8	1.5	1.9	1.3	1.0	1.6
七月	July	1.3	2.0	1.4	1.9	1.0	0.9	1.7
八月	August	1.3	1.7	1.2	1.3	0.7	0.7	1.9
九月	September	1.3	1.5	1.3	1.5	0.8	0.8	1.6
十月	October	1.0	1.2	1.2	1.3	0.7	0.6	1.3
十一月	November	1.1	1.6	1.6	1.3	1.1	0.5	1.4
十二月	December	1.1	1.4	1.6	1.1	1.1	0.5	1.4

1-10 国有土地使用权出让、划拨情况

Basic Statistics on Lease and Administrative Allocation of Use Right of State-Owned Land

项　　目	Item	2000	2005	2006	2007	2008	2009	2010	2011	2012
国有土地使用权出让	**Lease of the Use Right of State-owned Land**									
出让地块(宗)	Land leased (item)	202	312	316	333	278	297	386	474	581
协议	Agreement	200	241	225	171	119	100	173	133	80
招标	Invitation for Bid				1	3		3		
拍卖	Auction	2	8	7	3	5	1	11		
挂牌交易	Listed Transaction		63	84	158	149	196	199	341	500
出让面积（公顷）	Area of Totally Leased Land (hectare)	3115	986	1208	843	809	1047	1364	1386	1853
土地使用权出让总收入（万元）	**Total Revenue from Leasing of the Use Right(10 000 yuan)**	**38428**	**89039**	**156231**	**267666**	**309181**	**284405**	**358098**	**334069**	**218817**
国有土地使用权划拨	**Administrative Allocation of the Use Right of State-owned Land**									
划拨地块（宗）	Land Allocated (item)	113	100	90	100	102	79	108	253	154
划拨面积（公顷）	Area of Land Allocated(hectare)	12543	835	259	388	455	1721	1027	1426	1617

注：本表数据来源市国土资源局。

1-11 国民经济和社会发展总量与速度指标

指 标	Item	总量指标			
		1995	2000	2005	2008
人口与就业	**Population and Employment**				
人口	**Population**				
年底总人口(万人)	Population at the Year-end (10 000 persons)	648.21	688.01	741.73	772.30
非农业人口	Non-agricultural Population	255.71	285.79	333.14	363.87
农业人口	Agriculturral Population	392.50	402.22	408.59	408.43
男性人口	Male	334.75	355.18	382.02	395.54
女性人口	Female	313.46	332.83	359.71	376.76
就业	**Employment**				
全社会从业人员数(万人)	Employment(10 000 persons)	372.60	389.10	415.83	448.05
#全部单位在岗职工人数	Number of Employed Staff and Workers	141.17	109.62	119.73	126.89
城镇登记失业人数(万人)	Registered Unemployed in Urban Areas(10 000 persons)	5.92	3.85	8.45	9.40
宏观经济	**Macroeconomic Indicator**				
国民经济核算	**National Accounts**				
生产总值(亿元)	Gross Domestic Product(100 mil. yuan)	330.35	646.13	1313.93	2318.14
第一产业	Primary Industry	41.40	44.65	66.01	103.45
第二产业	Secondary Industry	135.33	277.13	540.50	981.58
工业	Industry	112.50	218.44	420.00	721.40
第三产业	Tertiary Industry	153.62	324.35	707.42	1233.11
#最终消费	Total Consumption	239.64	413.43	766.62	1182.61
资本形成总额	Total Investment	151.55	287.82	839.01	1837.86
固定资产投资	**Investment in Fixed Assets**				
全社会固定资产投资总额(亿元)	Total Investment in Fixed Assets(100 mil. yuan)	103.42	232.37	835.10	1906.36
一、城镇	Urban Area	88.50	203.01	776.33	1786.60
#房地产	Real Estate	21.65	51.85	225.23	540.26
二、农村	Rural Area	14.92	29.36	58.77	119.76
在固定资产投资中:国有经济	State-Owned	69.08	159.60	373.70	694.89
集体经济	Collective-Owned	9.78	14.65	59.23	246.89
个体经济	Self-employed Individual	11.13	24.40	79.04	50.43
其他经济	Other	13.43	33.72	323.13	914.15
财政	**Public Finance**				
地方财政一般预算收入(亿元)	General Budgetary Revenue of Local Government (100 mil. yuan)	18.21	46.80	72.92	145.61
地方财政一般预算支出(亿元)	General Budgetary Expenditure of Local Government (100 mil. yuan)	18.42	52.00	97.61	226.99
总收入					
物价指数(上年=100)	**Price Indices(preceding year=100)**				
商品零售价格指数	Retail Price Index	114.6	98.7	99.7	105.4
居民消费价格指数	Consumer Price Index	117.0	100.2	100.3	106.0
工业生产者出厂价格指数	Producer Price Indices (PPI) for Manufactured Goods	110.8	99.4	103.9	103.7
利用外资	**Utilization of Foreign Capital**				
利用外资签定协议额(万美元)	Amount of Foreign Capital for Utilization Through Signed Contracts or Agreements(USD 10 000)	28956	54123	121499	118230
外商实际直接投资额(万美元)	Amount of Foreign Capital Actually Utilized (USD 10 000)	18653	15633	57113	114738

注：国民经济核算2004—2008年为全国第二次经济普查修订数据。
2009年及以前年份财政收支为一般预算收支与基金预算收支之和。
由于2010年固定资产投资起报点的变化，指数和平均增长速度为可比口径计算。

Principal Aggregate Indicators on National Economic and Social Development and Their Related Indices and Growth Rates

Aggregate Data				速度指标（%）				Indices and Growth Rates		
				指数Index（2012比以下各年） (2012 as percentage of the following years)				平均增长速度 Average Annual Growth Rate		
2009	2010	2011	2012	2000	2005	2010	2011	2001-2005	2006-2010	2011-2012
781.67	782.73	791.83	795.98	115.7	107.3	101.7	100.5	1.5	1.1	0.8
370.66	374.64	391.31	392.04	137.2	117.7	104.6	100.2	3.1	2.4	2.3
411.01	408.09	400.52	403.94	100.4	98.9	99.0	100.9	0.3	-0.02	-0.5
399.28	398.80	402.52	397.58	111.9	104.1	99.7	98.8	1.5	0.9	-0.2
382.39	383.93	389.31	398.40	119.7	110.8	103.8	102.3	1.6	1.3	1.9
462.52	477.58	495.99	514.57	132.2	123.7	107.7	103.7	1.3	2.8	3.8
129.62	130.70	154.33	155.28	141.7	129.7	118.8	100.6	1.8	1.8	9.0
10.02	10.46	10.37	9.60	249.4	113.6	91.8	92.6	17.0	4.4	-4.2
2724.08	3241.69	3862.58	4366.10	481.1	255.6	127.2	111.8	13.5	15.0	12.8
110.38	140.06	173.14	195.59	191.0	154.8	113.1	106.0	4.3	6.5	6.3
1144.75	1406.72	1674.31	1881.75	536.6	264.6	128.5	111.8	15.2	15.5	13.3
816.92	1003.57	1189.61	1328.71	513.3	257.2	130.6	112.4	14.8	14.5	14.3
1468.95	1694.91	2015.13	2288.76	476.4	258.5	127.2	112.2	13.0	15.2	12.8
1403.10	1598.51	1856.91	2092.97	340.4	222.3	121.3	109.9	8.9	12.9	10.1
2281.91	2835.42	3264.83	3783.10	924.0	348.5	122.7	113.2	21.5	23.2	10.8
2500.13	3250.56	3346.26	4243.43	2305.6	641.5	164.8	126.8	29.2	31.2	28.4
2367.58	3104.92	3207.97	4107.54	2586.4	676.3	169.1	128.0	50.8	31.9	30.0
696.34	842.34	996.81	1281.90	2472.3	569.2	152.2	128.6	34.1	30.2	23.4
132.55	145.64	138.29	135.89	462.8	231.2	93.3	98.3	14.9	19.9	-3.4
932.91	1348.76	1204.80	1661.22	1314.2	561.3	155.5	137.9	18.5	29.3	24.7
289.91	326.44	258.15	194.71	1678.0	415.0	75.3	75.4	32.2	40.7	-13.2
97.86	54.73	74.64	82.72	428.0	132.1	190.8	110.8	26.5	-7.1	38.1
1179.45	1520.63	1808.67	2304.78	8629.6	900.5	191.4	127.4	57.1	36.3	38.3
181.40	241.86	318.55	396.96	848.2	544.4	164.1	124.6	9.3	27.1	28.1
276.85	371.62	494.58	597.49	1149.0	612.1	160.8	120.8	13.4	30.7	26.8
99.5	102.7	104.4	102.3							
99.7	103.5	105.6	102.8							
99.9	102.3	102.5	100.5							
60027	119689	120083	360264	665.6	296.5	301.0	300.0	17.6	-0.3	73.5
121872	156653	200522	247800	1585.1	433.9	158.2	123.6	29.6	22.4	25.8

1-11 续表1

指　标	Item	总量指标			
		1995	2000	2005	2008
产　业	**Industry**				
农业	**Agriculture**				
耕地面积(万亩)	Cultivated Areas(10 000 hectares)	463.97	443.37	400.17	390.77
乡村劳动力资源总数（万人）	Total Number of Rural Labor Source (10 000 persons)	213.80	240.76	255.93	256.17
农林牧渔及服务业总产值 (亿元)	Gross Output Value of Farming Forestry, Animal Husbandry and Fishery(100 mil yuan)	75.46	74.37	106.54	168.27
主要农产品产量(万吨)	Output of Major Farm Products(10 000 tons)				
粮　食	Grain	175.30	201.90	205.50	214.40
奶　类	Milk	13.29	24.59	42.22	58.97
油　料	Oil-bearing Crops	2.17	1.34	1.16	1.15
蔬　菜	Vegetables	133.60	162.14	195.70	221.53
水　果	Fruits	24.10	34.35	51.28	71.69
肉　类	Meat	12.78	14.75	18.20	11.54
水产品	Aquatic Products	0.85	1.14	0.94	1.25
工业	**Industry**				
全部工业总产值（亿元）	Gross industrial Output Value(100 mil. yuan)	405.90	639.48	1308.56	2388.14
规模以上工业企业主要经济指标	Principal Indicators of Industrial Enterprises of State Ownership and Non-state-owned Above Designated Size (100 mil. yuan)				
工业增加值（亿元）	Value Added of Industrial(100 mil. yuan)		130. 18	314.01	605.25
资产总计（亿元）	Total Assets(100 mil. yuan)		958.05	1503.85	2426.13
主营业务收入（亿元）	Revenue from Principal Business(100 mil. yuan)		420.42	980.97	1928.05
利润总额（亿元）	Profits(100 mil. yuan)		16.11	28.72	84.89
从业人员年平均人数 （万人）	Annual Average Employers(10 000 persons)		43.25	37.92	40.17
主要工业产品产量	Output of Major Industrial Products				
布(万米)	Cloth(10 000 m)	30332	24818	27012	22721
机制纸及纸板(吨)	Machine-Made Paper(ton)	364400	54711	221865	442758
家用电冰箱(台)	Household Refrigerators(unit)	13000	5860	25407	100854
发电量(亿千瓦时)	Electricity(100 million kwh)	22.00	19.00	48.00	71.69
钢材(吨)	Steel Products(ton)	314400	100000	240182	478819
汽车(万辆)	Motor Vehicle (10 000 units)	0.3	0.9	4.1	26.8
建筑业	**Construction**				
建筑业企业从业人数(人)	Number of Employed Persons(person)		136718	158311	400740
建筑业总产值(亿元)	Gross Output Value(100 mil. yuan)	42.55	105.93	326.65	915.19
房屋建筑施工面积 (万平方米)	Floor Space of Buildings under Construction (10 000 sq.m)	601.70	793.30	1801.20	3133.90
房屋建筑竣工面积 (万平方米)	Floor Space of Buildings Completed (10 000 sq.m)	177.15	336.80	569.01	1056.53

continued 1

Aggregate Data				速度指标（%）				Indices and Growth Rates		
2009	2010	2011	2012	指数Index（2012比以下各年）(2012 as percentage of the following years)				平均增长速度 Average Annual Growth Rate		
				2000	2005	2010	2011	2001-2005	2006-2010	2011-2012
387.89	383.32	377.10	369.91	83.4	92.4	96.5	98.1	-2.0	-0.9	-1.8
255.00	256.36	260.97	259.06	107.6	101.2	101.1	99.3	1.2	0.04	0.5
178.70	227.10	272.66	308.36	197.3	157.3	113.0	106.0	5.1	6.8	16.5
218.20	221.70	182.04	192.55	95.4	93.7	86.9	105.8	0.4	1.5	-6.8
61.82	63.37	64.80	66.64	271.0	157.8	105.2	102.8	11.4	8.5	2.5
1.12	1.20	1.17	1.02	76.1	87.9	85.0	87.2	-2.8	0.7	-7.8
242.41	253.10	261.66	277.80	171.3	142.0	109.8	106.2	3.8	5.3	4.8
78.96	84.78	91.14	93.21	271.4	181.8	109.9	102.3	8.3	10.6	4.9
12.62	13.65	14.46	15.17	102.8	83.4	111.1	104.9	4.2	-5.6	5.4
1.30	1.19	1.18	1.40	122.8	148.9	117.6	118.6	-3.8	4.8	8.5
2827.07	3562.88	4093.32	4656.08	666.9	341.5	130.8	113.8	14.3	21.2	14.3
700.13	862.28	1012.58	1132.44							
2913.56	3592.13	3975.38	4775.92	498.5	317.6	133.0	120.1	9.4	19.0	15.3
2384.52	3011.19	3381.27	3758.50	894.0	383.1	124.8	111.2	18.5	25.1	11.7
177.20	245.37	172.94	167.77	1041.4	584.2	68.4	97.0	12.3	53.6	-17.3
43.42	47.11	50.42	49.23	113.8	129.8	104.5	97.6	-2.6	4.4	2.2
22202	23810	16344	14300	57.8	53.1	60.2	87.5	1.7	-2.5	-22.4
476258	495966	497882	276000	504.0	124.4	55.6	55.4	32.3	17.5	-16.8
92146	107571	72218	157652	2690.3	620.5	146.6	218.3	34.1	33.5	21.1
83.21	96.94	95.01	99.48	523.6	207.3	102.6	104.7	20.4	15.1	1.3
1105074	1107663	184753	313000	313.0	130.3	28.3	169.4	19.2	35.8	-47.2
50.7	65.2	55.7	54.2	6018.9	1321.2	83.1	97.3	35.4	73.9	-8.9
461080	539000	372088	391199	286.1	247.1	72.6	105.1	3.0	27.8	-14.8
1296.58	1820.35	1619.09	1874.23	1769.3	573.8	103.0	115.8	25.3	41.0	1.5
3947.01	4592.57	6218.70	7531.07	949.3	418.1	164.0	121.1	17.8	20.6	28.1
1209.88	1391.91	2392.39	1985.31	589.5	348.9	142.6	83.0	11.1	19.6	19.4

1-11 续表2

指 标	Item	总量指标			
		1995	2000	2005	2008
交通运输	**Transportation**				
货运量(万吨)	Freight Traffic(10 000 tons)	9590	6999	12051	27560
铁 路	Railways	3317	3101	540	605
公 路	Highways	6268	3890	11505	26949
民用航空	Civil Aviation	5	8	6	6
客运量(万人次)	Passenger Traffic(10 000 persons-times)	9069	8068	10479	26501
铁 路	Railways	2678	2130	1796	2680
公 路	Highways	6128	5578	8294	23175
民用航空	Civil Aviation	263	360	389	646
邮电通信业	**Post and Telecommunication Services**				
邮电业务总量(亿元)	Total Business Revenue(100 mil. yuan)	7.65	46.16	132.04	264.67
函 件(万件)	Number of Letters Delivered(10 000 pieces)	14647	8230	9526	5638
本地电话局用交换机容量 (万门)	Capacity of Local Office Telephone Exchanges (10 000 line)	58.3	204.8	457.3	462.5
本地固定电话年末用户(万户)	Local fixed telephone end users (million)	30.79	141.28	321.48	306.88
城市电话用户	Urban Telephone Subscribers	29.15	124.26	271.40	268.49
乡村电话用户	Rural Telephone Subscribers	0.84	17.02	50.08	38.39
移动电话用户(万户)	Number of Mobile Telephone Subscribers (10 000 subscribers)		73.10	419.96	737.76
互联网年末宽带用户(万户)	Number of Subscribers of Intemet Services (10 000 subscribers)			33.93	81.40
国内商业	**Domestic Trade**				
社会消费品零售总额 (亿元)	Total Retail Sales of Consumer Goods (100 mil. yuan)	186.60	360.42	670.56	1176.58
对外经济贸易	**Foreign Trade**				
进出口总额(万美元)	Total Exports and Imports(USD 10 000)	137510	173696	390146	704029
出口额	Exports	110163	106062	263441	447113
进口额	Imports	27347	67634	126705	256916
国际旅游	**International Tourism**				
国际旅游者人数(万人次)	Number of International Tourists(10 000 persons)	41.35	65.03	77.56	63.20
国际旅游收入(亿元)	Foreign Exchange Earnings from Tourism (10 000yuan)	10.38	22.41	33.54	28.72
金融业	**Financial Intermediation**				
金融机构（不含外资）人民币存款余额(亿元)	Balance of Deposits in Domestic Funded Financial Institutions (100 mil. yuan)	359.51	1335.63	3599.70	5788.43
金融机构（不含外资）人民币贷款余额 (亿元)	Balance of Loans in Domestic Funded Financial Institutions (100 mil. yuan)	334.50	972.52	2158.10	3267.89

注：2006年铁路数据按新口径统计；
2006年国际互联网络用户改为互联网宽带用户。

continued 2

Aggregate Data				速度指标（%） Indices and Growth Rates						
2009	2010	2011	2012	指数Index（2012比以下各年） (2012 as percentage of the following years)				平均增长速度 Average Annual Growth Rate		
				2000	2005	2010	2011	2001-2005	2006-2010	2011-2012
30606	34323	39231	44924	641.9	372.8	130.9	114.5	11.5	23.3	14.4
614	706	823	825	26.6	152.8	116.9	100.2	-29.5	5.5	8.1
29986	33610	38399	44082	1133.2	383.2	131.2	114.8	24.2	23.9	14.5
6	7	9	17	212.5	283.3	242.9	188.9	-5.6	3.1	55.8
28693	30294	33375	36154	448.1	345.0	119.3	108.3	5.4	23.7	9.2
2585	2781	2861	2919	137.0	162.5	105.0	102.0	-3.4	9.1	2.5
25271	26536	29358	30893	553.8	372.5	116.4	105.2	8.3	26.2	7.9
837	977	1156	2342	650.6	602.1	239.7	202.6	1.6	20.2	54.8
298.92	323.11	200.50	216.20	468.4	163.7	66.9	107.8	23.4	19.6	-18.2
6128	8176	3061	2769	33.6	29.1	33.9	90.5	3.0	-3.0	-41.8
441.1	449.0	441.5	878.3	428.9	192.1	195.6	198.9	17.4	-0.4	39.9
289.10	261.77	270.36	311.02	220.1	96.7	118.8	115.0	17.9	-4.0	9.0
253.28	228.27	238.34	277.43	223.3	102.2	121.5	116.4	16.9	-3.4	10.2
35.82	33.50	32.02	33.59	197.4	67.1	100.3	104.9	24.1	-7.7	0.1
1120.06	1423.08	1614.15	1803.54	2467.2	429.5	126.7	111.7	41.9	27.6	12.6
116.79	146.18	184.10	202.31		596.3	138.4	109.9		33.9	17.6
1381.12	1637.04	1965.98	2263.86	628.1	337.6	138.3	115.2	13.2	19.5	17.6
724618	1039273	1260179	1301446	749.3	333.6	125.2	103.3	17.6	21.6	11.9
333114	531729	582662	729878	688.2	277.1	137.3	125.3	20.0	15.1	17.2
391504	507544	677517	571568	845.1	451.1	112.6	84.4	13.4	32.0	6.1
67.29	84.18	100.23	115.35	177.4	148.7	137.0	115.1	3.6	1.7	17.1
31.05	42.40	51.28	59.89	267.2	178.6	141.3	116.8	8.4	4.8	18.8
7457.71	8863.36	10350.80	12044.68	901.8	334.6	135.9	116.4	21.9	19.7	16.6
4436.50	6420.72	7496.25	8559.24	880.1	396.6	133.3	114.2	17.3	24.4	15.5

1-11 续表3

指 标	Item	总量指标			
		1995	2000	2005	2008
保险公司保费收入(亿元)	insurance premium income (100 million Yuan)	4.70	13.58	44.94	101.45
保险公司赔款及给付支出金额(亿元)	insurance and compensation paid to Amount (100 million Yuan)	1.70	1.39	9.50	25.92
教育、科技、文化	**Education, Science and Technology and Culture**				
教育	**Education**				
专任教师数(人)	Full-time Teachers(person)				
#普通高等学校	Institutions of Higher Education	15914	15679	29498	38926
普通中等专业教育学校	Regular Specialized Secondary Schools	2533	3172	2130	1904
普通中等教育学校	Regular Secondary Education Schools	21984	26230	31094	31425
小 学	Primary Schools	30270	30215	29647	30382
在校学生数(万人)	Students Enrollment(10 000 person)				
#普通高等学校	Institutions of Higher Education	11.67	19.41	53.06	66.68
普通中等专业教育学校	Regular Specialized Secondary Schools	3.74	6.02	6.16	8.06
普通中等教育学校	Regular Secondary Education Schools	32.32	48.31	55.74	52.80
小 学	Primary Schools	79.36	77.81	60.47	54.66
科技	**Science and Technology**				
认定的高新技术企业(个)	Hi-tech Enterprises (unit)				
企事业单位累计授权专利数（件）	Accumulated patents awarded(unit)	3164	6139	11670	19256
文化	**Culture**				
图书馆总藏量(千册件)	Total Collections in Library (1000 Volume-time)	2830	3214	3671	4040
文化馆、站（个）	Cultural Centers or Stations (unit)	201	251	192	197
电视节目制作时间(小时)	Time for TV Programs Production(hour)	5738	11871	27377	26897
家庭、生活、环境	**Family, People's Livelihood and Environment**				
家庭	**Family**				
家庭总户数 (万户)	Total Number of Households(10 000 household)	171.25	187.08	203.04	216.52
城镇居民平均每户家庭人口(人)	Average Household Size in Urban Areas(person)	3.88	2.99	2.93	2.82
农村居民平均每户家庭人口(人)	Average Household Size in Rural Areas(person)	4.60	4.30	4.22	4.03
婚姻	**Marriages and Divorces**				
结婚对数(对)	Register Number of Marriages(couple)	47236	46415	49962	77912
离婚对数(对)	Number of Divorces(couple)	4296	5161	12747	15722
居住	**Housing**				
城镇居民人均现住房总建筑面积(平方米)	Per Capita Total Building Area of Urban Residents' Houses(sq.m)	13.05	14.82	16.38	26.32
农村居民人均居住面积(平方米)	Per Capita Net Floor Space of Rural Residents(sq.m)	21.77	28.31	36.73	54.97

注：2008年及以前图书馆总藏量为图书馆藏书量。

2005年以前城镇居民人均现住房总建筑面积为城镇人均住房使用面积。

continued 3

Aggregate Data				速度指标（%）				Indices and Growth Rates		
2009	2010	2011	2012	指数Index（2012比以下各年）(2012 as percentage of the following years)				平均增长速度 Average Annual Growth Rate		
				2000	2005	2010	2011	2001-2005	2006-2010	2011-2012
122.11	129.38	162.57	173.21	1275.5	385.4	133.9	106.5	27.0	23.6	15.7
25.16	26.39	37.14	47.55	3420.9	500.5	180.2	128.0	46.9	22.7	34.2
40605	42098	42734	44487	283.7	150.8	105.7	104.1	13.5	7.4	2.8
1720	1845	1723	1595	50.3	74.9	86.4	92.6	-7.7	-2.8	-7.0
31415	31506	31675	31526	120.2	101.4	100.1	99.5	3.5	0.3	0.03
30334	29944	29900	29651	98.1	100.0	99.0	99.2	-0.4	0.2	-0.5
70.31	73.30	76.60	80.70	415.8	152.1	110.1	105.4	22.3	6.7	4.9
7.44	6.75	6.11	5.43	90.2	88.1	80.4	88.9	0.5	1.9	-10.3
50.63	48.89	47.20	45.33	93.8	81.3	92.7	96.0	2.9	-2.6	-3.7
52.52	51.56	51.39	50.85	65.4	84.1	98.6	98.9	-4.9	-3.1	-0.7
	827	978	917			110.9	93.8			5.3
23962	31999	41273	53118	865.3	455.2	166.0	128.7	13.7	22.4	28.8
4324	4465	4907	6123	190.5	166.8	137.1	124.8	2.7	4.0	17.1
197	197	196	197	78.5	102.6	100.0	100.5	-5.2	0.6	...
27131	29626	43925	30091	253.5	109.9	101.6	68.5	18.2	1.6	0.8
221.51	226.71	234.34	239.54	128.0	118.0	105.7	102.2	1.7	2.2	2.8
2.84	2.81	2.83	2.76	92.3	94.2	98.2	97.5	-0.4	-0.8	-0.9
4.07	3.94	3.97	4.09	95.1	96.9	103.8	103.0	-0.4	-1.4	1.9
88138	83645	94398	89877	193.6	179.9	107.5	95.2	1.5	10.9	3.7
15796	19060	19421	18579	354.2	143.4	95.9	94.1	19.8	8.4	-2.1
28.40	28.70	28.90	32.98	222.5	201.3	114.9	114.1	2.0	11.9	7.2
56.73	66.73	67.00	78.00	275.5	212.4	116.9	116.4	5.3	12.7	8.1

1-11 续表4

指 标	Item	总量指标			
		1995	2000	2005	2008
生活	**People's Livelihood**				
城镇居民人均可支配收入(元)	Per Capita Annual Disposable Income of Urban Households (yuan)	4153	6364	9628	15207
农村居民人均纯收入(元)	Per Capita Net Income of Rural Residents(yuan)	1353	2344	3460	5212
城乡居民人民币储蓄存款余额(亿元)	Savings Deposit of Urban and Rural Households (100 mil. yuan)	230.63	675.83	1716.76	2513.70
工资	**Wages and Welfare**				
在岗职工工资总额(亿元)	The Gross Salary of Workers (100 mil. yuan)	67.23	101.68	211.14	373.24
城镇非私营单位在岗职工年平均工资(元)	Aunual Average Wage of Stuff and Workers in Urban Non-privite Enterprises(yuan)	4763	9179	17728	29749
卫生	**Health Care**				
医院、卫生院(个)	Number of Hospitals(unit)	368	426	479	432
执业（助理）医师（人）	Licensed (Assistant) Doctors (person)	18846	18750	17730	18066
医院、卫生院床位数(张)	Number of Hospital Beds(unit)	28265	28697	30087	32998
市政建设	**City Construction**				
自来水供应量(万立方米)	Volume of Tap Water Supply(10 000 cu.m)	35885	30273	35776	36471
自来水供水管道长度(公里)	Length of Water Supply Pipelines(km)	1066	2237	2315	2385
城市天然气供气量 (万立方米)	Volume of Natural Gas Supply in Urban Areas (10 000 cu.m)	8419	11513	53202	84874
公交运营汽(电)车总数(辆)	Total Number of Public Buses and Trolley Buses(unit)	977	2573	4762	6123
道路长度(公里)	Length of Paved Roads(km)	835	975	1382	2115
绿地面积(公顷)	Areas of Green Land(hectare)	5603	4116	4867	9199
环境、灾害	**Environment and Disaster**				
工业废水排放量(万吨)	Volume of Waste Water up to the Standard for Discharge(10 000 tons)	12479	9145	16969	18304
火灾发生数(起)	Number of Fire Disasters(case)	426	1040	2664	1537
火灾事故损失额（万元）	Fire Loss(10 000 yuan)	742.1	472.4	1565.5	1907.7
交通事故发生数（起）	Number of Traffic Accidents(case)	3065	4099	4903	2576
交通事故损失额（万元）	Loss of Traffic Accidents(10 000 yuan)	1103.2	1116.1	2024.4	522.8

continued 4

Aggregate Data				速度指标（%）				Indices and Growth Rates		
				指数Index（2012比以下各年）(2012 as percentage of the following years)				平均增长速度 Average Annual Growth Rate		
2009	2010	2011	2012	2000	2005	2010	2011	2001-2005	2006-2010	2011-2012
18963	22244	25981	29982	471.1	311.4	134.8	115.4	8.6	18.2	16.1
6275	7750	9788	11442	488.1	330.7	147.6	116.9	8.1	17.5	21.5
3084.20	3641.09	4155.65	4787.03	708.3	278.8	131.5	115.2	20.5	16.2	14.7
439.74	501.76	629.35	742.16	729.9	351.5	147.9	117.9	15.7	18.9	21.6
34032	37870	41679	44533	485.2	251.2	117.6	106.8	14.1	16.4	8.4
415	412	368	376	88.3	78.5	91.3	102.2	2.4	-3.0	-4.5
19284	18763	21551	23051	122.9	130.0	122.9	107.0	-1.1	1.1	10.8
34904	36796	37264	40585	141.4	134.9	110.3	108.9	1.0	4.1	5.0
38307	41089	38934	45792	151.3	128.0	111.4	117.6	3.4	2.8	5.6
1985	2416	2721	3208	143.4	138.6	132.8	117.9	0.7	0.9	15.2
95885	109052	120330	142263	1235.7	267.4	130.5	118.2	35.8	15.4	14.2
7039	7107	7462	7695	299.1	161.6	108.3	103.1	13.1	8.3	4.1
2296	2662	2755	3119	319.9	225.7	117.2	113.2	7.2	14.0	8.2
9553	12140	13680	15196	369.2	312.2	125.2	111.1	3.4	20.1	11.9
13168	13840	13148	10224	111.8	60.3	73.9	77.8	13.2	-4.0	-14.1
1485	1825	1920	2568	246.9	96.4	140.7	133.8	20.7	-7.3	18.6
1850.6	2224.2	1587.2	1206.5	255.4	77.1	54.2	76.0	27.1	7.3	-26.3
2702	2323	2264	2446	59.7	49.9	105.3	108.0	3.6	-13.9	2.6
851.7	736.6	611.9	1011.1	90.6	49.9	137.3	165.2	12.6	-18.3	17.2

1-12 国民经济和社会发展结构指标

Structural Indicators on National Economic and Social Development

单位: % (%)

指　　标	Item	1995	2000	2005	2008	2009	2010	2011	2012
人口与就业	**Population and Employment**								
人口	**Population**								
农业与非农业结构	Structure								
农业	Agriculture	60.55	58.46	55.09	52.88	52.58	52.14	50.58	50.75
非农业	Non-Agriculture	39.45	41.54	44.91	47.12	47.42	47.86	49.42	49.25
性别结构	Sexual Structure								
男	Male	51.64	51.62	51.50	51.22	51.08	50.95	50.83	49.95
女	Female	48.36	48.38	48.50	48.78	48.92	49.05	49.17	50.05
就业	**Employment**								
产业结构	Industrial Structure								
第一产业	Primary Industry	41.17	37.78	32.78	28.50	26.40	24.55	24.41	22.33
第二产业	Secondary Industry	29.43	27.57	27.46	29.10	28.45	30.45	30.51	31.55
第三产业	Tertiary Industry	29.40	34.65	39.76	42.40	45.15	45.00	45.08	46.12
宏观经济	**Macro Economy**								
国民经济核算	**National Accounting**								
生产总值产业结构	Industrial Structure								
第一产业	Primary Industry	12.53	6.91	5.02	4.46	4.05	4.32	4.48	4.48
第二产业	Secondary Industry	40.97	42.89	41.14	42.34	42.02	43.39	43.35	43.10
第三产业	Tertiary Industry	46.50	50.20	53.84	53.20	53.93	52.29	52.17	52.42
生产总值支出结构	Structure of Gross Domestic by Expenditures								
最终消费	Total Consumption	72.54	63.99	58.35	51.02	51.51	49.31	48.07	47.93
资本形成总额	Total Investment	45.88	44.55	63.85	79.28	83.77	87.47	84.52	86.65
货物和服务净出口	Net Export of Goods and Services	-18.42	-8.54	-22.20	-30.30	-35.28	-36.78	-32.60	-34.58
投　资	**Investment**								
全社会固定资产投资结构	Structure of Total Investment in Fixed Assets								
城乡结构	Urban and Rural Composition								
城镇	Urban Area	85.57	87.36	92.96	93.72	94.70	95.52	95.87	96.80
#房地产	Real Estate	20.93	22.31	26.97	28.34	27.85	25.91	29.79	30.21
农村	Rural Area	14.43	12.64	7.04	6.28	5.30	4.48	4.13	3.20
经济类型结构	Registion Status Composition								
国有单位	State-owned Enterprises Investment	66.79	68.68	44.75	36.45	37.31	41.49	36.00	39.15
集体单位	Collective-owned Enterprises Investment	9.46	6.30	7.09	12.95	11.60	10.04	7.71	4.59
个体经济	Self-employed Individual	10.76	10.50	9.46	2.65	3.91	1.68	2.23	1.95
其他经济	Other	12.99	14.51	38.69	47.95	47.18	46.78	54.05	54.31

1–12 续表1 continued 1

单位:% (%)

指 标	Item	1995	2000	2005	2008	2009	2010	2011	2012
财 政	**Government Finance**								
财政收入结构	Structure of Government Revenue								
#中 央	Central Government		31.94	58.30	39.49	39.68	37.28	35.78	32.37
地 方	Local Governments		68.06	41.70	44.87	45.32	47.36	49.02	52.71
产 业	**Industrial**								
农 业	**Agriculture**								
农林牧渔及服务业总产值结构	Structure of Gross Output Value of Farming,Forestry,Animal Husbandry, Fishery and Service								
农 业	Farming	68.03	69.23	61.69	56.85	59.42	63.36	63.42	62.69
林 业	Forestry	0.96	1.14	1.23	1.13	1.27	1.18	1.26	2.02
牧 业	Animal Husbandry	30.29	28.58	30.96	33.52	30.56	27.72	27.68	26.60
渔 业	Fishery	0.72	1.05	0.69	0.66	0.66	0.56	0.55	0.65
农林牧渔服务业	Farming,Forestry,Animal Husbandry and Fishery			5.43	7.84	8.09	7.18	7.09	8.04
工 业	**Industry**								
工业总产值经济类型结构	Structure of Gross Output Value of Industry by Registion Status								
国有经济	State-owned Enterprises	51.04	43.00	45.21	52.26	51.07	51.52	50.46	52.20
集体经济	Collective-owned Enterprises	40.98	32.76	5.16	1.85	1.38	1.22	0.92	0.81
其他经济类型	Others	7.98	24.24	49.63	45.89	47.55	47.26	48.62	46.99
工业总产值轻重结构	Structure of Gross Output Value of Industry by Ligth Industry and Heavy Industry								
轻工业	Light Industry	40.31	48.81	31.17	25.17	23.47	22.01	21.97	21.95
重工业	Heavy Industry	59.69	51.19	68.83	74.83	76.53	77.99	78.03	78.05
工业总产值规模结构	Structure of Gross Output Value of Industry by Size of Enterprises								
大型企业	Large Enterprises	38.80	36.29	35.46	43.85	43.54	42.11	41.15	48.46
中型企业	Medium-sized Enterprises	9.14	5.14	24.67	20.96	21.88	23.96	15.17	13.41
小型企业	Small Enterprises	52.06	58.57	39.87	35.19	34.58	33.93	43.68	38.13

注：本表2008年以后财政收入结构中地方指地方财政一般预算收入。

1–12 续表2 continued 2

单位: %　　(%)

指标	Item	1995	2000	2005	2008	2009	2010	2011	2012
建筑业	**Construction**								
建筑业总产值结构	Structure of Gross Output Value of Construction Industry								
土木工程建筑业	Civil Engineering Construction	86.27	88.50	56.59	59.14	67.14	68.61	53.75	47.57
房屋工程建筑	Building Construction	12.84	9.28	34.05	29.80	25.50	24.63	36.81	43.03
建筑安装业	Installation of Construction						4.39	6.70	6.49
装修装饰业	Decoration	0.89	2.21	1.08	1.67	1.50	0.82	0.90	1.14
其　他	Others		0.01	8.28	9.39	5.86	1.55	1.15	1.77
交通运输业	**Transportation**								
客运量结构	Structure of Freight Traffic								
铁 路	Railways	29.53	26.40	17.14	10.11	9.01	9.18	8.57	8.07
公 路	Highways	67.57	69.14	79.15	87.45	88.07	87.59	87.96	85.45
民用航空	Civil Aviation	2.90	4.46	3.71	2.44	2.92	3.23	3.46	6.48
货运量结构	Structure of Freight Traffic								
铁 路	Railways	34.59	44.31	4.48	2.20	2.01	2.06	2.10	1.84
公 路	Highways	65.36	55.58	95.47	97.78	97.97	97.92	97.88	98.12
民用航空	Civil Aviation	0.05	0.11	0.04	0.02	0.02	0.02	0.02	0.04
国内商业	**Domestic Trade**								
社会消费品零售总额结构	Composition of Retail Sales of Consumer Goods								
城镇	Urban Area	88.95	87.99	90.17	90.43	90.49	95.91	97.08	96.97
农村	Rural Area	11.05	12.01	9.83	9.57	9.51	4.09	2.92	3.03
国际旅游	**International Tourism**								
国际旅游人数结构	Structure of Tourists								
外国人	Foreigners	89.76	84.03	84.91	84.78	87.81	86.97	88.42	87.91
华侨及港澳台同胞	Overseas Chinese and Compatriots form Hong Kong, Macao and Taiwan	10.24	15.97	15.09	15.22	12.19	13.03	11.58	12.09
教育文化、卫生、人民生活	**Education and Culture，Health Care，People's Livelihood**								
教　育	**Education**								
在校学生结构	Structure of Student Enrollment								
#普通高等学校	Institutions of Higher Education	8.81	12.44	28.48	30.53	31.54	32.60	29.74	30.99
普通中等专业教育学校	Regular Specialized Secondary Schools	2.84	3.84	3.33	3.71	3.32	3.02	2.37	2.09
普通中等教育学校	Regular Secondary Education Schools	24.55	30.93	29.89	24.17	22.70	21.74	18.32	17.41
小学	Primary Schools	59.91	49.89	32.45	25.03	23.56	22.95	19.95	19.53

1–12 续表3 continued 3

单位: % (%)

指　　标	Item	1995	2000	2005	2008	2009	2010	2011	2012
专任教师结构	Full-time Teachers by Type								
#普通高等学校	Institutions of Higher Education	21.25	19.89	29.93	31.63	31.90	32.47	31.97	32.96
普通中等专业教育学校	Regular Specialized Secondary Schools	3.38	4.02	2.16	1.55	1.35	1.42	1.29	1.18
普通中等教育学校	Regular Secondary Education Schools	29.37	33.21	31.55	25.53	24.68	24.30	23.70	23.36
小学	Primary Schools	40.41	38.34	30.08	24.68	23.83	23.10	22.37	21.97
人民生活	**People's Livelihood**								
城镇居民消费结构	Consumption Structure of Urban Residents								
食　品	Food	44.68	36.46	37.04	36.40	32.43	31.29	31.29	32.48
衣　着	Clothing	12.67	8.13	9.03	10.25	10.98	11.11	12.27	12.17
家庭设备用品及服务	Household facilities,Articles and Services	13.75	11.33	4.73	6.33	7.28	7.56	8.11	7.87
医疗保健	Health Care	3.27	7.23	9.45	9.67	9.65	9.50	9.00	8.52
交通和通信	Transportation and Communication	5.58	6.93	9.67	10.37	11.33	12.06	12.81	14.26
教育文化娱乐服务	Recreation,Education and Culture Articles	9.05	13.74	17.18	14.35	14.34	14.66	14.26	14.33
居　住	Residence	6.49	11.23	9.10	8.81	8.86	9.33	8.26	8.47
杂项商品和服务	Articles for Daily Use and Others	4.51	4.95	3.80	3.82	5.13	4.49	4.00	1.91
农村居民消费结构	Consumption Structure of Rural Residents								
食品消费支出	Food	50.31	36.63	36.34	36.95	35.81	32.54	31.89	33.83
衣　着	Clothing	8.39	6.65	6.11	6.52	6.40	6.55	7.20	7.42
居　住	Residence	5.92	21.41	17.76	19.39	19.47	24.41	23.92	21.91
家庭设备用品及服务	Household facilities,Articles and Services	5.17	5.47	5.11	7.02	6.97	6.53	7.10	7.46
医疗保健	Health Care	1.78	6.93	8.19	8.05	8.50	8.54	8.65	8.85
交通和通讯	Transportation and Communication	8.09	4.21	8.19	7.84	9.83	8.45	9.01	10.19
文化娱乐用品及服务	Recreation,Education and Culture Articles	18.53	14.49	16.15	12.43	11.13	11.20	10.43	10.20
其它商品及服务	Articles for Daily Use and Others	1.81	4.21	2.15	1.80	1.89	1.78	1.80	0.14
卫　生	**Health Care**								
卫生技术人员结构	Medical Technical Personnel by Types								
执业（助理）医师	Licensed（Assistant） Doctors	45.42	44.82	41.96	38.09	37.34	33.16	35.17	34.46
注册护士	Registered Nurses	32.68	34.29	33.14	36.23	39.05	40.01	40.87	41.61
药　师	Junior Paramedics	8.78	8.31	7.30	5.74	5.45	5.36	5.10	5.05
技　师	Technicians	5.21	5.21	5.33	6.68	6.49	8.11	5.91	5.91
其　他	Others	7.91	7.37	12.27	13.26	11.67	13.36	12.95	12.97

1-13 国民经济和社会发展比例和效益指标

指　　标	Item	1995
人口与就业	**Population and Employment**	
人口	**Population**	
出生率(‰)	Birth Rate(‰)	11.95
死亡率(‰)	Death Rate(‰)	4.98
自然增长率(‰)	Natural Growth Rate(‰)	6.97
就业	**Employment**	
每一就业者负担人口	Dependency Ratio	1.7
三次产业就业者比例	Employment Ratio by Type of Industry	
(以第一产业为100)	(Employment in primary industry=100)	
第一产业	Primary Industry	100.0
第二产业	Secondary Industry	71.5
第三产业	Tertiary Industry	71.4
城镇登记失业率(%)	Unemployment Rate in Urban Areas(%)	3.1
宏观经济	**Macro Economy**	
国民核算	**National Accounting**	
三次产业增加值比例	Ratio of Value-added by Type of Industry	
(以第一产业为100)	(Employment in primary industry=100)	
第一产业	Primary Industry	100.0
第二产业	Secondary Industry	326.9
第三产业	Tertiary Industry	371.1
全社会劳动生产率(元／人)	Overall Labor Productivity(yuan/person)	8963
第一产业	Primary Industry	2698
第二产业	Secondary Industry	12404
第三产业	Tertiary Industry	14488
人均生产总值(元)	Per Capita GDP(yuan)	5131
固定资产投资	**Investment in Fixed Assets**	
全社会固定资产投资相当于生产总值比例(%)	Proportion of Investment in fixed Assets to GDP(%)	31.3
房屋建筑面积竣工率(%)	Rate of Floor Space of Buildings Completed in Construction(%)	33.4
固定资产交付使用率(%)	Rate of Fixed Assets Completed in Capital Construction and Put into Use(%)	70.7
建设项目建成投产率(%)	Rate of Projects Completed in Capital Construction and Put into Use(%)	43.7
财政	**Finance**	
财政总收入相当于生产总值比例(%)	Proportion of Local Government Revenue to GDP(%)	5.5
一般预算支出相当于生产总值比例(%)	Proportion of Local Government Expenditures to GDP(%)	5.6
利用外资	**Utilization of Foreign Capital**	
外商实际直接投资额相当于利用外资协议金额比例(%)	Proportion of Foreign Capital Actually Used to Total Amount of Foreign Capital for Utilization by Signed Contracts or Agreements (%)	64.4

注：本表财政收入数据2009年及以前为一般预算财政收入和基金收入之和。

Indicators on Proportions and Efficiency in National Economic and Social Development

2000	2003	2004	2005	2006	2007	2008	2009	2010	2011	2012
13.07	8.48	9.19	9.58	9.98	10.00	10.15	10.08	9.73	9.71	10.13
5.96	4.68	5.87	5.16	5.46	5.48	5.57	5.63	5.34	5.38	5.57
7.11	3.80	3.32	4.42	4.52	4.52	4.58	4.45	4.39	4.33	4.56
1.8	1.8	1.8	1.8	1.8	1.9	1.9	1.9	1.8	1.7	1.7
100.0	100.0	100.0	100.0	100.0	100.0	100.0	100.0	100.0	100.0	100.0
73.0	74.4	78.8	83.8	85.9	93.8	101.9	107.7	124.0	125.0	141.3
91.7	101.7	110.1	121.3	126.5	133.5	148.6	171.0	183.3	184.7	206.5
3.4	4.5	4.3	4.3	4.3	4.3	4.2	4.3	4.2	3.9	3.5
100.0	100.0	100.0	100.0	100.0	100.0	100.0	100.0	100.0	100.0	100.0
620.7	803.2	792.1	818.8	916.6	947.7	948.8	1037.1	1004.4	967.0	962.1
726.4	963.3	938.8	1071.7	1168.2	1202.5	1192.0	1330.8	1210.1	1163.9	1170.2
16367	23605	27069	31837	36730	43252	52422	59832	68965	79349	86410
2960	3501	4174	4747	5191	6148	7921	8830	11452	14530	16578
25443	36914	43199	47853	56073	64851	76899	87452	102992	112851	119979
24024	33502	37040	44024	48938	56870	67031	73674	80267	91908	110840
9484	13341	15294	16406	18890	22463	27794	32411	38343	45475	51166
36.0	50.5	58.7	65.8	72.4	81.4	82.2	91.8	100.3	86.6	97.2
42.0	33.8	24.4	28.1	26.1	29.0	16.9	16.0	6.9	10.0	8.7
74.0	62.7	42.8	52.8	46.6	49.8	40.5	42.8	38.4	40.4	42.4
44.2	39.9	41.5	54.2	47.0	40.6	53.3	72.5	53.9	54.9	56.1
7.3	7.7	7.8	6.6	6.5	7.1	10.9	12.2	15.8	16.8	17.2
8.0	8.2	8.1	8.1	9.1	9.9	14.5	15.4	11.5	12.8	13.7
28.88	26.52	35.24	47.01	45.18	77.49	97.05	203.03	130.9	167.0	68.8

1-13 续表1

指 标	Item	1995
能 源	**Energy**	
单位生产总值能耗降低率（%）	Decreasing Rate of Energy Consumption per Unit GDP(%)	
规模以上工业单位工业增加值能耗降低率（%）	Decreasing Rate of Energy Consumption per Unit Industrial value-added of Industry Above Designated Size(%)	
单位生产总值电耗降低率（%）	Decreasing Rate of Electricity Consumption per Unit GDP(%)	
产 业	**Industries**	
农业	**Agriculture**	
人均耕地面积(公顷)	Per Capita Cultivated Land(hectare)	0.08
农业从业者人均耕地面积(公顷)	Cultivated Land per Agricultural Laborer(hectare)	0.20
每公顷耕地农业机械总动力(千瓦)	Total Power of Agricultural Machinery per Hectare of Cultivated Land(kw)	5.23
每公顷耕地化肥施用量(公斤)	Chemical Fertilizer Consumption per Hectare of Cultivated Land(kg)	536
每公顷耕地生产的农业总产值(元)	Agricultural Output Value per Hectare of Cultivated Land(yuan)	24396
每个农林牧渔及服务业劳动力农产品生产量(公斤)	Output of Farm Products per Farming,Forestry,Animal Husbandry,Fishery and Service Husbandry and Fishery Laborer (kg)	
粮食	Grain	1150
蔬菜	Vegetables	877
禽蛋	Poultry Eggs	93
肉类	Meat	84
水产品	Aquatic Products	6
每公顷播种面积农产品产量(公斤)	Output of Farm Crops per Hectare of Sown Area(kg)	
粮食	Grain	3806
油料	Oil-bearing Crops	1753
蔬菜	Vegetables	34800
规模以上工业企业经济效益	**Economic Benefit of Industrial Enterprises above Designated Size**	
总资产贡献率（%）	Ratio of Total Assets to Industrial Output Value (%)	
资产负债率（%）	Assets-Liability Ratio (%)	
流动资产周转次数（次/年）	Rate of Annual Turnover Working Capitals(times/year)	
成本费用利润率（%）	Ratio of Profits to Cost (%)	
产品销售率（%）	Proportion of Industrial Products Sold(%)	
全员劳动生产率（元/人）	Overall Labor Productivity (yuan/person)	
建筑业	**Construction**	
机械装备率(元／人)	Value of Machinery per Laborer(yuan/person)	5990
产值利润率(%)	Ratio of Per-tax Profits to Gross Output Value (%)	3.5
全员劳动生产率(元／人)(按总产值计算)	Overall Labor Productivity(yuan/person) (in terms of gross output value per employee)	37689
邮电通信业	**Post and Communication Services**	
电话普及率(含移动电话）(部/百人)	Access to Telephones, National(include mobilphone) (set/100 persons)	7.9
#移动电话普及率(部/百人)	Access to Mobilphones (set/100 persons)	0.48
国内商业	**Domestic Trade**	
人均批发零售和住宿餐饮业消费品零售额(元)	Per Capita Retail Sales of Wholesale,Retail Trade and Accommodation Catering Trade (yuan)	1979

continued 1

2000	2003	2004	2005	2006	2007	2008	2009	2010	2011	2012
				4.15	5.75	6.65	5.56	2.06	3.56	3.51
				3.04	12.56	13.43	10.48	12.18	15.44	10.52
				4.48	6.94	6.93	5.33	1.00	4.43	2.92
0.07	0.07	0.07	0.07	0.06	0.06	0.06	0.06	0.06	0.06	0.06
0.20	0.19	0.19	0.22	0.23	0.25	0.21	0.21	0.22	0.22	0.22
6.78	7.54	7.93	8.39	8.63	8.99	10.41	10.12	10.48	11.50	12.10
664	725	780	794	819	843	867	891	922	953	987
25161	30357	35862	39937	43261	51361	64593	69106	88869	108457	125041
1382	1213	1392	1493	1569	1433	1695	1792	1901	1567	1700
1110	1167	1287	1421	1536	1549	1752	1990	2171	2253	2452
95	89	84	86	92	74	86	96	106	108	115
101	114	122	132	145	77	91	104	117	124	134
8	7	7	7	7	9	10	11	10	10	12
4342	4182	4656	4796	5025	4452	5102	5206	5349	4764	5045
1526	1532	1758	1821	1880	1934	2008	1956	2004	1988	1987
37797	36657	35002	35231	35916	33677	35723	38344	39667	40475	42607
	7.0	6.9	8.4	7.8	10.2	8.6	11.3	12.2	8.6	7.7
65.0	61.3	65.2	65.0	64.3	64.6	62.6	61.1	57.6	57.7	59.4
1.0	1.1	1.2	1.3	1.4	1.6	1.5	1.7	1.7	1.5	1.5
4.2	5.7	5.0	3.1	5.5	7.3	4.6	8.1	8.8	5.2	4.5
97.1	96.3	97.9	97.5	98.2	96.8	96.1	97.6	97.1	97.4	96.7
29496	58801	66752	82815	97561	129706	150641	161289	188483	194105	230032
6805	9453	13240	13332	13502	9079	12026	11928	9461	28669	12216
3.4	4.1	4.4	4.8	4.5	5.2	6.0	6.3	4.4	4.4	2.8
74347	132981	163414	206337	241887	203994	226669	285854	321340	334172	479232
31.2	69.1	88.8	100.0	111.1	117.9	124.7	167.1	199.0	221.3	247.2
10.62	33.67	48.29	56.62	66.99	80.02	88.09	132.79	168	189.58	210.87
4027	6956	7859	8795	9437	10932	13840	16432	19363	23145	26529

1-13 续表2

指　　标	Item	1995
对外经济贸易	**Foreign Trade**	
进出口总额相当于生产总值比例(%)	Proportion of Total Imports & Exports to GDP(%)	34.76
国际旅游	**International Tourism**	
每一来华游客花费(元)	Expenditure per International Tourist in China(yuan)	2511
金融	**Finance and Insurance**	
金融机构存款相当于生产总值比例(%)	Bank Deposits as Percentage of GDP(%)	108.83
金融机构贷款相当于生产总值比例(%)	Bank Loans as Percentage of GDP(%)	101.26
教育、科技、文化	**Education, Science and Technology and Culture**	
教育	**Education**	
毕业率(%)	Graduation Rate(%)	
小学	Primary Schools	
初中	Junior Schools	
学校教师负担系数	Student-teacher Ratio(in percentage)	
高等学校	Colleges and Universities	6.83
中等学校	Secondary Schools	14.42
小学	Primary Schools	26.22
文化(个)	**Culture (unit)**	
每百万人有艺术表演团体	Number of Troupes per Million Persons	3.39
每百万人有公共图书馆	Number of Public Libraries per Million Persons	2.31
家庭、生活、环境	**Family, People's Livelihood and Environment**	
家庭	**Family**	
城市居民家庭	Urban Households	
平均每户就业面（%）	Percentage of Employees Per Household (%)	55.90
每一就业者负担人数(人)	Persons Supported by Each Laborer (person)	1.79
农村居民家庭	Rural Households	
平均每一劳动力负担人口（人）	Persons Supported by Each Laborer(person)	1.58
卫生	**Health Care**	
每千人医院数(个)	Number of Hospitals per 1000 Persons(unit)	0.06
每千人医生数(人)	Number of Doctors per 1000 Persons(person)	2.91
每千人医院床位数(张)	Number of Hospital Beds per 1000 Persons(unit)	4.36
市政建设	**City Construction**	
城市自来水普及率(%)	Percentage of Households with Access to Tap Water(%)	
城市用燃气普及率(%)	Percentage of Households with Access to Tap Gas (%)	
人均公园绿地面积(平方米)	Public Green Areas per 10 000 Persons(sq. m)	3.80

continued 2

2000	2003	2004	2005	2006	2007	2008	2009	2010	2011	2012
22.25	20.19	23.29	24.79	22.01	22.21	21.97	18.17	21.20	20.56	18.74
3445	3584	4212	4324	4353	4242	4544	4614	5037	5116	5192
206.71	281.61	277.73	283.41	275.92	259.80	264.31	279.84	278.99	267.98	275.87
150.51	206.43	186.17	169.91	159.11	152.16	149.22	166.65	203.30	194.07	196.04
								100.4	100.2	100.2
								99.7	100.6	98.7
12.38	19.87	16.69	17.99	17.36	16.97	17.13	17.32	17.41	17.92	18.14
17.84	18.52	18.78	18.47	20.51	19.99	18.97	18.27	17.78	16.40	16.42
25.75	22.69	21.71	20.38	19.78	18.61	17.99	17.32	17.22	18.06	17.15
3.20	3.07	3.03	2.56	2.31	2.16	2.15	2.13	1.53	3.52	2.22
2.18	1.95	2.07	2.02	1.82	1.81	1.79	1.78	1.77	1.76	1.75
45.73	48.00	48.80	47.44	48.30	47.77	47.87	53.20	53.70	54.80	54.00
2.19	2.08	2.05	2.11	2.07	2.09	2.09	1.88	1.86	1.83	1.85
1.57	1.56	1.56	1.60	1.59	1.57	1.50	1.50	1.50	1.50	1.50
0.03	0.04	0.04	0.04	0.04	0.04	0.03	0.03	0.03	0.03	0.03
2.35	2.02	2.04	2.39	2.19	2.08	2.16	2.29	2.21	2.53	2.70
3.83	3.94	3.91	3.75	3.46	3.42	3.65	3.84	4.04	4.23	4.58
98.95	99.04	99.09	99.00	99.09	100.01	111.22	100.00	98.77	99.95	100.00
81.51	91.23	91.20	91.30	92.62	98.60	97.66	98.15	97.02	97.46	98.19
5.12	5.35	5.03	5.63	7.59	7.61	7.80	7.90	9.11	9.89	10.22

1-14 平均每天主要社会经济活动

指　　标	Item	1995	2000
一、每天创造的财富	**Daily Production**		
生产总值(万元)	Gross Domestic Product(10 000 yuan)	9050.7	17702.2
第一产业	Primary Industry	1134.3	1223.3
第二产业	Secondary Industry	3707.7	7592.6
工业	Industry	3082.2	5984.7
建筑业	Construction	625.5	1608.0
第三产业	Tertiary Industry	4208.8	8886.3
#交通运输、仓储及邮政业	Transport, Storage, Post & Telecommunication Services	674.0	1709.3
批发和零售业	Wholesale and Retail Trade		
住宿和餐饮业	Hotels and Catering Services		
财政总收入(万元)	Total Government Revenue(10 000 yuan)	498.8	1304.0
财政一般预算支出(万元)	Government General Budgetary Expenditures(10 000 yuan)	504.7	1274.1
粮食(吨)	Grain(ton)	4801	5532
奶类(吨)	Milk(ton)	364	674
蔬菜(吨)	Vegetables(ton)	3660	4442
肉类(吨)	Meat(ton)	350	404
水产品(吨)	Aquatic Products(ton)	23	31
布(万米)	Cloth(10 000 m)	83.0	77.0
发电量(万千瓦小时)	Electricity(10 000 kwh)	610.0	534.0
钢材(吨)	Steel(ton)	861	274
汽车(辆)	Motor Vehicle(unit)	8	25
二、每天消费量	**Daily National Consumption**		
最终消费(万元)	Final Consumption Expenditure(10 000 yuan)	6565.5	11326.9
社会消费品零售总额(万元)	Total Retail Sales of Consumer Goods (10 000 yuan)	5112.3	9874.5
三、每天其他经济活动	**Other Daily Economic Activities**		
资本形成总额(万元)	Gross Capital Formation(10 000 yuan)	4152.1	7885.5
#固定资本形成	Fixed Capital Formation		
存货增加	Changes in Stock		
竣工住宅面积(平方米)	Floor Space of Buildings Completed (sq.m)	6927	14930
货运量(万吨)	Freight Traffic(10 000 tons)	26.3	19.2
客运量(万人次)	Passenger Traffic(10 000 person-times)	24.8	22.1
邮电业务总量(万元)	Business Volume of Postal and Telecommunications Services(10 000 yuan)	209.6	1264.7
进出口总额(万美元)	Total Value of Imports and Exports (USD 10 000)	110.2	475.9
出口额	Exports	82.5	290.6
进口额	Imports	27.7	185.3
外商实际直接投资额(万美元)	Foreign Capital Actually Used(USD 10 000)	51.1	42.8
国际旅游人数(人次)	Number of Tourists from Abroad(person-time)	1134	1782
四、每天人口变动和婚姻	**Daily Population Changes and Marriages**		
出　生(人)	Births(person)	211	247
死　亡(人)	Deaths(person)	88	113
结　婚(对)	Marriages(couple)	129	129
离　婚(对)	Divorces(couple)	12	14

注：本表财政收入数据2009年及以前为一般预算财政收入和基金收入之和。

Selected Indicators on Average Daily Social and Economic Activities

2005	2006	2007	2008	2009	2010	2011	2012
35998.1	42162.7	50866.6	63510.7	74632.3	88813.4	105824.1	119619.2
1808.5	1929.9	2260.6	2834.3	3024.1	3837.3	4743.6	5358.6
14808.2	17689.0	21423.0	26892.6	31363.0	38540.3	45871.5	51554.8
11506.9	13540.3	16300.0	19764.4	22381.4	27495.1	32592.1	36403.0
3301.4	4148.8	5123.0	7128.2	8981.6	11045.2	13279.5	15151.8
19381.4	22543.8	27183.0	33783.8	40245.2	46435.9	55209.0	62705.8
1816.4	2029.6	2307.1	2716.7	3030.1	3416.2	4044.9	4587.9
4032.9	4567.7	5356.4	6655.1	8028.8	9256.4	11477.8	13323.8
1381.9	1431.0	1920.3	2346.6	2576.7	2837.8	3405.2	3754.0
2300.6	2638.6	3433.6	6517.8	9080.0	13991.5	17805.0	20632.1
2819.6	3689.0	4771.4	8679.2	11509.0	10181.4	13550.0	16369.6
5631	5831	5180	5874	5978	6074	4987	5275
1157	1292	1447	1616	1694	1736	1775	1826
5362	5709	5601	6069	6641	6934	7169	7611
499	538	280	316	346	374	396	416
26	27	34	34	36	33	32	38
74.0	72.6	76.7	62.3	60.8	65.2	44.8	39.1
1316.3	1830.1	1946.3	1964.1	2279.7	2655.9	2603.0	2725.5
658	1960	2157	1312	3028	3035	506	857
112	282	468	734	1389	1787	1525	1484
21003.3	23861.1	27266.3	32400.3	38441.1	43794.8	50874.2	57341.6
18371.5	21505.5	25649.6	32235.1	37838.9	44850.4	53862.5	62023.6
22986.6	28637.5	39766.3	50352.3	62518.1	77682.7	89447.4	103646.6
20918.4	26404.9	34795.6	45315.3	58878.9	72237.8	83395.6	97509.0
2068.2	2232.6	4970.7	5037.0	3639.2	5444.9	6051.8	6137.5
16400	15975	25466	18998	22537	12287	23601	24762
33.0	32.4	41.4	75.5	83.9	94.0	107.5	123.1
28.7	30.8	34.2	72.6	78.6	83.0	91.4	99.1
3617.7	5116.7	6212.7	7256.4	8189.6	8852.3	5494.8	5923.6
1068.9	1138.1	1468.9	1928.9	1985.3	2847.3	3452.5	3565.6
721.8	747.6	951.0	1225.0	912.6	1456.8	1596.3	1999.7
347.1	390.5	517.9	703.9	1072.6	1390.5	1856.2	1565.9
156.5	225.9	305.7	314.4	333.9	429.2	549.4	678.9
2125	2376	2740	1732	1844	2306	2746	3160
210	223	226	232	232	225	226	237
63	122	124	127	130	124	125	130
137	184	185	213	241	229	259	246
35	35	43	43	43	52	53	51

1-15 各区县国民经济和社会发展主要指标（2012年）

指　标	Item	新城区 Xincheng	碑林区 Beilin	莲湖区 Lianhu
一、年底总人口（常住人口）（万人）	Population at the Year-end Permanent population(10 000 persons)	59.44	62.08	70.25
二、生产总值（亿元）	Gross Domestic Product(100 mil. yuan)	428.92	466.96	479.40
第一产业	Primary Industry			
第二产业	Secondary Industry	174.54	92.89	212.22
工业	Industry	103.68	12.48	140.47
第三产业	Tertiary Industry	254.38	374.07	267.18
三、全社会固定资产投资总额（亿元）	Total Investment in Fixed Assets(100 mil. yuan)	353.50	376.45	473.49
#城镇	Urban Area	353.50	376.45	473.49
#房地产	Real Estate	86.72	169.57	140.65
四、财政一般预算收入（亿元）	Local Financial Revenue(100 mil. yuan)	26.99	33.03	34.74
财政一般预算支出（亿元）	Local Financial Expenditure(100 mil. yuan)	21.24	17.94	23.53
五、农林牧渔及服务业总产值（亿元）	Gross Output Value of Farming Forestry Animal Husbandry and Fishery(100 mil yuan)			
主要农产品产量（万吨）	Output of Major Farm Products(10 000 tons)			
粮食	Grain			
蔬菜	Vegetables			
瓜果	Fruits class			
水果	Fruits			
肉类	Meat			
奶类	Milk			
六、规模以上工业总产值（亿元）	Gross industrial Output Value(100 mil. yuan)	307.70	18.46	459.41
七、建筑业总产值（亿元）	Gross Output Value(100 mil. yuan)	240.03	461.38	156.42
房屋建筑施工面积（万平方米）	Floor Space of Buildings under Construction (10 000 sq.m)	1145.85	2542.69	1115.96
房屋建筑竣工面积（万平方米）	Total Retail Sales of Consumer Goods (100 mil. yuan)	200.84	717.10	240.50
八、社会消费品零售总额（亿元）	Floor Space of Buildings Completed(100 mil. yuan)	392.96	392.32	323.21
九、城镇居民人均可支配收入（元）	Per Capita Annual Disposable Income of Urban Households (yuan)	30658	31268	31195
农村居民人均纯收入（元）	Per Capita Net Income of Rural Residents(yuan)			
十、医疗机构数（个）	Number of Health Care Institutions(unit)	307	328	346
卫生技术人员（人）	Number of Medical Technical Personnel (person)	10725	10580	8854
床位数（张）	Number of Beds(unit)	6637	6325	5444

Principal Indicators of National Economy and Social Development by Region (2012)

灞桥区 Baqiao	未央区 Weiyang	雁塔区 Yanta	阎良区 Yanliang	临潼区 Lintong	长安区 Chang'an	蓝田县 Lantian	周至县 Zhouzhi	户　县 Huxian	高陵县 Gaoling
60.16	81.46	118.89	28.23	66.45	109.54	51.88	57.00	56.10	33.81
233.30	518.06	838.91	141.49	211.53	340.90	95.73	78.28	142.13	228.16
16.08	2.24	2.34	19.70	29.63	30.06	24.45	25.39	25.37	20.33
134.69	265.08	311.46	75.16	120.43	160.16	35.21	21.07	75.66	184.14
113.79	189.88	183.97	62.42	109.91	122.60	21.73	16.04	65.20	167.50
82.53	250.74	525.11	46.63	61.47	150.68	36.07	31.82	41.10	23.69
236.36	568.99	956.06	154.52	152.20	406.99	99.54	89.14	140.33	235.87
227.48	563.57	949.53	133.66	141.47	398.88	81.30	65.66	116.61	225.93
63.89	207.83	448.11	13.42	6.83	99.93	4.21	3.85	13.33	23.58
34.50	16.85	25.00	8.09	8.01	24.72	2.67	2.10	5.58	9.53
20.80	16.93	18.50	14.00	24.21	36.54	19.25	25.23	21.32	16.28
24.56	3.65	3.28	29.05	46.82	45.37	40.15	41.28	40.71	33.49
6.11	1.57		8.13	35.17	36.88	28.98	24.32	31.37	20.02
26.56	4.52	2.51	65.73	39.34	53.00	15.04	17.98	27.52	25.60
0.97	0.17		21.02	6.42	4.15	7.24	0.31	5.05	0.97
9.26	0.87	0.57	6.40	4.63	7.45	11.87	37.96	9.06	5.14
0.73	0.22	0.15	0.63	4.10	2.05	1.87	2.80	1.87	0.76
6.41	2.22	0.09	9.47	34.78	2.19	3.98	1.31	2.98	3.22
278.37	684.55	587.65	219.31	341.01	354.65	41.60	17.08	93.55	663.99
20.26	363.99	451.23	19.95	12.13	39.01	15.04	5.90	11.90	76.99
109.08	500.38	1075.80	81.58	120.85	168.47	128.25	48.39	114.11	379.66
35.95	96.00	241.22	31.01	80.78	47.41	44.43	22.68	29.61	197.77
55.01	318.57	439.52	26.78	55.93	127.86	40.89	27.49	44.67	18.67
28688	30103	31934	31026	24568	26493	19957	20025	22520	23462
13278	14562	14800	13403	10685	11107	7824	7733	9654	10673
537	265	477	158	469	785	631	476	585	212
3962	4435	12123	1864	2287	4038	1494	2130	2794	1613
2094	3148	8171	1402	1911	3226	1005	1235	2414	1227

主 要 统 计 指 标 解 释

行政区划 指国家对行政区域的划分。根据有关法规规定，我国的行政区域划分如下：（1）全国分为省、自治区、直辖市；（2）省、自治区分为自治州、县、自治县、市；（3）自治州分为县、自治县、市；（4）县、自治县分为乡、民族乡、镇；（5）直辖市和较大的市分为区、县；（6）国家在必要时设立的特别行政区。

气候 指地球与大气之间长期能量交换与质量交换所形成的一种自然环境状态，它是多种因素综合作用的结果。气候既是人类生活和生产的环境要素之一，又是供给人类生活和生产的重要资源。气温、降水、湿度等气象要素的多年平均值是用来描述一个地区气候状况的主要参数，而各种气象要素某年、某月的平均值（或总量）则可以反映出该时期天气气候状况的重要特征。

自然资源 指人类可以直接从自然界获得，并用于生产和生活的物质资源。自然资源一般可以分成可再生资源和非再生资源两大类。可再生资源指在较短时间内可以再生、可以循环利用的资源，包括土地资源、水资源、气候资源、生物资源和海洋资源等。非再生资源指在使用后不能再生的资源，包括矿产资源和地热能源。

土地资源 土地指陆地的表层部分，它主要由岩石、岩石的风化物和土壤构成。土地资源按利用类型可以分为农用地、建筑用地和未利用地。农用地包括耕地、园地、林地、牧草地和水面。建筑用地包括居民点及工矿用地、交通用地和水利设施用地。未利用地指农用地和建筑用地以外的土地，包括滩涂、荒漠、戈壁、冰川和石山等。

耕地面积 指经过开垦用以种植农作物并经常进行耕耘的土地面积。包括种有作物的土地面积、休闲地、新开荒地和抛荒未满三年的土地面积。

森林面积 指由乔木树种构成，郁闭度0.2以上（含0.2）的林地或冠 宽度10米以上的林带的面积，即有林地面积。森林面积包括天然起源和人工起源的针叶林面积、阔叶林面积、针阔混交林面积和竹林面积，不包括灌木林地面积和疏林地面积。

林业用地面积 指生长乔木、竹类、灌木、沿海红树林等林木的土地面积，包括有林地、灌木林、疏林地、未成林造林地、迹地、苗圃等。

水资源总量 指评价区内降水形成的地表和地下产水总量，即地表产流量与降水入渗补给地下水量之和，不包括过境水量。

地表水资源量 指评价区内河流、湖泊、冰川等地表水体中可以逐年更新的动态水量，即当地天然河川径流量。

地下水资源量 指评价区内降水和地表水对饱水岩土层的补给量，包括降水入渗补给量和河道、湖库、渠系、渠灌田间等地表水体的入渗补给量。

气温 指空气的温度，我国一般以摄氏度（℃）为单位表示。气象观测的温度表是放在离地面约1.5米处通风良好的百叶箱里测量的，因此，通常说的气温指的是离地面1.5米处百叶箱中的温度。其统计计算方法为：

月平均气温是将全月各日的平均气温相加，除以该月的天数而得。

年平均气温是将12个月的月平均气温累加后除以12而得。

降水量 指从天空降落到地面的液态或固态（经融化后）水，未经蒸发、渗透、流失而在地面上积聚的深度。其统计计算方法为：

月降水量是将全月各日的降水量累加而得。

年降水量是将12个月的月降水量累加而得。

日照时数 指太阳实际照射地面的时间。其统计方法与降水量相同。

平均增长速度 平均增长速度表明社会经济现象在一个较长的时期内逐期平均增长变化的程度，它不能根据各个环比增长速度直接求得，但与平均发展速度之间存在着一定的数量关系：平均增长速度＝平均发展速度－1。

平均发展速度 是一种根据环比发展速度计算的序时平均数,由于各时期对比的基础不同，所以计算平均发展速度不能采用一般的序时平均数的计算方法，计算方法分为水平法和累计法。水平法，又称几何平均法，即将环比发展速度按连乘法用几何平均数公式计算。累计法，也称方程法，根据一段时期内各年发展水平总和与基期水平的关系，列出方程式计算平均发展速度。水平法着重考虑最后一年所达到的发展水平；累计法着重考虑整个时期累计发展水平的总量。

本《年鉴》内所列的平均增长速度，除固定资产投资用“累计法”计算外，其余均用“水平法”计算。从某年到某年平均增长速度的年份，均不包括基期年在内。如建国六十年以来的平均增长速度是以1949年为基期计算的，则写为1950-2009年平均增长速度，其余类推。

Explanatory Notes on Main Statistical Indicators

Divisions of Administrative Areas refers to the division of administrative areas by the State. The relative laws stipulate that (1)the whole country is divided into provinces, autonomous regions and municipalities directly under the Central Government;(2)provinces and autonomous regions are further divided into autonomous prefectures, counties, autonomous counties and cities; (3)autonomous prefectures are further divided into counties, autonomous counties and cities; (4)counties and autonomous counties are further divided into townships, ethnic townships and towns; (5)municipalities directly under the Central Government and large cities are divided into districts and counties, (6)the State shall, when necessary, establish special administrative regions.

Climate refers to the natural environmental status formed by the long-term exchange of energy and mass between the earth and the atmosphere, and is the result of interaction of many factors. Climate is both one of the environment factors and also the important resources for living and production activities of the human being. The average values across several years of meteorological factors such as temperature, rainfall and humidity are used as important parameters to describe the climate of a region, while the average values (or total values)of a given year or month of meteorological factors reflect the key characteristics of climate for that period of time.

Natural Resources refer to material resources that could be obtained from the nature by human being and used for production and living. Natural resources in general can be classified as renewable resources and non-renewable resources. Renewable resources refer to resources that could be renewed and recycled during a relatively short period of time, including land resource, water resource, climate resource, biology resource and marine resource. Non-renewable resources include resources that could not be renewed, such as minerals and geothermal resource.

Land Resource Land refers to the surface of the earth, consisting of mainly rocks and its whethering and earth. Land resource can be classified, by its utilization, as land for agriculture, land for construction and unused land. Land for agriculture includes cultivated land, plantation land, forestland, grassland and waters. Land for construction includes land for residential purpose, for manufacturing and mining, for transportation and for water-conservancy projects. Unused land refers to land other than land for agriculture and.construction, including beaches, deserts, Gobi, glaciers and rock mountains.

Area of Cultivated Land refers to area of land reclaimed for the regular cultivation of various farm crops, including crop-cover land, fallow, newly reclaimed land and land laid idle for less than 3 years.

Forest Area refers to the area of trees and bamboo grow with canopy density above 0.2, the area of shrubby tree according to regulations of the government, the area of forest land inside farm land and the area of trees planted by the side of villages, farm houses and along roads and rivers.

Area of Afforested Land refers to area for land for trees bamboo, bushes and mangrove, including forest-covered land, bush-covered land, sparse forest land, land planned for afforestation and nurseries of young trees.

Total Water Resources refers to total volume of water resources measured as run-off for surface water from rainfall and recharge for groundwater in a given area, excluding transit water.

Surface Water Resources refers to total renewable resources which exist in rivers, lakes, glaciers and other collectors from rainfall and are measured as run-off of rivers.

Groundwater Resources refers to replenishment of aquifers with rainfall and surface water.

Temperature refers to the air temperature. China uses centigrade as the unit. The thermometry used for weather observation is put in a breezy shutter, which is 1.5 meters high from the ground. Therefore, the commonly used temperature refers to the temperature in the breezy shutter 1.5 meters away from the ground. The calculation method is as follows:

Monthly average temperature is the summation of average daily temperature of one month divided by the actual days of that particular month.

Annual average temperature is the summation of monthly average of a year divided by 12 months.

Volume of Precipitation refers to the deepness of liquid state or solid state (thawed)water falling from the sky to the ground that has not been evaporated, infiltrated or run off. The calculation method is as follows:

Monthly precipitation is the summation of daily precipitation of a month.

Annual precipitation is the summation of 12 months precipitation of a year.

Sunshine Hours refer to the actual hours of sun irradiating the earth. The calculation method is the same as that of the precipitation.

Average Annual Growth Rate shows the average growth rate of social and economic development during a longer period. It can not be directly calculated by chain based growth rate. The relation is:

Average Annual Growth Rate=Average Speed of Development 1

Average speed of development is the time series average of speed which calculated by chain based.Because the reference bases during the different periods are not same, average speed of development can not be calculated by the general method. Level approach and accumulative approach for calculating average speed of development rate are applied. The "level approach" , or the method of calculating the geometric average, is derived by the formula of geometric average of the chain-based speeds of development, or comparing the level of the last year of the interval with that of the beginning year; the other is called the "accumulative approach" or the "algebraic average" , "equation" method, which is derived by the summation of the actual figure of each year in the interval divided by the figure in the base year. The level approach focuses on the level of the last year, while the accumulative approach emphasizes the aggregate development in the duration.

The average annual growth rates listed in the Yearbook are calculated by the level approach except for the growth rate of investment in fixed assets. The base year is not listed in the duration for which average annual growth rates are computed. For instance, the average annual growth rate of the 60 years since 1949 is shown as the average annual growth rate of 1950-2009 without showing the base year 1949.

2

基本单位

BASIC UNIT

资料整理：王亚丽　张利民　张　奇

Data management:Wang Yali　Zhang Limin　Zhang Qi

第二部分　基本单位

一、简要说明

本章资料主要包括法人单位、产业活动单位和企业一套表调查单位数等资料，由西安市统计局普查中心提供。

二、主要指标

法人单位数（个）	103977	比上年增长　18.9%
产业活动单位数（个）	113604	比上年增长　18.2%
规模以上工业企业数（个）	966	
限额以上批发零售住宿餐饮业企业数（个）	1080	
资质内建筑业企业数（个）	396	
房地产开发经营企业数（个）	672	
重点服务业企业数（个）	570	

2　BASIC UNIT

Ⅰ.Brief Introduction

This chapter consists of unified data Enterprises and Industrial Active Units and Investigation Unit in "Enterprises of a table", provided by Xian Bureau of Statistic's Census Centre.

Ⅱ.Major Indicators

		Increase over Preceding Year
Number of Enterprises (unit)	103977	18.9%
Number of Industrial Active Units (unit)	113604	18.2%
Number of Industrial Enterprises above designed size (unit)	966	
Number of Enterprises about Wholesale、Retail、Accommodation and Catering above designed size (unit)	1080	
Number of Qualified Construction Enterprises (unit)	396	
Number of Real Estate Development Enterprises (unit)	672	
Number of Key Service Enterprises (unit)	570	

2-1 按登记注册类型分法人单位数（2012年）

Impersonal Entities Grouped by Status of Registion（2012）

单位：个 (unit)

分　组	Classify	法人单位数 Number of Enterprises	企业 Enterprises
总　计	**Total**	**103977**	**91812**
#非公有制经济	Non-public sectors of the economy	86549	85752
按登记注册类型分	**Grouped by Status of Registion**		
（一）内资	Domestic Funded Enterprises	103121	90964
国有	State-owned Enterprises	6650	1926
集体	Collective-owned Enterprises	2382	1606
股份合作	Cooperative Enterprises	407	378
联营	Joint Ownership Enterprises	238	219
国有联营	State Joint Ownership Enterprises	31	27
集体联营	Collective Joint Ownership Enterprises	82	74
国有与集体联营	Joint State-collective Ownership Enterprises	21	17
其他联营	Other Joint Ownership Enterprises	104	101
有限责任公司	Limited Liability Corporations	35026	34910
国有独资公司	State Sole Funded Corporations	179	178
其他有限责任公司	Other Limited Liability Corporations	34847	34732
股份有限公司	Share-holding Corporations Limited	1285	1276
私营	Private Enterprises	47240	46611
私营独资企业	Private-funded Enterprises	11102	10664
私营合伙	Private Partnership Enterprises	2191	2116
私营有限责任公司	Private Limited Liability Corporations	31031	30923
私营股份有限公司	Private Share-holding Corporations Ltd.	2916	2908
其他	Other Domestic Funded Enterprises	9893	4038
（二）港、澳、台商投资企业	Enterprises with Funds from Hong Kong, Macao and Taiwan	284	281
与港、澳、台商合资经营	Joint-venture with Funds from Hong Kong,Macao and Taiwan	106	105
与港、澳、台商合作经营	Cooperative Enterprises with Funds from Hong Kong Macau and Taiwan	15	15
港澳台商独资经营	Enterprises with Sole Investment from Hong Kong Macau and Taiwan	143	141
港澳台商投资股份有限公司	Share-holding Corporations Ltd. with funds from Hong Kong, Macao & Taiwan	18	18
其他港澳台商投资	Other Enterprises with Funds from Hong Kong, Macao and Taiwan	2	2
（三）外商投资	Foreign Funded Enterprises	572	567
中外合资经营	Sino-foreign Joint Ventures	225	225
中外合作经营	Sino-Foreign Cooperation Enterprises	20	18
外资企业	Foreign Owned Enterprises	283	280
外商投资股份有限公司	Limited Company Funded by Foreign Investment	40	40
其他外商投资	Other Foreign Funded Enterprises	4	4

2-2 按国民经济行业分法人单位数（2012年）

Impersonal Entities by Sector（2012）

单位：个 (unit)

行业	Scetor	法人单位数 Number of Enterprises	企业 Enterprises
总计	**Total**	**103977**	**91812**
（一）农、林、牧、渔业	Agriculture,Forestry,Animal Husbandry and Fishery	2094	1676
农业	Farming	1137	911
林业	Forestry	213	189
畜牧业	Animal Husbandry	473	374
渔业	Fishery	30	26
农、林、牧、渔服务业	Services in Support of Agriculture	241	176
（二）采矿业	Mining	314	314
煤炭开采和洗选业	Mining and Washing of Coal	13	13
石油和天然气开采业	Extraction of Petroleum and Natural Gas	28	28
黑色金属矿采选业	Mining of Ferrous Metal Ores	13	13
有色金属矿采选业	Mining of Non-ferrous Metal Ores	40	40
非金属矿采选业	Mining and Processing of Nonmetal Ores	76	76
开采辅助活动	Mining auxiliary activities	94	94
其他采矿业	Other Mining	50	50
（三）制造业	Manufacturing	13797	13797
农副食品加工业	Processing of Food from Agricultural Products	362	362
食品制造业	Manufacture of Foods	380	380
酒、饮料和精制茶制造业	Alcohol,Beverage and Refined tea industry	129	129
烟草制品业	Manufacture of Tobacco	4	4
纺织业	Manufacture of Textile	142	142
纺织服装、服饰业	Textile, Garments industry	183	183
皮革、毛皮、羽毛及其制品和制鞋业	Leather, Fur, Feather and its Froducts and Footwear	37	37
木材加工和木、竹、藤、棕、草制品业	Timber Processing,Bamboo,Cane,Palm Fiber and Straw Products	152	152
家具制造业	Manufacture of Furniture	386	386
造纸及纸制品业	Manufacture of Paper and Paper Products	312	312
印刷和记录媒介复制业	Printing,Reproduction of Recording Media	565	565
文教、工美、体育和娱乐用品制造业	Cultural and Educational, Arts and Crafts,Sports and Entertainment manufacturing Industrial	211	211
石油加工、炼焦和核燃料加工业	Processing of Petroleum, Coking, Processing of Nuclear Fuel	62	62
化学原料和化学制品制造业	Manufacture of Raw Chemical Materials and Chemical Products	695	695

2-2 续表1 continued 1

单位：个 (unit)

行 业	Scetor	法人单位数 Number of Enterprises	企业 Enterprises
医药制造业	Manufacture of Medicines	388	388
化学纤维制造业	Manufacture of Chemical Fibers	21	21
橡胶和塑料制品业	Manufacture of Rubber and Manufacture of Plastics	403	403
非金属矿物制品业	Manufacture of Non-metallic Mineral Products	1123	1123
黑色金属冶炼和压延加工业	Smelting and Pressing of Ferrous Metals	316	316
有色金属冶炼和压延加工业	Smelting and Pressing of Non-ferrous Metals	153	153
金属制品业	Manufacture of Metal Products	954	954
通用设备制造业	Manufacture of General Purpose Machinery	1598	1598
专用设备制造业	Manufacture of Special Equipment	1461	1461
汽车制造业	Manufacture of Motor Vehicle	167	167
铁路、船舶、航空航天	Railways,Shipbuilding,Aerospace and Other		
和其他运输设备制造业	Transportation Equipment Manufacturing Industry	294	294
电气机械和器材制造业	Manufacture of Electric Equipment and Machinery	1438	1438
计算机、通信和其他	Manufacture of Communication Equipment,	1074	1074
电子设备制造业	Computers and other Electronic Equipment	89	89
仪器仪表制造业	Manufacture of Measuring Instruments and Machinery	522	522
其他制造业	Other Manufacturing	119	119
废弃资源综合利用	Recycling and Disposal of Waste	57	57
金属制品、机械和设备修理业	Metal Products,Machinery and Equipment Repair Industry	89	89
（四）电力、燃气及水的生产供应业	Production and Distribution of Electricity,Gas and Water	267	266
电力、热力生产和供应业	Production and Supply of Electric Power and Heat Power	150	149
燃气生产和供应业	Gas mining and supplying industry	44	44
水的生产和供应业	Production and Supply of Water	73	73
（五）建筑业	Construction	7513	7513
房屋建筑业	Construction of Building	1182	1182
土木工程建筑业	Civil Engineering	952	952
建筑安装业	Architectural Installation	1387	1387
建筑装饰和其他建筑业	Architectural Decoration and Other Construction	3992	3992
（六）批发和零售业	Wholesale and Retail Trades	33654	33654
批发业	Wholesale Trade	18714	18714
零售业	Retail Trade	14940	14940

2-2 续表2 continued 2

单位：个 (unit)

行 业	Scetor	法人单位数 Number of Enterprises	企业 Enterprises
（七）交通运输、仓储和邮政业	Traffic, Transport, Storage and Post	1670	1641
铁路运输业	Transport Via Railway	30	30
道路运输业	Transport Via Road	967	945
水上运输业	Water Transport	1	1
航空运输业	Air Transport	52	49
管道运输业	Transport Via Pipeline	5	5
装卸搬运和运输代理服务业	Loading, Unloading, Portage and Other Transport Services	343	342
仓储业	Storage	206	203
邮政业	Post	66	66
（八）住宿和餐饮业	Hotels and Catering Services	2821	2810
住宿业	Hotels	1050	1047
餐饮业	Catering Services	1771	1763
（九）信息传输、软件和信息技术服务业	Information transmission, software and information technology services	3313	3293
电信、广播电视和卫星传输服务	Telecommunications, broadcasting and TV transmission and satellite services	180	178
互联网和相关服务	internet and relevant services	591	588
软件和信息技术服务	Software and Information Technology Service	2542	2527
（十）金融业	Financial Intermediation	958	931
货币金融服务	Monetary and Financial Services	223	203
资本市场服务	Capital Market Services	373	372
保险业	Insurance	144	142
其他金融业	Other Financial Intermediation	218	214
（十一）房地产业	Real Estate	6205	6177
房地产业	Real Estate	6205	6177
（十二） 租赁和商务服务业	Leasing and Business Services	10093	9856
租赁业	Leasing	781	778
商务服务业	Business Services	9312	9078
（十三）科学研究和技术服务业	Scientific Research, Technical Sevice	4537	3980
研究与试验发展	Research and Experimental Development	366	271
专业技术服务业	Professional Technical Services	2331	2067
科技推广和应用服务业	Services of Science and Technology Exchanges and Promotion	1840	1642

2-2 续表3 continued 3

单位：个 (unit)

行业	Scetor	法人单位数 Number of Enterprises	企业 Enterprises
（十四）水利、环境和公共设施管理业	Management of Water Conservancy, Environment and Public Facilities	776	613
水利管理业	Management of Water Conservancy	117	52
生态保护和环境治理业	Environmental Management	92	75
公共设施管理业	Management of Public Facilities	567	486
（十五）居民服务、修理和其他服务业	Services to Households and Other Services	3343	3265
居民服务业	Services to Households	829	778
机动车、电子产品和日用产品修理业	The repair service industry for motor vehicle、electronic products and Household and personal product	995	992
其他服务业	Other Services	1519	1495
（十六）教育	Education	2894	317
教育	Education	2894	317
（十七）卫生和社会工作	Health, Social Security	2152	140
卫生	Health	2045	129
社会工作	Social	107	11
（十八）文化、体育和娱乐业	Culture, Sports and Entertainment	1829	1566
新闻和出版业	Journalism and Publishing Activities	151	102
广播、电视、电影和影视录音制作业	Broadcasting, Movies, Television and Audiovisual Activities	245	217
文化艺术业	Cultural and Art Activities	528	378
体育	Sports Activities	124	96
娱乐业	Entertainment	781	773
（十九）公共管理、社会保障和社会组织	Public Management and Social Organizaion	5747	3
中国共产党机关	Organs of Communist Party of China	168	
国家机构	Government Agencies	1542	
人民政协、民主党派	People's Pc~litical Consultative Conference and Democratic Parties	27	
社会保障	Social Security	35	2
群众团体、社会团体和其他成员组织	Mass organizations、social groups and other members of the organization	692	1
基层群众自治组织	Grass-roots Mass Self-Government Organizations	3283	
（二十）国际组织	International Organizations		
国际组织	International Organizations		

2-3 按行政区划分法人单位数（2012年）

Impersonal Entities by Region（2012）

单位：个 (unit)

区 县	Region	法人单位数 Number of Enterprises	企业 Enterprises
总 计	Total	103977	91812
新城区	Xincheng	6753	6022
碑林区	Beilin	11048	10419
莲湖区	Lianhu	11175	10464
灞桥区	Baqiao	4445	3777
未央区	Weiyang	16778	16208
雁塔区	Yanta	33754	32627
阎良区	Yanliang	1681	1322
临潼区	Lintong	2339	1334
长安区	Chang'an	5441	3976
蓝田县	Lantian	2268	954
周至县	Zhouzhi	2784	1234
户 县	Huxian	3345	1870
高陵县	Gaoling	2166	1605

2-4 按登记注册类型分产业活动单位数（2012年）

Industrial Active Units by Status of Registion（2012）

单位：个 (unit)

分　组	Classify	产业活动单位数 Number of Industrial Active Units	企业 Enterprises
总计	**Total**	**113604**	**98651**
按登记注册类型分	Grouped by Status of Registion		
（一）内资	Domestic Funded Enterprises	112214	97270
国有	State-owned Enterprises	9557	2783
集体	Collective-owned Enterprises	3272	1914
股份合作	Cooperative Enterprises	728	696
联营	Joint Ownership Enterprises	279	256
国有联营	State Joint Ownership Enterprises	38	33
集体联营	Collective Joint Ownership Enterprises	92	82
国有与集体联营	Joint State-collective Ownership Enterprises	24	19
其他联营	Other Joint Ownership Enterprises	125	122
有限责任公司	Limited Liability Corporations	37104	36984
国有独资公司	State Sole Funded Corporations	206	205
其他有限责任公司	Other Limited Liability Corporations	36898	36779
股份有限公司	Share-holding Corporations Limited	2388	2377
私营	Private Enterprises	48658	48019
私营独资企业	Private-funded Enterprises	11302	10857
私营合伙	Private Partnership Enterprises	2241	2165
私营有限责任公司	Private Limited Liability Corporations	32074	31964
私营股份有限公司	Private Share-holding Corporations Ltd.	3041	3033
其他	Other Enterprises	10228	4241

2-4 续表 continued

单位：个 (unit)

分　组	Classify	产业活动单位数 Number of Industrial Active Units	企业 Enterprises
（二）港、澳、台商投资企业	Enterprises with Funds from Hong Kong,Macao and Taiwan	479	476
与港、澳、台商合资经营	Joint-venture with Funds from Hong Kong,Macao and Taiwan	136	135
与港、澳、台商合作经营	Cooperative Enterprises with Funds from Hong Kong Macau and Taiwan	36	36
港澳台商独资经营	Enterprises with Sole Investment from Hong Kong Macau and Taiwan	283	281
港澳台商投资股份有限公司	Share-holding Corporations Ltd. with funds from Hong Kong, Macao & Taiwan	21	21
其他港澳台商投资	Other Enterprises with Funds from Hong Kong,Macao and Taiwan	3	3
（三）外商投资	Foreign Funded Enterprises	911	905
中外合资经营	Sino-foreign Joint Ventures	280	280
中外合作经营	Sino-Foreign Cooperation Enterprises	23	21
外资企业	Foreign Owned Enterprises	542	538
外商投资股份有限公司	Limited Company Funded by Foreign Investment	59	59
其他外商投资	Other Foreign Funded Enterprises	7	7

2-5 按国民经济行业分产业活动单位数（2012年）

Industrial Active Units by Sector（2012）

单位：个 (unit)

行 业	Scetor	产业活动单位数 Number of Industrial Active Units	企业 Enterprises
总计	**Item**	**113604**	**98651**
（一）农、林、牧、渔业	Agriculture,Forestry,Animal Husbandry and Fishery	2108	1690
农业	Farming	1143	917
林业	Forestry	215	191
畜牧业	Animal Husbandry	477	378
渔业	Fishery	30	26
农、林、牧、渔服务业	Services in Support of Agriculture	243	178
（二）采矿业	Mining	330	330
煤炭开采和洗选业	Mining and Washing of Coal	13	13
石油和天然气开采业	Extraction of Petroleum and Natural Gas	31	31
黑色金属矿采选业	Mining of Ferrous Metal Ores	13	13
有色金属矿采选业	Mining of Non-ferrous Metal Ores	40	40
非金属矿采选业	Mining and Processing of Nonmetal Ores	77	77
开采辅助活动	Mining auxiliary activities	106	106
其他采矿业	Mining of Other Ores	50	50
（三）制造业	Manufacturing	14120	14120
农副食品加工业	Processing of Food from Agricultural Products	377	377
食品制造业	Manufacture of Foods	384	384
酒、饮料和精制茶制造业	Alcohol,Beverage and Refined tea industry	134	134
烟草制品业	Manufacture of Tobacco	4	4
纺织业	Manufacture of Textile	146	146
纺织服装、服饰业	Textile, Garments industry	185	185
皮革、毛皮、羽毛及其制品和制鞋业	Manufacture of Leather, Fur, Feather and Related Products	38	38
木材加工和木、竹、藤、棕、草制品业	Processing of Timber,Manufacture of Wood,Bamboo,Rattan, Plam and Straw Products	160	160
家具制造业	Manufacture of Furniture	395	395
造纸及纸制品业	Manufacture of Paper and Paper Products	316	316
印刷和记录媒介复制业	Printing,Reproduction of Recording Media	577	577
文教、工美、体育和娱乐用品制造业	Manufacture of Articles For Culture,Education and Sport Activities	214	214
石油加工、炼焦和核燃料加工业	Processing of Petroleum, Coking, Processing of Nuclear Fuel	62	62
化学原料和化学制品制造业	Manufacture of Raw Chemical Materials and Chemical Products	709	709

2-5 续表1 continued 1

单位：个 (unit)

行业	Scetor	产业活动单位数 Number of Industrial Active Units	企业 Enterprises
医药制造业	Manufacture of Medicines	396	396
化学纤维制造业	Manufacture of Chemical Fibers	23	23
橡胶和塑料制品业	Manufacture of Rubber	408	408
非金属矿物制品业	Manufacture of Non-metallic Mineral Products	1145	1145
黑色金属冶炼和压延加工业	Smelting and Pressing of Ferrous Metals	318	318
有色金属冶炼和压延加工业	Smelting and Pressing of Non-ferrous Metals	155	155
金属制品业	Manufacture of Metal Products	972	972
通用设备制造业	Manufacture of General Purpose Machinery	1630	1630
专用设备制造业	Manufacture of Special Equipment	1504	1504
汽车制造业	Manufacture of Motor Vehicle	183	183
铁路、船舶、航空航天和其他运输设备制造业	Railways,Shipbuilding,Aerospace and Other Transportation Equipment Manufacturing Industry	307	307
电气机械和器材制造业	Manufacture of Electric Equipment and Machinery	1460	1460
计算机、通信和其他电子设备制造业	Manufacture of Communication Equipment, Computers and other Electronic Equipment	1105	1105
仪器仪表制造业	Manufacture of Measuring Instruments and Machinery	539	539
其他制造业	Other Manufacturing	122	122
废弃资源综合利用业	Recycling and Disposal of Waste	58	58
金属制品、机械和设备修理业	Metal Products,Machinery and Equipment Repair Industry	94	94
（四）电力、燃气及水的生产供应业	Production and Distribution of Electricity,Gas and Water	281	278
电力、热力生产和供应业	Production and Supply of Electric Power and Heat Power	159	156
燃气生产和供应业	Gas mining and supplying industry	46	46
水的生产和供应业	Production and Supply of Water	76	76
（五）建筑业	Construction	7855	7855
房屋建筑业	Construction of Building	1338	1338
土木工程建筑业	Civil Engineering	997	997
建筑安装业	Architectural Installation	1419	1419
建筑装饰和其他建筑业	Architectural Decoration and Other Construction	4101	4101
（六）批发和零售业	Wholesale and Retail Trades	35940	35940
批发业	Wholesale Trade	19123	19123
零售业	Retail Trade	16817	16817

2-5 续表2 continued 2

单位：个 (unit)

行业	Scetor	产业活动单位数 Number of Industrial Active Units	企业 Enterprises
（七）交通运输、仓储和邮政业	Traffic, Transport, Storage and Post	2098	2045
铁路运输业	Transport Via Railway	34	34
道路运输业	Transport Via Road	1088	1048
水上运输业	Water Transport	4	3
航空运输业	Air Transport	55	52
管道运输业	Transport Via Pipeline	7	7
装卸搬运和运输代理服务业	Loading, Unloading, Portage and Other Transport Services	383	382
仓储业	Storage	222	218
邮政业	Post	305	301
（八）住宿和餐饮业	Hotels and Catering Services	3306	3292
住宿业	Hotels	1152	1147
餐饮业	Catering Services	2154	2145
（九）信息传输、软件和信息技术服务业	Information Transmission, Computer Services and Software	3610	3586
电信、广播电视和卫星传输服务	Telecom & Other Information Transmission Services	310	308
互联网和相关服务	internet and relevant services	619	615
软件和信息技术服务	Software and Information Technology Service	2681	2663
（十）金融业	Financial Intermediation	2565	2518
货币金融服务	Monetary and Financial Services	1498	1464
资本市场服务	Capital Market Services	426	425
保险业	Insurance	409	402
其他金融业	Other Financial Intermediation	232	227
（十一）房地产业	Real Estate	6383	6344
房地产业	Real Estate	6383	6344
（十二）租赁和商务服务业	Leasing and Business Services	10518	10177
租赁业	Leasing	806	803
商务服务业	Business Services	9712	9374
（十三）科学研究和技术服务业	Scientific Research, Technical Sevice and	4767	4114
研究与试验发展	Geologic Prospecting	378	281
专业技术服务业	Professional Technical Services	2443	2145
科技推广和应用服务业	Services of Science and Technology Exchanges and Promotion	1946	1688

2-5 续表3 continued 3

单位：个 (unit)

行 业	Scetor	产业活动单位数 Number of Industrial Active Units	企业 Enterprises
（十四）水利、环境和公共设施管理业	Management of Water Conservancy, Environment and	894	630
水利管理业	Public Facilities	159	52
生态保护和环境治理业	Ecological protection and environmental governance industry	94	75
公共设施管理业	Management of Public Facilities	641	503
（十五）居民服务、修理和其他服务业	Services to Households and Other Services	3728	3625
居民服务业	Services to Households	1121	1056
机动车、电子产品和日用产品修理业	The repair service industry for motor vehicle、electronic products and Household and personal product	1024	1021
其他服务业	Other Services	1583	1548
（十六）教育	Education	3564	332
教育	Education	3564	332
（十七）卫生和社会工作	Health, Social Security and Social Welfare	2487	156
卫生	Health	2373	145
社会工作	social work	114	11
（十八）文化、体育和娱乐业	Culture, Sports and Entertainment	1921	1616
新闻和出版业	Journalism and Publishing Activities	169	112
广播、电视、电影和影视录音制作业	Broadcasting, Movies, Television and Audiovisual Activities	256	226
文化艺术业	Cultural and Art Activities	558	381
体育	Sports Activities	143	113
娱乐业	Entertainment	795	784
（十九）公共管理、社会保障和社会组织	Public Management and Social Organizaion	7129	3
中国共产党机关	Organs of Communist Party of China	181	
国家机构	Government Agencies	2745	
人民政协、民主党派	Chinese People's Political Consultative Conference、democratic parties	27	
社会保障	Social Security	48	2
群众团体、社会团体和其他成员组织	Non-Government Organizations, Social Organizations and Religion Organizations	818	1
基层群众自治组织	Grass-roots Mass Self-Government Organizations	3310	
（二十）国际组织	International Organizations		
国际组织	International Organizations		

2-6 按行政区划分产业活动单位数（2012年）

Industrial Active Units by Region（2012）

单位：个 (unit)

区 县	Region	产业活动单位数 Number of Enterprises	企业 Enterprises
总 计	**Total**	**113604**	**98651**
新城区	Xincheng	7751	6815
碑林区	Beilin	12426	11700
莲湖区	Lianhu	12219	11378
灞桥区	Baqiao	4859	4145
未央区	Weiyang	17469	16865
雁塔区	Yanta	35626	34150
阎良区	Yanliang	1897	1484
临潼区	Lintong	3021	1544
长安区	Chang'an	5809	4207
蓝田县	Lantian	2989	1102
周至县	Zhouzhi	3189	1339
户 县	Huxian	3870	2204
高陵县	Gaoling	2479	1718

2-7 按统计机构分企业一套表调查单位数（2012年）

Number of Survey Units by Statistical Agencies of "One Table" (2012)

单位：个 (unit)

区县、开发区	Region	规模以上工业 Industrial Enterprises above designed size	限额以上批发零售住宿餐饮业 Above wholesale and retail accommodation and catering industry	资质内建筑业 Qualified Construction Enterprises	房地产开发经营企业 Real Estate Development Enterprises	重点服务业 Key Service Enterprises
全市	Total	966	1080	396	672	570
新城区	Xincheng	16	141	32	53	25
碑林区	Beilin	15	166	40	71	84
莲湖区	Lianhu	38	128	34	65	46
灞桥区	Baqiao	113	53	32	30	11
未央区	Weiyang	27	59	30	57	19
雁塔区	Yanta	41	115	102	73	49
阎良区	Yanliang	56	16	15	25	6
临潼区	Lintong	40	18	13	7	10
长安区	Chang'an	33	45	20	39	13
蓝田县	Lantian	22	10	9	10	2
周至县	Zhouzhi	28	12	7	16	8
户　县	Huxian	54	23	6	15	6
高陵县	Gaoling	33	22	6	26	9
高新技术开发区	GaoXin	196	112	15	44	144
经济技术开发区	JingKai	149	116	31	47	80
曲江新区	Qujiang		14		37	42
浐灞生态区	Chanba Eco-District		1		28	4
阎良国家航空技术产业基地	Aviation Industry Base	14			10	
国家民用航天产业基地	Aerospace Base	17	2	1	13	2
国际港务区	International Trade &Logistic Park				1	5
沣东新城	FengDongXinCheng	51	27	3	5	5
其他	other	23				

2-8 按行政区划分企业一套表调查单位数（2012年）

Number of Survey Units by Region of "One Table " (2012)

单位：个 (unit)

区　县	Region	规模以上工业 Industrial Enterprises above designed size	限额以上批发零售住宿餐饮业 Above wholesale and retail accommodation and catering industry	资质内建筑业 Qualified Construction Enterprises	房地产开发经营企业 Real Estate Development Enterprises	重点服务业 Key Service Enterprises
全市	Total	966	1080	396	672	570
新城区	Xincheng	21	140	31	57	26
碑林区	Beilin	16	168	41	72	89
莲湖区	Lianhu	46	127	35	66	48
灞桥区	Baqiao	118	53	32	45	19
未央区	Weiyang	167	203	63	122	103
雁塔区	Yanta	199	234	115	147	222
阎良区	Yanliang	72	16	15	35	6
临潼区	Lintong	40	18	13	7	10
长安区	Chang'an	101	53	23	55	19
蓝田县	Lantian	24	10	9	9	2
周至县	Zhouzhi	28	12	7	16	8
户　县	Huxian	55	23	6	15	6
高陵县	Gaoling	79	23	6	26	12

注：本表为2012年企业一套表年报数。

2-9 按国民经济行业（GB/T4754-2002）分法人单位数（2012年）

Impersonal Entities by Sector（GB/T4754-2002）（2012）

单位：个 (unit)

行　业	Scetor	法人单位数 Number of Enterprises	企业 Enterprises
总计	**Total**	**103977**	**91812**
（一）农、林、牧、渔业	Agriculture,Forestry,Animal Husbandry and Fishery	2151	1678
农业	Farming	1048	847
林业	Forestry	244	219
畜牧业	Animal Husbandry	471	372
渔业	Fishery	29	25
农、林、牧、渔服务业	Services in Support of Agriculture	359	215
（二）采矿业	Mining	310	310
煤炭开采和洗选业	Mining and Washing of Coal	19	19
石油和天然气开采业	Extraction of Petroleum and Natural Gas	101	101
黑色金属矿采选业	Mining of Ferrous Metal Ores	13	13
有色金属矿采选业	Mining of Non-ferrous Metal Ores	36	36
非金属矿采选业	Mining and Processing of Nonmetal Ores	75	75
其他采矿业	Mining of Other Ores	66	66
（三）制造业	Manufacturing	13917	13917
农副食品加工业	Processing of Food from Agricultural Products	368	368
食品制造业	Manufacture of Foods	374	374
饮料制造业	Manufacture of Beverages	128	128
烟草加工业	Manufacture of Tobacco	4	4
纺织业	Manufacture of Textile	164	164
纺织服装、鞋、帽制造业	Manufacture of Textile Wearing Apparel, Footwarc and Caps	162	162
皮革、毛皮、羽毛（绒）及其制造业	Manufacture of Leather, Fur, Feather and Related Products	32	32
木材加工及竹、藤、棕、草制品业	Processing of Timber,Manufacture of Wood,Bamboo,Rattan, Plam and Straw Products	152	152
家具制造业	Manufacture of Furniture	383	383
造纸及纸制品业	Manufacture of Paper and Paper Products	312	312
印刷业、记录媒介的复制	Printing,Reproduction of Recording Media	563	563
文教体育用品制造业	Manufacture of Articles For Culture,Education and Sport Activities	55	55
石油加工、炼焦及核燃料加工业	Processing of Petroleum, Coking, Processing of Nuclear Fuel	61	61
化学原料及化学制品制造业	Manufacture of Raw Chemical Materials and Chemical Products	698	698

2-9 续表1 continued 1

单位：个 (unit)

行业	Scetor	法人单位数 Number of Enterprises	企业 Enterprises
医药制造业	Manufacture of Medicines	386	386
化学纤维制造业	Manufacture of Chemical Fibers	22	22
橡胶制品业	Manufacture of Rubber	100	100
塑料制品业	Manufacture of Plastics	307	307
非金属矿物制品业	Manufacture of Non-metallic Mineral Products	1110	1110
黑色金属冶炼及压延加工业	Smelting and Pressing of Ferrous Metals	149	149
有色金属冶炼及压延加工业	Smelting and Pressing of Non-ferrous Metals	169	169
金属制品业	Manufacture of Metal Products	937	937
通用设备制造业	Manufacture of General Purpose Machinery	1821	1821
专用设备制造业	Manufacture of Special Equipment	1582	1582
交通运输设备制造业	Manufacture of Transport Equipment	488	488
电气机械及器材制造业	Manufacture of Electric Equipment and Machinery	1449	1449
通信设备、计算机及其他电子设备制造业	Manufacture of Communication Equipment, Computers and other Electronic Equipment	1064	1064
仪器仪表及文化、办公用机械制造业	Manufacture of Measuring Instruments and Machinery for Cultural Activity and Office Work	546	546
工艺品及其他制造业	Manufacture of Artwork and Other Manufacturing	273	273
废弃资源和废旧材料回收加工业	Recycling and Disposal of Waste	58	58
（四）电力、燃气及水的生产供应业	Production and Distribution of Electricity,Gas and Water	266	265
电力、热力的生产和供应业	Production and Supply of Electric Power and Heat Power	150	149
燃气生产和供应业	Gas mining and supplying industry	44	44
水的生产和供应业	Production and Supply of Water	72	72
（五）建筑业	Construction	7516	7516
房屋和土木工程建筑业	Construction of Building & Civil Engineering	2108	2108
建筑安装业	Architectural Installation	1458	1458
建筑装饰业	Architectural Decoration	2782	2782
其他建筑业	Other Construction	1168	1168
（六）交通运输、仓储及邮政业	Traffic, Transport, Storage and Post	1660	1631
铁路运输业	Transport Via Railway	29	29
道路运输业	Transport Via Road	863	843
城市公共交通业	Urban Public Traffic	93	91

2-9 续表2 continued 2

单位：个 (unit)

行 业	Scetor	法人单位数 Number of Enterprises	企业 Enterprises
水上运输业	Water Transport		
航空运输业	Air Transport	52	49
管道运输业	Transport Via Pipeline	5	5
装卸搬运和其他运输业	Loading, Unloading, Portage and Other Transport Services	349	348
仓储业	Storage	207	204
邮政业	Post	62	62
（七）信息传输、计算机服务和软件业	Information Transmission, Computer Services and Software	3742	3721
电信传输和其他信息传输服务业	Telecom & Other Information Transmission Services	636	632
计算机服务业	Computer Services	1621	1612
软件业	Software Industry	1485	1477
（八）批发和零售业	Wholesale and Retail Trades	33654	33654
批发业	Wholesale Trade	18698	18698
零售业	Retail Trade	14956	14956
（九）住宿和餐饮业	Hotels and Catering Services	2821	2810
住宿业	Hotels	1048	1045
餐饮业	Catering Services	1773	1765
（十）金融业	Financial Intermediation	687	659
银行业	Bank	74	70
证券业	Security Activities	128	127
保险业	Insurance	143	141
其他金融业	Other Financial Intermediation	342	321
（十一）房地产业	Real Estate	6205	6177
房地产业	Real Estate	6205	6177
（十二）租赁和商务服务业	Leasing and Business Services	10411	10171
租赁业	Leasing	787	784
商务服务业	Business Services	9624	9387
（十三）科学研究、技术服务和地质勘查业	Scientific Research, Technical Sevice and Geologic Prospecting	4412	3909
研究与试验发展	Research and Experimental Development	370	273
专业技术服务业	Professional Technical Services	2029	1853
科技交流和推广服务业	Services of Science and Technology Exchanges and Promotion	1858	1654
地质勘查业	Geologic Prospecting	155	129

2–9 续表3 continued 3

单位：个 (unit)

行 业	Scetor	法人单位数 Number of Enterprises	企业 Enterprises
（十四）水利、环境和公共设施管理业	Management of Water Conservancy, Environment and Public Facilities	768	604
水利管理业	Management of Water Conservancy	110	44
环境管理业	Environmental Management	171	132
公共设施管理业	Management of Public Facilities	487	428
（十五）居民服务和其他服务业	Services to Households and Other Services	3357	3275
居民服务业	Services to Households	961	906
其他服务业	Other Services	2396	2369
（十六）教育	Education	2884	313
教育	Education	2884	313
（十七）卫生、社会保障和社会福利业	Health, Social Security and Social Welfare	2157	111
卫生	Health	2016	99
社会保障业	Social Security	35	3
社会福利	Social Welfare	106	9
（十八）文化、体育和娱乐业	Culture, Sports and Entertainment	1351	1091
新闻出版	Journalism and Publishing Activities	147	99
广播、电视、电影和音像业	Broadcasting, Movies, Television and Audiovisual Activities	233	206
文化艺术业	Cultural and Art Activities	553	404
体育	Sports Activities	57	26
娱乐业	Entertainment	361	356
（十九）公共管理和社会组织	Public Management and Social Organizaion	5708	
中国共产党机关	Organs of Communist Party of China	168	
国家机构	Government Agencies	1539	
人民政协和民主党派	People's Political Consultative Conference and Democratic Parties	27	
群众团体、社会团体和宗教组织	Non-Government Organizations, Social Organizations and Religion Organizations	691	
基层群众自治组织	Grass-roots Mass Self-Government Organizations	3283	
（二十）国际组织	International Organizations		

2-10 按国民经济行业（GB/T4754-2002）分产业活动单位数（2012年）

Industrial Active Units by Sector（GB/T4754-2002）（2012）

单位：个 (unit)

行　业	Scetor	产业活动单位数 Number of Industrial Active Units	企业 Enterprises
总计	**Total**	**113604**	**98651**
（一）农、林、牧、渔业	Agriculture,Forestry,Animal Husbandry and Fishery	2220	1727
农业	Farming	1089	888
林业	Forestry	246	221
畜牧业	Animal Husbandry	475	376
渔业	Fishery	29	25
农、林、牧、渔服务业	Services in Support of Agriculture	381	217
（二）采矿业	Mining	326	326
煤炭开采和洗选业	Mining and Washing of Coal	19	19
石油和天然气开采业	Extraction of Petroleum and Natural Gas	116	116
黑色金属矿采选业	Mining of Ferrous Metal Ores	13	13
有色金属矿采选业	Mining of Non-ferrous Metal Ores	36	36
非金属矿采选业	Mining and Processing of Nonmetal Ores	76	76
其他采矿业	Mining of Other Ores	66	66
（三）制造业	Manufacturing	14247	14247
农副食品加工业	Processing of Food from Agricultural Products	383	383
食品制造业	Manufacture of Foods	378	378
饮料制造业	Manufacture of Beverages	133	133
烟草加工业	Manufacture of Tobacco	4	4
纺织业	Manufacture of Textile	169	169
纺织服装、鞋、帽制造业	Manufacture of Textile Wearing Apparel, Footware and Caps	163	163
皮革、毛皮、羽毛（绒）及其制造业	Manufacture of Leather, Fur, Feather and Related Products	33	33
木材加工及竹、藤、棕、草制品业	Processing of Timber,Manufacture of Wood,Bamboo,Rattan, Plam and Straw Products	160	160
家具制造业	Manufacture of Furniture	392	392
造纸及纸制品业	Manufacture of Paper and Paper Products	316	316
印刷业、记录媒介的复制	Printing,Reproduction of Recording Media	574	574
文教体育用品制造业	Manufacture of Articles For Culture,Education and Sport Activities	56	56
石油加工、炼焦及核燃料加工业	Processing of Petroleum, Coking, Processing of Nuclear Fuel	61	61
化学原料及化学制品制造业	Manufacture of Raw Chemical Materials and Chemical Products	712	712

2-10 续表1 continued 1

单位：个 (unit)

行 业	Scetor	产业活动单位数 Number of Industrial Active Units	企业 Enterprises
医药制造业	Manufacture of Medicines	394	394
化学纤维制造业	Manufacture of Chemical Fibers	24	24
橡胶制品业	Manufacture of Rubber	102	102
塑料制品业	Manufacture of Plastics	310	310
非金属矿物制品业	Manufacture of Non-metallic Mineral Products	1132	1132
黑色金属冶炼及压延加工业	Smelting and Pressing of Ferrous Metals	150	150
有色金属冶炼及压延加工业	Smelting and Pressing of Non-ferrous Metals	171	171
金属制品业	Manufacture of Metal Products	953	953
通用设备制造业	Manufacture of General Purpose Machinery	1857	1857
专用设备制造业	Manufacture of Special Equipment	1628	1628
交通运输设备制造业	Manufacture of Transport Equipment	525	525
电气机械及器材制造业	Manufacture of Electric Equipment and Machinery	1471	1471
通信设备、计算机及其他电子设备制造业	Manufacture of Communication Equipment, Computers and other Electronic Equipment	1094	1094
仪器仪表及文化、办公用机械制造业	Manufacture of Measuring Instruments and Machinery for Cultural Activity and Office Work	565	565
工艺品及其他制造业	Manufacture of Artwork and Other Manufacturing	278	278
废弃资源和废旧材料回收加工业	Recycling and Disposal of Waste	59	59
（四）电力、燃气及水的生产供应业	Production and Distribution of Electricity,Gas and Water	280	277
电力、热力的生产和供应业	Production and Supply of Electric Power and Heat Power	159	156
燃气生产和供应业	Gas mining and supplying industry	46	46
水的生产和供应业	Production and Supply of Water	75	75
（五）建筑业	Construction	7856	7856
房屋和土木工程建筑业	Construction of Building & Civil Engineering	2308	2308
建筑安装业	Architectural Installation	1491	1491
建筑装饰业	Architectural Decoration	2854	2854
其他建筑业	Other Construction	1203	1203
（六）交通运输、仓储及邮政业	Traffic, Transport, Storage and Post	2079	2026
铁路运输业	Transport Via Railway	32	32
道路运输业	Transport Via Road	975	937
城市公共交通业	Urban Public Traffic	102	100

2-10 续表2 continued 2

单位：个 (unit)

行 业	Scetor	产业活动单位数 Number of Industrial Active Units	企业 Enterprises
水上运输业	Water Transport	3	2
航空运输业	Air Transport	55	52
管道运输业	Transport Via Pipeline	7	7
装卸搬运和其他运输业	Loading, Unloading, Portage and Other Transport Services	386	385
仓储业	Storage	223	219
邮政业	Post	296	292
（七）信息传输、计算机服务和软件业	Information Transmission, Computer Services and Software	4041	4015
电信传输和其他信息传输服务业	Telecom & Other Information Transmission Services	791	784
计算机服务业	Computer Services	1689	1679
软件业	Software Industry	1561	1552
（八）批发和零售业	Wholesale and Retail Trades	35933	35933
批发业	Wholesale Trade	19103	19103
零售业	Retail Trade	16830	16830
（九）住宿和餐饮业	Hotels and Catering Services	3301	3287
住宿业	Hotels	1149	1144
餐饮业	Catering Services	2152	2143
（十）金融业	Financial Intermediation	2292	2244
银行业	Bank	1345	1327
证券业	Security Activities	178	177
保险业	Insurance	408	401
其他金融业	Other Financial Intermediation	361	339
（十一）房地产业	Real Estate	6381	6342
房地产业	Real Estate	6381	6342
（十二） 租赁和商务服务业	Leasing and Business Services	10833	10490
租赁业	Leasing	810	807
商务服务业	Business Services	10023	9683
（十三）科学研究、技术服务和地质勘查业	Scientific Research, Technical Sevice and Geologic Prospecting	4616	4035
研究与试验发展	Research and Experimental Development	382	283
专业技术服务业	Professional Technical Services	2109	1920
科技交流和推广服务业	Services of Science and Technology Exchanges and Promotion	1968	1701
地质勘查业	Geologic Prospecting	157	131

2-10 续表3 continued 3

单位：个 (unit)

行 业	Scetor	产业活动单位数 Number of Industrial Active Units	企业 Enterprises
（十四）水利、环境和公共设施管理业	Management of Water Conservancy, Environment and Public Facilities	886	621
水利管理业	Management of Water Conservancy	152	44
环境管理业	Environmental Management	220	133
公共设施管理业	Management of Public Facilities	514	444
（十五）居民服务和其他服务业	Services to Households and Other Services	3736	3629
居民服务业	Services to Households	1256	1187
其他服务业	Other Services	2480	2442
（十六）教育	Education	3555	329
教育	Education	3555	329
（十七）卫生、社会保障和社会福利业	Health, Social Security and Social Welfare	2503	126
卫生	Health	2342	114
社会保障业	Social Security	48	3
社会福利	Social Welfare	113	9
（十八）文化、体育和娱乐业	Culture, Sports and Entertainment	1442	1141
新闻出版	Journalism and Publishing Activities	167	111
广播、电视、电影和音像业	Broadcasting, Movies, Television and Audiovisual Activities	243	214
文化艺术业	Cultural and Art Activities	583	407
体育	Sports Activities	64	32
娱乐业	Entertainment	385	377
（十九）公共管理和社会组织	Public Management and Social Organizaion	7077	
中国共产党机关	Organs of Communist Party of China	181	
国家机构	Government Agencies	2742	
人民政协和民主党派	People's Political Consultative Conference and Democratic Parties	27	
群众团体、社会团体和宗教组织	Non-Government Organizations, Social Organizations and Religion Organizations	817	
基层群众自治组织	Grass-roots Mass Self-Government Organizations	3310	
（二十）国际组织	International Organizations		

主要统计指标解释

企业（单位）登记注册类型 是以在工商行政管理机关登记注册的各类企业为划分对象，以工商行政管理部门对企业登记注册的类型为依据，将企业登记注册类型分为内资企业、港澳台商投资企业和外商投资企业三大类。内资企业包括国有企业、集体企业、股份合作企业、联营企业、有限责任公司、股份有限公司、私营公司和其他企业；港澳台商投资企业和外商投资企业分别包括合资经营企业、合作经营企业、独资经营企业和股份有限公司。对不在工商行政管理部门进行登记注册的行政机关、事业单位和社会团体，主要按其经费来源和管理方式进行划分。

国有企业 指企业全部资产归国家所有，并按《中华人民共和国企业法人登记管理条例》规定登记注册的非公司制的经济组织。不包括有限责任公司中的国有独资公司。

集体企业 指企业资产归集体所有，并按《中华人民共和国企业法人登记管理条例》规定登记注册的经济组织。

股份合作企业 指以合作制为基础，由企业职工共同出资入股，吸收一定比例的社会资产投资组建，实行自主经营，自负盈亏，共同劳动，民主管理，按劳分配与按股分红相结合的一种集体经济组织。

联营企业 指两个及两个以上相同或不同所有制性质的企业法人或事业单位法人，按自愿、平等、互利的原则，共同投资组成的经济组织。联营企业包括国有联营企业、集体联营企业、国有与集体联营企业和其他联营企业。

有限责任公司 指根据《中华人民共和国公司登记管理条例》规定登记注册，由两个以上、五十个以下的股东共同出资，每个股东以其所认缴的出资额对公司承担有限责任，公司以其全部资产对其债务承担责任的经济组织。有限责任公司包括国有独资公司以及其他有限责任公司。

股份有限公司 指根据《中华人民共和国公司登记管理条例》规定登记注册，其全部注册资本由等额股份构成并通过发行股票筹集资本，股东以其认购的股份对公司承担有限责任，公司以其全部资产对其债务承担责任的经济组织。

私营企业 指由自然人投资设立或由自然人控股，以雇佣劳动为基础的营利性经济组织。包括按照《公司法》、《合伙企业法》、《私营企业暂行条例》规定登记注册的私营有限责任公司、私营股份有限公司、私营合伙企业和私营独资企业。

其他企业 指上述企业之外的其他内资经济组织。

与港澳台商合资经营企业 指港澳台地区投资者与内地企业依照《中华人民共和国中外合资经营企业法》及有关法律的规定，按合同规定的比例投资设立、分享利润和分担风险的企业。

与港澳台商合作经营企业 指港澳台地区投资者与内地企业依照《中华人民共和国中外合作经营企业法》及有关法律的规定，依照合作合同的约定进行投资或提供条件设立、分配利润和分担风险的企业。

港澳台商独资经营企业 指依照《中华人民共和国外资企业法》及有关法律的规定，在内地由港澳台地区投资者全额投资设立的企业。

港澳台商投资股份有限公司 指根据国家有关规定，经原外经贸部依法批准设立，其中港、澳、台商的股本占公司注册资本的比例达25%以上的股份有限公司。凡其中港、澳、台商的股本占公司注册资本的比例小于25%的，属于内资企业中的股份有限公司。

中外合资经营企业 指外国企业或外国人与中国内地企业依照《中华人民共和国中外合资经营企业法》及有关法律的规定，按合同规定的比例投资设立、分享利润和分担风险的企业。

中外合作经营企业 指外国企业或外国人与中国内地企业依照《中华人民共和国中外合作经营企业法》及有关法律的规定，依照合作合同的约定进行投资或提供条件设立、分配利润和分担风险的企业。

外资企业 指依照《中华人民共和国外资企业法》及有关法律的规定，在中国内地由外国投资者全额投资设立的企业。

外商投资股份有限公司 指根据国家有关规定，经原外经贸部依法批准设立，其中外资的股本占公司注册资本的比例达25%以上的股份有限公司。凡其中外资股本占公司注册资本的比例小于25%的，属于内资企业中的股份有限公司。

行政机关、事业单位和社会团体 参照企业登记注册类型，主要按其经费来源和管理方式划分。具体规定如下：

（1）行政机关：包括国家机关和政党机关，原则上均列为“国有”。但有特殊规定的，如供销社等，则列为“集体”。

（2）事业单位：包括经国家机构编制部门和有关业务主管部门批准成立的各类事业单位，不包括实行企业化管理的事业单位。事业单位的划分办法如下：

①由国家财政预　拨款或列入财政预　外资金管理以及经费主要来源于国有主管部门或国有上级单位的事业单位，列为“国有”。

②经费主要来源于集体单位的事业单位，列为“集体”。

③公民个人（或个人合伙）开办的事业单位，列为“私营”。

④上述以外的其他事业单位，如果其经费来源不明确，按管理方式进行归类。

（3）社会团体：包括经民政部门批准成立以及未纳入社会团体管理条例范围的工会、妇联等各类社会团体。社会团体的划分办法如下：

①未纳入民政部社会团体管理条例范围的工会、妇联、共青团、青联、工商联、科协、侨联等社会团体，国家拨款设立的基金会或基金管理组织以及经费主要来源于国有业务主管部门或国有上级单位的社会团体，列为“国有”。

②经费主要来源于集体单位的社会团体，列为“集体”。

③公民个人（或个人合伙）开办的社会团体，划为“私营”。

④上述以外的其他社会团体，如果其经费来源不明确，改按管理方式进行归类。

Explanatory Notes on Main Statistical Indicators

Registration Status of Enterprises Enterprises are classified into 3 categories, namely domestic-funded enterprises, enterprises with investment from Hong Kong, Macau and Taiwan, and enterprises with foreign investment, according to the registration status of an enterprise in industrial and commercial administration agencies. Domestic-funded enterprises include State- owned enterprises, collective-owned enterprises, cooperative enterprises, joint ownership enterprises, limited liability corporations, share-holding corporations Ltd., private enterprises and other enterprises. Included in the enterprises with investment from Hong Kong, Macau and Taiwan and enterprises with foreign investment are joint-venture enterprises, cooperative enterprises, sole investment enterprises and share-holding corporations Ltd. For government agencies, institutions and social organizations which are not registered in industrial and commercial administration agencies, they are classified mainly by their sources of funding and manner of management.

State–owned Enterprises refer to non-corporation economic units where the entire assets are owned by the State and which have been registered in accordance with the Regulation of the People's Republic of China on the Management of Registration of Corporate Enterprises. Not included from this category are solely State-funded corporations in the limited liability corporations.

Collective–owned Enterprises refer to economic units where the assets are owned collectively and which have been registered in accordance with the Regulation of the People's Republic of China on the Management of Registration of Corporate Enterprises.

Cooperative Enterprises refer to a form of collective economic units (enterprises)where capitals come mainly from employees as their shares, with certain proportion of capital from the outside, where production is organized on the basis of independent operation, independent accounting for profits and losses, joint work, democratic management, and a distribution system that integrates remuneration according to work with dividend according to capital share.

Joint Ownership Enterprises refer to economic units established by two or more corporate enterprises or corporate institutions of the same or different ownership, through joint investment on the basis of voluntary participation, equality, and mutual benefits. They include State joint ownership enterprises; collective joint ownership enterprises; joint State-collective enterprises; and other joint ownership enterprises.

Limited Liability Corporations refer to economic units established with investment from 2-50 investors and registered in accordance with the Regulation of the People's Republic of China on the Management of Registration of Corporations, each investor bearing limited liability to the corporation depending on its share of investment, and the corporation bearing liability to its debt to the maximum of its total assets. Limited liability corporations include solely State-funded limited liability corporations and other limited liability corporations.

Share–holding Corporations Ltd. refer to economic units registered in accordance with the Regulation of the People's Republic of China on the Management of Registration of Corporations, with total registered capital divided into equal shares and raised through issuing stocks. Each investor bears limited liability to the corporation depending on the holding of shares, and the corporation bears liability to its debt to the maximum of its total assets.

Private Enterprises refer to profit-making economic units invested and established by natural persons, or controlled by natural persons using employed labour~ Included in this category are private limited liability corporations, private share-holding corporations Ltd., private partnership enterprises and private-funded enterprises registered in accordance with the Company Law, the Law on Partnership Business and Interim Regulations on Private Enterprises.

Other Domestic–funded Enterprises refer to domestic-funded economic units other than those mentioned above.

Joint Venture Enterprises with Funds from Hong Kong, Macau and Taiwan are enterprises established by investors from Hong Kong, Macau and Taiwan with enterprises in the mainland of China in accordance with the Law of the People's Republic of China on Sino-foreign Equity Joint Ventures and other relevant laws, where the establishment of the investment and the sharing of profits and risks are stipulated under joint venture contracts.

Cooperative Enterprises with Funds from Hong Kong, Macan and Taiwan established by investors from Hong Kong, Macau and Taiwan with enterprises in the mainland of China in accordance with the Law of the People's Republic of China on Sino-foreign Contractual Joint Venture and other relevant laws, where the investment or provision of facilities and the sharing of profits and risks are stipulated under cooperative contracts.

Enterprises with Sole (exclusive)Investment from

Hong Kong, Macau and Taiwan refer to enterprises established in the mainland of China with exclusive investment from investors from Hong Kong, Macau and Taiwan in accordance with the Law of the People's Republic of China on Wholly Foreign-owned Enterprises and other relevant laws.

Share–holding Corporations Ltd. with Investment from Hong Kong, Macau and Taiwan refer to share- holding corporations Ltd. established with the approval from the former Ministry of Foreign Trade and Economic Relations in line with relevant State regulations, where the share of investment from Hong Kong, Macau or Taiwan businessmen exceeds 25% of the total registered capital of the corporation. In case the share of investmentfrom Hong Kong, Macau or Taiwan is less than 25% of thetotal registered capital, the enterprise is to be classified as domestic-funded share-holding corporation Ltd.

Joint Venture Enterprises with Foreign Investment refer to enterprises jointly established byforeign enterprises or foreigners with enterprises in themainland of China in accordance with the Law of thePeople's Republic of China on Sino-foreign Equity JointVentures and other relevant laws, where the sharing ofinvestment, profits and risks is stipulated under contract.

Cooperative Enterprises with Foreign Investment refer to enterprises jointly established by foreign enterprises or foreigners with enterprises in the mainland of China in accordance with the Law of the People's Republic of China on Sino-foreign Contractual Joint Venture and other relevant laws, where the investment or provision of facilities and the sharing of profits and risks are stipulated under cooperative contracts.

Enterprises with Sole (exclusive)Foreign Investment refer to enterprises established in the mainland of China with exclusive investment from foreign investors in accordance with the Law of the People's Republic of China on Wholly Foreign-owned Enterprises and other relevant laws.

Share–holding Corporations Ltd. with Foreign Investment refer to share-holding corporations Ltd. established with the approval from the former Ministry of Foreign Trade and Economic Relations in line with relevant State regulations, where the share of investment from foreign investors exceeds 25% of the total registered capital of the corporation. In case the share of foreign investment is less than 25% ofthe total registered capital, the enterprise is to be classified as domestic-funded share-holding corporation Ltd.

Government Agencies, Institutions and Social Organizations are classified into the following categories by source of funds and manner of management taking reference of thc registration status of enterprises:

(1)Government agencies: include State and party agencies, classified in principle as State-owned. There are exceptions, such as supply and marketing cooperatives which are classified as collective-owned.

(2)Institutions: include institutions of various types established with the approval by organization and staffing departments of the government, but exclude institutions where enterprise management system is introduced. Institutions are further classified as follows:

(a)Institutions for which their main budgets are from government budget appropriations or extra-budget funds, or allocated from the budget of their competent government agencies. Such institutions are classified as state-owned.

(b)Institutions for which their budget mainly come from collective units. Such institutions are classified as collective-owned.

(c)Social institutions established by individual or a group of citizens, which are classified as private.

(d)Institutions other than those mentioned above for which their sources of budget are not clear. Such institutions are classified by the manner of management.

(3)Social organizations: include social organizations established with the approval from the Ministry of Civil Affairs, and organizations that are not covered by social organization management regulations such as trade unions, women's federations etc.. Social organizations are further classified as follows:

(a)Social organizations that are not covered by social organization management regulations of the Ministry of Civil Affairs such as trade unions, women federations, communist youth leagues, youth associations, industrial and commerce associations, scientist associations, overseas Chinese associations, etc., foundations and fund management organizations established with funds from the state, and social organizations whose funds mainly come from the budget of their competent government agencies. Such institutions are classified as State-owned.

(b)Social organizations for which their budget mainly come from collective units. Such institutions are classified as collective-owned.

(c)Social organizations established by individual or a group of citizens, which are classified as private.

(d)Social organizations other than those mentioned above for which their sources of budget are not clear. Such organizations are classified by the manner of management.

3 国民经济核算

NATIONAL ECONOMIC ACCOUNTS

资料整理：吴　羽　徐　枫
Data management:Wu Yu Xu Feng

第三部分 国民经济核算

一、简要说明

本章资料包括西安生产总值、构成和指数，分区县生产总值等。根据国家统计局的统一要求，为保持GDP数据的历史可比性，根据国家统计局和陕西省统计局《年度GDP历史数据修订办法》，对2005—2007年度GDP历史数据进行了修订；人均GDP按户籍人口计算，2005年以后按常住人口计算。资料由西安市统计局国民经济核算处提供。

二、主要指标

生产总值（亿元）	4366.10	比上年增长	11.8%
第一产业	195.59	比上年增长	6.0%
第二产业	1881.75	比上年增长	11.8%
第三产业	2288.76	比上年增长	12.2%
人均生产总值（元/人）	51166	比上年增长	11.3%

3 NATIONAL ECONOMIC ACCOUNTS

Ⅰ.Brief Introduction

The data in this chapter consists of composition and indices of the GDP in Xi'an and GDP by region, etc. According to the request of National Bureau of Statistic, in order to keep the history GDP data comparable, the GDP of 2005 - 2007 had been adjusted based on Adjusting Method of yearly GDP released by National Bureau of Statistic and Shaan'xi Provincial Bureau of Statistic. Per capital GDP had been calculated on register population, and after 2005 was calculated on permanent population. Data in this chapter is provided by National Economic Accounting Division of the XI'an Bureau of Statistics.

Ⅱ.Major Indicators

		Increase over Preceding Year
Gross Domestic Product(100 mil. yuan)	4366.10	11.8%
Primary Industry	195.59	6.0%
Secondary Industry	1881.75	11.8%
Tertiary Industry	2288.76	12.2%
Per Capita Gross Domestic Product (yuan/person)	51166	11.3%

3-1 主要年份生产总值

Gross Domestic Product in Representative Years

(本表按当年价格计算)　　(Data in the table are calculated at current prices)
单位：亿元　　(100 million yuan)

年　份 Year	生产总值 Gross Domestic Product	第一产业 Primary Industry	第二产业 Secondary Industry	工业 Industry	建筑业 Construction	第三产业 Tertiary Industry	人均生产总值(元/人) Per Capita Gross Domestic Product (yuan/person)
1952	3.37	1.59	0.88	0.77	0.11	0.90	135
1965	12.76	2.62	7.22	6.71	0.51	2.92	323
1970	17.76	3.13	10.96	10.46	0.50	3.67	412
1975	21.33	4.14	12.63	12.07	0.56	4.56	448
1978	25.35	4.83	14.59	13.87	0.72	5.93	513
1980	31.66	4.73	18.69	17.12	1.57	8.24	623
1983	35.89	5.22	20.14	17.60	2.54	10.53	674
1984	44.14	7.45	24.17	22.53	1.64	12.52	817
1985	57.58	8.76	30.83	25.80	5.03	17.99	1049
1986	65.78	9.59	33.86	28.55	5.31	22.33	1178
1987	80.16	10.73	37.69	31.90	5.79	31.74	1409
1988	99.22	11.47	46.58	40.24	6.34	41.17	1711
1989	109.38	12.78	48.91	43.23	5.68	47.69	1861
1990	116.51	13.94	50.15	44.43	5.72	52.42	1932
1991	136.14	17.17	57.06	50.56	6.50	61.91	2224
1992	164.85	18.78	69.22	61.33	7.89	76.85	2662
1993	229.56	22.58	110.88	98.88	12.00	96.10	3661
1994	289.82	31.68	128.27	110.53	17.74	129.87	4563
1995	330.35	41.40	135.33	112.50	22.83	153.62	5131
1996	406.95	46.94	161.63	132.52	29.11	198.38	6246
1997	488.82	51.33	197.97	161.97	36.00	239.52	7424
1998	525.85	51.91	216.32	175.00	41.32	257.62	7906
1999	577.29	45.53	243.35	194.00	49.35	288.41	8599
2000	646.13	44.65	277.13	218.44	58.69	324.35	9484
2001	734.86	45.87	312.90	246.90	66.00	376.09	10628
2002	826.68	47.77	353.58	280.20	73.38	425.33	11831
2003	946.66	50.72	407.38	324.88	82.50	488.56	13341
2004	1102.39	60.21	476.92	383.46	93.46	565.26	15294
2005	1313.93	66.01	540.50	420.00	120.50	707.42	16406
2006	1538.94	70.44	645.65	494.22	151.43	822.85	18890
2007	1856.63	82.51	781.94	594.95	186.99	992.18	22463
2008	2318.14	103.45	981.58	721.40	260.18	1233.11	27794
2009	2724.08	110.38	1144.75	816.92	327.83	1468.95	32411
2010	3241.69	140.06	1406.72	1003.57	403.15	1694.91	38343
2011	3862.58	173.14	1674.31	1189.61	484.70	2015.13	45475
2012	4366.10	195.59	1881.75	1328.71	553.04	2288.76	51166

注：2005年以后人均GDP按平均常住人口计算，根据全国第二次经济普查结果，对2005-2007年生产总值及人均GDP进行了修订。

3-2 主要年份生产总值指数（上年＝100）

Indices of Gross Domestic Product in Representative Years(preceding year = 100)

(本表按可比价格计算) (Data in the table are calculated at constant prices)

年份	Year	生产总值 Gross Domestic Product	第一产业 Primary Industry	第二产业 Secondary Industry	工业 Industry	建筑业 Construction	第三产业 Tertiary Industry	人均生产总值(元/人) Per Capita Gross Domestic Product (yuan/person)
1952		103.6	92.2	137.5	136.2	166.7	123.7	
1965		126.1	134.1	133.0	132.2	160.8	106.7	
1970		122.0	109.4	140.0	138.3	179.4	100.1	
1975		103.8	92.6	107.1	106.5	109.0	107.5	
1978		101.7	101.6	99.4	99.2	119.9	108.2	
1980		111.5	83.3	119.7	118.1	151.1	116.5	
1985		112.6	107.5	111.8	107.0	121.9	116.9	
1986		111.4	107.7	108.4	107.5	109.8	118.8	
1987		113.6	100.8	109.1	110.8	101.5	126.6	
1988		111.4	81.2	115.5	118.8	91.0	114.7	
1989		106.7	103.0	104.5	106.1	88.6	110.8	
1990		105.2	103.0	102.5	103.3	92.9	109.6	
1991		109.8	118.6	108.6	108.6	108.4	108.6	108.2
1992		115.6	109.4	118.1	118.1	118.2	115.0	114.3
1993		123.9	112.5	142.7	143.7	135.6	108.4	122.3
1994		110.3	98.4	110.6	106.8	141.3	113.2	108.8
1995		110.0	104.5	112.1	108.1	136.6	108.6	108.5
1996		114.9	106.8	118.8	117.1	126.8	111.7	113.5
1997		114.4	109.1	116.7	116.4	117.8	112.4	113.2
1998		113.3	106.5	117.5	116.1	123.4	108.8	112.1
1999		112.2	97.4	115.7	114.0	122.8	110.1	111.2
2000		113.0	103.5	115.1	113.8	120.1	111.5	111.4
2001		113.1	102.5	115.3	116.3	111.8	112.6	111.4
2002		113.3	103.1	115.0	116.4	109.3	113.0	112.1
2003		113.5	101.8	117.5	115.7	125.0	111.2	111.7
2004		113.5	106.7	115.9	115.5	117.3	112.0	111.7
2005		114.0	107.5	112.3	110.3	120.0	116.3	112.2
2006		114.0	107.1	113.7	112.3	118.7	114.9	112.9
2007		115.6	104.5	115.7	114.9	118.4	116.4	113.9
2008		116.3	107.6	116.4	115.7	118.9	116.9	115.3
2009		114.5	106.3	114.0	111.7	121.2	115.5	113.7
2010		114.5	106.9	118.0	118.1	117.6	112.5	113.8
2011		113.8	106.7	114.9	116.2	111.7	113.4	113.2
2012		111.8	106.0	111.8	112.4	110.3	112.2	111.3
平均每年增长	**Yearly Average Growth Rates**							
“一五”时期	**The First Five-Year Plan Period**	**15.8**	**5.9**	**37.7**	**31.8**	**64.7**	**16.9**	
“二五”时期	**The Second Five-Year Plan Period**	**2.0**	**-3.7**	**2.5**	**6.7**	**-13.5**	**8.4**	
1963--1965年	**Readjust Period**	**14.2**	**16.1**	**23.4**	**22.8**	**36.6**	**0.3**	
“三五”时期	**The Third Five-Year Plan Period**	**7.1**	**0.1**	**11.7**	**11.1**	**12.8**	**5.4**	
“四五”时期	**The Fourth Five-Year Plan Period**	**5.0**	**4.0**	**5.3**	**6.6**	**-2.9**	**5.0**	
“五五”时期	**The Fifth Five-Year Plan Period**	**6.0**	**-0.7**	**6.5**	**5.8**	**22.4**	**10.1**	
“六五”时期	**The Sixth Five-Year Plan Period**	**10.7**	**7.9**	**10.4**	**7.9**	**20.8**	**12.9**	
“七五”时期	**The Seventh Five-Year Plan Period**	**9.6**	**-1.3**	**7.9**	**9.2**	**-4.1**	**15.9**	
“八五”时期	**The Eighth Five-Year Plan Period**	**13.8**	**8.5**	**17.8**	**16.3**	**27.4**	**10.7**	**12.3**
“九五”时期	**The Ninth Five-Year Plan Period**	**13.6**	**4.6**	**16.8**	**15.5**	**22.1**	**10.9**	**12.3**
“十五”时期	**The Tenth Five-Year Plan Period**	**13.5**	**4.3**	**15.2**	**14.8**	**16.5**	**13.0**	**11.8**
“十一五”时期	**The Eleventh Five-Year Plan Period**	**15.0**	**6.5**	**15.5**	**14.5**	**19.0**	**15.2**	**13.9**

注：根据全国第二次经济普查结果，对2005-2007年生产总值指数进行了修订。

3-3 主要年份生产总值指数（1952年=100）

Indices of Gross Domestic Product in Representative Years(1952= 100)

(本表按可比价格计算) (Data in the table are calculated at constant prices)

年份 Year	生产总值 Gross Domestic Product	第一产业 Primary Industry	第二产业 Secondary Industry	工业 Industry	建筑业 Construction	第三产业 Tertiary Industry
1952	100	100	100	100	100	100
1965	341.6	173.3	1048.3	1016.5	1492.1	329.2
1970	481.6	174.3	1821.0	1723.0	2716.6	428.6
1975	614.2	211.9	2362.5	2368.8	2348.6	547.9
1978	678.7	231.3	2560.8	2557.5	2904.6	643.8
1980	821.4	204.2	3237.2	3138.4	6445.0	885.2
1983	988.4	222.5	3846.2	3481.7	10593.4	1154.4
1984	1213.6	278.2	4748.8	4290.2	13612.5	1388.7
1985	1366.8	299.1	5310.6	4589.2	16586.9	1632.4
1986	1523.1	322.3	5756.7	4933.0	18215.7	1928.9
1987	1730.0	324.9	6280.6	5463.8	18496.2	2441.6
1988	1926.3	263.7	7256.6	6491.5	16826.0	2801.2
1989	2054.8	271.6	7583.1	6888.1	14899.4	3104.6
1990	2162.5	279.7	7772.7	7115.4	13841.6	3403.6
1991	2374.4	331.7	8441.2	7727.4	15004.3	3696.3
1992	2744.8	362.9	9969.1	9126.0	17735.0	4250.7
1993	3400.8	408.2	14225.9	13114.1	24048.7	4607.8
1994	3751.1	401.8	15733.8	14005.8	33980.8	5216.0
1995	4126.2	419.9	17637.6	15140.3	46417.8	5664.6
1996	4741.0	448.5	20953.5	17729.3	58857.7	6327.4
1997	5423.7	489.3	24452.7	20636.9	69334.4	7112.0
1998	6145.1	521.1	28731.9	23959.4	85558.7	7737.9
1999	6894.8	507.6	33242.8	27313.8	105066.1	8519.4
2000	7791.1	525.4	38262.5	31083.1	126184.3	9499.1
2001	8811.7	538.5	44116.7	36149.6	141074.1	10696.0
2002	9983.7	555.2	50734.2	42078.1	154194.0	12086.5
2003	11331.5	265.2	59612.7	48684.4	192742.5	13440.2
2004	12861.3	603.1	69091.1	56230.5	226086.9	15053.0
2005	14661.9	648.3	77589.3	62022.2	271304.3	17506.6
2006	16714.6	694.3	88219.0	69650.9	322038.2	20115.1
2007	19322.1	725.5	102069.4	80028.9	381293.3	23414.0
2008	22471.6	780.6	118808.8	92593.5	453357.7	27371.0
2009	25730.0	829.8	135442.0	103426.9	549469.5	31613.5
2010	29460.9	950.1	155081.1	122147.2	646176.1	36197.5
2011	33513.2	1013.8	178177.0	141935.0	721778.7	41045.6
2012	37469.9	1074.6	199290.7	159578.0	796465.0	46062.0

3-4 主要年份生产总值构成

Composition of Gross Domestic Product in Representative Years

(本表按当年价格计算) (Data in the table are calculated at current prices)

单位：% (%)

年 份	Year	生产总值 Gross Domestic Product	第一产业 Primary Industry	第二产业 Secondary Industry	工业 Industry	建筑业 Construction	第三产业 Tertiary Industry
1952		100	47.18	26.11	22.85	3.26	26.71
1965		100	20.53	56.58	52.59	3.99	22.89
1970		100	17.62	61.71	58.90	2.81	20.67
1975		100	19.41	59.21	56.59	2.62	21.38
1978		100	19.05	57.55	54.71	2.84	23.40
1980		100	14.94	59.03	54.07	4.96	26.03
1985		100	15.22	53.54	44.81	8.73	31.24
1986		100	14.58	51.47	43.40	8.07	33.95
1987		100	13.38	47.02	39.80	7.22	39.60
1988		100	11.56	46.95	40.56	6.39	41.49
1989		100	11.68	44.72	39.52	5.20	43.60
1990		100	11.96	43.05	38.13	4.92	44.99
1991		100	12.61	41.91	37.14	4.77	45.48
1992		100	11.39	41.99	37.20	4.79	46.62
1993		100	9.84	48.30	43.07	5.23	41.86
1994		100	10.93	44.26	38.14	6.12	44.81
1995		100	12.53	40.97	34.05	6.92	46.50
1996		100	11.53	39.72	32.56	7.16	48.75
1997		100	10.50	40.50	33.13	7.37	49.00
1998		100	9.87	41.14	33.28	7.86	48.99
1999		100	7.89	42.15	33.61	8.54	49.96
2000		100	6.91	42.89	33.81	9.08	50.20
2001		100	6.24	42.58	33.60	8.98	51.18
2002		100	5.78	42.77	33.89	8.88	51.45
2003		100	5.36	43.03	34.32	8.71	51.61
2004		100	5.46	43.26	34.78	8.48	51.28
2005		100	5.02	41.14	31.96	9.18	53.84
2006		100	4.58	41.95	32.11	9.84	53.47
2007		100	4.44	42.12	32.04	10.08	53.44
2008		100	4.46	42.34	31.12	11.22	53.20
2009		100	4.05	42.02	29.99	12.03	53.93
2010		100	4.32	43.39	30.96	12.43	52.29
2011		100	4.48	43.35	30.80	12.55	52.17
2012		100	4.48	43.10	30.43	12.67	52.42
	Yearly Average Growth Rates						
"一五"时期	**The First Five-Year Plan Period**	**100**	**32.88**	**43.92**	**32.40**	**11.52**	**23.20**
"二五"时期	**The Second Five-Year Plan Period**	**100**	**18.08**	**58.63**	**52.01**	**6.62**	**23.29**
1963--1965年	**Readjust Period**	**100**	**19.36**	**55.38**	**51.56**	**3.82**	**25.26**
"三五"时期	**The Third Five-Year Plan Period**	**100**	**18.60**	**57.33**	**55.08**	**2.25**	**24.07**
"四五"时期	**The Fourth Five-Year Plan Period**	**100**	**20.46**	**59.59**	**57.04**	**2.55**	**19.95**
"五五"时期	**The Fifth Five-Year Plan Period**	**100**	**18.41**	**57.69**	**54.39**	**3.30**	**23.90**
"六五"时期	**The Sixth Five-Year Plan Period**	**100**	**16.03**	**55.01**	**48.61**	**6.40**	**28.96**
"七五"时期	**The Seventh Five-Year Plan Period**	**100**	**12.42**	**46.11**	**39.99**	**6.12**	**41.47**
"八五"时期	**The Eighth Five-Year Plan Period**	**100**	**11.44**	**43.52**	**37.70**	**5.82**	**45.04**
"九五"时期	**The Ninth Five-Year Plan Period**	**100**	**9.09**	**41.45**	**33.34**	**8.11**	**49.46**
"十五"时期	**The Tenth Five-Year Plan Period**	**100**	**5.49**	**42.47**	**33.62**	**8.85**	**52.04**
"十一五"时期	**The Eleventh Five-Year Plan Period**	**100**	**4.34**	**42.47**	**31.09**	**11.38**	**53.19**

3-5 各区县生产总值（2012年）

Gross Domestic Product by Region (2012)

单位：亿元　　(100 million yuan)

区　县	Region	生产总值 Gross Domestic Product	第一产业 Primary Industry	第二产业 Secondary Industry	工业 Industry	第三产业 Tertiary Industry
新城区	Xincheng	428.92		174.54	103.68	254.38
碑林区	Beilin	466.96		92.89	12.48	374.07
莲湖区	Lianhu	479.40		212.22	140.47	267.18
灞桥区	Baqiao	233.30	16.08	134.69	113.79	82.53
未央区	Weiyang	518.06	2.24	265.08	189.88	250.74
雁塔区	Yanta	838.91	2.34	311.46	183.97	525.11
阎良区	Yanliang	141.49	19.70	75.16	62.42	46.63
临潼区	Lintong	211.53	29.63	120.43	109.91	61.47
长安区	Chang'an	340.90	30.06	160.16	122.60	150.68
蓝田县	Lantian	95.73	24.45	35.21	21.73	36.07
周至县	Zhouzhi	78.28	25.39	21.07	16.04	31.82
户　县	Huxian	142.13	25.37	75.66	65.20	41.10
高陵县	Gaoling	228.16	20.33	184.14	167.50	23.69

3–6 各区县生产总值指数（2012年）（上年＝100）

Indices of Gross Domestic Product by Region (2012) (preceding year = 100)

区 县	Region	生产总值 Gross Domestic Product	第一产业 Primary Industry	第二产业 Secondary Industry	工业 Industry	第三产业 Tertiary Industry
新城区	Xincheng	111.5		110.6	110.1	112.2
碑林区	Beilin	113.2		115.2	110.0	112.7
莲湖区	Lianhu	111.5		109.9	109.0	112.9
灞桥区	Baqiao	113.8	106.5	113.7	113.4	115.2
未央区	Weiyang	109.5	91.7	107.3	108.9	112.2
雁塔区	Yanta	111.4	90.4	110.2	114.3	112.1
阎良区	Yanliang	112.2	106.4	113.5	113.8	112.4
临潼区	Lintong	112.2	105.1	114.0	113.7	112.7
长安区	Chang'an	113.2	106.1	113.9	113.5	113.8
蓝田县	Lantian	111.0	106.3	113.0	110.6	111.8
周至县	Zhouzhi	111.0	106.8	113.1	111.5	112.2
户 县	Huxian	109.5	106.5	109.7	109.4	110.7
高陵县	Gaoling	118.0	106.4	119.4	118.8	115.2

3-7 各区县生产总值构成（2012年）

Composition of Gross Domestic Product by Region (2012)

单位：%　　(%)

区　县	Region	生产总值 Gross Domestic Product	第一产业 Primary Industry	第二产业 Secondary Industry	第三产业 Tertiary Industry
新城区	Xincheng	100		40.7	59.3
碑林区	Beilin	100		19.9	80.1
莲湖区	Lianhu	100		44.3	55.7
灞桥区	Baqiao	100	6.9	57.7	35.4
未央区	Weiyang	100	0.4	51.2	48.4
雁塔区	Yanta	100	0.3	37.1	62.6
阎良区	Yanliang	100	13.9	53.1	33.0
临潼区	Lintong	100	14.0	56.9	29.1
长安区	Chang'an	100	8.8	47.0	44.2
蓝田县	Lantian	100	25.5	36.8	37.7
周至县	Zhouzhi	100	32.4	26.9	40.7
户　县	Huxian	100	17.8	53.2	29.0
高陵县	Gaoling	100	8.9	80.7	10.4

3–8 主要年份分行业增加值

Value-added by Sector in Representative Years

单位：亿元 (100 million yuan)

指　标	Item	2004	2005	2006	2007	2008	2009	2010	2011	2012
生产总值	**Gross Domestic Product**	**1102.39**	**1313.93**	**1538.94**	**1856.63**	**2318.14**	**2724.08**	**3241.69**	**3862.58**	**4366.10**
第一产业	Primary Industry	60.21	66.01	70.44	82.51	103.45	110.38	140.06	173.14	195.59
第二产业	Secondary Industry	476.92	540.50	645.65	781.94	981.58	1144.75	1406.72	1674.31	1881.75
工业	Industry	383.46	420.00	494.22	594.95	721.40	816.92	1003.57	1189.61	1328.71
建筑业	Construction	93.46	120.50	151.43	186.99	260.18	327.83	403.15	484.70	553.04
第三产业	Tertiary Industry	565.26	707.42	822.85	992.18	1233.11	1468.95	1694.91	2015.13	2288.76
交通运输、仓储及邮政业	Transportation,Storage,Post andTelecommunications	55.10	66.30	74.08	84.21	99.16	110.60	124.69	147.64	167.46
批发和零售业	Wholesale and Retail Trades	125.12	147.20	166.72	195.51	242.91	293.05	337.86	418.94	486.32
住宿和餐饮业	Accommodation and Catering Trade	35.89	50.44	52.23	70.09	85.65	94.05	103.58	124.29	137.02
金融、保险业	Banking and Insurance	61.49	75.00	96.50	128.50	160.84	198.47	226.42	256.57	311.61
房地产业	Real Estate	39.05	52.48	62.32	75.26	92.97	124.98	158.86	187.99	201.14
其他服务业	Others Services	248.61	316.00	371.00	438.61	551.58	647.80	743.50	879.70	985.21

3–9 主要年份分行业增加值指数（上年＝100）

Indices of Value -added by Sector in Representative Years(preceding year＝100)

(本表按可比价格计算) (Data in the table are calculated at constant prices)

指　标	Item	2005	2006	2007	2008	2009	2010	2011	2012
生产总值	**Gross Domestic Product**	**114.0**	**114.0**	**115.6**	**116.3**	**114.5**	**114.5**	**113.8**	**111.8**
第一产业	Primary Industry	107.5	107.1	104.5	107.6	106.3	106.9	106.7	106.0
第二产业	Secondary Industry	112.3	113.7	115.7	116.4	114.0	118.0	114.9	111.8
工业	Industry	110.3	112.3	114.9	115.7	111.7	118.1	116.2	112.4
建筑业	Construction	120.0	118.7	118.4	118.9	121.2	117.6	111.7	110.3
第三产业	Tertiary Industry	116.3	114.9	116.4	116.9	115.5	112.5	113.4	112.2
交通运输、仓储及邮政业	Transportation,Storage,Post andTelecommunications	113.2	112.3	110.3	108.4	105.0	111.5	112.5	110.0
批发和零售业	Wholesale and Retail Trades	112.7	112.5	112.9	115.0	119.7	112.3	118.8	113.5
住宿和餐饮业	Accommodation and Catering Trade	136.1	116.6	117.3	111.6	106.6	107.2	113.4	105.5
金融保险业	Banking and Insurance	109.3	107.3	126.7	113.6	121.4	110.7	107.2	124.8
房地产业	Real Estate	112.9	117.5	119.7	107.6	131.6	118.6	111.5	106.4
其他服务业	Others Services	117.7	117.7	116.3	122.5	113.2	112.7	113.4	110.5

3-10 主要年份三次产业贡献率

Share of the Contributions of the Three Strata of Industry to the Increase of the GDP in Representative Years

单位：%　　　　(%)

年 份 Year	生产总值 Gross Domestic Product	第一产业 Primary Industry	第二产业 Secondary Industry	第三产业 Tertiary Industry
2006	100	2.5	40.2	57.3
2007	100	1.4	41.4	57.2
2008	100	2.0	41.4	56.6
2009	100	1.7	39.5	58.8
2010	100	1.7	50.7	47.6
2011	100	2.1	47.0	50.9
2012	100	2.1	44.1	53.8

3-11 主要年份三次产业拉动率

Contribution of the Three Strata of Industry to GDP Growth in Representative Years

单位：%　　　　(%)

年 份 Year	生产总值 Gross Domestic Product	第一产业 Primary Industry	第二产业 Secondary Industry	第三产业 Tertiary Industry
2006	14.0	0.4	5.7	7.9
2007	15.6	0.2	6.4	9.0
2008	16.3	0.3	6.8	9.2
2009	14.5	0.2	5.7	8.6
2010	14.5	0.3	7.4	6.8
2011	13.8	0.3	6.5	7.0
2012	11.8	0.2	5.2	6.4

3-12 主要年份支出法生产总值

Gross Domestic Product by Expenditure Approach in Representative Years

(本表按当年价格计算) (Data in the table are calculated at current prices)

单位：亿元 (100 million yuan)

年 份 Year	生产总值 Gross Domestic Product	最终消费 Final Consumption Expenditures	资本形成总额 Total Investment	货物和服务净出口 Net Export of Goods and Services
1992	164.85	148.09	68.61	-51.85
1993	229.56	172.60	113.48	-56.52
1994	289.82	200.88	131.97	-43.03
1995	330.35	239.64	151.55	-60.84
1996	406.95	272.46	170.35	-35.86
1997	488.82	317.61	182.30	-11.09
1998	525.85	343.15	200.96	-18.26
1999	577.29	377.89	257.65	-58.25
2000	646.13	413.43	287.82	-55.12
2001	734.86	456.78	328.59	-50.51
2002	826.68	505.57	385.45	-64.34
2003	946.66	541.73	507.87	-102.94
2004	1102.39	689.24	649.93	-236.78
2005	1313.93	766.62	839.01	-291.70
2006	1538.94	870.93	1045.27	-377.26
2007	1856.63	995.22	1451.47	-590.06
2008	2318.14	1182.61	1837.86	-702.33
2009	2724.08	1403.10	2281.91	-960.93
2010	3241.69	1598.51	2835.42	-1192.24
2011	3862.58	1856.91	3264.83	-1259.16
2012	4366.10	2092.97	3783.10	-1509.97

3-13 主要年份支出法生产总值指数（上年＝100）

Indices of Gross Domestic Product by Expenditure Approach in Representative Years (preceding year = 100)

年 份 Year	生产总值 Gross Domestic Product	最终消费 Final Consumption Expenditures	资本形成总额 Total Investment
1992	115.6	114.4	116.0
1993	123.9	103.1	124.9
1994	110.3	104.9	116.4
1995	110.0	110.0	114.6
1996	114.9	102.1	105.8
1997	114.4	108.2	106.6
1998	113.3	114.9	108.1
1999	112.2	114.8	123.6
2000	113.0	109.9	116.2
2001	113.1	108.5	111.2
2002	113.3	109.7	117.1
2003	113.5	108.8	129.6
2004	113.5	109.8	123.7
2005	114.0	107.7	127.0
2006	114.0	109.4	120.1
2007	115.6	109.5	135.2
2008	116.3	116.9	120.2
2009	114.5	118.4	122.6
2010	114.5	110.5	118.7
2011	113.8	110.4	108.4
2012	111.8	109.9	113.2

3-14 支出法生产总值及指数（2012年）

Gross Domestic Product and Indices by Expenditure Approach（2012）

单位：亿元 (100 million yuan)

指　标	Item	2012	指数（上年=100）Indices (preceding year= 100)
生产总值	**Gross Domestic Product**	**4366.10**	**111.8**
(一)最终消费	Final Consumption Expenditures	2092.97	109.9
1. 居民消费	Resident Consumption Expenditures	1612.48	113.2
农村居民	Village Residents	203.23	111.7
城镇居民	Urban Residents	1409.25	113.5
2. 政府消费	Government Consumption Expenditures	480.49	99.8
(二)资本形成总额	Gross Total Capital Formation	3783.1	113.2
1. 固定资本形成总额	Fixed Capital	3559.08	114.4
2. 存货增加	Change of Goods in Stock	224.02	97.2
(三)货物和服务净出口	Net Export of Goods and Services	-1509.97	112.6

3-15 分行业资本形成总额（2012年）

Gross Capital Formation by Sector (2012)

单位：亿元 (100 million yuan)

指　标	Item	2012
资本形成总额	**Total Investment**	**3783.10**
一、固定资本形成总额	**Gross Fixed Capital Formation**	3559.08
1、住宅	Residential Buildings	1445.18
2、非住宅建筑物	Non-residential Buildings	1585.80
3、机器和设备	Machinery and Equipment	217.21
4、土地改良支出	Land Reform Expenditure	4.33
5、矿藏勘探费	Cost of Mineral Deposits Prospecting	0.38
6、计算机软件	Computer Sofiwares	98.10
7、其他	Others	208.08
二、存货增加	**Change of Goods in Stock**	**224.02**
1、农林牧渔业	Agriculture, Forestry, Animal Husbandry and Fishery	1.64
2、工业	Industry	68.70
3、建筑业	Construction	35.88
4、交通运输、仓储及邮政业	Transportation, Storage and Post	5.72
5、批发和零售业	Wholesale and Retail Trades	16.94
6、住宿和餐饮业	Hotels and Catering Services	-0.11
7、房地产业	Real Estate	93.51
8、其他	Others	1.74

3-16 最终消费支出（2012年）

Final Consumption Expenditures (2012)

单位：亿元 (100 million yuan)

指　标	Item	2012
最终消费支出（亿元）	**Final Consumption Expenditures**	**2092.97**
一、居民消费支出	**Resident Consumption Expenditures**	**1612.48**
（一）农村居民	Rural Residents	203.23
1. 食品类支出	Food Expenditures	65.52
2. 衣着类支出	Clothing Expenditures	14.37
3. 居住类支出	Residence Expenditures	17.14
4. 家庭设备、用品及服务类支出	Household Facilities, Articles and Services Expenditures	20.58
5. 医疗保健类支出	Medical Care Expenditures	20.63
6. 交通和通信类支出	Transportion and Communication Expenditures	12.42
7、文化教育娱乐及服务支出	Culture. Education and Entertainment Expenditures	19.75
8、银行中介服务支出	Indirect Calculated Expenditures of Financial lntermediation Services	7.78
9. 保险服务消费支出	Insurance Services Consumption Expenditures	0.42
10. 自有住房服务虚拟类支出	Virtual Expenditures of Private Housing Services	21.11
11. 其他商品和服务类支出	Other goods and services Expenditures	3.51
（二）城镇居民	Urban Residents	1409.25
1. 食品类支出	Food Expenditures	420.59
2. 衣着类支出	Clothing Expenditures	157.58
3. 居住类支出	Residence Expenditures	109.66
4. 家庭设备、用品及服务类支出	Household Facilities, Articles and Services Expenditures	101.87
5. 医疗保健类支出	Medical Care Expenditures	110.33
6. 交通和通信类支出	Transportion and Communication Expenditures	184.65
7. 文化教育娱乐及服务支出	Culture, Education and Entertainment Expenditures	185.61
8. 银行中介服务支出	Indirect Calculated Expenditures of Financial Intermediation Services	35.98
9.保险服务消费支出	Insurance Services Consumption Expenditures	4.13
10.自有住房服务虚拟支出	Virtual Expenditures of Private Housing Services	29.37
11. 实物收入消费支出	Physical goods Consumption Expenditures	9.40
12. 其他商品和服务支出	Other goods and services Expenditures	60.08
二、政府消费支出	**Government Consumption Expenditures**	**480.49**

3-17 居民总消费水平（2012年）

Consumption of Residents (2012)

指　标	Item	2012	指数（上年=100） Indices (preceding year=100)
一、按当年价格计算（元/人）	**Calculated at Current Prices (yuan/person)**		
全体居民消费水平	Per Capita Consumption of All Residents	18897	115.6
农村居民	Farmer	8158	119.3
城镇居民	Non-Farmer	23324	113.8
二、按可比价格计算（元/人）	**Calculated at Comparable Prices (yuan/person)**		
全体居民消费水平	Per Capita Consumption of All Residents	17532	112.7
农村居民	Farmer	7509	116.0
城镇居民	Non-Farmer	21665	110.9
三、常住居民年平均人口（万人）	**Average Annual Population of Residents (10 000 persons)**	**853.32**	**100.5**

3-18 主要年份非公有制经济增加值

The Added Value of Non-public-owned Economic in Representative Years

单位：亿元　　　　(100 million yuan)

年　份 Year	非公有制经济增加值 the Added Value of Non-public-owned Economic	第一产业 Primary Industry	第二产业 Secondary Industry	第三产业 Tertiary Industry	非公有制经济增加值占GDP比重(%) the Added Value of Non-public-owned Economic Percentage to GDP	第一产业 Primary Industry	第二产业 Secondary Industry	第三产业 Tertiary Industry
2005	568.45	20.86	232.66	314.93	43.26	31.60	43.05	44.52
2006	684.66	26.27	279.06	379.33	44.46	37.29	43.22	46.04
2007	854.26	25.25	365.24	463.77	46.01	30.60	46.71	46.74
2008	1103.96	36.42	468.58	598.96	47.62	35.21	47.74	48.57
2009	1327.49	36.32	542.37	748.80	48.73	32.90	47.38	50.98
2010	1611.28	42.66	665.90	902.72	49.70	30.46	47.34	53.26
2011	1952.78	52.93	814.44	1085.41	50.56	30.57	48.64	53.86
2012	2244.25	59.79	902.29	1282.17	51.40	30.57	47.95	56.02

3-19 主要年份五大主导产业增加值

Value-added of the Five Leading Industries in Representative Years

单位：亿元 (100 million yuan)

年 份 Year	五大主导产业增加值（剔除重复） Value-added of Five Leading Industries	高新技术产业增加值 High-Tech Industry	装备制造业增加值 Manufacture of Equipment	旅游业增加值 Tourism	文化产业增加值 Culture Industry	现代服务业增加值 Modem Services
2004	429.37	78.70	154.28	83.14	46.01	209.23
2005	536.08	100.46	179.88	99.90	60.46	272.51
2006	654.05	119.37	218.10	120.37	77.93	332.65
2007	839.20	142.45	280.12	148.53	99.98	416.26
2008	1084.89	199.23	344.61	189.86	127.44	734.95
2009	1324.33	296.68	392.27	226.82	151.02	881.20
2010	1622.99	361.92	485.53	275.35	190.62	1056.73
2011	1963.85	432.43	566.78	329.02	250.70	1270.12
2012	2271.88	510.82	679.71	385.03	334.68	1428.08

注：五大主导产业增加值为剔除产业间重复计算部分，各产业增加值为包含产业间重复计算部分。
2012年文化产业增加值为年快报数据。

3-20 主要年份五大主导产业增加值占GDP比重

Proponions of Value-added of the Five Leading Industhes to GDP in Representave Years

单位：% (%)

年 份 Year	五大主导产业增加值（剔除重复） Value-added of Five Leading Industries	高新技术产业增加值 High-Tech Industry	装备制造业增加值 Manufacture of Equipment	旅游业增加值 Tourism	文化产业增加值 Culture Industry	现代服务业增加值 Modem Services
2004	38.9	7.1	14.0	7.5	4.2	19.0
2005	40.8	7.6	13.7	7.6	4.6	20.7
2006	42.5	7.8	14.2	7.8	5.1	21.6
2007	45.2	7.7	15.1	8.0	5.4	22.4
2008	46.8	8.6	14.9	8.2	5.5	31.7
2009	48.6	10.9	14.4	8.3	5.5	32.3
2010	50.1	11.2	15.0	8.5	5.9	32.6
2011	50.8	11.2	14.7	8.5	6.5	32.9
2012	52.0	11.7	15.6	8.8	7.7	32.7

注：五大主导产业增加值为剔除产业间重复计算部分，各产业增加值为包含产业间重复计算部分。根据全国第二次经济普查结果，对2005-2008年各产业增加值数据进行了修订。

主要统计指标解释

生产总值（GDP） 是按市场价格计算的一个地区（或国家）所有常住单位在一定时期内生产活动的最终成果。生产总值有三种表现形态，即价值形态、收入形态和产品形态。从价值形态看，它是所有常住单位在一定时期内生产的全部货物和服务价值超过同期中间投入的全部非固定资产货物和服务价值的差额，即所有常住单位的增加值之和；从收入形态看，它是所有常住单位在一定时期内创造并分配给常住单位和非常住单位的初次收入分配之和；从产品形态看，它是所有常住单位在一定时期内最终使用的货物和服务价值与货物和服务净出口价值之和。在实际核算中，生产总值有三种计算方法，即生产法、收入法和支出法。三种方法分别从不同的方面反映生产总值及其构成。

三次产业 是根据社会生产活动历史发展的顺序对产业结构的划分，产品直接取自自然界的部门称为第一产业，对初级产品进行再加工的部门称为第二产业，为生产和消费提供各种服务的部门称为第三产业。它是世界上较为通用的产业结构分类，但各国的划分不尽一致。

三产业的划分是世界上较为常用的产业结构分类，但各国的划分不尽一致。我国的三次产业划分是：

第一产业：农业（包括农业、林业、畜牧业、渔业和农林牧渔服务业）。

第二产业：工业（包括采矿业，制造业，电力气及水的生产和供应业）和建筑业。

第三产业：除第一、第二产业以外的其他各业。

劳动者报酬 指劳动者因从事生产活动所获得的全部报酬。包括劳动者获得的各种形式的工资、奖金和津贴，既包括货币形式的，也包括实物形式的，还包括劳动者所享受的公费医疗和医药卫生费、上下班交通补贴、单位支付的社会保险费、住房公积金等。

生产税净额 指生产税减生产补贴后的余额。生产税指政府对生产单位从事生产、销售和经营活动以及因从事生产活动使用某些生产要素（如固定资产、土地、劳动力）所 收的各种税、附加费和规费。生产补贴与生产税相反，指政府对生产单位的单方面转移支出，因此视为负生产税，包括政策亏损补贴、价格补贴等。

固定资产折旧 指一定时期内为弥补固定资产损耗按照规定的固定资产折旧率提取的固定资产折旧，或按国民经济核算统一规定的折旧率虚拟计算的固定资产折旧。它反映了固定资产年当期生产中的转移价值。各类企业和企业化管理的事业单位的固定资产折旧是指实际计提的折旧费；不计提折旧的政府机关、非企业化管理的事业单位和居民住房的固定资产折旧是按照统一规定的折旧率和固定资产原值计算的虚拟折旧。原则上，固定资产折旧应按固定资产当期的重置价值计算，但是目前我国尚不具备对全社会固定资产进行重估价的基础，所以暂时只能采用上述办法。

营业盈余 指常住单位创造的增加值扣除劳动者报酬、生产税净额和固定资产折旧后的余额。它相当于企业的营业利润加上生产补贴，但要扣除从利润中开支的工资和福利等。

支出法国内生产总值 是从最终使用的角度反映一个国家（或地区）一定时期内生产活动最终成果的一种方法，包括最终消费支出、资本形成总额及货物和服务净出口三部分。计算公式为：

支出法国内生产总值二最终消费支出+资本形成总额+货物和服务净出口

最终消费支出 指常住单位为满足物质、文化和精神生活的需要，从本国经济领土和国外购买的货物和服务的支出。它不包括非常住单位在本国经济领土内的消费支出。最终消费支出分为居民消费支出和政府消费支出。

居民消费支出 指常住住户在一定时期内对于货物和服务的全部最终消费支出。居民消费支出除了直接以货币形式购买的货物和服务的消费支出外，还包括以其他方式获得的货物和服务的消费支出，即所谓的虚拟消费支出。居民虚拟消费支出包括如下几种类型：单位以实物报酬及实物转移的形式提供给劳动者的货物和服务；住户生产并由本住户消费了的货物和服务，其中的服务仅指住户的自有住房服务和付酬的家庭雇员提供的家庭和个人服务；金融机构提供的金融媒介服务。

政府消费支出 指政府部门为全社会提供的公共服务的消费支出和免费或以较低的价格向居民住户提供的货物和服务的净支出，前者等于政府服务的产出价值减去政府单位所获得的经营收入的价值，后者等于政府部门免费或以较低价格向居民住户提供的货物和服务的市场价值减去向住户收取的价值。

资本形成总额 指常住单位在一定时期内获得减去处置的固定资产和存货的净额，包括固定资本形成总额和存货增加两部分。

固定资本形成总额 指常住单位在一定时期内获得的固定资产减处置的固定资产的价值总额。固定资产是通过生产活动生产出来的，且其使用年限在一年以上、单位价值在规定标准以上的资产，不包括自然资产。可分为有形固定资本形成总额和无形固定资本形成总额。有形固定资本形成总额包括一定时期内完成的建筑工程、安装工程和设备工器具购置（减处置）价值，以及土地改良、新增役、种、奶、毛、娱乐用牲畜和新增经济林木价值。无形固定资本形成总额包括矿藏的勘探、计算机软件等获得减处置。

存货增加 指常住单位在一定时期内存货实物量变动的市场价值，即期末价值减期初价值的差额，再扣除当期由于价格变动而产生的持有收益。存货增加可以是正值，也可以是负值，正值表示存货上升，负值表示存货下降。存货包括生产单位购进的原材料、燃料和储备物资等存货，以及生产单位生产的产成品、在制品和半成品等存货。

货物和服务净出口 指货物和服务出口减货物和服务进口的差额。出口包括常住单位向非常住单位出售或无偿转让的各种货物和服务的价值；进口包括常住单位从非常住单位购买或无偿得到的各种货物和服务的价值。由于服务活动的提供与使用同时发生，一般把常住单位从非常住单位得到的服务作为进口，非常住单位从常住单位得到的服务作为出口。货物的出口和进口都按离岸价格计算。

Explanatory Notes on Main Statistical Indicators

Gross Domestic Product (GDP) refers to the final products at market prices produced by all resident units in a country (or a region) during a certain period of time. Gross domestic product is expressed in three different perspectives, namely value, income, and products respectively. GDP in its value perspective refers to the total value of all goods and services produced by all resident units during a certain period of time, minus the total value of input of goods and services of the nature of non-fixed assets; in other words, it is the sum of the value-added of all resident units. GDP from the perspective of income includes the primary income created by all resident units and distributed to resident and non-resident units. GDP from the perspective of products refers to the value of all goods and services for final demand by all resident units plus the net exports of goods and services during a given period of time. In the practice of national accounting, gross domestic product is calculated from three approaches, namely production approach, income approach and expenditure approach, which reflect gross domestic product and its composition from different angles.

For a region, it is called as Gross Regional Product(GRP) or regional GDP.

Three Strata of Industry Classification of economic activities into three strata of industry is a common practice in the world, although the grouping varies to some extent from country to country. In China economic activities are categorized into the following three strata of industry:

Primary industry refers to agriculture, forestry, animal husbandry and fishery and services in support of these industries.

Secondary industry refers to mining and quarrying, manufacturing, production and supply of electricity, water and gas, and construction.

Tertiary industry refers to all other economic activities not included in the primary or secondary industries.

Compensation of Employees refers to the total payment of various forms to employees for the productive activities they are engaged in. It includes wages, bonuses and allowances, which the employees earn in cash or in kind. It also includes the free medical services provided to the employees and the medicine expenses, transport subsidies and social insurance, and housing fund paid by the employers.

Net Taxes on Production refers to taxes on production less subsidies on production. The taxes on production refers to the various taxes, extra charges and fees levied on the production units on their production, sale and business activities as well as on the use of some factors of production, such as fixed assets, land and labour in the production activities they are engaged in. In contrast to taxes on production, subsidies on production refer to the unilateral government transfer to the production units and are therefore regarded as negative taxes on production. They include subsidies on the loss due to implementation of government policies, price subsidies, etc.

Depreciation of Fixed Assets refers to the depreciation of fixed assets in a given period, drawn in accordance with the stipulated depreciation rate for the purpose of compensating the wear-and-tear loss of the fixed assets or the depreciation of fixed assets imputed in accordance with the stipulated unified depreciation rate in the national economic accounting system. It reflects the value of transfer of the fixed assets in the production of the current period. The depreciation of fixed assets in various enterprises and institutions managed as enterprises refers to the depreciation expenses actually drawn. In government agencies and institutions not managed as enterprises which do not draw the depreciation expenses, as well as for the houses of residents, the depreciation of fixed assets is the imputed depreciation, which is calculated in accordance with the stipulated unified depreciation rate. In principle, the depreciation of fixed assets should be calculated on the basis of the re-purchased value of the fixed assets. However, currently the conditions in China do not facilitate the revaluation of all the fixed assets. Therefore, only the above-mentioned methods can be adopted at present.

Operating Surplus refers to the balance of the value added created by the resident units after deducting the labourers remuneration, net taxes on production and the depreciation of fixed assets. It is equivalent to the business profit of the enterprises plus subsidies to production, but the wages and welfare expenses paid from the profits should be deducted.

GDP by Expenditure Approach refers to the method of measuring the final results of production activities of a country (region) during a given period from the perspective of final uses. It includes final consumption expenditure, gross capital formation and net export of goods and services. The formula for computation is.:

GDP by expenditure approach = final consumption expenditure + gross capital formation + net export of goods and services

Final Consumption Expenditure refers to the total expenditure of resident units for purchases of goods and services from both the domestic economic territory and abroad to meet the needs of material, cultural and spiritual life. It does not include the expenditure of non-resident units on consumption in the economic territory of the country. The final consumption expenditure is broken down into household consumption expenditure and government consumption expenditure.

Household Consumption Expenditure refers to the total expenditure of resident households on the final consumption of goods and services. In addition to the consumption of goods and services bought by the households directly with money, the household consumption expenditure also includes expenditure on goods and services obtained by the households in other ways, i.e. the so-called imputed consumption expenditure, which includes the following: (a) the goods and services provided to households by employers in the form of payment in kind and transfer in kind; (b) goods and services produced and consumed by the households themselves, in which the services refer to the owner-occupied housing and services offered by payed family employees; (c) financial intermediate services provided by financial institution.

Government Consumption Expenditure refers to the consumption expenditure spent for the provision of public services provided by the government to the whole country and the net expenditure on the goods and services provided by the government to households free of charge or at reduced prices. The former equals to the output value of the government services minus the value of operating income obtained by the government departments. The latter equals to the market value of the goods and services provided by the government free of charge or at reduced prices to the households minus the value received by the government from the households.

Gross Capital Formation refers to the fixed assets acquired less disposals and the net value of inventory, thus including gross fixed capital formation and changes in inventories.

Gross Fixed Capital Formation refers to the value of acquisitions less those disposals of fixed assets during a given period. Fixed assets are the assets produced through production activities with unit value above a specified amount and which could be used for over one year. Natural assets are not included. Gross fixed capital formation can be categorized into total tangible fixed capital formation and total intangible fixed capital formation. Total tangible fixed capital formation includes the value of the construction projects and installation projects completed and the equipment, apparatus and instruments purchased (less those disposed) as well as the value of land improved, the value of draught animals, breeding stock and animals for milk, for wool and for recreational purposes and the newly increased forest with economic value. Total intangible fixed capital formation includes the prospecting of minerals and the acquisition of computer software minus the disposal of them.

Changes in Inventories refers to the market value of the change in the physical volume of inventory of resident units during a given period, i.e. the difference between the values at the beginning and at the end of the period minus the gains due to the change in prices. The changes in inventories can have a positive or a negative value. A positive value indicates an increase in inventory while a negative value indicates a decrease in inventory. The inventory includes raw materials, fuels and reserve materials purchased by the production units as well as the inventory of finished products, semi-finished products and work-in-progress.

Net Export of Goods and Services refers to the exports of goods and services subtracting the imports of goods and services. Exports include the value of various goods and services sold or gratuitously transferred by resident units to non-resident units. Imports include the value of various goods and services purchased or gratuitously acquired resident units from non-resident units. Because the provision of services and the use of them happen simultaneously, the acquisition of services by resident units from abroad is usually treated as import while the acquisition of services by non-resident units in this country is usually treated as export. The exports and imports of goods are calculated at FOB.

4 人口、从业人员与职工工资

POPULATION, EMPLOYMENT AND WAGES

资料整理：王义龙　张　静
Data management:Wang Yilong Zhang Jing

第四部分　人口、从业人员与职工工资

一、简要说明

本章资料包括主要年份人口、分区县户籍和常住人口及变动、从业人员及劳动报酬等。户籍人口数为公安年报数，1991年以前年份市区数未包括临潼、长安。主要数据由西安市统计局人口就业处提供。

二、主要指标

年末户籍人口（万人）	795.98	比上年增长	0.52%
人口自然增长率（‰）	4.56	比上年增长	0.23个千分点
常住人口（万人）	855.29	比上年增长	0.46%
男女性别比（以女性为100）	105.56	比上年下降	0.06个百分点
户籍人口密度（人／平方公里）	787	比上年增加	4人/平方公里
城镇非私营单位在岗职工年平均工资（元）	45846	比上年增长	10.0%

4　POPULATION,EMPLOYMENT AND WAGES

Ⅰ.Brief Introduction

This chapter consists of the data about ragistered population and permanent resident population consequent years, population of all the districts and counties and the correspondent changes, the employed and their wages. The registered population data are from the annual report of the Xi'an Bureau of Public Security, with Lintong, Chang'an not included before 1991. The population data is provided primarily by Population & Employment Division of the Xi'an Bureau of Statistics.

Ⅱ.Major Indicators

		Increase over Preceding Year
Total registered Population of Year-end(10 000 persons)	795.98	0.52%
Natural Growth Rate(‰)	4.56	0.23 thousands of points
Permanent Population(10 000 persons)	855.29	0.46%
Sex Ratio (Female=100)	105.56	-0.06 percentage points
Density of Population (person/sq.km)	787	4
Aunual Average Wage of Stuff and Workers in Urban Non-privite Enterprises(yuan)	45846	10.0%

4-1 主要年份人口数、人口密度和人口发展情况

Population, Population Density and Population Development in Representative years

单位：万人 (10 000 persons)

年份 Year	总人口 Total population	市区 Urban Area	女性人口数 Number of Female	非农业人口数 Non-Agricultural Population	人口密度（人/平方公里） Density of Population (person/sq.km)	总人口指数（上年为100） Total Population Index (100 for preceding year) 全市 Whole City	市区 Urban Area
1952	252.92	92.42	118.81	57.61	254	102.6	103.1
1965	400.05	179.88	190.72	136.39	401	102.5	103.4
1970	435.12	188.12	210.47	139.12	436	101.9	101.4
1978	498.10	210.15	241.82	159.98	499	101.7	102.7
1980	511.91	221.19	249.26	172.85	513	101.4	102.6
1985	553.11	245.76	268.40	201.90	554	101.6	102.2
1986	563.97	251.80	273.30	205.92	565	102.0	102.5
1987	574.46	257.69	278.12	210.25	575	101.9	102.3
1988	585.85	264.94	283.68	216.99	587	102.0	102.8
1989	597.36	270.80	289.44	222.54	598	102.0	102.2
1990	608.89	275.69	295.29	226.98	610	101.9	101.8
1991	615.48	419.29	298.13	230.85	617	101.1	152.1
1992	623.20	429.54	301.92	236.45	624	101.3	102.4
1993	630.91	435.41	305.30	240.85	632	101.2	101.4
1994	639.45	442.30	309.17	248.35	641	101.4	101.6
1995	648.21	448.65	313.46	255.71	645	101.4	101.4
1996	654.87	454.68	316.60	261.28	653	101.0	101.3
1997	662.06	461.17	320.18	267.52	663	101.1	101.4
1998	668.22	466.31	323.20	271.75	669	100.9	101.1
1999	674.50	463.56	326.12	276.14	676	100.9	99.4
2000	688.01	483.10	332.83	285.79	689	102.0	104.2
2001	694.84	489.88	336.04	292.62	696	101.0	101.4
2002	702.59	497.38	339.51	300.05	704	101.1	101.5
2003	716.58	510.26	346.26	312.88	718	102.0	102.6
2004	725.01	516.30	350.85	318.50	717	101.2	101.2
2005	741.73	533.21	359.71	333.14	734	102.3	103.3
2006	753.11	540.97	365.74	343.78	745	101.5	101.5
2007	764.25	549.19	371.84	353.85	756	101.5	101.5
2008	772.30	554.73	376.76	363.87	764	101.1	101.0
2009	781.67	561.58	382.39	370.66	773	101.2	101.2
2010	782.73	562.65	383.93	374.64	774	100.1	100.2
2011	791.83	568.77	389.31	391.31	783	101.2	101.1
2012	795.98	572.76	398.40	392.04	787	100.5	100.7

注：人口部分均为公安年报数据，系户籍人口。1991年以前年份，市区数未包括临潼、长安。

4-2 主要年份人口自然变动情况

Natural Population Movements in Representative Years

单位：万人 (10 000 persons)

年份 Year	出生 Birth 人数 Population	出生 Birth 出生率(‰) Birth Rate (‰)	死亡 Death 人数 Population	死亡 Death 死亡率(‰) Death Rate (‰)	自然增长率(‰) Natural Growth Rate (‰)	迁入人口 Immigrant population	迁出人口 Emigrant population
1985	8.95	16.30	3.01	5.48	10.82	11.60	8.74
1986	10.14	18.15	2.78	4.97	13.18	11.79	8.39
1987	9.76	17.14	2.83	4.97	12.17	12.58	9.26
1988	9.42	16.24	2.89	4.98	11.26	13.54	8.97
1989	11.78	19.92	3.04	5.13	14.79	12.73	10.15
1990	12.40	20.55	3.45	5.72	14.83	11.82	9.86
1991	8.73	14.25	3.26	5.33	8.92	8.98	6.09
1992	8.98	14.49	3.39	5.48	9.01	13.94	9.54
1993	9.25	14.75	3.37	5.38	9.37	11.50	8.33
1994	8.08	12.71	3.16	4.97	7.74	13.40	8.59
1995	7.69	11.95	3.21	4.98	6.97	14.41	8.85
1996	7.26	11.15	3.41	5.24	5.91	11.94	8.88
1997	6.84	10.38	3.12	4.75	5.63	12.58	8.62
1998	6.40	9.62	3.10	4.66	4.96	10.89	8.36
1999	6.19	9.22	3.88	5.78	3.44	12.58	9.23
2000	8.90	13.07	4.06	5.96	7.11	17.12	9.23
2001	5.11	7.39	2.89	4.19	3.20	15.16	10.83
2002	5.34	7.64	3.08	4.41	3.23	13.90	9.41
2003	6.02	8.48	3.32	4.68	3.80	20.60	9.15
2004	6.63	9.19	4.23	5.87	3.32	15.56	10.19
2005	7.67	9.58	4.13	5.16	4.42	22.61	9.46
2006	8.13	9.98	4.45	5.46	4.52	17.23	11.75
2007	8.27	10.00	4.53	5.48	4.52	19.90	14.01
2008	8.47	10.15	4.65	5.57	4.58	18.49	15.04
2009	8.47	10.08	4.73	5.63	4.45	16.84	13.14
2010	8.23	9.73	4.51	5.34	4.39	14.09	13.50
2011	8.25	9.71	4.57	5.38	4.33	14.21	11.74
2012	8.64	10.13	4.75	5.57	4.56	12.55	13.10

注：2004年以前为公安年报数据。迁入人口和迁出人口为公安年报数据。2010年出生、死亡、自然增长率根据第六次人口普查数据推算得出。2005-2009、2011-2012年出生、死亡、自然增长率为人口变动抽样调查数据。

4-3 全市及各区县人口数和户数（2012年）

Population and Households by Region（2012）

单位：万人　　　　　　　　　　　　　　　　　　　　　　　　　　　　(10 000 persons)

区　县	Region	总户数（万户）Number of Households (10 000 households)	总人口 Total Population	非农业人口 Non-agriculture	按性别划分 Grouped by Sex 男 Male	女 Female	迁入人口(人) Immigrant population (person)	迁出人口(人) Emigrant population (person)
全　市	**Total**	**239.54**	**795.98**	**398.40**	**403.94**	**392.04**	**125546**	**131044**
新城区	Xincheng	17.00	50.47	50.47	25.60	24.87	4568	2123
碑林区	Beilin	20.79	71.18	71.18	36.64	34.54	17276	27214
莲湖区	Lianhu	22.01	64.44	64.44	32.52	31.92	7056	6978
灞桥区	Baqiao	17.40	52.40	24.81	25.86	26.54	7497	4044
未央区	Weiyang	17.48	55.54	41.07	27.66	27.88	15216	8134
雁塔区	Yanta	24.29	80.82	70.40	40.47	40.35	25787	36575
阎良区	Yanliang	7.61	25.68	8.83	12.94	12.74	2134	1527
临潼区	Lintong	19.88	70.59	11.81	35.71	34.88	4151	4167
长安区	Chang'an	29.02	101.64	17.04	50.81	50.83	14552	9477
蓝田县	Lantian	18.58	64.67	5.78	33.53	31.14	4818	7305
周至县	Zhouzhi	17.52	67.13	6.33	35.45	31.68	7640	12178
户　县	Huxian	18.29	59.94	12.41	31.03	28.91	6012	7161
高陵县	Gaoling	9.67	31.48	13.83	15.72	15.76	8839	4161

注：本表均为公安年报数据。

4-4 全市及各区县常住人口数和人口变动情况（2012年）

Permanent Population and Population Changes by Region（2012）

单位：万人 (10 000 persons)

区 县	Region	常住人口 Permanent Population	城镇 Urban	出生率（‰） Birth Rate（‰）	死亡率（‰） Death Rate（‰）	自然增长率（‰） Natural Growth Rate（‰）
全 市	**Total**	**855.29**	**611.62**	**10.13**	**5.57**	**4.56**
新城区	Xincheng	59.44	59.44	7.15	3.70	3.45
碑林区	Beilin	62.08	62.08	7.55	4.10	3.45
莲湖区	Lianhu	70.25	70.25	8.61	5.15	3.46
灞桥区	Baqiao	60.16	55.67	10.74	6.09	4.65
未央区	Weiyang	81.46	74.25	10.88	5.47	5.41
雁塔区	Yanta	118.89	118.89	9.05	4.54	4.51
阎良区	Yanliang	28.23	15.59	9.71	5.45	4.26
临潼区	Lintong	66.45	21.25	11.05	5.53	5.52
长安区	Chang'an	109.54	61.00	11.08	6.36	4.72
蓝田县	Lantian	51.88	14.08	12.25	7.54	4.71
周至县	Zhouzhi	57.00	16.47	13.14	7.63	5.51
户 县	Huxian	56.10	21.88	10.59	5.88	4.71
高陵县	Gaoling	33.81	20.77	10.57	5.95	4.62

注：本表数据均为人口变动抽样调查数据。

4-5 主要年份常住人口数

Permanent Population in Representative Years

单位：万人 (10 000 persons)

年 份 Year	年末常住人口 Permanent population (year-end)	城镇 Urban	农村 Rural
2000	741.14	450.36	290.78
2005	806.81	510.55	296.26
2006	822.52	530.94	291.58
2007	830.54	548.99	281.55
2008	837.52	565.16	272.36
2009	843.46	581.40	262.06
2010	847.41	584.71	262.70
2011	851.34	596.79	254.55
2012	855.29	611.62	243.67

注：2000年常住人口为普查数据。2010年常住人口为年末常住人口数，根据第六次人口普查数据推算得出。2005-2009、2011-2012年常住人口为人口变动抽样调查数据。

4-6 主要年份社会从业人数

Number of Social Laborers in Representative Years

单位：万人 (10 000 persons)

年 份 Year	合 计 Total	一、按城乡分 Grouped by Urban area and Rural area					二、按三次产业分 Grouped by Industry		
		1.城镇 Urban	国有经济 State-owned Enterprises	集体经济 Collective-owned Enterprises	其他经济 Others	2.乡村 Village	第一产业 Primary Industry	第二产业 Secondary Indusyry	第三产业 Tertiary Industry
1985	296.80	129.07	96.80	29.07	3.20	167.73	135.89	98.61	62.30
1986	299.45	132.82	101.28	28.43	3.11	166.63	127.46	100.61	71.38
1987	312.16	138.56	104.58	30.72	3.26	173.60	130.36	107.75	74.05
1988	327.76	142.24	106.46	30.73	5.05	185.52	138.87	108.12	80.77
1989	332.65	145.65	108.80	30.44	6.41	187.00	142.21	106.40	84.04
1990	343.06	147.93	110.95	29.78	7.20	195.13	149.64	106.74	86.68
1991	347.65	149.48	111.87	29.80	7.81	198.17	152.24	108.19	87.22
1992	357.51	151.67	113.19	29.97	8.51	205.84	154.75	110.22	92.54
1993	363.70	155.72	112.98	29.77	12.97	207.98	154.02	114.02	95.66
1994	364.56	154.88	113.39	27.97	13.52	209.68	153.51	108.53	102.52
1995	372.60	158.80	113.79	25.58	19.43	213.80	153.39	109.67	109.54
1996	379.29	164.54	113.29	24.82	26.43	214.75	153.43	109.17	116.69
1997	385.14	169.52	112.44	23.52	33.56	215.62	153.23	109.46	122.45
1998	393.95	177.20	106.06	21.50	49.64	216.75	153.00	110.45	130.50
1999	400.43	180.27	105.08	20.50	54.69	220.16	154.64	110.58	135.21
2000	389.10	176.45	103.46	18.40	54.59	212.65	147.03	107.26	134.81
2001	389.30	177.94	100.47	17.10	60.37	211.36	145.09	108.96	135.25
2002	397.16	181.85	100.54	16.90	64.41	215.31	143.04	111.62	142.50
2003	404.92	183.23	94.51	16.78	71.94	221.69	146.67	109.09	149.16
2004	409.57	187.53	93.43	15.41	78.69	222.04	141.81	111.70	156.06
2005	415.83	192.53	93.27	14.47	84.79	223.30	136.31	114.20	165.32
2006	422.15	196.16	84.46	14.41	97.29	225.99	135.10	116.09	170.96
2007	436.36	214.27	90.58	11.88	111.81	222.09	133.33	125.06	177.97
2008	448.05	224.20	90.17	10.60	123.43	223.85	127.87	130.23	189.95
2009	462.52	239.39	90.83	7.63	140.93	223.13	122.13	131.57	208.82
2010	477.58	252.54	94.01	5.48	153.05	225.04	117.27	145.40	214.91
2011	495.99	265.43	91.62	5.33	168.48	230.56	121.05	151.33	223.61
2012	514.57	287.65	95.33	5.10	187.22	226.92	114.92	162.35	237.30

注：第一产业从业人员中包括城镇农林牧渔及服务业企业人员。

4-7 按国民经济行业分从业人数（2012年）

单位：万人

行业	Sector	合计 Total
总计	**Total**	**514.57**
（一）农、林、牧、渔业	Agriculture ,Forestry,Animal Husbandry and Fishery	114.92
（二）采矿业	Mining	0.70
（三）制造业	Manufacturing	99.75
（四）电力、燃气及水的生产供应业	Production and Distribution of Electricity,Gas and Water	1.68
（五）建筑业	Construction	60.22
（六）批发和零售业	Wholesale and Retail Trades	60.94
（七）交通运输、仓储和邮政业	Traffic,Transport,Storage and Post	27.30
（八）住宿和餐饮业	Hotels and Catering Services	25.82
（九）信息传输、软件和信息技术服务业	Information Transmission,Software and Information Technology Services	8.13
（十）金融业	Financial Intermediation	6.03
（十一）房地产业	Real Estate	8.61
（十二） 租赁和商务服务业	Leasing and Business Services	12.66
（十三）科学研究和技术服务业	Scientific Research and Technical Services	13.49
（十四）水利、环境和公共设施管理业	Management of Water Conservancy, Environment and Public Facilities	2.56
（十五）居民服务、修理和其他服务业	Services to Households, Repairs and Other Services	16.30
（十六）教育	Education	25.78
（十七）卫生和社会工作	Health and Social Work	14.02
（十八）文化、体育和娱乐业	Culture, Sports and Entertainment	3.80
（十九）公共管理、社会保障和社会组织	Public Administration, Social Security and Social Organizations	11.86
（二十）国际组织	International Organizations	

Number of Employed Persons Grouped by Sector（2012）

(10 000 persons)

国有经济 State-owned Enterprises	集体经济 Collective-owned Enterprises	城镇其他经济 Urban Other Enterprises	城镇私营经济及个体劳动者 Urban Private Enterprises and Individual Labors	乡镇劳动者 Rural and Urban Labors
95.33	**5.10**	**65.16**	**122.06**	**226.92**
0.35		0.01	1.27	113.29
0.04		0.08	0.58	
20.11	0.79	25.63	28.06	25.16
0.62		0.93	0.13	
12.61	2.13	9.64	8.13	27.71
2.34	0.27	7.80	37.94	12.59
7.78	0.07	0.97	5.06	13.42
1.23	0.06	3.95	12.27	8.31
2.06	0.04	3.14	1.98	0.91
1.53	0.19	3.31	0.09	0.91
1.38	0.24	3.01	3.98	
0.49	0.72	1.40	6.06	3.99
8.58	0.06	1.70	2.57	0.58
2.14	0.01	0.22	0.19	
0.34	0.39	0.46	7.23	7.88
15.94	0.02	1.06	4.44	4.32
6.19	0.11	0.45	1.04	6.23
1.36		1.40	1.04	
10.24				1.62

4-8　全部单位从业人员情况（2012年）

单位：人

分　组	Classify	单位从业人员 Employed Persons	女　性 Female
总　计	**Total**	**1655884**	**604034**
一、按机构类型分组	**Grouped by Organization Type**		
#企业	Enterprises	1259071	425660
机关	Institutions	99152	31357
事业	Agencies and Organizations	294735	145703
二、按国民经济行业分组	**Grouped by Economic Sector**		
（一）农、林、牧、渔业	Agriculture ,Forestry,Animal Husbandry and Fishery	3533	948
（二）采矿业	Mining	1177	187
（三）制造业	Manufacturing	465420	148272
（四）电力、燃气及水的生产供应业	Production and Distribution of Electricity,Gas and Water	15533	4868
（五）建筑业	Construction	243865	38686
（六）批发和零售业	Wholesale and Retail Trades	104133	48974
（七）交通运输、仓储和邮政业	Traffic,Transport,Storage and Post	88049	28391
（八）住宿和餐饮业	Hotels and Catering Services	52311	30277
（九）信息传输、软件和信息技术服务业	Information Transmission,Software and Information Technology Services	52360	26853
（十）金融业	Financial Intermediation	50328	27064
（十一）房地产业	Real Estate	46335	18472
（十二） 租赁和商务服务业	Leasing and Business Services	26074	8916
（十三）科学研究和技术服务业	Scientific Research and Technical Services	103443	31306
（十四）水利、环境和公共设施管理业	Management of Water Conservancy, Environment and Public Facilities	23666	11366
（十五）居民服务、修理和其他服务业	Services to Households, Repairs and Other Services	11836	4838
（十六）教育	Education	170185	86546
（十七）卫生和社会工作	Health and Social Work	67556	43257
（十八）文化、体育和娱乐业	Culture, Sports and Entertainment	27595	12409
（十九）公共管理、社会保障和社会组织	Public Administration, Social Security and Social Organizations	102485	32404
（二十）国际组织	International Organizations		

Basic Facts on All Employed Persons（2012）

(persons)

在岗职工合计 Total Fully Employed Staff and Workers	其他从业人员 Other Employed Persons	单位从业人员平均人数 Average Employment	在岗职工 Fully Employed Staff and Workers	其他从业人员 Other Employed Persons
1552803	**103081**	**1730999**	**1618823**	**112176**
1182829	76242	1328624	1242514	86110
87987	11165	102068	90812	11256
279419	15316	297274	282822	14452
3350	183	3535	3355	180
1177		1203	1203	
451846	13574	503594	489686	13908
14720	813	15609	14828	781
201103	42762	269721	217443	52278
101747	2386	103255	100864	2391
85014	3035	92584	89489	3095
51243	1068	53352	52255	1097
52154	206	48538	48328	210
48396	1932	54531	52797	1734
42842	3493	48192	44631	3561
25530	544	25905	25368	537
98562	4881	102397	97588	4809
21614	2052	23711	21679	2032
11534	302	11848	11548	300
162250	7935	173444	165626	7818
62600	4956	66860	62439	4421
26037	1558	27322	25777	1545
91084	11401	105398	93919	11479

4–9 国有单位从业人员情况（2012年）

单位：人

分 组	Classify	单位从业人员 Employed Persons	女 性 Female
总 计	**Total**	**953301**	**349080**
一、按机构类型分组	**Grouped by Organization Type**		
#企业	Enterprises	563161	174202
机关	Institutions	99152	31357
事业	Agencies and Organizations	290988	143521
二、按国民经济行业分组	**Grouped by Economic Sector**		
（一）农、林、牧、渔业	Agriculture ,Forestry,Animal Husbandry and Fishery	3451	912
（二）采矿业	Mining	417	39
（三）制造业	Manufacturing	201085	56885
（四）电力、燃气及水的生产供应业	Production and Distribution of Electricity,Gas and Water	6169	1930
（五）建筑业	Construction	126283	21547
（六）批发和零售业	Wholesale and Retail Trades	23418	10963
（七）交通运输、仓储和邮政业	Traffic,Transport,Storage and Post	77774	24772
（八）住宿和餐饮业	Hotels and Catering Services	12253	7169
（九）信息传输、软件和信息技术服务业	Information Transmission,Software and Information Technology Services	20592	14389
（十）金融业	Financial Intermediation	15323	7650
（十一）房地产业	Real Estate	13798	6019
（十二） 租赁和商务服务业	Leasing and Business Services	4908	2052
（十三）科学研究和技术服务业	Scientific Research and Technical Services	85785	25211
（十四）水利、环境和公共设施管理业	Management of Water Conservancy, Environment and Public Facilities	21371	10145
（十五）居民服务、修理和其他服务业	Services to Households, Repairs and Other Services	3354	1165
（十六）教育	Education	159382	80681
（十七）卫生和社会工作	Health and Social Work	61909	39370
（十八）文化、体育和娱乐业	Culture, Sports and Entertainment	13606	5798
（十九）公共管理、社会保障和社会组织	Public Administration, Social Security and Social Organizations	102423	32383
（二十）国际组织	International Organizations		

Basic Facts on Persons Employed by State-owned Units（2012）

(persons)

在岗职工合计 Total Fully Employed Staff and Workers	其他从业人员 Other Employed Persons	单位从业人员平均人数 Average Employment	在岗职工 Fully Employed Staff and Workers	其他从业人员 Other Employed Persons
886901	**66400**	**1005537**	**935816**	**69721**
522915	40246	609971	565633	44338
87987	11165	102068	90812	11256
275999	14989	293498	279371	14127
3268	183	3453	3273	180
417		417	417	
192776	8309	225658	217693	7965
5612	557	6280	5726	554
106390	19893	144304	120116	24188
23129	289	22385	22105	280
75535	2239	82772	80477	2295
11510	743	12460	11700	760
20546	46	17106	17063	43
14682	641	17617	17062	555
11327	2471	15852	13296	2556
4526	382	4865	4491	374
81534	4251	84907	80749	4158
19337	2034	21353	19348	2005
3144	210	3349	3141	208
152836	6546	162612	156143	6469
57071	4838	61267	56964	4303
12239	1367	13544	12195	1349
91022	11401	105336	93857	11479

4-10 城镇集体单位从业人员情况（2012年）

单位：人

分 组	Classify	单位从业人员 Employed Persons	女性 Female
总 计	**Total**	**50999**	**13579**
一、按机构类型分组	**Grouped by Organization Type**		
#企业	Enterprises	50227	13166
机关	Institutions		
事业	Agencies and Organizations	772	413
二、按国民经济行业分组	**Grouped by Economic Sector**		
（一）农、林、牧、渔业	Agriculture ,Forestry,Animal Husbandry and Fishery		
（二）采矿业	Mining		
（三）制造业	Manufacturing	7870	3509
（四）电力、燃气及水的生产供应业	Production and Distribution of Electricity,Gas and Water	38	16
（五）建筑业	Construction	21180	3426
（六）批发和零售业	Wholesale and Retail Trades	2735	1006
（七）交通运输、仓储和邮政业	Traffic,Transport,Storage and Post	713	286
（八）住宿和餐饮业	Hotels and Catering Services	561	345
（九）信息传输、软件和信息技术服务业	Information Transmission,Software and Information Technology Services	392	102
（十）金融业	Financial Intermediation	1923	986
（十一）房地产业	Real Estate	2398	831
（十二） 租赁和商务服务业	Leasing and Business Services	7195	496
（十三）科学研究和技术服务业	Scientific Research and Technical Services	645	184
（十四）水利、环境和公共设施管理业	Management of Water Conservancy, Environment and Public Facilities	109	42
（十五）居民服务、修理和其他服务业	Services to Households, Repairs and Other Services	3923	1594
（十六）教育	Education	162	112
（十七）卫生和社会工作	Health and Social Work	1122	636
（十八）文化、体育和娱乐业	Culture, Sports and Entertainment	33	8
（十九）公共管理、社会保障和社会组织	Public Administration, Social Security and Social Organizations		
（二十）国际组织	International Organizations		

Basic Facts on Persons Employed by Urban Collective-owned Units（2012）

(persons)

在岗职工合计 Total Fully Employed Staff and Workers	其他从业人员 Other Employed Persons	单位从业人员 平均人数 Average Employment	在岗职工 Fully Employed Staff and Workers	其他从业人员 Other Employed Persons
48648	**2351**	**50921**	**48545**	**2376**
47905	2322	50149	47802	2347
743	29	772	743	29
7410	460	7901	7425	476
38		38	38	
20347	833	21020	20193	827
2117	618	2732	2108	624
696	17	712	695	17
551	10	544	534	10
392		414	414	
1803	120	1884	1756	128
2247	151	2378	2226	152
7193	2	7156	7154	2
645		629	629	
109		107	107	
3832	91	4092	4001	91
162		162	162	
1074	48	1119	1071	48
32	1	33	32	1

4-11 其他经济类型单位从业人员情况（2012年）

单位：人

分组	Classify	单位从业人员 Employed Persons	女性 Female
总 计	**Total**	**651584**	**241375**
一、按机构类型分组	**Grouped by Organization Type**		
#企业	Enterprises	645683	238292
机关	Institutions		
事业	Agencies and Organizations	2975	1769
二、按国民经济行业分组	**Grouped by Economic Sector**		
（一）农、林、牧、渔业	Agriculture ,Forestry,Animal Husbandry and Fishery	82	36
（二）采矿业	Mining	760	148
（三）制造业	Manufacturing	256465	87878
（四）电力、燃气及水的生产供应业	Production and Distribution of Electricity,Gas and Water	9326	2922
（五）建筑业	Construction	96402	13713
（六）批发和零售业	Wholesale and Retail Trades	77980	37005
（七）交通运输、仓储和邮政业	Traffic,Transport,Storage and Post	9562	3333
（八）住宿和餐饮业	Hotels and Catering Services	39497	22763
（九）信息传输、软件和信息技术服务业	Information Transmission,Software and Information Technology Services	31376	12362
（十）金融业	Financial Intermediation	33082	18428
（十一）房地产业	Real Estate	30139	11622
（十二） 租赁和商务服务业	Leasing and Business Services	13971	6368
（十三）科学研究和技术服务业	Scientific Research and Technical Services	17013	5911
（十四）水利、环境和公共设施管理业	Management of Water Conservancy, Environment and Public Facilities	2186	1179
（十五）居民服务、修理和其他服务业	Services to Households, Repairs and Other Services	4559	2079
（十六）教育	Education	10641	5753
（十七）卫生和社会工作	Health and Social Work	4525	3251
（十八）文化、体育和娱乐业	Culture, Sports and Entertainment	13956	6603
（十九）公共管理、社会保障和社会组织	Public Administration, Social Security and Social Organizations	62	21
（二十）国际组织	International Organizations		

Basic Facts on Persons Employed by Other Units（2012）

(persons)

在岗职工合计 Total Fully Employed Staff and Workers	其他从业人员 Other Employed Persons	单位从业人员平均人数 Average Employment	在岗职工 Fully Employed Staff and Workers	其他从业人员 Other Employed Persons
617254	**34330**	**674541**	**634462**	**40079**
612009	33674	668504	629079	39425
2677	298	3004	2708	296
82		82	82	
760		786	786	
251660	4805	270035	264568	5467
9070	256	9291	9064	227
74366	22036	104397	77134	27263
76501	1479	78138	76651	1487
8783	779	9100	8317	783
39182	315	40348	40021	327
31216	160	31018	30851	167
31911	1171	35030	33979	1051
29268	871	29962	29109	853
13811	160	13884	13723	161
16383	630	16861	16210	651
2168	18	2251	2224	27
4558	1	4407	4406	1
9252	1389	10670	9321	1349
4455	70	4474	4404	70
13766	190	13745	13550	195
62		62	62	

4-12 主要年份单位从业人员数及工资总额

Number of Employed Persons and Remuneration in Representative Years

年 份 year	单位从业人员 （万人） Number of Employed Persons (10 000 persons)	从业人员工资总额 （万元） Remuneration of Employed Persons (10 000 yuan)	城镇非私营单位 从业人员平均工资(元) Aunual Average Wage of Employees in Urban Non-privite Units(yuan)
1978	67.19	4.71	713
1980	91.76	7.31	859
1985	127.04	14.17	1148
1986	132.78	16.87	1311
1987	135.48	19.13	1446
1988	137.56	22.81	1702
1989	139.86	25.64	1873
1990	141.55	29.48	2133
1991	142.86	26.88	2276
1992	144.51	30.80	2545
1993	146.03	43.25	2999
1994	142.37	58.87	4172
1995	141.17	67.23	4763
1996	140.60	75.64	5407
1997	138.89	80.83	5785
1998	138.78	82.85	6900
1999	115.88	90.13	7764
2000	112.45	103.80	9179
2001	113.93	123.12	10786
2002	115.77	138.88	12138
2003	116.68	155.95	13504
2004	118.15	184.63	15473
2005	123.66	215.67	17728
2006	125.10	250.87	20475
2007	129.40	319.23	25012
2008	130.85	379.29	29749
2009	135.64	450.48	34032
2010	140.38	520.88	37870
2011	154.33	658.73	41679
2012	165.59	770.86	44533

4-13 全部单位从业人员工资总额（2012年）

Total Wages of All Employed Persons（2012）

单位：万元 （10 000yuan）

分 组	Classify	单位从业人员工资总额 Total Wages of Employment	在岗职工工资总额 Total Wages of Employed Staff and Workers
总 计	**Total**	**7708589**	**7421603**
一、按机构类型分组	**Grouped by Organization Type**		
#企业	Enterprises	5577485	5348205
机关	Institutions	483647	466374
事业	Agencies and Organizations	1640015	1600320
二、按国民经济行业分组	**Grouped by Sector**		
（一）农、林、牧、渔业	Agriculture ,Forestry,Animal Husbandry and Fishery	11258	11153
（二）采矿业	Mining	4029	4029
（三）制造业	Manufacturing	1961852	1923462
（四）电力、燃气及水的生产供应业	Production and Distribution of Electricity, Gas and Water	86487	85043
（五）建筑业	Construction	966357	836422
（六）批发和零售业	Wholesale and Retail Trades	355013	350215
（七）交通运输、仓储和邮政业	Traffic,Transport,Storage and Post	451443	440146
（八）住宿和餐饮业	Hotels and Catering Services	142112	139809
（九）信息传输、软件和信息技术服务业	Information Transmission,Software and Information Technology Services	307382	306664
（十）金融业	Financial Intermediation	412536	401849
（十一）房地产业	Real Estate	181042	174610
（十二） 租赁和商务服务业	Leasing and Business Services	88832	87772
（十三）科学研究和技术服务业	Scientific Research and Technical Services	699109	680382
（十四）水利、环境和公共设施管理业	Management of Water Conservancy, Environment and Public Facilities	70987	66874
（十五）居民服务、修理和其他服务业	Services to Households, Repairs and Other Services	29742	29300
（十六）教育	Education	946667	930715
（十七）卫生和社会工作	Health and Social Work	379525	360704
（十八）文化、体育和娱乐业	Culture, Sports and Entertainment	111563	107501
（十九）公共管理、社会保障和社会组织	Public Administration, Social Security and Social Organizations	502652	484955
（二十）国际组织	International Organizations		

4-13 续表 continued

单位：万元 (10 000 yuan)

分 组	Classify	其他从业人员劳动报酬 Remuneration of Other Employed Persons	城镇非私营单位从业人员平均工资（元） Aunual Average Wage of Employees in UrbanNon-privite Units(yuan)
总 计	**Total**	**286986**	**44533**
一、按机构类型分组	**Grouped by Organization Type**		
#企业	Enterprises	229280	41979
机关	Institutions	17273	47385
事业	Agencies and Organizations	39695	55168
二、按国民经济行业分组	**Grouped by Sector**		
（一）农、林、牧、渔业	Agriculture ,Forestry,Animal Husbandry and Fishery	105	31846
（二）采矿业	Mining		33489
（三）制造业	Manufacturing	38390	38957
（四）电力、燃气及水的生产供应业	Production and Distribution of Electricity, Gas and Water	1445	55409
（五）建筑业	Construction	129936	35828
（六）批发和零售业	Wholesale and Retail Trades	4798	34382
（七）交通运输、仓储和邮政业	Traffic,Transport,Storage and Post	11297	48760
（八）住宿和餐饮业	Hotels and Catering Services	2303	26637
（九）信息传输、软件和信息技术服务业	Information Transmission,Software and Information Technology Services	718	63328
（十）金融业	Financial Intermediation	10688	75652
（十一）房地产业	Real Estate	6432	37567
（十二） 租赁和商务服务业	Leasing and Business Services	1060	34291
（十三）科学研究和技术服务业	Scientific Research and Technical Services	18728	68274
（十四）水利、环境和公共设施管理业	Management of Water Conservancy, Environment and Public Facilities	4112	29938
（十五）居民服务、修理和其他服务业	Services to Households, Repairs and Other Services	442	25103
（十六）教育	Education	15953	54581
（十七）卫生和社会工作	Health and Social Work	18821	56764
（十八）文化、体育和娱乐业	Culture, Sports and Entertainment	4062	40833
（十九）公共管理、社会保障和社会组织	Public Administration, Social Security and Social Organizations	17698	47691
（二十）国际组织	International Organizations		

4-14 国有单位从业人员工资总额（2012年）

Total Wages of Persons Employed by State-owned Units（2012）

单位：万元 （10 000yuan）

分组	Classify	单位从业人员工资总额 Total Wages of Employment	在岗职工工资总额 Total Wages of Employed Staff and Workers
总计	**Total**	**4775583**	**4590140**
一、按机构类型分组	**Grouped by Organization Type**		
#企业	Enterprises	2669464	2539990
机关	Institutions	483647	466374
事业	Agencies and Organizations	1622472	1583776
二、按国民经济行业分组	**Grouped by Sector**		
（一）农、林、牧、渔业	Agriculture ,Forestry,Animal Husbandry and Fishery	11109	11004
（二）采矿业	Mining	1734	1734
（三）制造业	Manufacturing	864246	843071
（四）电力、燃气及水的生产供应业	Production and Distribution of Electricity, Gas and Water	28186	27029
（五）建筑业	Construction	557673	487581
（六）批发和零售业	Wholesale and Retail Trades	65503	64863
（七）交通运输、仓储和邮政业	Traffic,Transport,Storage and Post	405747	397048
（八）住宿和餐饮业	Hotels and Catering Services	31130	29601
（九）信息传输、软件和信息技术服务业	Information Transmission,Software and Information Technology Services	108829	108776
（十）金融业	Financial Intermediation	130664	126490
（十一）房地产业	Real Estate	54073	50228
（十二） 租赁和商务服务业	Leasing and Business Services	20842	20124
（十三）科学研究和技术服务业	Scientific Research and Technical Services	590193	574228
（十四）水利、环境和公共设施管理业	Management of Water Conservancy, Environment and Public Facilities	64275	60230
（十五）居民服务、修理和其他服务业	Services to Households, Repairs and Other Services	9709	9351
（十六）教育	Education	910716	897817
（十七）卫生和社会工作	Health and Social Work	356733	338234
（十八）文化、体育和娱乐业	Culture, Sports and Entertainment	61661	57870
（十九）公共管理、社会保障和社会组织	Public Administration, Social Security and Social Organizations	502559	484862
（二十）国际组织	International Organizations		

4-14 续表 continued

单位：万元 (10 000 yuan)

分组	Classify	其他从业人员劳动报酬 Remuneration of Other Employed Persons	城镇非私营单位从业人员平均工资（元） Aunual Average Wage of Employees in UrbanNon-privite Units(yuan)
总　计	**Total**	**185443**	**47493**
一、按机构类型分组	**Grouped by Organization Type**		
#企业	Enterprises	129473	43764
机关	Institutions	17273	47385
事业	Agencies and Organizations	38696	55281
二、按国民经济行业分组	**Grouped by Sector**		
（一）农、林、牧、渔业	Agriculture ,Forestry,Animal Husbandry and Fishery	105	32172
（二）采矿业	Mining		41585
（三）制造业	Manufacturing	21176	38299
（四）电力、燃气及水的生产供应业	Production and Distribution of Electricity, Gas and Water	1157	44882
（五）建筑业	Construction	70092	38646
（六）批发和零售业	Wholesale and Retail Trades	640	29262
（七）交通运输、仓储和邮政业	Traffic,Transport,Storage and Post	8700	49020
（八）住宿和餐饮业	Hotels and Catering Services	1530	24984
（九）信息传输、软件和信息技术服务业	Information Transmission,Software and Information Technology Services	54	63621
（十）金融业	Financial Intermediation	4174	74169
（十一）房地产业	Real Estate	3845	34111
（十二）　租赁和商务服务业	Leasing and Business Services	718	42841
（十三）科学研究和技术服务业	Scientific Research and Technical Services	15965	69511
（十四）水利、环境和公共设施管理业	Management of Water Conservancy, Environment and Public Facilities	4045	30101
（十五）居民服务、修理和其他服务业	Services to Households, Repairs and Other Services	358	28990
（十六）教育	Education	12898	56005
（十七）卫生和社会工作	Health and Social Work	18499	58226
（十八）文化、体育和娱乐业	Culture, Sports and Entertainment	3791	45527
（十九）公共管理、社会保障和社会组织	Public Administration, Social Security and Social Organizations	17698	47710
（二十）国际组织	International Organizations		

4-15 城镇集体单位从业人员工资总额（2012年）

Total Wages of Persons Employed by Urban Collective-owned Units in Towns and Cities（2012）

单位：万元 （10 000yuan）

分 组	Classify	单 位 从业人员 工资总额 Total Wages of Employment	在岗职工 工资总额 Total Wages of Employed Staff and Workers
总 计	**Total**	**152703**	**148734**
一、按机构类型分组	**Grouped by Organization Type**		
#企业	Enterprises	149894	145975
机关	Institutions		
事业	Agencies and Organizations	2809	2760
二、按国民经济行业分组	**Grouped by Sector**		
（一）农、林、牧、渔业	Agriculture ,Forestry,Animal Husbandry and Fishery		
（二）采矿业	Mining		
（三）制造业	Manufacturing	25975	25135
（四）电力、燃气及水的生产供应业	Production and Distribution of Electricity, Gas and Water	180	180
（五）建筑业	Construction	67622	65941
（六）批发和零售业	Wholesale and Retail Trades	5813	5023
（七）交通运输、仓储和邮政业	Traffic,Transport,Storage and Post	2349	2251
（八）住宿和餐饮业	Hotels and Catering Services	1439	1422
（九）信息传输、软件和信息技术服务业	Information Transmission,Software and Information Technology Services	2183	2183
（十）金融业	Financial Intermediation	10901	10666
（十一）房地产业	Real Estate	7001	6869
（十二） 租赁和商务服务业	Leasing and Business Services	13533	13530
（十三）科学研究和技术服务业	Scientific Research and Technical Services	3709	3709
（十四）水利、环境和公共设施管理业	Management of Water Conservancy, Environment and Public Facilities	185	185
（十五）居民服务、修理和其他服务业	Services to Households, Repairs and Other Services	6325	6243
（十六）教育	Education	647	647
（十七）卫生和社会工作	Health and Social Work	4686	4601
（十八）文化、体育和娱乐业	Culture, Sports and Entertainment	155	151
（十九）公共管理、社会保障和社会组织	Public Administration, Social Security and Social Organizations		
（二十）国际组织	International Organizations		

4-15 续表 continued

单位：万元 (10 000 yuan)

分 组	Classify	其他从业人员劳动报酬 Remuneration of Other Employed Persons	城镇非私营单位从业人员平均工资（元） Aunual Average Wage of Employees in UrbanNon-privite Units(yuan)
总 计	**Total**	**3969**	**29988**
一、按机构类型分组	**Grouped by Organization Type**		
#企业	Enterprises	3919	29890
机关	Institutions		
事业	Agencies and Organizations	50	36391
二、按国民经济行业分组	**Grouped by Sector**		
（一）农、林、牧、渔业	Agriculture ,Forestry,Animal Husbandry and Fishery		
（二）采矿业	Mining		
（三）制造业	Manufacturing	840	32875
（四）电力、燃气及水的生产供应业	Production and Distribution of Electricity, Gas and Water		47342
（五）建筑业	Construction	1681	32171
（六）批发和零售业	Wholesale and Retail Trades	790	21278
（七）交通运输、仓储和邮政业	Traffic,Transport,Storage and Post	98	32994
（八）住宿和餐饮业	Hotels and Catering Services	17	26456
（九）信息传输、软件和信息技术服务业	Information Transmission,Software and Information Technology Services		52725
（十）金融业	Financial Intermediation	236	57862
（十一）房地产业	Real Estate	133	29442
（十二） 租赁和商务服务业	Leasing and Business Services	3	18912
（十三）科学研究和技术服务业	Scientific Research and Technical Services		58962
（十四）水利、环境和公共设施管理业	Management of Water Conservancy, Environment and Public Facilities		17243
（十五）居民服务、修理和其他服务业	Services to Households, Repairs and Other Services	82	15456
（十六）教育	Education		39957
（十七）卫生和社会工作	Health and Social Work	86	41878
（十八）文化、体育和娱乐业	Culture, Sports and Entertainment	4	46909
（十九）公共管理、社会保障和社会组织	Public Administration, Social Security and Social Organizations		
（二十）国际组织	International Organizations		

4-16 其他经济类型单位从业人员工资总额（2012年）

Total Wages of Persons Employed by Other Units（2012）

单位：万元 （10 000yuan）

分 组	Classify	单 位 从业人员 工资总额 Total Wages of Employment	在岗职工 工资总额 Total Wages of Employed Staff and Workers
总 计	**Total**	**2780303**	**2682729**
一、按机构类型分组	**Grouped by Organization Type**		
#企业	Enterprises	2758128	2662239
机关	Institutions		
事业	Agencies and Organizations	14733	13785
二、按国民经济行业分组	**Grouped by Sector**		
（一）农、林、牧、渔业	Agriculture ,Forestry,Animal Husbandry and Fishery	149	149
（二）采矿业	Mining	2295	2295
（三）制造业	Manufacturing	1071631	1055257
（四）电力、燃气及水的生产供应业	Production and Distribution of Electricity, Gas and Water	58121	57833
（五）建筑业	Construction	341062	282900
（六）批发和零售业	Wholesale and Retail Trades	283697	280329
（七）交通运输、仓储和邮政业	Traffic,Transport,Storage and Post	43347	40848
（八）住宿和餐饮业	Hotels and Catering Services	109543	108786
（九）信息传输、软件和信息技术服务业	Information Transmission,Software and Information Technology Services	196370	195705
（十）金融业	Financial Intermediation	270971	264693
（十一）房地产业	Real Estate	119968	117513
（十二） 租赁和商务服务业	Leasing and Business Services	54456	54118
（十三）科学研究和技术服务业	Scientific Research and Technical Services	105208	102445
（十四）水利、环境和公共设施管理业	Management of Water Conservancy, Environment and Public Facilities	6527	6460
（十五）居民服务、修理和其他服务业	Services to Households, Repairs and Other Services	13709	13707
（十六）教育	Education	35304	32250
（十七）卫生和社会工作	Health and Social Work	18106	17870
（十八）文化、体育和娱乐业	Culture, Sports and Entertainment	49747	49480
（十九）公共管理、社会保障和社会组织	Public Administration, Social Security and Social Organizations	93	93
（二十）国际组织	International Organizations		

4-16 续表 continued

单位：万元 (10 000 yuan)

分 组	Classify	其他从业人员劳动报酬 Remuneration of Other Employed Persons	城镇非私营单位从业人员平均工资(元) Aunual Average Wage of Employees in UrbanNon-privite Units(yuan)
总 计	**Total**	**97574**	**41218**
一、按机构类型分组	**Grouped by Organization Type**		
#企业	Enterprises	95888	41258
机关	Institutions		
事业	Agencies and Organizations	948	49046
二、按国民经济行业分组	**Grouped by Sector**		
（一）农、林、牧、渔业	Agriculture ,Forestry,Animal Husbandry and Fishery		18134
（二）采矿业	Mining		29193
（三）制造业	Manufacturing	16374	39685
（四）电力、燃气及水的生产供应业	Production and Distribution of Electricity, Gas and Water	288	62556
（五）建筑业	Construction	58162	32670
（六）批发和零售业	Wholesale and Retail Trades	3368	36307
（七）交通运输、仓储和邮政业	Traffic,Transport,Storage and Post	2499	47634
（八）住宿和餐饮业	Hotels and Catering Services	757	27149
（九）信息传输、软件和信息技术服务业	Information Transmission,Software and Information Technology Services	665	63308
（十）金融业	Financial Intermediation	6278	77354
（十一）房地产业	Real Estate	2455	40040
（十二） 租赁和商务服务业	Leasing and Business Services	339	39222
（十三）科学研究和技术服务业	Scientific Research and Technical Services	2763	62397
（十四）水利、环境和公共设施管理业	Management of Water Conservancy, Environment and Public Facilities	68	28996
（十五）居民服务、修理和其他服务业	Services to Households, Repairs and Other Services	2	31107
（十六）教育	Education	3055	33088
（十七）卫生和社会工作	Health and Social Work	237	40470
（十八）文化、体育和娱乐业	Culture, Sports and Entertainment	267	36193
（十九）公共管理、社会保障和社会组织	Public Administration, Social Security and Social Organizations		14984
（二十）国际组织	International Organizations		

4-17 主要年份城镇登记失业人数及失业率

Registered Unemployed Persons and Unemployment Rate in Urban Area in Representative Years

年 份 year	城镇登记失业人数(万人) Real Number of Registered Unemployed Persons (10 000 persons)	城镇登记失业率(%) Registered Unemployment in Urban Area (%)
2002		3.7
2003		4.5
2004	8.29	4.3
2005	8.45	4.3
2006	8.74	4.3
2007	8.77	4.3
2008	9.40	4.2
2009	10.02	4.3
2010	10.46	4.2
2011	10.37	3.9
2012	9.60	3.5

4-18 按国民经济行业(GB/T4754-2002)分单位从业人员（2012年）

Number of Employed Persons by Sector（GB/T4754--2002）（2012）

单位：人 (persons)

行 业	Scetor	2012
总 计	**Total**	**1655884**
按国民经济行业分组	**Grouped by Sector**	
（一）农、林、牧、渔业	Agriculture ,Forestry,Animal Husbandry and Fishery	3533
（二）采矿业	Mining	1177
（三）制造业	Manufacturing	465420
（四）电力、燃气及水的生产供应业	Production and Distribution of Electricity,Gas and Water	15533
（五）建筑业	Construction	243865
（六）交通运输、仓储及邮政业	Traffic,Transport,Storage and Post	88049
（七）信息传输、计算机服务和软件业	Information Transmission,Computer Service and Software	52360
（八）批发和零售业	Wholesale and Retail Trades	104133
（九）住宿和餐饮业	Hotels and Catering Services	52311
（十）金融业	Financial Intermediation	50328
（十一）房地产业	Real Estate	46335
（十二）租赁和商务服务业	Leasing and Business Services	26074
（十三）科学研究、技术服务和地质勘察业	Scientific Research,Technical Service and Geologic Prospecting	103443
（十四）水利、环境和公共设施管理业	Management of Water Conservancy, Environment and Public Facilities	23666
（十五）居民服务和其他服务业	Services to Households, Repairs and Other Services	11836
（十六）教育	Education	170185
（十七）卫生、社会保障和社会福利业	Health,Social Security and Social Welfare	67781
（十八）文化、体育和娱乐业	Culture, Sports and Entertainment	27595
（十九）公共管理和社会组织	Public Management and Social Organization	102260

主要统计指标解释

人口数 指一定时点、一定地区范围内的有生命的个人的总和。年度统计的年末人口数，指每年12月31日24时的人口数。

常住人口 指实际经常居住在某地区一定时间（半年以上，含半年）的人口。常住人口包括户口在本辖区人也在本辖区居住的人，户口在本辖区之外但在户口登记地半年以上的人，户口待定（无户口和口袋户口）的人，户口在本辖区但离开本辖区半年以下的人。

城镇人口和乡村人口 城镇人口是指居住在城镇范围内的全部常住人口；乡村人口是除上述人口以外的全部人口。

出生率（又称粗出生率） 指在一定时期内（通常为一年）平均每千人所出生的人数的比率，一般用千分率表示。其计算公式为：

出生率＝年出生人数 / 年平均人数 × 1000‰

式中：出生人数指活产婴儿，即胎儿脱离母体时（不管怀孕月数），有过呼吸或其他生命现象。年平均人数指年初、年底人口数的平均数，也可用年中人口数代替。

死亡率（又称粗死亡率） 指在一定时期内（通常为一年）一定地区的死亡人数与同期内平均人数（或期中人数）之比，一般用千分率表示。本资料中的死亡率指年死亡率，其计算公式为：

死亡率＝年死亡人数 / 年平均人数 × 1000‰

人口自然增长率 指在一定时期内（通常为一年）人口自然增加数（出生人数减死亡人数）与该时期内平均人数（或期中人数）之比，一般用千分率表示。计算公式为：

人口自然增长率＝（本年出生人数—本年死亡人数）/ 年平均人数 × 1000‰。

从业人员 指在16周岁及以上，从事一定社会劳动并取得劳动报酬或经营收入的人员。这一指标反映了一定时期内全部劳动力资源的实际利用情况，是研究我国基本国情国力的重要指标。

单位从业人员 指在各级国家机关、政党机关、社会团体及企业、事业单位中工作，取得工资或其他形式的劳动报酬的全部人员。包括在岗职工、再就业的离退休人员、民办教师以及在各单位中工作的外方人员和港澳台方人员、兼职人员、借用的外单位人员和第二职业者。不包括离开本单位仍保留劳动关系的职工。各单位的就业人员反映了各单位实际参加生产或工作的全部劳动力。

城镇私营和个体就业人员 城镇私营就业人员指在工商管理部门注册登记，其经营地址设在县城关镇（含城关镇）以上的私营企业就业人员；包括私营企业投资者和雇工。城镇个体就业人员指在工商管理部门注册登记，并持有城镇户口或在城镇长期居住，经批准从事个体工商经营的就业人员；包括个体经营者和在个体工商户劳动的家庭帮工和雇工。

国有单位 指资产归国家所有的经济组织。包括按《中华人民共和国企业法人登记管理条例》规定登记注册的非公司制的经济组织，以及中央、地方各级国家机关、事业单位和社会团体。

集体单位 指生产资料归集体所有，并按《中华人民共和国企业法人登记管理条例》规定登记注册的经济组织。

其他单位 包括股份合作单位、联营单位、有限责任公司、股份有限公司、港澳台商投资单位以及外商投资单位等其他登记注册类型单位。

在岗职工 指在本单位工作并由单位支付工资的人员，以及有工作岗位，但由于学习、病伤产假等原因暂未工作，仍由单位支付工资的人员。

职工工资总额 指各单位在一定时期内直接支付给本单位全部职工的劳动报酬总额。工资总额的计算原则应以直接支付给职工的全部劳动报酬为根据。各单位支付给职工的劳动报酬以及其他根据有关规定支付的工资，不论是计入成本的还是不计入成本的，不论是按国家规定列入计征奖金税项目的，还是未列入计征奖金税项目的，不论是以货币形式支付的还是以实物形式支付的，均包括在工资总额内。

职工平均工资 指企业、事业、机关单位的职工在一定时期内平均每人所得的货币工资额。它表明一定时期职工工资收入的高低程度，是反映职工工资水平的主要指标。计算公式为：

职工平均工资＝报告期实际支付的全部职工工资总额/报告期全部职工平均人数

城镇登记失业人员 指有非农业户口，在一定的劳动年龄内，有劳动能力，无业而要求就业，并在当地就业服务机构进行求职登记的人员。

城镇登记失业率 指城镇登记失业人数同城镇从业人数与城镇从业人数与城镇登记失业人数之和的比。计算公式为：

$$\text{城镇登记失业率}=\frac{\text{城镇登记失业人数}}{\text{（城镇单位就业人员–使用的农村劳动力–聘用的离退休人员–聘用的港澳台及外方人员）+不在岗职工+城镇私营业主+城镇个体户主+城镇私营企业及个体就业人员+城镇登记失业人数}}\times 100\%$$

Explanatory Notes on Main Statistical Indicators

The annual statistics on total population is taken at midnight, the 31st of December, not including residents in Taiwan province, Hong Kong SAR and Macao SAR and Chinese national residing abroad.

Permanent population refers to the population of actual habitual residence in a certain area in a certain period of more than six months time, including six months. Permanent population include the accounts in this area which are also living in this area, accounts outside this area but with more than half a year of household registration, accounts to be determined including people without accounts or pockets of accounts, and accounts in the area but leaving this area less than six months.

Urban Population and Rural Population Urban population refers to all people residing in cities and towns, while rural population refers to population other than urban population.

Birth Rate (or Crude Birth Rate) refers to the ratio of the number of births to the average population (or mid-period population) during a certain period of time (usually a year), expressed in ‰. Birth rate in the chapter refers to annual birth rate. The following formula is used:

$$\text{Birth Rate}=\frac{\text{Number of Births}}{\text{Annual Average Population}}\times 1000‰$$

Number of births in the formula refers to live births, i.e. when a baby has breathed or showed any vital phenomena regardless of the length of pregnancy.

Annual average population is the average of the number of population at the beginning of the year and that at the end of the year. Sometimes it is substituted by the mid-year population.

Death Rate (or Crude Death Rate) refers to the ratio of the number of deaths to the average population (or mid-period population) during a certain period of time (usually a year), expressed in ‰. Death rate in the chapter refers to annual death rate. The following formula is used:

$$\text{DeathRate}=\frac{\text{Number of Deaths}}{\text{Annual Average Population}}\times 1000‰$$

Natural Growth Rate of Population refers to the ratio of natural increase in population (number of births minus number of deaths) in a certain period of time (usually a year) to the average population (or mid-period population) of the same period, expressed in ‰ . The following formula is applied:

Natural Growth Rate of Population =(Number of Births-Number of Deaths)/Annual Average Population× 1000‰

Employed Persons refer to persons aged 16 and over who are engaged in gainful employment and thus receive remuneration payment or earn business income. This indicator reflects the actual utilization of total labour force during a certain period of time and is often used for the research on China's economic situation and national power.

Persons Employed in Various Units refer to all the persons working in government agencies of various levels, political and party organizations, social organizations, enterprises and institutions, and receiving wages or other forms of payment. They include fully-employed staff and workers, re-employed retirees, teachers in the schools run by the local people, foreigners and Chinese compatriots from Hong Kong, Macao, and Taiwan working in various units, part-time employees, employees of other units working temporarily at current posts, and employees holding the second job, but do not include persons who have left their working units while keeping their labour contract (employment relation) unchanged. This indicator reflects the total number of laborers actually engaged in production or other operations in various units.

Persons Employed in Private Enterprises and Self- Employed Individuals in Urban Areas Persons employed in private enterprises refer to the persons employed in the private enterprises which have been registered at the departments of industrial and commercial administration for which the business operation are situated at a county town (i.e. a town where the county government is located), or at urban areas with administrative hierarchy higher than a county town. The self-employed individuals in urban areas refer to persons who hold the certificates of residence in urban areas or have resided in the urban areas for a long time and have been registered at the departments of industrial and commercial administration and approved to be engaged in individual industrial or commercial business, including self-employed persons as well as helpers and hired labourers who work in individual households.

State-owned Units refer to economic units whose assets are owned by the state, including non-corporation units registered according to Regulation of the People's Republic of China on the Registration of Enterprises and

Corporations, state organs, institutions and social organizations at the central-level and local levels.

Collective-owned Units refer to economic units registered according to Regulation of the People's Republic of China on the Registration of Enterprises and Corporations where the means of production are collectively owned.

Units of Other Types of Ownership refer to units registered with other types of ownership, including cooperative units, joint ownership units, limited liability corporations, share holding corporations, units funded by entrepreneurs from Hong Kong, Macao, and Taiwan, and foreign- funded units.

Employed Staff and Workers refer to persons who work in, and receive wages from their working units, including persons who have their work posts but are temporarily absent from work for reasons of study or on sick, injury or maternal leave and still receive wages from their working units.

Total Wage Bill refers to the total remuneration payment to employed persons in various units during a certain period of time. The calculation of total wage bill is based on the total remuneration payment to employed persons . Therefore, all the wages and salaries and other payments to employed persons are included in the total wage bill regardless of sources, reckoning the cost of production or not, category, listing as items of premium taxation or not, and forms, paying in cash or in kind.

Average Wage refers to the average wage in money terms per person during a certain period of time for employed persons in enterprises, institutions, and government agencies, which reflects the general level of wage income during a certain period of time and is calculated as follows:

$$\text{AverageWage} = \frac{\text{TotalWage Billof Employed Personsat Reference Time}}{\text{Average Number of Persons Employedat Reference Time}}$$

Registered Unemployed Persons in Urban Areas refer to the persons with non-agricultural household registration at certain working ages (16 years old to retirement age), who are capable of working, unemployed and willing to work, and have been registered at the local employment service agencies to apply for a job.

Registered Unemployment Rate in Urban Areas refers to the ratio of the number of the registered unemployed persons to the sum of the number of persons employed in various units (minus the employed rural labour force, re-employed retirees, and Hong Kong, Macao, Taiwan or foreign employees), laid-off staff and workers in urban units, owners of private enterprises in urban areas, owners of self-employed individuals in urban areas, employees of private enterprises in urban areas, employee of self-employed individuals in urban areas, and the registered unemployed persons in urban areas. The formula is as follows:

$$\text{Registered Unemployment rate in urban areas} = \frac{\text{numberof registered urban unemployed persons}}{\begin{array}{c}\text{number of persons employed in}\\ \text{urbanunits-employed rurallabour force}\\ \text{re-employed retirees - HongKong,}\\ \text{Macao,Taiwan or foreign employees}\\ \text{+ laid-off staff and workers+owners of}\\ \text{urban private Enterprises+ owners of}\\ \text{urbanself-employed Individuals + employees}\\ \text{ofurbanprivate Enterprises+employees of}\\ \text{urbanself- employed Individuals+ registered}\\ \text{unemployed persons in urbanareas}\end{array}} \times 100\%$$

5 固定资产投资

INVESTMENT IN FIXED ASSETS

资料整理：赵　晖　令润翠　王　峰　康　敏
Data management: Zhao Hui Ling Runcui Wang Feng Kang Min

第五部分　固定资产投资

一、简要说明

本章资料主要包括全社会固定资产投资、城镇投资、房地产开发投资、城乡集体固定资产投资和城乡私人建房投资以及分区县情况，由西安市统计局固定资产投资处提供。2011年固定资产投资增速基数为按2011年统计制度中投资项目新标准调整的2010年固定资产投资。除2012年房地产开发经营情况(5-23表)为年报数据外,其他(5-18)、(5-19)、(5-20)、(5-21)、(5-22)均为快报数据。

二、主要指标

全社会固定资产投资（亿元）	4243.43	比上年增长	26.8%
#国有经济单位	1661.22	比上年增长	37.9%
集体经济单位	194.71	比上年增长	-24.6%
#城镇投资	4107.54	比上年增长	28.0%
房地产开发	1281.90	比上年增长	28.6%
全市新增固定资产（亿元）	1765.05	比上年增长	36.1%
全市竣工住宅面积（万平方米）	1189.04	比上年增长	38.0%

5　INVESTMENT IN FIXED ASSETS

Ⅰ.Brief Introduction

This chapter consists of primarily the data on fixed asset investment, investment of urban units, real estate development investment, urban and rural area collective fixed asset investment, urban and rural area private housing investment and the classified data of the districts and the counties on real estate development investment, provided by Fixed Asset Investment Division of the Xi'an Bureau of Statistics. The base of growth rate of fixed assets in 2011 is the national asset investment in 2010 adiusted by the new standards of the project to invest in 2011 statistical system.

Ⅱ.Major Indicators

		Increase over Preceding Year
Investment Fulfilled In Fixed Assets(100 mil. Yuan)	4243.43	26.8%
State-owned Enterprises	1661.22	37.9%
Collective-owned Enterprises	194.71	-24.6%
Investment of Urban Units	4107.54	28.0%
Real Estate Development	1281.90	28.6%
Investment Fulfilled Newly Increased FixedAssets(100 mil. yuan)	1765.05	36.1%
Total Floor Space of Building Completed(10 000 sq.m)	1189.04	38.0%

5-1 主要年份按城乡分全社会固定资产投资

Total Investment in Fixed Assets in the Whole Country by Rural and Urban Areas in Representative Years

单位：亿元 (100 million yuan)

年　份 Year	全社会固定资产投资合计 Total	城镇 Urban Area	房地产开发 Real Estate	农村 Rural Area
1979	4.08	3.01		1.07
1980	6.12	4.48		1.64
1981	5.59	4.56		1.03
1982	9.49	8.02		1.47
1983	10.46	9.17		1.29
1984	12.89	10.69		2.20
1985	18.44	14.44		4.00
1986	22.15	18.54		3.61
1987	27.05	23.15		3.90
1988	29.14	24.43		4.71
1989	28.30	23.85		4.45
1990	26.39	23.10	0.91	3.29
1991	30.76	25.55	2.01	5.21
1992	38.48	32.85	3.32	5.63
1993	75.06	66.65	7.39	8.41
1994	85.57	73.47	12.02	12.10
1995	103.42	88.50	21.65	14.92
1996	114.38	96.98	24.66	17.40
1997	116.90	95.17	24.68	21.73
1998	154.80	138.68	38.21	16.12
1999	197.31	172.64	44.30	24.67
2000	232.37	203.01	51.85	29.36
2001	287.72	256.95	67.42	30.77
2002	338.15	307.24	79.37	30.91
2003	478.10	445.74	124.82	32.36
2004	646.69	612.03	169.67	34.66
2005	835.10	776.33	225.23	58.77
2006	1066.62	971.84	285.76	94.78
2007	1435.33	1340.59	387.33	94.74
2008	1906.36	1786.60	540.26	119.76
2009	2500.13	2367.58	696.34	132.55
2010	3250.56	3104.92	842.34	145.64
2011	3346.26	3207.97	996.81	138.29
2012	4243.43	4107.54	1281.90	135.89

5-2 主要年份按经济类型分全社会固定资产投资

Total Investment in Fixed Assets in the Whole Country by Registion Stares in Representative Years

单位：亿元 (100 million yuan)

年 份 Year	合计 Total	国有经济 State-owned	集体经济 Collective-owned	个体经济 Self-employed Individual	其他经济 Others
1985	18.44	13.96	1.36	3.12	
1986	22.15	18.05	0.97	3.13	
1987	27.05	22.18	1.50	3.37	
1988	29.14	23.72	1.86	3.56	
1989	28.30	23.22	1.46	3.62	
1990	26.39	22.21	1.44	2.74	
1991	30.76	24.42	2.26	4.08	
1992	38.48	32.04	1.45	4.99	
1993	75.06	59.66	3.03	6.55	5.82
1994	85.57	64.71	4.14	10.09	6.63
1995	103.42	69.08	9.78	11.13	13.43
1996	114.38	80.66	8.73	12.50	12.49
1997	116.90	77.46	10.21	15.11	14.12
1998	154.80	113.07	7.89	10.59	23.25
1999	197.31	136.50	13.62	16.22	30.97
2000	232.37	159.60	14.65	24.40	33.72
2001	287.72	175.58	14.67	38.57	58.90
2002	338.15	200.06	13.70	44.68	79.71
2003	478.10	264.83	22.33	73.43	117.51
2004	646.69	329.14	40.06	48.95	228.54
2005	835.10	373.70	59.23	79.04	323.13
2006	1066.62	401.14	110.68	107.33	447.47
2007	1435.33	476.78	207.08	183.09	568.38
2008	1906.36	694.89	246.89	50.43	914.15
2009	2500.13	932.91	289.91	97.86	1179.45
2010	3250.56	1348.76	326.44	54.73	1520.63
2011	3346.26	1204.80	258.15	74.64	1808.67
2012	4243.43	1661.22	194.71	82.72	2304.78

注：集体经济：包括城镇集体和农村集体。
个体经济：包括私营个体投资及城镇工矿区私人建房和农村私人建房。

5-3 主要年份按产业分全市固定资产投资

Total Investment in Fixed Assets in the Whole City by Three Strata of Industry in Representative Years

单位：亿元 (100 million yuan)

年 份 Year	合计 Total	第一产业 Primary Industry	第二产业 Secondary Industry	工业 Industry	第三产业 Tertisry Industry
1979	3.01	0.06	1.24	1.20	1.71
1980	4.48	0.06	2.09	1.99	2.33
1981	4.56	0.11	2.10	1.83	2.35
1982	8.02	0.04	4.07	3.63	3.91
1983	9.17	0.11	4.97	4.41	4.09
1984	10.69	0.19	4.56	3.99	5.94
1985	14.44	0.18	7.22	6.45	7.04
1986	18.54	0.16	8.98	8.37	9.40
1987	23.15	0.19	11.81	11.26	11.15
1988	24.43	0.15	11.95	11.20	12.33
1989	23.85	0.13	11.94	11.50	11.78
1990	23.10	0.25	11.03	10.59	11.82
1991	25.55	0.27	12.48	11.95	12.80
1992	32.85	0.10	15.60	14.73	17.15
1993	66.65	0.07	24.50	22.44	42.08
1994	73.47	0.03	27.04	25.85	46.40
1995	88.50	0.14	28.80	27.71	59.56
1996	96.98	0.13	25.96	24.24	70.89
1997	95.17	0.24	23.65	21.66	71.28
1998	138.68	0.48	35.33	29.86	102.87
1999	172.64	0.94	39.88	36.40	131.82
2000	203.01	0.76	57.21	54.37	145.04
2001	256.95	0.86	63.31	61.28	192.78
2002	307.24	4.29	74.34	68.45	228.61
2003	445.74	3.34	83.25	78.41	359.15
2004	612.03	3.38	97.69	95.67	510.96
2005	776.33	5.26	144.25	140.44	626.82
2006	971.84	10.04	213.43	206.48	748.37
2007	1340.59	10.20	297.53	286.61	1032.86
2008	1786.60	23.75	369.74	356.12	1393.11
2009	2367.58	24.46	458.44	442.70	1884.68
2010	3104.92	39.83	556.10	498.62	2508.99
2011	3207.97	43.10	474.73	390.30	2690.14
2012	4165.99	99.34	671.92	578.17	3394.73

5-4 全市固定资产投资(2012年)

Total Investment in Fixed Assets in the Whole City (2012)

单位：万元 (10 000 yuan)

指　标	Item	合计 Total	房地产开发 Real Estate
一、本年完成投资	**Investment Completed This Year(10 000 yuan)**	**41659924**	**12819013**
#住宅	Residential Buildings	12158138	10116672
（一）按登记注册类型分	**Grouped by Registion Status**		
内资	Domestic Funded Enterprises	39415441	11687139
国有	State-owned Enterprises	16086985	966589
集体	Collective-owned Enterprises	1827753	118183
股份合作	Cooperative Enterprises	109553	31459
联营	Joint Ownership Enterprises	170400	10379
国有联营	State Joint Ownership Enterprises	119378	
集体联营	Collective Joint Ownership Enterprises	9820	
国有与集体联营	Joint State-collective Ownership Enterprises	29460	8437
其他联营	Other Joint Ownership Enterprises	11742	1942
有限责任公司	Limited Liability Corporations	13726913	7563840
国有独资公司	State-funded Corporations	405853	123276
其他有限责任公司	Other Limited Liability Corporations	13321060	7440564
股份有限公司	Stock Limited Corporation	1054875	276405
私营	Private Enterprises	5291753	2682735
私营独资	Private-funded Enterprises	871177	117710
私营合伙	Private Limited Liability Corporations	127974	22771
私营有限责任公司	Private Limited Liability Corporations	4089150	2431809
私营股份有限公司	Private Share Holding Corporations	203452	110445
其他	Other	1147209	37549
港澳台商投资	Enterprises Funded by Hong Kong, Macao and Taiwan	716030	390554
与港澳台合资经营	Joint-venture Enterprises	275921	62169
与港澳台合作经营	Cooperative Enterprises	20068	20068
港澳台独资	Wholly Funded from Hong Kong,Macao and Taiwan	405441	308317
港澳台投资股份有限公司	Share-holding Corporations Ltd.	9700	
其他港澳台投资		4900	

5-4 续表1 continued 1

单位：万元 (10 000 yuan)

指 标	Item	合计 Total	房地产开发 Real Estate
外商投资	Foreign Owned Enterprises	1528453	741320
中外合资经营	Joint-venture Enterprises	305179	245018
中外合作经营	Cooperation Enterprises	157618	133780
外资企业	Foreign Funded Enterprises	717229	362522
外商投资股份有限公司	Share-holding Corporations Ltd. With Foreign Funds	327419	
其他外商投资		21008	
（二）按隶属关系分	**Grouped by Jurisdiction of Management**	**41659924**	**12819013**
中央	Central	1681280	371918
省属	Provincial	4103421	791482
市属	Municipal	35875223	11655613
（三）按建设性质分	**Grouped by Type of Construction**	**26148224**	
新建	New Construction	21651399	
扩建	Expansion	1685922	
改建和技术改造	Reconstruction	2810903	
（四）按构成分	**Grouped by Composition**	**41659924**	**12819013**
1. 建筑工程	Construction Projects	30391089	9301747
2. 安装工程	Installment Projects	3877377	1331586
3. 设备、工器具购置	Purchasing of Equipment and Instruments	3311375	143591
4. 其他费用	Others	4080083	2042089

5-4 续表2 continued 2

单位：万元 (10 000 yuan)

指 标	Item	合计 Total	房地产开发 Real Estate
二、构成(%)	**Proportion (%)**		
（一）按登记注册类型分组	**Grouped by Status**		
#国有经济	State-owned	39.9	8.5
集体经济	Collective-owned	5.0	2.1
（二）按隶属关系分组	**Grouped by Jurisdiction of Management**		
中央	Central	4.0	2.9
省属	Provincial	9.8	6.2
市属	Municipal	86.2	90.9
（三）按建设性质分	**Grouped by Type of Construction**		
新建	New Construction	52.0	
扩建	Expansion	4.0	
改建和技术改造	Reconstruction	6.7	
（四）按构成分	**Grouped by Composition of Funds**		
1. 建筑工程	Construction Projects	73.0	72.6
2. 安装工程	Installation Projects	9.3	10.4
3. 设备、工器具购置	Purchasing of the Equipment and Instruments	7.9	1.1
4. 其他	Others	9.8	15.9
三、本年新增固定资产（万元）	**Newly Increase in Fixed Assets(10 000 yuan)**	**17650473**	**3580256**
四、房屋面积（万平方米）	**Floor Space (10 000 sq.m)**		
本年施工房屋面积	Floor Space of Buildings Under Construction This Year	14093.91	9947.89
住宅	Residential Buildings	9565.84	8294.92
本年竣工房屋面积	Floor Space of Buildings Completed This Year	1626.25	1063.70
住宅	Residential Buildings	1189.04	903.82
五、竣工房屋价值（万元）	**Value of the Building Completed (10 000 yuan)**	**4932669**	**3105722**
住宅	Residential Buildings	3455499	2600362

5-5 按国民经济行业分全市固定资产投资（2012年）

Investment in Fixed Assets in the Whole City by Sector (2012)

单位：万元 (10 000 yuan)

行　业	Scetor	2012
本年完成固定资产投资	**Grouped by Sector (10 000 yuan)**	**41659924**
（一）农、林、牧、渔业	Agriculture,Forestry,Animal Husbandry and Fishery	993367
（二）采矿业	Mining	21100
（三）制造业	Manufacturing	4823480
农副食品加工业	Processing of Food from Agricultural Products	127361
食品制造业	Manufacture of Foods	347936
酒、饮料和精制茶制造业	Wine, soft drinks and refined tea industry	29940
烟草制品业	Tobacco Processing	
纺织业	Textile Industry	28975
纺织服装、服饰业	Textile, apparel industry	2205
皮革、毛皮、羽毛及其制品和制鞋业	Leather, Fur, Feather (eiderdown) and Their Products Industry	
木材加工和木、竹、藤、棕、草制品业	Timber Processing,Bamboo,Cane,Palm Fiber and Straw Products	16660
家具制造业	Furniture Manufacturing	78950
造纸及纸制品业	Papermaking and Paper products	38490
印刷和记录媒介复制业	Printing,Record Medium Reproduction	69178
文教、工美、体育和娱乐用品制造业	Culture, education, Craft art, sports and entertainment goods manufacturing industry	
石油加工、炼焦和核燃料加工业	Petroleum Refining, Ccoke Making and Nuclear Fuel Processing Industry	41965
化学原料和化学制品制造业	Raw Chemical Materials and Chemical Products	121218
医药制造业	Medical and Pharmaceutical Products	116139
化学纤维制造业	Chemical Fiber	
橡胶和塑料制品业	Rubber and plastic products industry	31395
非金属矿物制品业	Nonmetal Mineral Products	241863
黑色金属冶炼和压延加工业	Smelting and Pressing of Ferrous Metals	12720
有色金属冶炼和压延加工业	Smelting and Pressing of Nonferrou Metals	91951
金属制品业	Metal Products	155889

5-5 续表1 continued 1

单位：万元 (10 000 yuan)

行 业	Scetor	2012
通用设备制造业	General Equipment Manufacturing Industry	308429
专用设备制造业	Special Purpose Equipment	704071
汽车制造业	Automotive Manufacturing	763514
铁路、船舶、航空航天和其他运输设备制造业	Railroad, Marine, Aerospace and other Transportation Equipment Manufacturing	221195
电气机械和器材制造业	Electric Equipment and Machinery	412262
计算机、通信和其他电子设备制造业	Communication Equipment, Computer and Other Electronic Equipment Manufacturing Industry	466826
仪器仪表制造业	Instrument Manufacturing Industry	323055
其他制造业	Other Manufacturing	46482
废弃资源综合利用	Comprehensive Utilization of waste Resources	12386
金属制品、机械和设备修理业	Metal Products, Machinery and Equipment Repair Industry	12425
（四）电力、燃气及水的生产供应业	Production & Supply of Electricity,Gas & Water	937141
（五）建筑业	Construction	937464
（六）批发和零售业	Wholesale and Retail Trades	1210468
（七）交通运输、仓储和邮政业	Transport, Storage and Post	2928288
（八）住宿和餐饮业	Hotels and Catering Services	495665
（九）信息传输、软件和信息技术服务业	Information Transmission,Computer Service and Software	687847
（十）金融业	Financial Intermediation	247789
（十一）房地产业	Real Estate	20899157
（十二） 租赁和商务服务业	Leasing and Business Services	561134
（十三）科学研究和技术服务业	Scientific Research,Technical Service and Geologic Prospecting	696830
（十四）水利、环境和公共设施管理业	Management of Water Conservancy, Environment and Public Facilities	3257549
（十五）居民服务、修理和其他服务业	Services to Households, repairs and other services	332963
（十六）教育	Education	651315
（十七）卫生和社会工作	Health and social work	591415
（十八）文化、体育和娱乐业	Culture, Sports and Entertainment	287987
（十九）公共管理、社会保障和社会组织	Public administration, social security and social organizations	1098965
（二十）国际组织	International Organizations	

5-6 主要年份按资金来源及建设性质分全市固定资产投资

Total Investment in Fixed Assets in the Whole City by Sources of Funds and Type of Construction in Representative Years

单位：万元 (10 000 yuan)

指　标	Item	1995	2000	2001	2002	2003	2004	2005
一、投资总额(万元)	**Total Investment (10 000 yuan)**	**884994**	**2030122**	**2569496**	**3072442**	**4457381**	**6120324**	**7763283**
（一）按资金来源分	Grouped by Funds Source							
1. 国家预算内投资	State Budgetary Funds	69185	160982	256403	355960	365263	436496	728885
2. 国内贷款	Domestic Loans	216565	432282	672379	666146	1219234	1565246	1257175
3. 债券	Bonds	873	32460	6753	766	3278		
4. 利用外资	Utilization of Foreign Funds	80792	31622	54907	15192	47509	47401	40583
5. 自筹资金	Self-raising Funds	385047	875352	1121502	1392915	1733132	2629720	4001700
6. 其他资金	Others	132532	497424	457552	641463	1088965	1441461	1734940
（二）按构成分	Grouped by Composition of Funds							
1. 建筑安装工程	Construction and Installation Projects	527220	1404184	1698777	2119151	3067309	4127677	5086664
2. 设备、工器具购置	Purchasing of Equipment and Instruments	233730	382495	452602	552251	577240	708988	1021079
3. 其它费用	Others	124044	243443	418117	401040	812832	1283659	1655540
（三）按建设性质分	Grouped by Type of Construction							
#新建	New Construction	210926	533058	723957	874392	1294032	1874116	2907551
扩建	Expansion	180210	542510	581138	868603	1102914	1169537	1208430
改建	Reconstruction	157457	263657	344879	343184	447944	670229	782953
二、房屋施工面积（万平方米）	**Floor Space Under Construction**	**1070.58**	**1702.58**	**1767.13**	**2396.89**	**2716.18**	**3177.36**	**4030.38**

5-6 续表1 continued 1

单位：万元 (10 000 yuan)

指　标	Item	2006	2007	2008	2009	2010	2011	2012
一、投资总额(万元)	**Total Investment (10 000 yuan)**	**9718418**	**13405920**	**17865977**	**23675759**	**31049184**	**32079666**	**41659924**
（一）按资金来源分	Grouped by Funds Source							
1. 国家预算内投资	State Budgetary Funds	677145	670592	1555809	2562756	1649563	1480412	1851860
2. 国内贷款	Domestic Loans	1631689	1619218	2162957	3301919	4288663	3546561	4023452
3. 债券	Bonds							
4. 利用外资	Utilization of Foreign Funds	165390	183422	261325	144124	126802	89047	135147
5. 自筹资金	Self-raising Funds	5538393	8565573	12771844	15776565	18279153	19400468	28680236
6. 其他资金	Others	1705801	2367115	1114042	1890395	6705003	7563178	6969229
（二）按构成分	Grouped by Composition of Funds							
1. 建筑安装工程	Construction and Installation Projects	6486233	9165668	12864657	16337466	21690205	25553161	34268466
2. 设备、工器具购置	Purchasing of Equipment and Instruments	1409589	1858720	2024631	2619783	3094336	1911180	3311375
3. 其它费用	Others	1822596	2381532	2976689	4718510	6264643	4615325	4080083
（三）按建设性质分	Grouped by Type of Construction							
#新建	New Construction	3511432	5123975	6356716	8567540	14292899	16077747	21651399
扩建	Expansion	1101740	994841	2118013	3054929	2649749	1956527	1685922
改建	Reconstruction	1099304	1548130	1921664	2738799	2620997	2155112	2810903
二、房屋施工面积(万平方米)	**Floor Space Under Construction**	**4589.39**	**5759.28**	**6570.94**	**9571.25**	**11166.19**	**12353.11**	**14093.91**

5-7 主要年份市属固定资产投资

Investment In Fixed Assets of Municipal Units in Representative Years

单位：万元 (10 000 yuan)

指　标	Item	1995	2000	2001	2002	2003	2004	2005
一、投资总额	**Total Investment**	**432451**	**1263023**	**1539717**	**1848833**	**2978747**	**4355271**	**5788693**
#房地产开发	Real Estate	171291	473787	566557	702233	1114809	1492693	2062940
按经济类型分	Grouped by Type of Enterprises							
国有经济	State-owned Enterprises	258545	890546	894700	1006245	1586057	1884624	2198836
集体经济	Collective-owned Enterprises	5720	52893	62895	63877	142849	257226	258327
其他经济	Others	168186	319584	582122	778711	1249841	2213421	3331530
二、新增固定资产	**Newly Increased Fixed Assets**	**273324**	**953173**	**1159980**	**1295389**	**1812099**	**1962795**	**3011104**
三、房屋竣工面积（万平方米）	**Floor Space of the Building Completed(10 000sq.m)**	**202.52**	**509.48**	**535.98**	**537.44**	**631.89**	**606.23**	**767.70**
住宅（万平方米）	Residential Buildings	143.30	373.51	396.01	331.45	387.82	388.79	436.43

5-7 续表1 continued 1

单位：万元 (10 000 yuan)

指　标	Item	2006	2007	2008	2009	2010	2011	2012
一、投资总额（万元）	**Total Investment**	**7835681**	**10555849**	**14648360**	**19063075**	**25474854**	**26820029**	**35875223**
#房地产开发	Real Estate	2641871	3515719	4938202	6575526	8020893	9001953	11655613
按经济类型分	Grouped by Type of Enterprises							
国有经济	State-owned Enterprises	2591184	2972840	4480627	6527566	9306901	8750285	12264895
集体经济	Collective-owned Enterprises	363909	1366567	1646111	1614290	2253851	1897980	1932578
其他经济	Others	4880588	6216442	8521622	10921219	13914102	16171764	21677750
二、新增固定资产（万元）	**Newly Increased Fixed Assets**	**3495179**	**5279938**	**6488364**	**8380033**	**10423906**	**10663882**	**15376910**
三、房屋竣工面积（万平方米）	**Floor Space of the Building Completed(10 000sq.m)**	**914.80**	**1343.88**	**987.05**	**1359.46**	**668.49**	**1002.82**	**1450.29**
住宅（万平方米）	Residential Buildings	432.43	734.05	602.69	727.41	448.46	531.38	1069.61

5-8 市属固定资产投资（2012年）

Investment in Fixed Assets of Municipal Units (2012)

单位：万元 (10 000 yuan)

指　标	Item	城镇 Urban Area	房地产开发 Real Estate
一、本年完成投资	**Investment Completed This Year**	**35875223**	**11655613**
#住宅	Residential Buildings	10681158	9180031
（一）按登记注册类型分	**Grouped by Registion Status**		
内资	Domestic Funded Enterprises	33676431	10523739
国有	State-owned Enterprises	11924058	739559
集体	Collective-owned Enterprises	1821859	118183
股份合作	Cooperative Enterprises	100899	26119
联营	Joint Ownership Enterprises	161963	1942
国有联营	State Joint Ownership Enterprises	119378	
集体联营	Collective Joint Ownership Enterprises	9820	
国有与集体联营	Joint State-collective Ownership Enterprises	21023	
其他联营	Other Joint Ownership Enterprises	11742	1942
有限责任公司	Limited Liability Corporations	12310313	6683280
国有独资公司	State-funded Corporations	221459	8150
其他有限责任公司	Other Limited Liability Corporations	12088854	6675130
股份有限公司	Stock Limited Corporation	961517	245872
私营	Private Enterprises	5286953	2677935
私营独资	Private-funded Enterprises	871177	117710
私营合伙	Private Limited Liability Corporations	127974	22771
私营有限责任公司	Private Limited Liability Corporations	4084350	2427009
私营股份有限公司	Private Share Holding Corporations	203452	110445
其他	Other	1108869	30849
港澳台商投资	Enterprises Funded by Hong Kong, Macao and Taiwan	716030	390554
与港澳台合资经营	Joint Venture	275921	62169
与港澳台合作经营	Cooperation	20068	20068
港澳台独资	Sole-Funded	405441	308317
港澳台投资股份有限公司	Share-Holding Corporations Ltd.	9700	
其他港澳台投资	Investment From Hongkong,Macao,Taiwan	4900	
外商投资	Enterprises with Foreign Investment	1482762	741320
中外合资经营	Joint Venture	273179	245018
中外合作经营	Cooperation	157618	133780
外资企业	Sole-Funded	717229	362522

5-8 续表1 continued 1

单位：万元 (10 000 yuan)

指　标	Item	城镇 Urban Area	房地产开发 Real Estate
外商投资股份有限公司	Share-holding Corporations Ltd.	313728	
其他外商投资	Foreign Investment	21008	
（二）按建设性质分	**Grouped by Type of Construction**	**22241441**	
新建	New Construction	18361738	
扩建	Expansion	1408711	
改建和技术改造	Reconstruction	2470992	
（三）按构成分	**Grouped by Composition**	**35875223**	**11655613**
建筑工程	Construction Projects	26486300	8434489
安装工程	Installment Projects	3105897	1273453
设备、工器具购置	Purchasing of Equipment and Instruments	2593302	136911
其他费用	Others	3689724	1810760
二、本年完成投资额构成(%)	**the Constitution of Compeleted Investment this year (%)**		
（一）按登记注册类型分组	**Grouped by Status**		
# 国有经济	State-owned	34.2	6.4
集体经济	Collective-owned	5.4	1.3
（二）按建设性质分	**Grouped by Type of Construction**		
新建	New Construction	51.2	
扩建	Expansion	3.9	
改建和技术改造	Reconstruction	6.9	
（三）按构成分	**Grouped by Composition of Funds**		
建筑工程	Construction Projects	73.8	72.4
安装工程	Installation Projects	8.7	10.9
设备、工器具购置	Purchasing of the Equipment and Instruments	7.2	1.2
其他	Others	10.3	15.5
三、本年新增固定资产	**Newly Increase in Fixed Assets**	**15376910**	**3280080**
四、房屋面积（万平方米）	**Floor Space (10 000 sq.m)**		
本年施工房屋面积	Floor Space of Buildings Under Construction This Year	12522.16	9192.90
住宅	Residential Buildings	8568.45	7650.89
本年竣工房屋面积	Floor Space of Buildings Completed This Year	1450.29	967.42
住宅	Residential Buildings	1069.61	818.62
五、竣工房屋价值	**Value of the Building Completed**	**439.84**	**283.48**
住宅	Residential Buildings	315.04	236.55

5-9 按国民经济行业分市属固定资产投资（2012年）

Investment in Fixed Assets of Municipal Units by Sector (2012)

单位：万元 (10 000 yuan)

行 业	Scetor	2012
本年完成固定资产投资	**Grouped by Sector**	**35875223**
（一）农、林、牧、渔业	Agriculture,Forestry,Animal Husbandry and Fishery	993367
（二）采矿业	Mining	21100
（三）制造业	Manufacturing	3974551
农副食品加工业	Processing of Food from Agricultural Products	127361
食品制造业	Manufacture of Foods	347936
酒、饮料和精制茶制造业	Wine, soft drinks and refined tea industry	29940
烟草制品业	Tobacco Processing	
纺织业	Textile Industry	28975
纺织服装、服饰业	Textile, apparel industry	2205
皮革、毛皮、羽毛及其制品和制鞋业	Leather, Fur, Feather (eiderdown) and Their Products Industry	
木材加工和木、竹、藤、棕、草制品业	Timber Processing,Bamboo,Cane,Palm Fiber and Straw Products	16660
家具制造业	Furniture Manufacturing	78950
造纸及纸制品业	Papermaking and Paper products	38490
印刷和记录媒介复制业	Printing,Record Medium Reproduction	23884
文教、工美、体育和娱乐用品制造业	Culture, education, Craft art, sports and entertainment goods manufacturing industry	
石油加工、炼焦和核燃料加工业	Petroleum Refining, Ccoke Making and Nuclear Fuel Processing Industry	1465
化学原料和化学制品制造业	Raw Chemical Materials and Chemical Products	121218
医药制造业	Medical and Pharmaceutical Products	116139
化学纤维制造业	Chemical Fiber	
橡胶和塑料制品业	Rubber and plastic products industry	31395
非金属矿物制品业	Nonmetal Mineral Products	237117
黑色金属冶炼和压延加工业	Smelting and Pressing of Ferrous Metals	12720
有色金属冶炼和压延加工业	Smelting and Pressing of Nonferrou Metals	80234
金属制品业	Metal Products	155889

5-9 续表1 continued 1

单位：万元 (10 000 yuan)

行 业	Scetor	2012
通用设备制造业	General Equipment Manufacturing Industry	228429
专用设备制造业	Special Purpose Equipment	518707
汽车制造业	Automotive Manufacturing	612343
铁路、船舶、航空航天和其他运输设备制造业	Railroad, Marine, Aerospace and other Transportation Equipment Manufacturing	196906
电气机械和器材制造业	Electric Equipment and Machinery	291739
计算机、通信和其他电子设备制造业	Communication Equipment, Computer and Other Electronic Equipment Manufacturing Industry	386440
仪器仪表制造业	Instrument Manufacturing Industry	218116
其他制造业	Other Manufacturing	46482
废弃资源综合利用	Comprehensive Utilization of waste Resources	12386
金属制品、机械和设备修理业	Metal Products, Machinery and Equipment Repair Industry	12425
(四) 电力、燃气及水的生产供应业	Production & Supply of Electricity,Gas & Water	650552
(五) 建筑业	Construction	821701
(六) 批发和零售业	Wholesale and Retail Trades	1200368
(七) 交通运输、仓储和邮政业	Transport, Storage and Post	1937792
(八) 住宿和餐饮业	Hotels and Catering Services	329075
(九) 信息传输、软件和信息技术服务业	Information Transmission,Computer Service and Software	498778
(十) 金融业	Financial Intermediation	81045
(十一) 房地产业	Real Estate	18899031
(十二) 租赁和商务服务业	Leasing and Business Services	533885
(十三) 科学研究和技术服务业	Scientific Research,Technical Service and Geologic Prospecting	213996
(十四) 水利、环境和公共设施管理业	Management of Water Conservancy, Environment and Public Facilities	3162788
(十五) 居民服务、修理和其他服务业	Services to Households, repairs and other services	332963
(十六) 教育	Education	434310
(十七) 卫生和社会工作	Health and social work	468462
(十八) 文化、体育和娱乐业	Culture, Sports and Entertainment	256840
(十九) 公共管理、社会保障和社会组织	Public administration, social security and social organizations	1064619
(二十) 国际组织	International Organizations	

5-10 按资金来源及建设性质分市属固定资产投资（2012年）

Investment in Fixed Assets of Municipal Units by Sources of Funds and Type of Construction (2012)

指　标	Item	2012
投资总额（万元）	**Total Investment (10 000 yuan)**	**35875223**
一、按资金来源分	**Grouped by Funds Sources**	
1. 国家预算内资金	State Budgetary Funds	1540921
2. 国内贷款	Domestic Loans	3000149
3. 债券	Bonds	
4. 利用外资	Utilization of Foreign Funds	118201
5. 自筹资金	Self-raising Funds	25015498
6. 其他资金	Others	6200454
二、按建设性质分	**Grouped by Type of Construction**	
#新建	New Construction	18361738
扩建	Expansion	1408711
改建	Reconstruction	2470992
三、按构成分	**Grouped by Composition of Funds**	
1. 建筑工程	Construction Project	26486300
2. 安装工程	Installation Projects	3105897
3. 设备、工器具购置	Purchasing of Equipment and Instruments	2593302
4. 其他费用	Others	3689724
四、房屋施工面积（万平方米）	**Floor Space of Buildings Under Construction (10 000 sq.m)**	**12522.16**

5-11 全市固定资产投资资金来源（2012年）

Source of Funds for Total Fixed Assets Investment of Whole City (2012)

单位：万元 (10 000 yuan)

指标	Item	城镇 Urban Area	房地产开发 Real Estate
一、本年资金来源合计	**Total of Sources of Funds This Year**	**54571347**	**21688388**
1. 上年末结余资金	Balance of Last Year	6009897	4424873
2. 本年资金来源小计	Subtotal Funds This Year	48561450	17263515
(1) 国家预算资金	State Budgetary Funds	2129822	
(2) 国内贷款	Domestic Loans	4741321	2224414
(3) 债券	Bonds		
(4) 利用外资	Utilization of Foreign Funds	159385	24000
(5) 自筹资金	Self-raising Funds	33318548	8076423
(6) 其他资金来源	Others	8212374	6938678
二、本年各项应付款合计	**Total Sums of Money to be Paid This Year**	**3208714**	**2055721**

5-12 全市固定资产投资效果（2012年）

Achievements of Total Assets Investment of Whole City (2012)

指标	Item	城镇 Urban Area	房地产开发 Real Estate
一、建设项目投产率（%）	**Rate of Projects Put Into use(%)**	**56.1**	
施工项目个数（个）	Number of Constructing Projects (unit)	2277	
本年投产项目个数（个）	Number of Projects Put into Use (unit)	1277	
二、固定资产交付使用率（%）	**Rate of Fixed Assets Put into Use(%)**	**42.4**	**27.9**
本年新增固定资产（亿元）	Newly Increased Fixed Assets This Year(100 million yuan)	1765.10	358.00
本年完成投资（亿元）	Investment Completed This Year (100 million yuan)	4166.00	1281.90
三、建设周期（年）	**Construction Period (year)**	**3.6**	**5.5**
计划总投资（亿元）	Total Planned Investment(100 million yuan)	15105.60	7081.00
本年完成投资（亿元）	Investment Completed This Year (100 million yuan)	4166.00	1281.90
四、房屋建筑面积竣工率（%）	**Completion Rate of Buildings (%)**	**8.7**	**9.4**
本年施工房屋面积（万平方米）	Floor Space of the Constructing Buildings This Year (10 000 sq.m)	14093.90	9947.90
本年竣工房屋面积（万平方米）	Floor Space of the Buildings Completed This Year (10 000 sq.m)	1626.30	1063.70

5-13 分区县、开发区全社会固定资产投资额（2012年）

Investment Fulfilled in Fixed Assets by Region and Development Zone (2012)

单位：亿元 (100 million yuan)

区县、开发区	Region	全社会固定资产投资 Investment Fulfilled In Fixed Assets	城镇投资 Urban Area	房地产 Real Estate	农村集体 Rural Collective-owned Units	农村私人建房 Private Housing in Country
区县	**Region**	**4243.43**	**4107.54**	**1281.90**	**58.45**	**77.44**
新城区	Xincheng	353.50	353.50	86.72		
碑林区	Beilin	376.45	376.45	169.57		
莲湖区	Lianhu	473.49	473.49	140.65		
灞桥区	Baqiao	236.36	227.48	63.89	3.23	5.64
未央区	Weiyang	568.99	563.57	207.83		5.42
雁塔区	Yanta	956.06	949.53	448.11		6.53
阎良区	Yanliang	154.52	133.66	13.42	12.91	7.94
临潼区	Lintong	152.20	141.47	6.83	2.66	8.07
长安区	Chang'an	406.99	398.88	99.93	1.56	6.55
蓝田县	Lantian	99.54	81.30	4.21	8.40	9.84
周至县	Zhouzhi	89.14	65.66	3.85	13.69	9.79
户　县	Huxian	140.33	116.61	13.33	13.74	9.98
高陵县	Gaoling	235.87	225.93	23.58	2.25	7.68
开发区	Development Zones	**1553.07**	**1553.07**	**417.11**		
高新区	GaoXin	418.44	418.44	102.07		
经开区	JingKai	381.24	381.24	80.30		
曲江新区	Qujiang	356.10	356.10	131.83		
浐灞生态区	Chanba Eco-District	150.67	150.67	52.74		
航空基地	Aviation Industry Base	48.39	48.39	5.98		
航天基地	Aerospace Base	62.94	62.94	26.81		
国际港务区	International Trade&Logistic Park	58.16	58.16	3.85		
沣东新城	FengDongXinCheng	77.72	77.72	13.53		

5-14 主要年份全市新增固定资产及房屋竣工面积

Value of Newly Added Fixed Assets and Floor Spaces Completed of Municipal Units in Representative Years

年 份 Year	新增固定资产（亿元） Newly Increased Fixed Assets (10 000 yuan)	房屋竣工面积（万平方米） Floor Space of Buildings Completed (sq.m)	住 宅 Residential Buildings
1978	4.96	99.10	40.76
1980	4.64	164.87	100.15
1985	8.62	222.42	129.07
1986	13.40	272.95	155.91
1987	16.72	241.48	119.21
1988	16.82	211.83	102.43
1989	16.58	178.45	87.77
1990	20.30	211.88	111.05
1991	17.86	185.34	95.84
1992	22.33	204.75	112.66
1993	41.70	257.90	144.88
1994	55.37	282.91	184.49
1995	62.58	357.67	252.84
1996	60.04	332.18	249.52
1997	62.88	374.46	286.54
1998	80.23	382.80	275.63
1999	118.92	681.04	550.83
2000	150.16	714.83	544.95
2001	167.77	692.56	502.26
2002	198.97	773.28	486.13
2003	279.44	917.96	578.06
2004	261.95	776.59	498.33
2005	409.72	1131.41	598.61
2006	453.01	1199.45	583.10
2007	667.97	1672.16	929.50
2008	725.17	1113.31	693.42
2009	1013.44	1529.13	822.62
2010	1193.05	775.16	521.08
2011	1297.35	1231.91	861.44
2012	1765.05	1626.25	1189.04

5-15 全市按国民经济行业分房屋建筑面积（2012年）

单位：平方米 (sq.m)

行 业	Scetor	本年施工房屋面积 Floor Space of Buildings Under Construction This Year	住宅 Residential Residence
总 计	**Total**	**140939149**	**95658437**
（一）农、林、牧、渔业	Agriculture, Forestry, Animal Husbandry and Fishery	19850	
（二）采矿业	Mining		
（三）制造业	Manufacturing	8891883	441313
（四）电力、燃气及水的生产供应业	Generation and Supply of Electricity, Production and Supply of Gas and Water	158345	
（五）建筑业	Construction	620701	13700
（六）批发和零售业	Wholesale and Retail Trades	1749963	153210
（七）交通运输、仓储和邮政业	Transportation, Storage and Post	304241	12100
（八）住宿和餐饮业	Hotels and Catering Services	539603	100000
（九）信息传输、软件和信息技术服务业	Information Transmission, Computer Service and Software	113000	
（十）金融业	Financial Intermediation	135393	
（十一）房地产业	Real Estate	118633436	93259161
（十二） 租赁和商务服务业	Leasing and Business Services	687625	
（十三）科学研究和技术服务业	Scientific Research and Technical Service	1688530	63254
（十四）水利、环境和公共设施管理业	Management of Water Conservancy, Environment and Public Facilities	513775	22000
（十五）居民服务、修理和其他服务业	Services to Households, repairs and other services	616569	447329
（十六）教育	Education	2154007	440600
（十七）卫生和社会工作	Health and social work	1680887	94300
（十八）文化、体育和娱乐业	Culture, Sports and Entertainment	214763	
（十九）公共管理、社会保障和社会组织	Public administration, social security and social organizations	2216578	611470
（二十）国际组织	International Organizations		

Floors Space of Buildings Construction of Municipal Units by Sector (2012)

单位：平方米 (sq.m)

本年竣工房屋面积 Floor Space of Buildings Completed This Year	住 宅 Residential Residence	本年竣工房屋价值（万元） Value of Buildings Completed (10 000 yuan)	住 宅 Residential Residence
16262498	**11890418**	**4932669**	**3455499**
15500		5651	
713124	38300	166574	11145
72875		46388	
5920		800	
285682		43910	
28274	12000	10240	7300
65272		58902	
13384019	11210418	3857911	3205895
330000		200000	
143326		75900	
2912		800	
147329	147329	44198	44198
306320		50307	
91920		102877	
35000		8750	
635025	482371	259461	186961

5-16 分区县、开发区新增固定资产及房屋施工、竣工面积（2012年）

区县、开发区	Region	新增固定资产（亿元）Increased Fixed Assets (100 million yuan)	本年施工房屋面积（万平方米）Floor Space of Buildings Under Construction (10 000sq.m)	住宅 Residenctial Buildings
区县	**Region**	**1746.25**	**14093.91**	**9565.84**
新城区	Xincheng	96.00	870.81	692.77
碑林区	Beilin	299.36	1888.73	1432.49
莲湖区	Lianhu	237.23	1386.47	1002.52
灞桥区	Baqiao	75.29	791.60	541.00
未央区	Weiyang	152.58	2712.87	2073.25
雁塔区	Yanta	255.42	3521.35	2354.25
阎良区	Yanliang	68.97	317.12	135.30
临潼区	Lintong	100.14	133.33	88.86
长安区	Chang'an	149.21	1274.28	674.71
蓝田县	Lantian	87.10	98.75	52.23
周至县	Zhouzhi	37.40	128.93	62.37
户　县	Huxian	71.06	279.58	158.00
高陵县	Gaoling	116.49	690.09	298.10
开发区	**Development Zones**	**200.13**	**954.94**	**136.95**
高新区	GaoXin	72.85	602.06	
经开区	JingKai	32.51	85.41	44.73
曲江新区	Qujiang	63.56	44.88	35.81
浐灞生态区	Chanba Eco-District	5.47	6.54	
航空基地	Aviation Industry Base		12.32	
航天基地	Aerospace Base	14.06	188.74	56.41
国际港务区	International Trade&Logistic Park			
新城区	Xingcheng	11.67	15.00	

Newly Added Fixed Assets and Floor Space of Constructing and Completed Buildings by Region and Development Zone (2012)

本年竣工房屋面积（万平方米） Floor Space of Buildings Completed(10 000 sq.m)	住宅 Residenctial Buildings	本年竣工房屋价值（亿元） Value of Buildings Completed (100 million yuan)	住宅 Residenctial Buildings	商品房销售面积（万平方米） Floor Space of Houses Sales(sq.m) Houses(100 million yuan)	商品房销售额（亿元） Sales Income of Commercial Houses(100 million yuan)
1626.25	**1189.04**	**493.27**	**345.55**	**1538.91**	**858.53**
17.64	14.83	4.35	3.69	52.52	27.94
435.02	351.59	136.01	107.62	245.88	130.08
60.50	57.81	27.59	26.07	100.55	60.68
17.40	16.75	4.41	4.23	141.25	68.50
330.97	279.83	82.15	70.87	252.75	127.54
377.73	250.47	154.37	83.12	492.71	326.64
29.34	26.86	7.18	5.94	25.74	8.88
67.38	41.44	13.68	8.59	10.68	5.10
58.65	43.78	24.84	19.40	102.25	65.86
14.31		1.75		20.87	6.11
9.68	5.89	1.92	1.51	13.03	2.93
100.65	39.74	12.83	3.65	16.94	6.51
106.99	60.05	22.18	10.86	63.75	21.77
27.11	**20.81**	**9.15**	**6.52**		
14.73	14.73	4.42	4.42		
6.07	6.07	2.10	2.10		
6.30		2.63			

5-17 全市按行业分施工项目（2012年）

行 业	Scetor	本年新增固定资产（万元）Increased Fixed Assets This Year(10 000 yuan)
总计	**Total**	**17650473**
（一）农、林、牧、渔业	Agriculture, Forestry, Animal Husbandry and Fishery	879703
（二）采矿业	Mining	21100
（三）制造业	Manufacturing	2086579
（四）电力、燃气及水的生产供应业	Generation and Supply of Electricity, Production and Supply of Gas and Water	572262
（五）建筑业	Construction	647292
（六）批发和零售业	Wholesale and Retail Trades	649755
（七）交通运输、仓储和邮政业	Transportation, Storage and Post	637683
（八）住宿和餐饮业	Hotels and Catering Services	345708
（九）信息传输、软件和信息技术服务业	Information Transmission, Computer Service and Software	82338
（十）金融业	Financial Intermediation	19256
（十一）房地产业	Real Estate	7125235
（十二） 租赁和商务服务业	Leasing and Business Services	323653
（十三）科学研究和技术服务业	Scientific Research and Technical Service	370242
（十四）水利、环境和公共设施管理业	Management of Water Conservancy, Environment and Public Facilities	1956106
（十五）居民服务、修理和其他服务业	Services to Households, repairs and other services	335485
（十六）教育	Education	500476
（十七）卫生和社会工作	Health and social work	406743
（十八）文化、体育和娱乐业	Culture, Sports and Entertainment	206300
（十九）公共管理、社会保障和社会组织	Public administration, social security and social organizations	484557
（二十）国际组织	International Organizations	

Construction Project Grouped by Sector in the Whole City (2012)

施工项目个数（个）Number of Constructing Projects (unit)	本年新开工 Newly Started This Year	本年投产项目个数（个）Projects put into Use (unit)
2277	**1467**	**1277**
209	165	177
6	6	6
494	298	215
63	42	36
109	96	77
114	79	75
136	68	76
60	50	44
46	32	11
7	5	2
373	204	147
32	18	19
37	20	20
362	232	242
13	7	8
70	55	42
46	34	26
38	27	25
62	29	29

5-18 主要年份房地产开发投资主要指标

单位：万平方米

指 标	Item	1997	1998	1999	2000
本年完成投资额(亿元)	Investment Completed This Year(1 00 million yuan)	24.68	38.21	44.30	51.85
本年房屋施工面积	Floor Space of Buildings Under Construction This Year	451.47	678.87	793.46	763.18
#住宅	Residential Buildings	331.16	552.37	649.53	619.85
本年房屋竣工面积	Floor Space of Buildings Completed This Year	135.62	156.17	377.79	321.10
#住宅	Residential Buildings	120.33	133.33	352.28	295.55
本年房屋竣工价值(亿元)	Value of Floor Space of Buildings Completed(1 00 million yuan)	11.96	14.36	38.22	26.94
#住宅	Residential Buildings	9.63	11.00	33.02	22.97
商品房销售面积	Floor Space of Commercialized Buildings sold	78.45	117.11	296.97	212.92
#住宅	Residential Buildings	72.69	108.61	284.95	200.77
商品房销售额(亿元)	Total Sales of Commercialized Buildings(1 00 million yuan)	12.81	17.74	35.19	32.52
#住宅	Residential Buildings	11.39	15.46	32.35	29.46
商品房预售面积	Floor Space of Commercialized Buildings Presold	26.35	252.02	30.25	253.03
#住宅	Residential Buildings	23.27	246.77	27.34	253.03
商品房空置面积	Floor Space of Vacant Commercialized Buildings	58.71	32.52	62.38	36.41
#住宅	Residential Buildings	50.26	22.81	52.32	24.02
商品房出租面积	Floor Space of Commercialized Buildings Recenting	25.69	1.04	1.88	1.17
#住宅	Residential Buildings	22.87	0.01	0.15	0.02
本年新增固定资产(亿元)	Newly Increased Fixed Assets This Year(1 00 million yuan)	14.36	19.93	43.10	38.38

Main Indicators of Investment in Real Estate Development in Representative Years

(10 000 sq.m)

2001	2002	2003	2004	2005	2006	2007	2008	2009	2010	2011	2012
67.42	79.37	124.82	169.67	225.23	285.76	387.33	540.26	696.34	842.34	996.81	1281.90
743.78	1172.58	1343.12	1633.68	2174.29	2383.56	2915.95	3632.87	5708.63	6697.39	8247.69	9947.89
580.43	964.68	943.61	1204.01	1783.36	1890.27	2376.82	3079.13	4901.59	5777.71	7108.27	8294.92
316.24	329.71	339.67	380.84	361.62	399.64	483.30	443.96	542.81	463.65	631.03	1063.70
269.61	290.30	289.56	308.06	316.52	342.15	422.47	412.46	453.49	412.44	564.59	903.82
37.20	36.93	54.73	73.75	80.58	82.02	101.13	106.50	168.08	145.62	213.29	310.57
28.62	30.46	44.01	55.58	68.11	65.80	77.13	96.02	137.42	128.69	185.31	260.04
225.35	252.90	252.74	305.47	497.34	621.50	833.92	760.72	1256.02	1587.81	1778.02	1538.91
192.20	237.04	230.28	279.90	476.39	584.06	782.91	715.76	1202.12	1523.24	1674.85	1383.84
47.22	51.35	54.29	81.35	171.29	206.15	281.79	296.44	488.55	707.00	1091.31	1017.74
35.53	45.46	44.25	71.27	158.03	179.47	251.74	268.92	450.71	661.27	973.71	858.53
67.44	61.02	52.35	17.60	300.07	428.20	491.07	569.22	1125.44	1510.20	3105.76	2627.73
65.20	55.73	49.12	159.10	287.13	408.11	457.54	541.20	1095.17	1452.20	2826.79	2340.69
50.82	57.14	63.85	108.52	123.59	112.49	45.42	55.40	40.68	34.32	59.76	102.58
34.18	44.70	52.34	72.76	99.17	85.89	38.62	35.40	28.73	26.23	45.41	83.78
9.19	15.75	10.56	11.18	17.32	8.53	10.84	34.94	38.23	28.60	8.01	15.16
0.10	1.13	5.43	5.78	4.09	3.74	5.36	4.53	6.55	0.70	3.25	4.03
50.77	48.43	62.13	83.36	92.78	100.22	143.17	124.02	195.71	168.20	255.29	358.03

5-19 分区县、开发区房地产开发主要指标（2012年）

单位：万元

区县、开发区	Region	企业（单位）个数（个） Number of Enterprises (Unit)	本年完成投资 Investment Completed This Year	本年新增固定资产 Increased Fixed Assets This Year(10 000 yuan)
区　县	**Region**			
新城区	Xincheng	59	867201	48743
碑林区	Beilin	70	1689954	998667
莲湖区	Lianhu	68	1406482	58158
灞桥区	Baqiao	44	638881	62900
未央区	Weiyang	120	2078314	791378
雁塔区	Yanta	156	4481119	1129962
阎良区	Yanliang	35	134155	71805
临潼区	Lintong	7	68280	14500
长安区	Chang'an	52	999280	234828
蓝田县	Lantian	10	47862	2448
周至县	Zhouzhi	10	38466	23955
户　县	Huxian	15	133264	26283
高陵县	Gaoling	26	235755	116629
开发区	**Development Zones**			
高新区	GaoXin	41	1020683	580443
经开区	JingKai	46	802985	219024
曲江新区	Qujiang	35	1318307	541423
浐灞生态区	Chanba Eco-District	10	527390	34034
航空基地	Aviation Industry Base	13	59793	
航天基地	Aerospace Base	27	268095	129786
国际港务区	International Trade&Logistic Park	1	135309	
沣东新城	FengDongXinCheng	5	38545	

Main Indicators of Real Estate Development by Region and Development Zone (2012)

(10 000 yuan)

房屋施工面积（平方米）Floor Space of Buildings Under Constmction(sq.m)	住宅 Residenctial Buildings	房屋竣工面积（平方米）Floor Space of Buildings Completed(sq.m)	住宅 Residenctial Buildings	竣工房屋价值 Value of Buildings Completed	住宅 Residenctial Buildings
7376106	6241014	176358	148278	43499	36897
14129508	11391910	2819233	2146559	916969	664873
9733710	7976496	298995	292140	58155	57812
5731987	5000955	163981	157513	42080	40295
22830285	18252968	2696201	2413629	687814	613523
25656109	21852442	2752467	2277626	892649	767220
1919164	1353017	293379	268550	71805	59448
435258	435258	89729	89729	14500	14500
6576189	5637968	523487	437841	222075	193989
621751	589113	13059	11061	2448	1858
607946	559897	62656	58856	16195	15093
1015730	929975	135946	135946	26283	26283
2845184	2728232	611509	600491	111250	108571
8570746	6057947	1595317	1391191	576667	510908
7834813	5768535	635507	552092	183539	168330
8139690	7022381	1125668	851367	308556	247526
4497737	3813877	113507	110139	34034	33024
570552	198844				
3055828	2668716	196312	168552	129786	111971
1027348	998648				
100000	100000				

5-20 房地产开发投资主要指标（2012年）

Main Indicators of Investment in Real Estate Development (2012)

单位：万元 (10 000 yuan)

指　标	Item	全市合计 Total	#国有 State-owned	市区 Urban Area	市属 Municipal
一、企业（单位）个数（个）	**Number of Enterprises(unit)**	**672**	**48**	**612**	**619**
二、本年完成投资	**Investment Completed This Year**	**12819013**	**1089865**	**12369396**	**11658573**
按工程用途分	Grouped by Function				
住宅	Residential Buildings	10116672	884280	9715749	9182991
#别墅、高档公寓	Villas and Top-Grade Apartments	284544	37771	283401	284544
办公楼	Office Buildings	373553	32930	372837	353616
商业营业用房	Houses for Business Use	1097093	58679	1070579	1021134
其他	Others	1231695	113976	1210231	1100832
三、本年新增固定资产	**Increased Fixed Assets This Year**	**3580256**	**378537**	**3413389**	**3280080**
四、房屋施工面积（平方米）	**Floor Space of Buildings Under Construction (sq.m)**	**99478927**	**8307804**	**94459111**	**91947852**
#住宅	Residential Buildings	82949245	7524792	78208823	76527749
五、竣工房屋面积（平方米）	**Floor Space of Buildings Completed (sq.m)**	**10637000**	**1068258**	**9826889**	**9674157**
#住宅	Residential Buildings	9038219	958588	8242926	8186163
竣工房屋价值	Value of Buildings Completed	3105722	345153	2951994	2834773
#住宅	Residential Buildings	2600362	301054	2450415	2365483
六、商品房屋销售面积（平方米）	**Floor Space of Commercialized Buildings Sold(sq.m)**	**15389113**	**984496**	**14243259**	**13944131**
商品房销售额	Sales Income of Commercialized Buildings	10177400	737538	9790222	9304442

5-21 商品房销售情况(2012年)

Sales of Commercial Houses (2012)

指 标	Item	全市合计 Total	#国有 State-owned	市区 Urban Area	市属 Municipal
商品房销售面积（平方米）	**Floor Space of Commercialized Buildings Sold(sq.m)**	**15389113**	**984496**	**14243259**	**13944131**
现房销售面积	**Floor Space of Completed Apartment Sales**	**1550245**	**114011**	**1538830**	**1377218**
期房销售面积	**Floor Space of Forward Delivery Housing Sales**	**13838868**	**870485**	**12704429**	**12566913**
住宅	Residential Buildings	13838696	873609	12719101	12505581
#别墅、高档公寓	Villas and High-grade Apartments	481209	18950	457826	481209
办公楼	Office Buildings	569230	81886	566999	511997
商业营业用房	Houses for Business Use	707410	26778	683382	681808
其他	Others	273777	2223	273777	244745
商品房销售额（万元）	**Sales Income of Commercialized Buildings (10 000 yuan)**	**10177400**	**737538**	**9790222**	**9304442**
现房销售额	**Floor Space of Completed Apartment Sales**	**880463**	**116573**	**875806**	**799291**
期房销售额	**Floor Space of Forward Delivery Housing Sales**	**9296937**	**620965**	**8914416**	**8505151**
住宅	Residential Buildings	8585326	609952	8212153	7807534
#别墅高档公寓	Villas and High-grade Apartments	486989	22655	478548	486989
办公楼	Office Buildings	487949	77818	486989	448526
商业营业用房	Houses for Business Use	948843	48884	935798	904693
其他	Others	155282	884	155282	143689
商品房待售面积（平方米）	**Vacancy of Commercialized Buildings(sq.m)**	**1025787**	**230022**	**971077**	**935682**
#待售1年以上(1－3年)	Being Idle for One Year	566978	125124	566978	482756
待售3年以上（含3年）	Being Idle for Three Year	46039		46039	46039
住宅	Residence	837793	221556	783083	762151
#别墅高档公寓	Villas and High-grade Apartments	7447		7447	7447
办公楼	Office Buildings	24180		24180	24180
商业营业用房	Houses for Business Use	101928	3287	101928	92644
其他	Others	61886	5179	61886	56707
商品房出租面积（平方米）	**Floor Space of Commercialized Leased Buildings(sq.m)**	**151610**	**33327**	**143610**	**145610**
住宅	Residential Buildings	40290	32290	32290	40290
办公楼	Office Buildings	256		256	256
商业营业用房	Houses for Business Use	104064	1037	104064	98064
其他	Others	7000		7000	7000

5-22 房地产开发投资资金来源（2012年）

Source of Funds for Investment in Real Estate Development (2012)

单位：万元 (10 000 yuan)

指 标	Item	全市合计 Total	#国有 State-owned	市区 Urban Area	市属 Municipal
一.本年资金来源合计	**Total**	**21688388**	**1834373**	**21071966**	**19322307**
1. 上年末结余资金	Balance of Last Year	4424873	486525	4332909	3933574
2. 本年资金来源小计	Total Funds This Year	17263515	1347848	16739057	15388733
(1) 国内贷款	Domestic Loans	2224414	320034	2175766	1972213
#银行贷款	Bank Loan	1978501	304357	1932121	1770742
非银行金融机构贷款	Loans from financial Institutions except Bank	245913	15677	243645	201471
(2) 利用外资	Utilization of Foreign Funds	24000		24000	24000
#外商直接投资	Foreign Direct Investment	24000		24000	24000
(3) 自筹资金	Self-raising Funds	8076423	425468	7904791	7140369
#自有资金	Funds at the disposal of Enterprises	3157850	85309	3068973	2655246
(4) 其他资金	Others	6938678	602346	6634500	6252151
#定金及预收款	Earnest Money and Advance payment	4650920	353181	4515731	4239841
个人按揭贷款	Personal Mortgage loan	1741886	121006	1581270	1652059
二.本年各项应付款合计	**Total Sums of Money to be Paid This Year**	**2055721**	**215126**	**1902943**	**1853687**
#工程款	Project Fund	1239228	100915	1137145	1103253

5-23 房地产开发经营情况（2012年）

Running of Real Estate Development (2012)

单位：万元 (10 000 yuan)

指 标	Item	全市合计 Total	#国有 State-owned	市区 Urban Area	市属 Municipal
一、资产负债情况	**Assets and Liabilities**				
1. 资产总计	Total Assets	39575558	3975680	38599162	36374095
2. 负债总计	Total Liabilities	32097246	3281762	31238795	29410612
3. 所有者权益合计	Total Creditor's Equity	7478312	693918	7360367	6963483
#实收资本	Held Capital	13571745	445066	13436605	13219702
二、损益及分配情况	**Profit or Loss and the Distribution**				
1. 主营业务收入	Revenue from Principal Business	10785961	999243	10396919	10096097
土地转让收入	Revenue of Land Transferred	39954		28351	36423
商品房屋销售收入	Revenue of Commercial Houses Sold	10400430	969670	10024032	9821030
房屋出租收入	Revenue of Houses Leased	84277	4154	84005	81698
其他收入	Other Revenue	261300	25419	260531	156946
2. 主营业务成本	Cost of Principal Business	8063306	738989	7739962	7536614
3. 主营业务税金及附加	Taxes and Other Charges on Principal Business	702925	76040	681091	670800
4. 其他业务利润	Other Business Profit	53657	2094	53606	51756
5. 销售费用	Sales Expenditures	309616	31119	296535	263650
6. 管理费用	Management Cost	445224	27778	434225	415603
#税金	Tax	34250	2655	33500	29181
差旅费	Travel Expense	11035	433	10712	10335
工会经费	Labor Union Expenditure	1686	189	1666	1421
7. 财务费用	Fiscal Expenditure	90618	19738	88845	64472
#利息支出	Interest Exchange	68332	20334	67528	47364
8. 营业利润	Operating Profit	1262228	119920	1244264	1201369
投资收益	Investment Revenue	16183	463	16133	11830
营业外收入	Non-business Revenue	23567	1416	22902	22228
营业外支出	Non-business Expenditures	1256289	118967	1238939	1192399
9. 利润总额	Total Profit	216055	25231	215141	210299
10. 应付职工薪酬	Salary Payable	202972	31446	193002	185765

5-24 按国民经济行业（GB/T4754-2002）分全市固定资产投资（2012年）

Total Investment in Fixed Assets by Sector(GB/T4754-2002) (2012)

单位：万元 (10 000 yuan)

行 业	Scetor	2012
本年完成投资	**Grouped by Sector (10 000 yuan)**	**41659924**
（一）农、林、牧、渔业	Agriculture,Forestry,Animal Husbandry and Fishery	993367
（二）采矿业	Mining	21100
（三）制造业	Manufacturing	4823480
#农副食品加工业	Processing of Food from Agricultural Products	127361
食品制造业	Manufacture of Foods	347936
饮料制造业	Manufacture of Beverages	10982
石油加工业、炼焦及核燃料加工	Processing of Petroleum, Coking,Processing of Nuclear Fuel	41965
化学原料及化学制品制造	Manufacture of Raw Chemical Materials and Chemical Products	121218
医药制造	Manufacture of Medicines	116139
金属制品业	Manufacture of Metal Products	155889
通用设备制造业	Manufacture of General Purpose Machinery	308429
专用设备制造	Manufacture of Special Purpose Machinery	704071
交通运输设备制造业	Manufacture of Transport Equipment	221195
电气机械及器材制造业	Manufacture of Electrical Machinery and Equipment	412262
通信设备、计算机以及其他电子	Manufacture of Communication Equipment, Computers and Other Electronic Equipment	466826
仪器仪表以及文化办公用机械制造	Manufacture of Measuring Instruments and Machinery for Cultural Activity and Office Work	323055
（四）电力、燃气及水的生产供应业	Production & Supply of Electricity,Gas & Water	937141
（五）建筑业	Construction	937464
（六）交通运输、仓储及邮政业	Transport,Storage and Post	2928288
（七）信息传输、计算机服务和软件业	Information Transmission,Computer Service and Software	687847
（八）批发和零售业	Wholesale and Retail Trades	1210468
（九）住宿和餐饮业	Hotels and Catering Services	495665
（十）金融业	Financial Intermediation	247789
（十一）房地产业	Real Estate	20899157
（十二）租赁和商务服务业	Leasing and Business Services	561134
（十三）科学研究、技术服务和地质勘查业	Scientific Research,Technical Service and Geologic Prospecting	696830
（十四）水利、环境和公共设施管理业	Management of Water Conservancy, Environment and Public Facilities	3257549
（十五）居民服务和其他服务业	Services to Households and Other Services	332963
（十六）教育	Education	651315
（十七）卫生、社会保障和社会福利业	Health,Social Security and Social Welfare	591415
（十八）文化、体育和娱乐业	Culture, Sports and Entertainment	287987
（十九）公共管理和社会组织	Public Management and Social Organization	1098965

主要统计指标解释

全社会固定资产投资 是以货币形式表现的在一定时期内全社会建造和购置固定资产的工作量以及与此有关的费用的总称。该指标是反映固定资产投资规模、结构和发展速度的综合性指标，又是观察工程进度和考核投资效果的重要依据。全社会固定资产投资按登记注册类型可分为国有、集体、联营、股份制、私营和个体、港澳台商、外商、其他等。

城镇固定资产投资 指城镇各种登记注册类型的企业、事业、行政单位及个体户进行的计划总投资500万元及500万元以上的建设项目投资和房地产开发投资。县城及以上区域内发生的投资，县及县以上各级政府及主管部门直接领导、管理的建设项目和企业事业单位的投资均为城镇固定资产投资。

房地产开发投资 指各种登记注册类型的房地产开发公司、商品房建设公司及其他房地产开发法人单位和附属于其他法人单位实际从事房地产开发或经营活动的单位统一开发的包括统代建、拆迁还建的住宅、厂房、仓库、饭店、宾馆、度假村、写字楼、办公楼等房屋建筑物和配套的服务设施，土地开发工程（如道路、给水、排水、供电、供热、通讯、平整场地等基础设施工程）的投资；不包括单纯的土地交易活动。

农村投资 包括在农村区域范围内进行固定资产投资活动的企业、事业、行政单位及农户投资。

固定资产投资的资金来源 根据固定资产投资的资金来源不同，分为国家预算资金、国内贷款、利用外资、自筹资金和其他资金。

（1）国家预算资金：包括一般预算、政府性基金预算、国有资本经营预算和社保基金预算等资金。

（2）国内贷款：指报告期固定资产投资单位向银行及非银行金融机构借入的用于固定资产投资的各种国内借款，包括银行利用自有资金及吸收的存款发放的贷款、上级主管部门拨入的国内贷款、国家专项贷款、地方财政专项资金安排的贷款、国内储备贷款、周转贷款等。

（3）利用外资：指报告期收到的用于固定资产建造和购置的境外资金（包括设备、材料、技术在内）。包括对外借款（外国政府、国际金融组织贷款、出口信贷、外国银行商业贷款、对外发行债券和股票）、外商直接投资及外商其他投资。不包括我国自有外汇资金（国家外汇、地方外汇、留成外汇、调剂外汇和中国银行自有资金发行的外汇贷款等）。计算利用外资时，需要折算成人民币，折算中所使用的外汇汇率按现汇计算，即按使用外汇时的汇率计算。

（4）自筹资金：指固定资产投资单位报告期收到的，由各地区、各部门及企、事业单位筹集用于固定资产投资的预算外资金，包括中央各部门、各级地方和企、事业单位的自筹资金。

（5）其他资金：指在报告期收到的除以上各种资金之外其他用于固定资产投资的资金，包括企业或金融机构通过发行各种债券筹集到的资金、社会集资、个人资金、无偿捐赠的资金及其他单位拨人的资金等。

固定资产投资按国民经济行业分 根据现有企业、事业、行政单位和建设项目建成投产后的主要产品种类或主要用途及社会经济活动性质来确定国民经济行业。一般情况下，一个建设项目或一个企业、事业单位只能属于一种国民经济行业。

固定资产投资按隶属关系分 是按建设单位或企业、事业、行政单位的主管上级机关确定的。

（1）中央：是指中共中央、人大常委会和国务院各部、委、局、总公司以及直属机构直接领导的建设项目和企业、事业、行政单位。这些单位的固定资产投资计划由国务院各部门直接编制和下达，建设中所需物资、主要设备以及建设中的问题都由中央有关部门安排和解决。

（2）地方：是由省（自治区、直辖市）、地区（州、盟、省辖市）、县（旗、县级市）三级政府及业务主管部门直接领导和管理的建设项目、企业、事业、行政单位。地方项目还包括不隶属以上各级政府及主管部门的建设项目和企业、事业单位，如外商投资企业和无主管部门的企业等。

固定资产投资按建设性质分 根据整个建设项目情况来确定。建设项目的性质一般分为新建、扩建、改建和技术改造、单纯建造生活设施、迁建、恢复、单纯购置。房地产开发单位、农户投资不划分建设性质。

（1）新建：一般指从无到有开始建设的企业、事业和行政单位或建设项目。有的单位原有基础很小，经过建设后新增的固定资产价值超过该企、事业、行政单位原有固定资产价值（原值）三倍以上的也应作为新建。

（2）扩建：指在厂内或其他地点，为扩大原有产品的生产能力（或效益）或增加新的产品生产能力，而增建主要的生产车间（或主要工程）、分厂、独立的生产线。行政、事业单位在原单位增建业务用房（如学校增建教学用房、医院增建门诊部、病房等）也作为扩建。

现有企、事业单位为扩大原有主要产品生产能力或增加新的产品生产能力，增建一个或几个主要生产车间（或主要工程）、分厂，同时进行一些更新改造工程的，也应作为扩建。

（3）改建和技术改造：指现有企业、事业单位，对原有设施进行技术改造或更新（包括相应配套的辅助性生产、生活福利设施）的建设项目。现有企业、事业单位为适应市场变化的需要，而改变企业的主要产品种类（如军工企业转产民用品等）的建设项目，应作为改建。原有产品生产作业线由于各工序（车间）之间能力不平衡，为填平补齐充分发挥原有生产能力而增建不增加本企业主要产品设计能力的车间，也应作为改建。技术改造是指企业、事业单位在现有基础上，用先进的技术代替落后的技术，用先进的工艺和装备代替落后的工艺和装备，以改变企业落后的技术经济面貌，实现以内涵为主的扩大再生产，达到提高产品质量、促进产品更新换代、节约能源、降低消耗、扩大生产规模、全面提高社会经济效益的目的。技术改造具体包括以下内容：机器设备和工具的更新改造；生产工艺改革、节约能源和原材料的改造；厂房建筑和公共设施的改造；劳动条件和生产环境的改造等。

固定资产投资按构成分 固定资产投资活动按其工作内容和实现方式分为建筑安装工程，设备工具器具购置和其他费用三个部分。

（1）建筑安装工程（建筑安装工作量）：指各种房屋、建筑物的建造工程和各种设备、装置的安装工程。包括各种房屋建造工程；各种用途设备基础和各种工业窑炉的砌筑工程及金属结构工程；为施工而进行的各种准备工作和临时工程以及完工后的清理工作等；铁路、道路的铺设，矿井的开凿及石油管道的架设等；水利工程；防空地下建筑等特殊工程；列入房屋丁程预算内的暖气、卫生、通风、照明、煤气等设备的价值及装设油饰工程；列入建筑工程预算内的各种管道（蒸汽、压缩空气、石油、给排水等管道）、电力、电讯电缆导线等的敷设工程；以及各种机械设备的安装下程；为测定安装工程质量，对设备进行的试运工作；房地产开发单位进行的商品房屋开发建设工程、土地开发工程。

在建筑安装工程中，不包括被安装设备本身的价值。

（2）设备工具器具购置：指建设单位或企、事业单位购置或自制的，达到固定资产标准的设备、工具、器具的价值。新建单位及扩建单位的新建车间，按照设计或计划要求购置或自制的全部设备、工具、器具，不论是否达到固定资产标准均计入“设备工具器具购置”中。

（3）其他费用：指在固定资产建造和购置过程中发生的，除上述几项内容以外的各种应分摊计入固定资产的费用。

施工项目 指报告期内所有施工的建设项目个数，包括本年新开工的项目和以前年度开工在本年继续施工的建设项目。凡是报告期内施过工的建设项目，不论施工时间长短，均作为施工项目统计。施工项目个数可以反映一定时期固定资产投资的实际规模，与同期全部建成投产项目个数相比，可以从建设速度的角度反映固定资产投资的效果。

全部建成投产项目 指报告期内按设计文件规定的全部生产能力（或效益）建成投产，经验收合格交付使用的建设项目。

新增生产能力（或工程效益） 指通过固定资产投资活动而增加的设计能力（或工程效益）。主要指标包括建设规模、本年施工规模、自开始建设累计新增生产能力（或工程效益）、本年新增生产能力（或工程效益）等。

建设规模 指建设项目或工程设计文件中规定的全部设计能力（或工程效益）。包括已经建成投产和尚未建成投产的工程的生产能力（或工程效益）。

本年施工规模 指报告期内施工的单项工程的设计能力（或工程效益），即全部建设规模中在本年正式施工的部分。

自开始建设累计新增生产能力（或工程效益） 指自开始建设至本年底止建成投产的全部单项工程累计的新增生产能力（或工程效益）。

本年新增生产能力（或工程效益） 指在本年度内按照新增生产能力（或工程效益）的计算条件和标准，实际建成投入生产或交付使用的生产能力（或工程效益）。

施工房屋面积 指报告期内施工的全部房屋（包括地下室、半地下室以及配套房屋）建筑面积。包括本期新开工的面积和上期开工跨入本期继续施工的房屋面积，以及上期已停建在本期恢复施工的房屋面积。本期竣工和本期施工后又停缓建的房屋，其建筑面积仍计入本期房屋施工面积中。

竣工房屋面积 指在报告期内房屋建筑按照设计要求已经全部完工，达到住人和使用条件，经验收鉴定合格（或达到竣工验收标准），可正式移交使用单位的各栋房屋建筑面积的总和。

新增固定资产 指报告期内交付使用的固定资产价值。包括本年内建成投入生产或交付使用的工程投资和达到固定资产标准的设备、工具、器具的投资及有关应摊入的费用。该指标是表示固定资产投资成果的价值指标，也是反映建设进度，计算固定资产投资效果的重要指标。

项目建成投产率 指一定时期内全部建成投产项目个数与同期施工项目个数的比率。该指标是从建设单位建设速度的角度反映投资效果的指标。

固定资产交付使用率 指一定时期新增固定资产与同期完成投资额的比率。该指标是反映固定资产动用速度，衡量建设过程中宏观投资效果的综合指标。由于新增固定资产是较长时期内形成的结果，而投资额则是当年完成的，因此，该指标一般适宜于反映较长时期内固定资产的动用情况。

商品房销售面积 指报告期内出售商品房屋的合同总面积（即双方签署的正式买卖合同中所确定的建筑面积）。由现房销售建筑面积和期房销售建筑面积两部分组成。

商品房销售额 指报告期内出售商品房屋的合同总价款（即双方签署的正式买卖合同中所确定的合同总价）。该指标与商品房销售面积同口径，由现房销售额和期房销售额两部分组成。

经济适用房 指根据经济适用房计划安排建设的政策性住宅。经济是指房屋建筑造价和销售价格低于一般商品住宅；适用是指适合中低收入家庭购买使用。经济适用房主要是由地方政府统一下达投资计划，房地产公司开发，对外销售；用地一般采用行政划拨或招标投标方式，免收土地出让金；对各种经批准的收费减半征收，开发利润不超过3%；销售价格实行政府指导价。该指标可以分析房地产投资结构，反映中低收入家庭商品住宅的供求平衡情况。

Explanatory Notes on Main Statistical Indicators

Total Investment in Fixed Assets in the Whole Country refers to the volume of activities in construction and purchases of fixed assets of the whole country and related fees, expressed in monetary terms during the reference period. It is a comprehensive indicator which shows the size, structure and growth of the investment in fixed assets, providing a basis for observing the progress of construction projects and evaluating results of investment. Total investment in fixed assets in the whole country includes, by type of ownership, the investment by State-owned units, collective-owned units, joint ownership units, share-holding units, private units individuals as well as investments by entrepreneurs from Hong Kong, Macao and Taiwan, foreign investors and others.

Urban Investment in Fixed Assets refers to construction projects involving a total planned investment of 5000 000 yuan and over by enterprises of various types of ownership, institutions, administrative units and individuals in urban areas, investment in real estate development. In other words, all investments that take place in county towns and urban areas, investment in construction projects under the direct leadership and management of government agencies at and above county levels and investments by enterprises and institutions at and above county levels are covered in urban investment in fixed assets.

Investment in Real Estate Development refers to investment by real estate development companies, commercialized buildings construction companies and other real estate development units of various types of ownership in the construction of buildings, such as residential buildings, factory buildings, warehouses, hotels, guesthouses, holiday villages, office buildings, and the complementary service facilities and land development projects, such as roads, water supply, water drainage, power supply, heating supply, telecommunications, land leveling and other infrastructural projects. It does not include activities in pure land transactions.

Investment in Rural Areas refers to investment in fixed assets by enterprises, institutions, administrative units and households in rural areas.

Sources of Funds for Investment in Fixed Assets are categorized as funds from the State budget, domestic loans, foreign investment, self-raised funds, and others, depending on the sources of investment.

(1) Fund from the State budget consists of budgetary appropriation and loans from the State budget. More specifically, it includes, from the budget of the central government, capital construction fund (operation fund and non-operational fund), special expenses, loans from repayment, discount fund, expenses on innovation and trial production of new products, expenses on urban construction, expenses on temporary construction from business departments, development fund for less developed areas, as well as local budgetary fund transferred from the central budget.

(2) Domestic loans refer to loans of various forms borrowed by investing units from banks and non-bank financial institutions during the reference period for the purpose of investment in fixed assets, including loans issued by banks from their self-owned funds and deposit, loans appropriated by higher authorities, special loans by government, loans arranged by local government from special funds, domestic reserve loan, and working loan.

(3) Foreign investment refers to overseas funds received during the reference period for the construction and purchase of investment in fixed assets (covering equipment, materials and technology), including foreign borrowings (loans from foreign governments and international financial institutions, export credit, commercial loans from foreign banks, issue of bonds and stocks overseas), foreign direct investment and other foreign investments. Excluded from this category is capital in foreign exchanges owned by China (foreign exchanges owned by the central and local governments, foreign exchanges retained by enterprises, foreign exchanges by enterprises through the regulating mechanism, loans in foreign exchanges issued by the Bank of China with its own fund, etc). In calculating the utilization of foreign capital, foreign currencies are converted into Chinese Renminbi applying the current exchange rate when the foreign capitals are actually used.

(4) Self-raised funds refer to extra-budgetary funds for investment in fixed assets received during the reference period by investing units from central government ministries, local governments, enterprises and institutions, including their self-raised funds.

(5) Others refer to funds for investment in fixed assets received from sources other than those listed above, including capital raised through issuing bonds by

enterprises or financial institutions, funds raised from individuals and through donations, and funds transferred from other units.

Investment in Fixed Assets by Sector The classification of construction projects by sector is determined by enterprises, institutions, administrative units and the major products or the purpose of the projects of existing enterprises, institutional and administrative units when they are put into production or use, and by the nature of their social economic activities. In general, one project or one enterprise or institution can only be classified into one sector.

Investment in Fixed Assets by Jurisdiction of Management refers to the classification of investment by the competent authorities under which investment is made by construction units, enterprises, institutions or administrative units.

(1) Central investment refers to the investment in projects or by enterprises, institutions or administrative units which are under the direct leadership and management of the State Council and of the national commissions, ministries, agencies and State-owned large corporations. Various ministries and departments of the State Council prepare and implement plans for investment in fixed assets by those departments, and arrange and ensure the supply of materials and key equipment required for the projects.

(2) Local investment refers to the investment in projects or by enterprises, institutions or administrative units which are under the direct leadership and management of departments under the provincial, prefecture and county governments. Also included are projects by foreign-invested enterprises and enterprises without competent managing authorities.

Investment in Fixed Assets by Type of Construction Construction projects in general can be classified, by the type of construction, into new construction, expansion, reconstruction and technical transformation, purely construction of living facilities, moving, restoration and purely purchasing. However, investment by type of construction is not applied to investment by real-estate development units and investment by rural households.

(1) New construction in general refers to construction projects, which start from scratch, of enterprises, institutions, administrative agencies. In case the size of the existing unit is quite small, and the value of newly added fixed assets is more than three times of the original value, the expansion will be considered as new construction.

(2) Expansion refers to construction of new major production workshop, branch factory or independent production line within a factory or in other locations, for the purpose of increasing the production capacity (or improving efficiency) or adding new production capacity. Newly constructed accommodation for the operation of institutions and administrative organizations (such as newly constructed buildings for teaching in schools, buildings for clinics or wards in hospitals, etc.) are also classified as expansion.

Also included in expansion are investments by existing enterprises or institutions in building major production line(s) or branch factory(ies) along with some work on innovation, for the purpose of expanding the production capacity of original products or producing new products.

(3) Reconstruction and technical transformation refers to construction projects by existing enterprises or institutions in innovation or technical transformation of the old facilities (including auxiliary production equipment and welfare facilities). Also considered as reconstruction is the construction of new workshops by the existing enterprises or institutions to change the variety of products to meet the market demand (such as the production of civil products by defence industries), or to bring the designed production capacity into full play through a more balanced production process on production lines. Technical transformation refers to replacement of old technology or equipment by new technology or equipment, in order to expand the reproduction through improvement of technology contents in production, to improve product quality, to promote new products to save energy,to reduce consumption, to expand the production scale and to improve overall social-economic efficiency. Contents of technical transformation include: updating of machinery, equipment and tools; reforming production process by using energy or materials saving technology; construction of factory workshops and transformation of public facilities; improvement of working conditions and environment, etc.

Investment in Fixed Assets by Structure By their

contents and the mode of implementation, investment activities are classified into 3 categories, i.e. construction and installation, purchase of equipment and instrument, and other expenses.

(1) Construction and installation (work volume of construction and installation) refers to the construction of houses and buildings and the installation of various kinds of equipment and instruments. They include construction of houses; equipment foundations, industrial kilns and stoves, and metal structure work; preparation works and temporary works for project construction, and clearing up works post project construction; pavement of railways and roads, drilling of mines and putting up of oil pipes; construction of water conservancy; construction of underground air-raid shelters and construction of other special projects; value of equipment for heating, sanitation, ventilation, lighting, gas, painting, etc. that are covered by the budget of housing projects; laying out of various pipelines (for steam, compressed air, petroleum, tap water and sewage) and wiring and cabling for electric power and for communications; installation of various machinery and equipment; testing operation for pre- testing the quality of installation projects, and land and other development work conducted by real estate developers for commercialized housing.

The value of equipment installed is itself not included in the value of construction and installation projects.

(2) Purchase of equipment and instruments refers to the total value of equipment, tools, and instruments purchased or self-produced which come up to the cut-off point for fixed assets by the construction units or investing enterprises or institutions. Equipment, tools and instruments purchased or self-produced for new workshops by newly established or expanded units are categorized as "purchase of equipment and instruments" no matter whether they come up to the cut-off point for fixed assets.

(3) Other expenses refer to expenses arising during the construction or purchase of fixed assets other than those mentioned above.

Projects under Construction refer to number of all projects with construction activities newly started in current year or left-over from the previous year in the reference period. All projects that have construction activities undertaken during the reference period are reported as projects under construction irrespective of the length of construction work. The number of projects under construction can reflect the actual size of investment in fixed assets during a given period, and when compared with the number of projects completed and put into use during the same period, it demonstrates the results of investment in fixed assets from the angle of the speed of the construction.

Projects Completed and Put into Use refer to projects have been completed in accordance with the design documents, resulting in forming production capacity (efficiency) and have been checked and accepted after relevant tests, and have been formally delivered for use.

Newly Increased Production Capacity (or Project Efficiency) refers to the increase in design capacity (or project efficiency) through investment in fixed assets. The main indicators include: construction scale, scale of projects under construction in current year, the accumulated newly increased production capacity (project efficiency) since the start of the projects and the newly increased production capacity (project efficiency) of current year.

Construction Scale refers to the total designed production capacity (project efficiency) of the construction projects in accordance with the design document, including those have been put into operation and those that have not been completed.

Scale of Projects under Construction in Current Year refers to the designed production capacity (project efficiency) of a single project under construction in the reference period, i.e. the part of the total scale of project which is officially under construction in current year.

The Accumulated Newly Increased Production Capacity (project efficiency) since the Start of the Projects refers to the accumulated newly increased production capacity of all the single projects which have been put into use from the beginning of the projects till the end of current year.

The Newly Increased Production Capacity (project efficiency) of Current Year refers to the production capacity (project efficiency) that has been completed and put into operation in current year according to the calculation conditions and standards on newly increased production capacity (project efficiency).

Floor Space of Buildings under Construction refers to the total floor space of all the buildings (including basement, semi-basement and auxiliary buildings), including the effective area and the area occupied by the structure. This indicator is one of the important indicators in physical terms to reflect the scale and accomplishment of the construction industry and also an important basis for monitoring the progress, Calculating the cost, analyzing the efficiency and studying the supply of building materials in relation to the construction projects.

Floor Space Completed refers to the floor space of all buildings completed in the reference period, which have been appraised and accepted (or come up to the designed standards) and have been transferred to owner units.

Newly Increased Fixed Assets refer to the value of fixed that has been put into use, including investment in projects that have been completed and put into operation in current year and the investment in equipment, tools and appliance that meet the standard of fixed assets and fees that should be apportioned. This is an indicator that demonstrates the results of investment in fixed assets in monetary terms, and an important indicator to reflect the speed of construction and to calculate the efficiency of investment.

Rate of Construction Projects Completed and Put into Use refers to the ratio of the number of construction projects completed and put into use in a certain period of time to the number of projects under construction in the same period. This reflects the investment efficiency from the perspective of the speed of projects construction.

Rate of Projects of Fixed Assets Completed and Put into Operation refers to the ratio of the newly increased fixed assets to the total investment made in the same period. This is a comprehensive indicator reflecting the speed of the employment of fixed assets and the investment efficiency at the macro-level. As the newly increase fixed assets is the result of a long period while the investment is completed in the current year, this indicator is expected to be used to reflect the employment of fixed assets over a long period of time.

6 财　政

GOVERNMENT FINANCE

资料整理：刘　婷
Data management:Liu Ting

第六部分　财政

一、简要说明

本章资料主要包括地方财政收入、支出总额构成及分区县情况，由西安市统计局综合处根据西安市财政局提供资料整理。

二、主要指标

财政总收入（亿元）	753.07	比上年增长	15.9%
一般预算收入（亿元）	396.96	比上年增长	24.6%
一般预算支出（亿元）	597.49	比上年增长	20.8%

6　GOVERNMENT FINANCE

Ⅰ.Brief Introduction

This chapter consists of primarily data on regional revenue, expenditure of the municipal government, regional revenue and expenditure of the districts and the counties. The data are provided by the Xi'an Bureau of Finance and are compiled by Integration division of the Xi'an Bureau of Statistics.

Ⅱ.Major Indicators

		Increase over Preceding Year
Total Government Revenue(100 mil. Yuan)	753.07	15.9%
General Budgetary Revenue(100 mil. Yuan)	396.96	24.6%
Ordinary Budgetary Expenditures(100 mil. Yuan)	597.49	20.8%

6-1 主要年份地方财政一般预算收入及支出

General Budgetary Local Government Revenue and Expenditure in Representative Years

单位：亿元 （100 million yuan）

年 份 Year	地方财政一般预算收入 General Budgetary Revenue of Local Government	地方财政一般预算支出 General Budgetary Expenditure of Local Government
2000	46.80	52.00
2001	51.45	57.30
2002	54.50	63.80
2003	72.90	76.60
2004	75.30	87.30
2005	72.92	97.61
2006	85.89	119.22
2007	112.92	161.25
2008	145.61	226.99
2009	181.40	276.85
2010	241.86	371.62
2011	318.55	494.58
2012	396.96	597.49

注：本表数据来源：市财政局。

6-2 财政收入（2012年）

Government Revenue（2012）

单位：万元　　　　(10 000 yuan)

指　　标	Item	2012
财政总收入	**Total Government Revenue**	**7530710**
#一般预算收入	**General Budgetary Revenue**	**3969597**
一、税收收入	**Total Tax Revenue**	**3220756**
1. 增值税	Value Added Tax	253997
2. 营业税	Business Tax	1287594
3. 企业所得税	Corporate Income Tax	283752
4. 企业所得税退税	Return for Corporate Income Tax	
5. 个人所得税	Individual Income Tax	91729
6. 资源税	Resource Tax	335
7. 固定资产投资方向调节税	Tax on Adjustment of the Orientation of Investment in Fixed Assets	
8. 城市维护建设税	City Maintenance and Construction Tax	244300
9. 房产税	House Property Tax	120677
10. 印花税	Stamp Tax	79102
11. 城镇土地使用税	Urban Land Use Tax	79745
12. 土地增值税	Land Appreciation Tax	259461
13. 车船税	Tax on the Use of Vehicles and Ships	46099
14. 耕地占用税	Farm Land Occupatian Tax	218738
15. 契税	Deed Tax	255227
16. 其他收入	Other Tax Revenue	
二、非税收入	**Total Non-tax Revenue**	**748841**
1. 专项收入	Special Program Receipts	115116
2. 行政性收费收入	Charge of Adminnistrative and Institutional Units	342329
3. 罚没收入	Penalty Receipts	99329
4. 国有资本经营收入	State-owned Assets Profit	6084
5. 国有资源（资产）有偿使用收入	Revenue for the use of State-owned Assets (Resources)	184281
6. 其他收入	Other Revenue	1702
政府性基金收入	**Governmental Fund Revenue**	**4128887**

注：本表数据来源：市财政局。

6-3 地方财政支出（2012年）

Government Expenditures（2012）

单位：万元　　　　（10 000 yuan）

指　标	Item	2012
一、政府性基金支出	**Governmental Fund Revenue Expenditure**	**4235010**
二、一般预算支出	**General Budgetary Expenditure**	**5974937**
1. 一般公共服务支出	Expenditure for General Public Services	685296
2. 国防支出	Expenditure for National Defense	7997
3. 公共安全支出	Expenditure for Public Security	326250
4. 教育支出	Expenditure for Education	1080419
5. 科学技术支出	Expenditure for Science and Technology	59301
6. 文化体育与传媒支出	Expenditure for Cultural, sports and the media	140745
7. 社会保障和就业支出	Expenditure for Social Safety Net and Employment Effort	678208
8. 医疗卫生支出	Expenditure for Medical and Health Care	414573
9. 节能环保支出	Expenditure for Energy Saving and Environment Protection	141454
10. 城乡社区事务支出	Expenditure for Urban and Rural Community Affairs	753364
11. 农林水事务支出	Expenditure for Agriculture, Forestry and Water Conservancy	451053
12. 交通运输支出	Expenditure for Transportation	264490
13. 资源勘探电力信息等事务支出	Expenditure for Mining ,Electricity and Information	304762
14. 商业服务业等事务支出	Expenditure for Commerce and Services	59182
15. 金融监管等事务支出	Expenditure for Financial Supervision	23735
16. 地震灾后恢复重建支出	Expenditure for Post-earthquake Recovery and Reconstruction	215
17. 国土资源气象等事务支出	Expenditure for Land Recources and Meteorological Affairs	31410
18. 住房保障支出	Expenditure for Housing Support	397262
19. 粮油物资管理事务支出	Material Reserves Management Affairs Spending	24056
20. 储备事务支出	Expenditure for Reserve	
21. 国债还本付息支出	Expenditure for National Debt and Interest(10 000yuan)	46982
22. 其它支出	Other Expenditure	84183

注：本表数据来源：市财政局。

6-4 各区县、开发区财政一般预算收入（2012年）

General Budgetary Revenue by Region and Development Zone（2012）

单位：万元 （10 000 yuan）

区县、开发区	Region	一般预算收入 General Budgetary Revenue	税收收入 Tax Revenue	增值税 Value Added Tax	营业税 Business Revenue	企业所得税 Corporate Income Tax
全市	**Total**	**3969597**	**3220756**	**253997**	**1287594**	**283752**
市本级合计	**Sum of city level**	**492461**	**305674**	**28946**	**52987**	**49943**
区、县合计	**Region**	**2318206**	**1909914**	**152208**	**855376**	**136489**
新城区	Xincheng	269944	175986	12337	73220	28675
碑林区	Beilin	330285	289819	26337	129077	32247
莲湖区	Lianhu	347437	250330	30873	124177	15997
雁塔区	Yanta	344958	318130	15575	168792	22462
灞桥区	Baqiao	168539	151501	7471	71674	5101
未央区	Weiyang	250009	237325	17986	111048	16144
阎良区	Yanliang	80905	69806	5902	15365	1575
临潼区	Lintong	80065	74714	11380	19710	3658
长安区	Chang'an	247228	169004	7383	72405	6155
蓝田县	Lantian	26721	20402	712	12408	497
周至县	Zhouzhi	21001	17601	956	10597	200
户　县	Huxian	55773	46667	7093	17271	1193
高陵县	Gaoling	95341	88629	8203	29632	2585
开发区合计	**Sum of Development Zones**	**1158930**	**1005168**	**72843**	**379231**	**97320**
高新区	GaoXin	577477	452140	47054	138818	66068
经开区	JingKai	239105	227219	21829	111033	15890
曲江新区	Qujiang	211200	205409	536	83940	10863
浐灞生态区	Chanba Eco-District	82001	77851	1144	28407	2301
航空基地	Aviation Industry Base	4489	4222	238	1899	209
航天基地	Aerospace Base	22634	19691	344	9440	726
国际港务区	International Trade&Logistic Park	8639	8275	38	3155	211
沣东新城	FengDongXinCheng	13385	10361	1660	2539	1052

注：本表数据来源：市财政局。

6-4 续表1 continued 1

单位：万元 (10 000 yuan)

区县、开发区	Region	税收收入 Tax Revenue					
		个人所得税 Individual Income Tax	资源税 Resource Tax	城市维护建设税 City Maintenance and Construction Tax	耕地占用税 Farm Land Occupation Tax	契税 Deed Tax	其他各项税收收入 Other Tax Revenue
全市	**Total**	**91729**	**335**	**244300**	**218738**	**255227**	**585084**
市本级合计	**Sum of city level**	**14046**		**13972**		**90000**	**55780**
区、县合计	**Region**	**53868**	**332**	**150365**	**215480**	**43048**	**302748**
新城区	Xincheng	6605	2	14354	1832		38961
碑林区	Beilin	19104		25302			57752
莲湖区	Lianhu	6716		25607	165		46795
雁塔区	Yanta	8731		23458	41684		37428
灞桥区	Baqiao	960		10018	38960		17317
未央区	Weiyang	4149		19130	28322		40546
阎良区	Yanliang	1614		4326	18916	9072	13036
临潼区	Lintong	1293	16	7610	16290	7290	7467
长安区	Chang'an	3423	6	10685	31500	13468	23979
蓝田县	Lantian	111	219	1214	2075	1475	1691
周至县	Zhouzhi	74	46	932	2827	732	1237
户　县	Huxian	371	43	3240	8959	2730	5767
高陵县	Gaoling	717		4489	23950	8281	10772
开发区合计	**Sum of Development Zones**	**23815**	**3**	**79963**	**3258**	**122179**	**226556**
高新区	GaoXin	15995		42451		47000	94754
经开区	JingKai	5215	3	22220		10372	40657
曲江新区	Qujiang	1457		8669		40275	59669
浐灞生态区	Chanba Eco-District	702		3755		18479	23063
航空基地	Aviation Industry Base	47		464		707	658
航天基地	Aerospace Base	246		1198		2334	5403
国际港务区	International Trade&Logistic Park	52		332		3012	1475
沣东新城	FengDongXinCheng	101		874	3258		877

6-4 续表2

单位：万元

区县、开发区	Region	非税收入 Non-tax Revenue	专项收入 Special Program Receipts	行政事业性收费收入 Charge of Adiministrative and Institutional Units
全市	**Total**	**748841**	**115116**	**342329**
市本级合计	**Sum of city level**	**186787**	**18941**	**93308**
区、县合计	**Region**	**408292**	**61968**	**165967**
新城区	Xincheng	93958	5816	4717
碑林区	Beilin	40466	10509	16080
莲湖区	Lianhu	97107	10493	59091
雁塔区	Yanta	26828	10066	9247
灞桥区	Baqiao	17038	4395	6464
未央区	Weiyang	12684	8109	2180
阎良区	Yanliang	11099	920	8568
临潼区	Lintong	5351	2617	1065
长安区	Chang'an	78224	3250	49752
蓝田县	Lantian	6319	738	3084
周至县	Zhouzhi	3400	607	1150
户　县	Huxian	9106	1933	2785
高陵县	Gaoling	6712	2515	1784
开发区合计	**Sum of Development Zones**	**153762**	**34207**	**83054**
高新区	GaoXin	125337	17258	78129
经开区	JingKai	11886	9294	1030
曲江新区	Qujiang	5791	3655	782
浐灞生态区	Chanba Eco-District	4150	1494	2133
航空基地	Aviation Industry Base	267	199	37
航天基地	Aerospace Base	2943	513	529
国际港务区	International Trade&Logistic Park	364	142	55
沣东新城	FengDongXinCheng	3024	1652	359

continued 2

（10 000 yuan）

罚没收入 Penalty Receipts	国有资本经营收入 State-owned Assets Profit	国有资源(资产)有偿使用收入 The Revenues of the Compensation for the Use of State-owned Resoures(Assants)	其他收入 Other Income	基金收入 Fund Revenue
99329	**6084**	**184281**	**1702**	**4128887**
56978	**773**	**16622**	**165**	**898332**
37298	**3611**	**137911**	**1537**	**939402**
4202	3	79220		1993
4399	3608	4676	1194	3926
4160		23074	289	191912
4495		3020		2353
2601		3578		173177
985		1410		14969
1153		458		9046
1073		542	54	6716
7964		17258		348982
1628		869		10343
1234		409		17047
1814		2574		28946
1590		823		129992
5053	**1700**	**29748**		**2291153**
1927		28023		317818
789		773		173174
871		483		1205673
408		115		302136
26		5		24516
127	1700	74		97700
153		14		75522
752		261		94614

6-5 各区县、开发区财政一般预算支出（2012年）

单位：万元

区县、开发区	Region	一般预算支出 Ordinary Budgetary Expenditures	一般公共服务支出 General Public Services	国防支出 Expenditure for National Defense	公共安全支出 Expenditure for Public Safety
全市	**Total**	**5974937**	**685296**	**7997**	**326250**
市本级合计	**Sum of city level**	**2371008**	**212304**	**5862**	**144289**
区、县合计	**Region**	**2757616**	**344497**	**2066**	**167192**
新城区	Xincheng	212440	37168	153	16104
碑林区	Beilin	179421	27818	355	19872
莲湖区	Lianhu	235296	33788	200	19187
雁塔区	Yanta	208047	24760	185	20643
灞桥区	Baqiao	169283	20125	201	10990
未央区	Weiyang	184981	27902	234	14737
阎良区	Yanliang	139962	18819		7810
临潼区	Lintong	242058	23774		8556
长安区	Chang'an	365362	46209	266	14955
蓝田县	Lantian	192513	16972	194	7389
周至县	Zhouzhi	252265	18083	74	6706
户　县	Huxian	213234	21721	99	11624
高陵县	Gaoling	162754	27358	105	8619
开发区合计	**Sum of Development Zones**	**846313**	**128495**	**69**	**14769**
高新区	GaoXin	363000	39029	69	5020
经开区	JingKai	159240	23067		4959
曲江新区	Qujiang	159703	27908		526
浐灞生态区	Chanba Eco-District	67751	16636		179
航空基地	Aviation Industry Base	9470	2780		
航天基地	Aerospace Base	28924	3793		1910
国际港务区	International Trade&Logistic Park	10247	3305		
沣东新城	FengDongXinCheng	47978	11977		2175

注：本表数据来源：市财政局。

Ordinary Budgetary Expenditures by Region and Development Zone（2012）

（10 000 yuan）

教育支出 Expenditure for Education	科学技术支出 Expenditure for Science and Technology	文化体育与传媒支出 Expenditure for Culture,Sport and Media	社会保障和就业支出 Expenditure for Social Safety Net and Employment Effort	医疗卫生支出 Expenditure for Medical and Health Care	节能环保支出 Expenditure for Energy Saving and Environment Protection
1080419	**59301**	**140745**	**678208**	**414573**	**141454**
189581	**28976**	**62058**	**328373**	**171633**	**103401**
813473	**17108**	**28667**	**342277**	**240017**	**27552**
54064	1891	441	21958	8513	148
44355	1464	997	40685	11401	437
62134	1961	1313	41125	13865	325
56728	1970	971	23225	16738	95
56821	1128	1256	27494	15075	1155
58149	1451	2425	16420	13870	550
36000	1000	1463	14677	11220	1250
80576	419	3043	23534	25042	4871
98180	2511	5551	43086	36794	1819
68652	355	2022	26094	24267	3438
91049	500	3086	23358	27712	6543
69570	665	3580	23232	19454	2610
37195	1793	2519	17389	16066	4311
77365	**13217**	**50020**	**7558**	**2923**	**10501**
21988	13167	3106	666	27	1613
14819	50		496		2016
9650		36521		85	1905
10060		10393			2484
200					600
600			115		875
310					925
19738			6281	2811	83

6-5 续表1

单位：万元

区县、开发区	Region	一般预算支出 Ordinary Budgetary Expenditures 城乡社区事务支出 Expenditure for Urban and Rural Community Affairs	农林水事务支出 Expenditure for Agriculture,Foresty Water Conservancy	交通运输支出 Expenditure for Industry,Commerce and Banking	资源勘探电力信息等事务支出 Expenditure for Mining,Electricity and Information
全市	**Total**	**753364**	**451053**	**264490**	**304762**
市本级合计	**Sum of city level**	**253416**	**172898**	**210870**	**109279**
区、县合计	**Region**	**332451**	**270795**	**52117**	**9487**
新城区	Xincheng	63827	190	729	275
碑林区	Beilin	23511	112	582	306
莲湖区	Lianhu	52227	148	425	397
雁塔区	Yanta	51537	4513	916	490
灞桥区	Baqiao	7974	15563	4036	361
未央区	Weiyang	35975	4584	1969	401
阎良区	Yanliang	21777	13362	3273	2900
临潼区	Lintong	10637	43497	7781	537
长安区	Chang'an	37614	47847	13018	1048
蓝田县	Lantian	1665	29350	5259	267
周至县	Zhouzhi	6444	52601	4011	95
户　县	Huxian	10898	31827	6206	1968
高陵县	Gaoling	8365	27201	3912	442
开发区合计	**Sum of Development Zones**	**167497**	**7360**	**1503**	**185996**
高新区	GaoXin	113775		1000	140329
经开区	JingKai	10941	145		21552
曲江新区	Qujiang	27585	5889	503	
浐灞生态区	Chanba Eco-District	6153	200		14847
航空基地	Aviation Industry Base				3266
航天基地	Aerospace Base	5473			6000
国际港务区	International Trade&Logistic Park	450			2
沣东新城	FengDongXinCheng	3120	1126		

continued 1

(10 000 yuan)

商业服务业等事务支出 Expenditure for Commerce and Services	金融监管等事务支出 Expenditure for Financial Supervision	地震灾后恢复重建支出 Expenditure for Post-earthquake Reconstruction	国土资源气象等事务支出 Expenditure for Land Recources and Meteorological Affairs	住房保障支出 Expenditure for Housing Support	粮油物资管理事务支出 Material Reserves Management Affairs Spending
59182	**23735**	**215**	**31410**	**397262**	**24056**
34931	**19715**		**5934**	**270077**	**19883**
19211	**1043**	**215**	**21927**	**56557**	**4173**
561			1521	4845	12
1305			598	3305	18
738	42		597	6422	25
359			1955	2961	
697			1822	3829	108
1326			1785	3074	32
778	470		626	3527	307
2313	11		1449	5149	259
3546			4056	7225	1417
905	318		1631	3286	250
3947	50		1847	5016	244
1784	53	215	1248	5189	916
952	99		2792	2729	585
5040	**2977**		**3549**	**70628**	
1008	77		102	21650	
30				22975	
252				14781	
50	2900		3447	402	
				624	
				8150	
3700				1466	
				580	

6-5 续表2 continued 2

单位：万元 （10 000 yuan）

区县、开发区	Region	一般预算支出 Ordinary Budgetary Expenditure		基金支出
		国债还本付息支出 Expenditure for National Debt and Interst	其他支出 Other Expenditure	Fund Expenditure
全市	**Total**	**46982**	**84183**	**4235010**
市本级合计	**Sum of city level**	**10873**	**16655**	**1086856**
区、县合计	**Region**	**1694**	**5097**	**905646**
新城区	Xincheng	40		2924
碑林区	Beilin		2300	7207
莲湖区	Lianhu	42	335	169976
雁塔区	Yanta	1		14147
灞桥区	Baqiao	48	600	139446
未央区	Weiyang	97		15294
阎良区	Yanliang	144	559	15301
临潼区	Lintong	195	415	18208
长安区	Chang'an	204	16	313993
蓝田县	Lantian	138	61	25746
周至县	Zhouzhi	356	543	29630
户　县	Huxian	216	159	17316
高陵县	Gaoling	213	109	136458
开发区合计	**Sum of Development Zones**	**34415**	**62431**	**2242508**
高新区	GaoXin	88	286	291663
经开区	JingKai	45	58145	249516
曲江新区	Qujiang	34098		1141633
浐灞生态区	Chanba Eco-District			284883
航空基地	Aviation Industry Base		2000	27521
航天基地	Aerospace Base	8	2000	93489
国际港务区	International Trade&Logistic Park	89		70322
沣东新城	FengDongXinCheng	87		83481

主要统计指标解释

财政收入 指国家财政参与社会产品分配所取得的收入，是实现国家职能的财力保证。主要包括：

（1）各项税收：包括国内增值税、国内消费税、进口货物增值税和消费税、出口货物退增值税和消费税、营业税、企业所得税、个人所得税、资源税、城市维护建设税、房产税、印花税、城镇土地使用税、土地增值税、车船税、船舶吨税、车辆购置税、关税、耕地占用税、契税、烟叶税等。

（2）非税收入：包括专项收入、行政事业性收费、罚没收入和其他收入。

财政支出 指国家财政将筹集起来的资金进行分配使用，以满足经济建设和各项事业的需要。主要包括：

（1）一般公共服务：指政府提供基本公共管理与服务的支出，包括人大事务、政协事务、政府办公厅（室）及相关机构事务、发展与改革事务、统计信息事务、财政事务、税收事务、审计事务、海关事务、人力资源事务、纪检监察事务、人口与计划生育事务、商贸事务、知识产权事务、工商行政管理事务、国土资源事务、海洋管理事务、测绘事务、地震事务、气象事务、民族事务、宗教事务、港澳台侨事务、档案事务、共产党事务、民主党派事务及工商联事务、群众团体事务、彩票事务等。

（2）外交：指政府外交事务支出，包括外交行政管理、驻外机构、对外援助、国际组织、对外合作与交流、边界勘界联检等方面的支出。

（3）国防：指政府用于国防方面的支出，包括用于现役部队、预备役部队、民兵、国防科研事业、专项工程、国防动员等方面的支出。

（4）公共安全：指政府维护社会公共安全方面的支出，包括武装警察、公安、国家安全、检察、法院、司法行政、监狱、劳教、国家保密、缉私警察等。

（5）教育：指政府教育事务支出，包括教育行政管理、 前教育、小 教育、初中教育、普通高中教育、普通高等教育、初等职业教育、中专教育、技校教育、职业高中教育、高等职业教育、广播电视教育、留 生教育、特殊教育、干部继续教育、教育机关服务等。

（6）科 技术：指用于科 技术方面的支出，包括科 技术管理事务、基础研究、应用研究、技术研究与开发、科技条件与服务、社会科 、科 技术普及、科技交流与合作等。

（7）文化教育与传媒：指政府在文化、文物、体育、广播影视、新闻出版等方面的支出。

（8）社会保障和就业：指政府在社会保障与就业方面的支出，包括社会保障和就业管理事务、民政管理事务、财政对社会保险基金的补助、补充全国社会保障基金、行政事业单位离退休、企业改革补助、就业补助、抚恤、退役安置、社会福利、残疾人事业、城市居民最低生活保障、其他城镇社会救济、农村社会救济、自然灾害生活救助、红十字事务等。

（9）医疗卫生：指政府医疗卫生方面的支出，包括医疗卫生管理事务支出、医疗服务支出、医疗保障支出、疾病预防控制支出、卫生监督支出、妇幼保健支出、农村卫生支出等。

（10）环境保护：指政府环境保护支出，包括环境保护管理事务支出、环境监测与监察支出、污染治理支出、自然生态保护支出、天然林保护工程支出、退耕还林支出、风沙荒漠治理支出、退牧还草支出、已垦草原退耕还草、能源节约利用、污染减排、可再生能源和资源综合利用等支出。

（11）城乡社区事务：指政府城乡社区事务支出，包括城乡社区管理事务支出、城乡社区规划与管理支出、城乡社区公共设施支出、城乡社区住宅支出、城乡社区环境卫生支出、建设市场管理与监督支出等。

（12）农林水事务：指政府农林水事务支出，包括农业支出、林业支出、水利支出、扶贫支出、农业综合开发支出等。

（13）交通运输：指政府交通运输和邮政业方面的支出，包括公路运输支出、水路运输支出、铁路运输支出、民用航空运输支出、邮政业支出等。

（14）工业商业金融等事务：指政府对工业、商业及金融等方面的支出，包括采掘业支出、制造业支出、建筑业支出、工业和信息产业监管支出、国有资产监管支出、商业流通事务支出、金融业监管支出、旅游业管理与服务支出等。

中央财政收入和地方财政收入 指按现行分税制财政体制划分的中央本级收入和地方本级收入。属于中央财政的收入包括关税，进口货物增值税和消费税，出口货物退增值税和消费税，消费税，铁道部门、各银行总行、各保险公司总公司等集中交纳的营业税和城市维护建设税，增值税75%部分，纳入共享范围的企业所得税60%部分，未纳入共享范围的中央企业所得税、中央企业上交的利润，个人所得税60%部分，车辆购置税，船舶吨税，证券交易印花税97%部分，海洋石油资源税，中央非税收入等。属于地方财政的收入包括营业税（不含铁道部门、各银行总行、各保险公司总公司集中交纳的营业税），地方企业上交利润，城市维护建设税（不含铁道部门、各银行总行、各保险公司总公司集中交纳的部分），房产税，城镇土地使用税，土地增值税，车船税，耕地占用税，契税，烟叶税，印花税，增值税25%部分，纳入共享范围的企业所得税40%部分，个人所得税40%部分，证券交易印花税3%部分，海洋石油资源税以外的其他资源税，地方非税收入等。

中央财政支出和地方财政支出 指根据政府在经济和社会活动中的不同职责，划分中央和地方政府的责权，按照政府的责权划分确定的支出。中央财政支出包括一般公共服务，外交支出，国防支出，公共安全支出，以及中央政府调整国民经济结构、协调地区发展、实施宏观调控的支出等。地方财政支出包括一般公共服务，公共安全支出，地方统筹的各项社会事业支出等。

Explanatory Notes on Main Statistical Indicators

Government Revenue refers to income for the government finance through participating in the distribution of social products. It is the financial guarantee to ensure government functioning. The contents of government revenue include the following main items:

(1) Various tax revenues, including domestic value added tax (VAT), domestic consumption tax, VAT and consumption tax from imports, VAT and consumption tax rebate for exports, business tax, corporate income tax, individual income tax, resource tax, city maintenance and construct tax, house property tax, stamp tax, urban land use tax, land appreciation tax, tax on vehicles and boat operation, ship tonnage tax, vehicle purchase tax, tariffs, farm land occupation tax, deed tax, and tobacco leaf tax, etc.

(2) Non-tax revenue, including special program receipts, charge of administrative and institutional units, penalty receipts and others non-tax receipts.

Government Expenditure refers to the distribution and use of the funds which the government finance has raised, so as to meet the needs of economic construction and various causes. It includes the following main items:

(1) Expenditure for general public services: It refers to the spending on the basic public management and services which provided by governments, including the expense on affairs of People' s Congress, affairs of People' s Political Consultative Conference, affairs of government general office and relative institutions, affairs of development and reform, affairs of statistics, affairs of finance, affairs of taxation, affairs of audit, affairs of customs, affairs of human resources and social security, affairs of discipline inspection and supervision, affairs of population and family planning, affairs of commerce and trade, affairs of intellectual property, affairs of administration for industry and commerce, affairs of land and resources, affairs of oceanic administration, affairs of surveying and mapping, affairs of earthquake, ethnic affairs, religious affairs, affairs of Hong Kong, Macao, Taiwan, and Overseas Chinese, affairs of archives administration, affairs of Chinese Communist Party, affairs of democratic parties and federation of industry and commerce, affairs of mass organization, and affairs of lottery, etc.

(2) Expenditure for foreign affairs: It refers to the spending of government on foreign affairs, including the expense on administration of foreign affairs, missions overseas, external assistance, international organizations, foreign cooperation and communication, surveying and joint inspection on borderline, etc.

(3) Expenditure for national defence: It refers to the spending of government on national defence, including the expense on active force, reserve force, militia, scientific research on national defence, special projects, mobilization of national defence, etc.

(4) Expenditure for public security: It refers to the spending of government on maintaining social and public security, including the expense on armed police force, public security, state security, prosecution, courts, justice, prison, labour education and rehabilitation, protection of state secrecy, anti-smuggling police, etc.

(5) Expenditure for education: It refers to the spending of government on education, including the expense on the administration of education, pre-primary education, primary education, secondary education, high school education, regular higher education, primary vocational education, secondary vocational education, technical school education, vocational high school education and higher vocational education, radio and television education, student abroad education, special education, on the job training of cadres, education authorities services, etc.

(6) Expenditure for science and technology: It refers to the spending of government on science and technology (S&T), including the expense on the administration of S&T, basic research, applied research, research and development, conditions and services of S&T, popularization of social science, science and technology, exchanges and cooperation of S&T, etc.

(7) Expenditure for culture, sport and media: It refers to the spending of government on culture, cultural heritage, sports, radio, film, television, press and publication, etc.

(8) Expenditure for social safety net and employment effort: It refers to the spending of government on social safety net and employment,

including the expense on administration of social safety net and employment, civil affairs, budgetary subsidy on the social insurance funds, subsidy on National Social Security Fund, retirees of administrative units andinstitutions, subsidy on enterprise reform, subsidy on employment effort, pension, placement of ex-serviceman, social welfare, the handicapped undertakings, the system of cost of living allowances for urban residents, other urban social relief, rural social relief, living relief of natural disasters, affairs of Red Cross Society, etc.

(9) Expenditure for medical and health care: It refers to the spending of government on medical and health care, including the expense on administration of medical and health care, medical services, health care, disease prevention and control, health inspection and supervision, women and children's health, rural health care, etc.

(10) Expenditure for environment protection: It refers to the spending of government on environment protection, including the expense on administration of environment protection, environment monitoring and supervision, pollution control, natural ecology protection, project of virgin forests protection, reforesting farmland, controlling the sources of dust storms, returning pastureland to grassland, returning pastureland to grassland, returning cultivated land to grassland, energy conservation, emissions reduction, comprehensive utilization of renewable energy and resources, etc.

(11) Expenditure for urban and rural community affairs: It refers to the spending of government on urban and rural community affairs, including the expense on administration of urban and rural community, planning and management of urban and rural community, public facilities of urban and rural community, housing of urban and rural community, sanitation of urban and rural community, management and supervision on the construction market, etc.

(12) Expenditure for agriculture, forestry and water conservancy: It refers to the spending of government on agriculture, forestry and water conservancy, including the expense on agriculture, forestry, water conservancy, poverty alleviation, comprehensive agricultural development, etc.

(13) Expenditure for transportation: It refers to the spending of government on transportation and postal services, including the expense on road transportation, waterway transportation, railway transportation, civil aviation transportation, and postal services.

(14) Expenditure for industry, commerce and banking: It refers to the spending of government on industry, commerce and banking, including the expense on mining, manufacturing, construction, industry and information technology supervision and administration, State-owned assets supervision and administration, commerce and circulation affairs, financial intermediation supervision and administration, tourism administration and service, etc.

Revenue of the Central Government and Revenue of the Local Governments refers to the revenue collected by the Central Government and that by the local governments as defined by the decentralized taxation system. In accordance with this system, the revenue of the Central Government includes tariff, VAT and consumption tax from imports, VAT and consumption tax rebate for exports, consumption tax, business tax and city maintenance and construct tax from the Ministry of Railways, head offices of banks, head offices of insurance company, which are handed over to the government in a centralized way, 75% of the value added tax, 60% the share part of the corporate income tax, unshared part of corporate income tax of the central enterprises, profit handed in by the central enterprises, 60% of individual income tax, vehicle purchase tax, ship tonnage tax, 97% of stamp tax on securities transactions, resource tax on the offshore petroleum resources. The revenue of the local governments includes business tax (excluding the part of the Ministry of Railways, head offices of banks, head offices of insurance company, which are handed over to the government in a centralized way), profit handed in by the local enterprises, city maintenance and construct tax (excluding the part of the Ministry of Railways, head offices of banks, head offices of insurance company, which are handed over to the government in a centralized way), house property tax, urban land use tax, land appreciation tax, tax on vehicles and boat operation, farm land occupation tax, deed tax, and tobacco leaf tax, stamp tax, 25% of the value added tax, 40% the share part of the corporate income tax, 40% of individual income tax, 3% of stamp tax on securities transactions, resource tax other than the tax on offshore petroleum resources, local non-tax revenue, etc.

Expenditure of the Central Government and Expenditure of the Local Governments according to the different functions of the Central Government and local governments in economic and social activities, the rights of affairs administration are demarcated between those of the Central Government and those of local governments; and the classification of the expenditure between the Central Government and local governments are made on the basis of the classification of the rights of affairs administration between them. The expenditure of the Central Government includes the expenditure for general public services, expenditure for foreign affairs, expenditure for public security, and the expenditure of the Central Government for adjusting the national economic structure; coordinating the development among different regions; and exercising macroeconomic regulation. The expenditure of the local governments includes mainly the expenditure for general public services, expenditure for public security, and expenditures for social development which are planed by local governments, etc.

7 物价指数

PRICE INDICES

资料整理：周　文　王　晶　王　茹
Data management:Zhouwen WangJing Wangru

第七部分　物价指数

一、简要说明

本章资料主要包括居民消费、零售、工业产品出厂、主要原材料购进、土地交易、　地产销售、租赁以及固定资产投资和建筑安装工程等价格指数，由国家统计局西安调查队提供。

二、主要指标

商品零售价格总指数（上年=100）	102.3	比上年下降	1.1个百分点
居民消费价格总指数（上年=100）	102.8	比上年下降	2.8个百分点

7　PRICE INDICES

Ⅰ.Brief Introduction

This chapter consists of primarily data on price indices of residents consumption, retail, industrial products dispatching sales, primary raw material purchasing, land deal, real estate selling, leasing, fixed asset investment and construction installation projects, provided by Fixed Asset NBS Survey Office in Xi'an.

Ⅱ.Major Indicators

		Increase over Preceding Year
Retail Price Index(the price preceding year=100)	102.3	−1.1 percentage points
Consumer Price Index(the price preceding year=100)	102.8	−2.8 percentage points

7-1 主要年份各种价格指数

Price Indices in Representative Years

(以上年价格为100) (the price of preceding year= 100)

年 份 Year	居民消费价格指数 Consumer Price Index	商品零售价格指数 Retail Price Index	工业生产者出厂价格指数 Producer Price Indices (PPI) for Manufactured Goods	工业生产者购进价格指数 Purchasing Price Indices for Industrial Producers	固定资产投资价格指数 Price Index for Investment in Fixed Assets
1980	108.7	109.3			
1981	102.4	102.7			
1982	100.9	101.0			
1983	102.6	102.0			
1984	104.7	104.8			
1985	109.7	109.3			
1986	108.5	107.4			
1987	110.6	111.4			
1988	122.8	123.2			
1989	118.3	117.8			
1990	102.5	100.9			
1991	109.4	108.3			
1992	112.2	112.4			
1993	117.2	112.8	102.5	104.3	
1994	128.5	126.2	132.2	115.0	
1995	117.0	114.6	110.8	113.1	
1996	110.9	107.9	100.7	103.8	
1997	106.0	101.5	98.6	102.5	
1998	97.9	95.5	94.4	97.5	
1999	96.8	97.4	97.5	96.9	100.8
2000	100.2	98.7	99.4	102.4	102.1
2001	99.9	98.9	99.3	101.0	101.3
2002	98.6	98.5	98.2	98.4	101.2
2003	100.5	100.0	101.5	105.3	102.4
2004	102.3	101.9	102.7	110.4	103.3
2005	100.3	99.7	103.9	109.6	102.4
2006	101.6	101.5	103.2	106.1	102.0
2007	104.7	103.7	101.9	106.2	103.5
2008	106.0	105.4	103.7	108.5	110.5
2009	99.7	99.5	99.9	100.7	97.9
2010	103.5	102.7	102.3	106.3	103.8
2011	105.6	104.4	102.5	108.8	105.4
2012	102.8	102.3	100.5	97.2	101.9

7-2 居民消费价格指数（2012年）

Residents Consumer Price Indices (2012)

(以上年价格为100) (the price of preceding year= 100)

指　标	Item	2012
居民消费价格总指数	**Consumer Price Index**	**102.8**
非食品价格指数	Non-foodstuff Price Index	101.6
服务项目价格指数	Price Index of Service	101.7
工业品价格指数	Ex-factory Price Indices of Industrial Products	101.5
扣除食品烟酒和能源价格指数	Price Index with Food,Tobacco,Liquor and Energy Excluded	101.5
扣除鲜菜鲜果总指数	Price Index with Fresh Vegetables and Fruits Excluded	102.6
消费品价格指数	Price Index of Consumer Goods	103.1
一、食品	**Food**	**105.2**
1. 粮食	Grain	104.7
2. 淀粉及制品	Starches and Processed Products	109.0
3. 干豆类及豆制品	Beans and Bean Products	98.9
4. 油脂	Oil or Fat	107.2
5. 肉禽及其制品	Meat,Poultry and Processed Products	103.0
6. 蛋	Eggs	98.1
7. 水产品	Aquatic Products	111.6
8. 菜	Vegetables	109.6
9. 调味品	Flavouring	102.4
10. 糖	Carbohydrate	105.4
11. 茶及饮料	Tea and Beverages	108.6
12. 干鲜瓜果	Dried and Fresh Melons and Fruits	99.1
13. 糕点饼干面包	Cake,Biscuit and Bread	106.7
14. 液体乳及乳制品	Milk and Its Product	101.9
15. 在外用膳食品	Dining Out	106.7
16. 其他食品	Other Food	109.1
二、烟酒	**Tobacco and Liquor**	**103.8**
1. 烟草	Tobacco	100.2
2. 酒	Liquor	111.0
三、衣着	**Clothing**	**102.1**
1. 服装	Garments	101.9
2. 衣着材料	Clothing Material	100.0
3. 鞋袜帽	Footgear and Hats	102.7
4. 衣着加工服务费	Clothing Manufacturing Services	105.1

7-2 续表 continued

(以上年价格为100) (the price of preceding year= 100)

指 标	Item	2012
四、家庭设备用品及维修服务	**Household facilities,Articles and Services**	**102.4**
1. 耐用消费品	Durable Consumer Goods	101.3
2. 室内装饰品	Interior Decorations	102.3
3. 床上用品	Bed Articles	104.6
4. 家庭日用杂品	Daily Use Household Articles	102.2
5. 家庭服务及加工维修服务	Household Service and Maintenance Renovation	106.0
五、医疗保健和个人用品	**Health Care and Personal Articles**	**104.2**
1. 医疗保健	Health Care	104.1
(1)医疗器具及用品	Medical Instrument Articles	107.8
(2)中药材及中成药	Traditional Chinese Medicine	111.6
(3)西药	Western Medicine	101.0
(4)保健器具及用品	Health Care Appliances and Articles	102.0
(5)医疗保健服务	Health Care Services	100.0
2. 个人用品及服务	Personal Articles and Services	104.4
六、交通和通讯	**Transportation and Communication**	**98.9**
1. 交通	Transportation	102.1
(1)交通工具	Transportation Facility	99.6
(2)车用燃料及零配件	Fuels and Parts	102.2
(3)车辆使用及维修费	Fees for Vehicles Use and Maintenance	101.3
(4)市区公共交通费	Incity Traffic Fare	100.0
(5)城市间交通费	Intercity Traffic Fare	105.6
2. 通信	Communication	95.9
(1)通信工具	Telecommunication Facility	71.4
(2)通信服务	Telecommunication Service	99.7
七、娱乐教育文化用品及服务	**Recreation,Education and Culture Articles**	**101.0**
1. 文娱用耐用消费品及服务	Durable Consumer Goods for Cultural and Recreational Use and Services	91.9
2. 教育	Education	101.4
3. 文化娱乐用品类	Cultural and Recreational Articles	103.1
4. 旅游	Touring	104.9
八、居住	**Residence**	**101.3**
1. 建房及装修材料	Building and Building Decoration Materials	99.7
2. 住房租金	Rental Housing	100.9
3. 自有住房	Private Housing	100.1
4. 水、电、燃料	Water, Electricity and Fuels	102.8

7-3 商品零售价格指数（2012年）

Retail Price Indices (2012)

(以上年价格为100) (the price of preceding year= 100)

指　标	Item	2012
商品零售价格总指数	**Retail Price Indices**	**102.3**
一、食品	**Food**	**105.0**
1. 粮食	Grain	104.5
2. 淀粉及制品	Starches and Processed Products	109.0
3. 干豆类及豆制品	Beans and Bean Products	97.8
4. 油脂	Oil or Fat	107.2
5. 肉禽及其制品	Meat,Poultry and Processed Products	102.7
6. 蛋	Eggs	98.0
7. 水产品	Aquatic Products	111.6
8. 菜	Vegetables	109.6
9. 调味品	Flavouring	102.9
10. 糖	Carbohydrate	103.9
11. 干鲜瓜果	Dried and Fresh Melons and Fruits	99.1
12. 糕点饼干面包	Cake,Biscuit and Bread	106.0
13. 液体乳及乳制品	Milk and Its Product	102.0
14. 在外用膳食品	Dining Out	107.5
15. 其他食品	Other Food and Manufacturing Services	109.1
二、饮料、烟酒	**Beverages,Tobacco and Liquor**	**107.4**
1. 茶及饮料	Tea and Beverages	111.8
2. 烟草	Tobacco	100.1
3. 酒	Liquor	111.1
三、服装、鞋帽	**Garments,Shoes and Hats**	**102.2**
1. 服装	Garments	101.9
2. 鞋袜帽	Footgear and Hats	102.9
3. 其他	Others	110.9
四、纺织品	**Textiles**	**103.5**
1. 衣着材料	Cotton Cloth	100.0
2. 床上用品	Blend Cloth	105.2
五、家用电器及音像器材	**Household Appliances,Music and Video Equipment**	**95.9**
1. 家庭设备	Household facility	100.2
2. 文娱用耐用消费品	Durable Consumer Goods on Cultural and Recreational Use	89.4
3. 专业音像器材类	Music and Video Equipment	97.8

7-3 续表 continued

(以上年价格为100) (the price of preceding year= 100)

指 标	Item	2012
六、文化办公用品	**Cultural and Office Appliances**	**98.5**
七、日用品	**Articles for Daily Use**	**102.0**
1. 日用百货	General Merchandise for Daily Use	99.9
2. 日用杂品	Miscellaneous for Daily Use	102.0
3. 洗涤用品	Daily Use Articles For Washing	104.1
4. 其他日用品	Other Daily Articles	102.2
八、体育娱乐用品	**Sports and Recreation Articles**	**100.5**
1. 体育用品	Sports Goods	101.1
2. 娱乐用品	Receration Goods	100.1
九、交通通信用品	**Transportation and Communication Goods**	**96.3**
1. 交通运输机械	Transportation Machinery	99.7
2. 通信器材	Communication Machinery	77.6
十、家具	**Furniture**	**102.7**
十一、化妆品	**Cosmetics**	**103.5**
十二、金银珠宝	**Gold,Silver and Jewelry**	**96.3**
十三、中西药品及医疗保健用品	**Traditional Chinese and Western Medicines And Health Care Articles**	**104.0**
1. 医疗器具及用品	Medical Apparatus and Article	107.8
2. 中药材及中成药	Traditional Chinese Medicinal Materials and Medicines	111.1
3. 西药	Western Medicine	101.0
4. 保健器具及用品	Health Care Apparatus and Article	101.2
十四、书报杂志及电子出版物	**Books,Newspapers,Magazines and Electronic Publications**	**100.8**
1. 教材及参考书	Teaching Materials and Reference Books	100.0
2. 书报杂志	Books, Newspapers and Magazines	102.5
3. 电子音像制品	Electronic Audio-video Products	100.0
十五、燃料	**Fuel**	**102.0**
1、煤炭及制品	Coal and Its Products	103.4
2、石油及制品	Oil and Its Products	101.8
十六、建筑材料及五金电料	**Building Materials and Hardware**	**100.2**
1. 建筑装潢材料	Building Decoration Materials	99.3
2. 五金电料	Hardware	103.6

7–4 主要年份工业生产者出厂价格指数

(上年价格=100)

类 别	Classify	1997	1998	1999	2000
全部工业品	**Total Industry Products**	**98.6**	**94.4**	**97.5**	**99.4**
按轻重工业分	Grouped by Light Industry and Heavy Industry				
轻工业	Light Industry	98.2	91.1	95.9	97.8
以农产品为原料	Using Farm Products as Raw Materials	99.2	89.5	95.2	99.2
以非农产品为原料	Using Non-farm Products as Raw Materials	96.8	93.4	97.0	95.5
重工业	Heavy Industry	99.0	97.3	98.9	100.8
采掘	Mining & Quarrying		104.1	101.5	97.5
原料	Raw Materials	101.0	100.7	102.3	107.7
加工	Processing	97.9	95.6	98.0	98.4
按用途分	Grouped by Use				
生产资料	Means of Production	99.6	96.6	98.3	100.5
采掘	Mining & Quarrying		104.1	101.5	97.5
原料	Raw Materials	100.9	100.6	100.2	106.4
加工	Processing	98.9	94.7	97.6	98.7
生活资料	Consumer Goods	97.0	91.4	96.5	97.3
食品	Food	108.2	97.8	95.8	94.4
衣着	Clothing	93.0	83.9	95.2	101.6
一般日用品	Articles for Daily Use	91.6	95.1	97.6	96.9
耐用消费品	Durable Consumer Goods	99.7	95.4	98.0	95.9
按工业部门分	Grouped by Industrial Sector				
1. 冶金工业	Metallurgical Industry	99.2	97.5	91.2	98.2
2. 电力工业	Power Industry	111.3	111.2	109.3	109.6
3. 煤炭及炼焦工业	Coal and Coking Industry	98.9	98.5	96.3	100.5
4. 石油工业	Petroleum Industry			107.1	134.2
5. 化学工业	Chemical Industry	91.8	92.9	96.6	96.7
6. 机械工业	Machine Manufacturing Industry	98.8	94.6	98.1	98.0
7. 建筑材料工业	Building Materials Industry	98.2	99.3	96.7	98.5
8. 森林工业	Timber Industry	107.6	104.5	97.9	98.9
9. 食品工业	Food Industry	106.8	95.3	95.5	94.3
10. 纺织工业	Textiles Industry	94.3	82.6	93.7	103.4
11. 缝纫工业	Tailoring Industry	100.1	97.3	99.1	103.5
12. 皮革工业	Leather Industry	91.2	96.8	98.0	99.2
13. 造纸工业	Paper Industry			95.3	96.7
14. 文教艺术用品工业	Cultural,Educational & Handicrafts Articles			96.7	96.4
15. 其它工业	Other Industry	109.5	109.2	98.9	104.8

注：经国务院批准，2011年起国家统计局进行统计方法制度改革，新的工业生产者价格调查方案中把“工业品价格统计”改称为“工业生产者价格统计”，相应地将“工业品出厂价格指数”和“原材料、燃料、动力购进价格指数”改为“工业生产者出厂价格指数”和“工业生产者购进价格指数”。

Producer Price Indices (PPI) for Manufactured Goods in Representative Years

(the price of preceding year= 100)

2001	2002	2003	2004	2005	2006	2007	2008	2009	2010	2011	2012
99.3	**98.2**	**101.5**	**102.7**	**103.9**	**103.2**	**101.9**	**103.7**	**99.9**	**102.3**	**102.5**	**100.5**
99.6	98.4	101.3	103.4	99.9	100.2	101.8	103.7	100.6	102.5	107.0	100.4
99.0	98.4	104.5	108.7	97.3	100.1	103.3	106.0	98.9	104.0	109.3	100.3
100.6	98.6	99.9	100.8	101.2	100.2	100.8	102.1	101.8	101.4	100.9	100.5
99.2	98.2	101.6	101.9	107.9	105.5	101.9	103.8	99.3	102.2	101.6	100.5
94.8	101.3	103.4	140.5	107.9	100.6	111.6	122.3	90.0	150.2	102.6	101.8
101.1	101.3	111.2	109.0	114.2	111.8	104.9	110.8	99.5	108.9	111.2	108.6
98.5	97.7	100.1	100.6	106.7	104.2	101.2	101.9	99.4	100.8	100.1	99.2
99.1	98.0	101.8	102.7	105.3	104.2	101.3	103.4	99.3	102.2	101.9	100.3
94.8	101.3	103.4	140.5	107.9	100.6	111.6	122.3	90.0	150.2	102.6	101.8
101.1	101.0	108.1	106.6	111.3	111.6	104.8	110.2	99.7	109.0	111.3	108.7
98.5	97.4	100.9	102.0	104.3	103.0	100.6	102.0	99.3	101.0	100.3	98.9
99.9	99.1	100.5	102.5	100.4	100.4	103.5	104.7	101.4	102.5	104.5	100.8
99.6	101.2	101.0	103.6	100.3	100.4	105.3	106.6	100.3	103.3	109.5	101.6
99.4	100.8	99.4	102.7	102.0	103.3	104.6	105.1	102.7	101.2	111.9	99.4
101.9	97.9	101.2	101.2	101.3	100.8	100.1	102.7	102.6	101.2	101.5	101.5
97.0	98.1	97.2	98.3	99.1	99.4	100.7	100.7	103.9	101.9	99.5	99.0
97.2	98.7	103.8	107.1	103.9	106.5	103.2	104.8	92.0	105.8	116.3	100.7
102.4	100.0	103.2	104.1	110.6	107.9	105.5	110.0	109.0	101.2	104.7	111.2
110.3	106.7	136.8	131.4	97.1	95.4	106.8	104.8	101.7	110.6	109.3	101.5
96.6	100.7	118.6	110.5	121.7	117.6	104.8	115.6	96.7	114.2	108.4	108.2
100.5	99.2	100.2	100.8	103.2	100.8	101.1	104.1	102.6	100.8	104.2	100.3
98.3	97.6	99.8	100.6	104.9	103.4	101.0	101.7	99.9	100.9	99.5	99.0
100.6	99.6	99.7	100.0	98.6	98.9	98.9	101.8	101.9	99.9	100.6	99.6
98.1	98.9	100.1	100.2	101.6	101.6	101.1	101.1	101.1	101.7	105.2	103.2
99.8	101.1	102.8	107.5	98.3	99.0	106.1	109.3	98.3	104.3	110.1	101.7
97.5	94.9	117.3	119.1	89.9	102.4	98.4	99.7	97.5	108.9	107.2	88.7
100.0	101.1	100.2	103.6	100.8	103.5	104.6	105.1	102.6	101.3	113.4	99.4
101.0	101.8	98.7	99.6	101.2	100.0	99.0	99.6	99.7	99.6	98.0	99.9
102.3	95.0	96.9	100.2	101.2	100.0	100.1	104.5	98.4	100.4	103.4	99.2
101.1	103.4	97.5	96.5	98.1	100.1	99.1	99.2	102.2	99.9	100.7	106.0
107.1	99.4	103.3	105.0	103.4	105.7	111.4	104.3	99.7	100.5	104.3	101.2

7-5 主要年份工业生产者购进价格指数

Purchasing Price Indices for Industrial Producers in Representative Years

(上年价格=100) (the price of preceding year= 100)

指　标	Item	2000	2001	2002	2003	2004	2005
全部原材料	**Total of Raw Materials**	**102.4**	**101.0**	**98.4**	**105.3**	**110.4**	**109.6**
(一)燃料、动力类	Fuel and Power	105.0	101.8	100.9	105.7	109.4	123.5
(二)黑色金属材料类	Ferrous Metals	102.7	102.1	98.5	107.4	117.4	107.6
#钢材	Steel	103.4	102.4	97.9	106.0	114.8	107.5
(三)有色金属材料和电线类	Non-ferrous Metals and Electric Wires	105.2	95.5	96.8	105.8	114.1	107.8
(四)化工原料类	Raw Chemical Materials	104.6	102.5	97.9	102.4	106.3	106.1
(五)木材及纸浆类	Timber and Paper Pulp	101.2	102.8	99.4	101.2	100.3	108.2
(六)建筑材料及非金属矿类	Building Materials and Non-metal ores	100.3	99.7	98.6	99.6	110.4	99.3
(七)其它工业原材料及半成品类	Other Industrial Raw Materials and Semi-Products	98.8	100.8	98.9	102.5	111.2	106.1
(八)农副产品类	Agricultural Products	100.4	102.8	98.2	113.7	112.7	100.9
(九)纺织原料类	Textile Materials	98.0	96.8	90.6	103.4	103.9	97.6

7-5 续表 continued

(上年价格=100) (the price of preceding year= 100)

指　标	Item	2006	2007	2008	2009	2010	2011	2012
全部原材料	**Total of Raw Materials**	**106.1**	**106.2**	**108.5**	**100.7**	**106.3**	**108.8**	**97.2**
(一)燃料、动力类	Fuel and Power	112.6	107.0	109.8	105.1	108.6	113.5	102.3
(二)黑色金属材料类	Ferrous Metals	99.2	104.8	111.3	99.2	103.1	102.9	93.4
#钢材	Steel	98.5	104.9	111.7	98.7	103.5	102.9	93.3
(三)有色金属材料和电线类	Non-ferrous Metals and Electric Wires	116.5	110.7	99.1	93.9	113.6	118.9	93.0
(四)化工原料类	Raw Chemical Materials	101.6	105.6	111.4	95.0	103.9	108.1	87.7
(五)木材及纸浆类	Timber and Paper Pulp	111.7	105.9	106.5	102.6	101.1	105.4	100.9
(六)建筑材料及非金属矿类	Building Materials and Non-metal ores	100.7	104.0	104.8	106.8	102.1	102.9	97.4
(七)其它工业原材料及半成品类	Other Industrial Raw Materials and Semi-Products	104.3	108.8	110.6	101.4	108.1	109.4	100.3
(八)农副产品类	Agricultural Products	107.2	107.2	108.9	99.6	106.5	107.4	103.4
(九)纺织原料类	Textile Materials	101.5	100.5	99.8	97.6	104.6	107.0	89.1

7-6 土地交易价格指数（2012年）

Transactions Price Indices of Land (2012)

(上年价格=100) (the price of preceding year= 100)

指　标	Item	2012
土地交易	**Transactions Price Indices of Land**	**100.6**
一、居住用地	**Land for Residential Building Use**	**100.3**
（一）经济适用住房用地	Economically Affordable Housing	100.0
（二）商品住宅用地	Commercialized Housing	100.3
1. 普通住宅用地	General Residential Buildings	100.4
2. 高档住宅用地	Luxury Residential Buildings	100.1
二、工业用地	**Land for Industry and Storage Use**	**101.6**
三、商业营业用地	**Land for Business,Tourism and Entertainment**	**101.0**
四、其他用地	**Land for Other Uses**	**100.3**

7-7 住宅销售价格指数（2012年）

Selling Price Indices of Residential Buildings (2012)

(上年价格=100) (the price of preceding year= 100)

指　标	Item	2012
新建住宅	**Newly Residential Buildings**	**100.5**
一、保障性住房	guaranteed house	
二、新建商品住宅	New commodity residential house	100.5
（一）90平方米及以下	90 square meters and less	100.5
（二）90-144平方米	90-144 square metre	100.7
（三）144平方米以上	144 square meters and more	99.9
二手住宅	**Second-hand Residential Buildings**	**98.6**
一、90平方米及以下	90 square meters and the following	99.6
二、90-144平方米	90-144 square metre	98.0
三、144平方米以上	144 square meters	98.5

7-8 住宅租赁和物业服务价格指数（2012年）

Lease and Property Service Price Index (2012)

(上年价格=100) (the price of preceding year= 100)

指　标	Item	2012
住宅租赁	**Renting Price Indices of Residential Buildings**	**100.8**
一、经济适用住房	Economical Affordable Housing	100.0
二、廉租房	Tenement House	100.0
三、商品住宅	Commercialized Residential Buildings	100.8
（一）普通住宅	General Residential Buildings	101.9
（二）高档住宅	Luxury Residential Buildings	100.6
物业服务	**Property Services**	100.0
一、经济适用住房	Economical Affordable Housing	100.0
二、商品住宅	Commercialized Residential Buildings	100.0
（一）普通住宅	General Residential Buildings	100.0
（二）高档住宅	Luxury Residential Buildings	100.0

7-9 主要年份固定资产投资价格指数

Price Indices for Investment in Fixed Assets in Representative Years

(上年价格=100) (the price of preceding year= 100)

指　标	Item	2000	2004	2005	2006	2007	2008	2009	2010	2011	2012
固定资产投资价格指数	**Price Indices for Investment in Fixed Assets**	**102.1**	**103.3**	**102.4**	**102.0**	**103.5**	**110.5**	**97.9**	**103.8**	**105.4**	**101.9**
建筑安装、装饰工程	Construction,Installation and Decoration	103.9	104.6	102.3	102.6	104.9	114.9	97.1	105.5	107.2	102.6
设备、工器具购置	Purchase of Equipment and Instruments	97.9	100.5	104.5	100.8	100.7	101.0	98.6	100.0	100.6	99.1
其他费用	Others	100.0	100.6	100.5	100.5	100.6	101.9	100.9	100.8	102.8	102.7

主 要 统 计 指 标 解 释

居民消费价格指数 是反映一定时期内城乡居民所购买的生活消费品和服务项目价格变动趋势和程度的相对数，是对城市居民消费价格指数和农村居民消费价格指数进行综合汇总计算的结果。通过该指数可以观察和分析消费品的零售价格和服务项目价格变动对城乡居民实际生活费支出的影响程度。

商品零售价格指数 是反映一定时期内城乡商品零售价格变动趋势和程度的相对数。商品零售价格的变动与国家的财政收入、市场供需的平衡、消费与积累的比例关系有关。因此，该指数可以从一个侧面对上述经济活动进行观察和分析。

工业生产者出厂价格指数 是反映一定时期内全部工业产品出厂价格总水平的变动趋势和程度的相对数，包括工业企业售给本企业以外所有单位的各种产品和直接售给居民用于生活消费的产品。该指数可以观察出厂价格变动对工业总产值及增加值的影响。

工业生产者购进价格指数 是反映工业企业作为生产投入，而从市场和能源、原材料生产企业购买原材料、燃料和动力产品价格的变动趋势和程度的统计指标，是扣除工业企业物质消耗成本中的价格变动影响的重要依据。

固定资产投资价格指数 是反映一定时期内固定资产投资品及取费项目的价格变动趋势和程度的相对数。固定资产投资额是由建筑安装工程投资完成额、设备工器具购置投资完成额和其他费用投资完成额三部分组成的。编制固定资产投资价格指数应首先分别编制上述三部分投资的价格指数，然后采用加权算术平均法求出固定资产投资价格总指数。

该指数可以准确地反映固定资产投资中涉及的各类投资品和取费项目价格变动趋势和变动幅度，消除按现价计算的固定资产投资指标中的价格变动因素，真实地反映固定资产投资的规模、速度、结构和效益，为国家科学地制定、检查固定资产投资计划并提高宏观调控水平，为完善国民经济核算体系提供科学的、可靠的依据。

Explanatory Notes on Main Statistical Indicators

Consumer Price Indices reflect the trend and degree of changes in prices of consumer goods and services purchased by urban and rural households during a given period. They are obtained by combining Consumer Price Indices of Urban Household and Consumer Price Indices of Rural Household. The Indices enable the observation and analysis of the degree of impact of the changes in the prices of retailed goods and services on the actual living expenses of urban and rural residents.

Retail Price Indices reflect the trend and degree of change in retail prices of commodities during a given period. The change in retail prices of commodities is related to government revenue, the equilibrium of market supply and demand, and the ratio of consumption to accumulation. Therefore, the retail price indices are useful from an oblique perspective for observing and analyzing the changes of the above economic activities.

Producer Price Indices (PPI) for Manufactured Goods reflect the trend and degree of changes in general ex-factory prices of all manufactured goods during a given period, including sales of manufactured goods by an industrial enterprise to all units outside the enterprise, as well as sales of consumer goods to residents. It can be used to analyze the impact of ex-factory prices on gross output value and value-added of the industrial sector.

Purchasing Price Indices for Industrial Producers reflect changes in the level and degree of prices paid by industrial enterprises when they purchase production input such as raw materials, fuels and power from the market or from other energy or raw materials producing enterprises. These indices provide an important basis for measuring the material consumption of industrial enterprises after removing the influence of price changes.

Price Indices for Investment in Fixed Assets reflect the trend and degree of changes in prices of investment goods and projects in fixed assets during a given period. The investment in fixed assets consists of three components, namely the investment in construction and installation, the investment in purchases of equipment and instrument, and the investment in other items. Price indices for investment in fixed assets are calculated as the weighted arithmetic mean of the price indices for the three components of investment in fixed assets.

Removing the factor of price change in the aggregates of investment at current prices, this indicator shows the changes in the prices of commodities and fees involved in the investment of fixed assets, and can be used to observe the actual size, growth, structure, and efficiency of investment in fixed assets and provides reliable and scientific data for government planning, management, decision-making, and further improving the current national accounting system.

8 人民生活

PEOPLE´S LIVELIHOOD

资料整理：冯军魁　贾薪蓉　赵兰莉
Data management:Feng Junkui　Jia Xinrong　Zhao Lanli

第八部分　人民生活

一、简要说明

本章资料主要内容包括城乡居民家庭基本情况、主要商品购买数量、耐用消费品拥有数量等，由西安市统计局人口就业处提供。

二、主要指标

城镇居民人均可支配收入（元）	29982	比上年增长	15.4%
城镇居民人均消费性支出（元）	21434	比上年增长	11.0%
农村居民人均纯收入（元）	11442	比上年增长	16.9%
农村居民人均生活消费支出（元）	7774	比上年增长	15.9%

8　PEOPLE'S LIVELIHOOD

Ⅰ.Brief Introduction

Data in this chapter reflects situation of the people's daily life of Xi'an city. It consists of mainly basic condition of urban and rural households, volume of primary commodity purchasing, possession of endurable goods, etc. The data come from Population & Employment Division of the Xi'an Bureau of Statistics.

Ⅱ.Major Indicators

		Increase over Preceding Year
Per Capita Annual Disposable Income of Urban Households (yuan)	29982	15.4%
Per Capita Annual Consumption Expenditure of Urban Households (yuan)	21434	11.0%
Per Capita Living Expenditure Built(yuan)	11442	16.9%
Per Capita Net Income of Rural Residents(yuan)	7774	15.9%

8-1 主要年份城乡居民家庭人均收入及恩格尔系数

Per Capita Annual Income and Engel's Coefficient of Urban and Rural Households in Representative Years

年 份 Year	城镇居民家庭人均可支配收入 Per Capita Annual Disposable Income of Urban Households		农村居民家庭人均纯收入 Per Capita Annual Net Income of Rural Households		城镇居民家庭恩格尔系数（%） Engel's Coefficient of Urban Households	农村居民家庭恩格尔系数（%） Engel's Coefficient of Rural Households
	绝对数（元） Value(yuan)	指数（1980年=100） Indax (1980 year= 100)	绝对数（元） Value(yuan)	指数（1978年=100） Indax (1978 year= 100)		
1978			140			
1979						
1980	414		190	135.7	53.3	53.3
1981	446	107.7	207	147.9	52.9	53.7
1982	479	115.6	254	181.4	55.1	56.7
1983	509	122.9	245	175.0	55.1	58.4
1984	540	130.3	299	213.6	54.9	51.7
1985	719	173.5	351	250.7	49.5	48.5
1986	911	219.8	390	278.6	49.9	47.9
1987	1034	249.7	434	310.0	50.6	50.3
1988	1142	275.6	482	344.3	44.9	47.5
1989	1344	324.3	530	378.6	51.7	48.2
1990	1518	366.5	610	435.7	53.1	49.5
1991	1619	390.9	707	505.0	51.6	46.7
1992	1992	481.0	783	559.3	52.5	50.9
1993	2661	642.5	870	621.4	46.4	46.0
1994	3517	849.1	1078	770.0	45.2	50.1
1995	4153	1002.5	1353	966.4	44.7	50.3
1996	5023	1212.6	1586	1132.9	42.6	49.9
1997	5344	1290.1	1846	1318.6	40.7	49.2
1998	5670	1368.7	2052	1465.7	39.8	42.4
1999	5999	1448.3	2203	1573.6	36.3	39.1
2000	6364	1536.5	2344	1674.3	36.5	36.6
2001	6705	1618.8	2490	1778.6	34.8	33.9
2002	7184	1734.3	2641	1886.4	34.4	31.1
2003	7748	1870.7	2838	2027.1	34.8	37.6
2004	8544	2062.8	3143	2245.0	36.1	35.7
2005	9628	2324.5	3460	2471.4	37.0	36.3
2006	10905	2632.9	3808	2720.0	34.4	36.8
2007	12662	3057.0	4399	3142.1	36.6	38.2
2008	15207	3671.4	5212	3722.9	36.4	37.0
2009	18963	4578.2	6275	4482.3	32.4	35.8
2010	22244	5370.4	7750	5535.7	31.3	32.5
2011	25981	6272.6	9788	6991.4	31.3	31.9
2012	29982	7238.5	11442	8172.9	32.5	33.8

8-2 主要年份城乡居民人民币储蓄存款

Savings Deposit of Urban and Rural Households in Representative Years

单位：亿元 (100 million yuan)

年 份 Year	年末余额 Balance at Ycar-end	指数（上年=100） Index (preccding year=100)
1978	3.72	
1980	5.48	113.0
1981	6.36	116.1
1982	7.76	122.0
1983	10.02	129.1
1984	14.7	146.7
1985	16.7	113.6
1986	23.1	138.3
1987	32.13	139.1
1988	32.51	101.2
1989	45.78	140.8
1990	62.23	135.9
1991	78.64	126.4
1992	96.09	122.2
1993	124.61	129.7
1994	174.19	139.8
1995	230.63	132.4
1996	394.02	170.8
1997	358.78	91.1
1998	499.68	139.3
1999	586.4	117.4
2000	675.83	115.3
2001	800.86	118.5
2002	988.04	123.4
2003	1210.56	122.5
2004	1432.86	118.4
2005	1716.76	119.8
2006	1950.53	113.6
2007	2002.38	102.7
2008	2513.7	125.5
2009	3084.2	122.7
2010	3641.09	118.1
2011	4155.65	114.1
2012	4787.03	115.2

8-3 各区县城乡居民人均收入

Per Capita Income of Urban and Rural Households by Region

区 县	Region	城镇居民人均可支配收入 Per Capita Disposable Income of Urban Households				农村居民人均纯收入 Per Capita net Income of Rural Households			
		绝对数（元）Value(yuan)			2012年指数（上年＝100）	绝对数（元）Value(yuan)			2012年指数（上年＝100）
		2010	2011	2012	Index(preceding year=100)(2012)	2010年	2011	2012	Index(preceding year=100)(2012)
全 市	**Total**	**22244**	**25981**	**29982**	**115.4**	**7750**	**9788**	**11442**	**116.9**
新城区	Xincheng	22554	26498	30658	115.7				
碑林区	Beilin	22998	27025	31268	115.7				
莲湖区	Lianhu	22940	26962	31195	115.7				
灞桥区	Baqiao	21162	24817	28688	115.6	8849	11291	13278	117.6
未央区	Weiyang	22184	26041	30103	115.6	9712	12383	14562	117.6
雁塔区	Yanta	23517	27601	31934	115.7	9863	12585	14800	117.6
阎良区	Yanliang	22927	26839	31026	115.6	8969	11426	13403	117.3
临潼区	Lintong	18213	21271	24568	115.5	7156	9109	10685	117.3
长安区	Chang'an	19557	22918	26493	115.6	7389	9421	11107	117.9
蓝田县	Lantian	14874	17309	19957	115.3	5316	6704	7824	116.7
周至县	Zhouzhi	14877	17353	20025	115.4	5238	6615	7733	116.9
户 县	Huxian	16761	19532	22520	115.3	6549	8265	9654	11.7
高陵县	Gaoling	17377	20313	23462	115.5	7106	9053	10673	117.9

8-4 主要年份城镇居民家庭及收支基本情况

Basic Conditions of Urban Households in Representative Years

指　　标	Item	2001	2002	2003	2004
一.平均每户家庭人口（人）	**Average Household Size(person)**	**3.03**	**3.01**	**3.04**	**2.99**
二. 平均每户就业人数（人）	**Average Number of Employed Persons Per Housedhold (person)**	**1.38**	**1.47**	**1.46**	**1.46**
三. 平均每户就业面（%）	**Proportion Percentage of Employment Per Housedhold (%)**	**45.6**	**48.8**	**48.00**	**48.80**
四. 平均每一就业者负担人数（人）	**Number of Dependents per Emplyee(person)**	**2.19**	**2.05**	**2.08**	**2.05**
五. 年人均家庭总收入（元）	**Per Capita Annual Income(yuan)**	**6743.12**	**7670.67**	**8315.13**	**9150.65**
#可支配收入	Disposable Income	6704.86	7183.54	7748.38	8544.03
（一）工资性收入	Income from Wages and Salaries	4288.09	5075.62	5443.21	6050.38
（二）经营性收入	Net Business Income	135.27	159.03	111.83	251.37
（三）财产性收入	Income from Properties	49.35	60.90	194.17	186.95
（四）转移性收入	Income from Transfer	2270.41	2375.12	2565.92	2661.95
六. 年人均家庭总支出（元）	**Annual Actual Expenditure Per Capita (yuan)**	**6678.56**	**7819.74**	**8610.43**	**9312.05**
（一）消费性支出	Consumption Expenditure	5815.66	6419.21	6805.30	7427.82
1.食品	Food	2023.91	2205.38	2371.02	2685.10
2.衣着	Clothing	485.93	540.52	574.56	611.03
3.家庭设备用品及服务	Facilities,Articles and Services	628.91	467.36	403.24	493.33
4.医疗保健	Health Care and Medical Services	406.13	535.52	602.31	641.77
5.交通和通信	Transport and Communication Services	453.12	567.96	630.48	688.22
6.教育文化娱乐服务	Education,Receration and Cultural Services	908.07	1126.68	1230.60	1252.55
7.居住	Residence	531.45	783.56	779.32	813.14
8.杂项商品和服务	Miscellaneous Goods and Services	378.14	192.23	213.77	242.68
（二）购房和建房支出	Purchase and Construction Expenditure of Houses	289.31	415.08	532.19	590.33
（三）转移性支出	Transfer Expenditure	573.59	567.81	786.70	768.01
（四）财产性支出	Property Expenditure				
（五）社会保障支出	Social Services Expenditure		417.64	486.24	525.89
七. 人均期末手存现金（元）	**Cash Reserves at Hand at the end of Year Per Capita (yuan)**	**550.39**	**587.82**	**810.60**	**882.65**

8-4 续表1 continued 1

指 标	Item	2005	2006	2007	2008
一.平均每户家庭人口（人）	**Average Household Size(person)**	**2.93**	**2.90**	**2.91**	**2.82**
二. 平均每户就业人数（人）	**Average Number of Employed Persons Per Housedhold (person)**	**1.39**	**1.40**	**1.39**	**1.35**
三. 平均每户就业面（%）	**Proportion Percentage of Employment Per Housedhold (%)**	**47.44**	**48.28**	**47.77**	**47.87**
四. 平均每一就业者负担人数（人）	**Number of Dependents per Emplyee(person)**	**2.11**	**2.07**	**2.09**	**2.09**
五. 年人均家庭总收入（元）	**Per Capita Annual Income(yuan)**	**10387.44**	**11708.43**	**13421.45**	**16365.67**
#可支配收入	Disposable Income	9627.89	10905.39	12662.03	15206.89
（一）工资性收入	Income from Wages and Salaries	6926.28	7622.92	8897.30	10944.90
（二）经营性收入	Net Business Income	163.66	345.70	375.68	410.70
（三）财产性收入	Income from Properties	193.20	317.87	208.80	241.24
（四）转移性收入	Income from Transfer	3104.30	3421.94	3939.67	4768.83
六. 年人均家庭总支出（元）	**Annual Actual Expenditure Per Capita (yuan)**	**10030.64**	**12033.94**	**12257.69**	**14380.69**
（一）消费性支出	Consumption Expenditure	7899.81	8986.87	10097.95	12015.81
1.食品	Food	2926.32	3093.12	3696.57	4374.24
2.衣着	Clothing	712.98	783.93	950.50	1232.12
3.家庭设备用品及服务	Facilities,Articles and Services	373.36	582.85	597.11	761.02
4.医疗保健	Health Care and Medical Services	746.67	695.09	847.80	1161.86
5.交通和通信	Transport and Communication Services	763.56	922.99	1145.90	1246.34
6.教育文化娱乐服务	Education,Receration and Cultural Services	1357.50	1666.93	1466.55	1724.63
7.居住	Residence	719.00	946.87	1027.90	1058.11
8.杂项商品和服务	Miscellaneous Goods and Services	300.42	295.09	365.62	457.49
（二）购房和建房支出	Purchase and Construction Expenditure of Houses	722.35	1273.52	524.62	262.31
（三）转移性支出	Transfer Expenditure	745.24	1043.44	933.52	1042.50
（四）财产性支出	Property Expenditure		1.89	9.33	23.30
（五）社会保障支出	Social Services Expenditure	663.24	728.22	692.27	1036.77
七. 人均期末手存现金（元）	**Cash Reserves at Hand at the end of Year Per Capita (yuan)**	**1121.29**	**1525.31**	**1563.07**	**1296.10**

8-4 续表2 continued 2

指 标	Item	2009	2010	2011	2012
一.平均每户家庭人口（人）	**Average Household Size(person)**	**2.84**	**2.81**	**2.83**	**2.76**
二. 平均每户就业人数（人）	**Average Number of Employed Persons Per Housedhold (person)**	**1.51**	**1.51**	**1.55**	**1.49**
三. 平均每户就业面（%）	**Proportion Percentage of Employment Per Housedhold (%)**	**53.20**	**53.70**	**54.8**	**54.00**
四. 平均每一就业者负担人数（人）	**Number of Dependents per Emplyee(person)**	**1.88**	**1.86**	**1.83**	**1.85**
五. 年人均家庭总收入（元）	**Per Capita Annual Income(yuan)**	**20299.12**	**23879.86**	**27710.24**	**32032**
#可支配收入	Disposable Income	18963.31	22243.63	25981.45	29982
（一）工资性收入	Income from Wages and Salaries	13562.24	15733.57	18240.83	20937
（二）经营性收入	Net Business Income	715.99	979.22	1442.33	1843
（三）财产性收入	Income from Properties	357.26	506.47	639.65	971
（四）转移性收入	Income from Transfer	5663.63	6660.60	7387.43	8281
六. 年人均家庭总支出（元）	**Annual Actual Expenditure Per Capita (yuan)**	**17619.36**	**20597.76**	**23991.29**	**26524**
（一）消费性支出	Consumption Expenditure	14250.78	16543.21	19305.83	21434
1.食品	Food	4621.40	5176.55	6041.18	6961
2.衣着	Clothing	1564.44	1837.40	2368.64	2608
3.家庭设备用品及服务	Facilities,Articles and Services	1037.98	1250.86	1565.74	1686
4.医疗保健	Health Care and Medical Services	1375.57	1572.40	1737.36	1826
5.交通和通信	Transport and Communication Services	1614.68	1995.20	2472.58	3056
6.教育文化娱乐服务	Education,Receration and Cultural Services	2043.52	2424.51	2753.85	3072
7.居住	Residence	1262.83	1542.76	1594.54	1816
8.杂项商品和服务	Miscellaneous Goods and Services	730.36	743.53	771.94	410
（二）购房和建房支出	Purchase and Construction Expenditure of Houses	606.42	639.83	1125.88	853
（三）转移性支出	Transfer Expenditure	1517.15	1907.40	1961.60	2429
（四）财产性支出	Property Expenditure	23.09	53.55	119.38	38
（五）社会保障支出	Social Services Expenditure	1221.92	1453.77	1478.60	1769
七. 人均期末手存现金（元）	**Cash Reserves at Hand at the end of Year Per Capita (yuan)**	**2553.73**	**4727.95**	**6295.60**	**6001**

8-5 城镇居民家庭基本情况（2012年）

Basic Conditions of Urban Households（2012）

指　　标	Item	2012
一、人均可支配收入（元）	**Per Capita Disposable Income(yuan)**	**29982.00**
二、家庭人口数（人/户）	**Number of Family Members (Person/Household)**	**2.76**
（一）有收入者人数	Family Members Earning Income	2.08
1.就业人口数	Family Members Employed	1.49
(1)国有经济单位职工人数	Employed by State-Owned Enterprises	0.84
(2)城镇集体经济单位职工人数	Employed by Urban Collective Enterprises	0.05
(3)其他经济类型单位职工人数	Employed by Other Units	0.10
(4)城镇个体或私营企业主人数	Personnel of Urban Individual Business	0.10
(5)城镇个体或私营企业被雇人数	Employed by Self-Employers	0.22
(6)离退休再就业人员数	Re-Employed Resigned and Retired Personnel	0.07
(7)其它就业人员数	Others	0.11
2.离退休人数	Resigned and Retired	0.56
3.其它有收入者人数	Others	0.03
（二）无收入者人数	Family Members Without Income	0.68
三、非家庭人口在家用餐人次数	**None-Family Members Eating At Home**	**4.91**
（人次/户）	**(Person-Times/Household)**	
四、家庭人口在外用餐人次数	**Family Members Eating Outside**	**9.77**
（人次/户）	**(Person-Times/Household)**	

8-6 城镇居民家庭年人均收入情况（2012年）

Statistics on Per Capita Annual Income of Urban Residents（2012）

单位：元 （yuan）

项　　目	Iterm	总平均 Total
一、家庭总收入	**Total Family Income**	**32032**
#可支配收入	Disposable Income	29982
（一）工薪收入	Income from Wages and Salaries	20937
#工资及补贴收入	Wages and Subsidies	20564
（二）经营净收入	Net Income from Business	1843
（三）财产性收入	Income from Properties	971
#利息收入	Interest Income	126
出租房屋收入	House Rents	594
（四）转移性收入	Transfer Income	8281
#养老金或离退休金	Pensions	6859
提取住房公积金	Withdrawal of Housing Funds	72
记帐补贴	Book-Keeping Allowances	209
二、出售财物收入	**Income from Sales Of Property**	**33**
（一）出售住房收入	Sales of Housing	29
（二）出售其它物品收入	Sales of Other Properties	4
三、借贷收入	**Income For Savings and Credit**	**9998**

8-7 城镇居民家庭年人均支出情况（2012年）

Statistics on Per Capita Annual Living Expenditure of Urban Households（2012）

单位：元 （yuan）

项　　目	Item	总平均 Total
一.家庭总支出	**Total Expenditures**	**26524**
（一）消费支出	Consumption Expenditures	21434
#服务性消费支出	Consumption on Service	5992
1.食品	Food	6961
2.衣着	Clothing	2608
3.家庭设备用品及服务	Household Facilities,Articles and Service	1686
4.医疗保健	Health Care and Medical Service	1826
5.交通和通信	Transport and Communications	3056
6.教育文化娱乐服务	Education,Receration and Cultural Services	3072
7.居住	Residence	1816
8.杂项商品和服务	Miscellaneous Goods and Services	410
（二）购房与建房支出	Expenditures on House Purchasing/Construction	854
（三）转移性支出	Transfer Expenditures	2429
（四）财产性支出	Property Expenditures	38
（五）社会保障支出	Expenditures on Social Security	1769
二.借贷支出	**Expenditures on Loans and Debts**	**10953**

8-8 城镇居民家庭年人均消费性支出情况（2012年）

Statistics on Per Capita Annual Consumption Expenditure of Urban Households（2012）

单位：元 (yuan)

项　　目	Item	总平均 Total
消费支出（元）	**Consumption Expenditures**	**21434**
#服务性消费支出	Consumption on services	5992
食品	**Food**	**6961**
一. 粮油类	Grains and oil	856
1.粮食	Grain	534
2.淀粉及薯类	Starches and Tubers	66
3.干豆类及豆制品	Bean and Bean Products	88
4.油脂类	Oil or Fats	168
二. 肉禽蛋水产品类	Meat,Poultry,Egg and Aquatic Products	1146
1.肉类	Meat	696
2.禽类	Poultry	148
3.蛋类	Egg	109
4.水产品类	Aquatic Products	193
三. 蔬菜类	Vegetables	602
1.鲜菜	Fresh Vegetables	543
2.干菜	Dried Vegetables	41
3.菜制品	Vegetable Products	18
四. 调味品	Flavouring	112
五. 糖烟酒饮料类	Sugar,Tobacco,Liquor and Beverage	863
1.糖类	Sugar	66
2.烟草类	Tobacco	363
3.酒类	Liquor	252
4.饮料	Beverage	182
六. 干鲜瓜果类	Dried and Fresh Melons &Fruits	651
七. 糕点、奶及奶制品	Cakes, Milk and Processed Products	523
1.糕点	Cakes	191
2.奶及奶制品	Milk and Its Products	332
八. 其它食品	Other Food	241
九. 饮食服务	Catering Services	1967
1.食品加工服务费	Charge for Food Processing Services	4
2.在外饮食	Foods Consumed outside	1963

8-8 续表1 continued 1

单位：元 (yuan)

项目	Item	总平均 Total
非食品类	**Non-food**	
一. 衣着	**Clothing**	**2608**
（一）服装	Garments	1855
（二）衣着材料	Cloth Materials	24
（三）鞋类	Shoes	617
（四）其它衣着用品	Others	101
（五）衣着加工服务费	Tailoring and Laundering	11
二. 家庭设备用品及服务	**Household Facilities,Articles and Services**	**1686**
（一）耐用消费品	Durable Consumer Goods	726
1.家具	Furniture	231
2.家庭设备	Household Facilities	495
（二）室内装饰品	Interior Decorations	51
（三）床上用品	Bed Articles	149
（四）家庭日用杂品	Daily Use Household Articles	643
（五）家具材料	Furniture Materials	25
（六）家庭服务	Household Services	92
三. 医疗保健	**Medicine and Medical Services**	**1826**
（一）医疗器具	Medical Appliances and Articles	14
（二）保健器具	Health Care Articles	70
（三）药品费	Medicines	719
（四）滋补保健品	Tonic	166
（五）医疗费	Medical Care Services	823
（六）其他	Others	34
四. 交通和通讯	**Transportation ,Post and Telecommumication Services**	**3056**
（一）交通	Trasportation	2185
1.家庭交通工具	Family Vehicles	1193
2.车辆用燃料及零配件	Fuel and Accessories	405
3.交通工具服务支出	Expenditure on Maintenance of Vehicles	235
4.交通费	Transport Servi	352

8-8 续表2 continued 2

单位：元 (yuan)

项　目	Item	总平均 Total
（二）通信	Telecommumication	871
1.通信工具	Telecommunication Tools	261
2.通信服务	Telecommunication Services	610
五. 教育文化娱乐服务	**Recreation,Culture and Education Services**	**3072**
（一）文化娱乐用品	Recreating Goods	648
（二）文化娱乐服务	Recreation and Culture Services	1152
（三）教育	Education	1272
六. 居住	**Residence**	**1816**
（一）住房	Housing	694
1.租赁房房租	House Renting	87
2.住房装潢支出	Home Decorate Expenditure	446
3.维修用建筑材料	Building Material for Repair	88
4.其他	Others	73
（二）水电燃料及其它	Water,Electricity,Fuel and Others	939
1.水	Water	88
2.电	Electricity	338
3.燃料	Fuel	205
4.取暖费	Heating Cost	274
5.其他	Others	34
（三）居住服务费	Cost on Housing Service	183
1.物业管理费	Housing Management	156
2.维修服务费	Expenditures on House Maintenance	11
3.其它	Others	16
七. 杂项商品和服务	**Miscellaneous Commodities and Services**	**410**
（一）杂项商品	Miscellaneous Commodities	284
1.金银珠宝饰品	Jewel	118
2.手表	Watches	14
3.理发美容用具	Hair-care	9
4.化妆品	Cosmetics	97
5.其它杂品	Others	46
（二）服务	Services	126
1.旅馆住宿费	Rent for Hotels	24
2.理发洗澡费	Hair-cutting and Bathing	36
3.美容费	Cosmetic	30
4.其它服务	Others	36

8-9 主要年份城镇居民家庭年人均购买主要商品数量

商品名称	Name of Commodities	2000	2001	2002	2003
食用植物油（市斤）	Vegetable Oil(500g)	10	9.1	9.9	9.4
猪　肉（市斤）	Pork (500g)	13.7	12	12.9	13.6
牛　肉（市斤）	Beef(500g)	1.7	1.6	1.4	1.5
羊　肉（市斤）	Mutton (500g)	0.7	0.5	0.8	1.0
鸡（市斤）	Chicken (500g)	4.4	3.6	3.7	4.0
鲜　蛋（市斤）	Eggs (500g)	12.3	10.8	11.4	11.9
鱼（市斤）	Fish(500g)	3.7	3.8	4.5	5.2
鲜　菜（市斤）	Fresh Vegetables (500g)	107	104.5	112.3	109.7
白　酒（市斤）	Liquor(500g)	0.9	1.0	1.0	1.0
果　酒（市斤）	Fruit Wine (500g)	0.2	0.3	0.3	0.2
啤　酒（市斤）	Beer (500g)	3.0	3.6	4.7	4.0
糕　点（市斤）	Cake(500g)	4.6	4.2	4.8	5.3
鲜乳品（市斤）	Fresh Dairy Products (500g)	12	12.8	18.9	21.8
奶　粉（市斤）	Milk Powder (500g)	0.6	0.6	0.6	0.7
服　装(件)	Clothes(unit)	5.1	5.6	6.6	6.5
鞋(双)	Shoes(pair)	2.4	2.5	2.6	2.7
水（吨）	Water(ton)	25.7	24.5	28.6	28.8
电（度）	Electricity (degree)	307.5	309.7	390.8	385.3
煤　炭(公斤)	Coal (kg)	62	61.7	51.8	45.1
罐装液化石油气（公斤）	Liquified Petroleum Gas (kg)	17.9	14.5	13.3	12.2
管道天燃气（立方米）	Piping Gas (cu.m)	26.1	26.4	35.1	39

Per Capita Annual Purchases of Principal Goods in Urban Household in Representative Years

2004	2005	2006	2007	2008	2009	2010	2011	2012
9.4	12.3	10.1	10.2	11.5	10.2	9.5	9.7	167.2
12.5	15	13.6	12.8	19	12.6	13.1	12.9	13.9
2.0	2.6	2.4	1.9	2.1	2.7	3.2	3.3	2.7
1.1	1.1	0.8	0.8	0.7	1.0	1.1	1.0	1.0
3.5	5.0	3.8	4.1	6.3	4.2	4.4	4.6	4.3
10.4	14.1	11.8	11.1	13.2	10.7	11	11.1	11.2
4.3	5.6	4.6	5.3	6.1	5.0	5.1	5.5	5.1
113.4	132.5	110.9	113.9	126.5	111.7	111.7	113.1	118
1.4	1.3	1.3	1.5	0.9	1.1	1.2	1.1	1.1
0.2	0.2	0.3	0.2	0.2	0.3	0.4	0.4	0.4
4.0	6.5	6.3	4.6	3.8	5.2	5.3	4.8	3.8
5.4	6.6	5.9	6.5	11.3	8.1	8.2	7.9	8.0
20.4	28	25	25.3	16.9	19.6	20.2	19.7	19.7
0.7	0.6	0.5	0.7	0.9	0.6	0.6	0.5	1.0
6.8	6.9	7.1	9.0	6.9	8.7	9.2	9.3	10.5
2.8	2.8	2.8	2.8	3.2	4.2	3.7	3.9	3.9
26.5	26.1	22.9	22.8	22.2	27.1	28.4	27.2	30.4
435.6	449.5	444.9	460.6	439.3	523.1	589.9	591.8	606.8
51.4	33.9	46	66.5	70.4	34.3	30.5	21.9	28.3
12.7	9.8	7.5	6.9	8.1	7.5	5.6	4.8	3.4
38.4	58.2	46.4	38.8	33.2	45.2	54.2	70.4	77.8

8-10 城镇居民家庭居住情况（2012年）

Conditions of Dwellings of Urban Households（2012）

住房情况	Accommodation data	2012
一、家庭居住人口数（人/户）	**Number of Persons Per Household(person/household)**	**2.75**
二、现住房总建筑面积（平方米/人）	**Building Area of Living Houses(sq.m/person)**	**32.98**
三、房屋产权（合计）（%）	**Proportion of Property Right of Houses(%)**	
租赁公房	Public Houses Rent	5.93
租赁私房	Private Houses Rent	5.28
原有私房	Originally Self-owned Houses	2.84
房改私房	Present Self-owned Houses	39.84
商品房	Commercial Houses	37.55
其他	Others	8.56
四、住宅建筑式样（合计）（%）	**Proportion of Patterns of Residential Building(%)**	
单栋住宅	Flats With Complete Facilities	2.24
四居室	4 Rooms	3.15
三居室	3 Rooms	37.41
二居室	2 Rooms	50.22
一居室	1 Rooms	3.49
普通楼房	Ordinary Storeyed Building	3.03
平房及其他	Single-storey Houses and Others	0.46
五、装修状况（合计）（%）	**Proportion of Decoration Condition(%)**	
有装修	Decorated	73.67
未装修	Undecorated	26.33
如果装修过，最近一次装修花费（元/户）	Expenditure of Latest Decoration(yuan/household)	30140.99
六、现有住房按市场价估计值（元/户）	**Estimated Market Price of Present Houses(yuan/household)**	**359937.93**
七、租赁房房租（元/户）	**Expenditure of Rent Houses(yuan/household)**	**72.77**
八、现住房房租折算（元/户）	**Rent of Self-owned Houses(yuan/household)**	**1046.48**
九、购房总金额（元/户）	**Total Expenditure on Purchase of Houses(yuan/household)**	**117776.23**
购房实际支出金额	Expenditure on Purchase Practice of Houses	111282.56
十、饮水情况（合计）（%）	**Proportion of Water Drinking(%)**	
自来水	Tap Water	93.43
矿泉水	Mineral Water	2.70
纯净水	Pure Water	3.54
井、河水	Well Water and River Water	0.26
其他	Others	0.07

8-10 续表 continued

住房情况	Accommodation data	2012
十一、用水情况（合计）（%）	**Proportion of Water Use Condition(%)**	
独用自来水	Moloply Use of Tap Water	98.42
公用自来水	Public Tap Water	1.12
井、河水	Well Water and River Water	0.46
其他	Others	
十二、卫生设备（合计）（%）	**Proportion of Sanitary Facilities(%)**	
无卫生设备	Without Sanitary Facilities	0.33
有厕所浴室	With Bathroom and Lavatory	90.77
有厕所无浴室	With Lavatory but without Bathroom	7.58
公用	Common-used Sanitary Facilities	1.32
十三、取暖设备（合计）（%）	**Proportion of Heating Facilities(%)**	
无取暖设备	Without Heating Facilities	4.54
空调设备	Air-conditioner	16.27
暖气	Central Heating	68.28
其他	Others	10.92
十四、炊用燃料使用情况（合计）（%）	**Proportion of Cooking Fuels(%)**	
管道天燃气	Pipeline Gas	68.24
罐装液化石油	Liquefied Gas	18.83
煤炭	Coal	9.57
其他燃料	Others	2.27
十五、除了现住房，还有几处其它住房（套/户）	**Other Living Houses besides Present Living House (unit/household)**	0.24
出租房	Houses for Rent	0.15
偶尔居住房	Houses Seldom Living in	0.05
其它用途房	Houses for other Purposes	0.03

8-11 城镇居民家庭每百户主要耐用消费品年末拥有量

商品名称	Commodity Names	2000	2001	2002	2003
摩托车（辆）	Motorcycle (unit)	5.0	6.0	8.7	10.2
家用汽车（辆）	Car (unit)			0.3	0.3
洗衣机（台）	Washing Machine (unit)	96.7	97.7	97.3	95.7
电冰箱（台 ）	Refrigerator (unit)	91.0	91.3	95.7	91.8
彩色电视机（台）	Color TV Set (unit)	124.0	123.7	128.3	127.0
家用电脑（台）	Computer (unit)	11.7	15.7	19.0	23.9
组合音响（套）	Hi-Fi System (set)	16.7	19.3	23.0	22.9
摄像机（台）	Pick-up Camera (unit)	1.0	0.3	1.0	1.7
照相机（架）	Camera (set)	46.3	47.3	48.0	48.3
钢琴（架）	Piano (set)	1.3	0.3	1.7	2.0
其它中高档乐器（件）	Other High-Grade Musical Instruments (unit)	2.3	3.7	6.7	5.9
微波炉（台）	Oven (unit)	18.0	27.7	39.3	42.2
空调器（台）	Air Conditioner (unit)	51.3	54.3	75.0	82.4
淋浴热水器（台）	Shower(unit)	52.3	52.3	63.7	70.0
健身器材（件）	Health Care Equipment (unit)	3.3	3.0	1.7	2.6
消毒碗柜（台）	Disinfecting Cupboard(unit)			1.7	4.7
洗碗机（台）	Dishwasher (unit)				
固定电话（部）	Telephone (unit)	81.3	86.0	88.0	87.1
移动电话（部）	Hand Telephone (unit)	7.6	19.3	48.3	74.4

Number of Durable Consumer Goods Owned Every 100 Urban Households in Representative Years

2004	2005	2006	2007	2008	2009	2010	2011	2012
9.1	8.6	8.9	5.4	7.9	7.6	8.0	8.3	11.0
0.3	0.6	0.9	2.0	4.0	9.0	13.3	16.7	24.3
98.3	101.1	101.1	98.9	95.3	98.8	100.3	100.8	100.4
91.2	90.9	94.4	95.7	89.2	95.0	97.1	97.7	96.5
134.0	134.0	136.0	134.5	119.9	126.7	128.7	129.9	122.5
31.7	20.3	37.1	45.6	54.0	68.8	76.1	82.0	86.2
20.0	34.0	20.6	24.8	19.0	25.2	27.7	28.0	22.7
1.1	3.1	4.3	4.8	7.7	9.7	11.1	11.8	12.0
44.3	49.7	47.7	50.1	39.9	52.1	57.7	62.0	65.3
2.0	1.4	1.7	1.1	2.4	2.4	2.7	2.5	3.0
7.1	11.4	12.9	6.0	4.7	5.3	5.3	5.8	7.4
47.1	52.0	52.9	56.4	52.7	62.1	66.4	68.4	66.2
92.6	99.7	102.9	116.0	104.0	119.7	129.5	135.1	146.7
74.9	110.3	71.4	74.1	70.9	79.9	82.3	84.1	91.8
2.9	6.9	3.4	4.0	4.3	4.8	5.0	5.5	6.6
7.1	29.4	6.0	7.4	5.5	7.8	8.5	8.9	8.6
			0.6	0.6	0.3	0.8	0.8	1.3
85.7	88.0	79.1	75.2	67.4	72.8	71.5	69.9	60.9
102.0	119.7	144.3	162.3	162.1	185.3	196.4	207.1	226.0

8-12 主要年份农村居民家庭基本情况

指 标	Item	1998	1999	2000
一、调查户数(户)	**Households Surveyed(household)**	**460**	**460**	**500**
二、调查人口(人)	**Residents Surveyed(person)**			
1. 常住人口	Average Number of Permanent Residents	2028	2024	2147
2. 整半劳动力	Average Number Able-bodied and Semi-able-bodied Laborers Per Households	1279	1296	1371
3. 平均每个劳动力负担人口	Persons Supported by Each Laborers	1.59	1.56	1.57
三、平均每人全年收入(元)	**Per Capita Annual Income(yuan)**			
1. 总收入	Total Revenue	2597.24	2711.55	2929.23
2. 纯收入	Net Income	2052.07	2202.73	2343.76
3. 现金收入	Cash Income	2087.96	2288.00	2513.14
4. 可支配收入	Disposable Income			2225.13
四、按人均纯收入分组(%)	**Grouped by Per Capita Annual Net Income(%)**			
户数占总户数比重	Percentage of Households			
1000元以下	Below 1000 yuan			
1000-2000元	1000-2000 yuan			
2000-3000元	2000-3000 yuan			
3000-4000元	3000-4000 yuan			
4000-5000元	4000-5000 yuan			
5000元以上	Over 5000 yuan			
五、农民家庭房屋情况	**Rural Household Housing Condition**			
1. 年末人均住房价值(元)	Average Value of Living House Per Capita of Year-end(yuan)	4813.50	4850.32	5398.21
2. 年末人均住房面积(平方米)	Average Floor Space of Living House Per Capita at Year-end(sq.m)	27.32	26.80	28.31
3. 年内人均新建房屋面积(平方米)	Percapita Space of Building Newly Built Within the year (sq.m)	1.33	2.03	1.58
4. 年内人均新建房屋价值(元)	Percapita Value of Building Newly Built Within the Year(yuan)	308.01	304.40	408.07
六、生活消费支出总计(元)	**Per Capita Living Expenditure Built(yuan)**	**1564.81**	**1492.43**	**1605.36**
1.食品消费支出	Food	663.75	584.18	587.97
2.衣着	Clothing	120.76	112.83	106.80
3.居住	Residence	327.56	247.45	343.71
4.家庭设备用品及服务	Household Facilities,Articles and Services	87.43	97.79	87.89
5.医疗保健	Medical and Health Care Services	72.72	94.60	111.25
6.交通通讯	Transport and Communications	51.99	62.45	67.51
7.文化娱乐用品及服务	Culture,Educational and Recreational Articles and Services	196.96	230.09	232.61
8.其它商品及服务	Other Commodities and Services	43.64	63.04	67.62

Basic Indicators of Rural Households In Representative Years

2001	2002	2003	2004	2005	2006	2007	2008	2009	2010	2011	2012
770	**770**	**750**	**710**	**720**	**700**	**700**	**900**	**940**	**940**	**940**	**930**
3214	3212	3102	2920	3040	2935	2924	3628	3828	3704	3732	3801
2008	2017	1993	1873	1904	1841	1863	2422	2557	2469	2570	2621
1.60	1.59	1.56	1.56	1.60	1.59	1.57	1.50	1.50	1.50	1.50	1.50
3185.54	3370.82	3571.71	3889.12	4495.44	4968.93	5605.12	6746.04	7961.26	9737	11910	14087
2490.27	2641.44	2837.83	3142.78	3459.60	3808.38	4398.64	5212.14	6275.22	7750	9788	11442
2747.00	2965.92	3042.02	3299.16	3940.24	4466.49	4969.58	6249.34	7297.58	9265	11278	13719
2357.30	2560.58	2729.88	3021.25	3353.43	3562.80	4167.18	4983.23	6008.41	7369		10727
	11.69	10.00	5.49	5.14	3.57	2.57	1.89	1.70	1.06		
	28.57	26.67	22.40	18.33	14.57	7.57	7.33	3.83	2.45		
	27.92	26.00	28.45	25.00	22.43	15.14	13.78	7.98	5.74		
	15.45	16.13	19.30	20.70	19.43	21.00	13.00	12.55	6.91		
	5.97	10.00	9.01	11.94	13.57	17.72	14.00	12.87	11.28		
	10.40	11.20	15.35	18.89	26.43	36.00	50.00	61.07	72.55		
6286.53	6883.06	7354.40	7780.97	9052.30	10878.22	13145.27	20476.11	24500.32	32059	37103	56470
29.72	32.54	33.90	34.66	36.73	40.05	42.92	54.97	56.73	67	63	78
1.81	2.20	0.98	1.13	1.13	1.82	2.03	1.80	2.62	4	2	3
475.33	484.18	239.47	309.07	365.97	746.64	787.03	784.68	1349.27	2380	1591	2641
1676.42	**1782.14**	**1802.75**	**2276.65**	**2602.68**	**2708.87**	**3380.80**	**3938.09**	**4771.06**	**5633**	**6705**	**7774**
567.62	553.78	677.03	812.47	945.76	996.75	1289.61	1455.22	1708.35	1833	2138	2630
105.53	115.02	113.15	133.97	159.09	174.81	205.85	256.92	305.46	369	483	577
409.90	444.92	314.04	478.37	462.21	488.47	768.16	763.44	928.87	1375	1604	1703
74.29	83.64	98.59	104.93	133.11	152.83	191.26	276.61	332.52	368	476	580
115.92	136.18	128.47	173.89	213.04	216.67	257.14	316.95	405.62	481	580	688
88.83	115.14	143.45	191.89	213.12	236.97	256.27	308.85	469.06	476	604	792
241.31	275.38	296.80	340.88	420.45	387.51	352.98	489.68	531.23	631	699	793
73.02	58.08	31.22	40.25	55.90	54.86	59.53	70.42	89.95	100	121	11

8-13 主要年份农村居民家庭人均总收入和纯收入

单位：元

指 标	Item	2005	2006
一、全年总收入	**Annul Total Revenue**	**4495.44**	**4968.92**
1. 工资性收入	Wages Income	1292.69	1498.79
2. 家庭经营收入	Household Business Income	2612.18	2799.09
3. 财产性收入	Property Income	330.42	388.00
4. 转移性收入	Transfer Income	260.15	283.04
二、全年纯收入	**Annul Net Income**	**3459.60**	**3808.38**
1. 工资性收入	Wages Income	1292.69	1498.79
2. 家庭经营纯收入	Household Business Net Income	1629.54	1661.10
（1）第一产业收入	Income from Primary Industry	982.81	992.79
（2）第二产业收入	Income from Secondary Industry	143.16	166.33
（3）第三产业收入	Income from Tertiary Industry	503.57	501.98
3. 财产性收入	Property Income	330.42	388.00
4. 转移性收入	Transfer Income	206.95	260.49

Per Capita Annual Total Revenue and Net Income of Rural Households In Representative Years

(yuan)

2007	2008	2009	2010	2011	2012
5605.13	**6746.04**	**7961.25**	**9736.93**	**11910**	**14087**
1751.84	2161.42	2587.24	3307.61	4282	4946
3063.28	3595.63	4109.86	4734.60	5347	6599
449.52	553.35	738.95	1025.49	1417	1637
340.49	435.64	525.20	669.23	864	906
4398.64	**5212.14**	**6275.22**	**7750.35**	**9788**	**11442**
1751.84	2161.42	2587.24	3307.61	4282	4946
1887.68	2092.35	2469.83	2826.61	3413	4133
1168.79	1232.01	1431.38	1532.79	1740	1794
177.99	241.48	257.74	290.73	375	591
540.90	618.86	780.71	1003.09	1298	1749
449.52	553.35	738.95	1025.49	1418	1637
309.60	405.02	479.20	590.64	675	726

8-14 全市及各区县农村居民家庭人均总收入和纯收入(2012年)

单位：元

指 标	Item	西安市 Xi'an	灞桥区 Baqiao	未央区 Weiyang
一、全年总收入	**Annual Total Revenue**	**14087**	**15066**	**17082**
1. 工资性收入	Income from Wages and Salaries	4946	6065	6326
2. 家庭经营收入	Income from Household Operations	6599	4997	3405
3. 财产性收入	Income from Properties	1637	2889	6033
4. 转移性收入	Income from Transfers	905	1115	1318
二、全年纯收入	**Annual Net Income**	**11442**	**13278**	**14562**
1. 工资性收入	Wages Income	4946	6065	6326
2. 家庭经营纯收入	Household Business Net Income	4133	3321	1425
（1）第一产业收入	Income from Primary Industry	1794	-511	38
（2）第二产业收入	Income from Secondary Industry	591	1212	314
（3）第三产业收入	Income from Tertiary Industry	1748	2620	1073
3. 财产性收入	Property Income	1637	2889	6033
4. 转移性收入	Transfer Income	726	1003	778
三、可支配收入	**Disposable Income**	**10727**	**12673**	**13483**

Per Capita Annual Total Revenue and Net Income of Rural Households in Whole City and Regions(2012)

(yuan)

雁塔区 Yanta	阎良区 Yanliang	临潼区 Lintong	长安区 Chang'an	蓝田县 Lantian	周至县 Zhouzhi	户 县 Huxian	高陵县 Gaoling
16052	**20315**	**13635**	**12800**	**8844**	**9922**	**13680**	**12785**
5715	3804	5130	5830	4230	2956	5179	4657
3321	14389	7051	5298	4070	6314	7753	6203
6618	886	226	427	-65	242	38	1122
398	1236	1228	1245	609	410	710	803
14800	**13403**	**10685**	**11107**	**7824**	**7733**	**9654**	**10673**
5715	3804	5130	5830	4230	2956	5179	4657
2091	7681	4345	3787	3192	4231	3908	4192
-1	4009	2834	754	1748	2915	1991	1298
1417	880	463	220	462	410	248	479
675	2792	1048	2813	982	906	1669	2415
6618	886	226	427	-65	242	38	1122
376	1032	984	1063	467	304	529	702
13839	**12772**	**10040**	**10481**	**7523**	**7044**	**8681**	**9989**

8-15 全市及各区县农村居民家庭基本情况（2012年）

指　标	Item	西安市 Xi'an	灞桥区 Baqiao	未央区 Weiyang
一、调查户数（户）	**Number of Households Surveyed (household)**	**930**	**100**	**80**
二、常住人口（人）	**Permanent Residents(person)**	**3801**	**417**	**321**
1. 6岁及以下	6 Year-old and Below	223	26	32
2. 7-15岁人口	7-15 Year-old	345	40	25
3. 16-60岁人口	16-60 Year-old	2781	311	247
4. 61岁以上人口	61 Year-old and Above	452	40	17
三、整半劳动力(人)	**Able-bodied and Semi-able-bodied Labourer(person)**	**2621**	**278**	**225**
四、常住人口外出从业人数(人)	**Permanent Residents Employed in Other Places Outside(person)**	**531**	**60**	**18**
五、劳动力文化程度(人)	**Labourer Literacy(person)**	**2133**	**237**	**164**
1. 不识字或识字很少	Illiterates or Semi-illiterates	22	1	6
2. 小学文化程度	Primary Schools	194	14	2
3. 初中文化程度	Junior Secondary Schools	1190	126	90
4. 高中程度	Senior Secondary Schools	479	54	32
5. 中专程度	Specialized Secondary Schools	102	13	14
6. 大专及以上	Universities and Colleges and Above	146	29	20
六、人均耕地经营面积（亩）	**Area of Cultivated Land Managed per Capita(mu)**	**0.83**	**0.56**	**0.01**

Basic Conditions of Rural Households in Whole City and Regions(2012)

雁塔区 Yanta	阎良区 Yanliang	临潼区 Lintong	长安区 Chang'an	蓝田县 Lantian	周至县 Zhouzhi	户 县 Huxian	高陵县 Gaoling
80	**80**	**100**	**100**	**90**	**100**	**100**	**100**
295	**334**	**437**	**377**	**331**	**457**	**417**	**415**
18	11	24	20	17	26	19	30
22	34	37	40	37	40	34	36
241	254	314	256	228	337	313	280
14	35	62	61	49	54	51	69
217	**214**	**316**	**245**	**241**	**315**	**305**	**265**
32	**17**	**128**	**12**	**46**	**50**	**90**	**78**
127	**63**	**292**	**217**	**231**	**266**	**304**	**232**
		1	3	2	2	7	0
1	2	47	40	21	32	26	9
53	30	173	117	166	128	166	141
37	28	57	37	29	79	62	64
13	2	6	13	7	8	17	9
23	1	8	7	6	17	26	9
	1.1	**1.35**	**1.02**	**1.05**	**1.24**	**0.7**	**0.89**

8-16 全市及各区县农村居民家庭人均全年总支出（2012年）

单位：元

指　标	Item	西安市 Xi'an	灞桥区 Baqiao	未央区 Weiyang
全年总支出	**Annual Total Expenditure**	**10964**	**10003**	**14658**
一、家庭经营费用支出	**Expenditure for Household Business**	**2146**	**808**	**1657**
#农业支出	Farming	1100	351	1
牧业支出	Animal Husbandry	383	315	
二、购置生产用固定资产支出	**Purchasing Productive Fixed Assets**	**141**	**28**	**1**
三、建造生产性固定资产雇工支出	**Expenditure on Labor Hiring on Building of Productive Fixed Assets**	**3**		
四、税费支出	**Expenditure for Tax and Fee**	**5**		**1**
五、生活消费支出	**Expenditure for Living Consumption**	**7774**	**8449**	**11382**
六、财产性支出	**Expenditure for Property**	**4**		
七、转移性支出	**Expenditure for Transfer**	**891**	**718**	**1617**

8-17 全市及各区县农村居民家庭人均生产情况（2012年）

单位：公斤

指　标	Item	西安市 Xi'an	灞桥区 Baqiao	未央区 Weiyang
粮食产量	Output of Grain	676		
#小麦	Wheat	346		
玉米	Corn	324		
大豆	Soybean	2		
棉花产量	Output of Cotton	6		
油料产量	Output of Oil-bearing Crops			
蔬菜产量	Output of Vegetables	177		
水果产量	Output of Fruits	86		

Per Capita Annual Total Expenditure of Rural Households in Whole City and Regions(2012)

(yuan)

雁塔区 Yanta	阎良区 Yanliang	临潼区 Lintong	长安区 Chang'an	蓝田县 Lantian	周至县 Zhouzhi	户 县 Huxian	高陵县 Gaoling
12021	**15724**	**12702**	**9848**	**6499**	**8725**	**11515**	**8665**
617	**6708**	**2490**	**1394**	**731**	**1839**	**3365**	**1847**
1	6473	993	879	356	1015	417	839
	218	455	66	86	37	2261	98
6	**2**	**657**	**14**	**186**	**213**	**146**	**26**
				39	**1**		
		1		**3**	**21**	**12**	**3**
10415	**8178**	**8665**	**7633**	**5098**	**5857**	**6837**	**6004**
	14	**9**			**16**		
983	**822**	**880**	**807**	**442**	**778**	**1155**	**785**

Output of Major Farm Crops Per Capita by Rural Householdsin Whole City and Regions(2012)

(kg)

雁塔区 Yanta	阎良区 Yanliang	临潼区 Lintong	长安区 Chang'an	蓝田县 Lantian	周至县 Zhouzhi	户 县 Huxian	高陵县 Gaoling
	3164	649	542	912	174	745	790
	1642	318	288	464	78	385	405
	1498	307	253	448	96	360	386
					13		
	65						
	912	234			14	17	606
	32	61			564	62	4

8-18 全市及各区县农村居民家庭人均出售产品情况（2012年）

单位：公斤

指　标	Item	西安市 Xi'an	灞桥区 Baqiao	未央区 Weiyang
粮食	Grain	402	31	
棉花	Cotton	6		
油料	Oil-bearing Corps			
蔬菜	Vegetables	194		
水果	Fruits	140	182	11
肉猪及猪肉	Fattened Hogs & Pork	29		
菜牛及牛肉	Beef Cattle & Beef	1		
菜羊及羊肉	Mutton Sheep & Mutton			
蛋类	Poultry Eggs			
奶类	Milks	23	36	

8-19 全市及各区县农村居民家庭人均粮食收支情况（2012年）

单位：公斤

指　标	Item	西安市 Xi'an	灞桥区 Baqiao	未央区 Weiyang
一、粮食收入合计	**Total Grain Income**	**783**	**175**	**106**
1. 家庭经营生产	Self-produced	677	1	
2. 购入	Purchased	104	174	105
3. 借入	Borrowed			
4. 收回借出粮	Grains Taken Back	2		
5. 其它粮食收入	Other Grain Income			1
二、粮食支出合计	**Total Grain Expenditure**	**579**	**206**	**105**
1. 主食用粮	Staple Food	144	101	105
2. 其它生活用粮	Other Living Uses			
3. 出售	Sold Out	402	31	
4. 种籽	Seeds	10	8	
5. 饲料	Fodder	23	66	
6. 借出	Lent Out			
7. 归还借粮	Grains Returned			
8. 其它粮食支出	Other Grain Expenditure			
三、年末粮食结存调查数	**Year-end Grain Deposite Balance**	**196**	**77**	**15**

Per Capita Product Sold by Rural Households in Whole City and Regions(2012)

(kg)

雁塔区 Yanta	阎良区 Yanliang	临潼区 Lintong	长安区 Chang'an	蓝田县 Lantian	周至县 Zhouzhi	户 县 Huxian	高陵县 Gaoling
	921	803	401	517	293	224	738
	71						
	918	332	24	15	32	15	600
	21	59	6	40	831	60	4
	30	21		6	27	180	3
	2			6			
				1			
			3				
	97	78	5	2			4

Per Capita Annual Income and Expenditure of Grains of Rural Households in Whole City and Regions(2012)

(kg)

雁塔区 Yanta	阎良区 Yanliang	临潼区 Lintong	长安区 Chang'an	蓝田县 Lantian	周至县 Zhouzhi	户 县 Huxian	高陵县 Gaoling
93	**3263**	**739**	**600**	**976**	**280**	**906**	**896**
	3162	649	542	912	193	747	790
93	101	83	58	64	87	159	106
		7					
93	**1203**	**920**	**606**	**825**	**418**	**460**	**881**
93	225	109	187	293	119	125	115
	921	803	401	517	294	224	738
	37	8	8	10	3	6	16
	20	0	10	5	2	105	12
	179	**483**	**189**	**379**	**159**	**203**	**196**

8-20　全市及各区县农村居民家庭人均购买商品（2012年）

单位：元

商品名称	Commodity Names	西安市 Xi'an	灞桥区 Baqiao	未央区 Weiyang
一、食品	Food	1786	2175	2613
二、衣着类	Clothing	575	673	803
三、居住	Residence	1133	1070	2555
四、家用设备和日用品	Household Facilities and Articles	552	485	567
五、交通、通讯类	Transport,post and Telecommunication	545	676	568
六、文教	Cultural and Edueation	279	151	261
七、医疗保健类	Health Care and Medical Services	215	149	266
八、其他杂项商品	Other Commodities and Services	122	99	171

8-21　全市及各区县农村居民家庭人均主要食品消费量（2012年）

单位：公斤

食品名称	Food Names	西安市 Xi'an	灞桥区 Baqiao	未央区 Weiyang
一、粮食	Grain	144	101	105
#小麦	Wheet	103	43	82
二、油脂类	Oil or Fat	9	12	8
三、蔬菜及菜制品	Vegetable and Its Products	191	88	92
四、瓜果类	Melons and Fruits	19	10	19
五、水果类	Fruits	29	20	32
六、肉禽及制品	Meat,Poultry and Their Products	11	14	14
七、蛋类及蛋制品	Eggs and Its Products	7	8	8
八、奶及奶制品	Milk and Dairy Products	10	10	14
九、酒	Liquor	5	4	5

Per Capita Purchase of Commodities in Rural Households in Whole City and Regions(2012)

(yuan)

雁塔区 Yanta	阎良区 Yanliang	临潼区 Lintong	长安区 Chang'an	蓝田县 Lantian	周至县 Zhouzhi	户 县 Huxian	高陵县 Gaoling
3080	1457	1594	1515	1248	1356	1363	1877
901	685	615	431	348	463	525	424
460	899	1783	999	977	905	1253	457
603	1100	817	494	287	320	541	378
334	754	891	570	333	593	311	345
374	1079	324	155	65	112	209	199
325	95	352	151	343	151	196	161
310	61	137	105	47	130	82	117

Per Capita Average Food Consumption of Rural Households in Whole City and Regions(2012)

(kg)

雁塔区 Yanta	阎良区 Yanliang	临潼区 Lintong	长安区 Chang'an	蓝田县 Lantian	周至县 Zhouzhi	户 县 Huxian	高陵县 Gaoling
93	225	109	187	293	119	125	115
55	154	83	114	235	97	95	89
9	9	10	9	9	8	8	9
93	1297	86	93	59	90	53	99
11	17	11	7	5	11	10	86
28	18	15	124	9	13	18	21
17	10	9	11	8	11	14	9
8	7	6	6	6	8	5	7
15	6	12	12	9	5	8	9
7	6	5	6	3	3	3	5

8-22 全市及各区县农村居民家庭每百户耐用消费品年末拥有量（2012年）

指 标	Item	西安市 Xi'an	灞桥区 Baqiao	未央区 Weiyang
大型家具（件）	Large Furnitures (unit)			
洗衣机(台)	Washing Machine(unit)	99	91	110
电风扇（台）	Electric Fan(unit)			
电冰箱（台）	Refrigerator(unit)	79	90	99
空调机（台）	Air Conditioner(unit)	69	66	141
热水器（台）	Water Heater(unit)	71	74	95
自行车(辆)	Bicycle (unit)	117	90	93
摩托车(辆)	Motorcycle(unit)	36	17	10
生活用汽车（辆）	Automobile(unit)	18	18	54
电话机（部）	Telephone (unit)	298	283	358
移动电话（部）	Mobile Phone(unit)	255	244	285
彩色电视机（台）	Color TV Set(unit)	125	106	151
黑白电视机（台）	Black-white TV Set(unit)	2	1	
影碟机（台）	Video Disc Player (unit)	37	54	16
照相机（架）	Camera(set)	21	25	16
家用计算机(台)	Computer(unit)	45	47	90

8-23 全市及各区县农村居民家庭人均住房情况（2012年）

指 标	Item	西安市 Xi'an	灞桥区 Baqiao	未央区 Weiyang
一、年末住房面积（平方米）	**Floor Space of Houses at the End of Year (sq.m)**	**78**	**111**	**176**
二、住房类型（平方米）	**Pattern of Houses(sq.m)**	**78**	**111**	**176**
1. 楼房面积	Floor Space of Storied Building	66	110	174
2. 砖瓦平房面积	Floor Space of Single-storey Building	12	1	2
3. 其它	Others			
三、年末住房价值（元）	**Value of Houses at the End of Year (yuan)**	**56470**	**57434**	**104903**
四、年内新建（购）房屋面积（平方米）	**Floor Space Of Newly-Built Purchased Houses (sq.m)**	**3**	**11**	
年内新建（购）房屋价值（元）	Value of Houses of Newly-Built Purchased (yuan)	2641	10576	

Year-end Possession of Durable Consumer Goods Per 100 Rural Households in Whole City and Regions(2012)

雁塔区 Yanta	阎良区 Yanliang	临潼区 Lintong	长安区 Chang'an	蓝田县 Lantian	周至县 Zhouzhi	户 县 Huxian	高陵县 Gaoling
93	101	100	92	93	102	102	109
100	85	82	72	38	55	81	97
143	54	44	35	9	22	84	109
100	89	57	63	18	56	86	82
71	129	119	128	68	120	186	146
9	53	60	37	22	74	30	39
43	6	8	11	3	8	9	25
395	269	278	231	241	281	344	323
314	244	244	214	183	259	292	275
153	140	79	126	106	123	143	140
8	0	1	1	3	0	2	
48	31	51	20	24	32	56	37
83	13	7	16	4	3	36	19
103	43	12	31	13	19	55	52

Per Capita Housing Conditions of Rural Households in Whole City and Regions (2012)

雁塔区 Yanta	阎良区 Yanliang	临潼区 Lintong	长安区 Chang'an	蓝田县 Lantian	周至县 Zhouzhi	户 县 Huxian	高陵县 Gaoling
225	**68**	**46**	**51**	**42**	**41**	**49**	**73**
225	**68**	**46**	**51**	**42**	**41**	**49**	**73**
225	62	13	43	19	29	47	48
	6	33	8	23	12	2	25
222306	**550525**	**21848**	**45002**	**30133**	**33767**	**21912**	**32457**
4		**2**	**5**		**2**	**2**	**5**
2224		1505	3628		2515	1128	3199

主要统计指标解释

一、城镇住户

城镇家庭人口 指居住在一起，经济上合在一起共同生活的家庭成员。凡计算为家庭人口的成员其全部收支都包括在本家庭中。

城镇就业面 指就业人口占家庭人口的百分比。

城镇就业者负担人数 指家庭人口与就业人口之比。

城镇家庭总收入 指家庭成员得到的工薪收入、经营净收入、财产性收入、转移性收入之和，不包括出售财物收入和借贷收入。

城镇家庭可支配收入 指家庭成员得到可用于最终消费支出和其它非义务性支出以及储蓄的总和，即居民家庭可以用来自由支配的收入。它是家庭总收入扣除交纳的个人所得税、个人交纳的社会保障支出以及记账补贴后的收入。计算公式为：

可支配收入=家庭总收入—交纳个人所得税—个人交纳的社会保障支出—记账补贴

城镇家庭总支出 指除借贷支出以外的全部家庭支出。包括消费性支出、购房建房支出、转移性支出、财产性支出、社会保障支出。

城镇家庭消费性支出 指家庭用于日常生活的支出，包括食品、衣着、居住、家庭设备用品及服务、医疗保健、交通和通信、娱乐教育文化服务、其他商品和服务等八大类支出。

恩格尔系数 指食物支出金额在消费性总支出金额中所占的比例。计算公式为：

$$恩格尔系数=\frac{食品支出金额}{消费性总支出金额}\times 100\%$$

二、农村住户

农村住户 指农村常住户。农村常住户指长期（一年以上）居住在乡镇（不包括城关镇）行政管理区域内的住户，以及长期居住在城关镇所辖行政村范围内的农村住户。户口不在本地而在本地居住一年及以上的住户也包括在本地农村常住户范围内；有本地户口，但举家外出谋生一年以上的住户，无论是否保留承包耕地都不包括在本地农村住户范围内。

常住人口 指全年经常在家或在家居住6个月以上，而且经济和生活与本户连成一体的人口。外出从业人员在外居住时间虽然在6个月以上，但收入主要带回家中，经济与本户连为一体，仍视为家庭常住人口；在家居住，生活和本户连成一体的国家职工、退休人员也为家庭常住人口。但是现役军人、中专及以上（走读生除外）的在校学生、以及常年在外（不包括探亲、看病等）且已有稳定的职业与居住场所的外出从业人员，不算家庭常住人口。家庭常住人口主要作为计算农村住户平 每人收入、消费和积累水平及分析家庭人口状况的依据。

整、半劳动力 整劳动力指男子18周岁到50周岁，女子18周岁到45周岁；半劳动力指男子16周岁到17周岁，51周岁到60周岁；女子16周岁到17周岁，46周岁到 55周岁，同时具有劳动能力的人。虽然在劳动年龄之内，但已丧失劳动能力的人，不应算为劳动力；超过劳动年龄，但能经常参加劳动，计入半劳动力数内。常住人口中的职工，若这些职工为劳动力，就包括在本户的整半劳动力中。

总收入 指调查期内农村住户和住户成员从各种来源渠道得到的收入总和。按收入的性质划分为工资性收入、家庭经营收入、财产性收入和转移性收入。

工资性收入 指农村住户成员受雇于单位或个人，靠出卖劳动而获得的收入。

家庭经营收入 指农村住户以家庭为生产经营单位进行生产筹划和管理而获得的收入。农村住户家庭经营活动按行业划分为农业、林业、牧业、渔业、工业、建筑业、交通运输业邮电业、批发和零售贸易餐饮业、社会服务业、文教卫生业和其他家庭经营。

财产性收入 指金融资产或有形非生产性资产的所有者向其他机构单位提供资金或将有形非生产性资产供其支配，作为回报而从中获得的收入。

转移性收入 指农村住户和住户成员无须付出任何对应物而获得的货物、服务、资金或资产所有权等，不包括无偿提供的用于固定资本形成的资金。一般情况下，是指农村住户在二次分配中的所有收入。

现金收入 指农村住户和住户成员在调查期内得到以现金形态表现的收入。按来源分成工资性收入、家庭经营现金收入、财产性收入、转移性收入。

纯收入 指农村住户当年从各个来源得到的总收入相应地扣除所发生的费用后的收入总和。计算方法：

纯收入＝总收入—税费支出—家庭经营费用支出—生产性固定资产折旧—赠送农村内部亲友支出

纯收入主要用于再生产投入和当年生活消费支出，也可用于储蓄和各种非义务性支出。 “农民人纯收入”是按人口平 的纯收入水平，反映的是一个地区农村居民的平 收入水平。

总支出 指农村住户用于生产、生活和再分配的全部支出。包括家庭经营费用支出、购置生产性固定资产支出、税费支出、生活消费支出、财产性支出和转移性支出。

Explanatory Notes on Main Statistical Indicators

I. Urban Households

Population of Urban Households refer to members of households living and sharing economically together in the urban areas. All the income and expenditure of all the members of such households are included in the income and expenditure of the household.

Proportion of Urban Employment refers to the proportion of employed population to the population of urban households.

Number of Dependents per Urban Employee refers to the ratio between number of persons in an urban household and the number of employed persons.

Total Income of Urban Households refers to the sum of wage and salary; net business income; income from properties; and income from transfers of members of the households. Income from selling of properties and income from borrowing are not included..

Disposable Income of Urban Households refers to the actual income at the disposal of members of the households which can be used for final consumption, other non-compulsory expenditure and savings. This equals to total income minus income tax, personal contribution to social security and subsidy for keeping diaries in being a sample household. The following formula is used:

Disposable income = total household income - income tax - personal contribution to social security - subsidy for keeping diaries for a sampled household

Total Expenditure of Urban Households refers to all expenditure of households except expenditure on lending. It includes expenditure on consumption; on purchasing or building houses; on transfers; on properties; and on social security.

Consumption Expenditure of Urban Households refers to total expenditure of households for consumption in daily life, including expenditure on the eight categories of food; clothing; housing; household appliances and services; health care and medical services; transport and communications; recreation, education and cultural services; and miscellaneous goods and services.

Expenditure of Urban Households on Consumption of Services refers to expenditure of households on various kinds of non-commercial services provided by society.

Engel's Coefficient refers to the percentage of expenditure on food in the total consumption expenditure, using the following formula:

$$\text{Engel's Coefficient} = \frac{\text{expenditure on food}}{\text{total consumption expenditure}} \times 100\%$$

II. Rural Household

Rural Households refer to usual resident households in rural areas. Usual resident households in rural areas are households residing on a long term basis(for more than one year) in the areas under the administration of township governments (not including county towns), and in the areas under the administration of villages in county towns. Households residing in the current addresses for over one year with their household registration in other places are still considered as resident households of the locality. For households with their household registration in one place but all members of the households having moved away to make a living in another place for over one year, they will not be included in the rural households of the area where they are registered, irrespective of whether they still keep their contracted land.

Usual Resident Population refers to persons staying at home regularly or for over 6 months during a year and integrated with the household economically and in terms of living.. Members of the household staying away from the household for over 6 months but keeping a close economic relation with the household by sending the majority of income to the household are regarded as usual resident of the household. Government staff and workers or retirees living as close members of the household are also considered as usual resident. However, servicemen, students of secondary technical schools or schools of higher education and persons with stable jobs and residence outside the household (excluding those visiting relatives or seeking medical service) are not included as resident population of the household. Resident population is used in calculating incomc, consumption, accumulation on per capita basis of rural households and in analyzing composition of rural households.

Full/Semi Labour Force Full labour force refers to persons capable of work, aged 18-50 for males and 18-45 for females. Semi labour force refers to persons capable of work, aged 16-17 and 51-60 for males and 16-17 and 46-55 for females. Persons at their working ages but not capable of work are not to be included as labour force. Persons not at working ages but participating regularly in work are included in semi labour force. For staff and workers who are usual residents, are included as full or semi labour force of the household if they are in the labour force.

Total Income refers to the sum of income earned from various sources by the rural households and their members during the reference period, and is classified as income from wages and salaries, income from household operations, income from properties and income from transfers.

Income from Wages and Salaries refers to income from labour earned by the members of rural households employed by other units or individuals.

Income from Household Operations refers to income by the rural households as units of production and operation. Operations by rural households are classified according to their economic activities namely agriculture, forestry, animal husbandry, fishery, manufacturing, construction, transportation, post and telecommunications, wholesale, retail and catering, social service, culture, education, health, and other household operations.

Income from Properties refers to the income received as returns by owners of financial assets or tangible non-productive assets by providing capitals or tangible non-productive assets to other institutional units.

Income from Transfers refers to the receipt by rural households and their members of goods, services, capital or rights of assets without giving or repaying accordingly, excluding capital provided to them for the formation of fixed assets. In general, it refers to all income received by rural households through redistribution.

Cash Income refers to income received by rural households and their members in the form of cash during the reference period. It is classified, by source of income, into income from wages and salaries, cash income from household operations, income from properties and income from transfers.

Net Income refers to the total income of rural households from all sources minus all corresponding expenses. The formula for calculation is as follows:

Net income = total income - taxes and fees paid - household operation expenses - taxes and fees depreciation of fixed assets for production - gifts to non-rural relatives

Net income is mainly used as input for reinvestment in production and as consumption expenditure of the year, and also used for savings and non-compulsory expenses of various forms. "Per capita net income of farmers" is the level of net income averaged by population, reflecting the average income level of rural households in a given area.

Total Expenditure refers to total expenses of rural households on production, consumption and redistribution, including expenditure on household operations; purchase of productive fixed assets; taxes and fees; expenses on household consumption; expenses on properties; and expenses on transfers.

9 城市公用事业

URBAN PUBLIC UTILITIES

资料整理：郝 静

Data management:Hao jing

第九部分 城市公用事业

一、简要说明

本章资料主要包括城市供水、供燃气、供热、公共交通、市政设施、市政设施水平、城市规模及用地状况、园林绿地、环境卫生等情况，由西安市统计局社会科技处根据西安市建委、市交通局及地铁办提供的数据整理。

二、主要指标

人均公园绿地面积（平方米）	10.22	比上年同口径增长	9.9%
人均城市道路面积（平方米）	17.54	比上年同口径增长	10.5%
用水普及率（%）	100	比上年同口径增加	
燃气普及率（%）	98.19	比上年同口径增加	0.69个百分点

9 URBAN PUBLIC UTILITIES

Ⅰ.Brief Introduction

Data in this chapter reflects basic condition of urban public utilities of Xi'an City. Data on public utilities primarily consist of urban water supply, gas sales, urban heating, public transportation, municipal facilities, level of municipal construction, scale of the city, condition of land utilization, parks, greenbelt and environmental sanitation. Data in this chapter is compiled by Social Science & Technology Division of Xi'an Bureau of Statistics according to the data provided by Committee of Urban Construction of Xi'an, Xi'an Burean of Transportation and Xi'an Metro office.

Ⅱ.Major Indicators

		Increase over Preceding Year
Per Capita Public Green Areas (sq.m)	10.22	9.9%
Per Captia Area of Roads (sq.m)	17.54	10.5%
Water-Consuming Popularization (%)	100	
Gas-Consuming Popularization (%)	98.19	0.69 percentage points

9-1 城市供水

Urban Water Supply

指　标	Item	2000	2008	2009	2010	2011	2012
年末水厂个数（个）	Number of Water Factory at Year-end (units)	8	9	9	9	15	15
供水综合生产能力（万立方米/日）	Total Volume of Water Supply (10 000 cu.m/day)	139.9	180.5	190.0	197.4	197.4	200.33
# 地下水	Groundwater	73.9	52.4	55.3	55.8	54.8	57.04
年末供水管道总长度（公里）	Length of Water Supply Pipelines at Year-end (kms)	2237	2385	1985	2416	2721	3208
全年供水总量（万立方米）	Total Annual Volume of Water Supply (10 000 cu.m)	30273	36471	38307	41089	38934	45792
#生产运营用水	For Productive Use	6486	6292	6414	6267	5484	5334
居民家庭用水	For Residential Use	10949	17510	18513	20944	19945	24704
用水人口（万人）	Population with Access to Tap Water (10 000 persons)	257.0	374.1	357.6	410.9	394.1	406.32

注：本表数据来源于市建委。
2009年部门统计制度变化，年末供水管道总长度和用水人口数调整。
2010年后数据为全市口径，2009年以前数据为市区口径。

9-2 城市供燃气

Gas Supply in Urban Area

指　标	Item	2000	2008	2009	2010	2011	2012
一、天然气	**Natural Gas**						
管道长度（公里）	Total Length of Gas Pipelines (km)	480	3540	3932	4488	4500	5075.19
供气总量（万立方米）	Total Gas Supply(10 000 cu.m)	11513	84874	95885	109052	120330	142263
#家庭用量	Residential Households	2808	13767	15473	20989	22868	27760.63
用气人口（万人）	Population with Access to Gas (10 000 persons)	79.5	246.7	285.0	333.0	356.0	371.54
二、液化石油气	**Liquefied Petroleum Gas**						
供气总量（吨）	Total Gas Supply (tons)	43304	74164	74913	11469	5920	4529.70
# 家庭用量	Residential Households	43303	46342	46275	7376	4352	4254
用气人口（万人）	Population with Access to Gas (10 000 persons)	101.6	81.9	50. 5	31.2	28.6	27.44

注：本表数据来源于市建委。
2010年后数据为全市口径，2009年以前数据为市区口径。

9-3 城市供热

Heating in Urban Area

指 标	Item	2000	2008	2009	2010	2011	2012
供热能力	Heating Capacity						
蒸气（吨/小时）	Steam (tons/hour)	766	1063	2118	2235	2075	3073. 00
热水（兆瓦）	Hot Water (megawatts)	405	11085	11467	3531	4570	5401. 94
供热总量(万吉焦)	Volume Supplied (10 000 gigajoules)						
蒸气	Steam	126	1192	1541	1674	1421	1616.98
热水	Hot Water	202	896	1220	2570	2901	2443.57
管道长度（公里）	Length of Pipelines (km)						
蒸气	Steam	221	97	209	180	167	187.07
热水	Hot Water	133	179	289	361	500	516.18
供热面积（万平方米）	Heated Area (10 000sq.m)	854	3179	5178	6094	6524	8512.84
#住宅	Residential Buildings	536	2616	4325	5009	5226	7328.16

注：本表数据来源于市建委。
2010年后数据为全市口径，2009年以前数据为市区口径。

9-4 城市公共交通

Urban Public Traffic

指 标	Item	2000	2008	2009	2010	2011	2012
运营车辆（辆）	Operating Vehicles (units)	2573	6123	7039	7107	7462	7695
标准运营车辆（标台）	Standard Vehicles (units)	2509	6416	7833	8139	8598	8925.6
公交客运总量（万人次）	Total of Bus Passenger(10 000 person-times)	44570	139924	161782	162400	175234	175241
公交客运收入（万元）	Bus Passenger Transport Income (10 000 yuan)				129397	141505	135505
出租汽车数（辆）	Number of Taxis (units)	10277	11879	12786	12786	13839	14139
地铁运营线路长度（公里）	Length of Subway Lines in Operation(km)						19.87
地铁客运量（万人次）	Total of Subway Passenger(10 000 person-times)						5911.64

注：本表数据来源于市交通局和地铁办。

9-5 市政设施

Municipal Facilities

指　标	Item	2000	2008	2009	2010	2011	2012
一、道路长度（公里）	**Length of Roads (km)**	**975**	**2115**	**2296**	**2662**	**2755**	**3119.30**
二、道路面积（万平方米）	**Area of Roads (10 000 sq.m)**	**1263**	**4722**	**5057**	**5965**	**6259**	**7126.56**
三、人行道面积（万平方米）	**Area of Sidewalks (10 000 sq.m)**	**636**	**1470**	**1517**	**1834**	**1867**	**2105.31**
四、桥梁数（座）	**Number of Bridges (units)**	**79**	**305**	**314**	**347**	**402**	**422**
#立交桥	Overpasses	22	71	71	71	91	97
五、路灯盏数（盏）	**Number of Street Lights (units)**	**27516**	**266442**	**271444**	**291754**	**311991**	**329881**
六、排水管道长度（公里）	**Length of Drainage Pipelines (km)**	**835**	**2562**	**2848**	**3765**	**4043**	**4435.92**
七、污水年排放量（万立方米）	**Annual Discharge Volume of Sewage (10 000 cu.m)**	**23543**	**21886**	**31394**	**34706**	**36673**	**40302.70**
八、污水处理厂处理能力（万立方米/日）	**Daily Disposal Capacity of Sewage (10 000 cu.m/day)**	**29**	**77.5**	**80**	**106.5**	**111.6**	**128.1**
九、污水年处理量（万立方米）	**Yearly Disposal Capacity of Sewage Disposal Plant (10 000 cu.m)**	**5441**	**13003**	**20386**	**25088**	**31512**	**35463**
十、防洪堤长度（公里）	**Length of Flood Control Dikes (km)**	**1.6**	**119**	**119**	**168**	**168**	**188**

注：本表数据来源于市建委。
2010年后数据为全市口径，2009年以前数据为市区口径。

9-6 城市设施水平

Urban Municipal Facilities

指　标	Item	2000	2008	2009	2010	2011	2012
一、人均日生活用水量（升）	**Per Capita Daily Consumption of Tap Water For Residential Use (liters)**	**241.5**	**179.7**	**198.4**	**186.2**	**185.2**	**220.96**
二、用水普及率(%)	**Water-Consuming Popularization (%)**	**99**	**111.2**	**100**	**98.8**	**100**	**100**
三、每万人拥有公共交通车辆（标台）	**Number of Public Transport Vehicles Per 10 000 Population (units)**	**10.2**	**19.1**	**22.9**	**23.8**	**21.8**	**22.4**
四、燃气普及率(%)	**Gas-Consuming Popularization (%)**	**81.5**	**97.7**	**98.2**	**97**	**97.5**	**98.19**
五、人均城市道路面积（平方米）	**Per Captia Area of Roads (sq.m)**	**5.1**	**14**	**14.8**	**15.4**	**15.9**	**17.54**
六、建成区排水管道密度（公里/平方公里）	**Density of Drainage Pipelines in Developed Areas (km/sq.km)**	**4.5**	**8**	**10.1**	**9.5**	**9.7**	**9.83**
七、污水处理率(%)	**Rate of Sewerage Disposal (%)**	**23.1**	**65.1**	**81**	**84**	**85.9**	**89.51**
八、园林绿化	**Afforestation and Parks and Gardens**						
人均公园绿地面积（平方米）	Per Capita Public Green Areas (sq.m)	5.1	7.8	7.9	9.1	9.9	10.22
建城区绿地率（%）	Rate of Green Areas in Developed Areas (%)	19.7	31.9	40.4	29.2	30.9	31.2
九、生活垃圾无害化处理率(%)	**Rate of No Harm Disposal of Garbage (%)**	**90.9**	**90.4**	**90.3**	**93.9**	**93.7**	**94.93**

注：本表数据来源于市建委。
由于用水人口包括不在城市辖区内但已经使用城市供水的人口，故有些年份用水普及率有大于100%。
2010年后数据为全市口径，2009年以前数据为市区口。

9-7 城市规模及用地情况

City Scale and Land Use

单位：平方公里 (sq.km)

指　标	Item	2000	2008	2009	2010	2011	2012
建成区面积	Area of the Constructed Regions	187	273	283	395	415	451.38
城市建设用地	Land use for Construction	175	370	277	336	349	376.39

注：本表数据来源于市建委。
2010年后数据为全市口径，2009年以前数据为市区口径。

9-8 城市园林绿化

Urban Parks,Gardens and Green Areas in Cities

指　标	Item	2000	2008	2009	2010	2011	2012
一、公园个数（个）	**Number of Parks (units)**	**47**	**54**	**55**	**68**	**66**	**72**
二、公园面积（公顷）	**Area of Parks (hectares)**	**880**	**1233**	**1241**	**1335**	**1478**	**1529**
三、园林绿地面积（公顷）	**Total Area of Parks,Gardens and Green Areas (hectares)**	**4116**	**9199**	**9553**	**12140**	**13680**	**15196**
#公园绿地面积	Public Green Areas	1263	2625	2700	3526	3898	4154
四、年末绿化覆盖面积（公顷）	**Coverage Space of Green Areas at year-end (hectares)**	**6542**	**11616**	**12059**	**15646**	**17325**	**19017**
五、建成区绿化覆盖率（%）	**Coverage of Green Areas in Developed Areas (%)**	**33.3**	**40.3**	**40.4**	**37.5**	**38.96**	**39.53**

注：本表数据来源于市建委。
2006年统计制度变化，"公共绿地面积"改为"公园绿地面积"。
2010年数据为全市口径，2009年以前数据为市区口径。

9-9 城市环境卫生

Urban Environment Sanitation

指 标	Item	2000	2008	2009	2010	2011	2012
清扫面积（万平方米）	Area Under Cleaning Program (10 000 sq.m)	1739	4218	5285	6290	6411	6952
清运生活垃圾（万吨）	Volume of Residential Garbage Disposal (10 000 tons)	98	152	179	237	265	287.32
清运粪便（万吨）	Volume of Excrement and Urine Disposal (10 000 tons)	5	4	3	3	4	2.99
公共厕所（座）	Number of Public Lavatories (units)	430	1131	1131	1257	1493	1594
市容环卫专用车辆（台）	Special Vehicles of Environmental Sanitation (units)	330	716	939	1042	1200	1279

注：本表数据来源于市建委。
2010年后数据为全市口径，2009年以前数据为市区口径。

9-10 市区及县供水（2012年）

Urban Water Supply (2012)

指 标	Item	西安 Xi'an	市区 City	蓝田 Lantian	周至 ZhouZhi	户县 Huxian	高陵 GaoLing
年末水厂个数（个）	Number of Water Factory at Year-end (units)	15	11	1	1	1	1
供水综合生产能力（万立方米/日）	Total Volume of Water Supply (10 000 cu.m/day)	200.33	190.17	2.6	1.8	3.12	2.64
# 地下水	Groundwater	57.04	54.55		1.8	0.55	0.14
年末供水管道总长度（公里）	Length of Water Supply Pipelines at Year-end (km)	3207.73	2788.88	113	50	75.85	180
全年供水总量（万立方米）	Total Annual Volume of Water Supply (10 000 cu.m)	45791.8	43848.1	578.77	441.9	684.19	238.80
#生产运营用水	For Productive Use	5334.28	5123.35	56.99	11.42	132.52	10
居民家庭用水	For Residential Use	24703.7	23484.7	284.3	347	416.35	171.40
用水人口（万人）	Population with Access to Tap Water (10 000 persons)	406.32	353.42	14.43	8.05	16.54	13.88

注：本表数据来源于市建委。
2009年部门统计制度变化，年末供水管道总长度和用水人口数调整。

9-11 市区及县供燃气（2012年）

Gas Supply in Urban Area (2012)

指 标	Item	西安 Xi'an	市区 City	蓝田 Lantian	周至 ZhouZhi	户县 Huxian	高陵 GaoLing
一、天然气	**Natural Gas**						
管道长度（公里）	Total Length of Gas Pipelines (km)	5075.19	4881.17	31	30	54	79.02
供气总量（万立方米）	Total Gas Supply(10 000 cu.m)	142263	138050	658.53	2.65	1300	2252
#家庭用量	Residential Households	27760.6	25293.1	590	2.55	375	1500
用气人口（万人）	Population with Access to Gas (10 000 persons)	371.54	353.41	2.22	1.2	7.94	6.77
二、液化石油气	**Liquefied Petroleum Gas**						
供气总量（吨）	Total Gas Supply (tons)	4529.7		1500.2	1175.5	1485	369
# 家庭用量	Residential Households	4254		1275	1172	1456	351
用气人口（万人）	Population with Access to Gas (10 000 persons)	27.44		7.22	5.8	8.02	6.40

注：本表数据来源于市建委。

9-12 市区及县供热（2012年）

Heating in Urban Area (2012)

指 标	Item	西安 Xi'an	市区 City	蓝田 Lantian	周至 ZhouZhi	户县 Huxian	高陵 GaoLing
供热能力	Heating Capacity						
蒸气（吨/小时）	Steam (tons/hour)	3073	2843			230	
热水（兆瓦）	Hot Water (megawatts)	5401.94	5062.94				339
供热总量(万吉焦)	Volume Supplied(10 000 gigajoules)						
蒸气	Steam	1616.98	1583.98			33	
热水	Hot Water	2443.57	2323.59				119.98
管道长度（公里）	Length of Pipelines (km)						
蒸气	Steam	187.07	175.07			12	
热水	Hot Water	516.18	493.28				22.9
供热面积（万平方米）	Heated Area (10 000sq.m)	8512.84	8216.78			50	246.06
#住宅	Residential Buildings	7328.16	7040.84			50	237.32

注：本表数据来源于市建委。

9-13 市区及县市政设施（2012年）

Municipal Facilities in Urban Area (2012)

指 标	Item	西安 Xi'an	市区 City	蓝田 Lantian	周至 ZhouZhi	户县 Huxian	高陵 GaoLing
一、道路长度（公里）	Length of Roads (km)	3119.3	2829.47	66.8	34	105.44	83.59
二、道路面积（万平方米）	Area of Roads (10 000 sq.m)	7126.56	6332.79	112.56	74	338.14	269.07
三、人行道面积（万平方米）	Area of Sidewalks (10 000 sq.m)	2105.31	1849.75	50.12	32	84.57	88.87
四、桥梁数（座）	Number of Bridges (units)	422	404	10	2	3	3
#立交桥	Crossroads	97	92			3	2
五、路灯盏数（盏）	Number of Street Lights (units)	329881	308969	1576	4500	6076	8760
六、排水管道长度（公里）	Length of Drainage Pipelines (km)	4435.92	4022.04	66.72	42.48	116.68	188
七、污水年排放量（万立方米）	Annual Discharge Volume of Sewage (10 000 cu.m)	40302.7	38188	463.5	344	1140	167.2
八、污水处理厂处理能力（万立方米/日）	Daily Disposal Capacity of Sewage (10 000 cu.m/day)	128.1	121.5	1.5	1.1	3	1
九、污水年处理量（万立方米）	Yearly Disposal Capacity of Sewage Disposal Plant (10 000 cu.m)	35463	33797	345	258	944	119
十、防洪堤长度（公里）	Length of Flood Control Dikes (km)	188	139	20	22		7

注：本表数据来源于市建委。

9-14 市区及县市政设施水平(2012年）

Urban Municipal Facilities in Urban Area (2012)

指 标	Item	西安 Xi'an	市区 City	蓝田 Lantian	周至 ZhouZhi	户县 Huxian	高陵 GaoLing
一、人均日生活用水量（升）	Per Capita Daily Consumption of Tap Water For Residential Use (liters)	220.96	241.76	93.26	142.09	79.65	38
二、用水普及率(%)	Water-Consuming Popularization (%)	100	100	100	100	100	100
三、每万人拥有公共交通车辆（标台）	Number of Public Transport Vehicles Per 10 000 Population (units)	22.4					
四、燃气普及率（%）	Gas-Consuming Popularization (%)	98.19	100	65.42	86.96	96.49	94.88
五、人均城市道路面积（平方米）	Per Captia Area of Roads (sq.m)	17.54	17.92	7.8	9.19	20.44	19.39
六、建城区排水管道密度(公里/平方公里)	Density of Drainage Pipelines (km/sq.km)	9.83	10.73	5.56	4.45	5.11	5.88
七、污水处理率(%)	Rate of Sewerage Disposal (%)	89.51	90.1	74.43	75	82.81	71.17
八、园林绿化	Afforestation and Parks and Gardens						
人均公园绿地面积（平方米）	Per Capita Public Green Areas (sq.m)	10.22	10.8	3.74	11.3	5.44	7.2
建城区绿地率（%）	Rate of Green Areas in Developed Areas(%)	31.2	33.3	17.58	17.07	26.72	19.09
九、生活垃圾无害化处理率(%)	Rate of No Harm Disposal of Garbage (%)	94.93	99.84			100	100

注：本表数据来源于市建委。

主要统计指标解释

供水综合生产能力 指按供水设施取水、净化、送水、出厂输水干管等环节设计能力计算的综合生产能力。包括在原设计能力的基础上，经挖、革、改增加的生产能力。计算时，以四个环节中最薄弱的环节为主确定能力。

年末供水管道长度 指从送水泵至用户水表之间所有管道的长度。不包括新安装尚未使用、水厂内以及用户建筑物内的管道。

全年供水总量 指报告期供水企业（单位）供出的全部水量。包括有效供水量和漏损水量。

生活用水量 包括公共服务用水和居民家庭用水。公共服务用水指为城市社会公共生活服务的用水。包括行政事业单位、部队营区和公共设施服务、社会服务业、批发零售业、住宿餐饮业以及其他公共服务业等单位的用水。居民家庭用水指城市范围内所有居民家庭的日常生活用水。包括城市居民、农民家庭、公共供水站用水。

用水普及率 指城市用水人口数与城市人口总数的比率。计算公式：

$$\text{用水普及率}=\frac{\text{城市用水人口数}}{\text{城市人口总数}}\times 100\%$$

供气管道长度 指报告期末从气源厂压缩机的出口或门站出口至各类用户引入管之间的全部已经通气投入使用的管道长度。不包括煤气生产厂、输配站、液化气储存站、灌瓶站、储配站、气化站、混气站、供应站等厂（站）内的管道。

全年供气总量 指全年燃气企业（单位）向用户供应的燃气数量。包括销售量和损失量。

燃气普及率 指报告期末使用燃气的城市人口数与城市人口总数的比率。计算公式为：

$$\text{燃气普及率}=\frac{\text{城市使用燃气人口数}}{\text{城市人口总数}}\times 100\%$$

城市供热能力 指供热企业（单位）向城市热用户输送热能的设计能力。

城市供热总量 指在报告期供热企业（单位）向城市热用户输送全部蒸汽和热水的总热量。

城市供热管道长度 指从各类热源到热用户建筑物接人口之间的全部蒸汽和热水的管道长度。不包括各类热源厂内部的管道长度。

年末道路长度 指年末道路长度和与道路相通的桥梁、隧道的长度，按车行道中心线计算。在统计时只统计路面宽度在3.5米（含3.5米）以上的各种铺装道路，包括开放型工业区和住宅区道路在内。

城市桥梁 指为跨越天然或人工障碍物而修建的构筑物。包括跨河桥、立交桥、人行天桥以及人行地下通道等。按使用年限分为永久性桥和半永久性桥。

城市排水管道长度 指所有排水总管、干管、支管、检查井及连接井进出口等长度之和。

城市污水日处理能力 指 水处理厂（或 水处理装置）每昼夜处理 水量的设计能力。

城市园林绿地面积 指报告期末用作园林和绿化的各种绿地面积。包括公园绿地、生产绿地、防护绿地、附属绿地和其他绿地的面积。

公园绿地 城市中向公众开放的以游憩为主要功能，有一定的游憩设施和服务设施，同时兼有健全生态、美化景观、防灾减灾等综合作用的绿化用地。包括综合公园、社区公园、专类公园、带状公园和街旁绿地。其中综合公园、专类公园和带状公园面积之和为公园面积。

清扫保洁面积 指报告期末对城市道路和公共场所（主要包括城市行车道、人行道、车行隧道、人行过街地下通道、道路附属绿地、地铁站、高架路、人行过街天桥、立交桥、广场、停车场及其他设施等）进行清扫保洁的面积。一天清扫多次的，按清扫保洁面积最大的一次计算。

市容环卫专用车辆 指用于环境卫生作业、监察的专用车辆和设备，包括用于道路清扫、冲洗、洒水、除雪、垃圾粪便清运、市容监察以及与其配套使用的车辆和设备。

每万人拥有公共交通车辆 指报告期末城区内每万人平均拥有的公共交通车辆标台数。计算公式：

$$\text{每万人拥有公共交通车辆}=\frac{\text{公共交通运营车标台数}}{\text{城市人口总数}}$$

Explanatory Notes on Main Statistical Indicators

Production Capacity of Water Supply refers to the designed overall production capacity of water facilities, covering the four segments of water collection, purification, conveyance, and outflow through trunk pipelines. Increased capacity through transformation and innovation projects is included as well. The capacity is determined mainly on the weakest of the above-mentioned four segments.

Length of Water Supply Pipelines at Year–end refers to the total length of all the pipelines between the water pumps and the user water meters, excluding pipelines newly installed but not used yet, pipeline in the water factory,and pipeline in the user's buildings.

Annual Volume of Water Supply refers to the total volume of water supplied by water-works (units) during the reference period, including both the effective water supply and loss during the water supply.

Consumption of Water for Residential Use refers to water consumption of households for daily life and water consumption of public service facilities. The latter refers to water consumption for urban public services, including the consumption of government agencies and public institutions, military barracks, public facilities, wholesale and retail trades, accommodation and catering industry and other units providing public services. Household water consumption refers to consumption of water for daily life of all households within the boundary of cities, including households of urban residents and farmers, and public water supply stations.

Coverage Rate of Urban Population with Access to Tap Water refers to the ratio of the urban population with access to tap water to the total urban population. The formula is:

$$\text{Coverage of urban population with access to tap water} = \frac{\text{Urban population with access to tap water}}{\text{Urban population}} \times 100\%$$

Length of Gas Pipelines refers to the total length of pipelines in use between the outlet of the compressor of gas-work or outlet of gas stations and the leading pipe of users, excluding pipelines within gasworks, delivery stations, LPG storage stations, refilling stations, gas-mixing stations and supply stations.

Volume of Gas Supply refers to the total volume of gas provided to users by gas-producing enterprises (units) in a year, including the volume sold and the volume lost.

Coverage Rate of Urban Population with Access to Gas refers to the ratio of the urban population with access to gas to the total urban population at the end of the reference period. The formula is:

$$\text{Coverage rate of urban population with access to gas} = \frac{\text{Urban population with access to gas}}{\text{Urban population}} \times 100\%$$

Heating Capacity in Urban Areas refers to the designed capacity of heating enterprises (units) in supplying heating energy to urban users during the reference period.

Quantity of Heat Supplied in Urban Areas refers to the total quantity of heat from steam and hot water supplied to urban users by heating enterprises (units) during the reference period.

Length of Urban Heating Pipelines refers to the total length of steam or hot water pipelines for sources of heat to the leading pipelines of the buildings of the users, excluding internal pipelines in heat generating enterprises

Length of Paved Roads at Year–end refers to the length of roads with paved surface including bridges and tunnels connected with roads by the end of the year. Length of the roads is measured by the central lines for vehicles for paved roads with a width of 3.5 meters and over, including roads in open-ended factory compounds and residential quarters.

Urban Bridges refer to bridges built to cross over natural or man-made barriers, including bridges over rivers, overpasses for traffic and for pedestrians, underpasses for pedestrians, etc. Both permanent and semi-permanent bridges are included.

Length of Urban Sewage Pipes refers to the total length of general drainage, trunks, branch and inspection wells, connection wells, inlets and outlets, etc.

Daily Disposal Capacity of Urban Sewage refers to the designed 24-hour capacity of sewage disposal by the sewage treatment works or facilities.

Area of Parks and Green Land refers to the total area occupied for green projects at the end of the reference period, including park green land, production green land, protection green land, green land attached to institutions, and other green areas.

Park Green Area refers to green areas open to the public for amusement and rest with the facilities of amusement, rest and services. Its function includes perfecting ecology, beautifying landscape, and preventing and reducing disaster. Park green areas include comprehensive park, community park, topic park, belt- shaped park and green area nearby street. Total areas of comprehensive park, topic park and belt-shaped is the area of park.

Area Cleaned refers to the area which are regularly cleaned, as at the end of the reference period, at urban roads and public places (mainly including urban roadways, pedestrian walkways, vehicular tunnels, pedestrian underpasses, underground railway stations, lifted roads, pedestrians walk bridges, overpasses, plazas, carparks and other facilities). Ifthere are several times of cleaning in a day at a location, the area of that time of cleaning with the largest area cleaned will be taken.

Vehicles Dedicated to Urban Cleanliness and Environmental Sanitation refer to vehicles and facilities dedicated for use in the operation, management and monitoring of environmental hygiene work. They include vehicles for road cleaning, washing, showering, ice removal, disposal of garbage and human wastes, cleanliness monitoring and related activities.

Public Transportation Vehicles per 10000 Population refers to the number of public transportation vehicles, at the end of the reference period, per 10000 population in the city district. The formula for calculation is:

$$\frac{\text{PublicTransportation Vehicles}}{\text{per 10000 Population}} = \frac{\text{Number of Public Transportation Vehicles}}{\text{City District Population}}$$

10 环境保护

ENVIRONMENT PROTECTION

资料整理：郝　静
Data management:Hao Jing

第十部分　环境保护

一、简要说明

本章资料反映环境保护、工业污染排放及处理利用情况、危险废物集中处置情况、生活及其他污染情况和工业污染治理项目建设情况，由西安市统计局社会科技处根据西安市环保局提供的数据资料整理。

二、主要指标

工业用水重复利用率（%）	68.29	比上年增加	21.29个百分点
工业固体废物综合利用率（%）	95.92	比上年减少	1.38个百分点
全年环境空气达到二级以上天数（天）	306	比上年增加	1天

注：因2011年环保年报统计口径变化，故与往年不可比。

10 ENVIRONMENT PROTECTION

Ⅰ.Brief Introduction

This chapter contain information that reflect environment protection, discharge and treatment of industrial pollutant, centralized treatment of dangerous wastes, domestic pollution and other pollution, construction of projects of industrial pollution treatment. Data in this chapter is compiled by Social & Science and Technology Division of the Xi'an Bureau of Statistics according to the reported data from Environment Protection Administration department of the municipal government.

Ⅱ.Major Indicators

		Increase over Preceding Year
Percentage of Industrial Water Recycled (%)	68.29	21.29percentage points
Percentage of Industrial Solid Waste Utilized (%)	95.92	-1.38percentage points
Days of Air Quality up to the secondarylevels（day）	306	1

Note: Because of the 2011 annual report of environmental protection statistical caliber changed,it was not compared with previous years.

10-1　城市环境保护(2012年）

Urban Environmental Protection (2012)

指　标	Item	2012
一、饮用水环境	**Potable Water Environment**	
全市饮用水水质达标率(%)	Compliance Rate of the City's Potable Water Quality (%)	100
二、大气环境	**Atmospheric Environment**	
1、可吸入颗粒物浓度年平均值(毫克/立方米)	Annual Average Concentration of Particulate Matters(mg/cu.m)	0.118
二氧化硫浓度年平均值	Annual Average Concentration of Sulphur Dioxide	0.040
二氧化氮浓度年平均值	Annual Average Concentration of Nitrogen Dioxide	0.042
2、全年环境空气质量达标天数(天)	Days of Air Quality up to the Standards(days)	306
全年环境空气质量达标率(%)	Annual compliance rate of Ambient Air Quality(%)	83.61
三、声环境	**Voice**	
1、功能区噪声平均值(dB(A))	Average Noise Value of Functional Districts(dB(A))	60.0
0类区	Class 0	53.7
1类区	Class 1	56.9
2类区	Class 2	58.5
3类区	Class 3	64.4
4类区	Class 4	66.5
2、道路交通噪声平均值(dB(A))	Average Noise Value of Road Traffic(dB(A))	68.2
3、区域噪声平均值(dB(A))	Average Noise Value of Region(dB(A))	55.3
四、环境污染治理	**Environmental pollution treatment**	
当年完成环保验收项目环境保护投资（亿元）	Year Completed Investment in Environmental Protection Projects of Environmental acceptance(100 million yuan)	8.23

注：本表数据来源于市环保局。

10-2 主要年份工业“三废”排放及处理利用情况

指 标	Item	2000	2006	2007
一、工业废水排放量（万吨）	**Volume of Waste Water Discharge (10 000 tons)**	**9145**	**16389**	**19069**
工业废水处理量（万吨）	Volume of Industrial Wastewater Disposal (10 000 tons)			
废水治理设施数（套）	Number of Facilities for Treatment of Waste Water (sets)			
二、工业废气排放量（亿立方米）	**Total Volume of Industrial Waste Gas Emission (100 million cu.m)**	**275.97**	**642.51**	**1149.41**
废气治理设施数（套）	Number of Facilities for Treatment of Waste Gas(sets)		466	846
三、工业固体废物产生量（万吨）	**Volume of Industrial Solid Wastes Produced (10 000 tons)**	**107**	**161**	**193**
工业固体废物处置量（万吨）	Volume of Industrial Solid Wastes Treated (10 000 tons)	20	5	6
工业固体废物综合利用量（万吨）	Volume of Industrial Solid Waste Utilized (10 000 tons) in a Comprehensive Way	63	143	171
工业固体废物综合利用率（%）	Percentage of Volume of Industrial Solid Waste Utilized in a Comprehensive Way(%)	58.88	89.07	88.48
四、工业锅炉（台/蒸吨）	**Industrial Boilers (units/tons)**			

注：本表数据来源于市环保局。

2010年全国统一进行了污染源普查动态更新调查工作，“十二五”的环境统计体系与污染源普查体系相衔接，与“十一五”环境统计口径不同。

Discharge and Treatrment of Waste Gas, Water & Solid Wastes in Repersentative Years

2008	2009	2010	2011	2012
18304	**13168**	**13840.00**	**13148.00**	**10223.73**
		10673.52	12632.38	9089.04
		267	314	312
1519.18	**737.24**	**791.56**	**1018.46**	**1043.31**
920	852	816	745	649
220	**246**	**267.29**	**279.00**	**259.14**
5	4.85	3.56	6.00	9.24
215	241	262	271.00	248.58
97.78	97.83	98.05	97.30	95.92
		503/8785	**576/13466**	**567/14565**

10–3　工业污染排放及处理利用情况（2012年）

Discharge and Treatment of Industrial Pollution (2012)

指　标	Item	2012
一、被调查企业基本情况	**Basic condition of Enterprises investigated**	
1. 企业数（个）	Number of Enterprises (units)	483
2. 工业总产值（亿元）（当年价格）	Gross Industry Output Value (100 millian yuan)	2040.94
3. 工业锅炉数（台/蒸吨）	Industrial Boilers (units/tons)	567/14565
4. 工业炉窑数（座）	Number of Industrial Grates (items)	748
二、工业废水	**Industrial Waste Water**	
1. 工业用水总量（万吨）	Total Volume of Industrial Water (10 000 tons)	48643.35
#取水量	Volume of Fresh Water	15424.89
重复用水量	Volume of Water Recycled	33218.46
2. 工业用水重复利用率（%）	Percentage of Industrial Water Recycled (%)	68.29
3. 废水治理设施数（套）	Number of Facilities for Treatment of Waste Water (sets)	312
4. 废水治理设施处理能力（万吨/日）	Disposal Capacity of Facilities for Treatment of Waste Water (10 000 tons/day)	41.23
5. 废水治理设施运行费用（万元）	Operating Expense of Facilities for Treatment of Waste Water (10 000 yuan)	12323.50
6. 工业废水排放量（万吨）	Volume of Industrial Waste Water Discharged (10 000 tons)	10223.73
三、工业废气	**Industrial Waste Gas**	
1. 煤炭消费量（万吨）	Total Coal Consumption (10 000 tons)	837.65
2. 燃料油消费量（不含车船用）（万吨）	Fuel Oil Consumption (10 000 tons)	1.61
3. 天然气消费量（亿立方米）	Natural Gas Consumption (100 millian cu.m)	1.60
4. 工业废气排放总量（亿立方米）	Total Volume of Industrial Waste Gas Emission (100 millian cu.m)	1043.31
5. 废气治理设施数（套）	Number of Facilities for Treatment of Waste Gas (sets)	649
6. 废气治理设施处理能力（万立方米/时）	Disposal Capacity of Facilities for Treatment of Waste Gas (10 000 cu.m./h)	3124. 50
7. 废气治理设施设备运行费用（万元）	Operating Expense of Facilities for Treatment of Waste gas(10 000 yuan)	28076.10
8. 二氧化硫产生量（吨）	Volume of Sulphur Dioxide Removed (tons)	172845.26
9. 二氧化硫排放量（吨）	Volume of Sulphur Dioxide Emission (tons)	83062.90
10. 氮氧化物产生量（吨）	Production of nitrogen oxides(tons)	47392.70
11. 氮氧化物排放量（吨）	Nitrogen oxide emissions(tons)	41857.70
12. 烟（粉）尘产生量（吨）	Tobacco (powder) dust production(tons)	1305183.29
13. 烟（粉）尘排放量（吨）	The smoke (powder) dust emissions(tons)	17462.58
四、工业固体废物	**Industrial Solid Waste**	
1. 工业固体废物产生量（万吨）	Volume of Industrial Solid Waste Produced (10 000tons)	259.14
2. 工业固体废物综合利用量（万吨）	Volume of Industrial Solid Waste Utilized (10 000tons)	248.58
3. 工业固体废物综合利用率（%）	Percentage of Industrial Solid Waste Utilized (%)	95.92
4. 工业固体废物贮存量（万吨）	Volume of Industrial Solid Waste Accumulated (10 000tons)	1.54
5. 工业固体废物处置量（万吨）	Volume of Industrial Solid Waste Treated (10 000tons)	9.24
6. 工业固体废物倾倒丢弃量（万吨）	Volume of Industrial Solid Waste Discharged (10 000tons)	0.006

注：本表数据来源于市环保局。

10-4 城市污水排放及处理情况（2012年）

Discharge and Treatment of City Sewage(2012)

指　标	Item	2012
一、污水处理厂数（座）	**Number of Sewage Treatment Works(units)**	**24**
污水处理厂处理能力（万吨/日）	Daily Disposal Capacity of Sewage(10 000 tons/day)	134.93
二、污水处理	**Sewgae Disposal**	
污水实际处理量(万吨)	Volume of Sewgae Disposal(10 000 tons)	29015.32
#生活污水处理量	Volume of Domestic Sewgae Disposal	27456.07
工业污水处理量	Volume of Industrial Sewage Disposal	1559.25
三、再生水	**Recycled water**	
生产量(万吨)	Production(10 000 tons)	47376.00
利用量(万吨)	Utilization(10 000 tons)	716.02
四、化学需氧量去除量（吨）	**Volume of COD Removed (tons)**	**81211.19**
五、氨氮去除量（吨）	**Volume of Ammonia and Nitrogen Removed(tons)**	**7923.35**
六、总磷去除量（吨）	**Volume of Total Phosphorus Removed(tons)**	**1115.55**
七、污泥产生量（万吨）	**Volume of Sludge Produced(10 000 tons)**	**19.88**
八、污泥处置量（万吨）	**Volume of Sludge Disposal(10 000 tons)**	**19.88**
九、污泥倾倒丢弃量（吨）	**Dumping sludge discards (tons)**	
十、本年运行费用（万元）	**Operating Expense(10 000 yuan)**	**27586.85**

注：本表数据来源于市环保局。

10-5 危险废物（医疗废物）集中处理情况(2012年）

Condition of Collected Dangerous Wastes Treated (2012)

指 标	Item	2012
一.危险废物集中处理（置）厂数（个）	**Number of Colleted Dangerous Wastes Treated Plants(items)**	**2**
二.医疗废物集中处理（置）厂数（个）	**The number of Manufacturing Plants of Medical waste treatment (units)**	
三.危险废物设计处置能力（吨/日）	**Design hazardous waste disposal capacity (tons / day)**	**55**
四.实际处置危险废物量（吨）	**The actual amount of hazardous waste disposal (tons)**	**13543.42**
五.危险废物综合利用量（吨）	**Volume of Dangerous Wastes Utilized in a Comprehensive Way (tons)**	**540**
六.焚烧残渣流向（千克）	**Flow Direction of Residuum after Burning (kg)**	
1. 焚烧残渣量	Volume of Residuum after Burning	406303
2. 焚烧残渣安全填进处理量	Secure landfill disposal incineration residues	406303
3. 焚烧飞灰产生量	Fly ash production	70425. 78
4. 焚烧飞灰安全填进处理量	Fly ash landfill disposal safety	70425. 78
七.当年运行费用（万元）	**Operating Expenses in Current year(10 000 yuan)**	**2229.33**

注：本表数据来源于市环保局。

10-6 生活及其他污染情况（2012年）

Domestic Pollution and Other conditions (2012)

指 标	Item	2012
一.基本情况	**Basic Condition**	
1. 生活天然气消费量（万立方米）	Volume of Living natural gas consumption (10 000 cu.m)	69407.00
2. 生活用水总量（万吨）	Volume of Living water (10 000 tons)	42183.00
二.污染排放情况	**Discharge of Pollutant**	
1. 城镇生活污水排放量（万吨）	Volume of Urban Domestic Sewage Discharged(10 000 tons)	29823.64
2. 生活污水处理量（万吨）	Volume of Domestic Sewgae Disposal(10 000 tons)	26569.89
3. 生活CDD产生量（吨）	Volume of Life CDD production (tons)	141026.51
4. 生活CDD排放量（吨）	Volume of Life CDD emissions (tons)	62360.87
5. 生活氨氮产生量（吨）	Volume of Ammonia and Nitrogen in Urban Domestic Sewage Produced (tons)	18264.09
6. 生活氨氮排放量（吨）	Volume of Ammonia and Nitrogen in Urban Domestic Sewage Discharged (tons)	10550.33
7. 二氧化硫排放量（吨）	Volume of Domestic and Other Sulphur Dioxide Emission (tons)	20569. 90
8. 氨氮化物排放量（吨）	Volume of Ammonia and Nitrogen in Urban Domestic Sewage Discharged (tons)	11401.19
9. 烟尘排放量（吨）	Volume of Soot Emission (tons)	12624.40

注：本表数据来源于市环保局。

10–7 工业污染治理项目建设情况（2012年）

Condition of Anti-Industrial-Pollution Projects (2012)

指　标	Item	2012
一、工业企业数（个）	**Number of Industrial Enterprises (units)**	**13**
二、老工业污染源项目治理本年施工总数（个）	**The total number of construction projects of Old industrial pollution sources control this year(units)**	**13**
#工业废水治理项目	Treatment of Waste Water	4
工业废气治理项目	Treatment of Waste Gas	2
工业固体废物治理项目	Treatmen of Solid Wastes	3
三、老工业污染源项目治理本年竣工总数（个）	**The Total Number of Old Industrial Pollution Control Projects Completed this year(units)**	**17**
#工业废水治理项目	Treatment of Waste Water	4
工业废气治理项目	Treatment of Waste Gas	6
工业固体废物治理项目	Treatmen of Solid Wastes	3
四、老工业污染源治理项目本年完成投资(万元)	**Investment completed in Old industrial pollution control projects this Year(10 000 yuan)**	**15333.18**
#废水治理项目	Treatment of Waste Water	2850.78
废气治理项目	Treatment of Waste Gas	11802.50
固体废物治理项目	Treatmen of Solid Wastes	292.86
五、老工业污染源治理项目本年投资来源(万元)	**Source of Investment in Old industrial pollution control projects this Year(10 000 yuan)**	**15333.18**
#排污费补助	Pollution Charges Subsidies	153.60
政府其他补助	Other Government Subsidies	1020
企业自筹	Self-raising Funds	14159.58
六、"三同时"项目竣工验收数（个）	**number of "Three simultaneous" project completion and acceptance (a)**	**5**
七、"三同时"竣工验收项目实际环保投资(万元)	**"Three simultaneous" actual environmental investment completed and accepted (10 000 yuan)**	**4960.00**
八、"三同时"项目废水治理新增处理能力（万吨/日）	**"Three simultaneous"Add processing capacity of wastewater treatment (10 000 tons / day)**	**0.51**
九、"三同时"项目废气治理新增处理能力（万立方米/时）	**"Three simultaneous"Add processing capacity of Exhaust treatment (10 000 cu.m/h)**	**130.00**

注：本表数据来源于市环保局。
"三同时"指建设项目中防治污染的措施，必须与主体工程同时设计，同时施工，同时投产使用。

10-8 各区县、开发区环境保护基本情况（2012年）

区县、开发区	Region	本年完成环保验收项目环保投资额（万元）Investment Completed in accepted Environmental projects this year (10 000 yuan)	工业二氧化硫排放量（吨）Volume of Industrial Sulphur Dioxide Discharged (tons)
全　市	**Total**	**82328**	**83062.9**
市本级	city	50367	
新城区	Xincheng	2257	155.6
碑林区	Beilin		1653.3
莲湖区	Lianhu	3800	4689.1
灞桥区	Baqiao	989.5	15727.2
未央区	Weiyang	1392.4	2527.8
雁塔区	Yanta	3793.9	768.5
阎良区	Yanliang	343	2574.9
临潼区	Lintong	3588.2	2747.2
长安区	Chang'an	3145.4	2676.5
蓝田县	Lantian	399	612.8
周至县	Zhouzhi	986	269.5
户　县	Huxian	719	6967.2
高陵县	Gaoling	550.7	1092
高新开发区	Gaoxinkaifaqu	4438.9	1074.9
经济开发区	Jingjikaifaqu	4671	2954.8
浐东新城	Fendongxincheng	250	36014.5
航天基地	Hangtianjidi	637	557.2

注：本表数据来源于市环保局。

环境统计中污水处理厂个数包含部分大学园区及部分大型小区的污水处理厂。

Condition of Environment Protection by Regions (2012)

工业化学 需氧量排放量 （吨） Volume of COD Removed (tons)	垃圾处理站数 （座） Number of Rubbish Disposal Works (units)	污水处理厂数 （个） Number of Sewage Treatment Works (units)
24381.0	**5**	**24**
313.3		
27.2		
1039.5		1
1122.7	2	2
2852		2
107.7		1
92.5	1	1
1117.6		2
139.1		7
49.2		2
155.3		1
5720.6		2
155.9	2	1
1273.5		1
699.5		
9165.3		1
350.1		

主要统计指标解释

工业用水 指工矿企业在生产过程中用于制造、加工、冷却、空调、净化、洗涤等方面的用水，按新水取用量计，不包括企业内部的重复利用水量。

工业废水排放量 指经过企业厂区所有排放口排到企业外部的工业废水量。包括生产废水、外排的直接冷却水、超标排放的矿井地下水和与工业废水混排的厂区生活污水，不包括外排的间接冷却水（清污不分流的间接冷却水应计算在内）。

直接排入海的 指经企业位于海边的排放口，直接排入海的废水量。直接排放指废水经过工厂的排污口直接排入海，而未经过城市下水道或其他中间体，也不受其他水体的影响。

工业废水排放达标量 指报告期内废水中各项污染物指标都达到国家或地方排放标准的外排工业废水量，包括未经处理外排达标的，经废水处理设施处理后达标排放的，以及经污水处理厂处理后达标排放的。

生活污水排放量 指城镇居民每年排放的生活污水。用人均系数法测算。测算公式为：

$$\text{生活污水排放量} = \text{城镇生活污水排放系数} \times \text{市镇非农业人口} \times 365$$

生活污水中化学需氧量（COD）排放量 指城镇居民每年排放的生活污水中的COD的量。用人均系数法测算。测算公式为：

$$\text{城镇生活污水中COD产生系数} = \text{城镇牛活污水中COD排放量} \times \text{市镇非农业人口} \times 365$$

化学需氧量（COD） 指用化学氧化剂氧化水中有机污染物时所需的氧量。COD值越高，表示水中有机污染物污染越重。

工业废气排放量 指报告期内企业厂区内燃料燃烧和生产工艺过程中产生的各种排入大气的含有污染物的气体的总量，以标准状态（273K，101325Pa）计算。测算公式为：

$$\text{工业废气排放量} = \text{燃料燃烧过程中废气排放量} + \text{生产工艺过程中废气排放量}$$

生活及其他SO_2排放量 以生活及其他煤炭消费量和其含硫量为基础，根据以下公式计算：

$$\text{生活及其他}SO_2\text{排放量} = \text{生活及其他煤炭消费量} \times \text{含硫量} \times 0.8 \times 2$$

工业SO_2排放量 指报告期内企业在燃料燃烧和生产工艺过程中排入大气的SO_2总量，计算公式为：

$$\text{工业}SO_2\text{排放量} = \text{燃料燃烧过程中}SO_2\text{排放量} + \text{生产工艺过程中}SO_2\text{排放量}$$

工业烟尘排放量 指企业厂区内燃料燃烧过程中产生的烟气中夹带的颗粒物排放量。

生活及其他烟尘排放量 指除工业生产活动以外的所有社会、经济活动及公共设施的经营活动中燃烧所排放的烟尘纯重量。以生活及其他煤炭消费量为基础进行测算。

工业粉尘排放量 指企业在生产工艺过程中排放的能在空气中悬浮一定时间的固体颗粒物排放量。如钢铁企业的耐火材料粉尘、焦化企业的筛焦系统粉尘、烧结机的粉尘、石灰窑的粉尘、建材企业的水泥粉尘等。不包括电厂排入大气的烟尘。

工业固体废物产生量 指报告期内企业在生产过程中产生的固体状、半固体状和高浓度液体状废弃物的总量，包括危险废物、冶炼废渣、粉煤灰、炉渣、煤矸石、尾矿、放射性废物和其他废物等；不包括矿开采的剥离废石和掘进废石（煤矸石和呈酸性或碱性的废石除外）。酸性或碱性废石指采掘的废石其流经水、雨淋水的pH值小于4或pH值大于10.5者。

危险废物 指列入国家危险废物名录或根据国家规定的危险废物鉴别标准和鉴别方法认定的，具有爆炸性、易燃性、易氧化性、毒性、腐蚀性、易传染疾病等危险特性之一的废物。

工业固体废物综合利用量 指报告期内企业通过回收、加工、循环、交换等方式，从固体废物中提取或者使其转化为可以利用的资源、能源和其他原材料的固体废物量（包括当年利用往年的工业固体废物贮存量），如用作农业肥料、生产建筑材料、筑路等。综合利用量由原产生固体废物的单位统计。

工业固体废物综合利用率 指工业固体废物综合利用量占丁业固体废物产生量（包括综合利用往年贮存量）的百分率。计算公式为：

$$\text{工业固体废物综合利用率} = \frac{\text{工业固体废物综合利用量}}{\text{工业固体废物产生量+综合利用往年贮存量}} \times 100\%$$

工业固体废物贮存量 指报告期内企业以综合利用或处置为目的，将固体废物暂时贮存或堆存在专设的贮存设施或专设的集中堆存场所内的数量。专设的固体废物贮存场所或贮存设施必须有防扩散、防流失、防渗漏、防止污染大气、水体的措施。

工业固体废物处置量 指报告期内企业将固体废物焚烧或者最终置于符合环境保护规定要求的场所，并不再回取的工业固体废物量（包括当年处置往年的工业固体废物贮存量）。处置方式有填埋（其中危险废物应安全填埋）、焚烧、专业贮存场（库）封场处理、深层灌注、回填矿井及海洋处置（经海洋管理部门同意投海处置）等。

工业固体废物排放量 指报告期内企业将所产生的固体废物排到固体废物污染防治设施、场所以外的数量，不包括矿 开采的剥离废石和掘进废石（煤矸石和呈酸性或碱性的废石除外）。

“三废”综合利用产品产值 指报告期内利用“三废”作为主要原料生产的产品价值（现行价）；已经销售或准备销售的应计算产品价值，留作生产自用的不应计算产品价值。

生活垃圾清运量 指报告期内收集和运送到各生活垃圾处理厂（场）和生活垃圾最终消纳点的生活垃圾数量。生活垃圾指城市日常生活或为城市日常生活提供服务的活动中产生的固体废物以及法律行政规定的视为城市生活垃圾的固体废物。包括：居民生活垃圾、商业垃圾、集市贸易市场垃圾、街道清扫垃圾、公共场所垃圾和机关、学校、厂矿等单位的生活垃圾。

生活垃圾无害化处理率 指报告期生活垃圾无害化处理量与生活垃圾产生量的比率。在统计上，由于生活垃圾产生量不易取得，可用清运量代替。计算公式为：

$$\text{生活垃圾无害化处理率} = \frac{\text{生活垃圾无害化处理量}}{\text{生活垃圾产生量}} \times 100\%$$

Explanatory Notes on Main Statistical Indicators

Water Use by Industry refers to new withdrawals of water, excluding reuse of water within enterprises.

Waste Water Discharged by Industry refers to the volume of waste water discharged by industrial enterprises through all their outlets, including waste water from production process, directly cooled water, groundwater from mining wells which does not meet discharge standards and sewage from households mixed with waste water produced by industrial activities, but excluding indirectly cooled water discharged (It should be included if the discharge is not separated from waste water).

Waste Water Directly Discharged into Sea refers to the volume of waste water directly discharged into sea through outlets of enterprises situated by sea without going through municipal sewerage networks or any other intermediates or being affected by any other water bodies.

Industrial Waste Water Meeting Discharge Standards refers to volume of industrial waste water discharge which, with or without treatment, reaches national or local standards with regard to all pollutants.

Urban Non-industrial Waste Water Discharge refers to annual discharge of non-industrial waste water by urban households. It is estimated by per capita coefficient using the formula:

$$\begin{array}{c}\text{Urban non-industrial}\\ \text{waste water discharge}\end{array} = \begin{array}{c}\text{urban non-industrial waste}\\ \text{water discharge coefficient}\end{array} \times \begin{array}{c}\text{urban non-alagricultur}\\ \text{population}\end{array} \times 365$$

Volume of Chemical Oxygen Demand (COD) Generated by Urban Non-industrial Waster Water refers to chemical oxygen demand generated through the annual discharge of non-industrial waste water by urban households. It is estimated as:

$$\begin{array}{c}\text{Volume of chemical oxygen}\\ \text{demand (cod) generated}\\ \text{by urban non-industrial}\\ \text{waster water}\end{array} = \begin{array}{c}\text{Coefficient of COD}\\ \text{generated through urban}\\ \text{non-industrial waste water}\end{array} \times \begin{array}{c}\text{urban}\\ \text{non-agricultural}\\ \text{population}\end{array} 365$$

Chemical Oxygen Demand (COD) refers to the amount of oxygen required when chemical oxidants are used to oxidize organic pollutants in water. A higher value of COD corresponds to more serious pollution by organic pollutants.

Industrial Waste Air Emission refers to the discharge into atmosphere of waste air containing pollutants generated from fuel burning and production processes in enterprises within a given period of time. It is calculated at standard status (273K, 101325Pa) as:

$$\begin{array}{c}\text{Industrial waste}\\ \text{air emission}\end{array} = \begin{array}{c}\text{tnoissimehrough}\\ \text{fuel burning}\end{array} + \begin{array}{c}\text{tnoissimehrough}\\ \text{production process}\end{array}$$

SO_2 Emission through Non-industrial and Other Activities is calculated on the basis of consumption of coal by households and other activities and the sulphur content of coal with the following formula:

$$\begin{array}{c}SO_2\text{ emission}\\ \text{through non-}\\ \text{industrial and}\\ \text{other activities}\end{array} = \begin{array}{c}\text{of coalby}\\ \text{households}\\ \text{andother}\\ \text{activities}\end{array} \times \begin{array}{c}\text{sulphur}\\ \text{content}\end{array} \times 0.8 \times 2$$

SO_2 Emission through Industrial Activities refers to volume of sulphur dioxide emission from fuel burning and production process by enterprises during a given period of time. It is calculated as:

$$\begin{array}{c}SO_2\text{ emission}\\ \text{through industrial}\\ \text{activities}\end{array} = \begin{array}{c}SO_2\text{emIssIon from}\\ \text{fuel burning}\end{array} + \begin{array}{c}SO_2\text{ emission from}\\ \text{production process}\end{array}$$

Industrial Soot Emission refers to the volume of soot in smoke emitted in the process of fuel burning in the premises of enterprises.

Soot Emission by Consumption and Others refers to the net volume of soot emitted by fuel burning from all social and economic activities and operations of public facilities other than industrial activities. It is calculated on the basis of coal consumption by households and others.

Industrial Dust Emission refers to volume of dust emitted by production process of enterprises and suspended in the air for a given period of time, including dust from refractory material of iron and steel works, dust from coke-screening systems and sintering machines of coke plants, dust from lime kilns and dust from cement production in building material enterprises, but excluding soot and dust emitted from power plants.

Industrial Solid Wastes Produced refers to total volume of solid, semi-solid and high concentration liquid residues produced by industrial enterprises from production process in a given period of time, including hazardous wastes, slag, coal ash, gangue, tailings, radioactive residues and other wastes, but excluding stones stripped or dug out in mining - gangue and acid or alkaline stones not included (a stone is acid or alkaline according to the pH value of the water being below 4 or above 10.5 when the stone is in, or soaked by water).

Hazardous Wastes refers to those included in the national hazardous wastes catalogue or specified as any one of the following properties in the national hazardous wastes identification standards: explosive, ignitable, oxidizable, toxic, corrosive or liable to cause infectious diseases or lead to other dangers.

Industrial Solid Wastes Utilized refers to volume of solid wastes from which useful materials can be extracted or which can be converted into usable resources, energy or other materials by means of reclamation, processing, recycling and exchange (including utilizing in the year the stocks of industrial solid wastes of the previous year). Examples of such utilizations include fertilizers, building materials and road materials. The information shall be collected by the producing units of the wastes.

Rate of Utilization of Industrial Solid Wastes refers to the percentage of industrial solid wastes utilized over industrial solid wastes produced (including stocks of the previous years). It is calculated as:

$$\text{Rate of utilization of industrial solid wastes} = \frac{\text{volume of industrial solid wastes utilized}}{\text{industrial solid wastes produced} + \text{stock of previous years}} \times 100\%$$

Stock of Industrial Solid Wastes refers to the volume of solid wastes placed in special facilities or special sites for purposes of utilization or disposal. The sites or facilities should take measures against dispersion, loss, seepage, and air and water contamination.

Industrial Solid Wastes Disposed refers to the quantity of industrial solid wastes which are burnt or placed ultimately in the sites meeting the requirements for environmental protection and not salvaged or recycled (including disposition in the year of those wastes of previous years). The disposition includes landfill (Safe landfills should be conducted for hazardous wastes), incineration, containment spaces, deep underground disposal, backfill in mining pits and disposal at sea.

Industrial Solid Wastes Discharged refers to the volume of industrial solid wastes discharged by producing enterprises to disposal facilities or to other sites. The wastes exclude stones stripped or dug from mining (gangue and acid or alkaline waste stones not included).

Output Value of Products Made from Waste Gas, Waste Water and Solid Wastes refers to the current value of products with waste gas, waste water and solid wastes as main materials of production. Products sold and ready to sell shall be included while those produced for own use shall not be included.

Consumption Wastes Transported refers to volume of consumption wastes collected and transported to disposal factories or sites. Consumption wastes are solid wastes produced from urban households or from service activities for urban households, and solid wastes regarded by laws and regulations as urban consumption wastes, including those from households, commercial activities, markets, cleaning of streets, public sites, offices, schools, factories, mining units and other sources.

Ratio of Consumption Wastes Treated refers to consumption wastes treated over that produced. In practical statistics, as it is difficult to estimate, the volume of consumption wastes produced is replaced with that transported. It is calculated as:

$$\text{Ratio of consumption wastes treated} = \frac{\text{consumption wastes treated}}{\text{consumption wastes produced}} \times 100\%$$

11 农 业

AGRICULTURE

资料整理：张喜兰　马秋娟　薛　丰
Data management:Zhang Xilan　Ma Qiujuan　Xue Feng

第十一部分　农业

一、简要说明

本章资料主要包括农村基本情况、农业生产条件与生产情况、耕地、农林牧渔及服务业产值、主要农产品产量以及各区县农业生产和农村经济效益主要指标，由西安市统计局农村处提供。

二、主要指标

年末耕地面积（万亩）	369.91	比上年下降	1.9%
农林牧渔及服务业总产值（亿元）	308.36	比上年增长	6.0%
农作物播种面积（万亩）	701.33	比上年下降	0.4%
粮食产量（万吨）	192.54	比上年下降	5.8%

11　AGRICULTURE

Ⅰ.Brief Introduction

Data in this chapter reflects basic condition of agriculture production of Xi'an city. It is primarily consist of basic condition of rural area, condition of agriculture production, plow land, production value of farming, forestry, animal husbandry and fishery, gross yield of primary produce and primary indicators of agriculture production and rural area economic performance. The data are provided and compiled by Rural Area Division of the Xi'an Bureau of Statistics.

Ⅱ.Major Indicators

		Increase over Preceding Year
Cultivated Area Year-end(10 000 mu)	369.91	-1.9%
Gross Output Value of Farming, Forestry, Animal Husbandry, Fishery and Service(100 mil. Yuan)	308.36	6.0%
Sown Area of Crops(10 000 mu)	701.33	-0.4%
Grain Output(10 000 tons)	192.54	-5.8%

11-1 主要年份农村户数、人口和劳动力情况

Grass-roots Households, Population and Labor Resources in Rural Area

指　　标	Item	2000	2005	2007	2008	2009	2010	2011	2012
一、乡村户数（万户）	**Number of Households (10 000 households)**	**98.77**	**101.50**	**100.85**	**101.02**	**101**	**101.43**	**102.59**	**101.92**
二、农村劳动力和从业人员情况	**Rural Population and Employment**								
1. 乡村劳动力资源总数（万人）	Total Number of Rural Labor Source (10 000 persons)	240.76	255.93	254.06	256.17	255	256.36	260.97	259.06
2. 乡村从业人员数（万人）	Rural Laborers(10 000 persons)	212.65	223.30	222.09	223.85	223.13	225.04	230.56	226.92
#女性	Female	99.07	103.22	101.83	103.11	102.76	103.25	109.61	107.63
#农业	Laborers of Farming	146.07	137.69	131.96	126.46	121.78	116.58	116.15	113.29
三、自来水受益村数（个）	**Number of Villages Benefited from（unit） the Tap Water System(unit)**	**1527**	**1756**	**1881**	**1934**	**2058**	**2184**	**2400**	**2545**
通汽车村数（个）	**Number of Villages Accessible by motor Vehicles（unit）**	**2785**	**2952**	**2973**	**2996**	**2989**	**2989**	**2978**	**2936**
通电话村数（个）	**Number of Villages Accessible by Telephone（unit）**	**2885**	**3101**	**3129**	**3086**	**3071**	**3052**	**3033**	**2974**

11-2 各区县乡村从业人员数（2012年）

Number of Labours in Families by Region（2012）

单位：万人 (10 000 persons)

区 县	Region	乡村劳动力资源总数 Total Number of Rural Labor Source	乡村从业人员数合计 Rural Laborers Total	#女性 Female	#农林牧渔业 Farming,Forestry Animal Husbandry and Fishery
合 计	**Total**	**259.06**	**226.92**	**107.63**	**113.29**
新城区	Xincheng				
碑林区	Beilin				
莲湖区	Lianhu				
灞桥区	Baqiao	18.76	15.77	6.52	5.89
未央区	Weiyang	13.31	8.80	4.15	2.26
雁塔区	Yanta	6.73	5.38	2.51	0.21
阎良区	Yanliang	10.78	9.55	4.58	5.01
临潼区	Lintong	36.07	32.32	15.31	17.18
长安区	Chang'an	54.47	49.10	20.88	20.67
蓝田县	Lantian	34.57	33.90	21.84	21.56
周至县	Zhouzhi	40.19	34.66	14.57	19.17
户 县	Huxian	33.29	28.47	13.20	16.36
高陵县	Gaoling	10.89	8.97	4.07	4.98

11-3 主要年份耕地面积

Area of Cultivated Land in Representatives Years

单位：万亩 (10 000 mu)

年 份 Year	年末实有耕地面积 Cultivated Area Year-end	水田 Paddy Field	水浇地 Irrigable Land
1970	554.09	18.20	297.05
1975	538.35	20.34	349.13
1978	530.96	16.70	370.46
1980	526.29	17.45	372.96
1985	508.88	17.63	328.10
1990	495.32	17.97	311.91
1992	485.30	16.44	298.19
1993	479.04	14.36	304.49
1994	471.44	13.98	299.58
1995	463.97	17.04	278.01
1996	451.50	14.21	283.76
1997	456.62	11.90	290.49
1998	455.15	11.18	282.23
1999	450.74	11.31	281.96
2000	443.37	10.26	284.04
2001	431.69	9.00	274.73
2002	424.46	7.98	275.96
2003	413.84	6.65	263.75
2004	404.87	6.59	254.04
2005	400.17	5.55	254.04
2006	395.79	5.33	263.75
2007	391.77	4.80	255.95
2008	390.77	4.64	255.36
2009	387.89	4.39	260.71
2010	383.32	4.03	257.43
2011	377.10	3.80	253.46
2012	369.91	3.32	248.97

11-4 各区县耕地面积（2012年）

单位：亩

区 县	Region	年末实有耕地面积 Cultivated Area Year-end	水田 Paddy Field	旱地 Dry Land	水浇地 Irrigable Land
合 计	**Total**	**3699119**	**33241**	**3665878**	**2489695**
新城区	Xincheng				
碑林区	Beilin				
莲湖区	Lianhu				
灞桥区	Baqiao	157665		157665	95869
未央区	Weiyang	22027		22027	22027
雁塔区	Yanta	8466		8466	6457
阎良区	Yanliang	236876		236876	228104
临潼区	Lintong	704906		704906	537059
长安区	Chang'an	663281	22530	640751	336406
蓝田县	Lantian	606000	8000	598000	173000
周至县	Zhouzhi	498850	1010	497840	361320
户 县	Huxian	572395	1701	570694	500800
高陵县	Gaoling	228653		228653	228653

Area of Cultivated Land by Region (2012)

(mu)

当年增加的耕地面积 Area of Newly Increased Cultivated Land	新开荒地面积 Area of Newly Reclamation of Wasteland	当年减少的耕地面积 Decrease in Cultivated Area in the Year	国家基建占地 Capital Construction	退耕改果、茶、桑面积 Area for Change into Fruit, Tea and Mulberry	退耕造林面积 Area for Change into Woods
12702	**5305**	**108125**	**68460**	**31939**	**1800**
		5370	3533		
		25673	21073	4600	
		7372	6513		850
209	14	4377	2718	1625	
		11089	10982	14	
483	172	23551	19495	1886	65
3399	926	4100	1843	2106	120
7359	4193	24524	2303	20822	765
230		886		886	
1022		1183			

11-5 主要年份农业机械拥有量（年末数）

指　标	Item	2004	2005	2006
农用机械总动力（千瓦）	**Total Power of Agricultural Machinery(kw)**	**2140737**	**2239001**	**2277584**
大中型拖拉机（台）	Large and Medium Tractors(unit)	7500	8415	8963
小型拖拉机（台）	Mini-tractors(unit)	27225	26326	23437
大中型拖拉机配套农具（台）	Number of Large and Medium Tractor Towing Farm Machinery(unit)	18446	19334	18724
小型拖拉机配套农具（台）	Mini-Tractor Towing Farm Machinery (unit)	47260	47883	30439
农用排灌柴油机（台）	Agricultural Diesel Engines(unit)	2522	2219	3547
农用排灌电动机（台）	Agricultural Motors(unit)	78542	79666	76614
农用水泵（台）	Agricultural Water Pump(unit)	74701	77567	73039
节水灌溉类机械（套）	Equipment in Water-saving Irrigation(set)	1141	1290	2656
联合收割机（台）	Combine Harvesters(unit)	4053	4802	5026
自走式机动割晒机（台）	Self-propelled Motorized Swather(unit)	3147	4226	1342
机动脱粒机（台）	Motorized Huller (unit)	13060	13870	5806
农用运输车（辆）	Agricultucal Transporter(unit)	42247	47348	50395

Possession of Agricultural Machinery in Representative Years（Number of year-end）

2007	2008	2009	2010	2011	2012
2348856	**2712616**	**2616053**	**2677334**	**2890247**	**2983979**
10431	11092	11479	14675	12585	12987
21555	19036	18406	14194	13008	11471
23487	25125	26575	29215	36209	32166
28780	26984	29039	24393	29624	27869
2709	2670	2691	3309	2639	2891
84416	85349	83243	79462	87461	87056
80722	80462	80174	77367	75426	80982
1991	1728	1799	1710	1733	2106
5294	5390	6155	6718	7854	8502
4918	2174	1220	208	187	
11585	23781	11960	13231	13407	14493
49576	54860	50671	51665	51838	51850

11-6 各区县农业机械拥有量（2012年）

指 标	Item	西安市 Xi' an	灞桥区 Baqiao	未央区 Weiyang
农用机械总动力（千瓦）	**Total Power of Agricultural Machinery(kw)**	**2983979**	**189822**	**53514**
大中型拖拉机（台）	Large and Medium Tractors(unit)	12987	461	232
小型拖拉机（台）	Mini-tractors(unit)	11471	16	11
大中型拖拉机配套农具（台）	Number of Large and Medium Tractor Towing Farm Machinery(unit)	32166	983	637
小型拖拉机配套农具（台）	Mini-Tractor Towing Farm Machinery (unit)	27869	50	13
农用排灌柴油机（台）	Agricultural Diesel Engines(unit)	2891		
农用排灌电动机（台）	Agricultural Motors(unit)	87056	3441	1167
农用水泵（台）	Agricultural Water Pump(unit)	80982	3381	1562
节水灌溉类机械（套）	Equipment in Water-saving Irrigation(set)	2106	30	155
联合收割机（台）	Combine Harvesters(unit)	8502	221	67
自走式机动割晒机（台）	Self-propelled Motorized Swather(unit)			
机动脱粒机（台）	Motorized Huller (unit)	14493	51	
农用运输车（辆）	Agricultucal Transporter(unit)	51850		561

Possession of Agricultural Machinery by Region（2012）

雁塔区 Yanta	阎良区 Yanliang	临潼区 Lintong	长安区 Chang'an	蓝田县 Lantian	周至县 Zhouzhi	户 县 Huxian	高陵县 Gaoling
42486	**183097**	**585501**	**446192**	**309612**	**447930**	**453429**	**272396**
65	960	2367	2376	1047	1423	2591	1465
19	771	1151	1534	2027	4332	1401	209
83	2841	6647	5237	2070	2191	6180	5297
51	1663	4306	5054	3362	8263	4135	972
		274	1720	525	312	60	
626	6617	18710	18860	3374	16542	13747	3972
601	6690	17964	12410	2331	18160	13899	3984
	414	166	947		264	130	
33	677	1788	1439	294	446	2622	915
	1274	5045	697	2015	2451	2420	540
813	2518	15715	7012	5057	9353	4238	6583

11-7 主要年份农业机械、化肥、水利、水电情况

指 标	Item	2000	2005	2006
一. 农业机械化水平（万亩）	**Statistics on Agricultural Machinery (10 000 mu)**			
当年机械耕地面积（实际）	Area Ploughed by Tractors	366.81	360.68	354.05
当年机械播种面积（作业）	Seeded Area by Tractors	482.74	485.62	519.00
当年机械收获面积（作业）	Harvest Area by Tractors	272.83	271.77	280.88
二. 农用化肥施用量（吨）	**Use of Agricultural Fertilizers and Insecticides(ton)**			
1.按实物量计算合计	Practicality Consumption	697243	749802	759882
氮肥	Nitrogenous Fertilizer	392366	411161	413514
磷肥	Phosphate Fertilizer	155480	161444	164781
钾肥	Potash Fertilizer	31841	34114	31414
复合肥	Compound Fertilizer	78620	115458	121124
2.按折纯量计算合计	Standard Consumption	196343	211790	216093
氮肥	Nitrogenous Fertilizer	102982	107645	110137
磷肥	Phosphate Fertilizer	18658	19368	19772
钾肥	Potash Fertilizer	15921	17055	15709
复合肥	Compound Fertilizer	39313	57009	59731
三. 农用塑料薄膜使用量（公斤）	**Plastic Sheet for Agricultural Use(kg)**	**1622198**	**1855383**	**1931527**
四. 农用柴油使用量（吨）	**Diesel Oil for Agricultural Use (ton)**	**52706**	**50832**	**49686**
五. 农药使用量（公斤）	**Pesticide (kg)**	**1559333**	**1427879**	**1471672**
六. 年末农村办沼气池（个）	**Number of Mash Gas Pond Managed by Village Government in Year-end(unit)**	**10199**	**12445**	**16211**
七. 农村水利化情况（万亩）	**Irrigation and Water Conservancy (10 000 mu)**			
有效灌溉面积	Effective Irrigation Area	335.97	280.10	276.58
旱涝保收面积	Stable-Harvesting Arable Land	294.06	255.37	253.66
机电排灌面积	Electrical Irrigation Area	249.11	223.74	214.03
八. 农村电气化情况	**Rural electrization**			
乡村及村以下办水电站（个）	Hydropower Station in Rural Areas(unit)	67	79	79
装机容量（千瓦）	Installed Power Generation Capacity(kw)	7236	13775	14252
发电量（万千瓦小时）	Generating Capacity (10 000 kwh)	1138	2239	2253
已配套机电井（眼）	Electricity Powered Well(unit)	50289	46505	46112

Agricultural Machinery,Chemical Fertilizers,Water Conservancy, Hydropower in Representative Years

2007	2008	2009	2010	2011	2012
361.62	404.42	413.70	367.32	427.03	425.40
521.36	539.81	544.86	548.28	507.55	529.99
296.06	313.11	342.82	403.50	413.93	428.28
762401	767980	776319	781072	785885	807900
408847	413397	414481	397975	398395	414339
160932	157145	153825	152943	151005	151967
34284	34149	33069	37715	38195	43356
124784	132481	142137	158062	163797	198238
220251	225949	230299	235532	239497	243281
109484	112000	112275	108868	110412	113662
19311	18855	18457	18315	18026	18061
17141	17077	16534	17997	18095	21267
62398	66247	71042	78811	81764	90291
2096169	**2122310**	**2141969**	**2450496**	**2533372**	**2683201**
50137	**51097**	**51346**	**61917**	**61637**	**57451**
1444867	**1465819**	**1325459**	**1243105**	**1242773**	**1252490**
26448	**36540**	**46737**	**50710**	**62208**	
276.28	274.48	273.17	281.28	262.32	267.84
247.99	249.31	247.60	234.15	214.62	211.31
210.51	211.01	213.42	224.60	200.36	198.66
76	76	75	44	44	46
24827	24827	25047	22325	22325	78848
10085	10477	10678	7268	7268	26447
45783	47032	46790	44310	40345	33959

11-8 各区县农业机械、化肥、水利、水电情况（2012年）

指 标	Item	西安市 Xi'an	灞桥区 Baqiao	未央区 Weiyang
一. 农业机械化水平（万亩）	**Statistics on Agricultural Machinery(10 000 mu)**			
当年机械耕地面积（实际）	Area Ploughed by Tractors	425.40	16.70	4.57
当年机械播种面积（作业）	Seeded Area by Tractors	529.99	20.76	3.46
当年机械收获面积（作业）	Harvest Area by Tractors	428.28	17.99	3.31
二. 农用化肥施用量（吨）	**Use of Agricultural Fertilizers and secticides(Ton)**			
1. 按实物量计算合计	Practicality Consumption	807900	25000	3635
氮肥	Nitrogenous Fertilizer	414339	10000	2384
磷肥	Phosphate Fertilizer	151967	600	454
钾肥	Potash Fertilizer	43356	2400	44
复合肥	Compound Fertilizer	198238	12000	753
2. 按折纯法计算合计	Standard Consumption	243281	10372	808
氮肥	Nitrogenous Fertilizer	113662	4600	563
磷肥	Phosphate Fertilizer	18061	72	29
钾肥	Potash Fertilizer	21267	1200	22
复合肥	Compound Fertilizer	90291	4500	194
三. 农用塑料薄膜使用量（公斤）	**Plastic Sheet for Agricultural Use(kg)**	2683201	202650	18235
四. 农用柴油使用量（吨）	**Diesel Oil for Agricultural Use (ton)**	57451	596	821
五. 农药使用量（公斤）	**Pesticide (kg)**	1252490	40000	6148
六. 年末农村办沼气池（个）	**Number of Mash Gas Pond Managed** by Village Government in Year-end(unit)			
七. 农村水利化情况（万亩）	**Irrigation and Water Conservancy (10 000 mu)**			
有效灌溉面积	Effective Irrigation Area	267.84	10.41	3.59
旱涝保收面积	Stable-Harvesting Arable Land	211.31	9.60	3.05
机电排灌面积	Electrical Irrigation Area	198.66	9.35	3.59
八. 农村电气化情况	**Rural electrization**			
乡村及村以下办水电站（个）	Hydropower Station in Rural Areas(unit)	46		
装机容量（千瓦）	Installed Power Generation Capacity(kw)	78848		
发电量（万千瓦小时）	Generating Capacity (10 000 kwh)	26447		
已配套机电井（眼）	Electricity Powered Well(unit)	33959	2029	430

Agricultural Machinery,Chemical Fertilizers,Water Conservancy, Hydropower by Region （2012）

雁塔区 Yanta	阎良区 Yanliang	临潼区 Lintong	长安区 Chang'an	蓝田县 Lantian	周至县 Zhouzhi	户　县 Huxian	高陵县 Gaoling
	22.54	52.31	111.68	54.80	66.81	53.08	42.91
	28.88	93.66	106.78	65.89	76.86	91.90	41.80
	21.83	82. 00	96.34	38.30	45.39	87.70	35.42
571	56375	148402	145115	94881	148682	106992	78247
328	26566	79260	82991	52005	62372	65749	32684
38	11573	43250	23850	19308	16085	15954	20855
91	4466	2626	6191	6158	9021	5147	7212
114	13770	23266	32083	17410	61204	20142	17496
148	19275	39101	30456	36350	46965	31941	27865
42	8768	20925	10416	22586	15321	17433	13008
4	1389	5230	2703	2286	1929	1916	2503
45	2233	1313	3090	3005	4231	2522	3606
57	6885	11633	14247	8473	25484	10070	8748
	1010871	216568	182231	175900	98648	491167	286931
194	2755	6522	14144	10120	3352	9994	8953
35	180812	332562	134425	78135	165040	63100	252233
2.18	22.89	51.88	33.73	21.60	51.61	49.44	20.51
	22.06	46.50	22.91	11.25	27.66	47.77	20.51
2.18	22.89	42.69	33.73	8.22	15.58	47.23	13.20
			7	6	26	7	
			5245	14270	54713	4620	
			773	3018	21060	1596	
	5414	7140	5943		70	9943	2990

11-9 主要年份农林牧渔及服务业总产值及指数

Gross Output Value of Farming,Forestry,Animal Husbandry,Fishery, Service and Related Indices in Representative Years

单位：万元 （10 000 yuan）

年 份 Year	农林牧渔及服务总产值（现价）Gross Output Value (At current prices)	农 业 Farming	林 业 Forestry	牧 业 Animal Husbandry	渔 业 Fishery	农林牧渔服务业 Service of Farming, Forestry, Animal Husbandry and Fishery	指数（上年=100）（可比价）Indices(preceding year= 100) (At cinstant prices)
1970	40617	35965	713	3896	43		111.2
1975	55322	47378	1509	6403	32		93.9
1978	65423	56519	1444	7427	33		104.7
1980	65322	54004	1177	10106	35		85.0
1985	134933	105888	2559	26186	300		106.4
1990	262073	191088	3134	65840	2011		102.5
1991	295620	208324	3362	81070	2864		108.6
1992	321155	219160	4225	94045	3725		108.6
1993	387068	261959	5031	115810	4268		112.8
1994	565056	359609	7819	192140	5488		102.4
1995	754597	513348	7185	228598	5466		106.8
1996	786003	552726	7573	219214	6490		102.1
1997	836201	585973	9226	233623	7379		110.3
1998	853279	625465	8146	212045	7623		107.5
1999	739905	530029	8883	194552	6441		100.7
2000	743712	514845	8482	212612	7773		104.3
2001	767511	527160	8427	223861	8063		102.8
2002	797444	539978	11378	238761	7327		103.0
2003	837857	551398	10550	269610	6299		101.5
2004	967946	580798	12773	314517	6728	53130	108.4
2005	1065437	657262	13086	329856	7340	57893	107.7
2006	1141484	686748	15188	346626	7017	85905	107.2
2007	1341450	798163	15845	410213	9051	108178	105.3
2008	1682725	956549	19031	564095	11084	131966	107.8
2009	1787032	1061756	22663	546191	11830	144592	106.5
2010	2270994	1438934	26787	629376	12830	163067	107.4
2011	2726608	1729295	34453	754593	14856	193411	106.6
2012	3083562	1933149	62291	820392	19877	247853	106.0

11-10 主要年份农林牧渔及服务业总产值指数

Related Indices of Gross Output Value of Farming,Forestry,Animal Husbandry,Fishery and Service in Representative Years

年 份 Year	农林牧渔及服务业总产值指数（上年=100）（可比价） Indices(preceding year= 100)(At constant prices)	农 业 Farming	林 业 Forestry	牧 业 Animal Husbandry	渔 业 Fishery	农林牧渔服务业 Service of Farming, Forestry, Animal Husbandry and Fishery
2005	107.7	108.0	98.7	107.3	112.6	107.9
2006	107.2	106.0	102.5	109.3	104.5	109.4
2007	105.3	106.4	101.3	102.4	106.3	108.7
2008	107.8	107.9	112.2	106.0	100.5	113.7
2009	106.5	105.4	121.3	106.8	107.4	110.2
2010	107.4	108.7	115.2	104.3	92.7	108.9
2011	106.6	108.2	105.7	102.9	102.1	107.7
2012	106.0	105.6	143.0	104.8	115.2	107.2

11-11 主要年份农林牧渔及服务业总产值构成

Gross Output Value and Its Composition of Farming, Forestry, Animal Husbandry,Fishery and Service at Current Price in Representative Years

年 份 Year	农林牧渔及服务业总产值(%) Service of Farming, Forestry, Animal Husbandry and Fishery(%)	农 业 Farming	林 业 Forestry	牧 业 Animal Husbandry	渔 业 Fishery	农林牧渔服务业 Service of Farming, Forestry, Animal Husbandry and Fishery
2005	100.0	61.7	1.2	31.0	0.7	5.4
2006	100.0	60.9	1.3	31.5	0.6	5.7
2007	100.0	59.5	1.2	30.6	0.7	8.0
2008	100.0	56.9	1.1	33.5	0.7	7.8
2009	100.0	59.4	1.3	30.5	0.7	8.1
2010	100.0	63.3	1.2	27.7	0.6	7.2
2011	100.0	63.4	1.3	27.7	0.5	7.1
2012	100.0	62.7	2.0	26.6	0.7	8.0

11-12 各区县农林牧渔及服务业总产值（2012年）

Gross Output Value of Farming, Forestry, Animal Husbandry, Fishery and Service by Region（2012）

单位：万元 (10 000 yuan)

区 县	Region	农林牧渔及服务业总产值 Gross Output Value	农 业 Farming	林 业 Forestry	牧 业 Animal Husbandry	渔 业 Fishery	农林牧渔服务业 Service of Farming, Forestry, Animal Husbandry and Fishery
合 计	**Total**	**3083562**	**1933149**	**62291**	**820392**	**19877**	**247853**
新城区	Xincheng						
碑林区	Beilin						
莲湖区	Lianhu						
灞桥区	Baqiao	245553	176663	1181	42554	2710	22445
未央区	Weiyang	36525	21321	13	10761	2363	2067
雁塔区	Yanta	32762	21438	151	7283		3890
阎良区	Yanliang	290460	209607	637	55943	299	23974
临潼区	Lintong	468170	231582	7858	187089	2704	38937
长安区	Chang'an	453711	304763	1145	106893	5497	35413
蓝田县	Lantian	401514	242972	22204	103124	3293	29921
周至县	Zhouzhi	412820	285713	26337	73897	728	26145
户 县	Huxian	407108	265463	1888	100804	1132	37821
高陵县	Gaoling	334939	173627	877	132044	1151	27240

11-13 各区县农林牧渔及服务业总产值指数和构成（2012年）

Gross Output Value and Its Composition of Farming, Forestry, Animal Husbandry,Fishery and Service at Current Price by Region（2012）

单位：%　　（%）

区 县	Region	农林牧渔及服务业总产值 Gross Output Value	农 业 Farming	林 业 Forestry	牧 业 Animal Husbandry	渔 业 Fishery	农林牧渔服务业 Service of Farming, Forestry, Animal Husbandry and Fishery
全市指数	**Total**	**106.0**	**105.6**	**143.0**	**104.8**	**115.2**	**107.2**
新城区	Xincheng						
碑林区	Beilin						
莲湖区	Lianhu						
灞桥区	Baqiao	106.4	107.9	106.8	101.2	105.8	106.3
未央区	Weiyang	92.4	98.3	80.0	79.9	171.5	76.8
雁塔区	Yanta	90.5	95.5	372.2	87.5	0.0	71.4
阎良区	Yanliang	106.6	106.4	113.5	106.6	104.5	109.1
临潼区	Lintong	104.9	106.4	89.9	103.1	112.8	109.2
长安区	Chang'an	106.2	106.3	82.5	107.0	124.9	101.8
蓝田县	Lantian	106.6	104.3	102.2	114.1	104.2	105.1
周至县	Zhouzhi	107.0	102.9	427.9	102.1	87.4	109.4
户 县	Huxian	106.8	106.6	155.7	104.6	105.7	113.8
高陵县	Gaoling	106.5	106.0	101.6	105.9	100.3	113.7
全市构成	**Total**	**100.0**	**62.7**	**2.0**	**26.6**	**0.7**	**8.0**
新城区	Xincheng						
碑林区	Beilin						
莲湖区	Lianhu						
灞桥区	Baqiao	100.0	72.0	0.5	17.3	1.1	9.1
未央区	Weiyang	100.0	58.4	0.0	29.5	6.5	5.6
雁塔区	Yanta	100.0	65.4	0.5	22.2	0.0	11.9
阎良区	Yanliang	100.0	72.2	0.2	19.3	0.1	8.2
临潼区	Lintong	100.0	49.5	1.7	39.9	0.6	8.3
长安区	Chang'an	100.0	67.2	0.3	23.5	1.2	7.8
蓝田县	Lantian	100.0	60.5	5.5	25.7	0.8	7.5
周至县	Zhouzhi	100.0	69.2	6.4	17.9	0.2	6.3
户 县	Huxian	100.0	65.2	0.5	24.7	0.3	9.3
高陵县	Gaoling	100.0	51.9	0.3	39.4	0.3	8.1

11-14 主要年份农林牧渔及服务业增加值

Value-Added of Farming, Forestry, Animal Husbandry, Fishery and Service in Representative Years

单位：万元 (10 000 yuan)

年份 Year	农林牧渔及服务业增加值 Farming,Forestry, Animal Husbandry, Fishery and Service	农业 Farming	林业 Forestry	牧业 Animal Husbandry	渔业 Fishery	农林牧渔服务业 Service of Farming, Forestry, Animal Husbandry and Fishery
1995	413981	329662	4413	76746	3160	
2000	446481	336777	4323	101353	4028	
2001	458720	342427	4258	108096	3939	
2002	477691	351358	6419	116591	3323	
2003	458378	312849	5473	137236	2820	
2004	582009	393349	6811	164572	2919	14358
2005	660148	444320	6888	169701	3373	35866
2006	704427	465823	8556	177431	3227	49390
2007	825053	538794	8420	210930	4467	62442
2008	1034471	639071	10592	301305	5598	77905
2009	1103793	698043	11958	303594	5913	84285
2010	1400575	935489	14362	349204	6503	95017
2011	1731398	1161249	18807	428169	7679	115494
2012	1955931	1297824	33973	465476	10115	148543

11-15 主要年份农林牧渔及服务业增加值指数

Indices of Value-Added of Farming, Forestry, Animal Husbandry, Fishery and Service in Representative Years

年份 Year	农林牧渔及服务业增加值指数（上年=100）（可比价） Farming,Forestry,Animal Husbandry,Fishery and Service	农业 Farming	林业 Forestry	牧业 Animal Husbandry	渔业 Fishery	农林牧渔服务业 Service of Farming, Forestry, Animal Husbandry and Fishery
2008	107.6	107.6	112.0	105.8	100.0	114.0
2009	106.3	103.6	114.6	111.2	106.3	108.8
2010	106.9	107.9	108.7	104.3	94.0	108.9
2011	106.7	108.1	106.1	102.8	102.7	108.1
2012	106.0	105.6	142.8	104.8	113.4	108.5

11-16 各区县农林牧渔及服务业增加值（2012年）

Value-Added of Farming, Forestry, Animal Husbandry, Fishery and Service by Region（2012）

单位：万元 (10 000 persons)

区县	Region	农林牧渔及服务业增加值 Farming,Forestry, Animal Husbandry, Fishery and Service	农业 Farming	林业 Forestry	牧业 Animal Husbandry	渔业 Fishery	农林牧渔服务业 Service of Farming, Forestry, Animal Husbandry and Fishery
合计	**Total**	**1955931**	**1297824**	**33973**	**465476**	**10115**	**148543**
新城区	Xincheng						
碑林区	Beilin						
莲湖区	Lianhu						
灞桥区	Baqiao	160774	120837	709	25575	1084	12569
未央区	Weiyang	22351	13645	3	6414	945	1344
雁塔区	Yanta	23406	15414	106	4778		3108
阎良区	Yanliang	197028	144210	325	37482	147	14864
临潼区	Lintong	296241	155152	4362	110372	1622	24733
长安区	Chang'an	300647	230244	641	44914	3549	21299
蓝田县	Lantian	244506	153060	12803	59674	1436	17533
周至县	Zhouzhi	253940	185982	13504	39165	386	14903
户县	Huxian	253698	169895	1038	62498	600	19667
高陵县	Gaoling	203340	109385	482	74604	346	18523

11-17 各区县农林牧渔及服务业增加值指数（2012年）

Indices of Value-Added of Farming, Forestry, Animal Husbandry, Fishery and Service by Region（2012）

（上年=100）（可比价） (preceding year = 100) (At constant prices)

区 县 Region	农林牧渔及服务业增加值指数（上年=100）（可比价） Farming,Forestry,Animal Husbandry,Fishery and Service	农 业 Farming	林 业 Forestry	牧 业 Animal Husbandry	渔 业 Fishery	农林牧渔服务业 Service of Farming, Forestry, Animal Husbandry and Fishery
合 计 Total	**106.0**	**105.6**	**142.8**	**104.8**	**113.4**	**108.5**
新城区 Xincheng						
碑林区 Beilin						
莲湖区 Lianhu						
灞桥区 Baqiao	106.5	107.9	106.8	101.1	105.8	106.3
未央区 Weiyang	91.7	98.2	100.0	79.9	171.5	76.8
雁塔区 Yanta	90.4	95.7	372.0	87.6	0.0	71.4
阎良区 Yanliang	106.4	106.2	113.4	106.4	105.0	109.3
临潼区 Lintong	105.1	106.4	90.0	103.1	112.9	109.2
长安区 Chang'an	106.1	105.4	82.5	107.7	125.6	109.6
蓝田县 Lantian	106.3	104.2	101.6	113.9	101.3	105.1
周至县 Zhouzhi	106.8	103.0	484.2	101.9	87.6	115.8
户 县 Huxian	106.5	106.4	155.5	104.5	105.7	113.7
高陵县 Gaoling	106.4	105.9	101.6	105.8	100.3	113.6

11-18 主要年份农作物播种面积

Sown Areas of Farm Crops In Representative Years

单位：万亩 (10 000 mu)

年 份 Year	总播种面积 Total Sown Area	粮 食 Grain Crops			棉 花 Cotton	油 料 Oil-bearing Crops	蔬 菜 Vegetables
			小 麦 Wheat	玉 米 Corn			
1980	835.43	706.35	324.17	273.14	81.23	10.01	24.02
1985	795.41	704.36	378.20	271.14	21.02	8.01	45.03
1990	816.41	731.42	387.20	282.14	15.02	12.00	51.03
1991	820.41	731.37	389.19	283.14	19.01	13.01	47.03
1992	820.65	715.50	384.60	273.60	26.70	16.20	54.60
1993	821.63	713.49	380.40	273.69	17.66	14.84	63.90
1994	821.10	719.00	375.90	272.40	19.70	13.80	59.90
1995	784.74	690.63	370.41	259.55	11.07	18.57	57.59
1996	797.40	709.00	366.30	286.80	7.70	18.80	55.50
1997	755.78	670.83	367.71	248.79	4.50	15.53	59.36
1998	789.99	705.03	370.17	285.45	3.56	14.69	60.95
1999	793.08	709.95	371.94	294.00	2.85	12.74	60.68
2000	784.94	697.55	369.89	283.70	2.48	13.46	64.35
2001	763.16	678.05	359.19	278.57	2.91	11.87	61.77
2002	751.10	655.59	350.64	271.95	2.63	11.40	67.71
2003	737.06	632.55	336.05	261.89	3.38	11.04	69.44
2004	753.83	630.63	311.52	286.50	4.94	9.74	77.55
2005	757.91	642.75	325.10	287.87	5.40	9.51	83.33
2006	769.49	648.00	313.23	307.89	6.09	8.58	87.03
2007	762.38	637.05	306.98	304.13	6.93	7.41	91.07
2008	756.06	630.31	319.39	286.69	6.35	8.59	93.02
2009	757.11	628.69	318.36	285.20	6.45	8.59	94.83
2010	751.74	621.71	317.18	279.93	6.26	8.98	95.71
2011	704.17	573.13	306.39	243.06	5.97	8.83	96.97
2012	701.33	572.50	305.34	242.20	5.00	7.70	97.82

注：2011年农作物播种面积为陕西省统计局依据(国统字办[2011]68号)文件调整数。

11-19 各区县主要农作物播种面积（2012年）

Sown Areas of Major Farm Crops by Region（2012）

单位：万亩 (10 000 mu)

区 县	Region	总播种面积 Total Sown Area	粮 食 Grain Crops	小 麦 Wheat	玉 米 Corn	棉 花 Cotton	油 料 Oil-bearing Crops	蔬 菜 Vegetables	瓜果类 Fruits Class
合 计	**Total**	**701.33**	**572.50**	**305.34**	**242.20**	**5.00**	**7.70**	**97.82**	**16.03**
新城区	Xincheng								
碑林区	Beilin								
莲湖区	Lianhu								
灞桥区	Baqiao	28.96	20.71	12.54	7.53	0.11	0.43	6.97	0.65
未央区	Weiyang	6.73	4.74	2.83	1.91			1.99	
雁塔区	Yanta	0.71							
阎良区	Yanliang	47.42	19.44	11.50	7.92	4.26	0.10	17.37	6.23
临潼区	Lintong	132.04	112.26	60.13	46.79	0.29	1.58	14.52	2.31
长安区	Chang'an	135.80	109.96	60.09	48.32	0.02	1.56	22.03	2.06
蓝田县	Lantian	113.47	98.56	50.59	33.84	0.32	2.54	8.57	2.69
周至县	Zhouzhi	88.16	78.08	40.49	35.68		1.03	8.85	0.13
户 县	Huxian	98.97	87.57	45.87	40.68		0.46	9.13	1.75
高陵县	Gaoling	49.07	41.18	21.29	19.53			7.68	0.21

11-20 主要年份农作物产品产量

Yield of Major Farm Crops in Representative Years

单位：万吨 (10 000 ton)

年份 Year	粮食作物 Grain Crops	夏粮 Summer Grain	小麦 Wheat	秋粮 Autumn Grain	稻谷 Rice	玉米 Corn	棉花 Cotton	油料 Oil-bearing Crops	油菜籽 Rapeseeds	蔬菜 Vegetables
1978	132.8	64.2	58.2	68.7	5.1	55.8	2.85	0.09	0.07	45.66
1979	145.7	81.8	74.2	63.9	4.5	53.4	2.63	0.33	0.29	49.11
1980	114.4	56.6	52.2	57.8	4.7	47.7	1.97	0.54	0.50	40.13
1981	116.1	78.7	74.3	37.4	3.4	31.5	1.36	0.76	0.75	34.06
1982	148.9	85.6	82.2	63.3	4.9	55.5	2.88	0.51	0.49	53.71
1983	148.1	81.8	79.6	66.3	4.8	58.5	0.85	0.36	0.34	46.99
1984	157.6	82.4	81.0	75.2	5.0	66.5	1.49	0.46	0.29	75.47
1985	150.1	76.1	74.8	74.0	5.1	65.1	0.49	0.75	0.39	86.44
1986	162.4	91.7	90.1	70.7	4.8	61.8	0.44	1.25	0.82	85.84
1987	171.2	87.0	85.2	84.2	5.0	74.3	0.47	1.57	1.22	95.16
1988	158.0	86.8	84.6	71.1	3.8	61.4	0.42	0.89	0.51	113.50
1989	173.6	93.5	91.2	80.2	4.7	70.4	0.55	1.33	0.94	129.32
1990	172.4	91.7	89.7	80.8	5.5	70.4	0.70	1.35	0.94	119.32
1991	178.8	91.1	89.2	87.7	5.0	77.5	0.97	1.20	0.74	117.41
1992	183.4	101.7	99.6	81.7	4.7	72.3	0.74	1.49	0.87	128.12
1993	190.0	101.1	99.0	88.9	4.9	78.6	0.75	1.40	1.00	145.80
1994	157.4	86.9	84.9	70.5	4.5	61.4	0.65	1.08	0.78	135.26
1995	175.3	99.8	97.4	75.5	3.4	67.8	0.29	2.17	1.90	133.60
1996	187.5	80.1	78.4	107.4	3.4	95.6	0.24	1.83	1.55	138.01
1997	190.5	114.3	112.3	76.3	3.5	69.4	0.17	1.86	1.65	142.11
1998	212.7	104.4	104.0	108.3	3.2	99.1	0.14	1.67	1.36	148.87
1999	204.4	95.5	94.4	108.9	2.9	99.7	0.15	1.30	1.00	153.24
2000	201.9	92.6	91.6	109.3	3.1	100.5	0.14	1.34	0.95	162.14
2001	197.1	98.1	97.2	98.9	2.7	91.3	0.17	1.23	0.90	152.80
2002	192.4	94.5	93.5	97.9	2.1	91.6	0.18	1.22	0.84	169.74
2003	176.3	98.2	96.7	78.2	1.6	72.3	0.22	1.13	0.70	169.67
2004	195.8	97.8	96.0	98.0	1.7	91.6	0.40	1.14	0.84	180.96
2005	205.5	100.0	99.1	105.5	1.6	99.3	0.45	1.16	0.89	195.70
2006	193.5	86.0	85.4	107.4	1.4	101.2	0.48	1.08	0.87	189.30
2007	189.1	77.3	76.7	111.8	1.5	105.6	0.59	0.96	0.77	204.30
2008	214.4	105.9	105.6	108.5	0.9	103.0	0.62	1.15	0.95	221.53
2009	218.2	103.0	102.1	115.2	0.9	109.5	0.63	1.12	0.93	242.41
2010	221.7	106.6	105.8	115.1	0.8	108.9	0.60	1.20	1.00	253.10
2011	182.0	90.5	89.7	91.5	0.7	85.3	0.56	1.17	0.95	261.66
2012	192.5	95.7	94.9	96.8	0.6	89.3	0.47	1.02	0.88	277.80

注：2011年农作物产品产量为陕西省统计局依据(国统字办[2011]70号)文件调整数。

11-21 各区县主要农作物产品产量（2012年）

Yield of Major Farm Crops by Region (2012)

单位：万吨 (10 000 tons)

区 县	Region	粮食作物 Grain Crops	夏粮 Summer Grain	小麦 Wheat	秋粮 Autumn Grain	稻谷 Rice	玉米 Corn
合 计	**Total**	**192.55**	**95.73**	**94.92**	**96.82**	**0.57**	**89.29**
新城区	Xincheng						
碑林区	Beilin						
莲湖区	Lianhu						
灞桥区	Baqiao	6.11	3.26	3.26	2.84		2.68
未央区	Weiyang	1.57	0.84	0.84	0.73		0.73
雁塔区	Yanta	0.00	0.00	0.00	0.00		0.00
阎良区	Yanliang	8.13	4.54	4.54	3.59		3.59
临潼区	Lintong	35.17	17.98	17.94	17.19		15.40
长安区	Chang'an	36.88	18.37	18.37	18.51	0.33	17.85
蓝田县	Lantian	28.98	12.99	12.91	15.99	0.20	11.57
周至县	Zhouzhi	24.32	12.24	11.81	12.07	0.04	11.88
户 县	Huxian	31.37	15.86	15.62	15.51		15.44
高陵县	Gaoling	20.02	9.65	9.65	10.38		10.17

11-21 续表 continued

单位：万吨 (10 000 tons)

区 县	Region	棉花 Cotton	油料 Oil-bearing Crops	油菜籽 Rapeseeds	蔬菜 Vegetables	瓜果类 Fruits Class
合 计	**Total**	**0.47**	**1.02**	**0.88**	**277.80**	**46.30**
新城区	Xincheng					
碑林区	Beilin					
莲湖区	Lianhu					
灞桥区	Baqiao	0.01	0.06	0.05	26.56	0.97
未央区	Weiyang				4.52	0.17
雁塔区	Yanta				2.51	
阎良区	Yanliang	0.40	0.01	0.01	65.73	21.02
临潼区	Lintong	0.03	0.17	0.15	39.34	6.42
长安区	Chang'an		0.28	0.26	53.00	4.15
蓝田县	Lantian	0.03	0.28	0.22	15.04	7.24
周至县	Zhouzhi		0.14	0.12	17.98	0.31
户 县	Huxian		0.08	0.07	27.52	5.05
高陵县	Gaoling				25.60	0.97

11-22 主要年份农作物单位面积产量

Yield of Farm Crops Per Unit Area in Representative Years

单位：公斤/亩 (kg/mu)

年 份 Year	粮食作物 Grain Crops	夏 粮 Summer Grain	小 麦 Wheat	秋 粮 Autumn Grain	玉 米 Corn	棉 花 Cotton	油 料 Oil-bearing Crops	油菜籽 Rapeseeds	蔬 菜 Vegetables
1990	236	232	232	241	249	46	103	101	2349
1992	256	259	259	253	264	28	92	101	2344
1993	266	260	260	274	287	42	94	107	2282
1994	219	226	226	211	225	33	79	84	2260
1995	254	263	263	243	261	27	117	128	2320
1996	265	214	214	321	333	32	86	100	2489
1997	284	305	306	257	279	38	76	129	2395
1998	302	278	279	328	347	40	114	121	2443
1999	288	253	254	327	339	52	102	106	2526
2000	289	247	248	338	354	55	102	112	2520
2001	291	270	271	314	328	60	104	113	2474
2002	293	266	267	326	337	70	107	115	2507
2003	279	287	288	269	276	67	102	110	2444
2004	310	308	308	313	320	81	117	129	2333
2005	320	304	305	336	345	84	121	132	2349
2006	299	273	273	323	329	80	125	135	2175
2007	297	250	250	341	347	85	129	132	2245
2008	340	330	331	350	359	97	134	137	2382
2009	347	320	321	375	384	97	131	131	2556
2010	357	333	334	381	389	94	130	131	2644
2011	318	293	293	347	351	95	133	134	2698
2012	336	310	311	367	369	94	132	130	2840

注：2011年农作物单产为陕西省统计局依据(国统字办[2011]72号)文件调整数。

11-23 各区县主要农作物单位面积产量（2012年）

The Output of Main Crops Per Unit Area by Region (2012)

单位：公斤/亩 (kg/mu)

区 县	Region	粮食作物 Grain Crops	夏 粮 Summer Grain	小 麦 Wheat	秋 粮 Autumn Grain	玉 米 Corn
合 计	**Total**	**336**	**310**	**311**	**367**	**369**
新城区	Xincheng					
碑林区	Beilin					
莲湖区	Lianhu					
灞桥区	Baqiao	295	260	260	349	356
未央区	Weiyang	331	298	298	380	380
雁塔区	Yanta					
阎良区	Yanliang	418	395	395	452	453
临潼区	Lintong	313	298	298	331	329
长安区	Chang'an	335	306	306	371	369
蓝田县	Lantian	294	252	255	340	342
周至县	Zhouzhi	311	294	292	331	333
户 县	Huxian	358	340	349	379	379
高陵县	Gaoling	486	453	453	522	521

11-23 续表 continued

单位：公斤/亩 (kg/mu)

区县	Region	棉花 Cotton	油料 Oil-bearing Crops	油菜籽 Rapeseeds	蔬菜 Vegetables	瓜果类 Fruits Class
合计	**Total**	**94**	**132**	**130**	**2840**	**2786**
新城区	Xincheng					
碑林区	Beilin					
莲湖区	Lianhu					
灞桥区	Baqiao	65	131	132	3810	3795
未央区	Weiyang				2270	
雁塔区	Yanta				3550	320
阎良区	Yanliang	95	118	113	3783	3818
临潼区	Lintong	90	106	104	2710	2873
长安区	Chang'an	80	179	182	2406	2054
蓝田县	Lantian	102	109	102	1756	2037
周至县	Zhouzhi		138	131	2031	1984
户县	Huxian	91	182	185	3015	3073
高陵县	Gaoling				3334	3381

11-24 设施农业生产情况（2012年）

Agricultural Production Facilities (2012)

指标	Item	种植面积（亩） planting area (mu)	产量（吨） outpot(ton)
一、蔬菜	**Vegetables**	**238795**	**1258775**
其中：芹菜	Celery	67760	351493
油菜	Rape	2518	5053
菠菜	Spinach	14206	35651
黄瓜	Cucumber	21400	104535
西红柿	Tomato	28016	96437
辣椒	Chilli	12769	40824
二、瓜果类	**Fruits class**	**99987**	**344586**
其中：草莓	Strawberry	4233	5867
三、花卉苗木	**Flower seedling wood**	**13802**	
四、食用菌	**Edible Fungi**	**2821**	**13055**
五、其他	**Others**	**23920**	
补充资料：蔬菜设施个数：93875（个）	Updates. Vegetable shed number (93875unit)		
蔬菜设施面积：153206（亩）	Vegetables awning area(153206mu)		

11-25 主要年份林业生产情况

Statistics on Forestry in Representative Years

指 标	Item	2000	2005	2007	2008	2009	2010	2011	2012
一.营林情况	**Afforestation**								
当年造林面积合计（万亩）	Build Forestry Areas(10 000 mu)	27.47	16.56	6.17	8.76	15.60	16.10	10.42	9.08
封山育林面积（万亩）	Hill-closeure for Afforestation Areas (t 0 000 mu)	18.78	18.65	23.97	30.19	37.40	55.10	41.30	41.90
零星四旁植树（万株）	Planting(10 000 plants)	731.00	1064.00	1176.00	952.00	931.00	509.20	536.70	579.20
育苗面积（万亩）	Raise Seedlings Areas(10 000 mu)	2.05	5.99	6.03	4.72	3.41	11.95	9.93	11.64
# 本年新育	New Seedling of Current Year	1.69	2.54	3.15	2.19	1.86	1.75	1.93	1.98
二.主要林产品产量（吨）	**Main Forestry Product(ton)**								
生漆	Lacquer	11	2	5	6	5	10	4	
核桃	Walnuts	997	3351	3349	4589	4306	7875	13235	15253
板栗	Chinese Chestnut	744	2076	2153	2728	3122	7736	8229	7654
花椒	Pepper	140	525	575	842	689	1420	889	879
三.村及村以下采伐木材（万立方米）	**Timber Harvested at or below Village Level (10 000 cu.m)**	**1.62**	**1.87**	**0.96**	**1.23**	**0.97**	**3.30**	**1.39**	**1.04**

注：2009年迹地更新面积改为更新造林面积；
2010年起，根据统计制度要求，林业统计数据取自林业部门。

11-26 各区县林业生产情况（2012年）

Statistics On Forestry by Region (2012)

区 县	Region	当年造林面积（亩） Build Forestry Areas in The Year (mu)	零星植树（万株） Planting (10 000 plants)	育苗面积（亩） Raise Seedlings Areas (mu)	核桃产量（吨） Output of Walnuts (ton)	板栗产量（吨） Output of Chinese Chestnut (ton)	村及村以下采伐木材（万立方） Timber Harvesting at\under Vallage level (10 000 cu.m)
合 计	**Total**	**90750**	**579.2**	**116430**	**15253**	**7654**	**1.04**
新城区	Xincheng						
碑林区	Beilin						
莲湖区	Lianhu						
灞桥区	Baqiao	5850	60.0		250		
未央区	Weiyang		33.0	2280			
雁塔区	Yanta		5.0	3390	50		
阎良区	Yanliang	1845	35.0	495			0.55
临潼区	Lintong	12375	72.0	1005	709	80	
长安区	Chang'an	11355	110.0	10335	425	230	
蓝田县	Lantian	26895	81.0	6300	5400	5040	0.07
周至县	Zhouzhi	20940	75.0	84870	8089	2184	0.02
户 县	Huxian	9840	78.2	5250	330	120	0.40
高陵县	Gaoling	1650	30.0	2505			

11-27 主要年份果业生产情况

Statistics on Fruits in Representative Years

指 标	Item	2000	2005	2007	2008	2009	2010	2011	2012
果园面积合计（万亩）	**Areas of Orchards (10 000 mu)**	**47.86**	**55.55**	**60.86**	**64.31**	**71.08**	**74.95**	**74.27**	**76.83**
苹果园	Apple Orchards	12.15	5.96	5.94	5.82	5.66	3.55	1.53	1.44
梨园	Pears Orchards	5.79	3.01	2.9	2.82	2.66	2.27	1.66	1.65
葡萄园	Grapes Orchards	1.89	3.02	3.18	3.55	4.59	4.83	4.91	5.46
桃园	Peach Orchards	3.47	8.66	8.87	8.75	8.48	7.68	6.87	6.78
猕猴桃园	Chinese Goosebeery Orchards	16.83	4.33	21.04	23.61	29.01	34.92	36.97	41.36
杏园	Apricot Orchards	0.62	2.5	2.65	2.78	2.97	3.62	3.6	3.59
柿子园	Presimmons Orchards	1.96	2.69	2.97	3.28	3.26	3.16	2.83	2.91
石榴园	Pomegranate Orchards				3.94	3.61	3.43	3.38	3.61
水果产量（吨）	**Output of Fruits (ton)**	**343551**	**512869**	**605075**	**716902**	**789587**	**847821**	**911361**	**932054**
苹果	Apple	89416	53387	52180	53194	53023	39130	34313	28675
梨	Pears	65459	57059	52869	55945	57929	55122	48026	47463
葡萄	Grapes	16647	30951	43621	50185	56731	64885	69003	75516
桃	Peach	27010	89755	124393	139058	146651	142051	137683	125857
猕猴桃	Chinese Goosebeery	96640	137853	146301	210393	233296	296023	357066	386336
杏	Apricot				39690	55535	48544	34340	57772
柿子	Persimmon				28540	34780	35287	31625	41211
石榴	Pomegranate				43701	42122	40211	34340	32329

11-28 各区县果业生产情况（2012年）

Area and Output of Fruits by Region (2012)

区 县	Region	果园面积（万亩） Area of Orchards(10 000 mu)	水果产量（吨） Output of Fruits(ton)
合 计	**Total**	**76.83**	**932054**
新城区	Xincheng		
碑林区	Beilin		
莲湖区	Lianhu		
灞桥区	Baqiao	7.18	92579
未央区	Weiyang	0.41	8720
雁塔区	Yanta	0.39	5700
阎良区	Yanliang	2.68	64018
临潼区	Lintong	4.77	46317
长安区	Chang'an	5.78	74497
蓝田县	Lantian	8.92	118651
周至县	Zhouzhi	38.72	379644
户 县	Huxian	5.10	90556
高陵县	Gaoling	2.88	51372

11-29 主要年份畜牧业生产情况

Statistics on Livestock Husbandry in Representative Years

指 标	Item	2005	2007	2008	2009	2010	2011	2012
一.大牲畜年末总头数（头）	**Large Animals In Stock at Year-end (head)**	**322521**	**181353**	**204723**	**208358**	**216043**	**212351**	**211852**
# 能繁殖母畜	Female Animals of Reprductive Ability	176682	110451	132772	136276	144104	143074	
# 役畜	Draught Animals	90717	39968	36069	42670	42243	32877	31866
1. 牛	Cattle	320773	180200	203596	207237	215072	211334	210819
# 能繁殖母畜	Female Animals of Reprductive Ability	176445	109970	132657	136143	144012	142977	
# 当年生仔畜	Newborn Livestock in the Year	72163	43313	41457	39403	40052	36093	
#肉牛	Farm Cattle			60490	63804	65447	62127	60233
#奶牛	Dairy Cattle	96498	96400	108164	112071	118747	117149	119888
2. 马（匹）	Horses	559	477	499	515	456	496	533
3. 驴	Donkeys	175	108	83	87	67	71	46
4. 骡	Mules	1014	568	545	519	448	450	454
二.猪年末头数（头）	**Hogs in Stock Year-end (head)**	**1472869**	**774534**	**864083**	**918734**	**943183**	**943987**	**966018**
# 能繁殖的母猪	Female Hogs of Reprductive Ability	123543	71600	85419	96522	106610	101332	103926
三.羊年末只数（只）	**Sheeps and Goats in Stock at Year-end(head)**	**532471**	**234900**	**263164**	**279463**	**294539**	**295995**	**284596**
1. 山羊	Goats	520354	226810	258287	274359	288738	288346	278738
# 奶山羊	Milch Goats	358733	177547	201007	229301	246442	245118	234643
2. 绵羊	Sheeps	12117	8090	4877	5104	5801	7649	5858
四.家禽年末存栏（万只）	**Poultry in Stock at Year-end (10 000 heads)**	**1373**	**849**	**920**	**981**	**1034**	**1154**	**1177**
五.年末养蜂箱数（箱）	**Honey (box)**	**24287**	**18371**	**22124**	**22779**	**22984**	**17567**	**17161**

11-30 各区县畜牧业生产情况（2012年）

Statistics On Livestock, Animal Husbandry by Region（2012）

区 县	Region	大牲畜年末头数（头） Large Animals In Stock at Year-end (head)	役畜 Draught Animals	牛（头） Cattle (head)	奶牛 Dairy Cattle	马（匹） Horses (head)	驴（头） Donkeys (head)	骡（头） Mutes (head)
合 计	**Total**	**211852**	**31866**	**210819**	**119888**	**533**	**46**	**454**
新城区	Xincheng							
碑林区	Beilin							
莲湖区	Lianhu							
灞桥区	Baqiao	12870	161	12854	12509	16		
未央区	Weiyang	5669		5669	5469			
雁塔区	Yanta	220		220	200			
阎良区	Yanliang	17789		17789	15755			
临潼区	Lintong	72488	7763	72488	64725			
长安区	Chang'an	8032	1297	7338	3974	326		368
蓝田县	Lantian	44175	12381	44175	2547			
周至县	Zhouzhi	31184	10028	31066	2879	80		38
户 县	Huxian	11090	31	11090	5842			
高陵县	Gaoling	8335	205	8130	5988	111	46	48

11-30 续表 continued

区 县	Region	猪（头） Hogs (head)	能繁殖的母猪 Female Hogs of Reprductive Ability	羊（只） Sheep and Goats (head)	山羊 Goats	奶山羊 Milch Goats	家禽（万只） Poultry (10 000 head)	蜂（箱） Honey (box)
合 计	**Total**	**966018**	**103926**	**284596**	**278738**	**234643**	**1176.72**	**17161**
新城区	Xincheng							
碑林区	Beilin							
莲湖区	Lianhu							
灞桥区	Baqiao	50186	5259	11974	11974	10533	43.77	330
未央区	Weiyang	27627	3631	570	570	440	6.40	
雁塔区	Yanta						2.50	
阎良区	Yanliang	38175	4392	54615	54615	54615	61.89	560
临潼区	Lintong	253800	22503	98212	98212	98212	270.50	1621
长安区	Chang'an	104764	9192	14684	12199	4420	287.10	3760
蓝田县	Lantian	80929	9766	70962	70962	46720	164.41	
周至县	Zhouzhi	205763	26163	12045	11890	2284	90.86	6580
户 县	Huxian	152885	16538	6614	6614	6467	135.30	4310
高陵县	Gaoling	51889	6482	14920	11702	10952	114.00	

11-31 主要年份畜产品和水产品产量

Output of Livestock Products and Aquatic Products in Representative Years

单位：吨 (ton)

年 份 Year	肉类总产量 Output of Meat	猪 肉 Pork	牛 肉 Beef	羊 肉 Mutton	禽 肉 Poultry
1990	63273	50646	4667	1931	5885
1991	72268	55086	5623	2162	9062
1992	88994	68134	6468	2460	11290
1993	93420	71274	7249	2220	12174
1994	106691	79433	8298	2350	15681
1995	127815	86513	11251	3731	23948
1996	91468	63750	5402	2578	19324
1997	106597	75381	6672	3468	20596
1998	134152	98974	8788	4710	21424
1999	130124	93859	9827	4147	21963
2000	147571	106137	12066	4766	23760
2001	157277	113353	11900	5153	20540
2002	161092	118634	11516	5394	20515
2003	165860	122759	13241	5180	19682
2004	171545	126404	13641	5874	18493
2005	182046	136503	14031	6106	18803
2006	108634	81199	8267	2841	13417
2007	102191	73254	8589	3111	14075
2008	115352	84654	9840	3335	16060
2009	126182	94490	10142	3677	17190
2010	136501	102296	10854	3875	18338
2011	144631	104816	11860	3645	19390
2012	151711	110506	12079	3697	20046

注：2010年起，根据统计制度要求，水产品产量及养殖面积统计数据取自水务部门。

11-31 续表 continued

单位：吨 (ton)

年 份 Year	奶类产量 Output of Milk	牛 奶 Cow Milk	禽 蛋 Poultry Eggs	蜂蜜（公斤） Honey(kg)	水产品 Output of Aquatic Products	养殖面积（万亩） Water Raise Areas (10 000 mu)
1990	82017	50528	55938	1035392	4259	2.55
1991	91006	57700	90558	1022797	4949	2.63
1992	100080	63586	104970	739275	6015	2.8
1993	111070	73897	125244	662049	7132	2.97
1994	145412	99025	146503	547808	7900	3.1
1995	132909	85753	141227	535891	8517	3.21
1996	133372	86103	138044	613290	8910	3.51
1997	150964	98078	156066	713918	10054	3.46
1998	174099	119719	142519	537304	10480	3.4
1999	209144	145191	135981	541613	11061	3.38
2000	245913	176155	138305	460598	11384	3.35
2001	255437	179977	132303	479839	12480	3.17
2002	288009	202826	134336	497530	12017	3.31
2003	336296	245407	128833	537805	9967	2.48
2004	384319	289564	117597	449765	9721	2.46
2005	422229	327961	118115	421052	9370	2.38
2006	471438	374813	97816	414271	11937	1.6
2007	528037	428462	98140	401761	12402	1.38
2008	589697	475681	108515	503031	12487	1.4
2009	618186	498394	116685	528731	13044	1.52
2010	633663	509178	123793	436759	11850	2.24
2011	647978	509777	125639	217632	11800	2.2
2012	666439	513337	129970	213174	14010	2.95

11-32 各区县主要畜产品和水产品产量（2012年）

Output of Major Livestock Products and Aquatic Products by Region（2012）

单位：吨 (tou)

区县	Region	肉类总产量 Output of Meat	猪肉 Pork	牛肉 Beef	羊肉 Mutton	禽肉 Poultry
合计	**Total**	**151711**	**110506**	**12079**	**3697**	**20046**
新城区	Xincheng					
碑林区	Beilin					
莲湖区	Lianhu					
灞桥区	Baqiao	7263	5464	742	142	800
未央区	Weiyang	2197	1943	140	3	30
雁塔区	Yanta	1493	1450	13		30
阎良区	Yanliang	6273	4237	590	516	865
临潼区	Lintong	41021	29073	3312	1470	4132
长安区	Chang'an	20472	13352	555	237	5617
蓝田县	Lantian	18719	10377	3632	949	2922
周至县	Zhouzhi	27951	24129	2112	190	1503
户县	Huxian	18694	15194	670	71	2386
高陵县	Gaoling	7628	5287	313	119	1761

11-32 续表 continued

单位：吨 (tou)

区 县	Region	奶类总产量 Output of Milk	牛 奶 Cow Milk	禽 蛋 Poultry Eggs	蜂 蜜 Honey(kg)	水产品 Aquatic Products	养殖面积（亩） Water Raise Areas(mu)
合 计	**Total**	**666439**	**513337**	**129970**	**213174**	**14010**	**29475**
新城区	Xincheng						
碑林区	Beilin						
莲湖区	Lianhu						
灞桥区	Baqiao	64080	56699	5597	8300	1505	2850
未央区	Weiyang	22163	22123	222		3000	4549
雁塔区	Yanta	880	880	242		100	255
阎良区	Yanliang	94734	64050	7112	15312	202	150
临潼区	Lintong	347760	278111	30426	43255	1865	5175
长安区	Chang'an	21868	17859	39697	65487	4546	9491
蓝田县	Lantian	39817	11741	6139		926	3615
周至县	Zhouzhi	13111	11920	9242	62394	828	2310
户 县	Huxian	29848	25810	17355	18426	803	900
高陵县	Gaoling	32178	24144	13938		235	180

11-33 农业科技、教育情况（2012年）

Agricultural Science and Technology Education（2012）

指 标	Item	2012
农业研究开发机构（个）	Agricultural research and development institutions (unit)	295
农业科技人员（人）	Agricultural scientific and technical personnel(persons)	3380
农业科研成果（个）	Agricultural scientific research achievements (unit)	30
农民技能培训人数（万人）	The number of peasants skills training(10000 persons)	18.6
良种推广面积（万亩）	Thoroughbred promotion area (10000 mu)	547.54
农业信息站（个）	information station of Agricultural (unit)	3104

11-34 主要年份农产品人均占有量

Per Capita Output of Major Farm Products in Representative Years

单位：公斤/人 (kg/ person)

年份 Year	粮食 Grain	棉花 Cotton	油料 Oil-bearing Crops	猪牛羊肉 Pork Beef and Mutton	禽蛋 Poultry Eggs	奶类 Milk	水果 Fruits	蔬菜 Vegetables
1978	266.7	5.7	0.2	5.4	0.9	3.3	6.8	91.7
1979	288.6	5.2	0.6	6.7	1.0	4.0	5.1	97.3
1980	223.5	3.8	1.1	5.9	1.2	4.1	6.9	78.4
1981	222.9	2.6	1.5	6.6	1.7	4.7	5.8	65.4
1982	281.5	5.5	1.0	4.9	2.7	5.6	5.9	101.6
1983	276.6	1.6	0.7	4.9	3.2	6.5	5.0	87.8
1984	289.4	2.7	0.8	4.8	6.2	8.7	4.8	138.6
1985	271.4	0.9	1.4	6.8	5.7	10.2	7.6	156.3
1986	288.0	0.8	2.2	7.8	6.4	12.1	9.6	152.2
1987	298.0	0.8	2.7	7.3	6.8	13.8	10.6	165.6
1988	269.7	0.7	1.5	8.0	8.9	15.6	11.1	193.7
1989	290.7	0.9	2.2	8.4	7.6	13.1	10.2	216.5
1990	298.7	1.2	2.1	9.4	9.2	14.2	11.5	196.0
1991	290.6	1.6	2.0	10.2	14.7	14.8	11.7	190.8
1992	294.3	1.2	2.4	12.4	16.8	16.2	17.3	205.6
1993	301.2	1.2	2.2	12.8	19.9	17.6	25.9	231.1
1994	246.1	1.0	1.7	14.1	22.9	22.7	28.0	211.5
1995	270.4	0.5	3.4	15.7	21.8	20.5	37.5	206.1
1996	286.3	0.4	3.2	11.0	21.1	20.4	43.9	210.8
1997	287.8	0.3	2.8	12.9	23.6	22.8	43.3	214.7
1998	318.3	0.2	2.5	16.8	21.3	26.1	50.0	222.8
1999	303.0	0.2	1.9	16.0	20.2	31.0	52.7	227.2
2000	293.5	0.2	1.9	17.9	20.1	35.7	49.9	235.7
2001	283.7	0.2	1.8	18.8	19.0	36.8	48.8	219.9
2002	273.8	0.3	1.7	19.3	19.1	41.0	53.5	241.6
2003	246.0	0.3	1.6	19.7	18.0	46.9	53.6	236.8
2004	270.1	0.6	1.6	20.1	16.2	53.0	63.9	249.6
2005	277.1	0.6	1.6	21.1	15.9	56.9	69.1	263.8
2006	256.9	0.6	1.4	12.3	13.0	62.6	73.5	251.4
2007	247.4	0.8	1.3	11.1	12.8	69.1	79.2	267.3
2008	256.0	0.7	1.4	11.7	13.0	70.4	85.6	264.5
2009	258.7	0.7	1.3	12.8	13.8	73.3	93.6	287.4
2010	261.8	0.7	1.4	13.8	14.6	74.8	100.1	298.9
2011	213.8	0.7	1.4	14.1	14.8	76.1	107.1	318.9
2012	225.6	0.6	1.2	14.8	15.2	78.1	109.2	325.6

11-35 主要年份农村经济效益指标

Main Indicators of Rural Economic Benefit in Representative Years

年份 Year	每一劳动力创造的 Average Labor Force Production 农林牧渔及服务业总产值（元） Gross Output Value of Farming,Forestry, Animal Husbandry, Fishery and Service (yuan)	粮食（公斤） Grain Crops(kg)	棉花（公斤） Cotton (kg)	油料（公斤） Oil-bearing Crops(kg)	每亩耕地种植业总产值（元） Output of Each Unit of Area Planting(yuan)	每百元物耗生产的总产值（元） Output per 100-Yuan of Material Consumed(yuan)
1978	504.7	1024.6	22.0	0.7	104.3	
1979	549.0	1096.5	19.8	2.3	116.0	
1980	483.1	846.1	14.5	4.0	99.2	
1981	502.8	840.5	9.9	5.5	105.4	
1982	631.5	1058.9	20.5	3.6	139.3	
1983	606.5	1053.2	6.1	2.6	124.1	
1984	850.7	1154.2	10.9	3.4	163.6	
1985	1020.1	1134.6	3.7	5.6	183.1	
1986	1132.2	1236.4	3.4	9.5	204.6	
1987	1280.3	1277.2	3.5	11.7	231.5	
1988	1558.4	1148.0	3.0	6.5	273.2	
1989	1605.3	1231.9	3.9	9.5	295.0	
1990	1766.3	1279.1	5.2	10.0	343.4	233.3
1991	1958.8	1326.6	7.2	8.9	380.4	238.4
1992	2093.7	1360.7	5.5	11.1	451.6	241.8
1993	2528.9	1409.7	5.6	10.4	546.8	240.1
1994	3705.0	1167.8	4.8	8.0	762.8	227.6
1995	4953.0	1300.6	2.2	16.1	1106.5	225.9
1996	5154.8	1391.2	1.8	13.6	1224.2	234.5
1997	5493.0	1413.4	1.3	13.8	1283.3	239.2
1998	5615.9	1578.1	1.0	12.4	1374.3	247.0
1999	4826.5	1516.6	1.1	9.7	1175.9	251.7
2000	5091.5	1498.0	1.0	9.9	1161.1	250.2
2001	5328.5	1462.4	1.3	9.1	1221.1	248.6
2002	5617.4	1427.5	1.3	9.1	1272.0	265.9
2003	5761.2	1308.1	1.6	8.4	1332.4	254.3
2004	6885.4	1452.7	3.0	8.5	1434.6	261.7
2005	7737.9	1524.7	3.3	8.6	1642.3	262.9
2006	8415.5	1435.7	3.6	8.0	1756.9	263.1
2007	10165.6	1403.0	4.4	7.1	2037.3	259.8
2008	13306.4	1695.4	4.9	9.1	2447.9	259.6
2009	14674.3	1791.7	5.1	9.2	2737.9	261.6
2010	19480.7	1901.3	5.1	10.0	3753.4	260.9
2011	23474.6	1567.2	4.9	10.1	4585.8	274.0
2012	27219.4	1699.6	4.2	10.1	5175.7	273.5

主要统计指标解释

农林牧渔业总产值 指以货币表现的农、林、牧、渔业全部产品和对农林牧渔业生产活动进行的各种支持性服务活动的价值总量，它反映一定时期内农林牧渔业生产总规模和总成果。1957年以前的农林牧渔业总产值中包括了厩肥和农民自给性手工业（如农民自制衣服、鞋、袜，自己从事粮食初步加工等）。1958年及以后，林业中增加了村及村以下竹木采伐产值；牧业中取消了厩肥产值；副业中取消了农民自给性手工业产值，增加了村及村以下办的工业产值；渔业中增加了海洋捕捞水产品产值。1980年及以后，在副业中增加了农民家庭兼营工业商品部分的产值。从1984年起村及村以下工业产值划归工业。从1993年起取消副业，将野生动物的捕猎划入牧业，野生植物采集和农民家庭兼营商品性工业划归农业。从2003年起，执行新的国民经济行业分类标准，农林牧渔业总产值中包括了农林牧渔服务业产值。林业中增加了森林采运业产值。农业中取消了家庭兼营商品性工业产值，将野生林产品的采集划归林业。第一次农业普查以后，由于畜牧业产品年报数据与普查数据之间存在一定的差距，根据农业普查结果对畜牧业年报数据进行了修正，对畜牧业产值进行了相应修正。

农林牧渔业总产值的计算方法通常是按农、林、牧、渔业产品及其副产品的产量分别乘以各自单位产品价格求得；少数生产周期较长，当年没有产品或产品产量不易统计的，则采用间接方法匡算其产值；然后将四业产品产值及农林牧渔服务业产值相加即为农林牧渔业总产值。

粮食产量 指全社会的产量。包括国有经济经营的、集体统一经营的和农民家庭经营的粮食产量，还包括工矿企业办的农场和其他生产单位的产量。粮食除包括稻谷、小麦、玉米、高粱、谷子及其他杂粮外，还包括薯类和豆类。其产量计算方法，豆类按去豆荚后的干豆计算；薯类（包括甘薯和马铃薯，不包括芋头和木薯）1963年以前按每4公斤鲜薯折1公斤粮食计算，从1964年开始改为按5公斤鲜薯折1公斤粮食计算。城市郊区作为蔬菜的薯类（如马铃薯等）按鲜品计算，并且不作粮食统计。其他粮食一律按脱粒后的原粮计算。1989年以前全国粮食产量数据主要靠全面报表取得，1989年开始使用抽样调查数据。

棉花产量 指全社会的产量。包括春播棉和夏播棉。产量按皮棉计算。不包括木棉。

油料产量 指全部油料作物的生产量。包括花生、油菜籽、芝麻、向日葵籽、胡麻籽（亚麻籽）和其他油料。不包括大豆、木本油料和野生油料。花生以带壳干花生计算。

水产品产量 指人工养殖的水产品和天然生长的水产品的捕捞量。包括海水的鱼类、虾蟹类、贝类和藻类以及内陆水域的鱼类、虾蟹类和贝类，不包括淡水生植物。水产品产量是通过各级水产和统计部门逐级上报取得数据。1995年及以前，贝类中牡蛎按鲜肉计算；蚶、蛤、蛙按5斤鲜品折1斤计算。1996年以后则统一按鲜品计算。

猪、牛、羊肉产量 指当年出栏并已屠宰、除去头蹄下水后带骨肉（即胴体重）的重量。包括全社会范围内的产量。1996年前为各级逐级上报数据。1996年第一次农业普查以后，由于畜牧业产品年报数据与普查数据之间存在一定的差距，根据普查结果对畜牧业年报数据进行了修正。1999年以后，国家统计局在部分地区开展了猪、牛、羊、禽等主要畜禽品种的抽样调查，并用抽样数据作为国家定案数据使用。未开展抽样调查的地区和品种，仍使用各级统计部门逐级上报数据。2007年，根据第二次农业普查结果，对2000-2006年畜牧业年报数据进行了修正。2008年，建立了主要畜禽监测调查制度，猪、牛、羊、禽等主要畜牧业数据均以抽样调查数为法定数据。

期初（末）畜禽存栏头（只）数 指报告期初（末）农村各种合作经济组织和国营农场、农民个人、机关、团体、学校、工矿企业、部队等单位以及城镇居民饲养的大牲畜、猪、羊、家禽等畜禽的存栏数。数据上报方式及数据调整情况同猪、牛、羊肉产量。

常用耕地 是指耕地总资源中专门种植农作物并经常进行耕种、能够正常收获的土地。包括当年实际耕种的熟地；弃耕、休闲不满三年，随时可以复耕的地；开荒利用三年以上的地。不包括临时种植农作物的坡度在25度以上的陡坡地；在河套、湖畔、库区临时开发的成片或零星土地；也不包括已列为国家和省（区、市）退耕计划但临时耕种的土地。

农作物播种面积 指实际播种或移植有农作物的面积。凡是实际种植有农作物的面积，不论种植在耕地上还是种植在非耕地上，均包括在农作物播种面积中。在播种季节基本结束后，因遭灾而重新改种和补种的农作物面积，也包括在内。它是反映我国耕地面积利用情况的一个重要指标。目前，农作物播种面积料、麻类、烟叶、蔬菜和瓜类、药材和其他农作物九大类。

主要包括粮食、棉花、油料、糖料、麻类、烟叶、蔬菜和瓜类、药材和其他农作物九大类。

有效灌溉面积 指具有一定的水源，地块比较平整，灌溉工程或设备已经配套，在一般年景下，当年能够进行正常灌溉的耕地面积。在一般情况下，有效灌溉面积应等于灌溉工程或设备已经配备，能够进行正常灌溉的水田和水浇地面积之和。它是反映我国耕地抗旱能力的一个重要指标。

农用化肥施用量 指本年内实际用于农业生产的化肥数量，包括氮肥、磷肥、钾肥和复合肥。化肥施用量要求按折纯量计算数量。折纯量是指把氮肥、磷肥、钾肥分别按含氮、含五氧化二磷、含氧化钾的百分之百成份进行折算后的数量。复合肥按其所含主要成分折算。公式为：

折纯量=实物量×某种化肥有效成份含量的百分比

农业机械总动力 指主要用于农、林、牧、渔业的各种动力机械的动力总和。包括耕作机械、排灌机械、收获机械、农用运输机械、植物保护机械、牧业机械、林业机械、渔业机械和其他农业机械【内燃机按引擎马力折成瓦（特）计算、电动机按功率折成瓦（特）计算】。不包括专门用于乡、镇、村、组办工业、基本建设、非农业运输、科学试验和教学等非农业生产方面用的动力机械与作业机械。这个指标的统计数据主要来源于农机部门。

Explanatory Notes on Main Statistical Indicators

Gross Output Value of Agriculture, Forestry, Animal Husbandry and Fishery refers to the total value of products of agriculture, forestry, animal husbandry and fishery, and total value of services in support of agriculture, forestry, animal husbandry and fishery activities. It reflects the total scale and results of agricultural production during a given period. Prior to 1957, China's gross agricultural output value included barnyard manure and handicraft products for self- consumption (clothes, shoes, stockings, and initial grain processing undertaken by peasants). Since 1958, cutting and felling of bamboo and trees by villages and other cooperative organizations under villages have been included in forestry; value of barnyard manure has been excluded from animal husbandry; self consumed handicrafts have not been included from sideline occupations, while the output value of industries run by villages and cooperative organizations under village has been included in sideline occupations; and the output value of fish catches by motor fishing boats has been added to fishery. Since 1980, the value of handicraft products made for sale by individuals in households has been added to sideline occupations. Since 1984, industries run by villages and under villages have been included in the sector of industry. Since 1993, the subdivision of sideline occupations has been cancelled, and the hunting of wild animals has been classified into animal husbandry, and the gathering of wild plants and commodity industry run by rural household have been included in farming. A new industrial classification of economic activities was introduced in 2003. Under the new classification, value of services to agriculture, forestry, animal husbandry and fishery is included in the gross output value of agriculture, value of wood felling and transport is included in forestry, value of industrial output by rural households is not included in agriculture, and the collection of wild forest products is taken from agriculture and included in forestry. The First Agriculture Census of China revealed some discrepancy between the production of animal products from the annual reports and that from the census. According to the result of the First Agriculture census, efforts were made to adjust the output value of animal husbandry to make the figures from the annual reports consistent with the census data.

Gross output value of agrieulture is obtained by multiplying the output of each product or by-product by its price, resulting in the output value of each single item. For a small number of products, annual output of which is not available or difficult to get due to the long production (growing) process involved, the output value is estimated through an indirect approach. The sum of output values of all products of agriculture, forestry, animal husbandry and fishery and services in support to those industries is then equal to the gross output value of agriculture.

Grain Output refers to the total output in the whole country including grains produced by State farms, collective units, rural households, as well as by farms affiliated to industrial and mining enterprises and other production units. Grain includes rice, wheat, corn, sorghum, millet and other miscellaneous grains as well as tubers and beans. Output of beans refers to dry beans without pods. The output of tubers (sweet potatoes and potatoes, not including taros and cassava) are converted into that of grain at the ratio 4:1, i.e. 4 kilograms of fresh tubers were equivalent to 1 kilogram of grain up to 1963. Since 1964 the ratio for conversion has been 5:1. Tubers supplied as vegetables (such as potatoes) in cities and suburbs are calculated as fresh vegetables and their output is not included in the output of grain. Output of all other grains refers to husked grain. Data on grain production before 1989 were obtained through the Comprehensive Statistical Reporting System. Since 1989, data from sample surveys are used.

Cotton Output refers to cotton production in the whole country including cotton planted in spring and in autumn. Output is measured as the weight of ginned cotton. Ceiba is not included.

Output of Oil–bearing Crops refers to the total production of oil-bearing crops of various kinds, including peanuts (dry, in shell), rapeseeds, sesame, sunflower seeds, flax seeds, and other oil-bearing crops. Soybeans, oil-bearing woody plants, and wild oil-bearing crops are not included.

Output of Aquatic Products refers to catches of both artificially cultured and naturally grown aquatic products, including fish, shrimps, crabs and shellfish in sea and inland water as well as seaweed. Freshwater plants are not included. Data on output of aquatic products are reported by aquatic product and statistical agencies level by level. Before 1995, among the shellfish, oyster was counted as fresh meat; 5 kilograms of ark shell, clams and frogs are equivalent to 1 kilogram of fresh aquatic products; they have all been counted as flesh aquatic products since 1996.

Output of Pork, Beef, and Mutton refers to the meat of slaughtered hogs, cattle, sheep and goats with head, feet, and offal taken away. Data refers to the production of the whole country. The First Agricultural Census of China in 1996 revealed some discrepancy between the production of animal products from the annual reports and that from the census. Efforts were made to adjust the output value of animal husbandry to make the figures from the annual reports consistent with the census data. Since 1999, the NBS conducted sample surveys for the major animal husbandry products, such as hogs, cattle, sheep and goats and fowls, and the data from sample surveys are used as national finalized data. Those products, which are not covered by the sample survey, are still reported by statistical agencies level by level. In 2007. the data on animal husbandry from 2000 to 2006 were revised according to the results of the Second Agriculture Census of China. In 2008, A Monitoring and Survey Program was set up on main livestock, the data on the main livestock such as hog, cattle, sheep and poultry became the official data based on the sampling survey.

Number of Livestock or Poultry in Stock at Beginning (or End) of Period refers to the total number of large animals, pigs, sheep, fowls, etc. raised by rural cooperative organizations, State farms, rural individuals, government agencies, schools, industrial and mining enterprises, army, and urban residents at the beginning (or end) of the reference period. Data reporting system and data adjustment are the same as that in the output of pork, beef and mutton.

Regularly Cultivated Land refers to farmland among the total land resources which is exclusively used for farming and is under regular cultivation with harvest in normal years. Included are currently cultivated land, land that has been abandoned or put in idle for less than 3 years and could be re-used for cultivation at any time, and new-claimed land that has been put into cultivation for more than 3 years. Excluded under this category are steep slope land over 25 degrees under temporary cultivation, land (large or small plots) that is claimed along river bends, lake sides or banks of reservoirs, as well as land that has been designated under the "Green for Grain" programmes of the state and provincial governments but is still temporarily under cultivation.

Sown Area of Crops refers to area of transplanted with crops regardless of being land sown or in cultivated area or non-cultivated area. Area of land re-sown due to lso included. This is an important indicator that can reflect the utilization condition of the cultivated land in China. At present, the sown area of crops mainly include the following 9 categories of crops: grain, cotton, oil-bearing crops, sugar crops, flax crops, tobacco, vegetables and melons, medicinal materials and other farm crops.natural disasters is also included. This is an important indicator that can reflect the utilization condition of the cultivated land in China. At present, the sown area of crops mainly include the following 9 categories of crops: grain, cotton, oil-bearing crops, sugar crops, flax crops, tobacco, vegetables and melons, medicinal materials and other farm crops.

Irrigated Area refers to area of land that are effectively irrigated, i.e. relatively level land, where there are water sources or complete sets of irrigation facilities to lift and move adequate water for irrigation purpose under normal conditions. Under normal situations, irrigated area is the sum of watered fields and irrigated fields where irrigation systems or equipment have been installed for regular irrigation purpose. This important indicator reflects drought resistance capacity of the cultivated land in China.

Consumption of Chemical Fertilizers in Agriculture refers to the quantity of chemical fertilizers applied in agriculture in the year, including nitrogenous fertilizer, phosphate fertilizer, potash fertilizer, and compound fertilizer. The consumption of chemical fertilizers is calculated in terms of volume of effective components by means of converting the gross weight of the respective fertilizers into weight containing effective component (e.g. nitrogen content in nitrogenous fertilizer, phosphorous pentoxide contents in phosphate fertilizer, and potassium oxide contents in potash fertilizer). Compound fertilizer is converted in regard to its major components. The formula is:

Volume of effective component= physical quantity × effective component of certain chemical fertilizer (%)

Total Power of Agricultural Machinery refers to total mechanical power of machinery used in agriculture, forestry, animal husbandry and fishery, including machinery for ploughing, irrigation and drainage, harvesting, transport, plant protection, animal husbandry, forestry and fishery and other agricultural machineries. (For the power of internal combustion engines, it is converted from its horsepower into watts while for electric motors the output power is converted into watts.) Machinery employed for non-agricultural purposes, such as the machines used in township-run and village-run industry, construction, non-agricultural transport, scientific experiments and teaching, are not included. Data are mainly from agricultural machinery agencies.

12 工 业

INDUSTRY

资料整理：赵 晖 王风玲 赵 博 陈小兵 李 玫 王 玥
Data management: Zhao Hui Wang Fengling Zhao Bo Chen Xiaobing Li Mei Wang Yue

第十二部分　工业

一、简要说明

本章资料包括全部工业总产值，规模以上工业企业单位数、总产值、主要经济指标等，由西安市统计局工业处提供。

二、主要指标

规模以上工业企业单位数（个）	970	
#大中型工业企业	226	
全部工业增加值（亿元）	1328.71	比上年增长　12.4%
#规模以上工业增加值	1132.25	比上年增长　13.0%

12　INDUSTRY

Ⅰ.Brief Introduction

Data in this chapter reflects gross industrial output value, number of industrial enterprises above designated size and gross product, primary economic. Data in this chapter are provided and compiled by Industry Division of the Xi'an Bureau of Statistics.

Ⅱ.Major Indicators

		Increase over Preceding Year
Number of Industrial Enterprises Above Designated Size(item)	970	
#Large-size and Medium-size Industrial Enterprises	226	
Value Added of Industry(100 mil. yuan)	1328.71	12.4%
#Value Added of Industry Above Designated Size	1132.25	13.0%

12-1 主要年份全部工业总产值

Gross Output Value of Industry In Representative Years

单位：万元 (10 000 yuan)

年 份 Year	全部工业总产值 Gross Industrial Output Value	工业总产值指数（上年=100） Index of Gross Industry Output Value (Preceding Year=100)	国有经济 State-owned Enterprises	集体经济 Collective-owned Enterprises	其他经济类型 Enterprises of Other Ownership
1952	23512	139.6	9917	464	13131
1962	120833	86.8	102103	17599	1131
1965	200416	132.1	183164	17252	
1970	333386	143.5	305303	28083	
1975	385509	106.1	332982	52527	
1978	483262	116.9	405376	77886	
1979	517483	106.6	438850	78633	
1980	531755	101.8	440139	91577	39
1981	524587	98.6	433740	90675	172
1982	549200	107.1	450308	98516	456
1983	603507	112.2	493773	108923	811
1984	674963	112.8	520593	153056	1314
1985	853196	120.4	632702	218893	1601
1986	976326	112.1	706380	267282	2664
1987	1142220	114.2	809186	328701	4341
1988	1429811	116.0	1012268	416217	1326
1989	1653472	106.1	1160877	486754	5814
1990	1771310	107.4	1196777	548605	25928
1991	2002727	110.0	1325242	604495	72990
1992	2300472	112.5	1488541	561369	250562
1993	3045988	121.7	1748145	1071122	226721
1994	3891584	120.6	1960533	1581321	349730
1995	4058952	108.7	2071755	1663536	323661
1996	5338510	133.4	2132140	2836176	370194
1997	5794532	121.8	1915536	2005610	1873386
1998	6738224	117.3	2593405	2077273	2067546
1999	7151528	117.1	2128243	2174220	2849065
2000	6394812	115.3	2749778	2094680	1550354
2001	7361510	116.4	3098431	2380910	1882169
2002	8379363	115.8	3472067	2312923	2594373
2003	9750800	115.1	4149015	1501372	4100413
2004	11853224	118.4	5414952	875412	5562860
2005	13085580	106.3	5916553	674900	6494127
2006	15573516	119.0	7527607	514810	7531099
2007	19798593	122.1	10179303	365329	9253961
2008	23881446	120.6	12479652	441987	10959807
2009	28270652	118.3	14440321	388777	13441554
2010	35628753	126.0	18353877	435206	16839669
2011	40933178	114.9	20654524	377199	19901455
2012	46560824	113.8	24303736	376427	21880661

12-1 续表 continued

单位：万元 (10 000 yuan)

年　份 Year	轻工业 Ligth Industry	重工业 Heavy Industry	大型工业 Large-size Industry Enterprises	中型工业 Medium-size Industry Enterprises	小型工业 Small-size Industry Enterprises
1952	20800	2712			
1962	68221	52618			
1965	98631	101785			
1970	124467	208919			
1975	167285	218224	145262	130592	109655
1978	220480	262782	168397	121813	193052
1979	243043	274440	189877	133759	193847
1980	283475	248280	193092	130053	208610
1981	309199	215388	178130	140810	205639
1982	303249	246031	213015	128597	207668
1983	315785	287722	245053	127164	231290
1984	321678	353285	241842	143165	289956
1985	401748	451448	333820	147488	371888
1986	458270	518056	401037	150644	424609
1987	516776	625452	472958	171698	497572
1988	699593	730210	615946	210089	603776
1989	712743	940729	696368	258414	698690
1990	787857	983453	716421	279098	775791
1991	897676	1105051	888052	303151	844524
1992	967104	1333368			
1993	1121957	1924031	1258137	384255	1403596
1994	1578875	2312709	1479613	390233	2021738
1995	1636219	2432733	1575030	371156	2112766
1996	2347887	2990623	1693985	358913	3285612
1997	2700085	3094447	1675521	274888	3844123
1998	3232681	3505543	1821556	308424	4608244
1999	3488547	3662981	1744637	337795	5069096
2000	3121419	3273393	2320973	328494	3745345
2001	3518054	3843456	2656010	368497	4337003
2002	3935764	4443599	3038828	398834	4941701
2003	4028859	5721941	2662073	2027256	5061471
2004	4211592	7641632	3595150	3237701	5020373
2005	4078417	9007163	4640325	3228553	5216702
2006	4510970	11062546	5970535	3414468	6188513
2007	7331719	12466874	8351303	4171131	7276159
2008	6010865	17870581	10472686	5005676	8403084
2009	6636464	21634188	12309192	6186395	9775065
2010	7841869	27786884	15002737	8537140	12088876
2011	8992547	31940631	16844272	6207660	17881246
2012	10218288	36342536	22563292	6243799	17753733

12-2 主要年份规模以上工业企业主要经济指标

Main Economic Indicators of all Industrial Enterprises above Designated Size in Representative Years

单位：亿元 (100 million yuan)

年 份 Year	企业单位数（个） Number of Enterprises (unit)	工业总产值（当年价） Gross Industrial Output Value (At Current Prices)	工业增加值（现价） Value-added of Industry	从业人员年平均人数（万人） Annual Average Employed Persons (10 000 persons)	资产合计 Total Assets
1998	793	350.38	99.20	51.71	810.56
1999	770	366.59	106.56	45.64	853.90
2000	816	417.97	130.18	43.25	958.05
2001	785	482.61	149.06	40.12	1054.36
2002	771	544.78	170.39	38.48	1065.76
2003	735	638.66	202.74	36.55	1195.69
2004	1066	830.06	254.17	38.08	1333.91
2005	902	981.02	314.01	37.92	1503.85
2006	904	1187.74	370.11	37.94	1651.67
2007	937	1577.05	499.96	38.55	1940.52
2008	1032	2007.85	605.25	40.17	2426.13
2009	1131	2468.27	700.13	43.42	2913.56
2010	1126	3130.15	862.28	47.11	3592.13
2011	891	3552.21	1012.58	50.42	3975.38
2012	970	4066.31	1132.44	49.23	4775.92

12-2 续表 continued

单位：亿元 (100 million yuan)

年 份 Year	负债合计 Total Liabilities	所有者权益合计 Owners' Equities	主营业务收入 Revenue from Principal Business	利润总额 Total Profits	利税总额 Total Pre-tax Profits
1998	548.68	261.88	346.84	1.26	14.82
1999	577.94	275.96	346.26	8.26	27.30
2000	622.46	323.72	420.42	16.11	36.29
2001	657.88	384.65	451.62	17.97	40.84
2002	643.78	412.27	541.64	25.43	51.31
2003	733.04	460.97	645.53	33.82	64.99
2004	869.30	464.60	812.46	38.57	74.23
2005	977.42	508.82	980.97	28.72	67.25
2006	1062.11	578.33	1183.51	61.46	110.23
2007	1254.01	686.51	1561.25	106.22	168.54
2008	1518.86	907.27	1928.05	84.89	168.63
2009	1779.38	1130.76	2384.52	177.20	280.68
2010	2069.29	1515.65	3011.19	245.37	373.56
2011	2295.49	1678.19	3381.27	172.94	312.78
2012	2835.55	1926.72	3758.56	167.77	320.57

12-3 各区县、开发区规模以上工业企业工业总产值（2012）

单位：亿元

区县、开发区	Region	单位数（个）Name of Enterprises (unit)	工业总产值 Gross Industrial Output Value	国有经济 State-owned Enterprises	集体经济 Collective-owned Enterprises
新城区	Xingcheng	22	307.67	114.27	
碑林区	Beilin	16	18.46	6.19	
莲湖区	Lianhu	46	459.41	199.50	0.24
灞桥区	Baqiao	118	278.37	25.54	8.56
未央区	Weiyang	168	684.55	147.27	5.11
雁塔区	Yanta	200	587.65	236.58	0.54
阎良区	Yanliang	72	219.31	9.64	0.91
临潼区	Lintong	40	341.01	7.73	
长安区	Chang'an	101	354.65	48.19	1.18
蓝田县	Lantian	24	41.60	6.44	0.79
周至县	Zhouzhi	28	17.08		0.75
户　县	Huxian	55	93.55	16.41	1.03
高陵县	Gaoling	80	662.99	19.31	7.39
在总计中：	Among of Total:				
高新区	GaoXin	196	731.31	197.88	
经济开发区	JingKai	149	991.06	18.67	7.39
航空基地	Aviation Industry Base	14	7.78	2.57	
航天基地	Aerospace Base	17	79.31	46.63	
沣东新城	Fengdongxincheng	51	178.20	126.55	3.93

Gross Output Value of Industrial Enterprises above Designated Size by Region and Development Zone (2012)

(100 million yuan)

其他经济类型 Enterprises of Other Ownership	轻工业 Ligth Industry	重工业 Heavy Industry	大型工业 Large-size Industry Enterprises	中型工业 Medium-size Industry Enterprises	小型工业 Small-size Industry Enterprises
193.40	68.50	239.17	281.61	17.06	9.00
12.27	7.94	10.52	3.39	8.48	6.59
259.67	55.30	404.11	390.34	47.52	21.55
244.27	43.64	234.73	40.19	17.52	220.66
532.17	154.76	529.79	353.65	119.91	210.99
350.53	95.38	492.27	303.69	128.99	154.97
208.76	47.54	171.77	129.54	11.63	78.14
333.28	132.64	208.37	158.15	41.65	141.21
305.28	34.88	319.77	241.37	54.14	59.14
34.37	11.78	29.82	5.35	11.18	25.07
16.33	10.85	6.23		0.93	16.15
76.11	54.02	39.53	37.79	22.16	33.60
636.29	28.43	634.56	425.48	143.22	94.29
533.43	108.81	622.50	295.84	161.96	273.51
965.00	140.12	850.94	557.74	210.41	222.91
5.21	0.83	6.95		2.99	4.79
32.68	0.60	78.71	49.67	23.86	5.78
47.72	14.02	164.18	135.64	22.68	19.88

12-4 规模以上工业企业主要工业产品产量（2012年）

Output of Major Industrial Products of Enterprises above Designated Size

产品名称	Name of Products	2012	比上年增长(%) Increase over Preceding Year (%)
铁矿石成品矿(万吨)	Iron Ore(10 000 ton)	2.7	8.5
发电量(亿千瓦小时)	Electricity Generation Volume(100 million kw.h)	99.5	4.7
火电	Thermal Power	98.7	5.2
水力发电	Hydroelectric Power	0.8	-32.8
自来水生产量(亿立方米)	Tap Water Production (100 million cu.m)	3.7	6.0
大米(万吨)	Rice (10 000 ton)	5.6	-1.9
小麦粉(万吨)	Wheat Flour (10 000 tons)	102.3	-5.1
精制食用植物油(万吨)	Edible Vegetable Oil (10 000 ton)	28.5	-9.1
鲜、冷藏肉（万吨）	Fresh/Frozen Meat(10 000 ton)	1.9	3.3
配混合饲料(万吨)	Mixed Feed(10 000 ton)	80.8	24.5
方便面(万吨)	Instant Noodle(10 000 ton)	9.2	-9.2
乳制品(万吨)	Dairy Products (10 000 ton)	124.4	12.3
液体乳(万吨)	Milk	115.8	12.0
罐头(万吨)	Canned Food (10 000 ton)		
饮料酒(万千升)	Beverage Wine (10 000 kiloliter)	45.6	-3.9
白酒（折65度，商品量）	Liquor (as 65 degree, amount of goods)	0.1	16.7
啤酒	Beer	45.5	-3.9
软饮料(万吨)	Soft Beverage (10 000 ton)	204.1	0.0
碳酸饮料类（汽水）	Carbonated Beverage	44.7	11.6
果汁和蔬菜汁饮料	Juice and Fruit Beverage	34.3	13.2
包装饮用水类	Canned Drinking Water	11.0	3821.4
纱(万吨)	Yarn (10 000 ton)	3.4	-13.5
1. 棉纱	Cotton Yarn	1.3	-27.7
2. 棉混纺纱	Blend Fabric	0.6	-34.5
3. 化学纤维纱	Pure Chemical-Fibre Yarn	1.6	17.3
布(亿米)	Cloth (100 million m)	1.4	-12.3
1. 棉布	Cotton Cloth	0.5	-34.7
2. 棉混纺布	Blend Fabric	0.3	-26.5
3. 化学纤维布	Pure Chemical-Fibre Cloth	0.7	22.4
无纺布(无纺织物)(万吨)	Non-textile fabrics(Non-extile stuff) (10 000 ton)		
服装（万件）	Garment (10 000 units)	1019.8	39.6
其中：梭织服装	Shuttle-Woven Garment	1017.9	40.1
皮革鞋靴（万双）	Leather Shoes (10 000 pairs)	173.4	22.5

12-4 续表1 continued1

产品名称	Name of Products	2012	比上年增长(%) Increase over Preceding Year (%)
人造板（万立方米）	Artificial Board (10 000 cu.m)	39.8	4.3
纤维板	Fibre Board	39.8	4.3
家具（件）	Furniture (unit)	131.1	29.2
木质家具	Wooden Furniture	114.0	38.4
软体家具	Soft Furniture (inc.: Sofa ,Mattress etc.)	10.8	-10.8
机制纸及纸板（外购原纸加工除外）（万吨）	Machine Made Paper(not including processing of procured base paper)(10 000 ton)	27.6	-31.1
其中：卫生用纸原纸	Body Paper of Sanitary Paper	0.3	-56.0
纸制品（万吨）	Paper-Made Products (10 000 ton)	8.4	-22.2
其中：瓦楞纸箱	Corrugated Paper	8.4	-22.2
单色印刷（万令）	Monochrom Printed products(10 000 reams)	143.2	31.1
多色印刷品（万对开色令）	Colored Printed products(10 000 reams)	898.2	-7.8
原油加工量（万吨）	Crude Oil Processing (10 000 ton)	217.5	42.0
汽油（万吨）	Petrol(10 000 ton)	34.4	73.2
柴油（万吨）	Diesel(10 000 ton)	62.4	48.8
燃料油（万吨）	Fuel Oil(10 000 ton)	13.9	16.7
石油沥青（万吨）	Petroleum Pitch (10 000 ton)	22.3	120.9
液化石油气（万吨）	Liquefied Petroleum Gas (10 000 ton)	6.7	48.8
石油焦（万吨）	Petroleum Coke (10 000 ton)	50.6	29.4
盐酸（含量31%以上）(万吨)	Salt Acid (Content over 31%) (10 000 ton)		
氢氧化钠（烧碱）(折100%)(万吨)	Caustic Soda (100%)(10 000 ton)		
碳化钙（电石）(折 300升／千克)(万吨)	Calcium Carbide Lonverted into(10 000 ton)		
化学农药原药(折有效成分100%)(万吨)	Chemical Pesticide(100% effective content)(10 000 ton)	0.4	100.0
涂料（万吨）	Construction Paint(10 000 ton)	1.4	-5.4
初级形态的塑料(塑料树脂及共聚物)（万吨）	Plastic,Resin and Copolymer (10 000 ton)		
合成洗涤剂（万吨）	Synthetic Detergents (10 000 ton)	11.6	33.5
合成洗衣粉（万吨）	Washing Power	3.6	63.3
化学原料药（万吨）	Chemical Medicine (10 000 ton)		
中成药（万吨）	Traditional Chinese Medicine (10 000 ton)	0.4	20.7
化学纤维（万吨）	Chemical Fiber	2.6	14.3
人造纤维（纤维素纤维）（万吨）	Man-made Fiber	2.6	14.3
塑料制品（万吨）	Plastic Product (10 000 ton)	10.3	31.6
塑料薄膜	Plastic Sheet	0.2	-69.6
农用薄膜	Agricultural Sheet	0.2	-69.6

12-4 续表2 continued2

产品名称	Name of Products	2012	比上年增长(%) Increase over Preceding Year (%)
水泥（万吨）	Cement (10 000 ton)	534.2	-8.7
硅酸盐水泥熟料（万吨）	Portland Cement Clinker (10 000 ton)	153.2	-23.3
窑外分解窑水泥熟料	Outside Decomposition of Kiln Cement Clinker	5.5	54.9
水泥混凝土电杆（万根）	Cement Pole(10 000 unit)	2.9	-17.7
商品混凝土(万立方米)	Ready-mixed Concrete (10 000 cu.m)	2455.0	26.3
沥青和改性沥青防水卷材（万平方米）	Asphalt and Modified Bitumen Membrane(10 000 sq.m)	2127.7	115.6
平板玻璃（万重量箱）	Plate Glass (10 000 wt.cases)		
钢化玻璃(万平方米)	Toughened Glass(10 000 sq.m)	27.5	-51.5
日用玻璃制品（万吨）	Glassware(10 000 ton)	0.8	-16.8
生铁（万吨）	Csat iron(10 000 ton)		
粗钢（万吨）	Thick Steel (10 000 ton)	0.9	-59.8
钢材（万吨）	Rolled-steel Final Products (10 000 ton)	31.3	67.2
中小型型钢	Rolled-steel Medium and Small	0.7	-25.0
盘条（线材）	Wire Rod	29.4	81.4
冷轧薄板	Non-hot-roll Thin Steel	0.1	-47.1
无缝钢管	Seamless Steel Pipe	1.0	4.4
焊接钢管	Welded Steel Pipes	0.1	-73.3
铁合金（万吨）	Ferroalloy (10 000 ton)	1.2	-20.3
铝材(万吨)	Aluminum Material (10 000 ton)	4.2	4.7
黄金（千克）	Gold (kg)	312.0	13.5
单晶硅（千克）	Monocrystalline Silicon (kg)	1356367.0	49.9
工业锅炉（蒸发量吨）	Industrial Boiler steam(ton)	1468.0	34.8
发动机（万千瓦）	Engine (10 000 kw)	66.3	-30.7
汽车发动机	Motor Engine	66.3	-30.7
金属切削机床(万台)	Metal-cutting Machines (10 000 unit)	0.4	2.3
泵(液体泵)(万台)	Pump (Liquid pump)(10 000 unit)	0.4	-2.8
风机（万台）	Fan(10 000 unit)	0.1	8.3
气体压缩机（万台）	Gas Compressor(10 000 unit)	594.5	-12.2
阀门（万吨）	Valves (10 000 ton)	0.1	-9.1
铸铁件（万吨）	Iron Castings (10 000 ton)	2.4	-28.6
铸钢件（万吨）	Steel Castings (10 000 ton)	0.9	2.3
锻件（万吨）	Forgings (10 000 ton)	0.7	-9.2
粉末冶金零件(万吨)	Powder Melallurgy Products(10 000 ton)		
矿山专用设备（万吨）	Mining Equipment (10 000 ton)	0.8	2.6
炼油、化工专用设备（万吨）	Oil Refining and Chemical Industry Machine(10 000 ton)	0.9	82.0

12-4 续表3 continued3

产品名称	Name of Products	2012	比上年增长(%) Increase over Preceding Year (%)
金属冶炼设备(冶炼设备)（吨）	Metal Smelting Equipments(ton)	14628.8	-36.4
金属轧制设备（吨）	Metal-rolling Machine(ton)	3757.9	-44.3
混凝土机械（台）	Concrete Machinery(unit)	325.0	-12.4
印刷专用设备（吨）	Printing Equipment(ton)	6450.0	6.3
环境保护专用设备(台、套)	Special Equipment for Environment Protection	125.0	-14.4
大气污染防治设备	Equipment for Preventing Atmospheric Pollution	77.0	-18.9
铁路货车（辆）	Freight(unit)	3219.0	-10.6
汽车（万辆）	Motor Vehicle(10 000unit)	54.2	-2.7
基本型乘用车（轿车）（万辆）	Basic Passenger Vehicles (10 000Cars)	36.6	-5.3
①排量≤1升	1.0L and Below Gas Displacement	4.8	-41.9
②1升<排量≤1.6升	1.0L-1.6L Gas Displacement(1.6L included)	28.0	-0.8
③1.6升<排量≤2.0升	1.6L-2.0L Gas Displacement(2.0L included)	3.6	73.7
④2.0升<排量≤2.5升	2.0L-2.5L Gas Displacement(2.5L included)		-97.9
多功能乘用车（MPV）	Multi-purpose Vehicles (MPV)	0.1	-54.2
运动型多用途乘用车	Sport Utility Vehicles	8.8	46.3
客车	Passenger Vehicles	0.9	-19.8
大型客车（车长>10）	Buses		-60.0
轻型客车（车长<7）	Large(40seats and above)	0.8	-15.8
载货汽车	Trucks	7.8	-19.5
改装汽车（万辆）	Refit Trucks (10 000 ton)unit)	1.1	-42.9
交流电动机（万千瓦）	Alternating Current Motor(10 000kw)	442.8	-21.6
变压器（万千伏安）	Transformer(10 000KVA)	10750.1	-5.9
高压开关板（面）	High-voltage Switch Panel(unit)	20643.0	85.7
低压开关板（万面）	Low-voltage Switch Panel(10 000 unit)	2.7	34.2
电力电缆(万千米)	Electric Power Cables(10 000 km)	1.2	56.0
通信及电子网络用电缆(万对千米)	Communication Cables(10 000 pair km)	1.2	-25.9
光缆(光纤通讯电缆)（万芯千米）	Cable (Optical Communication Cable) (10 000 Core.km)	334.8	113.3
绝缘制品(吨)	Insulating Products(ton)	5199.0	-11.1
家用电冰箱（万台）	Household refrigerator(10 000 unit)	15.8	118.3
电子计算机整机（万台）	Integrated Computer(10 000 unit)	1.1	-35.1
彩色显象管（万只）	Color kinescope(10 000 unit)	108.9	-42.9
半导体分立器件（亿只）	Semiconductor Discrete Device(100 million units)		
电子元件（亿只）	Electronic Components(100 million units)	9.9	-13.8
工业自动化调节仪表与控制系统（万台、套）	Automatization meter and system (10 000 unit)	4.9	0.4
电工仪器仪表（万台）	Electrical instrumentation (10 000 sets)	8.4	-26.8
分析仪器及装置（万台、套）	Analysis Instruments and Apparatus(10 000 sets)	4.7	-2.1

12-5 规模以上工业企业分行业工业增加值(2012年)

Value Added of Industrial Enterprises above Designated Size by Sector (2012)

单位：亿元 (100 million yuan)

行 业	Scetor	2012
总计	**Total**	**1132.25**
按工业行业大类分		
煤炭开采和洗选业	Mining and Washing of Coal	
石油和天然气开采业	Extraction of Petroleum and Natural Gas	
黑色金属矿采选业	Mining and Processing of Ferrous Metal Ores	0.09
有色金属矿采选业	Mining and Processing of Non-ferrous Metal Ores	
非金属矿采选业	Mining and Processing of Nonmetal Ores	
开采辅助活动	Mining Auxiliary Activities	20.28
其他采矿业	Mining of Other Ores	
农副食品加工业	Processing of Food from Agricultural Porducts	48.04
食品制造业	Manufacture of Foods	45.52
酒、饮料和精制茶制造业	Manufacture of Alcohol,Beverages and Tea	31.43
烟草制品业	Manufacture of Tobacco	0.61
纺织业	Manufacture of Textile	4.36
纺织服装、服饰业	Textile, Garments industry	4.24
皮革、毛皮、羽毛及其制品和制鞋业	Manufacture of Leather, Fur, Feather and Related Products	0.65
木材加工和木、竹、藤、棕、草制品业	Processing of Timber,Manufacture of Wood,Plam and Straw Products	3.15
家具制造业	Manufacture of Furniture	2.19
造纸及纸制品业	Manufacture of Paper and Paper Products	5.11
印刷和记录媒介复制	Printing,Reproduction of Recording Media	23.91
文教、工美、体育和娱乐用品制造业	Manufacture of Articles For Cultural,Educational and Sports Activities	1.39
石油加工业、炼焦和核燃料加工业	Processing of Petroleum, Cokeing,Processing of Nuclear and Nuclear Fuel	34.27
化学原料及化学制品制造业	Manufacture of Raw Chemical Materials and Chemical Products	39.40
医药制造业	Manufacture of Medicines	52.55
化学纤维制造业	Manufacture of Chemical Fibers	2.60
橡胶和塑料制品业	Manufacture of Rubber and Plastics	16.72
非金属矿物制品业	Manufacture of Non-metallic Mineral Products	59.10
黑色金属冶炼和压延加工业	Smelting and Pressing of Ferrous Metals	24.72
有色金属冶炼和压延加工业	Smelting and Pressing of Non-ferrous Metals	27.23
金属制品业	Manufacture of Metal Products	33.05
通用设备制造业	Manufacture of General Purpose Machinery	54.21
专用设备制造业	Manufacture of Special Equipment	80.15
汽车制造业	Manufacture of Motor Vehicle	188.25
铁路、船舶、航空航天和其他运输设备制造业	Railways,Shipbuilding,Aerospace and Other Transportation Equipment Manufacturing Industry	82.71
电气机械和器材制造业	Manufacture of Electric Equipment and Machinery	95.98
计算机、通讯和其他电子设备制造业	Manufacture of Communication Equipment, Computers and other Electronic Equipment	29.39
仪器仪表制造业	Manufacture of Measuring Instruments and Machinery	29.91
其他制造业	Manufacture of Other Manufacturing	
废弃资源综合利用业	Recycling and Disposal of Waste	2.90
金属制品、机械和设备修理业	Metal Products,Machinery and Equipment Repair Industry	1.64
电力、热力的生产和供应业	Production and Supply of Electric Power and Heat Power	71.74
燃气生产和供应业	Gas Mining and Supplying Industry	10.30
水的生产和供应业	Production and Supply of Water	4.46

12-6 各区县、开发区规模以上工业企业主要经济指标（2012年）

Main Economic Indicators of All Industrial Enterprises above Designated Size by Region and Development Zone (2012)

区县、开发区	Region	企业单位数（个）Number of Enterprises (unit)	从业人员年平均人数（万人）Annual Average Employers (10 000 persons)	资产合计（亿元）Total Assets (100 mill yuan)
新城区	Xingcheng	22	3.10	399.58
碑林区	Beilin	16	0.55	52.65
莲湖区	Lianhu	46	6.55	733.76
灞桥区	Baqiao	118	3.69	178.23
未央区	Weiyang	168	7.44	757.66
雁塔区	Yanta	200	8.78	993.47
阎良区	Yanliang	72	3.04	377.97
临潼区	Lintong	40	1.62	237.51
长安区	Chang'an	101	7.01	438.42
蓝田县	Lantian	24	0.52	55.90
周至县	Zhouzhi	28	0.31	11.56
户　县	Huxian	55	1.46	89.46
高陵县	Gaoling	80	5.17	449.76
在总计中：	Among of Total:			
高新区	GaoXin	196	11.44	1125.31
经济开发区	JingKai	149	8.37	779.75
航空基地	Aviation Industry Base	14	0.20	24.61
航天基地	Aerospace Base	17	1.22	138.33
沣东新城	Fengdongxincheng	51	1.79	88.86

12-6 续表1 continued1

单位：亿元 (100 million yuan)

区县、开发区	Region	负债合计 Total Liabilites	所有者权益合计 Total Owners' Equities	主营业务收入 Revenue from Principal Business	利润总额 Total Profits	利税总额 Total Pre-tax Profits
新城区	Xingcheng	265.46	134.11	307.11	4.37	19.75
碑林区	Beilin	31.14	21.51	21.40	1.69	3.55
莲湖区	Lianhu	347.92	385.84	426.90	19.92	37.46
灞桥区	Baqiao	91.43	81.74	274.96	32.26	45.29
未央区	Weiyang	416.43	338.12	711.45	24.32	60.79
雁塔区	Yanta	680.49	312.15	553.83	30.97	58.98
阎良区	Yanliang	236.15	141.05	222.04	9.16	11.10
临潼区	Lintong	135.80	101.51	292.61	11.98	19.11
长安区	Chang'an	231.19	206.64	315.71	12.23	24.74
蓝田县	Lantian	28.22	27.28	31.09	1.67	2.31
周至县	Zhouzhi	4.49	7.04	14.66	0.80	1.14
户　县	Huxian	59.16	30.19	83.75	1.16	4.56
高陵县	Gaoling	307.67	139.55	503.06	17.24	31.80
在总计中：	Among of Total:					
高新区	GaoXin	725.58	398.84	553.77	36.79	71.73
经济开发区	JingKai	491.36	282.76	816.51	39.32	64.38
航空基地	Aviation Industry Base	13.41	11.20	6.31	0.13	0.36
航天基地	Aerospace Base	61.69	76.52	78.04	6.28	7.37
沣东新城	Fengdongxincheng	63.85	24.98	178.84	−5.12	12.04

12-7 主要年份规模以上工业企业经济效益指标（2012）

Indicators of Economic Benefit of Industrial Enterprises above Designated Size in Representative Years(2012)

年 份 Year	总资产贡献率 (%) Ratio of Total Assets to Industrial Output Value (%)	资产负债率 (%) Assets-Liability Ratio (%)	流动资产周转次数 (次/年) Rate of Annual Turnover Working Capitals (times/year)	成本费用利润率 (%) Ratio of Profits to cost (%)	全员劳动生产率 (元/人.年) Overall Labor Productivity (yuan/person yea	产品销售率 (%) Proportion of Industrial Products Sold (%)
1998		67.7	0.9	-266.1	19185	95.3
1999		67.7	0.9	2.5	22878	95.9
2000		65.0	1.0	4.2	29496	97.1
2001	5.8	62.4	0.9	4.1	38267	96.7
2002	6.2	60.4	1.1	5.1	46940	96.7
2003	7.0	61.3	1.1	5.7	58801	96.3
2004	6.9	65.2	1.2	5.0	66752	97.9
2005	8.4	65.0	1.3	3.1	82815	97.5
2006	7.8	64.3	1.4	5.5	97561	98.2
2007	10.2	64.6	1.6	7.3	129706	96.8
2008	8.6	62.6	1.5	4.6	150641	96.1
2009	11.3	61.1	1.7	8.1	161289	97.6
2010	12.2	57.6	1.7	8.8	188483	97.1
2011	8.6	57.7	1.5	5.2	194105	97.4
2012	7.7	59.4	1.5	4.5	230032	96.7

12-8 规模以上工业企业主要经济指标（2012年）

单位：万元

分 组	Classify	企业单位数（个） Number of Enterprises (unit)	亏损企业 Loss Making Enterprises	工业总产值（当年价格） Gross Industrial Output Value (At Current Prices)
总计	**Total**	**970**	**167**	**40663123.7**
#市区	Urban Area	783	117	32510826.3
#亏损企业	Deficit Enterprises	167	167	4857426.9
按隶属关系分	**Grouped by Jurisdiction of Management**			
中央企业	Central Enterprises	80	11	12290628.9
省属企业	Provincial Enterprises	66	16	7857303.7
市属企业	Municipal Enterprises	824	140	20515191.1
按登记注册类型分组	**Grouped by Registion Status**			
内资企业	Domestic Investment Enterprises	858	140	33260425.7
国有	State-owned Enterprises	70	12	8370688.9
集体	Collective-owned Enterprises	23	1	264990.2
股份合作	Share-holding Corperative	10	1	157573.3
联营	Joint Ownership Enterprises	1		6034.4
国有联营	State Joint Ownership Enterprises			
集体联营	Collective Joint Ownership Enterprises	1		6034.4
国有与集体联营	Joint State-collective Ownership Enterprises			
其他联营	Other Joint Ownership Enterprises			
有限责任公司	Limited Liability Corporations	460	82	18671405.1
国有独资公司	State Sole Funded Enterprises	28	5	3468902.9
其他有限责任公司	Other Limited Liability Corporation	432	77	15202502.2
股份有限公司	Share-holding Corperation Ltd.	69	8	2863562.2
私营	Private Enterprises	218	35	2882143.8
私营独资	Private-funded Enterprises	25		358485.8
私营合伙	Private Partnership Enterprises	1		3568.7
私营有限责任公司	Private Limited Liability Corporations	178	31	2307374.6
私营股份有限公司	Private Share Holding Corporations	14	4	212714.7
其他	Other Domestic Funded Enterprises	7	1	44027.8
港澳台商投资	Enterprises with Funds from Hong Kong,Macao and Taiwan	26	11	333756.4
外商投资	Foreign Funded Enterprises	86	16	7068941.6
按轻重工业分	**Grouped by Light Industry and Heavy Industry**			
轻工业	Light Industry	267	45	7456524.6
重工业	Heavy Industry	703	122	33206599.1

Main Economic Indicators of All Industrial Enterprises above Designated Size (2012)

(10 000yuan)

工业销售产值（当年价） Value of Industry Products Sales (At Current Prices)	出口交货值 Export Delivery Value	从业人员年平均人数（人） Annual Average Employers (person)	资产总计 Total Assets	流动资产合计 Total Working Capitals	固定资产合计 Total Fixed Assets	固定资产原价 Origing Value of Fixed Assets	累计折旧 Accumulative Total Depreciation
39335118.2	**2268479.5**	**492309**	**47759163.1**	**26423062.3**	**16375268.2**	**22373512·0**	**8389004.0**
31514680.2	1778665.3	417691	41692374.1	23018565.8	14377124.2	19976484.7	7549666.8
4594207.2	75122.5	56445	7206297.7	2577394.2	3733794.4	5211972.6	1610985.3
12037981.1	703998.4	168121	22120029.0	11313260.7	9111177.0	12122615.1	4463540.3
7647885.9	491904.7	71050	6657795.7	3753923.7	1966739.5	2372570.5	855934.4
19649251.2	1072576.4	253138	18981338.4	11355877.9	5297351.7	7878326.4	3069529.3
32232756.4	1602638.9	406893	41683438.3	23387643.1	14113653.1	19225800.0	7257990.6
8241917.0	170509.9	93712	13926372.0	6183724.5	6635969.6	9105076.0	3075970.1
259790.2		5426	103615.5	62990.4	30459.0	36702.1	8847.5
153704.6	36.8	1828	146756.5	113228.4	17865.2	34439.7	17509.0
6034.4		103	4490.3	4094.1	362.1	823.7	734.2
6034.4		103	4490.3	4094.1	362.1	823.7	734.2
18197130.5	1298821.2	237835	21440368.1	13519131.5	5817457.0	7386948.8	2975225.9
3347222.6	285860.2	69097	6657475.4	4028309.6	2042528.3	2752547.4	1161908.1
14849907.9	1012961.0	168738	14782892.7	9490821.9	3774928.7	4634401.4	1813317.8
2621210.2	105722.8	34138	4310744.7	2448935.0	1114475.4	1878879.4	839425.5
2712654.8	26630.1	33109	1704722.3	1026165.2	482321.2	761907.0	333639.8
334888.4		2712	97336.2	48138.6	38030.4	46165.5	11411.2
3568.7		90	3548.0	2878.3	669.7	809.7	140.0
2166734.3	26590.2	27837	1340737.2	813101.1	384560.9	646404.0	309461.6
207463.4	39.9	2470	263100.9	162047.2	59060.2	68527.8	12627.0
40314.7	918.1	742	46368.9	29374.0	14743.6	21023.3	6638.6
321966.0	29939.0	6782	490039.5	173006.6	204424.4	281154.1	84260.2
6780395.8	635901.6	78634	5585685.3	2862412.6	2057190.7	2866557.9	1046753.2
7168251.8	225098.1	88134	4829513.7	2674086.8	1492956.8	2596599.6	1258115.2
32166866.4	2043381.4	404175	42929649.4	23748975.5	14882311.4	19776912.4	7130888.8

12-8 续表1

单位：万元

分组	Classify	负债合计 Total Liabilites	流动负债合计 Total Working Liabilities	非流动负债 Non-Working Liabilities
总计	**Total**	**28355470.1**	**21840098.4**	**6187456.6**
#市区	Urban Area	24360078.4	18553377.8	5556069.0
#亏损企业	Deficit Enterprises	5956104.3	3139435.3	2736751.1
按隶属关系分	**Grouped by Jurisdiction of Management**			
中央企业	Central Enterprises	13892768.7	9441447.4	4398384.7
省属企业	Provincial Enterprises	4015071.1	3246392.6	727184.5
市属企业	Municipal Enterprises	10447630.3	9152258.4	1061887.4
按登记注册类型分组	**Grouped by Registion Status**			
内资企业	Domestic Investment Enterprises	25084497.2	18883825.3	5896022.9
国有	State-owned Enterprises	9257762.0	5597417.6	3651191.3
集体	Collective-owned Enterprises	65693.9	41345.7	9159.2
股份合作	Share-holding Corperative	106016.8	100683.5	5316.4
联营	Joint Ownership Enterprises	3695.0	3695.0	
国有联营	State Joint Ownership Enterprises			
集体联营	Collective Joint Ownership Enterprises	3695.0	3695.0	
国有与集体联营	Joint State-collective Ownership Enterprises			
其他联营	Other Joint Ownership Enterprises			
有限责任公司	Limited Liability Corporations	12591366.1	10681439.1	1718935.4
国有独资公司	State Sole Funded Enterprises	3466087.2	2846179.6	619254.5
其他有限责任公司	Other Limited Liability Corporation	9125278.9	7835259.5	1099680.9
股份有限公司	Share-holding Corperation Ltd.	2197812.0	1708715.6	441797.5
私营	Private Enterprises	831392.3	721288.0	69042.9
私营独资	Private-funded Enterprises	43427.3	31673.2	8331.0
私营合伙	Private Partnership Enterprises	2828.2	1393.4	1434.8
私营有限责任公司	Private Limited Liability Corporations	700830.0	613999.3	51920.1
私营股份有限公司	Private Share Holding Corporations	84306.8	74222.1	7357.0
其他	Other Domestic Funded Enterprises	30759.1	29240.8	580.2
港澳台商投资	Enterprises with Funds from Hong Kong,Macao and Taiwan	243556.0	220161.5	21005.9
外商投资	Foreign Funded Enterprises	3027416.9	2736111.6	270427.8
按轻重工业分	**Grouped by Light Industry and Heavy Industry**			
轻工业	Light Industry	2489828.5	2188386.0	231430.4
重工业	Heavy Industry	25865641.6	19651712.4	5956026.2

continued1

(10 000yuan)

所有者权益合计 Total Owners' Equities	实收资本 Total Capital Hold	营业收入 Total Revenue	主营业务收入 Revenue from Principal Business	营业成本 Total Cost	主营业务成本 Cost of Principal Business	营业税金及附加 Taxs and Other Changes	主营业务税金及附加 Taxes and Other Charges on Principal Business
19267241.5	**8298132.7**	**38632905.9**	**37585629.5**	**33006727.4**	**31853310.7**	**375976.2**	**368346.8**
17226663.3	7075099.7	32086528.5	31260003.4	27245134.0	26210857.3	357435.5	350818.6
1245736.2	1669063.9	4615257.0	4519044.5	4167801.2	4096970.0	152202.4	152071.7
8225609.5	3512549.7	12923385.1	12661748.2	11557764.9	11034831.0	198616.3	197087.0
2623635.7	913933.3	6925181.6	6569842.9	5908138.6	5672778.4	21238.0	20929.9
8417996.3	3871649.7	18784339.2	18354038.4	15540823.9	15145701.3	156121.9	150329.9
16520074.4	6934530.8	31700033.8	30971027.7	27271060.0	26360906.8	295787.4	290879.5
4668489.7	2457114.4	8468599.6	8193748.4	7744554.7	7182994.2	185949.7	184775.8
29352.5	12548.0	254634.0	254629.3	220528.9	217804.5	956.2	955.6
40739.7	19946.4	118996.6	114316.1	102765.9	102237.8	225.9	225.9
795.3	1000.0	4399.1	4399.1	4168.1	4168.1	1.4	1.4
795.3	1000.0	4399.1	4399.1	4168.1	4168.1	1.4	1.4
8836420.2	3248552.1	17729241.3	17336083.3	15040988.0	14741946.0	78206.6	75360.7
3191385.6	786163.5	3530320.6	3389131.7	2891337.0	2785493.7	16998.7	16041.1
5645034.6	2462388.6	14198920.7	13946951.6	12149651.0	11956452.3	61207.9	59319.6
2104966.7	798141.7	2499349.2	2457129.3	1960242.1	1924384.8	13704.1	13664.9
823701.0	374528.2	2586272.6	2572898.3	2160239.7	2149945.4	16473.1	15624.8
38858.9	12813.7	339640.3	339330.0	288319.9	287608.5	1359.6	943.2
719.8	600.0	3568.7	3568.7	3019.7	3019.7	9.0	9.0
605328.4	299834.8	2059255.5	2047367.8	1737923.6	1728665.8	11036.0	10604.1
178793.9	61279.7	183808.1	182631.8	130976.5	130651.4	4068.5	4068.5
15609.3	22700.0	38541.4	37823.9	37572.6	37426.0	270.4	270.4
245255.2	248366.4	285287.0	278016.3	232803.6	225324.1	3515.6	3475.6
2501911.9	1115235.5	6647585.1	6336585.5	5502863.8	5267079.8	76673.2	73991.7
2302330.5	1106760.7	7007670.4	6888424.5	5597049.8	5461258.4	45394.0	43808.7
16964911.0	7191372.0	31625235.5	30697205.0	27409677.6	26392052.3	330582.2	324538.1

12-8 续表2

单位：万元

分 组	Classify	销售费用 Expenses for Sales	管理费用 Expenses for Management	财务费用 Financial cost
总计	**Total**	**1456698.6**	**2141123.7**	**501802.0**
#市区	Urban Area	1218232.3	1871369.9	418317.4
#亏损企业	Deficit Enterprises	87068.2	252980.7	227066.9
按隶属关系分	**Grouped by Jurisdiction of Management**			
中央企业	Central Enterprises	261510.3	860642.1	292583.2
省属企业	Provincial Enterprises	380739.1	304208.6	75564.8
市属企业	Municipal Enterprises	814449.2	976273.0	133654.0
按登记注册类型分组	**Grouped by Registion Status**			
内资企业	Domestic Investment Enterprises	980028.6	1880581.1	468538.4
国有	State-owned Enterprises	182617.0	487474.3	248561.6
集体	Collective-owned Enterprises	5826.0	9549.0	1870.5
股份合作	Share-holding Corperative	5031.3	5156.8	2985.4
联营	Joint Ownership Enterprises	83.0	124.3	20.0
国有联营	State Joint Ownership Enterprises			
集体联营	Collective Joint Ownership Enterprises	83.0	124.3	20.0
国有与集体联营	Joint State-collective Ownership Enterprises			
其他联营	Other Joint Ownership Enterprises			
有限责任公司	Limited Liability Corporations	572533.1	1091705.0	143396.0
国有独资公司	State Sole Funded Enterprises	91629.4	380265.5	21285.0
其他有限责任公司	Other Limited Liability Corporation	480903.7	711439.5	122111.0
股份有限公司	Share-holding Corperation Ltd.	127188.1	173278.7	39968.1
私营	Private Enterprises	86376.7	110410.4	31526.1
私营独资	Private-funded Enterprises	4996.1	7871.0	3366.9
私营合伙	Private Partnership Enterprises	251.3	219.4	42.2
私营有限责任公司	Private Limited Liability Corporations	72778.2	89392.4	25498.2
私营股份有限公司	Private Share Holding Corporations	8351.1	12927.6	2618.8
其他	Other Domestic Funded Enterprises	373.4	2882.6	210.7
港澳台商投资	Enterprises with Funds from Hong Kong,Macao and Taiwan	37565.4	27734.4	2764.2
外商投资	Foreign Funded Enterprises	439104.6	232808.2	30499.4
按轻重工业分	**Grouped by Light Industry and Heavy Industry**			
轻工业	Light Industry	639707.5	336931.8	47960.4
重工业	Heavy Industry	816991.1	1804191.9	453841.6

continued 2

(10 000yuan)

营业利润 Operating Profit	利润总额 Total Profits	亏损企业亏损额 Total Loss of Deficit Enterprises	利税总额 Total Pre-tax Profits	应付职工薪酬 Salary Payable	本年应交增值税 Value Added Tax Payable
1431463.2	**1677664.4**	**263660.1**	**3205728.2**	**3132576.0**	**1152087.6**
1223788.3	1468953.0	225329.3	2807688.2	2807368.0	981299.7
-278579.3	-263660.1	263660.1	21046.0	298265.7	132503.7
87931.6	209579.6	143185.5	745967.8	1475381.4	337771.9
249399.8	249372.2	17529.5	477538.5	426584.2	206928.3
1094131.8	1218712.6	102945.1	1982221.9	1230610.4	607387.4
1069809.0	1274602.6	206492.2	2459124.2	2630897.0	888734.2
-32453.7	63615.6	116378.8	545836.6	863188.0	296271.3
16019.5	15945.0	352.9	28476.5	19229.2	11575.3
-1448.0	2586.7	49.4	8130.9	4951.1	5318.3
2.1	0.2		13.7	274.1	12.1
2.1	0.2		13.7	274.1	12.1
734053.3	813057.1	70428.4	1307690.5	1422691.7	416426.8
130233.6	162035.5	26400.4	263825.8	460666.7	84791.6
603819.7	651021.6	44028.0	1043864.7	962025.0	331635.2
172535.7	200519.6	9678.5	289401.9	188677.0	75178.2
184067.7	181835.4	6232.5	281500.1	130057.2	83191.6
34290.4	33082.3		48027.1	10541.4	13585.2
27.1	32.5		131.6	314.4	90.1
127653.0	125283.4	4583.9	200708.9	107262.7	64389.5
22097.2	23437.2	1648.6	32632.5	11938.7	5126.8
-2967.6	-2957.0	3371.7	-1926.0	1828.7	760.6
-17192.9	-15462.2	30581.3	2135.2	31842.9	14081.8
378847.1	418524.0	26586.6	744468.8	469836.1	249271.6
365447.2	395446.3	20910.5	740858.2	465727.6	300017.9
1066016.0	1282218.1	242749.6	2464870.0	2666848.4	852069.7

12-8 续表3

单位：万元

分组	Classify	企业单位数（个） Number of Enterprises (unit)	亏损企业 Loss Making Enterprises	工业总产值（当年价格） Gross Industrial Output Value (At Current Prices)
按企业规模分	**Grouped by Size of Enterprises**			
大型企业	Large-size	65	9	23896867.9
中型企业	Medium-size	161	27	6243798.6
小型企业	Small-size	744	131	10522457.2
微型企业	Microenterprise			
按经济组织类型分组	**Grouped by Economic Type of Orgnization**			
独资企业	Appropratorship	153	22	10398747.2
合作、合伙企业	Partnership	20	2	215385.6
股份有限公司	Corporaton	87	12	3381884.6
有限责任公司	Limited Liability Company	710	131	26667106.3
按控股情况分	**Grouped by Cast strand**			
国有控股	State owned shares	213	36	24026547.9
集体控股	Collective shares	51	7	973806.5
私人控股	Private holdings	569	94	10282398.4
港澳台控股	Hong Kong and Macao Holdings	23	10	337054.7
外商投资	Foreign Investment	66	13	4272035.1
其他	Others	48	7	771281.1
按工业行业大类分	**Grouped by Sector**			
煤炭开采和洗选业	Mining and Washing of Coal			
石油和天然气开采业	Extraction of Petroleum and Natural Gas			
黑色金属矿采选业	Mining and Processing of Ferrous Metal Ores	1	1	2416.6
有色金属矿采选业	Mining and Processing of Non-ferrous Metal Ores			
非金属矿采选业	Mining and Processing of Nonmetal Ores			
开采辅助活动	Mining Auxiliary Activities	3		207660.1
其他采矿业	Mining of other Ores			
农副食品加工业	Processing of Food from Agricultural Porducts	47	6	1774701.3
食品制造业	Manufacture of Foods	32	5	1237426.3
酒、饮料和精制茶制造业	Manufacture of Alcohol,Beverages and Tea	13	4	761448.7
烟草制品业	Manufacture of Tobacco	1		7075.0
纺织业	Manufacture of Textile	14	3	177185.7
纺织服装、服饰业	Textile, apparel industry	7	1	130674.8
皮革、毛皮、羽毛及其制品和制鞋业	Leather fur feathers and its products and footwear	2		25965.8
木材加工和木、竹、藤、棕、草制品业	Processing of Timber,Manufacture of Wood,Plam and Straw Products	3		101467.1
家具制造业	Manufacture of Furniture	9	1	43431.4

continued 3

(10 000yuan)

工业销售产值（当年价）Value of Industry Products Sales (At Current Prices)	出口交货值 Export Delivery Value	从业人员年平均人数（人）Annual Average Employers (person)	资产总计 Total Assets	流动资产合计 Total Working Capitals	固定资产合计 Total Fixed Assets	固定资产原价 Origing Value of Fixed Assets	累计折旧 Accumulative Total Depreciation
23402149.2	1810885.0	307081	32995251.7	17409289.0	12488095.6	16902864.6	6271380.2
5848498.3	254470.8	93354	7201349.3	4199387.0	2093261.3	2803063.9	1061695.6
10084470.7	203123.7	91874	7562562.1	4814386.3	1793911.3	2667583.5	1055928.2
10178753.0	410159.6	118180	15403714.6	6866916.7	7271972.9	10031599.8	3403757.5
207743.7	1604.8	2892	209509.9	157296.7	34264.9	58108.7	25409.8
3065668.7	273150.1	38884	5022963.5	2866217.7	1350428.4	2176811.7	935710.2
25882952.8	1583565.0	332353	27122975.1	16532631.2	7718602.0	10106991.8	4024126.5
23480595.6	1380896.7	293674	34359031.3	18827728.1	12248736.9	16243526.4	5953058.3
948448.8	99165.0	14172	871484.1	468606.8	331901.6	734065.2	426428.5
9829035.4	268880.1	134831	8272069.6	4849036.6	2306354.7	3281243.2	1189882.1
321147.7	44844.5	5790	460711.7	165972.1	197144.4	262740.7	73069.9
4018021.1	453525.8	31600	2902437.8	1576847.8	1085897.9	1586647.1	664646.3
737869.6	21167.4	12242	893428.6	534870.9	205232.7	265289.4	81918.9
2384.2		112	2135.0	1554.0	433.0	1036.1	658.2
211028.7		800	1039519.1	574860.5	397324.3	576255.4	178931.1
1676452.3	844.6	9612	613859.0	379766.7	192471.6	313810.0	134929.6
1172344.1		11069	503461.5	275069.3	138437.8	256846.7	132996.8
839885.6	167283.4	8039	892068.8	435703.9	336739.1	522670.1	219039.1
7573.5		242	16055.2	13335.0	2136.4	4275.2	2138.8
164047.6	19047.9	12437	177292.3	99600.8	35364.0	80325.5	45369.7
129006.7		2033	133818.3	113806.8	17100.7	21069.6	4751.8
24206.1	75.2	1022	41752.3	19864.7	8136.8	10375.2	2238.5
95744.5		816	109602.3	54789.2	46470.9	81282.2	36498.6
40848.4		1242	36677.5	18839.5	7479.0	12174.5	7107.5

12-8 续表4

单位：万元

分 组	Classify	负债合计 Total Liabilites	流动负债合计 Total Working Liabilities	非流动负债 Non-Working Liabilities
按企业规模分	**Grouped by Size of Enterprises**			
大型企业	Large-size	20078034.7	14883377.2	5135570.2
中型企业	Medium-size	4009776.7	3252952.0	677190.1
小型企业	Small-size	4267658.7	3703769.2	374696.3
微型企业	Microenterprise			
按经济组织类型分组	**Grouped by Economic Type of Orgnization**			
独资企业	Appropratorship	9890486.2	6097724.3	3762607.9
合作、合伙企业	Partnership	148356.2	140066.2	7331.4
股份有限公司	Corporaton	2582959.6	2039627.9	493305.0
有限责任公司	Limited Liability Company	15733668.1	13562680.0	1924212.3
按控股情况分	**Grouped by Cast strand**			
国有控股	State owned shares	21267059.2	15626791.3	5539313.2
集体控股	Collective shares	408143.9	359507.0	21973.3
私人控股	Private holdings	4561156.7	4017613.9	380084.5
港澳台控股	Hong Kong and Macao Holdings	245846.2	223449.2	20008.4
外商投资	Foreign Investment	1375361.1	1160843.1	193644.3
其他	Others	497903.0	451893.9	32432.9
按工业行业大类分	**Grouped by Sector**			
煤炭开采和洗选业	Mining and Washing of Coal			
石油和天然气开采业	Extraction of Petroleum and Natural Gas			
黑色金属矿采选业	Mining and Processing of Ferrous Metal Ores	3703.1	1125.7	
有色金属矿采选业	Mining and Processing of Non-ferrous Metal Ores			
非金属矿采选业	Mining and Processing of Nonmetal Ores			
开采辅助活动	Mining Auxiliary Activities	286769.1	252337.9	31538.1
其他采矿业	Mining of other Ores			
农副食品加工业	Processing of Food from Agricultural Porducts	387707.1	375829.8	9056.6
食品制造业	Manufacture of Foods	237369.0	225354.8	11822.5
酒、饮料和精制茶制造业	Manufacture of Alcohol,Beverages and Tea	511385.5	464123.7	47261.7
烟草制品业	Manufacture of Tobacco	10334.3	9690.1	321.5
纺织业	Manufacture of Textile	77466.6	75921.7	1389.6
纺织服装、服饰业	Textile, apparel industry	102381.8	77350.2	3201.7
皮革、毛皮、羽毛及其制品和制鞋业	Leather fur feathers and its products and footwear	19430.6	13795.8	5334.8
木材加工和木、竹、藤、棕、草制品业	Processing of Timber,Manufacture of Wood,Plam and Straw Products	54249.7	27249.7	27000.0
家具制造业	Manufacture of Furniture	17815.4	12506.7	61.6

continued 4

(10 000yuan)

所有者权益合计 Total Owners' Equities	实收资本 Total Capital Hold	营业收入 Total Revenue	主营业务收入 Revenue from Principal Business	营业成本 Total Cost	主营业务成本 Cost of Principal Business	营业税金及附加 Taxs and Other Changes	主营业务税金及附加 Taxes and Other Charges on Principal Business
12907555.7	4777061.9	23007120.1	22395477.0	19972763.3	19134296.3	295076.3	292626.3
3149382.4	1669928.6	5851640.5	5495076.7	4822626.2	4575796.7	33398.8	30188.4
3210303.4	1851142.2	9774145.3	9695075.8	8211337.9	8143217.7	47501.1	45532.1
5489154.3	2948618.8	10445745.6	10152870.6	9374702.2	8757891.8	196416.9	194456.8
61153.2	47554.4	170055.3	164657.3	151534.5	150859.8	518.8	518.8
2424179.3	894969.9	2924655.2	2879323.9	2302030.9	2263002.5	18205.6	18166.4
11292754.7	4406989.6	25092449.8	24388777.7	21178459.8	20681556.6	160834.9	155204.8
13087828.1	5422930.8	23325876.9	22624602.4	20411196.4	19550244.4	248457.2	243864.7
454567.0	164763.0	914169.9	909545.1	764843.2	752170.7	3059.2	3045.2
3646998.0	1557337.8	9373566.9	9163581.4	7824257.6	7630929.8	98772.2	96753.1
213637.2	241570.9	284151.1	278804.1	240988.3	232006.2	3277.7	3218.2
1470924.7	690043.9	4011151.5	3889835.0	3166700.4	3099384.1	18872.2	18044.3
393286.5	221486.3	723989.6	719261.5	598741.5	588575.5	3537.7	3421.3
-1568.1	600.0	2010.3	2010.3	1904.1	1904.1	26.2	26.2
750643.1	513682.3	508105.6	496968.7	539466.1	505986.0	10868.2	10673.3
217335.1	109725.4	1556196.1	1547944.8	1453418.1	1450861.2	2165.8	2030.7
265611.1	125478.4	1149634.9	1132905.7	916957.8	871590.0	4508.3	4483.3
372824.8	148896.5	841928.9	826786.4	645194.8	625926.3	13420.1	13376.9
5637.6	1414.7	8385.4	8262.3	5160.6	5149.9	85.5	85.5
99412.6	34573.6	164800.3	163761.4	155469.7	154719.0	906.1	906.1
29227.7	24487.5	158709.1	158144.9	129048.6	128793.6	3225.2	3224.8
22321.7	7000.0	58513.3	26811.5	53563.1	22445.4	131.8	131.7
55180.8	16500.0	82731.6	79818.4	73253.6	73195.8	335.4	333.3
18827.8	10657.7	37009.2	36714.6	28455.4	28239.4	180.2	180.2

12-8 续表5

单位：万元

分 组	Classify	销售费用 Expenses for Sales	管理费用 Expenses for Management	财务费用 Financial cost
按企业规模分	**Grouped by Size of Enterprises**			
大型企业	Large-size	915208.1	1326127.0	362137.9
中型企业	Medium-size	250566.2	362820.4	73007.1
小型企业	Small-size	290924.3	452176.3	66657.0
微型企业	Microenterprise			
按经济组织类型分组	**Grouped by Economic Type of Orgnization**			
独资企业	Appropratorship	324904.3	578116.9	255795.6
合作、合伙企业	Partnership	5801.6	8779.3	3258.5
股份有限公司	Corporaton	143593.3	197426.7	53200.7
有限责任公司	Limited Liability Company	982399.4	1356800.8	189547.2
按控股情况分	**Grouped by Cast strand**			
国有控股	State owned shares	631411.4	1445362.3	371111.6
集体控股	Collective shares	41577.3	45829.4	10131.1
私人控股	Private holdings	357534.0	427969.1	85783.7
港澳台控股	Hong Kong and Macao Holdings	38069.6	27982.5	3076.1
外商投资	Foreign Investment	366495.9	146856.9	24492.3
其他	Others	21610.4	47123.5	7207.2
按工业行业大类分	**Grouped by Sector**			
煤炭开采和洗选业	Mining and Washing of Coal			
石油和天然气开采业	Extraction of Petroleum and Natural Gas			
黑色金属矿采选业	Mining and Processing of Ferrous Metal Ores	10.0	493.1	156.3
有色金属矿采选业	Mining and Processing of Non-ferrous Metal Ores			
非金属矿采选业	Mining and Processing of Nonmetal Ores			
开采辅助活动	Mining Auxiliary Activities	286.2	22128.6	-10879.8
其他采矿业	Mining of other Ores			
农副食品加工业	Processing of Food from Agricultural Porducts	38402.7	39375.2	15342.4
食品制造业	Manufacture of Foods	117806.2	41621.4	-1951.6
酒、饮料和精制茶制造业	Manufacture of Alcohol,Beverages and Tea	92598.6	31562.5	6504.4
烟草制品业	Manufacture of Tobacco	103.2	1937.0	-14.6
纺织业	Manufacture of Textile	2436.7	11332.9	549.1
纺织服装、服饰业	Textile, apparel industry	6233.8	7783.4	801.5
皮革、毛皮、羽毛及其制品和制鞋业	Leather fur feathers and its products and footwear	1023.7	2084.5	183.6
木材加工和木、竹、藤、棕、草制品业	Processing of Timber,Manufacture of Wood,Plam and Straw Products	2143.5	1801.8	2764.9
家具制造业	Manufacture of Furniture	2999.4	1844.5	499.5

continued 5

(10 000yuan)

营业利润 Operating Profit	利润总额 Total Profits	亏损企业亏损额 Total Loss of Deficit Enterprises	利税总额 Total Pre-tax Profits	应付职工薪酬 Salary Payable	本年应交增值税 Value Added Tax Payable
495481.5	645098.3	137201.4	1630781.2	2225317.8	690606.6
326129.1	387979.1	61119.9	608589.7	451929.1	187211.8
609852.6	644587.0	65338.8	966357.3	455329.1	274269.2
68308.8	175067.4	153603.5	746129.0	982596.1	374644.7
-4316.2	-267.4	3421.1	6510.9	7673.3	6259.5
198887.3	233285.2	11327.1	372387.1	214448.0	120896.3
1168583.3	1269579.2	95308.4	2080701.2	1927858.6	650287.1
472407.4	640638.0	178470.7	1495100.2	2183091.4	606005.0
48955.1	52277.0	2039.6	92634.2	62015.9	37298.0
587528.7	641300.4	25372.4	1019535.8	548037.9	279463.2
-26523.1	-24231.2	36636.9	-9897.7	27434.5	11055.8
296935.7	312878.8	18666.7	527773.9	260873.2	196022.9
52159.4	54801.4	2473.8	80581.8	51123.1	22242.7
-644.8	-634.0	634.0	-485.7	159.2	122.1
-31541.3	8636.6		44617.2	131766.4	25112.4
34564.2	39934.2	1487.7	65608.3	40510.0	23508.3
55694.5	56952.3	661.4	93375.7	47564.8	31915.1
56485.3	59995.3	6273.7	138741.3	51282.7	65325.9
1193.1	1194.2		1943.1	2252.4	663.4
-5637.1	-699.7	5688.0	5972.3	32691.4	5765.9
9886.8	11272.0	47.9	18633.4	9834.3	4136.2
1763.0	1853.6		2163.9	5357.4	178.5
2239.0	5926.0		15950.0	3500.6	9688.6
1651.5	1627.5	18.0	2910.5	3326.4	1102.8

12-8 续表6

单位：万元

分 组	Classify	企业单位数（个） Number of Enterprises (unit)	亏损企业 Loss Making Enterprises	工业总产值（当年价格） Gross Industrial Output Value (At Current Prices)
造纸及纸制品业	Manufacture of Paper and Paper Products	20	1	144535.5
印刷和记录媒介复制	Printing,Reproduction of Recording Media	19	4	508043.2
文教、工美、体育和娱乐用品制造业	Manufacture of Articles For Cultural,Educational and Sports Activities	6	1	45876.4
石油加工业、炼焦和核燃料加工业	Processing of Petroleum, Cokeing,Processing of Nuclear and Nuclear Fuel	8	1	2403745.4
化学原料及化学制品制造业	Manufacture of Raw Chemical Materials and Chemical Products	51	7	1128740.4
医药制造业	Manufacture of Medicines	50	8	1369557.6
化学纤维制造业	Manufacture of Chemical Fibers	2	1	100030.4
橡胶和塑料制品业	Manufacture of Rubber and Plastics	28	4	534530.2
非金属矿物制品业	Manufacture of Non-metallic Mineral Products	94	26	1576398.5
黑色金属冶炼和压延加工业	Smelting and Pressing of Ferrous Metals	24	6	551242.9
有色金属冶炼和压延加工业	Smelting and Pressing of Non-ferrous Metals	26	3	957391.1
金属制品业	Manufacture of Metal Products	60	9	1219928.6
通用设备制造业	Manufacture of General Purpose Machinery	62	12	1703911.4
专用设备制造业	Manufacture of Special Equipment	92	17	2189018.4
汽车制造业	Manufacture of Motor Vehicle	36	9	8063230.5
铁路、船舶、航空航天和其他运输设备制造业	Railways,Shipbuilding,Aerospace and Other Transportation Equipment Manufacturing Industry	48	8	3649580.4
电气机械和器材制造业	Manufacture of Electric Equipment and Machinery	91	9	3697744.0
计算机、通讯和其他电子设备制造业	Manufacture of Communication Equipment, Computers and other Electronic Equipment	54	9	1526592.2
仪器仪表制造业	Manufacture of Measuring Instruments and Machinery	34	2	1188771.3
其他制造业	Manufacture of Other Manufacturing	3		36637.4
废弃资源综合利用业	Recycling and Disposal of Waste			
金属制品、机械和设备修理业	Metal Products,Machinery and Equipment Repair Industry	3	1	20831.4
电力、热力的生产和供应业	Production and Supply of Electric Power and Heat Power	17	8	2824849.7
燃气生产和供应业	Gas Mining and Supplying Industry	7		677378.5
水的生产和供应业	Production and Supply of Water	3		75105.5

continued 6

(10 000yuan)

工业销售产值（当年价）Value of Industry Products Sales (At Current Prices)	出口交货值 Export Delivery Value	从业人员年平均人数（人）Annual Average Employers (person)	资产总计 Total Assets	流动资产合计 Total Working Capitals	固定资产合计 Total Fixed Assets	固定资产原价 Origing Value of Fixed Assets	累计折旧 Accumulative Total Depreciation
140743.7		4819	86419.8	45165.7	30425.6	42497.8	16158.1
489311.2	140.8	8872	604851.1	272580.0	240050.5	406868.9	199060.4
48394.9	9279.3	639	17447.9	8612.0	7951.7	9991.7	2436.3
2365809.8		5403	518269.0	269102.9	223993.8	281528.6	95851.0
1102216.3	130791.3	21485	1633212.6	870906.2	555774.3	1081223.6	575778.8
1295358.8	9302.9	16545	1026587.3	636622.2	235854.5	399349.3	191122.0
92868.8		400	73150.2	31230.7	38819.6	68660.8	38485.4
492889.5	3683.6	14674	587259.8	357687.3	127976.7	176545.3	65479.8
1536291.0		13768	948118.4	511554.2	366693.9	523059.9	198680.7
530881.4	5304.2	3759	282841.4	157032.6	106381.9	140862.6	34524.9
924514.2	56094.8	7433	839977.2	482120.5	215511.9	331649.4	138058.0
1171769.5	26070.4	24605	1661220.9	995151.7	561038.3	727896.6	283331.2
1649539.6	51176.7	17700	2709696.2	2144680.7	347422.1	507407.9	180033.3
1970205.5	118216.3	32539	2909067.0	1953644.0	671504.0	940455.6	326288.3
7871771.3	640883.5	93155	6339293.2	3443055.2	2185197.4	2490217.8	782848.9
3529932.5	509808.8	67211	7466581.4	4791455.1	1900893.0	2305507.8	1027035.5
3552294.5	242780.3	44016	4941959.0	3324376.9	1447766.7	1440012.4	505491.0
1420723.9	218911.5	27989	2606964.3	1542767.2	736446.7	937995.7	307686.1
1152377.4	58744.0	18982	1788177.7	1089932.4	495119.5	697664.0	326323.9
35683.6	40.0	623	24859.8	14791.4	7006.8	9917.4	3471.0
20662.4		337	18595.8	15218.9	2001.1	1766.6	900.5
2824300.4		12723	5641269.1	1031433.1	4138292.1	6072185.5	1954797.0
677950.8		4140	1311188.4	385807.0	457463.4	671600.7	224461.9
75105.5		3068	155914.3	60944.0	93589.1	228525.6	146040.3

12-8 续表7

单位：万元

分 组	Classify	负债合计 Total Liabilites	流动负债合计 Total Working Liabilities	非流动负债 Non-Working Liabilities
造纸及纸制品业	Manufacture of Paper and Paper Products	52830.6	38113.9	10303.4
印刷和记录媒介复制	Printing,Reproduction of Recording Media	248323.0	204856.5	38509.3
文教、工美、体育和娱乐用品制造业	Manufacture of Articles For Cultural,Educational and Sports Activities	5338.2	4762.7	
石油加工业、炼焦和核燃料加工业	Processing of Petroleum, Cokeing,Processing of Nuclear and Nuclear Fuel	377564.1	351530.1	26034.0
化学原料及化学制品制造业	Manufacture of Raw Chemical Materials and Chemical Products	838634.2	693492.6	130785.5
医药制造业	Manufacture of Medicines	454244.8	427393.1	26130.4
化学纤维制造业	Manufacture of Chemical Fibers	9338.3	9338.3	
橡胶和塑料制品业	Manufacture of Rubber and Plastics	414090.9	349228.5	50467.5
非金属矿物制品业	Manufacture of Non-metallic Mineral Products	483328.4	405797.4	26387.7
黑色金属冶炼和压延加工业	Smelting and Pressing of Ferrous Metals	197011.4	161743.5	17944.8
有色金属冶炼和压延加工业	Smelting and Pressing of Non-ferrous Metals	499495.3	424291.3	68788.1
金属制品业	Manufacture of Metal Products	973973.6	715560.2	248120.9
通用设备制造业	Manufacture of General Purpose Machinery	1619431.9	1522989.6	89666.3
专用设备制造业	Manufacture of Special Equipment	1409639.6	1257759.6	116387.1
汽车制造业	Manufacture of Motor Vehicle	3716369.3	3297234.2	374081.4
铁路、船舶、航空航天和其他运输设备制造业	Railways,Shipbuilding,Aerospace and Other Transportation Equipment Manufacturing Industry	4454640.6	3739157.4	707716.4
电气机械和器材制造业	Manufacture of Electric Equipment and Machinery	2481795.8	2124927.0	337148.1
计算机、通讯和其他电子设备制造业	Manufacture of Communication Equipment, Computers and other Electronic Equipment	1600622.3	1273911.2	278722.8
仪器仪表制造业	Manufacture of Measuring Instruments and Machinery	946968.3	778647.5	168228.7
其他制造业	Manufacture of Other Manufacturing	12837.5	12776.5	61.0
废弃资源综合利用业	Recycling and Disposal of Waste			
金属制品、机械和设备修理业	Metal Products,Machinery and Equipment Repair Industry	11405.7	11405.7	
电力、热力的生产和供应业	Production and Supply of Electric Power and Heat Power	5007944.2	1961260.0	3046684.0
燃气生产和供应业	Gas Mining and Supplying Industry	764194.6	490092.8	270008.5
水的生产和供应业	Production and Supply of Water	66835.3	48542.7	18292.6

continued 7

(10 000yuan)

所有者权益合计 Total Owners' Equities	实收资本 Total Capital Hold	营业收入 Total Revenue	主营业务收入 Revenue from Principal Business	营业成本 Total Cost	主营业务成本 Cost of Principal Business	营业税金及附加 Taxs and Other Changes	主营业务税金及附加 Taxes and Other Charges on Principal Business
33393.6	16014.4	144982.1	144496.7	128939.9	128793.3	499.3	496.7
355837.0	167400.7	497889.2	492700.7	368586.3	361828.6	4723.8	3754.3
11775.2	5768.9	45357.2	45356.8	33017.3	33017.3	352.0	352.0
140698.7	264112.4	2200184.5	2195847.8	1914858.5	1913725.9	135415.9	135315.7
789881.3	280013.8	1172415.3	1040692.2	939681.1	834673.4	4935.0	4474.5
569093.8	227681.1	1230212.7	1205278.3	679872.8	664195.8	11344.2	11290.0
63811.9	50800.0	92870.5	91809.1	74919.7	73861.0	368.3	368.3
165283.7	123722.7	475545.1	468487.5	398707.6	396088.2	2980.9	2284.1
456364.0	187483.0	1436546.9	1434920.7	1198309.0	1197051.1	8809.6	8804.4
79082.1	48210.3	575943.6	571681.8	518716.6	510508.8	2212.0	2209.0
340343.9	179217.2	798508.2	777595.7	679747.2	664129.8	3220.4	2824.2
676649.5	251643.5	1130822.5	1114746.4	955550.3	945773.4	4771.3	4585.9
1088397.1	181066.8	1539410.4	1526552.3	1190044.7	1181196.0	9338.3	8884.4
1484704.9	715888.7	1914913.1	1891438.9	1495557.8	1484205.7	17958.3	17872.6
2601841.4	801076.5	6814791.1	6439699.9	6089504.9	5804445.2	64246.8	63987.2
3011511.7	1024257.0	4169575.1	4106789.8	3553319.4	3507081.6	17884.2	17696.0
2434426.1	637413.0	3202079.7	3107248.0	2974570.9	2592072.1	17438.4	17000.3
1005755.8	549702.0	1632342.6	1598471.6	1395776.7	1361172.1	5687.6	4327.6
840648.7	431886.8	1165878.7	1146071.1	940414.7	931240.1	7785.7	7406.1
12022.2	4620.0	34980.8	34153.2	29944.7	29387.2	242.8	242.8
7190.0	4454.5	23692.4	23676.6	20596.3	18051.4	112.0	112.0
633324.9	830189.9	2979282.6	2907238.1	2783757.1	2738644.5	16452.5	16315.1
540670.8	271493.4	704950.2	665322.4	568808.7	545790.3	2529.5	1740.3
89079.0	51000.0	81706.7	75224.9	71633.3	67567.2	814.6	551.3

12-8 续表8

单位：万元

分 组	Classify	销售费用 Expenses for Sales	管理费用 Expenses for Management	财务费用 Financial cost
造纸及纸制品业	Manufacture of Paper and Paper Products	2454.2	3900.9	850.0
印刷和记录媒介复制	Printing,Reproduction of Recording Media	13957.9	51155.0	3245.9
文教、工美、体育和娱乐用品制造业	Manufacture of Articles For Cultural,Educational and Sports Activities	1150.3	1981.5	346.2
石油加工业、炼焦和核燃料加工业	Processing of Petroleum, Cokeing,Processing of Nuclear and Nuclear Fuel	10718.6	90539.4	7580.5
化学原料及化学制品制造业	Manufacture of Raw Chemical Materials and Chemical Products	56939.7	91139.3	14603.8
医药制造业	Manufacture of Medicines	322699.5	94951.7	15343.8
化学纤维制造业	Manufacture of Chemical Fibers	233.4	2803.5	-216.5
橡胶和塑料制品业	Manufacture of Rubber and Plastics	18269.8	22368.9	8447.9
非金属矿物制品业	Manufacture of Non-metallic Mineral Products	33428.2	39488.7	7652.6
黑色金属冶炼和压延加工业	Smelting and Pressing of Ferrous Metals	6487.8	12547.1	4926.1
有色金属冶炼和压延加工业	Smelting and Pressing of Non-ferrous Metals	12630.3	37442.8	21236.6
金属制品业	Manufacture of Metal Products	22646.7	85239.1	13031.1
通用设备制造业	Manufacture of General Purpose Machinery	52734.9	176680.1	-4048.5
专用设备制造业	Manufacture of Special Equipment	88341.0	154839.9	17155.2
汽车制造业	Manufacture of Motor Vehicle	201473.6	235372.8	39866.1
铁路、船舶、航空航天和其他运输设备制造业	Railways,Shipbuilding,Aerospace and Other Transportation Equipment Manufacturing Industry	90039.0	304249.1	45891.5
电气机械和器材制造业	Manufacture of Electric Equipment and Machinery	173528.5	241493.1	25937.3
计算机、通讯和其他电子设备制造业	Manufacture of Communication Equipment, Computers and other Electronic Equipment	32932.8	140866.9	16991.9
仪器仪表制造业	Manufacture of Measuring Instruments and Machinery	27064.0	123208.7	9479.0
其他制造业	Manufacture of Other Manufacturing	765.7	2398.0	195.8
废弃资源综合利用业	Recycling and Disposal of Waste			
金属制品、机械和设备修理业	Metal Products,Machinery and Equipment Repair Industry	1567.1	3118.1	192.0
电力、热力的生产和供应业	Production and Supply of Electric Power and Heat Power	2502.8	24733.3	223201.0
燃气生产和供应业	Gas Mining and Supplying Industry	16613.2	30113.5	15690.8
水的生产和供应业	Production and Supply of Water	3475.6	8527.4	246.2

continued 8

(10 000yuan)

营业利润 Operating Profit	利润总额 Total Profits	亏损企业亏损额 Total Loss of Deficit Enterprises	利税总额 Total Pre-tax Profits	应付职工薪酬 Salary Payable	本年应交增值税 Value Added Tax Payable
10090.3	10456.2	4.2	14390.1	13463.3	3434.6
60277.4	61547.1	2314.4	88262.9	67756.4	21992.0
5493.8	5492.0	48.9	6992.2	2717.0	1148.2
-49004.0	-47630.1	66872.3	103115.7	30243.4	15329.9
57517.7	64668.7	20650.1	98988.1	116586.8	29384.4
108472.3	108531.2	419.5	239730.6	132709.2	119855.2
14761.9	14733.5	343.9	18308.0	4430.2	3206.2
30683.5	31269.4	1078.3	49595.4	27612.8	15345.1
146977.7	151446.0	6374.3	229082.0	53253.7	68826.4
30675.0	30953.4	8444.5	45382.1	23717.5	12216.7
34168.2	42785.8	3831.1	67050.9	34788.9	21044.7
44122.6	52438.1	3179.2	79858.6	140120.5	22649.2
128429.9	136286.2	2972.3	203929.9	159304.4	58305.4
128430.4	140666.9	23022.7	231382.4	191901.4	72757.2
211302.9	224401.3	10708.2	430040.8	403673.2	141392.7
155571.3	190919.3	13739.2	266593.3	574598.5	57789.8
78764.9	101210.3	9534.9	231640.3	265599.7	112991.6
45806.8	70634.5	23413.8	96923.5	163184.0	20601.4
53921.9	62253.9	379.1	103901.7	135028.5	33862.1
1380.8	1436.7		2811.1	2534.6	1131.6
614.5	1174.0	15.3	2431.8	1874.7	1145.8
-61972.9	-39528.6	51503.2	108420.7	190780.9	131496.8
72275.5	72965.8		89642.2	47754.2	14146.9
-2953.4	2494.8		7823.9	20696.6	4514.5

12-9 规模以上国有及国有控股工业企业主要经济指标（2012年）

单位：万元

分 组	Classify	企业单位数（个） Number of Enterprises (unit)	亏损企业 Loss Making Enterprises	工业总产值（当年价格） Gross Industrial Output Value (At Current Prices)
总计	**Total**	**213**	**36**	**24026547.9**
#市区	Urban Area	178	30	18626872.9
#亏损企业	Deficit Enterprises	36	36	3385742.8
按隶属关系分	**Grouped by Jurisdiction of Management**			
中央企业	Central Enterprises	77	10	12234677.8
省属企业	Provincial Enterprises	40	7	6300182.3
市属企业	Municipal Enterprises	96	19	5491687.8
按轻重工业分	**Grouped by Light Industry and Heavy Industry**			
轻工业	Light Industry	40	6	1316684.7
重工业	Heavy Industry	173	30	22709863.2
按企业规模分	**Grouped by Size of Enterprises**			
大型企业	Large-size	44	8	17762086.2
中型企业	Medium-size	68	12	2409677.5
小型企业	Small-size	101	16	3854784.2
微型企业	Microenterprise			
按工业行业大类分	**Grouped by Sector**			
煤炭开采和洗选业	Mining and Washing of Coal			
石油和天然气开采业	Extraction of Petroleum and Natural Gas			
黑色金属矿采选业	Mining and Processing of Ferrous Metal Ores			
有色金属矿采选业	Mining and Processing of Non-ferrous Metal Ores			
非金属矿采选业	Mining and Processing of Nonmetal Ores			
开采辅助活动	Mining Auxiliary Activities	2		175160.0
其他采矿业	Mining of Other Ores			
农副食品加工业	Processing of Food from Agricultural Porducts	3	1	30664.6
食品制造业	Manufacture of Foods	5		352701.2
酒、饮料和精制茶制造业	Manufacture of Alcohol,Beverages and Tea	1		98484.4
烟草制品业	Manufacture of Tobacco	1		7075.0
纺织业	Manufacture of Textile	4	1	107240.5
纺织服装、服饰业	Textile, apparel industry			
皮革、毛皮、羽毛及其制品和制鞋业	Leather fur feathers and its products and footwear	1		25464.3
木材加工和木、竹、藤、棕、草制品业	Processing of Timber,Manufacture of Wood,Plam and Straw Products			
家具制造业	Manufacture of Furniture			

Economic Indicators of all State-owned and State-holding Share Industrial Enterprises above Designated Size (2012)

(10 000 yuan)

工业销售产值（当年价）Value of Industry Products Sales (At Current Prices)	出口交货值 Export Delivery Value	从业人员年平均人数（人）Annual Average Employers (person)	资产总计 Total Assets	流动资产合计 Total Working Capitals	固定资产合计 Total Fixed Assets	固定资产原价 Origing Value of Fixed Assets	累计折旧 Accumulative Total Depreciation
23480595.6	**1380896.7**	**293674**	**34359031.3**	**18827728.1**	**12248736.9**	**16243526.4**	**5953058.3**
18166339.0	919806.7	244239	30095966.9	16493728.1	10845243.2	14539604.2	5351871.6
3252679.5	20033.8	33548	5490225.5	1655985.2	3202025.8	4480460.0	1362156.0
11982065.8	701258.4	167022	22073868.2	11282818.9	9096556.7	12102405.7	4454689.4
6142127.7	475516.7	62331	5906964.1	3279863.4	1752061.9	2097197.7	714899.2
5356402.1	204121.6	64321	6378199.0	4265045.8	1400118.3	2043923.0	783469.7
1425842.0	19454.7	28933	1192576.9	594823.4	472526.1	917287.5	490435.6
22054753.6	1361442.0	264741	33166454.4	18232904.7	11776210.8	15326238.9	5462622.7
17446876.5	1319068.8	235020	26242865.4	14686041.4	9298666.6	11909782.9	4348834.2
2261044.0	45888.6	44359	3844635.1	2340734.4	1062204.1	1471207.8	546851.8
3772675.1	15939.3	14295	4271530.8	1800952.3	1887866.2	2862535.7	1057372.3
178528.6		126	986860.4	538800.3	388660.8	559700.2	171039.4
29558.4	844.6	942	52311.9	26662.8	24842.4	32344.0	7702.6
343786.5		2280	59119.5	24202.0	30364.1	50019.5	19685.2
249825.3		1272	157341.8	102033.6	21031.2	54029.6	33863.4
7573.5		242	16055.2	13335.0	2136.4	4275.2	2138.8
105403.9	18390.9	11295	115173.6	58973.1	22353.4	60760.0	38406.6
23704.6	75.2	887	39536.6	17854.7	7989.5	10180.3	2190.9

12-9 续表1

单位：万元

分组	Classify	负债合计 Total Liabilites	流动负债合计 Total Working Liabilities	非流动负债 Non-Working Liabilities
总计	**Total**	**21267059.2**	**15626791.3**	**5539313.2**
#市区	Urban Area	18354186.3	13302262.2	4991805.5
#亏损企业	Deficit Enterprises	4778635.2	2068871.5	2663669.2
按隶属关系分	**Grouped by Jurisdiction of Management**			
中央企业	Central Enterprises	13865085.5	9417845.6	4394303.3
省属企业	Provincial Enterprises	3554924.7	2819777.6	693683.6
市属企业	Municipal Enterprises	3847049.0	3389168.1	451326.3
按轻重工业分	**Grouped by Light Industry and Heavy Industry**			
轻工业	Light Industry	456225.5	403721.1	49726.5
重工业	Heavy Industry	20810833.7	15223070.2	5489586.7
按企业规模分	**Grouped by Size of Enterprises**			
大型企业	Large-size	16400601.5	11861133.3	4498882.0
中型企业	Medium-size	2397558.5	1859008.1	481662.2
小型企业	Small-size	2468899.2	1906649.9	558769.0
微型企业	Microenterprise			
按工业行业大类分	**Grouped by Sector**			
煤炭开采和洗选业	Mining and Washing of Coal			
石油和天然气开采业	Extraction of Petroleum and Natural Gas			
黑色金属矿采选业	Mining and Processing of Ferrous Metal Ores			
有色金属矿采选业	Mining and Processing of Non-ferrous Metal Ores			
非金属矿采选业	Mining and Processing of Nonmetal Ores			
开采辅助活动	Mining Auxiliary Activities	277021.0	245482.9	31538.1
其他采矿业	Mining of Other Ores			
农副食品加工业	Processing of Food from Agricultural Porducts	22100.8	22100.8	
食品制造业	Manufacture of Foods	34159.7	31518.0	2641.7
酒、饮料和精制茶制造业	Manufacture of Alcohol,Beverages and Tea	59450.7	59103.7	347.0
烟草制品业	Manufacture of Tobacco	10334.3	9690.1	321.5
纺织业	Manufacture of Textile	43702.6	42334.6	1368.0
纺织服装、服饰业	Textile, apparel industry			
皮革、毛皮、羽毛及其制品和制鞋业	Leather fur feathers and its products and footwear	18261.1	12626.3	5334.8
木材加工和木、竹、藤、棕、草制品业	Processing of Timber,Manufacture of Wood,Plam and Straw Products			
家具制造业	Manufacture of Furniture			

continued 1

(10 000 yuan)

所有者权益合计 Total Owners' Equities	实收资本 Total Capital Hold	营业收入 Total Revenue	主营业务收入 Revenue from Principal Business	营业成本 Total Cost	主营业务成本 Cost of Principal Business	营业税金及附加 Taxs and Other Changes	主营业务税金及附加 Taxes and Other Charges on Principal Business
13087828.1	**5422930.8**	**23325876.9**	**22624602.4**	**20411196.4**	**19550244.4**	**248457.2**	**243864.7**
11737638.6	4570037.3	18982471.9	18429078.1	16532342.0	15772790.6	238553.1	234315.0
711582.3	1060340.9	3382477.3	3299629.5	3024357.3	2969251.2	146359.4	146237.0
8207131.9	3503155.7	12871839.9	12610599.6	11508224.6	10988184.2	198264.4	196735.1
2351955.4	774991.9	5387292.6	5122209.3	4745603.8	4519993.2	14401.3	14121.9
2528740.8	1144783.2	5066744.4	4891793.5	4157368.0	4042067.0	35791.5	33007.7
736235.5	369189.3	1476791.1	1426419.4	1186112.6	1140930.1	16568.3	16066.3
12351592.6	5053741.5	21849085.8	21198183.0	19225083.8	18409314.3	231888.9	227798.4
9840461.0	3403874.4	16892802.8	16498059.9	14634951.3	14045420.4	211291.4	209319.0
1445434.1	923028.1	2396590.7	2154196.3	2012814.9	1808365.3	13236.9	11015.4
1801933.0	1096028.3	4036483.4	3972346.2	3763430.2	3696458.7	23928.9	23530.3
709839.4	510499.6	474956.1	464852.4	517046.5	483791.4	9795.8	9606.3
30211.1	12152.7	33469.6	33026.3	26450.7	26200.4	178.2	178.2
24959.8	23520.5	342648.9	340037.1	282406.9	280923.6	735.9	710.9
97891.1	28790.3	250404.1	249825.2	197447.1	196969.0	9290.5	9290.5
5637.6	1414.7	8385.4	8262.3	5160.6	5149.9	85.5	85.5
71470.9	8846.2	106708.8	105773.9	101586.6	100835.9	772.9	772.9
21275.5	6000.0	55406.4	23704.6	50975.5	19857.8	123.0	122.9

12-9 续表2

单位：万元

分组	Classify	销售费用 Expenses for Sales	管理费用 Expenses for Management	财务费用 Financial cost
总计	**Total**	**631411.4**	**1445362.3**	**371111.6**
#市区	Urban Area	479434.9	1262082.5	312483.6
#亏损企业	Deficit Enterprises	24664.3	169061.0	203066.4
按隶属关系分	**Grouped by Jurisdiction of Management**			
中央企业	Central Enterprises	260672.3	856854.0	292500.7
省属企业	Provincial Enterprises	186627.3	254563.5	58898.2
市属企业	Municipal Enterprises	184111.8	333944.8	19712.7
按轻重工业分	**Grouped by Light Industry and Heavy Industry**			
轻工业	Light Industry	80451.8	100322.3	566.8
重工业	Heavy Industry	550959.6	1345040.0	370544.8
按企业规模分	**Grouped by Size of Enterprises**			
大型企业	Large-size	516566.6	1153328.2	302716.8
中型企业	Medium-size	73548.0	182968.1	40978.7
小型企业	Small-size	41296.8	109066.0	27416.1
微型企业	Microenterprise			
按工业行业大类分	**Grouped by Sector**			
煤炭开采和洗选业	Mining and Washing of Coal			
石油和天然气开采业	Extraction of Petroleum and Natural Gas			
黑色金属矿采选业	Mining and Processing of Ferrous Metal Ores			
有色金属矿采选业	Mining and Processing of Non-ferrous Metal Ores			
非金属矿采选业	Mining and Processing of Nonmetal Ores			
开采辅助活动	Mining Auxiliary Activities	207.3	19381.1	-11030.6
其他采矿业	Mining of Other Ores			
农副食品加工业	Processing of Food from Agricultural Porducts	1611.7	1867.8	1170.4
食品制造业	Manufacture of Foods	35370.3	21272.8	11.7
酒、饮料和精制茶制造业	Manufacture of Alcohol,Beverages and Tea	13705.4	4377.6	-3189.2
烟草制品业	Manufacture of Tobacco	103.2	1937.0	-14.6
纺织业	Manufacture of Textile	1363.6	7938.5	207.3
纺织服装、服饰业	Textile, apparel industry			
皮革、毛皮、羽毛及其制品和制鞋业	Manufacture of Leather, Fur, Feather (eiderdown) and Related Products	881.8	1744.6	163.6
木材加工和木、竹、藤、棕、草制品业	Processing of Timber,Manufacture of Wood,Plam and Straw Products			
家具制造业	Manufacture of Furniture			

continued 2

(10 000 yuan)

营业利润 Operating Profit	利润总额 Total Profits	亏损企业亏损额 Total Loss of Deficit Enterprises	利税总额 Total Pre-tax Profits	应付职工薪酬 Salary Payable	本年应交增值税 Value Added Tax Payable
472407.4	**640638.0**	**178470.7**	**1495100.2**	**2183091.4**	**606005.0**
399063.5	575229.0	156745.8	1311858.2	1958207.9	498076.1
-188729.6	-178470.7	178470.7	74783.3	206314.2	106894.6
89667.5	210204.7	141515.5	743614.7	1467615.3	335145.6
134261.4	134460.2	9477.9	268248.2	311021.1	119386.7
248478.5	295973.1	27477.3	483237.3	404455.0	151472.7
96874.3	114083.0	4796.7	179305.3	155324.2	48654.0
375533.1	526555.0	173674.0	1315794.9	2027767.2	557351.0
393310.9	456284.7	137106.8	1084283.0	1618680.1	416706.9
67566.6	100963.9	26920.6	180218.4	229816.7	66017.6
11529.9	83389.4	14443.3	230598.8	334594.6	123280.5
-38263.5	1924.7		36168.9	126267.7	24448.4
2201.6	2187.6	366.5	3212.0	3843.7	846.2
2685.2	3000.4		8771.1	9590.3	5034.8
29799.3	30281.6		48381.5	14631.4	8809.4
1193.1	1194.2		1943.1	2252.4	663.4
-4981.6	-335.4	2172.2	4960.5	30289.3	4523.0
1754.3	1845.9		2074.1	4891.4	105.2

12-9 续表3

单位：万元

分 组	Classify	企业单位数（个） Number of Enterprises (unit)	亏损企业 Loss Making Enterprises	工业总产值（当年价格） Gross Industrial Output Value (At Current Prices)
造纸及纸制品业	Manufacture of Paper and Paper Products			
印刷和记录媒介复制	Printing,Reproduction of Recording Media	5		290184.4
文教、工美、体育和娱乐用品制造业	Manufacture of Articles For Cultural,Educational and Sports Activities			
石油加工业、炼焦和核燃料加工业	Processing of Petroleum, Cokeing,Processing of Nuclear and Nuclear Fuel	2	1	2161116.0
化学原料及化学制品制造业	Manufacture of Raw Chemical Materials and Chemical Products	15	3	468762.4
医药制造业	Manufacture of Medicines	5		85182.4
化学纤维制造业	Manufacture of Chemical Fibers	2	1	100030.4
橡胶和塑料制品业	Manufacture of Rubber and Plastics	3		232403.6
非金属矿物制品业	Manufacture of Non-metallic Mineral Products	6	1	64743.2
黑色金属冶炼和压延加工业	Smelting and Pressing of Ferrous Metals	3	1	135656.5
有色金属冶炼和压延加工业	Smelting and Pressing of Non-ferrous Metals	10	1	523548.2
金属制品业	Manufacture of Metal Products	12		800563.6
通用设备制造业	Manufacture of General Purpose Machinery	11	3	1188832.0
专用设备制造业	Manufacture of Special Equipment	22	4	1146843.7
汽车制造业	Manufacture of Motor Vehicle	10	1	5166143.5
铁路、船舶、航空航天和其他运输设备制造业	Railways,Shipbuilding,Aerospace and Other Transportation Equipment Manufacturing Industry	26	4	3422141.6
电气机械和器材制造业	Manufacture of Electric Equipment and Machinery	14	3	2220178.4
计算机、通讯和其他电子设备制造业	Manufacture of Communication Equipment, Computers and other Electronic Equipment	21	4	889327.2
仪器仪表制造业	Manufacture of Measuring Instruments and Machinery	8		890773.5
其他制造业	Manufacture of Other Manufacturing	2		17893.3
废弃资源综合利用业	Recycling and Disposal of Waste			
金属制品、机械和设备修理业	Metal Products,Machinery and Equipment Repair Industry			
电力、热力的生产和供应业	Production and Supply of Electric Power and Heat Power	12	7	2719913.0
燃气生产和供应业	Gas Mining and Supplying Industry	4		630415.5
水的生产和供应业	Production and Supply of Water	3		75105.5

continued 3

(10 000 yuan)

工业销售产值（当年价）Value of Industry Products Sales (At Current Prices)	出口交货值 Export Delivery Value	从业人员年平均人数（人）Annual Average Employers (person)	资产总计 Total Assets	流动资产合计 Total Working Capitals	固定资产合计 Total Fixed Assets	固定资产原价 Origing Value of Fixed Assets	累计折旧 Accumulative Total Depreciation
284364.1	104.0	4528	365895.8	156046.8	185631.4	300764.4	143768.4
2124315.0		1705	372304.4	187494.2	160999.1	220482.6	83172.7
460727.4	46950.6	14578	802343.9	384368.7	297395.8	437228.2	187595.6
85614.1		1916	53684.2	32383.2	16803.8	28926.8	12180.4
92868.8		400	73150.2	31230.7	38819.6	68660.8	38485.4
229821.8	3033.7	11797	422242.4	258458.2	75935.9	107854.1	40489.2
63473.0		1196	61999.0	46418.8	9176.2	14701.8	6208.8
128727.3	934.7	703	56541.8	40458.3	13221.3	18040.4	4819.0
509852.2	17219.8	3248	418897.3	255775.2	124734.9	137696.0	34583.5
766248.8	23821.1	19056	1372423.5	828898.1	480945.4	623863.2	252401.9
1149998.5	33429.7	10947	2267535.7	1829674.9	251435.0	369809.6	119508.8
986727.9	62696.0	16498	1662290.4	1195853.6	311221.9	459255.1	170866.4
5025028.6	465275.8	45484	3977569.2	2371061.1	1245835.8	1334402.3	426141.3
3313067.5	489418.7	63140	7168313.0	4576733.1	1855204.8	2234949.5	999324.6
2173797.6	159349.3	31024	3859419.3	2591405.1	1228960.3	1149643.1	394840.5
838586.9	44909.6	17555	1782673.3	1144732.3	375328.4	436459.8	156295.8
866321.9	14403.0	13455	1436509.6	810613.8	452611.5	638153.8	303439.7
17926.1	40.0	403	10427.9	7457.8	2488.3	3485.7	997.4
2719363.7		12239	5432871.3	911824.5	4099565.0	6025188.4	1946527.0
630278.1		3690	1179625.8	324034.2	431455.6	634126.4	210344.7
75105.5		3068	155914.3	60944.0	93589.1	228525.6	146040.3

12-9 续表4

单位：万元

分组	Classify	负债合计 Total Liabilites	流动负债合计 Total Working Liabilities	非流动负债 Non-Working Liabilities
造纸及纸制品业	Manufacture of Paper and Paper Products			
印刷和记录媒介复制	Printing,Reproduction of Recording Media	78821.4	63104.8	13869.0
文教、工美、体育和娱乐用品制造业	Manufacture of Articles For Cultural,Educational and Sports Activities			
石油加工业、炼焦和核燃料加工业	Processing of Petroleum, Cokeing,Processing of Nuclear and Nuclear Fuel	290155.8	284121.8	6034.0
化学原料及化学制品制造业	Manufacture of Raw Chemical Materials and Chemical Products	428903.5	355337.1	73245.7
医药制造业	Manufacture of Medicines	27594.4	27426.6	167.8
化学纤维制造业	Manufacture of Chemical Fibers	9338.3	9338.3	
橡胶和塑料制品业	Manufacture of Rubber and Plastics	323768.0	274849.4	48918.6
非金属矿物制品业	Manufacture of Non-metallic Mineral Products	38132.5	37604.8	497.4
黑色金属冶炼和压延加工业	Smelting and Pressing of Ferrous Metals	40734.9	37572.1	3162.8
有色金属冶炼和压延加工业	Smelting and Pressing of Non-ferrous Metals	272779.4	232731.8	40047.4
金属制品业	Manufacture of Metal Products	831816.7	594166.3	236462.9
通用设备制造业	Manufacture of General Purpose Machinery	1386577.3	1308991.3	77585.9
专用设备制造业	Manufacture of Special Equipment	895964.1	852850.7	42557.7
汽车制造业	Manufacture of Motor Vehicle	2285400.4	1928594.4	316224.6
铁路、船舶、航空航天和其他运输设备制造业	Railways,Shipbuilding,Aerospace and Other Transportation Equipment Manufacturing Industry	4302528.9	3592879.8	701921.0
电气机械和器材制造业	Manufacture of Electric Equipment and Machinery	1927270.5	1643209.9	284060.6
计算机、通讯和其他电子设备制造业	Manufacture of Communication Equipment, Computers and other Electronic Equipment	1233497.7	1001096.2	184413.4
仪器仪表制造业	Manufacture of Measuring Instruments and Machinery	784113.8	627074.2	156947.5
其他制造业	Manufacture of Other Manufacturing	5318.3	5257.3	61.0
废弃资源综合利用业	Recycling and Disposal of Waste			
金属制品、机械和设备修理业	Metal Products,Machinery and Equipment Repair Industry			
电力、热力的生产和供应业	Production and Supply of Electric Power and Heat Power	4863070.8	1837288.4	3025782.2
燃气生产和供应业	Gas Mining and Supplying Industry	709407.0	441897.0	267510.0
水的生产和供应业	Production and Supply of Water	66835.3	48542.7	18292.6

continued 4

(10 000 yuan)

所有者权益合计 Total Owners' Equities	实收资本 Total Capital Hold	营业收入 Total Revenue	主营业务收入 Revenue from Principal Business	营业成本 Total Cost	主营业务成本 Cost of Principal Business	营业税金及附加 Taxs and Other Changes	主营业务税金及附加 Taxes and Other Charges on Principal Business
287074.3	110524.1	300092.1	297401.0	208232.2	206377.3	3170.7	2957.1
82142.5	227994.2	2000068.1	1997816.5	1744609.4	1744604.5	134341.0	134340.3
373440.3	144296.8	550295.7	419670.2	445554.6	344991.9	2611.4	2301.1
26089.8	21402.2	74445.3	74324.1	50230.7	48100.1	280.5	280.5
63811.9	50800.0	92870.5	91809.1	74919.7	73861.0	368.3	368.3
98474.4	67670.4	222582.3	217921.2	184460.2	184160.6	1463.7	1346.2
23866.5	14079.7	64704.3	64324.9	57473.9	57283.4	949.8	949.8
15806.8	15237.7	128895.4	124685.4	119300.6	114760.9	249.4	246.6
146117.7	72988.9	384032.6	364925.3	311486.0	297449.9	972.8	972.8
540576.1	188066.5	730784.4	715723.5	619329.0	610329.1	2715.6	2533.4
880958.3	62830.3	1061539.2	1049963.7	786159.4	777630.1	6655.5	6518.4
762889.3	368953.2	937812.6	925370.5	744602.7	736495.6	7578.7	7520.9
1692168.8	515418.1	4163632.3	4006730.5	3725092.8	3599927.4	9414.0	9157.9
2865784.1	956123.4	3944735.7	3883314.0	3391960.2	3345744.6	16068.0	15892.3
1932146.7	342365.1	1826992.4	1737496.1	1792117.1	1414058.2	12785.1	12750.4
548591.6	246336.8	1039818.3	1028761.6	904530.2	890033.5	3988.3	2635.6
652395.6	352506.9	867081.7	853630.8	729099.8	721954.9	4626.5	4279.7
5109.5	2800.0	17223.3	17064.7	15229.4	15215.9	81.4	81.4
569800.7	791599.1	2896799.6	2824755.1	2716879.6	2671767.0	15881.9	15744.5
470218.8	228713.4	667785.1	628207.5	537221.7	514203.3	2458.2	1669.0
89079.0	51000.0	81706.7	75224.9	71633.3	67567.2	814.6	551.3

12-9 续表5

单位：万元

分 组	Classify	销售费用 Expenses for Sales	管理费用 Expenses for Management	财务费用 Financial cost
造纸及纸制品业	Manufacture of Paper and Paper Products			
印刷和记录媒介复制	Printing,Reproduction of Recording Media	9161.3	36604.6	47.9
文教、工美、体育和娱乐用品制造业	Manufacture of Articles For Cultural,Educational and Sports Activities			
石油加工业、炼焦和核燃料加工业	Processing of Petroleum, Cokeing,Processing of Nuclear and Nuclear Fuel	6762.9	82047.7	5762.6
化学原料及化学制品制造业	Manufacture of Raw Chemical Materials and Chemical Products	18629.5	52817.1	7922.0
医药制造业	Manufacture of Medicines	10159.0	5146.9	543.7
化学纤维制造业	Manufacture of Chemical Fibers	233.4	2803.5	-216.5
橡胶和塑料制品业	Manufacture of Rubber and Plastics	11566.3	10213.5	4992.6
非金属矿物制品业	Manufacture of Non-metallic Mineral Products	690.0	1718.8	87.1
黑色金属冶炼和压延加工业	Smelting and Pressing of Ferrous Metals	1181.7	4480.1	769.4
有色金属冶炼和压延加工业	Smelting and Pressing of Non-ferrous Metals	4258.6	24185.0	12341.5
金属制品业	Manufacture of Metal Products	12706.5	68890.1	10680.8
通用设备制造业	Manufacture of General Purpose Machinery	30392.3	149705.1	-7102.1
专用设备制造业	Manufacture of Special Equipment	40115.5	80432.6	8435.0
汽车制造业	Manufacture of Motor Vehicle	165196.7	168994.3	25410.6
铁路、船舶、航空航天和其他运输设备制造业	Railways,Shipbuilding,Aerospace and Other Transportation Equipment Manufacturing Industry	84971.2	283290.1	44248.1
电气机械和器材制造业	Manufacture of Electric Equipment and Machinery	127853.6	174810.6	13299.5
计算机、通讯和其他电子设备制造业	Manufacture of Communication Equipment, Computers and other Electronic Equipment	23896.2	90097.6	12867.0
仪器仪表制造业	Manufacture of Measuring Instruments and Machinery	9163.9	94618.9	7195.3
其他制造业	Manufacture of Other Manufacturing	458.7	626.4	61.8
废弃资源综合利用业	Recycling and Disposal of Waste			
金属制品、机械和设备修理业	Metal Products,Machinery and Equipment Repair Industry			
电力、热力的生产和供应业	Production and Supply of Electric Power and Heat Power	1503.5	18648.3	220980.9
燃气生产和供应业	Gas Mining and Supplying Industry	15791.7	28184.3	15219.6
水的生产和供应业	Production and Supply of Water	3475.6	8527.4	246.2

continued 5

(10 000 yuan)

营业利润 Operating Profit	利润总额 Total Profits	亏损企业亏损额 Total Loss of Deficit Enterprises	利税总额 Total Pre-tax Profits	应付职工薪酬 Salary Payable	本年应交增值税 Value Added Tax Payable
45600.8	46486.6		65846.7	50717.9	16189.4
-63536.7	-63260.5	66872.3	84542.7	12665.7	13462.2
18496.9	21849.4	18546.0	36166.4	84426.9	11705.6
9673.6	9876.5		12477.2	6844.1	2320.2
14761.9	14733.5	343.9	18308.0	4430.2	3206.2
9272.5	10079.0		16814.5	17611.1	5271.8
284.7	832.9	24.9	4040.0	5098.0	2257.3
604.1	500.7	1093.7	2371.2	4978.6	1621.1
18782.1	26685.0	1440.4	42149.8	19401.6	14492.0
19227.7	27154.3		40283.8	115424.4	10413.9
108470.8	115682.1	1242.0	163302.5	126531.4	40964.9
49920.3	56200.1	6834.7	99386.4	111198.9	35607.6
82711.9	73564.8	3984.5	172538.2	203807.7	89559.4
124924.3	158512.5	11328.2	223005.7	555865.6	48425.2
11834.9	30114.1	910.7	123504.7	199902.4	80605.5
9745.4	20366.6	13100.6	36896.5	110585.4	12541.6
16188.2	21786.2		49974.3	106756.6	23561.6
718.8	725.1		1331.0	1645.5	524.5
-66700.4	-44537.4	50210.1	102170.3	187065.9	130825.8
69990.6	70692.7		86655.2	45670.7	13504.3
-2953.4	2494.8		7823.9	20696.6	4514.5

12-10 规模以上股份制工业企业主要经济指标（2012年）

单位：万元

分 组	Classify	企业单位数（个）Number of Enterprises (unit)	亏损企业 Loss Making Enterprises	工业总产值（当年价格）Gross Industrial Output Value (At Current Prices)
总计	**Total**	**797**	**143**	**30048990.9**
#市区	Urban Area	428	75	17569735.4
#亏损企业	Deficit Enterprises	143	143	2013415.1
按隶属关系分	**Grouped by Jurisdiction of Management**			
中央企业	Central Enterprises	43	5	4893638.3
省属企业	Provincial Enterprises	50	13	7450053.1
市属企业	Municipal Enterprises	704	125	17705299.5
按轻重工业分	**Grouped by Light Industry and Heavy Industry**			
轻工业	Light Industry	227	41	6254068.7
重工业	Heavy Industry	570	102	23794922.2
按企业规模分	**Grouped by Size of Enterprises**			
大型企业	Large-size	44	5	15826133.9
中型企业	Medium-size	121	19	4886394.5
小型企业	Small-size	632	119	9336463.0
微型企业	microenterprise			
按工业行业大类分	**Grouped by Sector**			
煤炭开采和洗选业	Mining and Washing of Coal			
石油和天然气开采业	Extraction of Petroleum and Natural Gas			
黑色金属矿采选业	Mining and Processing of Ferrous Metal Ores	1	1	2416.6
有色金属矿采选业	Mining and Processing of Non-ferrous Metal Ores			
非金属矿采选业	Mining and Processing of Nonmetal Ores			
开采辅助活动	Mining Auxiliary Activities	2		41046.1
其他采矿业	Mining of Other Ores			
农副食品加工业	Processing of Food from Agricultural Porducts	42	6	1619182.6
食品制造业	Manufacture of Foods	27	5	664713.4
酒、饮料和精制茶制造业	Manufacture of Alcohol,Beverages and Tea	11	3	655583.3
烟草制品业	Manufacture of Tobacco			
纺织业	Manufacture of Textile	12	2	163097.0
纺织服装、服饰业	Textile, apparel industry	7	1	130674.8
皮革、毛皮、羽毛及其制品和制鞋业	Leather fur feathers and its products and footwear	1		501.5
木材加工和木、竹、藤、棕、草制品业	Processing of Timber,Manufacture of Wood,Plam and Straw Products	3		101467.1
家具制造业	Manufacture of Furniture	8	1	39190.8

Main Indicators of Share-holding Corporation Industrial Enterprises above Designated Size (2012)

(10 000 yuan)

工业销售产值（当年价） Value of Industry Products Sales (At Current Prices)	出口交货值 Export Delivery Value	从业人员年平均人数（人） Annual Average Employers (person)	资产总计 Total Assets	流动资产合计 Total Working Capitals	固定资产合计 Total Fixed Assets	固定资产原价 Origing Value of Fixed Assets	累计折旧 Accumulative Total Depreciation
28948621.5	**1856715.1**	**371237**	**32145938.6**	**19398848.9**	**9069030.4**	**12283803.5**	**4959836.7**
17046601.7	1059670.1	195630	15303843.0	9266306.2	4546459.8	5853841.2	2298142.6
1784101.8	49198.4	35639	2779079.1	1554207.1	704934.6	1018523.2	421971.6
4724473.0	538416.8	100713	9805282.8	6083232.8	2870065.5	3562733.0	1580671.4
7217001.8	487171.0	62017	6010942.9	3354664.9	1835207.2	2215956.6	806420.3
17007146.7	831127.3	208507	16329712.9	9960951.2	4363757.7	6505113.9	2572745.0
6015109.3	210152.2	71458	3985515.3	2150903.2	1263101.1	2202802.5	1083897.9
22933512.2	1646562.9	299779	28160423.3	17247945.7	7805929.3	10081001.0	3875938.8
15489830.9	1566095.7	223518	20048959.7	11804234.5	6141253.1	8150674.1	3295951.8
4515055.7	143905.4	68731	5335141.4	3278160.0	1338951.7	1745603.7	692238.2
8943735.0	146714.0	78988	6761837.5	4316454.4	1588825.6	2387525.7	971646.7
2384.2		112	2135.0	1554.0	433.0	1036.1	658.2
40730.0		800	59182.7	41286.5	9735.4	18247.9	8512.5
1522178.8	844.6	8441	505364.2	293570.3	179350.7	291336.2	125276.7
644242.3		6678	243854.8	86529.8	88159.8	161117.4	82720.8
723537.3	167283.4	6280	801551.2	400219.8	289442.7	441271.7	184937.0
152379.7	19047.9	12100	155321.3	91376.8	25648.7	66222.4	40981.9
129006.7		2033	133818.3	113806.8	17100.7	21069.6	4751.8
501.5		135	2215.7	2010.0	147.3	194.9	47.6
95744.5		816	109602.3	54789.2	46470.9	81282.2	36498.6
37518.0		1056	34162.6	17554.8	7082.5	11475.1	6804.6

12-10 续表1

单位：万元

分 组	Classify	负债合计 Total Liabilites	流动负债合计 Total Working Liabilities	非流动负债 Non-Working Liabilities
总计	**Total**	**18316627.7**	**15602307.9**	**2417517.3**
#市区	Urban Area	9162439.3	8053942.7	896484.1
#亏损企业	Deficit Enterprises	1875811.5	1503976.0	294723.1
按隶属关系分	**Grouped by Jurisdiction of Management**			
中央企业	Central Enterprises	5742624.7	4713008.3	983424.4
省属企业	Provincial Enterprises	3547722.9	2864897.8	642053.9
市属企业	Municipal Enterprises	9026280.1	8024401.8	792039.0
按轻重工业分	**Grouped by Light Industry and Heavy Industry**			
轻工业	Light Industry	2061599.7	1803242.9	191218.7
重工业	Heavy Industry	16255028.0	13799065.0	2226298.6
按企业规模分	**Grouped by Size of Enterprises**			
大型企业	Large-size	11603274.1	9849906.4	1694280.6
中型企业	Medium-size	2923322.8	2481928.3	370160.1
小型企业	Small-size	3790030.8	3270473.2	353076.6
微型企业	microenterprise			
按工业行业大类分	**Grouped by Sector**			
煤炭开采和洗选业	Mining and Washing of Coal			
石油和天然气开采业	Extraction of Petroleum and Natural Gas			
黑色金属矿采选业	Mining and Processing of Ferrous Metal Ores	3703.1	1125.7	
有色金属矿采选业	Mining and Processing of Non-ferrous Metal Ores			
非金属矿采选业	Mining and Processing of Nonmetal Ores			
开采辅助活动	Mining Auxiliary Activities	12679.9	9786.8	
其他采矿业	Mining of Other Ores			
农副食品加工业	Processing of Food from Agricultural Porducts	299551.2	290723.9	6006.6
食品制造业	Manufacture of Foods	122076.1	110501.0	11383.5
酒、饮料和精制茶制造业	Manufacture of Alcohol,Beverages and Tea	453962.3	409862.7	44099.5
烟草制品业	Manufacture of Tobacco			
纺织业	Manufacture of Textile	65218.3	63673.4	1389.6
纺织服装、服饰业	Textile, apparel industry	102381.8	77350.2	3201.7
皮革、毛皮、羽毛及其制品和制鞋业	Leather fur feathers and its products and footwear	1169.5	1169.5	
木材加工和木、竹、藤、棕、草制品业	Processing of Timber,Manufacture of Wood,Plam and Straw Products	54249.7	27249.7	27000.0
家具制造业	Manufacture of Furniture	17361.9	12054.8	60.0

continued 1

(10 000 yuan)

所有者权益合计 Total Owners' Equities	实收资本 Total Capital Hold	营业收入 Total Revenue	主营业务收入 Revenue from Principal Business	营业成本 Total Cost	主营业务成本 Cost of Principal Business	营业税金及附加 Taxs and Other Changes	主营业务税金及附加 Taxes and Other Charges on Principal Business
13716934.0	**5301959.5**	**28017105.0**	**27268101.6**	**23480490.7**	**22944559.1**	**179040.5**	**173371.2**
6067861.7	2179113.2	15370754.5	14955999.8	13228671.0	12948157.3	104006.7	101991.8
898816.8	768157.9	1701298.4	1618008.8	1567794.1	1509260.0	7988.6	7874.7
4061013.7	1296876.6	5458846.7	5354659.2	4634472.1	4569177.7	22036.0	21336.3
2444214.6	853427.5	6418653.1	6167789.6	5478687.1	5346582.0	18618.6	18318.4
7211705.7	3151655.4	16139605.2	15745652.8	13367331.5	13028799.4	138385.9	133716.5
1889382.5	918469.2	5831019.1	5762356.3	4677834.2	4619175.8	37027.7	36097.8
11827551.5	4383490.3	22186085.9	21505745.3	18802656.5	18325383.3	142012.8	137273.4
8436030.6	2511622.9	14981272.9	14506175.1	12693958.4	12325678.7	112233.0	110294.8
2369745.2	1130308.8	4411975.9	4210513.5	3562954.0	3457142.0	25048.5	22937.0
2911158.2	1660027.8	8623856.2	8551413.0	7223578.3	7161738.4	41759.0	40139.4
-1568.1	600.0	2010.3	2010.3	1904.1	1904.1	26.2	26.2
44395.9	4982.7	41379.4	40346.2	28913.7	28688.7	1124.5	1119.1
197198.7	100441.8	1435958.0	1431728.7	1349549.3	1347001.4	1951.0	1815.9
121297.3	74325.8	611486.4	604757.4	499338.2	493865.7	2073.9	2048.9
339730.5	118253.1	725565.9	712631.9	565696.3	550891.4	11084.4	11068.9
89689.9	17044.9	154459.8	153524.9	143739.7	142989.0	855.2	855.2
29227.7	24487.5	158709.1	158144.9	129048.6	128793.6	3225.2	3224.8
1046.2	1000.0	3106.9	3106.9	2587.6	2587.6	8.8	8.8
55180.8	16500.0	82731.6	79818.4	73253.6	73195.8	335.4	333.3
16766.4	9157.7	34048.0	33754.5	25830.1	25614.1	161.9	161.9

12-10 续表2

单位：万元

分组	Classify	销售费用 Expenses for Sales	管理费用 Expenses for Management	财务费用 Financial cost
总计	**Total**	**1125992.7**	**1554227.5**	**242747.9**
#市区	Urban Area	472273.7	693370.2	98385.2
#亏损企业	Deficit Enterprises	70463.6	122898.4	33847.2
按隶属关系分	**Grouped by Jurisdiction of Management**			
中央企业	Central Enterprises	112045.1	455276.1	59659.8
省属企业	Provincial Enterprises	370587.3	254489.0	68150.8
市属企业	Municipal Enterprises	643360.3	844462.4	114937.3
按轻重工业分	**Grouped by Light Industry and Heavy Industry**			
轻工业	Light Industry	514323.0	287903.0	46005.1
重工业	Heavy Industry	611669.7	1266324.5	196742.8
按企业规模分	**Grouped by Size of Enterprises**			
大型企业	Large-size	652323.6	897736.8	137236.0
中型企业	Medium-size	212647.3	258526.1	48642.1
小型企业	Small-size	261021.8	397964.6	56869.8
微型企业	microenterprise			
按工业行业大类分	**Grouped by Sector**			
煤炭开采和洗选业	Mining and Washing of Coal			
石油和天然气开采业	Extraction of Petroleum and Natural Gas			
黑色金属矿采选业	Mining and Processing of Ferrous Metal Ores	10.0	493.1	156.3
有色金属矿采选业	Mining and Processing of Non-ferrous Metal Ores			
非金属矿采选业	Mining and Processing of Nonmetal Ores			
开采辅助活动	Mining Auxiliary Activities	286.2	3311.7	149.2
其他采矿业	Mining of Other Ores			
农副食品加工业	Processing of Food from Agricultural Porducts	33851.2	36005.5	12405.5
食品制造业	Manufacture of Foods	50438.6	29575.5	1511.2
酒、饮料和精制茶制造业	Manufacture of Alcohol,Beverages and Tea	69348.2	24721.4	6453.2
烟草制品业	Manufacture of Tobacco			
纺织业	Manufacture of Textile	2303.4	9702.0	548.6
纺织服装、服饰业	Textile, apparel industry	6233.8	7783.4	801.5
皮革、毛皮、羽毛及其制品和制鞋业	Leather fur feathers and its products and footwear	141.9	339.9	20.0
木材加工和木、竹、藤、棕、草制品业	Processing of Timber,Manufacture of Wood,Plam and Straw Products	2143.5	1801.8	2764.9
家具制造业	Manufacture of Furniture	2999.3	1602.2	499.4

continued 2

(10 000 yuan)

营业利润 Operating Profit	利润总额 Total Profits	亏损企业亏损额 Total Loss of Deficit Enterprises	利税总额 Total Pre-tax Profits	应付职工薪酬 Salary Payable	本年应交增值税 Value Added Tax Payable
1367470.6	**1502864.4**	**106635.5**	**2453088.3**	**2142306.6**	**771183.4**
718358.2	761094.8	57794.5	1225132.1	1053182.5	360030.6
-114132.3	-106635.5	106635.5	-53795.6	177012.5	44851.3
161030.5	197733.5	37037.6	289054.1	723122.4	69284.6
242084.0	236207.2	14032.2	447351.9	380006.0	192526.1
964356.1	1068923.7	55565.7	1716682.3	1039178.2	509372.7
301501.6	325822.4	15848.5	611918.5	389791.4	249068.4
1065969.0	1177042.0	90787.0	1841169.8	1752515.2	522115.0
508451.0	568982.1	29553.5	1073581.2	1420144.7	392366.1
312287.7	354380.3	30187.2	521321.2	325907.0	141892.4
546731.9	579502.0	46894.8	858185.9	396254.9	236924.9
-644.8	-634.0	634.0	-485.7	159.2	122.1
7635.8	7620.4		9868.1	6189.9	1123.2
34235.6	35592.6	1487.7	55644.1	36910.2	18100.5
21787.8	21859.1	661.4	34195.4	22787.1	10262.4
52159.5	55404.5	4726.1	124741.5	43549.7	58252.6
-2432.3	2505.1	2316.3	8752.9	31961.3	5392.6
9886.8	11272.0	47.9	18633.4	9834.3	4136.2
8.7	7.7		89.8	466.0	73.3
2239.0	5926.0		15950.0	3500.6	9688.6
1576.4	1552.4	18.0	2664.8	2786.7	950.5

12-10 续表3

单位：万元

分　组	Classify	企业单位数（个） Number of Enterprises (unit)	亏损企业 Loss Making Enterprises	工业总产值（当年价格） Gross Industrial Output Value (At Current Prices)
造纸及纸制品业	Manufacture of Paper and Paper Products	14	1	72997.1
印刷和记录媒介复制	Printing,Reproduction of Recording Media	16	3	462215.6
文教、工美、体育和娱乐用品制造业	Manufacture of Articles For Cultural,Educational and Sports Activities	3	1	27805.1
石油加工业、炼焦和核燃料加工业	Processing of Petroleum, Cokeing,Processing of Nuclear and Nuclear Fuel	6		1210481.1
化学原料及化学制品制造业	Manufacture of Raw Chemical Materials and Chemical Products	46	6	1056843.6
医药制造业	Manufacture of Medicines	46	7	1266835.9
化学纤维制造业	Manufacture of Chemical Fibers	2	1	100030.4
橡胶和塑料制品业	Manufacture of Rubber and Plastics	22	4	284797.4
非金属矿物制品业	Manufacture of Non-metallic Mineral Products	83	25	1394832.7
黑色金属冶炼和压延加工业	Smelting and Pressing of Ferrous Metals	15	4	354419.5
有色金属冶炼和压延加工业	Smelting and Pressing of Non-ferrous Metals	23	3	899095.4
金属制品业	Manufacture of Metal Products	43	8	823413.4
通用设备制造业	Manufacture of General Purpose Machinery	52	12	1607672.7
专用设备制造业	Manufacture of Special Equipment	80	13	1622798.7
汽车制造业	Manufacture of Motor Vehicle	29	9	7903761.8
铁路、船舶、航空航天和其他运输设备制造业	Railways,Shipbuilding,Aerospace and Other Transportation Equipment Manufacturing Industry	35	6	3141441.2
电气机械和器材制造业	Manufacture of Electric Equipment and Machinery	73	8	1522671.6
计算机、通讯和其他电子设备制造业	Manufacture of Communication Equipment, Computers and other Electronic Equipment	45	7	1101393.5
仪器仪表制造业	Manufacture of Measuring Instruments and Machinery	29	2	816770.8
其他制造业	Manufacture of Other Manufacturing	2		24635.1
废弃资源综合利用业	Recycling and Disposal of Waste			
金属制品、机械和设备修理业	Metal Products,Machinery and Equipment Repair Industry	2		19128.6
电力、热力的生产和供应业	Production and Supply of Electric Power and Heat Power	8		168922.5
燃气生产和供应业	Gas Mining and Supplying Industry	7		677378.5
水的生产和供应业	Production and Supply of Water	2		70775.5

continued 3

(10 000 yuan)

工业销售产值（当年价） Value of Industry Products Sales (At Current Prices)	出口交货值 Export Delivery Value	从业人员年平均人数（人） Annual Average Employers (person)	资产总计 Total Assets	流动资产合计 Total Working Capitals	固定资产合计 Total Fixed Assets	固定资产原价 Origing Value of Fixed Assets	累计折旧 Accumulative Total Depreciation
72466.6		3038	36744.8	21565.5	13463.2	23941.1	12127.0
451072.9	104.0	7206	529576.7	232267.4	214118.6	354209.4	170308.9
27511.5	1899.1	386	8241.5	3584.3	3791.1	5464.0	2053.1
1212478.1		3961	262004.4	152316.1	108756.3	87848.6	17408.5
1028848.2	129474.7	19543	1466843.5	767421.5	511080.9	1024609.3	563375.6
1190073.1	2539.1	13489	904546.4	561680.7	202816.0	336231.7	160390.5
92868.8		400	73150.2	31230.7	38819.6	68660.8	38485.4
247359.0	1921.0	3112	204407.2	132513.6	61293.8	71131.5	26162.9
1361048.4		12054	833602.7	471305.5	308959.1	460926.7	170960.5
343115.0		2973	190967.8	96841.2	81846.1	103606.1	21804.3
871466.2	36834.5	7125	817839.7	465899.9	210845.9	321475.7	132550.3
793094.8	24375.4	18913	1162101.6	658572.3	446750.5	559028.4	220119.2
1555069.6	51176.7	16223	2637658.5	2085831.0	336542.2	491479.7	174837.2
1465000.6	77300.7	24708	2180074.3	1559951.0	413992.6	582549.4	218368.4
7715725.0	640883.5	91495	6280914.2	3407360.0	2163217.3	2457278.2	771776.6
3023689.2	494929.3	55367	6425947.5	4186459.9	1640159.5	1935124.0	855499.2
1405303.9	83431.0	13963	1158504.9	798942.4	235933.4	336125.8	136124.7
980081.4	69381.4	18095	1691714.9	1179088.7	327182.3	402461.5	142214.9
803822.5	55288.8	12044	1248435.8	768336.7	370105.7	441431.9	199773.4
23695.3		460	20624.0	10710.9	6933.9	9821.6	3448.1
18959.6		129	16615.3	13897.5	1597.6	899.2	436.6
168922.5		1086	499418.8	249124.5	167625.1	231752.4	64128.3
677950.8		4140	1311188.4	385807.0	457463.4	671600.7	224461.9
70775.5		2876	137607.4	55442.6	82164.6	212892.3	141831.5

12-10 续表4

单位：万元

分 组	Classify	负债合计 Total Liabilites	流动负债合计 Total Working Liabilities	非流动负债 Non-Working Liabilities
造纸及纸制品业	Manufacture of Paper and Paper Products	26900.0	20873.2	1613.5
印刷和记录媒介复制	Printing,Reproduction of Recording Media	202880.7	179585.3	19702.7
文教、工美、体育和娱乐用品制造业	Manufacture of Articles For Cultural,Educational and Sports Activities	2814.0	2814.0	
石油加工业、炼焦和核燃料加工业	Processing of Petroleum, Cokeing,Processing of Nuclear and Nuclear Fuel	169134.2	143134.2	26000.0
化学原料及化学制品制造业	Manufacture of Raw Chemical Materials and Chemical Products	731022.4	603359.2	117885.3
医药制造业	Manufacture of Medicines	419586.5	392796.3	26068.9
化学纤维制造业	Manufacture of Chemical Fibers	9338.3	9338.3	
橡胶和塑料制品业	Manufacture of Rubber and Plastics	119225.6	102820.5	2524.3
非金属矿物制品业	Manufacture of Non-metallic Mineral Products	468348.3	395903.5	24198.5
黑色金属冶炼和压延加工业	Smelting and Pressing of Ferrous Metals	122158.3	96503.3	13808.5
有色金属冶炼和压延加工业	Smelting and Pressing of Non-ferrous Metals	485344.2	413255.8	65672.6
金属制品业	Manufacture of Metal Products	625435.3	458358.5	160349.9
通用设备制造业	Manufacture of General Purpose Machinery	1580203.2	1484601.6	89013.0
专用设备制造业	Manufacture of Special Equipment	1098991.2	979241.7	84656.7
汽车制造业	Manufacture of Motor Vehicle	3676647.8	3263503.4	372462.0
铁路、船舶、航空航天和其他运输设备制造业	Railways,Shipbuilding,Aerospace and Other Transportation Equipment Manufacturing Industry	3869787.4	3286321.4	581182.3
电气机械和器材制造业	Manufacture of Electric Equipment and Machinery	604723.7	530575.8	55411.2
计算机、通讯和其他电子设备制造业	Manufacture of Communication Equipment, Computers and other Electronic Equipment	1021199.6	845225.3	127986.1
仪器仪表制造业	Manufacture of Measuring Instruments and Machinery	724460.1	568392.9	156067.2
其他制造业	Manufacture of Other Manufacturing	10750.7	10750.7	
废弃资源综合利用业	Recycling and Disposal of Waste			
金属制品、机械和设备修理业	Metal Products,Machinery and Equipment Repair Industry	10564.8	10564.8	
电力、热力的生产和供应业	Production and Supply of Electric Power and Heat Power	378459.7	266987.0	111472.6
燃气生产和供应业	Gas Mining and Supplying Industry	764194.6	490092.8	270008.5
水的生产和供应业	Production and Supply of Water	62103.3	43810.7	18292.6

continued 4

(10 000 yuan)

所有者权益合计 Total Owners' Equities	实收资本 Total Capital Hold	营业收入 Total Revenue	主营业务收入 Revenue from Principal Business	营业成本 Total Cost	主营业务成本 Cost of Principal Business	营业税金及附加 Taxs and Other Changes	主营业务税金及附加 Taxes and Other Charges on Principal Business
9768.6	9300.5	76746.8	76533.7	70205.5	70205.5	265.9	263.3
326004.9	157309.8	439888.9	436150.5	323497.8	317709.4	3128.8	2785.9
5427.5	3200.0	27511.7	27511.3	17216.0	17216.0	188.4	188.4
92870.1	51265.7	1054600.9	1052515.8	923440.6	922312.9	1422.5	1356.3
735741.8	263207.4	1009447.9	976688.9	797227.4	787913.9	4548.9	4096.9
481711.2	191534.3	1123513.4	1099138.4	614208.8	599039.1	10468.4	10415.2
63811.9	50800.0	92870.5	91809.1	74919.7	73861.0	368.3	368.3
83290.6	60054.3	233586.9	230903.4	196713.6	194393.8	1566.5	987.2
360055.2	170844.1	1268674.8	1267149.2	1061669.6	1060767.2	7092.1	7086.9
65690.9	23273.2	391784.6	387967.7	341386.7	337153.4	1854.6	1854.4
332495.1	173955.9	740689.3	719776.8	628039.2	612421.8	2746.2	2644.7
528443.9	194045.1	778236.0	766208.5	657717.1	649647.6	3549.3	3363.9
1055588.2	168145.8	1417918.4	1406129.7	1089750.5	1081582.8	8791.0	8337.1
1066360.8	478089.1	1416769.9	1401328.8	1098971.8	1092766.1	12681.7	12596.0
2583183.9	793815.6	6656758.5	6281888.3	5948947.6	5666655.8	63666.6	63407.0
2555731.4	795652.4	3620110.8	3569601.8	3110592.0	3070293.6	15394.1	15227.4
531391.0	304241.5	1402747.6	1389473.5	1215909.0	1205285.8	5025.7	4587.6
669929.1	359365.3	1143680.8	1116050.7	969092.7	942127.9	4144.0	3085.6
523415.1	234997.6	837106.0	822134.2	656277.4	650267.6	4406.5	4239.5
9873.2	3620.0	22918.5	22163.6	19066.8	18522.8	198.9	198.9
6050.5	4000.0	18959.6	18949.6	17917.3	15372.7	75.1	75.1
120958.9	129955.0	210920.3	152106.1	190452.5	153185.6	3302.5	3287.1
540670.8	271493.4	704950.2	665322.4	568808.7	545790.3	2529.5	1740.3
75504.1	43000.0	77257.3	70775.5	68601.2	64535.1	778.5	515.2

12-10 续表5

单位：万元

分 组	Classify	销售费用 Expenses for Sales	管理费用 Expenses for Management	财务费用 Financial cost
造纸及纸制品业	Manufacture of Paper and Paper Products	925.7	2277.3	753.2
印刷和记录媒介复制	Printing,Reproduction of Recording Media	10243.6	45440.5	2804.1
文教、工美、体育和娱乐用品制造业	Manufacture of Articles For Cultural,Educational and Sports Activities	883.6	1329.5	254.6
石油加工业、炼焦和核燃料加工业	Processing of Petroleum, Cokeing,Processing of Nuclear and Nuclear Fuel	9166.5	10322.9	2306.3
化学原料及化学制品制造业	Manufacture of Raw Chemical Materials and Chemical Products	54356.8	77240.6	12844.0
医药制造业	Clssify Manufacture of Medicines	300408.2	84865.3	13826.7
化学纤维制造业	Manufacture of Chemical Fibers	233.4	2803.5	-216.5
橡胶和塑料制品业	Manufacture of Rubber and Plastics	9175.3	13214.1	3308.1
非金属矿物制品业	Manufacture of Non-metallic Mineral Products	30646.6	30070.3	5933.3
黑色金属冶炼和压延加工业	Smelting and Pressing of Ferrous Metals	3469.7	7385.5	2965.2
有色金属冶炼和压延加工业	Smelting and Pressing of Non-ferrous Metals	8856.0	36066.0	20741.6
金属制品业	Manufacture of Metal Products	18048.3	63538.2	6330.9
通用设备制造业	Manufacture of General Purpose Machinery	48720.0	170295.8	-4220.1
专用设备制造业	Manufacture of Special Equipment	71133.3	111548.8	9509.8
汽车制造业	Manufacture of Motor Vehicle	198567.3	231500.8	39349.6
铁路、船舶、航空航天和其他运输设备制造业	Railways,Shipbuilding,Aerospace and Other Transportation Equipment Manufacturing Industry	79987.4	244555.6	40798.7
电气机械和器材制造业	Manufacture of Electric Equipment and Machinery	42634.4	63270.4	13249.1
计算机、通讯和其他电子设备制造业	Manufacture of Communication Equipment, Computers and other Electronic Equipment	26045.4	94700.1	11715.5
仪器仪表制造业	Manufacture of Measuring Instruments and Machinery	22646.1	95396.6	11836.6
其他制造业	Manufacture of Other Manufacturing	514.8	2067.2	165.0
废弃资源综合利用业	Recycling and Disposal of Waste			
金属制品、机械和设备修理业	Metal Products,Machinery and Equipment Repair Industry	705.0	1911.5	189.0
电力、热力的生产和供应业	Production and Supply of Electric Power and Heat Power	1049.4	11234.4	7043.4
燃气生产和供应业	Gas Mining and Supplying Industry	16613.2	30113.5	15690.8
水的生产和供应业	Production and Supply of Water	3206.6	7742.6	259.2

continued 5

(10 000 yuan)

营业利润 Operating Profit	利润总额 Total Profits	亏损企业亏损额 Total Loss of Deficit Enterprises	利税总额 Total Pre-tax Profits	应付职工薪酬 Salary Payable	本年应交增值税 Value Added Tax Payable
1562.6	1471.3	4.2	2851.9	6252.0	1114.7
58392.5	59700.0	2265.0	83512.9	60780.9	20684.1
4459.2	4489.9	48.9	5445.7	1630.3	767.4
17838.2	18939.2	0.0	23865.3	17493.4	3503.6
55853.7	60606.4	20617.3	93638.9	104291.2	28483.6
103362.3	103372.8	326.2	226381.7	120357.5	112540.5
14761.9	14733.5	343.9	18308.0	4430.2	3206.2
14995.5	16267.8	1078.3	25666.5	11435.9	7832.2
130546.5	132851.0	6349.4	200824.5	46438.4	60881.4
35604.7	35868.8	1528.1	48148.2	20121.0	10424.8
32217.1	40747.6	3831.1	63410.2	33747.7	19916.4
23612.2	29391.4	1963.0	48007.8	105301.6	15067.1
119611.4	127495.7	2972.3	191177.7	151313.5	54891.0
95787.3	100212.2	8197.3	164451.6	135081.6	51557.7
200517.5	213814.1	10708.2	410893.9	396582.6	133413.2
123188.2	149802.5	11123.3	212488.3	478358.7	47291.7
66480.9	75725.4	3050.2	114246.1	65420.6	33495.0
40316.4	57374.0	11761.1	78848.2	91731.2	17330.2
39007.0	44962.7	379.1	62416.2	47062.8	13047.0
875.1	929.6		1963.5	1585.4	835.0
669.2	1189.3		2102.9	935.9	838.5
-7611.2	-3228.6	10197.2	7640.5	16005.5	7566.6
72275.5	72965.8		89642.2	47754.2	14146.9
-3305.6	2076.2		7101.3	20049.5	4246.6

12-11　规模以上外商及港澳台商投资工业企业主要经济指标（2012年）

单位：万元

分　组	Classify	企业单位数（个） Number of Enterprises (unit)	亏损企业 Loss Making Enterprises	工业总产值（当年价格） Gross Industrial Output Value (At Current Prices)
总计	**Total**	**112**	**27**	**7402698.0**
#市区	Urban Area	100	22	6632177.5
#亏损企业	Deficit Enterprises	27	27	328694.1
按隶属关系分	**Grouped by Jurisdiction of Management**			
中央企业	Central Enterprises	4	1	152980.2
省属企业	Provincial Enterprises	10	3	1276375.8
市属企业	Municipal Enterprises	98	23	5973342.0
按登记注册类型分组	**Grouped by Type of Registration**			
港澳台商投资	Enterprises with Funds from Hong Kong, Macao &Taiwan	26	11	333756.4
与港澳台商合资经营	Cooperative Enterprises	14	7	129776.0
与港澳台商合作经营	Joint-venture Enterprises			
港澳台商独资	Enterprises with Sole Investment	11	4	172040.0
港澳台商投资股份有限公司	Share-holding Corporations Ltd. With their Investment	1		31940.4
其他港澳台投资	Other			
外商投资	Foreign Funded Enterprises	86	16	7068941.6
中外合资经营	Joint-venture Enterprises	58	11	5558550.6
中外合作经营	Cooperation Enterprises	1		4181.4
外资企业	Foreign Funded Enterprises	24	5	1232542.3
外商投资股份有限公司	Share-holding Corporations Ltd. With Foreign Funds	3		273667.3
其他外商投资	Other			
按轻重工业分	**Grouped by Light Industry and Heavy Industry**			
轻工业	Light Industry	41	10	3021254.8
重工业	Heavy Industry	71	17	4381443.2
按企业规模分	**Grouped by Size of Enterprises**			
大型企业	Large-size	13		4352113.5
中型企业	Medium-size	22	6	1448134.2
小型企业	Small-size	77	21	1602450.3
微型企业	microenterprise			
按工业行业大类分	**Grouped by Sector**			
煤炭开采和洗选业	Mining and Washing of Coal			
石油和天然气开采业	Extraction of Petroleum and Natural Gas			
黑色金属矿采选业	Mining and Processing of Ferrous Metal Ores			
有色金属矿采选业	Mining and Processing of Non-ferrous Metal Ores			
非金属矿采选业	Mining and Processing of Nonmetal Ores			
开采辅助活动	Mining Auxiliary Activities			
其他采矿业	Mining of Other Ores			

Economic Indicators of Foreign Fund Industrial Enterprises above Designated Size (2012)

(10 000 yuan)

工业销售产值（当年价）Value of Industry Products Sales (At Current Prices)	出口交货值 Export Delivery Value	从业人员年平均人数（人）Annual Average Employers (person)	资产总计 Total Assets	流动资产合计 Total Working Capitals	固定资产合计 Total Fixed Assets	固定资产原价 Origing Value of Fixed Assets	累计折旧 Accumulative Total Depreciation
7102361.8	**665840.6**	**85416**	**6075724.8**	**3035419.2**	**2261615.1**	**3147712.0**	**1131013.4**
6379751.6	660011.0	83148	5690072.0	2875750.9	2060160.3	2926881.4	1012106.1
301869.2	34060.3	6482	524428.1	208829.3	211583.3	299274.7	93632.2
145854.8	2740.0	1404	96289.4	59416.5	34848.3	79572.6	48201.6
1228530.7	186.5	6085	552845.8	325327.5	174355.2	225056.2	129858.9
5727976.3	662914.1	77927	5426589.6	2650675.2	2052411.6	2843083.2	952952.9
321966.0	29939.0	6782	490039.5	173006.6	204424.4	281154.1	84260.2
123477.5	2251.2	2705	203974.3	93089.1	33869.2	59750.0	28485.0
166468.5	27583.8	3554	247622.9	66113.1	159210.3	201655.8	47371.8
32020.0	104.0	523	38442.3	13804.4	11344.9	19748.3	8403.4
6780395.8	635901.6	78634	5585685.3	2862412.6	2057190.7	2866557.9	1046753.2
5395610.5	255902.4	63976	4137895.5	2107309.5	1482714.9	2013889.0	710954.0
4121.3	649.9	129	8346.2	7721.9	624.3	1012.3	388.0
1175688.9	212065.9	12776	1028768.0	505950.1	408303.6	642000.4	260156.9
204975.1	167283.4	1753	410675.6	241431.1	165547.9	209656.2	75254.3
2827426.8	200697.9	21424	1741488.2	980607.3	515131.8	890378.2	422748.4
4274935.0	465142.7	63992	4334236.6	2054811.9	1746483.3	2257333.8	708265.0
4227378.4	433614.7	63841	3839566.2	1772312.5	1521399.0	2123256.0	706839.1
1348360.6	137629.9	11301	1052493.2	534646.1	429450.8	521244.4	211007.9
1526622.8	94596.0	10274	1183665.4	728460.6	310765.3	503211.6	213166.4

12-11 续表1

单位：万元

分组	Classify	负债合计 Total Liabilites	流动负债合计 Total Working Liabilities	非流动负债 Non-Working Liabilities
总计	**Total**	**3270972.9**	**2956273.1**	**291433.7**
#市区	Urban Area	3089947.5	2788791.3	277893.7
#亏损企业	Deficit Enterprises	336658.7	302489.7	31780.5
按隶属关系分	**Grouped by Jurisdiction of Management**			
中央企业	Central Enterprises	35334.3	31252.9	4081.4
省属企业	Provincial Enterprises	315829.5	291913.5	23916.0
市属企业	Municipal Enterprises	2919809.1	2633106.7	263436.3
按登记注册类型分组	**Grouped by Type of Registration**			
港澳台商投资	Enterprises with Funds from Hong Kong, Macao &Taiwan	243556.0	220161.5	21005.9
与港澳台商合资经营	Cooperative Enterprises	108145.1	96981.9	11163.1
与港澳台商合作经营	Joint-venture Enterprises			
港澳台商独资	Enterprises with Sole Investment	116044.2	104620.7	9035.0
港澳台商投资股份有限公司	Share-holding Corporations Ltd. With their Investment	19366.7	18558.9	807.8
其他港澳台投资	Other			
外商投资	Foreign Funded Enterprises	3027416.9	2736111.6	270427.8
中外合资经营	Joint-venture Enterprises	2333326.9	2170259.7	142193.7
中外合作经营	Cooperation Enterprises	5057.1	5053.5	0.0
外资企业	Foreign Funded Enterprises	407558.8	322667.1	84891.4
外商投资股份有限公司	Share-holding Corporations Ltd. With Foreign Funds	281474.1	238131.3	43342.7
其他外商投资	Other			
按轻重工业分	**Grouped by Light Industry and Heavy Industry**			
轻工业	Light Industry	880560.8	807291.9	65626.6
重工业	Heavy Industry	2390412.1	2148981.2	225807.1
按企业规模分	**Grouped by Size of Enterprises**			
大型企业	Large-size	2167671.7	1973162.6	194508.8
中型企业	Medium-size	504510.6	452845.7	51664.8
小型企业	Small-size	598790.6	530264.8	45260.1
微型企业	microenterprise			
按工业行业大类分	**Grouped by Sector**			
煤炭开采和洗选业	Mining and Washing of Coal			
石油和天然气开采业	Extraction of Petroleum and Natural Gas			
黑色金属矿采选业	Mining and Processing of Ferrous Metal Ores			
有色金属矿采选业	Mining and Processing of Non-ferrous Metal Ores			
非金属矿采选业	Mining and Processing of Nonmetal Ores			
开采辅助活动	Mining Auxiliary Activities			
其他采矿业	Mining of Other Ores			

continued 1

(10 000 yuan)

所有者权益合计 Total Owners' Equities	实收资本 Total Capital Hold	营业收入 Total Revenue	主营业务收入 Revenue from Principal Business	营业成本 Total Cost	主营业务成本 Cost of Principal Business	营业税金及附加 Taxs and Other Changes	主营业务税金及附加 Taxes and Other Charges on Principal Business
2747167.1	**1363601.9**	**6932872.1**	**6614601.8**	**5735667.4**	**5492403.9**	**80188.8**	**77467.3**
2565124.4	1285821.1	6266065.6	6011793.2	5182529.0	4942096.4	78814.8	76093.3
186764.5	309965.0	281969.1	271938.4	274435.3	262467.6	2643.6	2635.8
60955.1	37194.0	141486.4	141089.8	121309.8	118416.3	734.3	734.3
218011.6	91735.4	1222091.3	1133134.3	860740.4	857111.6	6432.9	6404.3
2468200.4	1234672.5	5569294.4	5340377.7	4753617.2	4516876.0	73021.6	70328.7
245255.2	248366.4	285287.0	278016.3	232803.6	225324.1	3515.6	3475.6
94935.6	99555.8	88862.6	84920.0	68908.6	66624.9	709.1	696.8
131244.0	141310.6	168647.7	165580.0	144419.7	139414.2	2580.0	2552.3
19075.6	7500.0	27776.7	27516.3	19475.3	19285.0	226.5	226.5
2501911.9	1115235.5	6647585.1	6336585.5	5502863.8	5267079.8	76673.2	73991.7
1756070.5	759046.9	5215090.4	4920406.6	4330639.6	4144319.9	70883.2	68543.2
3289.1	3308.0	4549.5	4549.5	4008.2	4008.2	12.1	12.1
621209.2	324832.1	1214224.0	1199582.9	976879.0	930070.4	5571.4	5229.9
121343.1	28048.5	213721.2	212046.5	191337.0	188681.3	206.5	206.5
841296.4	407641.0	2821016.8	2765178.8	2163877.9	2100862.8	14430.0	14344.9
1905870.7	955960.9	4111855.3	3849423.0	3571789.5	3391541.1	65758.8	63122.4
1664036.1	634569.2	4105719.7	3867661.6	3331719.2	3104892.1	65688.2	64796.4
518779.3	319836.7	1336314.9	1267128.8	1131913.9	1127666.9	6862.3	5775.2
564351.7	409196.0	1490837.5	1479811.4	1272034.3	1259844.9	7638.3	6895.7

12-11 续表2

单位：万元

分 组	Classify	销售费用 Expenses for Sales	管理费用 Expenses for Management	财务费用 Financial cost
总计	**Total**	**476670.0**	**260542.6**	**33263.6**
#市区	Urban Area	471259.3	242746.4	30213.4
#亏损企业	Deficit Enterprises	22728.0	36285.9	6508.5
按隶属关系分	**Grouped by Jurisdiction of Management**			
中央企业	Central Enterprises	1024.5	6191.4	-88.8
省属企业	Provincial Enterprises	191637.3	41441.2	13610.1
市属企业	Municipal Enterprises	284008.2	212910.0	19742.3
按登记注册类型分组	**Grouped by Type of Registration**			
港澳台商投资	Enterprises with Funds from Hong Kong, Macao &Taiwan	37565.4	27734.4	2764.2
与港澳台商合资经营	Cooperative Enterprises	9154.4	12374.9	715.9
与港澳台商合作经营	Joint-venture Enterprises			
港澳台商独资	Enterprises with Sole Investment	26613.7	14202.9	1090.3
港澳台商投资股份有限公司	Share-holding Corporations Ltd. With their Investment	1797.3	1156.6	958.0
其他港澳台投资	Other			
外商投资	Foreign Funded Enterprises	439104.6	232808.2	30499.4
中外合资经营	Joint-venture Enterprises	327933.7	163328.5	19937.1
中外合作经营	Cooperation Enterprises	62.6	396.2	0.2
外资企业	Foreign Funded Enterprises	104851.5	59019.7	906.3
外商投资股份有限公司	Share-holding Corporations Ltd. With Foreign Funds	6256.8	10063.8	9655.8
其他外商投资	Other			
按轻重工业分	**Grouped by Light Industry and Heavy Industry**			
轻工业	Light Industry	392785.9	103403.4	18547.4
重工业	Heavy Industry	83884.1	157139.2	14716.2
按企业规模分	**Grouped by Size of Enterprises**			
大型企业	Large-size	390029.5	138779.7	23307.5
中型企业	Medium-size	39089.9	57896.2	2005.5
小型企业	Small-size	47550.6	63866.7	7950.6
微型企业	microenterprise			
按工业行业大类分	**Grouped by Sector**			
煤炭开采和洗选业	Mining and Washing of Coal			
石油和天然气开采业	Extraction of Petroleum and Natural Gas			
黑色金属矿采选业	Mining and Processing of Ferrous Metal Ores			
有色金属矿采选业	Mining and Processing of Non-ferrous Metal Ores			
非金属矿采选业	Mining and Processing of Nonmetal Ores			
开采辅助活动	Mining Auxiliary Activities			
其他采矿业	Mining of Other Ores			

continued 2

(10 000 yuan)

营业利润 Operating Profit	利润总额 Total Profits	亏损企业亏损额 Total Loss of Deficit Enterprises	利税总额 Total Pre-tax Profits	应付职工薪酬 Salary Payable	本年应交增值税 Value Added Tax Payable
361654.2	**403061.8**	**57167.9**	**746604.0**	**501679.0**	**263353.4**
266456.0	305438.7	51253.7	639343.0	476539.0	255089.5
-60108.8	-57167.9	57167.9	-47024.4	37752.0	7499.9
13633.3	14686.0	1670.0	21358.1	11412.4	5937.8
114823.5	114047.5	4563.4	202737.5	109043.7	82257.1
233197.4	274328.3	50934.5	522508.4	381222.9	175158.5
-17192.9	-15462.2	30581.3	2135.2	31842.9	14081.8
-3882.5	-3908.3	6899.1	700.6	12332.0	3899.8
-17594.2	-15900.1	23682.2	-4971.9	16212.7	8348.2
4283.8	4346.2		6406.5	3298.2	1833.8
378847.1	418524.0	26586.6	744468.8	469836.1	249271.6
310759.5	335147.0	13397.0	571601.2	385572.2	165571.0
70.2	70.2		160.7	305.0	78.4
68046.8	78324.6	13189.6	128760.7	73424.8	44864.7
-29.4	4982.2		43946.2	10534.1	38757.5
124962.6	129131.4	8814.9	316931.9	175683.0	173370.5
236691.6	273930.4	48353.0	429672.1	325996.0	89982.9
155695.4	185961.1		448057.9	359166.3	196408.6
111351.0	119198.9	31931.0	157249.8	79576.8	31188.6
94607.8	97901.8	25236.9	141296.3	62935.9	35756.2

12-11 续表3

单位：万元

分 组	Classify	企业单位数（个） Number of Enterprises (unit)	亏损企业 Loss Making Enterprises	工业总产值（当年价格） Gross Industrial Output Value (At Current Prices)
农副食品加工业	Processing of Food from Agricultural Porducts	4		157554.6
食品制造业	Manufacture of Foods	5	1	887861.1
酒、饮料和精制茶制造业	Manufacture of Alcohol,Beverages and Tea	8	4	631519.5
烟草制品业	Manufacture of Tobacco			
纺织业	Manufacture of Textile	1		2101.0
纺织服装、服饰业	Textile, apparel industry			
皮革、毛皮、羽毛及其制品和制鞋业	Leather fur feathers and its products and footwear			
木材加工和木、竹、藤、棕、草制品业	Processing of Timber,Manufacture of Wood,Plam and Straw Products			
家具制造业	Manufacture of Furniture			
造纸及纸制品业	Manufacture of Paper and Paper Products	2		29765.8
印刷和记录媒介复制	Printing,Reproduction of Recording Media	2	1	32939.0
文教、工美、体育和娱乐用品制造业	Manufacture of Articles For Cultural,Educational and Sports Activities	1		7380.2
石油加工业、炼焦和核燃料加工业	Processing of Petroleum, Cokeing,Processing of Nuclear and Nuclear Fuel	2		184451.9
化学原料及化学制品制造业	Manufacture of Raw Chemical Materials and Chemical Products	5	4	42394.6
医药制造业	Manufacture of Medicines	9	1	648953.6
化学纤维制造业	Manufacture of Chemical Fibers	1		96929.8
橡胶和塑料制品业	Manufacture of Rubber and Plastics	5	1	33322.9
非金属矿物制品业	Manufacture of Non-metallic Mineral Products	6		279766.6
黑色金属冶炼和压延加工业	Smelting and Pressing of Ferrous Metals	3	1	89999.4
有色金属冶炼和压延加工业	Smelting and Pressing of Non-ferrous Metals	3	1	59263.2
金属制品业	Manufacture of Metal Products	3	1	10143.3
通用设备制造业	Manufacture of General Purpose Machinery	5		103959.2
专用设备制造业	Manufacture of Special Equipment	9	3	369994.8
汽车制造业	Manufacture of Motor Vehicle	5	2	2444899.7
铁路、船舶、航空航天和其他运输设备制造业	Railways,Shipbuilding,Aerospace and Other Transportation Equipment Manufacturing Industry	5	1	98535.5
电气机械和器材制造业	Manufacture of Electric Equipment and Machinery	10	2	581859.9
计算机、通讯和其他电子设备制造业	Manufacture of Communication Equipment, Computers and other Electronic Equipment	9	2	288438.6
仪器仪表制造业	Manufacture of Measuring Instruments and Machinery	4	1	74142.8
其他制造业	Manufacture of Other Manufacturing	1		5891.0
废弃资源综合利用业	Recycling and Disposal of Waste			
金属制品、机械和设备修理业	Metal Products,Machinery and Equipment Repair Industry	2	1	18656.7
电力、热力的生产和供应业	Production and Supply of Electric Power and Heat Power	1		2102.3
燃气生产和供应业	Gas Mining and Supplying Industry	1		219871.0
水的生产和供应业	Production and Supply of Water			

continued 3

(10 000 yuan)

工业销售产值（当年价） Value of Industry Products Sales (At Current Prices)	出口交货值 Export Delivery Value	从业人员年平均人数（人） Annual Average Employers (person)	资产总计 Total Assets	流动资产合计 Total Working Capitals	固定资产合计 Total Fixed Assets	固定资产原价 Origing Value of Fixed Assets	累计折旧 Accumulative Total Depreciation
152699.4		1089	56919.7	32251.4	16827.2	30975.6	14148.4
839591.9		4921	333325.8	203147.2	60896.3	125875.8	69774.4
558790.7	167283.4	6224	718012.6	323611.8	312509.6	463802.8	183536.3
2101.0		75	9796.9	3996.7	1768.5	1819.6	51.1
30243.7		299	21913.8	8331.7	4228.5	7743.6	3712.1
33326.4	104.0	897	73144.5	27737.1	14010.1	27165.5	13520.5
7380.2	7380.2	170	4273.8	3939.3	334.5	475.0	140.5
181320.3		3401	104327.1	44482.5	59415.4	57029.3	11639.4
37423.2	2251.2	445	49784.7	43022.2	4683.7	9597.4	4690.2
626411.4	6846.3	6587	379566.8	275241.2	69033.2	152641.5	88048.5
89768.2		269	47403.8	27376.2	19006.2	57086.4	38238.8
29496.9	649.9	634	54683.4	40343.8	12702.8	15722.6	8546.4
273611.6		956	235411.8	81204.0	133702.8	165735.9	55840.4
90257.4	4369.5	506	39086.2	12857.9	24970.2	32478.2	7508.0
56419.4	19350.5	386	48555.3	38859.7	6569.8	16015.8	9446.0
10287.5	2685.4	512	26138.7	9605.6	14638.4	22892.0	8253.7
103329.2	15334.7	1397	111955.2	86816.5	19302.1	47949.5	30016.0
345835.3	41518.2	3750	357346.5	205844.7	111551.3	159574.0	51284.6
2419375.6	175396.6	42076	2087856.5	874796.0	879880.2	1045124.3	297817.7
90881.4	20390.1	698	100089.2	86151.7	10724.3	30498.7	19797.3
541655.3	25226.1	1812	198779.9	140574.2	39523.2	79933.2	40446.6
261464.2	148187.6	4777	559980.1	249952.4	291680.4	391513.3	122150.9
74123.8	28866.9	931	72504.3	56467.5	12014.2	21608.5	9594.3
5937.8		240	6192.1	3377.3	2415.4	3389.9	974.5
18656.7		282	15434.6	14020.1	639.3	1337.9	698.6
2102.3		65	10231.2	1456.2	7209.6	7589.0	379.4
219871.0		2017	353010.3	139954.3	131377.9	172136.7	40758.8

12-11　续表5

单位：万元

分　组	Classify	负债合计 Total Liabilites	流动负债合计 Total Working Liabilities	非流动负债 Non-Working Liabilities
农副食品加工业	Processing of Food from Agricultural Porducts	18191.0	18191.0	
食品制造业	Manufacture of Foods	149149.5	148704.1	445.3
酒、饮料和精制茶制造业	Manufacture of Alcohol,Beverages and Tea	443058.1	396586.1	46471.9
烟草制品业	Manufacture of Tobacco			
纺织业	Manufacture of Textile	3229.3	3229.3	
纺织服装、服饰业	Textile, apparel industry			
皮革、毛皮、羽毛及其制品和制鞋业	Leather fur feathers and its products and footwear			
木材加工和木、竹、藤、棕、草制品业	Processing of Timber,Manufacture of Wood,Plam and Straw Products			
家具制造业	Manufacture of Furniture			
造纸及纸制品业	Manufacture of Paper and Paper Products	6391.8	6391.8	
印刷和记录媒介复制	Printing,Reproduction of Recording Media	49547.1	38148.6	11398.5
文教、工美、体育和娱乐用品制造业	Manufacture of Articles For Cultural,Educational and Sports Activities	1734.5	1734.5	
石油加工业、炼焦和核燃料加工业	Processing of Petroleum, Cokeing,Processing of Nuclear and Nuclear Fuel	56797.7	36797.7	20000.0
化学原料及化学制品制造业	Manufacture of Raw Chemical Materials and Chemical Products	35377.3	31516.6	3860.7
医药制造业	Manufacture of Medicines	143426.0	140282.9	3143.0
化学纤维制造业	Manufacture of Chemical Fibers	8300.8	8300.8	
橡胶和塑料制品业	Manufacture of Rubber and Plastics	33746.6	33103.4	639.5
非金属矿物制品业	Manufacture of Non-metallic Mineral Products	48152.7	33177.1	3532.9
黑色金属冶炼和压延加工业	Smelting and Pressing of Ferrous Metals	39910.7	31684.7	8226.0
有色金属冶炼和压延加工业	Smelting and Pressing of Non-ferrous Metals	20978.9	13508.4	7470.4
金属制品业	Manufacture of Metal Products	11961.3	9572.8	
通用设备制造业	Manufacture of General Purpose Machinery	37144.3	36398.7	745.6
专用设备制造业	Manufacture of Special Equipment	139783.0	115850.2	23932.8
汽车制造业	Manufacture of Motor Vehicle	1301447.8	1249157.3	52290.4
铁路、船舶、航空航天和其他运输设备制造业	Railways,Shipbuilding,Aerospace and Other Transportation Equipment Manufacturing Industry	59599.9	55360.4	4239.5
电气机械和器材制造业	Manufacture of Electric Equipment and Machinery	103615.7	88562.7	5622.4
计算机、通讯和其他电子设备制造业	Manufacture of Communication Equipment, Computers and other Electronic Equipment	289432.6	214031.8	75400.7
仪器仪表制造业	Manufacture of Measuring Instruments and Machinery	29885.5	28439.4	1446.1
其他制造业	Manufacture of Other Manufacturing	3231.5	3231.5	
废弃资源综合利用业	Recycling and Disposal of Waste			
金属制品、机械和设备修理业	Metal Products,Machinery and Equipment Repair Industry	9190.0	9190.0	
电力、热力的生产和供应业	Production and Supply of Electric Power and Heat Power	5320.2	5320.2	
燃气生产和供应业	Gas Mining and Supplying Industry	222369.1	199801.1	22568.0
水的生产和供应业	Production and Supply of Water			

continued 4

(10 000 yuan)

所有者权益合计 Total Owners' Equities	实收资本 Total Capital Hold	营业收入 Total Revenue	主营业务收入 Revenue from Principal Business	营业成本 Total Cost	主营业务成本 Cost of Principal Business	营业税金及附加 Taxs and Other Changes	主营业务税金及附加 Taxes and Other Charges on Principal Business
37834.9	25039.3	180344.6	177744.9	167195.2	166539.7	350.0	309.1
184176.3	88817.5	835446.7	823450.6	666583.0	625780.0	2866.9	2866.9
267096.0	115746.5	560114.4	545660.5	431629.5	412873.8	3678.0	3634.8
6567.6	6528.7	2205.0	2101.0	1916.1	1916.1	9.7	9.7
15521.9	3302.5	28409.0	28409.0	22118.3	22118.3	151.6	151.6
23597.4	24437.9	29351.2	28811.2	21215.6	20903.0	244.3	244.3
2204.8	2038.9	7380.2	7380.2	6789.8	6789.8	110.6	110.6
47529.4	27840.6	139119.3	137796.0	115090.7	113963.0	900.7	801.2
14407.2	16231.7	36276.7	36242.2	30633.9	30633.9	384.8	384.8
236140.7	93229.6	632411.3	608417.7	329464.0	328894.0	6116.1	6115.1
39103.0	24800.0	89769.9	89769.9	71973.2	71973.2	368.3	368.3
20936.8	18358.0	27683.8	25688.9	23153.7	21243.9	136.0	136.0
183679.0	28402.0	277810.5	277810.5	226237.3	226237.3	2651.5	2651.5
-824.5	9549.4	90270.0	90246.4	85998.7	82351.3	454.8	454.8
27576.4	22181.3	57728.2	57709.6	52565.3	52545.3	423.9	129.2
14177.3	12279.8	13608.5	13367.1	10397.0	10396.9	55.7	55.7
74606.8	34997.1	123736.6	123289.3	107117.6	107092.6	267.6	267.6
206360.2	125951.1	346122.2	344126.1	300588.1	299665.7	1416.6	1402.9
767404.2	224966.2	2212523.2	1997468.3	1983998.5	1838597.8	53316.3	53316.3
40489.3	20214.8	92204.2	91280.9	61311.1	61303.5	1117.3	1104.8
80658.8	105230.6	531154.9	530173.3	495205.1	494573.5	936.6	560.5
270547.6	209436.1	261191.1	258567.4	243999.5	241175.7	1586.5	535.8
42618.8	18367.8	75045.1	74209.0	50200.5	50053.2	622.7	622.7
2960.5	1800.0	5161.0	5075.1	4351.5	4351.5	37.5	37.5
6244.5	3454.5	21686.7	21670.9	19127.7	16582.8	97.1	97.1
4911.0	400.0	2102.3	2102.3	1478.8	1478.8	6.5	6.5
130641.2	100000.0	254015.5	216033.5	205327.7	182369.3	1881.2	1092.0

12-11 续表5

单位：万元

分 组	Classify	销售费用 Expenses for Sales	管理费用 Expenses for Management	财务费用 Financial cost
农副食品加工业	Processing of Food from Agricultural Porducts	3571.8	3332.2	345.8
食品制造业	Manufacture of Foods	96179.9	29465.2	-3465.9
酒、饮料和精制茶制造业	Manufacture of Alcohol,Beverages and Tea	71588.7	20526.7	9411.5
烟草制品业	Manufacture of Tobacco			
纺织业	Manufacture of Textile	35.9	76.3	0.1
纺织服装、服饰业	Textile, apparel industry			
皮革、毛皮、羽毛及其制品和制鞋业				
木材加工和木、竹、藤、棕、草制品业	Processing of Timber,Manufacture of Wood,Plam and Straw Products			
家具制造业	Manufacture of Furniture			
造纸及纸制品业	Manufacture of Paper and Paper Products	659.0	615.9	-25.8
印刷和记录媒介复制	Printing,Reproduction of Recording Media	1973.5	2483.4	1719.1
文教、工美、体育和娱乐用品制造业	Manufacture of Articles For Cultural,Educational and Sports Activities	180.3	263.9	1.3
石油加工业、炼焦和核燃料加工业	Processing of Petroleum, Cokeing,Processing of Nuclear and Nuclear Fuel	2839.9	6256.0	763.8
化学原料及化学制品制造业	Manufacture of Raw Chemical Materials and Chemical Products	2582.0	3798.0	309.1
医药制造业	Manufacture of Medicines	215469.2	40047.9	10198.3
化学纤维制造业	Manufacture of Chemical Fibers	194.9	2234.7	-127.2
橡胶和塑料制品业	Manufacture of Rubber and Plastics	688.8	1961.8	286.0
非金属矿物制品业	Manufacture of Non-metallic Mineral Products	1475.2	7491.8	552.9
黑色金属冶炼和压延加工业	Smelting and Pressing of Ferrous Metals	2037.6	2050.0	1243.4
有色金属冶炼和压延加工业	Smelting and Pressing of Non-ferrous Metals	3894.5	2381.7	162.0
金属制品业	Manufacture of Metal Products	756.7	1982.7	26.3
通用设备制造业	Manufacture of General Purpose Machinery	5095.3	4837.9	594.2
专用设备制造业	Manufacture of Special Equipment	8758.8	25577.8	1699.1
汽车制造业	Manufacture of Motor Vehicle	26261.4	47019.0	12826.0
铁路、船舶、航空航天和其他运输设备制造业	Railways,Shipbuilding,Aerospace and Other Transportation Equipment Manufacturing Industry	1517.0	8858.7	827.2
电气机械和器材制造业	Manufacture of Electric Equipment and Machinery	12195.9	14157.1	1728.9
计算机、通讯和其他电子设备制造业	Manufacture of Communication Equipment, Computers and other Electronic Equipment	2289.3	12186.4	-3074.2
仪器仪表制造业	Manufacture of Measuring Instruments and Machinery	4674.4	5802.9	-251.0
其他制造业	Manufacture of Other Manufacturing	207.8	295.6	31.0
废弃资源综合利用业	Recycling and Disposal of Waste			
金属制品、机械和设备修理业	Metal Products,Machinery and Equipment Repair Industry	1303.2	3014.1	200.8
电力、热力的生产和供应业	Production and Supply of Electric Power and Heat Power	86.3	169.7	0.9
燃气生产和供应业	Gas Mining and Supplying Industry	10152.7	13655.2	-2720.0
水的生产和供应业	Production and Supply of Water			

continued 5

(10 000 yuan)

营业利润 Operating Profit	利润总额 Total Profits	亏损企业亏损额 Total Loss of Deficit Enterprises	利税总额 Total Pre-tax Profits	应付职工薪酬 Salary Payable	本年应交增值税 Value Added Tax Payable
4847.1	4689.8		7688.5	5501.4	2648.7
35748.0	37178.5	103.3	64405.0	28492.6	24359.6
26090.2	29035.2	6273.7	88198.9	34551.6	55485.7
166.9	166.9		190.6	158.4	14.0
7183.9	7437.5		8888.2	1307.2	1299.1
2132.5	2327.5	2018.7	4463.2	4144.8	1891.4
165.9	165.9		508.9	393.0	232.4
13285.5	14385.4		15992.1	16624.1	706.0
-1688.4	-2052.6	2104.1	-1319.8	2440.2	348.0
31343.8	30396.3	93.3	119315.7	92488.6	82803.3
15125.9	15077.4		18651.9	3466.1	3206.2
1463.5	1562.0	293.5	2888.3	2171.1	1190.3
44595.2	45230.8		57480.4	3793.9	9598.1
-573.0	-327.1	6563.5	2296.5	3590.7	2168.8
-674.1	-503.3	1440.4	996.6	2112.9	1076.0
191.0	276.7	1216.2	720.1	2194.1	387.7
4735.1	4899.9		7600.0	7202.3	2432.5
8621.6	13502.9	14054.1	29123.7	23903.1	14204.2
95681.5	117941.1	5763.2	207610.8	179953.9	36353.4
15983.6	16102.9	1126.5	22888.9	7272.5	5668.7
8078.0	8607.5	6669.3	13546.1	18948.0	4002.0
7555.1	13655.0	9359.3	17663.2	26741.4	2421.7
13996.8	14065.7	73.5	17667.5	6923.4	2979.1
213.1	218.0		483.4	696.3	227.9
451.4	1010.9	15.3	2020.1	1633.7	912.1
360.1	360.1		492.7	212.0	126.1
26574.0	27650.9		36142.5	24761.7	6610.4

12-12 规模以上大中型工业企业主要经济指标（2012年）

单位：万元

分组	Classify	企业单位数（个） Number of Enterprises (unit)	亏损企业 Loss Making Enterprises	工业总产值（当年价格） Gross Industrial Output Value (At Current Prices)
总计	**Total**	**226**	**36**	**30140666.5**
#市区	Urban Area	193	31	23655173.7
#亏损企业	Deficit Enterprises	36	36	3841617.9
按隶属关系分	**Grouped by Jurisdiction of Management**			
中央企业	Central Enterprises	49	10	11784360.7
省属企业	Provincial Enterprises	29	7	7383705.4
市属企业	Municipal Enterprises	148	19	10972600.4
按登记注册类型分组	**Grouped by Registion Status**			
国有	State-owned	40	8	8006979.7
集体	Collective-owned	5		116146.2
股份合作	Share-holding Corperative	1		115107.8
联营	Joint Ownership			
国有联营	State Joint Ownership Enterprises			
集体联营	Collective Joint Ownership Enterprises			
国有与集体联营	Joint State-collective Ownership Enterprises			
其他联营	Other Joint Ownership Enterprises			
有限责任公司	Limited Liability Corporations	93	15	13103675.3
国有独资公司	State Sole Funded Enterprises	21	4	3373758.1
其他有限责任公司	Other Limited Liability Corporation	72	11	9729917.2
股份有限公司	Share-holding Corperation Ltd.	36	3	2351496.4
私营	Private Enterprises	16	4	647013.4
私营独资	Private-funded Enterprises	1		34965.8
私营合伙	Private Partnership Enterprises			
私营有限责任公司	Private Limited Liability Corporations	12	3	530376.6
私营股份有限公司	Private Share Holding Corporations	3	1	81671.0
其他	Other Domestic Funded Enterprises			
港澳台商投资	Enterprises with Funds from Hong Kong,Macao and Taiwan	7	3	190068.4
外商投资	Foreign Funded Enterprises	28	3	5610179.3
按轻重工业分	**Grouped by Light Industry and Heavy Industry**			
轻工业	Light Industry	62	8	4496964.4
重工业	Heavy Industry	164	28	25643702.1
按企业规模分	**Grouped by Size of Enterprises**			
大型企业	Large-size	65	9	23896867.9
中型企业	Medium-size	161	27	6243798.6
小型企业	Small-size			
微型企业	microenterprise			

Economic Indicators of Large and Medium-sized Industrial Enterprises above Designated Size (2012)

(10 000 yuan)

工业销售产值（当年价）Value of Industry Products Sales (At Current Prices)	出口交货值 Export Delivery Value	从业人员年平均人数（人）Annual Average Employers (person)	资产总计 Total Assets	流动资产合计 Total Working Capitals	固定资产合计 Total Fixed Assets	固定资产原价 Origing Value of Fixed Assets	累计折旧 Accumulative Total Depreciation
29250647.5	**2065355.8**	**400435**	**40196601.0**	**21608676.0**	**14581356.9**	**19705928.5**	**7333075.8**
22951941.8	1603972.9	343699	35470342.3	19086251.9	12907047.6	17756117.4	6637816.4
3670139.0	39432.0	40236	5685038.3	1727064.2	3357359.1	4683847.6	1424917.9
11557528.3	692933.7	164142	21516713.9	11005835.9	8977389.2	11932878.6	4378590.7
7189652.8	473191.3	65166	6074732.3	3373811.4	1840900.4	2193570.0	794280.1
10503466.4	899230.8	171127	12605154.8	7229028.7	3763067.3	5579479.9	2160205.0
7885528.9	170469.9	89223	13583295.0	5956192.0	6563258.5	9004517.0	3046905.4
111409.9		3648	32915.1	19193.2	13441.2	13301.6	2230.2
114353.8		837	97786.3	81637.7	7434.7	16319.0	8884.3
12855211.2	1220319.5	192692	17356617.5	10929625.6	4885135.5	6116181.2	2507538.0
3255932.4	285725.3	68401	6331706.5	3933381.5	1945639.4	2644284.3	1121212.6
9599278.8	934594.2	124291	11024911.0	6996244.1	2939496.1	3471896.9	1386325.4
2125956.9	100832.6	29170	3673026.9	1986103.5	1008675.5	1717176.0	777345.5
582447.8	2489.2	9723	560900.8	328965.4	152561.7	193933.3	72325.4
28029.4		706	17048.7	12332.4	4671.0	4793.0	2120.9
473454.8	2489.2	7917	391075.4	219894.4	119623.1	157786.1	67117.9
80963.6		1100	152776.7	96738.6	28267.6	31354.2	3086.6
185349.3	16852.4	4118	262693.2	75575.9	156942.3	213768.4	56957.5
5390389.7	554392.2	71024	4629366.2	2231382.7	1793907.5	2430732.0	860889.5
4411269.5	188206.1	61769	3356089.7	1858447.3	1057220.5	1848292.0	893566.8
24839378.0	1877149.7	338666	36840511.3	19750228.7	13524136.4	17857636.5	6439509.0
23402149.2	1810885.0	307081	32995251.7	17409289.0	12488095.6	16902864.6	6271380.2
5848498.3	254470.8	93354	7201349.3	4199387.0	2093261.3	2803063.9	1061695.6

12-12 续表1

单位：万元

分组	Classify	负债合计 Total Liabilites	流动负债合计 Total Working Liabilities	非流动负债 Non-Working Liabilities
总计	**Total**	**24087811.4**	**18136329.2**	**5812760.3**
#市区	Urban Area	20941974.3	15615542.1	5234584.1
#亏损企业	Deficit Enterprises	4869861.2	2204353.6	2619413.2
按隶属关系分	**Grouped by Jurisdiction of Management**			
中央企业	Central Enterprises	13565695.2	9164396.3	4348454.6
省属企业	Provincial Enterprises	3627281.7	2905721.9	680578.2
市属企业	Municipal Enterprises	6894834.5	6066211.0	783727.5
按登记注册类型分组	**Grouped by Registion Status**			
国有	State-owned	9021601.9	5373207.5	3639994.2
集体	Collective-owned	24447.8	15863.0	8584.8
股份合作	Share-holding Corperative	85114.7	82064.7	3050.0
联营	Joint Ownership			
国有联营	State Joint Ownership Enterprises			
集体联营	Collective Joint Ownership Enterprises			
国有与集体联营	Joint State-collective Ownership Enterprises			
其他联营	Other Joint Ownership Enterprises			
有限责任公司	Limited Liability Corporations	10115419.7	8550019.4	1468947.6
国有独资公司	State Sole Funded Enterprises	3288567.5	2717447.2	570619.2
其他有限责任公司	Other Limited Liability Corporation	6826852.2	5832572.2	898328.4
股份有限公司	Share-holding Corperation Ltd.	1870348.2	1422895.1	421264.7
私营	Private Enterprises	298696.8	266271.2	24745.4
私营独资	Private-funded Enterprises	15883.0	9792.2	6090.8
私营合伙	Private Partnership Enterprises			
私营有限责任公司	Private Limited Liability Corporations	236608.8	213510.2	17445.3
私营股份有限公司	Private Share Holding Corporations	46205.0	42968.8	1209.3
其他	Other Domestic Funded Enterprises			
港澳台商投资	Enterprises with Funds from Hong Kong,Macao and Taiwan	122903.7	113110.9	9792.8
外商投资	Foreign Funded Enterprises	2549278.6	2312897.4	236380.8
按轻重工业分	**Grouped by Light Industry and Heavy Industry**			
轻工业	Light Industry	1718483.5	1523155.0	172882.5
重工业	Heavy Industry	22369327.9	16613174.2	5639877.8
按企业规模分	**Grouped by Size of Enterprises**			
大型企业	Large-size	20078034.7	14883377.2	5135570.2
中型企业	Medium-size	4009776.7	3252952.0	677190.1
小型企业	Small-size			
微型企业	microenterprise			

continued 1

(10 000 yuan)

所有者权益合计 Total Owners' Equities	实收资本 Total Capital Hold	营业收入 Total Revenue	主营业务收入 Revenue from Principal Business	营业成本 Total Cost	主营业务成本 Cost of Principal Business	营业税金及附加 Taxs and Other Changes	主营业务税金及附加 Taxes and Other Charges on Principal Business
16056938.1	**6446990.5**	**28858760.6**	**27890553.7**	**24795389.5**	**23710093.0**	**328475.1**	**322814.7**
14498897.8	5591581.2	23599831.3	22843727.0	20130806.6	19159118.9	314550.2	309754.3
812936.0	1143031.6	3750181.7	3689814.5	3359650.2	3309076.6	149098.7	148976.7
7949370.1	3382279.8	12324399.2	12071731.6	11022478.6	10508178.3	195372.1	193887.5
2429450.2	760653.8	6438544.7	6090994.5	5489441.1	5258445.4	18501.8	18209.1
5678117.8	2304056.9	10095816.7	9727827.6	8283469.8	7943469.3	114601.2	110718.1
4561686.7	2383142.1	8109573.5	7837690.9	7424669.9	6863997.0	183589.5	182423.9
8350.5	6844.7	113177.6	113177.6	106003.9	103282.7	270.4	270.4
12671.6	6544.5	80548.5	76526.5	71255.8	71246.8	11.3	11.3
7236643.0	2358421.1	12541292.7	12197058.8	10692916.2	10434502.2	56284.4	54233.7
3043136.7	738437.3	3343666.3	3208912.5	2720123.8	2619106.0	15632.2	14690.0
4193506.3	1619983.8	9197626.4	8988146.3	7972792.4	7815396.2	40652.2	39543.7
1794713.5	646594.5	2017768.0	1984685.9	1593812.6	1564684.1	10305.2	10266.0
260057.4	91037.7	554365.7	546623.6	443098.0	439821.2	5463.8	5037.8
1165.7	100.0	28029.4	27989.1	26444.8	26444.8	419.7	3.3
152320.1	56037.7	461364.0	454344.1	380669.1	377567.8	3976.1	3966.5
106571.6	34900.0	64972.3	64290.4	35984.1	35808.6	1068.0	1068.0
139789.4	132195.9	181720.8	178179.0	152340.5	146894.4	2758.8	2731.1
2043026.0	822210.0	5260313.8	4956611.4	4311292.6	4085664.6	69791.7	67840.5
1629630.7	659141.5	4417721.0	4310809.0	3386535.8	3276995.6	35974.8	34989.1
14427307.4	5787849.0	24441039.6	23579744.7	21408853.7	20433097.4	292500.3	287825.6
12907555.7	4777061.9	23007120.1	22395477.0	19972763.3	19134296.3	295076.3	292626.3
3149382.4	1669928.6	5851640.5	5495076.7	4822626.2	4575796.7	33398.8	30188.4

12-12 续表2

单位：万元

分 组	Classify	销售费用 Expenses for Sales	管理费用 Expenses for Management	财务费用 Financial cost
总计	**Total**	**1165774.3**	**1688947.4**	**435145.0**
#市区	Urban Area	986085.0	1486507.0	366927.0
#亏损企业	Deficit Enterprises	58723.8	185305.9	209029.2
按隶属关系分	**Grouped by Jurisdiction of Management**			
中央企业	Central Enterprises	253637.2	833714.6	290219.4
省属企业	Provincial Enterprises	371437.3	272612.1	67829.1
市属企业	Municipal Enterprises	540699.8	582620.7	77096.5
按登记注册类型分组	**Grouped by Registion Status**			
国有	State-owned	176257.6	465708.4	246005.9
集体	Collective-owned	2093.6	2913.1	458.6
股份合作	Share-holding Corperative	3973.1	2196.6	2600.8
联营	Joint Ownership			
国有联营	State Joint Ownership Enterprises			
集体联营	Collective Joint Ownership Enterprises			
国有与集体联营	Joint State-collective Ownership Enterprises			
其他联营	Other Joint Ownership Enterprises			
有限责任公司	Limited Liability Corporations	407465.2	848623.2	112296.6
国有独资公司	State Sole Funded Enterprises	88892.2	367914.8	19520.5
其他有限责任公司	Other Limited Liability Corporation	318573.0	480708.4	92776.1
股份有限公司	Share-holding Corperation Ltd.	109825.4	146042.5	37014.2
私营	Private Enterprises	37040.0	26787.7	11455.9
私营独资	Private-funded Enterprises	295.8	692.6	296.9
私营合伙	Private Partnership Enterprises			
私营有限责任公司	Private Limited Liability Corporations	32634.8	18443.5	9469.8
私营股份有限公司	Private Share Holding Corporations	4109.4	7651.6	1689.2
其他	Other Domestic Funded Enterprises			
港澳台商投资	Enterprises with Funds from Hong Kong,Macao and Taiwan	25951.6	14232.8	1876.3
外商投资	Foreign Funded Enterprises	403167.8	182443.1	23436.7
按轻重工业分	**Grouped by Light Industry and Heavy Industry**			
轻工业	Light Industry	530192.8	208822.0	30742.7
重工业	Heavy Industry	635581.5	1480125.4	404402.3
按企业规模分	**Grouped by Size of Enterprises**			
大型企业	Large-size	915208.1	1326127.0	362137.9
中型企业	Medium-size	250566.2	362820.4	73007.1
小型企业	Small-size			
微型企业	microenterprise			

continued 2

(10 000 yuan)

营业利润 Operating Profit	利润总额 Total Profits	亏损企业亏损额 Total Loss of Deficit Enterprises	利税总额 Total Pre-tax Profits	应付职工薪酬 Salary Payable	本年应交增值税 Value Added Tax Payable
821610.6	**1033077.4**	**198321.3**	**2239370.9**	**2677246.9**	**877818.4**
650428.4	866450.5	180973.5	1919688.5	2420782.4	738687.8
-206129.1	-198321.3	198321.3	58975.7	232079.7	108198.3
62381.4	179647.3	142472.1	699834.7	1441844.6	324815.3
231104.0	227274.0	9233.4	439107.1	391516.3	193331.3
528125.2	626156.1	46615.8	1100429.1	843886.0	359671.8
-36934.4	56589.5	109629.9	526874.5	840053.4	286695.5
1965.4	2407.8		8995.0	9920.8	6316.8
-3545.6	467.4		4705.7	2234.3	4227.0
444419.0	496900.2	47067.7	834179.4	1190879.1	280994.8
132055.9	159106.3	25690.7	255169.2	445602.5	80430.7
312363.1	337793.9	21377.0	579010.2	745276.6	200564.1
110154.3	134507.1	8344.9	201848.8	161432.4	57036.5
38505.5	37045.4	1347.8	57459.8	33983.8	14950.6
383.3	343.0		800.0	1293.3	37.3
24556.9	22565.9	122.8	38734.1	26839.3	12192.1
13565.3	14136.5	1225.0	17925.7	5851.2	2721.2
-12870.4	-11054.6	22466.0	1615.5	20411.1	9911.3
279916.8	316214.6	9465.0	603692.2	418332.0	217685.9
233040.6	258632.8	6532.4	537280.5	354600.8	242672.9
588570.0	774444.6	191788.9	1702090.4	2322646.1	635145.5
495481.5	645098.3	137201.4	1630781.2	2225317.8	690606.6
326129.1	387979.1	61119.9	608589.7	451929.1	187211.8

12-12 续表3

单位：万元

分 组	Classify	企业单位数（个） Number of Enterprises (unit)	亏损企业 Loss Making Enterprises	工业总产值（当年价格） Gross Industrial Output Value (At Current Prices)
按经济组织类型分组	**Grouped by Economic Type of Orgnization**			
独资企业	Appropratorship	63	12	9313030.3
合作、合伙企业	Partnership	1		115107.8
股份有限公司	Corporaton	41	4	2720136.7
有限责任公司	Limited Liability Company	121	20	17992391.7
按控股情况分	**Grouped by Cast strand**			
国有控股	State owned shares	115	20	21505339.7
集体控股	Collective shares	14	2	591320.9
私人控股	Private holdings	60	7	4378706.0
港澳台控股	Hong Kong and Macao Holdings	5	3	149028.0
外商投资	Foreign Investment	22	3	3096417.9
其他	Others	10	1	419854.0
按工业行业大类分	**Grouped by Sector**			
煤炭开采和洗选业	Mining and Washing of Coal			
石油和天然气开采业	Extraction of Petroleum and Natural Gas			
黑色金属矿采选业	Mining and Processing of Ferrous Metal Ores			
有色金属矿采选业	Mining and Processing of Non-ferrous Metal Ores			
非金属矿采选业	Mining and Processing of Nonmetal Ores			
开采辅助活动	Mining Auxiliary Activities	1		199114.1
其他采矿业	Mining of other Ores			
农副食品加工业	Processing of Food from Agricultural Porducts	7	1	897910.3
食品制造业	Manufacture of Foods	10	1	1012616.0
酒、饮料和精制茶制造业	Manufacture of Alcohol,Beverages and Tea	6	2	717067.4
烟草制品业	Manufacture of Tobacco			
纺织业	Manufacture of Textile	3	1	95359.0
纺织服装、服饰业	Textile, apparel industry	1		40500.0
皮革、毛皮、羽毛及其制品和制鞋业	Leather fur feathers and its products and footwear	1		25464.3
木材加工和木、竹、藤、棕、草制品业	Processing of Timber,Manufacture of Wood,Plam and Straw Products	1		85011.1

continued 3

(10 000 yuan)

工业销售产值（当年价）Value of Industry Products Sales (At Current Prices)	出口交货值 Export Delivery Value	从业人员年平均人数（人）Annual Average Employers (person)	资产总计 Total Assets	流动资产合计 Total Working Capitals	固定资产合计 Total Fixed Assets	固定资产原价 Origing Value of Fixed Assets	累计折旧 Accumulative Total Depreciation
9131407.1	355354.7	107349	14714713.6	6444643.8	7093717.4	9793331.7	3336001.5
114353.8		837	97786.3	81637.7	7434.7	16319.0	8884.3
2425690.2	268220.0	32413	4245714.9	2320758.4	1205645.1	1969509.2	862214.7
17579196.4	1441781.1	259836	21138386.2	12761636.1	6274559.7	7926768.6	3125975.3
21038252.0	1365892.1	279379	32356438.0	17637159.2	11806340.6	15698138.1	5767363.4
567319.2	99165.0	9672	631196.9	325295.9	268402.1	632957.6	384345.9
4210057.6	186442.4	74253	4376579.0	2257283.2	1346907.4	1743335.1	541951.1
144229.3	16748.4	3103	215732.2	55453.9	143784.8	189370.5	45717.1
2892968.8	379151.4	25966	2163508.9	1104279.3	871980.4	1257349.8	537191.5
397820.6	17956.5	8062	453146.0	229204.5	143941.6	184777.4	56506.8
202798.8		674	1032995.1	569634.2	396252.4	574562.7	178310.3
848414.2	844.6	4790	360610.5	242324.0	104948.4	154591.3	56964.2
957858.5		8356	377466.6	238701.8	101433.9	174071.7	81344.2
796683.6	167283.4	7006	857032.7	420574.1	322704.5	496438.3	204080.4
96960.5	15983.0	11075	107755.1	52674.3	21404.4	58305.1	36900.7
40126.9	0.0	1326	104941.7	94916.2	8472.2	10880.4	2945.0
23704.6	75.2	887	39536.6	17854.7	7989.5	10180.3	2190.9
80792.8	0.0	496	99420.9	50246.0	40832.7	61933.7	22788.3

12-12 续表4

单位：万元

分组	Classify	负债合计 Total Liabilites	流动负债合计 Total Working Liabilities	非流动负债 Non-Working Liabilities
按经济组织类型分组	**Grouped by Economic Type of Orgnization**			
独资企业	Appropratorship	9476099.8	5722429.8	3745269.6
合作、合伙企业	Partnership	85114.7	82064.7	3050.0
股份有限公司	Corporaton	2202846.7	1708039.8	466591.5
有限责任公司	Limited Liability Company	12323750.2	10623794.9	1597849.2
按控股情况分	**Grouped by Cast strand**			
国有控股	State owned shares	20027709.4	14540589.5	5389645.5
集体控股	Collective shares	276659.0	258306.0	18352.8
私人控股	Private holdings	2442139.6	2181037.9	223818.7
港澳台控股	Hong Kong and Macao Holdings	97973.0	88988.0	8985.0
外商投资	Foreign Investment	1015522.1	850975.6	164546.2
其他	Others	227808.3	216432.2	7412.1
按工业行业大类分	**Grouped by Sector**			
煤炭开采和洗选业	Mining and Washing of Coal			
石油和天然气开采业	Extraction of Petroleum and Natural Gas			
黑色金属矿采选业	Mining and Processing of Ferrous Metal Ores			
有色金属矿采选业	Mining and Processing of Non-ferrous Metal Ores			
非金属矿采选业	Mining and Processing of Nonmetal Ores			
开采辅助活动	Mining Auxiliary Activities	283837.3	249406.1	31538.1
其他采矿业	Mining of other Ores			
农副食品加工业	Processing of Food from Agricultural Porducts	253836.8	249375.5	4461.3
食品制造业	Manufacture of Foods	167921.0	162320.2	5600.7
酒、饮料和精制茶制造业	Manufacture of Alcohol,Beverages and Tea	491844.7	445025.7	46818.9
烟草制品业	Manufacture of Tobacco			
纺织业	Manufacture of Textile	40626.5	39258.5	1368.0
纺织服装、服饰业	Textile, apparel industry	88754.2	70254.2	0.0
皮革、毛皮、羽毛及其制品和制鞋业	Leather fur feathers and its products and footwear	18261.1	12626.3	5334.8
木材加工和木、竹、藤、棕、草制品业	Processing of Timber,Manufacture of Wood,Plam and Straw Products	48635.4	21635.4	27000.0

continued 4

(10 000 yuan)

所有者权益合计 Total Owners' Equities	实收资本 Total Capital Hold	营业收入 Total Revenue	主营业务收入 Revenue from Principal Business	营业成本 Total Cost	主营业务成本 Cost of Principal Business	营业税金及附加 Taxs and Other Changes	主营业务税金及附加 Taxes and Other Charges on Principal Business
5238490.7	2798514.3	9384963.3	9097338.6	8467221.3	7856025.5	191182.3	189571.6
12671.6	6544.5	80548.5	76526.5	71255.8	71246.8	11.3	11.3
2027044.5	707572.5	2306621.1	2270932.0	1823723.6	1794118.2	11725.4	11686.2
8778731.3	2934359.2	17086627.7	16445756.6	14433188.8	13988702.5	125556.1	121545.6
12325283.2	5000141.3	20926946.2	20271507.2	18304177.4	17470704.6	239542.1	235042.2
354421.1	121154.5	544413.3	540819.7	467714.1	455897.8	1468.7	1468.4
1925448.5	630865.9	3941292.7	3751296.1	3352104.9	3186307.4	69799.0	68777.8
117759.1	123043.2	144883.6	142045.5	126243.3	121237.8	2437.4	2409.7
1110925.2	460928.0	2880261.4	2767443.5	2193955.6	2134700.4	13115.3	13004.0
223101.0	110857.6	420963.4	417441.7	351194.2	341245.0	2112.6	2112.6
747050.9	511882.3	499875.7	488738.8	532972.0	499491.9	10816.1	10621.2
106773.6	55332.2	815690.6	810057.8	768835.1	768109.2	996.3	963.5
209545.4	85623.9	958285.7	943142.9	759683.9	715968.3	3944.2	3919.2
357329.5	116886.8	799607.7	784671.4	619533.6	600314.1	12904.5	12861.3
67128.5	5656.2	97956.1	97022.7	94534.3	93783.6	740.9	740.9
16187.5	16187.5	77008.8	77008.8	58662.0	58662.0	2766.6	2766.6
21275.5	6000.0	55406.4	23704.6	50975.5	19857.8	123.0	122.9
50785.4	12500.0	67577.9	64851.6	60672.4	60672.4	287.0	287.0

12-12 续表5

单位：万元

分　组	Classify	销售费用 Expenses for Sales	管理费用 Expenses for Management	财务费用 Financial cost
按经济组织类型分组	**Grouped by Economic Type of Orgnization**			
独资企业	Appropratorship	296830.3	530487.9	246666.1
合作、合伙企业	Partnership	3973.1	2196.6	2600.8
股份有限公司	Corporaton	121460.9	162207.3	49119.4
有限责任公司	Limited Liability Company	743510.0	994055.6	136758.7
按控股情况分	**Grouped by Cast strand**			
国有控股	State owned shares	591895.9	1366729.6	359407.5
集体控股	Collective shares	29531.1	26748.5	7265.1
私人控股	Private holdings	170264.6	151256.1	44127.9
港澳台控股	Hong Kong and Macao Holdings	23640.3	12026.0	926.0
外商投资	Foreign Investment	338275.8	106609.0	19412.8
其他	Others	12166.6	25578.2	4005.7
按工业行业大类分	**Grouped by Sector**			
煤炭开采和洗选业	Mining and Washing of Coal			
石油和天然气开采业	Extraction of Petroleum and Natural Gas			
黑色金属矿采选业	Mining and Processing of Ferrous Metal Ores			
有色金属矿采选业	Mining and Processing of Non-ferrous Metal Ores			
非金属矿采选业	Mining and Processing of Nonmetal Ores			
开采辅助活动	Mining Auxiliary Activities	78.9	21564.4	-10878.2
其他采矿业	Mining of other Ores			
农副食品加工业	Processing of Food from Agricultural Porducts	24212.4	9381.9	11008.5
食品制造业	Manufacture of Foods	111291.0	34697.7	-3074.4
酒、饮料和精制茶制造业	Manufacture of Alcohol,Beverages and Tea	83855.3	22087.1	6221.2
烟草制品业	Manufacture of Tobacco			
纺织业	Manufacture of Textile	794.5	6995.7	222.5
纺织服装、服饰业	Textile, apparel industry	5063.0	6122.1	554.0
皮革、毛皮、羽毛及其制品和制鞋业	Leather fur feathers and its products and footwear	881.8	1744.6	163.6
木材加工和木、竹、藤、棕、草制品业	Processing of Timber,Manufacture of Wood,Plam and Straw Products	1659.4	1380.6	2738.9

continued 5

(10 000 yuan)

营业利润 Operating Profit	利润总额 Total Profits	亏损企业亏损额 Total Loss of Deficit Enterprises	利税总额 Total Pre-tax Profits	应付职工薪酬 Salary Payable	本年应交增值税 Value Added Tax Payable
4417.5	109247.6	138580.6	639762.8	928960.9	339332.9
-3545.6	467.4		4705.7	2234.3	4227.0
128335.9	154875.9	9569.9	266345.5	180054.6	99744.2
692402.8	768486.5	50170.8	1328556.9	1565997.1	434514.3
410426.4	562783.7	164027.4	1356193.8	2084690.0	553868.0
12341.6	16077.8	560.1	37957.6	37131.7	20411.1
166401.3	206254.2	1640.3	388867.8	285704.5	112814.6
-17941.3	-16179.3	22466.0	-6415.9	14629.1	7326.0
214800.2	227704.0	9465.0	411433.5	221383.3	170614.2
35582.4	36437.0	162.5	51334.1	33708.3	12784.5
-32454.9	7728.1		43197.4	131075.2	24653.2
5539.0	8481.0	94.6	21164.6	16635.1	11687.3
46207.0	48016.5	146.3	80253.3	37402.0	28292.6
58960.1	62691.8	2857.9	139342.8	46576.1	63746.5
-5154.9	-947.4	2172.2	4164.9	28953.9	4371.4
3289.0	4617.3		9090.9	4580.0	1707.0
1754.3	1845.9		2074.1	4891.4	105.2
852.6	4672.7		14185.5	1795.8	9225.8

12-12 续表6

单位：万元

分组	Classify	企业单位数（个） Number of Enterprises (unit)	亏损企业 Loss Making Enterprises	工业总产值（当年价格） Gross Industrial Output Value (At Current Prices)
家具制造业	Manufacture of Furniture			
造纸及纸制品业	Manufacture of Paper and Paper Products	5		42554.5
印刷和记录媒介复制	Printing,Reproduction of Recording Media	10	1	415879.4
文教、工美、体育和娱乐用品制造业	Manufacture of Articles For Cultural,Educational and Sports Activities			
石油加工业、炼焦和核燃料加工业	Processing of Petroleum, Cokeing,Processing of Nuclear and Nuclear Fuel	2	1	1351419.6
化学原料及化学制品制造业	Manufacture of Raw Chemical Materials and Chemical Products	10	2	703415.0
医药制造业	Manufacture of Medicines	13	1	986312.4
化学纤维制造业	Manufacture of Chemical Fibers			
橡胶和塑料制品业	Manufacture of Rubber and Plastics	3		270286.9
非金属矿物制品业	Manufacture of Non-metallic Mineral Products	7	1	269988.2
黑色金属冶炼和压延加工业	Smelting and Pressing of Ferrous Metals	2	2	38823.6
有色金属冶炼和压延加工业	Smelting and Pressing of Non-ferrous Metals	7		622179.9
金属制品业	Manufacture of Metal Products	7	2	700331.7
通用设备制造业	Manufacture of General Purpose Machinery	6	2	1111003.6
专用设备制造业	Manufacture of Special Equipment	30	5	1611677.3
汽车制造业	Manufacture of Motor Vehicle	14	2	7805576.4
铁路、船舶、航空航天和其他运输设备制造业	Railways,Shipbuilding,Aerospace and Other Transportation Equipment Manufacturing Industry	17	2	3186631.9
电气机械和器材制造业	Manufacture of Electric Equipment and Machinery	17	2	2442433.7
计算机、通讯和其他电子设备制造业	Manufacture of Communication Equipment, Computers and other Electronic Equipment	25	5	1152125.9
仪器仪表制造业	Manufacture of Measuring Instruments and Machinery	10		1007235.4
其他制造业	Manufacture of Other Manufacturing			
废弃资源综合利用业	Recycling and Disposal of Waste			
金属制品、机械和设备修理业	Metal Products,Machinery and Equipment Repair Industry			
电力、热力的生产和供应业	Production and Supply of Electric Power and Heat Power	6	3	2658211.5
燃气生产和供应业	Gas Mining and Supplying Industry	4		623913.0
水的生产和供应业	Production and Supply of Water	1		67624.4

continued 6

(10 000 yuan)

工业销售产值（当年价） Value of Industry Products Sales (At Current Prices)	出口交货值 Export Delivery Value	从业人员年平均人数（人） Annual Average Employers (person)	资产总计 Total Assets	流动资产合计 Total Working Capitals	固定资产合计 Total Fixed Assets	固定资产原价 Origing Value of Fixed Assets	累计折旧 Accumulative Total Depreciation
39074.1		3015	24973.1	7000.3	16542.3	16879.0	4123.4
402976.4	104.0	7201	526256.4	237076.2	224759.2	375397.4	182514.8
1314618.6		4773	343942.3	150671.7	169459.5	241861.1	86427.1
695944.6	103125.7	17390	1151876.4	493934.1	499497.7	982546.8	529044.8
941371.9	3915.9	11464	656773.5	404353.1	149025.8	265716.4	128645.9
257313.5	3033.7	12068	446495.5	275744.9	79949.3	112628.2	41228.1
263784.0	0.0	3213	200454.0	97216.5	90335.1	104276.0	46538.6
31894.4	934.7	951	37190.6	21254.9	7408.7	9929.1	2520.4
598740.8	21489.0	5200	654640.5	359869.4	163952.3	200827.5	58163.2
677244.2	23385.0	18930	1354370.7	807152.3	467589.0	603928.2	243674.6
1071855.4	48764.4	11288	2166609.1	1711172.2	267530.1	403402.9	146232.3
1412053.2	109993.2	24508	2321506.4	1543288.1	539742.4	762462.9	273200.9
7620231.4	640672.4	89602	6073764.9	3259554.9	2123015.2	2364570.6	716758.0
3088283.3	480870.1	62994	6570781.4	4305585.8	1764953.8	2151477.6	973131.1
2380667.7	202342.2	36168	4278807.4	2828937.0	1329116.3	1269730.4	445770.9
1074730.4	199390.2	23414	2243182.0	1260091.9	688048.7	879141.8	289343.2
982202.5	43149.1	15406	1521723.1	890026.8	469655.2	662948.2	313851.1
2658211.5		11810	5284160.1	872342.3	4027572.9	5918897.4	1912227.1
624485.3		3685	1241396.2	347218.0	430487.6	642745.3	216138.2
67624.4		2745	117938.2	49260.3	68677.8	195598.2	138018.1

12-12 续表7

单位：万元

分组	Classify	负债合计 Total Liabilites	流动负债合计 Total Working Liabilities	非流动负债 Non-Working Liabilities
家具制造业	Manufacture of Furniture			
造纸及纸制品业	Manufacture of Paper and Paper Products	22028.1	11630.8	8618.8
印刷和记录媒介复制	Printing,Reproduction of Recording Media	190292.3	165545.8	22898.8
文教、工美、体育和娱乐用品制造业	Manufacture of Articles For Cultural,Educational and Sports Activities			
石油加工业、炼焦和核燃料加工业	Processing of Petroleum, Cokeing,Processing of Nuclear and Nuclear Fuel	263251.0	243217.0	20034.0
化学原料及化学制品制造业	Manufacture of Raw Chemical Materials and Chemical Products	546392.3	433190.7	113200.5
医药制造业	Manufacture of Medicines	257162.9	245309.5	11853.3
化学纤维制造业	Manufacture of Chemical Fibers			
橡胶和塑料制品业	Manufacture of Rubber and Plastics	344493.9	292176.8	48918.6
非金属矿物制品业	Manufacture of Non-metallic Mineral Products	76692.4	74671.3	2001.7
黑色金属冶炼和压延加工业	Smelting and Pressing of Ferrous Metals	28966.2	25803.4	3162.8
有色金属冶炼和压延加工业	Smelting and Pressing of Non-ferrous Metals	397121.8	340463.8	56657.9
金属制品业	Manufacture of Metal Products	791981.6	552858.7	238253.5
通用设备制造业	Manufacture of General Purpose Machinery	1261152.6	1184406.5	76746.1
专用设备制造业	Manufacture of Special Equipment	1089948.5	988458.2	90523.7
汽车制造业	Manufacture of Motor Vehicle	3583059.3	3174285.4	368191.6
铁路、船舶、航空航天和其他运输设备制造业	Railways,Shipbuilding,Aerospace and Other Transportation Equipment Manufacturing Industry	3952841.5	3336518.8	610839.6
电气机械和器材制造业	Manufacture of Electric Equipment and Machinery	2144712.0	1834386.0	310325.7
计算机、通讯和其他电子设备制造业	Manufacture of Communication Equipment, Computers and other Electronic Equipment	1440093.9	1132190.0	259915.7
仪器仪表制造业	Manufacture of Measuring Instruments and Machinery	792049.0	632433.7	159615.3
其他制造业	Manufacture of Other Manufacturing			
废弃资源综合利用业	Recycling and Disposal of Waste			
金属制品、机械和设备修理业	Metal Products,Machinery and Equipment Repair Industry			
电力、热力的生产和供应业	Production and Supply of Electric Power and Heat Power	4716505.2	1713426.9	3003078.3
燃气生产和供应业	Gas Mining and Supplying Industry	741557.5	469954.2	267510.0
水的生产和供应业	Production and Supply of Water	53792.4	35499.8	18292.6

continued 7

(10 000 yuan)

所有者权益合计 Total Owners' Equities	实收资本 Total Capital Hold	营业收入 Total Revenue	主营业务收入 Revenue from Principal Business	营业成本 Total Cost	主营业务成本 Cost of Principal Business	营业税金及附加 Taxs and Other Changes	主营业务税金及附加 Taxes and Other Charges on Principal Business
2828.6	6819.6	45336.5	45336.5	42033.4	42033.4	92.0	92.0
335963.8	141296.8	416025.7	411786.2	305417.0	301090.2	4083.1	3453.1
80685.2	227006.1	1280400.9	1276826.0	1103029.0	1101896.4	134827.5	134760.6
605484.1	177539.5	765823.3	635047.6	621445.3	517457.2	2836.7	2526.4
399610.6	130813.5	875312.7	850631.4	457380.3	456771.1	8644.2	8643.2
102001.6	76318.4	253297.6	248302.8	214791.4	214082.2	1933.2	1328.3
123761.7	28020.0	235099.4	234217.7	202641.7	201603.3	1237.8	1237.8
8224.3	8737.7	37241.1	33027.1	30327.6	25787.9	88.7	85.9
257518.7	122956.1	507873.3	488093.3	419421.9	406529.0	1671.8	1602.8
560154.4	175806.3	652133.4	636836.0	549970.6	541533.4	2532.3	2350.1
905456.5	81307.0	972891.7	962453.6	707184.7	699287.0	5897.8	5760.5
1216917.8	591437.2	1379576.0	1362798.1	1069296.7	1059972.8	11731.4	11701.4
2472705.4	728298.6	6548529.7	6180051.1	5872269.6	5592784.5	63016.9	62760.7
2617939.5	872035.4	3615927.9	3562026.5	3094895.9	3054452.6	14910.7	14735.8
2134095.3	426335.7	2056476.2	1968965.6	1958982.5	1582443.6	13758.3	13723.6
803084.0	424397.3	1306833.0	1275902.8	1155636.6	1121649.8	4278.6	2925.9
729113.8	367677.5	988642.8	972164.1	810310.5	802284.6	6400.3	6045.3
567655.0	773334.9	2808721.9	2760563.7	2625568.2	2589493.5	14870.8	14757.1
493515.7	237784.0	667393.5	628700.6	543650.5	520632.1	2338.3	1549.1
64145.8	39000.0	73815.1	67624.4	65267.3	61449.1	746.1	492.5

12-12 续表8

单位：万元

分组	Classify	销售费用 Expenses for Sales	管理费用 Expenses for Management	财务费用 Financial cost
家具制造业	Manufacture of Furniture			
造纸及纸制品业	Manufacture of Paper and Paper Products	782.2	820.2	546.7
印刷和记录媒介复制	Printing,Reproduction of Recording Media	11060.5	44074.5	1071.0
文教、工美、体育和娱乐用品制造业	Manufacture of Articles For Cultural,Educational and Sports Activities			
石油加工业、炼焦和核燃料加工业	Processing of Petroleum, Cokeing,Processing of Nuclear and Nuclear Fuel	4227.4	86268.3	6228.8
化学原料及化学制品制造业	Manufacture of Raw Chemical Materials and Chemical Products	40532.7	65755.3	11374.0
医药制造业	Manufacture of Medicines	263954.5	61601.1	11396.8
化学纤维制造业	Manufacture of Chemical Fibers			
橡胶和塑料制品业	Manufacture of Rubber and Plastics	12888.2	9920.1	5181.4
非金属矿物制品业	Manufacture of Non-metallic Mineral Products	13487.7	11668.4	510.9
黑色金属冶炼和压延加工业	Smelting and Pressing of Ferrous Metals	669.7	4122.1	411.4
有色金属冶炼和压延加工业	Smelting and Pressing of Non-ferrous Metals	5723.5	25514.8	17683.3
金属制品业	Manufacture of Metal Products	13625.8	66022.6	9930.7
通用设备制造业	Manufacture of General Purpose Machinery	33584.3	146086.6	-6303.2
专用设备制造业	Manufacture of Special Equipment	69591.3	122527.2	13880.4
汽车制造业	Manufacture of Motor Vehicle	193065.3	217993.9	38022.3
铁路、船舶、航空航天和其他运输设备制造业	Railways,Shipbuilding,Aerospace and Other Transportation Equipment Manufacturing Industry	75202.7	268840.8	40261.9
电气机械和器材制造业	Manufacture of Electric Equipment and Machinery	142420.0	199203.8	18646.0
计算机、通讯和其他电子设备制造业	Manufacture of Communication Equipment, Computers and other Electronic Equipment	25890.2	100430.9	16607.9
仪器仪表制造业	Manufacture of Measuring Instruments and Machinery	14919.5	105230.2	8413.4
其他制造业	Manufacture of Other Manufacturing			
废弃资源综合利用业	Recycling and Disposal of Waste			
金属制品、机械和设备修理业	Metal Products,Machinery and Equipment Repair Industry			
电力、热力的生产和供应业	Production and Supply of Electric Power and Heat Power	1396.6	14556.6	218738.7
燃气生产和供应业	Gas Mining and Supplying Industry	11783.8	27076.6	15675.6
水的生产和供应业	Production and Supply of Water	3132.1	7259.3	-89.1

continued 8

(10 000 yuan)

营业利润 Operating Profit	利润总额 Total Profits	亏损企业亏损额 Total Loss of Deficit Enterprises	利税总额 Total Pre-tax Profits	应付职工薪酬 Salary Payable	本年应交增值税 Value Added Tax Payable
871.1	871.1		1893.7	8526.7	930.6
55755.1	56798.6	67.7	80392.8	61258.4	19511.1
-54169.3	-52789.9	66872.3	94139.9	28765.9	12102.3
18626.2	23332.1	18112.9	41969.4	96796.5	15800.6
70403.5	70127.3	5.7	182471.1	113240.9	103699.6
10839.8	11730.0		18833.7	18035.0	5170.5
12229.5	18076.8	24.9	39630.1	10811.6	20315.5
-765.8	-526.7	1116.2	454.6	4925.3	892.6
25703.8	32410.7		48320.6	23089.9	14238.1
11472.7	19651.3	1387.5	30870.1	115584.5	8686.5
99091.4	105634.0	532.3	151445.6	124208.3	39913.8
89789.6	101455.0	19857.9	168837.4	151891.2	55651.0
190589.1	203531.8	4125.4	399930.9	385492.6	133382.2
122723.0	152574.4	8122.0	204798.8	539933.2	37313.7
30101.0	50503.7	6563.2	154785.0	225275.1	90523.0
13246.1	26983.5	21883.1	42266.5	138879.1	11004.4
38484.9	44692.5		77491.5	114202.7	26398.7
-57857.8	-39733.3	44379.2	96627.2	179072.4	121489.7
67959.8	68727.8		84014.1	45772.5	12948.0
-2475.3	1920.8		6724.4	19575.6	4057.5

12-13 规模以上高技术产业工业企业主要经济指标（2012年）

单位：万元

行 业	Scetor	企业单位数（个）Number of Enterprises (unit)	亏损企业 Loss Making Enterprises	工业总产值（当年价格）Gross Industrial Output Value (At Current Prices)
总计	**Total**	**126**	**15**	**6560931.7**
一、信息化学品制造	**Information Chemical Products**	**3**	**1**	**219835.4**
二、医药制造业	**Medicines Manufacturing**	**18**	**2**	**859967.9**
#化学药品制造业	Chemical Medicine Manufacturing	18	2	859967.9
三、航空航天器制造业	**Aviation and Aircrafts Manufacturing**	**12**		**2740239.4**
1、飞机制造业	Manufacture and Repairing of Aircrafts	8		2464316.2
2、航天器制造业	Aircrafts Manufacturing	4		275923.2
四、电子及通讯设备制造业	**Electronic and Communication Equipment**	**53**	**9**	**1519916.4**
1、通信设备制造业	Communication Equipment Manufacturing	12	1	270144.2
通信系统设备制造业	Communication system equipment manufacturing	10	1	265777.3
通信终端设备制造业	Communication Terminal Equipment	2		4366.9
2、雷达及配套设备制造业	Ruder Equipments	3		274702.0
3、广播电视设备制造业	Broadcast and Television Equipments	3		31889.4
4、电子器件制造业	Electronic Appliances Manufacturing	18	2	633242.7
电子真空器件制造业	Electronic Vacuum Appliances	2		40118.0
半导体分立器件制造	Semiconductor Discreting Appliances	9		473153.5
集成电路制造	Integrate Circuit	3	1	95476.0
光电子器件及其他	Photoelectron Appliances and Other	4	1	24495.2
电子器件制造	Electronic Appliances			
5、电子元件制造	Electronic Components Manufacturing	17	6	309938.1
五、电子计算机及办公设备制造业	**Computers and Office Equipment Manufacturing**	**1**		**6675.8**
六、医疗设备及仪器仪表制造业	**Medical Equipments and Meters**	**37**	**3**	**1196722.6**
1、医疗仪器设备及器械制造	Medical Equipments and Instruments	3	1	7951.3
2、仪器仪表制造业	Instruments and Meters	34	2	1188771.3
七、其他	**Others**	**2**		**17574.2**

Economic Indicators of High Technology Industry

Industrial Enterprises above Designated Size (2012)

(10 000 yuan)

工业销售产值（当年价） Value of Industry Products Sales (At Current Prices)	出口交货值 Export Delivery Value	从业人员年平均人数（人） Annual Average Employers (person)	资产总计 Total Assets	流动资产合计 Total Working Capitals	固定资产合计 Total Fixed Assets	固定资产原价 Origing Value of Fixed Assets	累计折旧 Accumulative Total Depreciation
6308542.3	**751589.7**	**110901**	**11507011.3**	**7119727.9**	**3276542.9**	**4386046.2**	**1948619.1**
222326.9	**57180.8**	**1894.0**	**354964.2**	**129708.7**	**218136.4**	**557663.8**	**339527.4**
824510.0	**3884.9**	**9989.0**	**524317.1**	**366906.8**	**110577.9**	**208883.7**	**103208.5**
824510.0	3884.9	9989.0	524317.1	366906.8	110577.9	208883.7	103208.5
2664587.1	**412868.5**	**51526.0**	**6192404.1**	**3964818.0**	**1707888.7**	**1973513.1**	**869671.0**
2397682.9	412788.5	45195.0	5535590.9	3639522.1	1493939.7	1694445.1	746077.9
266904.2	80.0	6331.0	656813.2	325295.9	213949.0	279068.0	123593.1
1415149.7	**218911.5**	**27847.0**	**2598843.8**	**1536408.2**	**735387.2**	**936315.6**	**307065.5**
262057.2	23164.7	3261.0	335994.0	275812.5	54857.9	56988.1	23005.1
258103.3	23164.7	3144.0	317243.5	268646.6	46450.3	48438.9	21223.1
3953.9		117.0	18750.5	7165.9	8407.6	8549.2	1782.0
263363.9	37593.1	5582.0	753943.3	504311.7	202108.2	235140.4	71511.3
28100.9	4367.0	540.0	31231.6	25018.2	4385.1	6203.7	1877.4
544515.7	139793.7	8648.0	952555.2	457848.8	337676.8	462259.8	146769.6
30060.1	12113.7	904.0	27219.6	19172.4	5935.7	9600.5	3664.8
401788.2	53001.7	3954.0	499138.1	336585.7	111765.3	140153.7	45423.3
89344.8	71877.8	2312.0	385782.7	77860.7	207138.9	297326.5	92559.2
23322.6	2800.5	1478.0	40414.8	24230.0	12836.9	15179.1	5122.3
317112.0	13993.0	9816.0	525119.7	273417.0	136359.2	175723.6	63902.1
5574.2		**142.0**	**8120.5**	**6359.0**	**1059.5**	**1680.1**	**620.6**
1160435.5	**58744.0**	**19301.0**	**1807857.1**	**1100562.5**	**502393.2**	**707007.3**	**328393.5**
8058.1		319.0	19679.4	10630.1	7273.7	9343.3	2069.6
1152377.4	58744.0	18982.0	1788177.7	1089932.4	495119.5	697664.0	326323.9
15958.9		**202.0**	**20504.5**	**14964.7**	**1100.0**	**982.6**	**132.6**

12-13 续表1

单位：万元

行业	Scetor	负债合计 Total Liabilites	流动负债合计 Total Working Liabilities	非流动负债 Non-Working Liabilities
总计	**Total**	**6569427.2**	**5473700.7**	**1037407.9**
一、信息化学品制造	**Information Chemical Products**	**125791.2**	**113424.3**	**12366.9**
二、医药制造业	**Medicines Manufacturing**	**216876.7**	**209999.2**	**6456.5**
#化学药品制造业	Chemical Medicine Manufacturing	216876.7	209999.2	6456.5
三、航空航天器制造业	**Aviation and Aircrafts Manufacturing**	**3656372.4**	**3086001.2**	**570371.2**
1、飞机制造业	Manufacture and Repairing of Aircrafts	3325804.3	2870671.2	455133.1
2、航天器制造业	Aircrafts Manufacturing	330568.1	215330.0	115238.1
四、电子及通讯设备制造业	**Electronic and Communication Equipment**	**1598674.9**	**1271963.8**	**278722.8**
1、通信设备制造业	Communication Equipment Manufacturing	197385.5	190306.9	4781.3
通信系统设备制造业	Communication system equipment manufacturing	188815.7	181770.1	4748.3
通信终端设备制造业	Communication Terminal Equipment	8569.8	8536.8	33.0
2、雷达及配套设备制造业	Ruder Equipments	506837.9	439936.3	66901.5
3、广播电视设备制造业	Broadcast and Television Equipments	22720.3	22330.1	390.2
4、电子器件制造业	Electronic Appliances Manufacturing	489283.6	325045.9	118547.0
电子真空器件制造业	Electronic Vacuum Appliances	10635.2	9501.0	1134.2
半导体分立器件制造	Semiconductor Discreting Appliances	292705.4	241468.4	51237.0
集成电路制造	Integrate Circuit	176356.8	65508.3	65157.8
光电子器件及其他电子器件制造	Photoelectron Appliances and Other Electronic Appliances	9586.2	8568.2	1018.0
5、电子元件制造	Electronic Components Manufacturing	382447.6	294344.6	88102.8
五、电子计算机及办公设备制造业	**Computers and Office Equipment Manufacturing**	**1947.4**	**1947.4**	
六、医疗设备及仪器仪表制造业	**Medical Equipments and Meters**	**959956.3**	**780859.3**	**169187.7**
1、医疗仪器设备及器械制造	Medical Equipments and Instruments	12988.0	2211.8	959.0
2、仪器仪表制造业	Instruments and Meters	946968.3	778647.5	168228.7
七、其他	**Others**	**9808.3**	**9505.5**	**302.8**

continued 1

(10 000 yuan)

所有者权益合计 Total Owners' Equities	实收资本 Total Capital Hold	营业收入 Total Revenue	主营业务收入 Revenue from Principal Business	营业成本 Total Cost	主营业务成本 Cost of Principal Business	营业税金及附加 Taxs and Other Changes	主营业务税金及附加 Taxes and Other Charges on Principal Business
4936436.8	**1907089.0**	**7145791.2**	**6928489.0**	**5805922.3**	**5637132.2**	**34077.7**	**32295.0**
229173.0	**66702.0**	**275857.1**	**179130.9**	**256303.2**	**162060.8**	**10.1**	**10.1**
307440.0	**113874.1**	**814348.9**	**790219.0**	**421186.0**	**420576.3**	**7907.7**	**7885.7**
307440.0	113874.1	814348.9	790219.0	421186.0	420576.3	7907.7	7885.7
2536031.7	**735434.1**	**3232851.7**	**3190460.5**	**2777825.9**	**2747783.0**	**12436.6**	**12415.5**
2209786.6	601038.4	2936279.5	2900834.3	2537440.4	2510837.8	11251.1	11238.6
326245.1	134395.7	296572.2	289626.2	240385.5	236945.2	1185.5	1176.9
999582.7	**545202.0**	**1626953.4**	**1593082.4**	**1393009.3**	**1358404.7**	**5642.4**	**4282.4**
138026.6	123488.6	297099.6	292885.8	232668.4	232199.2	1410.9	1109.3
127846.0	116718.1	293701.3	289487.5	230318.7	229849.5	1351.9	1050.3
10180.6	6770.5	3398.3	3398.3	2349.7	2349.7	59.0	59.0
247105.4	40247.8	422793.7	419193.5	345089.4	341602.4	301.6	301.6
8511.3	8000.0	26160.1	26119.0	23005.1	23005.1	206.2	206.2
463267.3	277952.2	565976.8	545516.6	525857.0	498860.7	2212.7	1154.3
16582.5	4180.0	27174.7	26532.2	21255.3	20807.8	231.2	231.2
206430.4	121369.8	427815.2	408303.2	398882.8	374589.1	1540.8	482.4
209425.8	122905.7	89285.0	89035.4	88424.5	86170.6	318.5	318.5
30828.6	29496.7	21701.9	21645.8	17294.4	17293.2	122.2	122.2
142672.1	95513.4	314923.2	309367.5	266389.4	262737.3	1511.0	1511.0
6173.1	**4500.0**	**5389.2**	**5389.2**	**2767.4**	**2767.4**	**45.2**	**45.2**
847340.1	**437186.8**	**1174363.0**	**1154179.1**	**945903.1**	**936612.6**	**7842.9**	**7463.3**
6691.4	5300.0	8484.3	8108.0	5488.4	5372.5	57.2	57.2
840648.7	431886.8	1165878.7	1146071.1	940414.7	931240.1	7785.7	7406.1
10696.2	**4190.0**	**16027.9**	**16027.9**	**8927.4**	**8927.4**	**192.8**	**192.8**

12-13 续表2

单位：万元

行　业	Scetor	销售费用 Expenses for Sales	管理费用 Expenses for Management	财务费用 Financial cost
总计	**Total**	**378624.8**	**562031.8**	**76099.8**
一、信息化学品制造	**Information Chemical Products**	**2101.3**	**10209.2**	**4082.2**
二、医药制造业	**Medicines Manufacturing**	**246306.9**	**55178.6**	**11812.8**
#化学药品制造业	Chemical Medicine Manufacturing	246306.9	55178.6	11812.8
三、航空航天器制造业	**Aviation and Aircrafts Manufacturing**	**69125.5**	**228692.3**	**32997.8**
1、飞机制造业	Manufacture and Repairing of Aircrafts	65299.3	198886.8	30300.3
2、航天器制造业	Aircrafts Manufacturing	3826.2	29805.5	2697.5
四、电子及通讯设备制造业	**Electronic and Communication Equipment**	**32584.5**	**139299.5**	**16889.6**
1、通信设备制造业	Communication Equipment Manufacturing	10094.0	38318.0	2450.9
通信系统设备制造业	Communication system equipment manufacturing	9728.3	37086.9	2451.3
通信终端设备制造业	Communication Terminal Equipment	365.7	1231.1	-0.4
2、雷达及配套设备制造业	Ruder Equipments	5493.4	34825.6	4488.6
3、广播电视设备制造业	Broadcast and Television Equipments	864.7	1497.0	498.0
4、电子器件制造业	Electronic Appliances Manufacturing	6302.1	29249.9	3545.7
电子真空器件制造业	Electronic Vacuum Appliances	1215.8	3172.8	51.1
半导体分立器件制造	Semiconductor Discreting Appliances	3916.6	17417.0	1349.7
集成电路制造	Integrate Circuit	694.7	4546.5	2022.0
光电子器件及其他电子器件制造	Photoelectron Appliances and Other Electronic Appliances	475.0	4113.6	122.9
5、电子元件制造	Electronic Components Manufacturing	9830.3	35409.0	5906.4
五、电子计算机及办公设备制造业	**Computers and Office Equipment Manufacturing**	**348.3**	**1567.4**	**102.3**
六、医疗设备及仪器仪表制造业	**Medical Equipments and Meters**	**28037.4**	**124515.3**	**10208.3**
1、医疗仪器设备及器械制造	Medical Equipments and Instruments	973.4	1306.6	729.3
2、仪器仪表制造业	Instruments and Meters	27064.0	123208.7	9479.0
七、其他	**Others**	**120.9**	**2569.5**	**6.8**

continued 2

(10 000 yuan)

营业利润 Operating Profit	利润总额 Total Profits	亏损企业亏损额 Total Loss of Deficit Enterprises	利税总额 Total Pre-tax Profits	应付职工薪酬 Salary Payable	本年应交增值税 Value Added Tax Payable
280985.2	**347150.5**	**24881.3**	**553703.2**	**889403.2**	**172475.0**
10.6	**2517.9**	**433.1**	**4185.0**	**11508.8**	**1657.0**
68377.7	**67870.9**	**189.8**	**176102.5**	**102863.3**	**100323.9**
68377.7	67870.9	189.8	176102.5	102863.3	100323.9
109244.1	**140256.8**		**168207.0**	**473789.9**	**15513.6**
90480.4	114223.2		139262.8	416209.8	13788.5
18763.7	26033.6		28944.2	57580.1	1725.1
45275.4	**69981.5**	**23413.8**	**95889.1**	**162348.4**	**20265.2**
11571.8	21040.3	385.4	28849.7	23623.6	6398.5
12266.0	18799.7	385.4	26287.7	23026.6	6136.1
-694.2	2240.6		2562.0	597.0	262.4
30932.0	35579.6		37396.2	47096.2	1515.0
248.2	383.8		1576.0	1871.5	986.0
9277.8	16665.0	10335.8	23049.9	46214.3	4172.2
1248.5	1799.1		2581.1	4935.9	550.8
13987.8	17317.5		21753.4	21170.9	2895.1
-5532.3	-2935.4	9725.2	-2386.4	15759.1	230.5
-426.2	483.8	610.6	1101.8	4348.4	495.8
-6754.4	-3687.2	12692.6	5017.3	43542.8	7193.5
531.4	**653.0**		**1034.4**	**835.6**	**336.2**
53839.9	**62164.3**	**844.6**	**104385.3**	**136124.8**	**34378.1**
-82.0	-89.6	465.5	483.6	1096.3	516.0
53921.9	62253.9	379.1	103901.7	135028.5	33862.1
3706.1	**3706.1**		**3899.9**	**1932.4**	**1.0**

12-14 规模以上工业企业主要经济效益指标（2012年）

行　业	Scetor	总资产贡献率（%）Ratio of Total Assets to Industrial Output Value (%)	资产负债率（%）Assets-Liability Ratio (%)
总计	**Total**	**7.7**	**59.4**
按工业行业大类分	**Grouped by Sector**		
煤炭开采和洗选业	Mining and Washing of Coal		
石油和天然气开采业	Extraction of Petroleum and Natural Gas		
黑色金属矿采选业	Mining and Processing of Ferrous Metal Ores	-15.5	173.5
有色金属矿采选业	Mining and Processing of Non-ferrous Metal Ores		
非金属矿采选业	Mining and Processing of Nonmetal Ores		
开采辅助活动	Mining Auxiliary Activities	3.2	27.6
其他采矿业	Mining of other Ores		
农副食品加工业	Processing of Food from Agricultural Porducts	13.0	63.2
食品制造业	Manufacture of Foods	18.1	47.2
酒、饮料和精制茶制造业	Manufacture of Alcohol,Beverages and Tea	16.2	57.3
烟草制品业	Manufacture of Tobacco	12.0	64.4
纺织业	Manufacture of Textile	3.5	43.7
纺织服装、服饰业	Textile, apparel industry	14.5	76.5
皮革、毛皮、羽毛及其制品和制鞋业	Leather fur feathers and its products and footwear	5.6	46.5
木材加工和木、竹、藤、棕、草制品业	Processing of Timber,Manufacture of Wood,Plam and Straw Products	17.1	49.5
家具制造业	Manufacture of Furniture	9.2	48.6
造纸及纸制品业	Manufacture of Paper and Paper Products	17.6	61.1
印刷和记录媒介复制业	Printing,Reproduction of Recording Media	15.1	41.1
文教、工美、体育和娱乐用品制造业	Manufacture of Articles For Cultural,Educational and Sports Activities	42.0	30.6

Main Indicators of Economic Benefit of Industrial Enterprises above Designated Size (2012)

流动资产周转率（次） Rate of Annual Turnover Working Capitals (times)	成本费用利润率（%） Ratio of Profits to Cost (%)	工业产品销售率（%） Proportion of Industrial Products Sold (%)	产值利税率（%） Ratio of Output Value to Profits and Tax (%)	每百元固定资产实现利税（元） Profit and Tax per 100 yuan of Fixed Assets (yuan)	每百元销售收入实现利税（元） Profit and Tax per 100 yuan of Sales Revenue (yuan)
1.5	**4.5**	**96.7**	**7.9**	**14.3**	**8.5**
1.3	-24.7	98.7	-20.1	-46.9	-24.2
0.9	1.6	101.6	21.5	7.7	9.0
4.1	2.6	94.5	3.7	20.9	4.2
4.2	5.3	94.7	7.5	36.4	8.2
1.9	7.7	110.3	18.2	26.5	16.8
0.6	16.6	107.1	27.5	45.5	23.5
1.7	-0.4	92.6	3.4	7.4	3.6
1.4	7.8	98.7	14.3	88.4	11.8
3.0	3.3	93.2	8.3	20.9	8.1
1.5	7.4	94.4	15.7	19.6	20.0
2.0	4.8	94.1	6.7	23.9	7.9
3.2	7.7	97.4	10.0	33.9	10.0
1.8	14.1	96.3	17.4	21.7	17.9
5.3	15.1	105.5	15.2	70.0	15.4

12-14 续表1

行 业	Scetor	总资产贡献率（%） Ratio of Total Assets to Industrial Output Value (%)	资产负债率（%） Assets-Liability Ratio (%)
石油加工、炼焦和核燃料加工业	Processing of Petroleum, Cokeing,Processing of Nuclear and Nuclear Fuel	21.2	72.9
化学原料和化学制品制造业	Manufacture of Raw Chemical Materials and Chemical Products	6.9	51.4
医药制造业	Manufacture of Medicines	24.0	44.3
化学纤维制造业	Manufacture of Chemical Fibers	24.7	12.8
橡胶和塑料制品业	Manufacture of Rubber and Plastics	9.8	70.5
非金属矿物制品业	Manufacture of Non-metallic Mineral Products	24.8	51.0
黑色金属冶炼和压延加工业	Smelting and Pressing of Ferrous Metals	17.7	69.7
有色金属冶炼和压延加工业	Smelting and Pressing of Non-ferrous Metals	10.2	59.5
金属制品业	Manufacture of Metal Products	5.5	58.6
通用设备制造业	Manufacture of General Purpose Machinery	7.3	59.8
专用设备制造业	Manufacture of Special Equipment	8.5	48.5
汽车制造业	Manufacture of Motor Vehicle	7.3	58.6
铁路、船舶、航空航天和其他运输设备制造业	Railways,Shipbuilding,Aerospace and Other Transportation Equipment Manufacturing Industry	4.3	59.7
电气机械和器材制造业	Manufacture of Electric Equipment and Machinery	5.2	50.2
计算机、通信和其他电子设备制造业	Manufacture of Communication Equipment, Computers and other Electronic Equipment	4.5	61.4
仪器仪表制造业	Manufacture of Measuring Instruments and Machinery	6.2	53.0
其他制造业	Manufacture of Other Manufacturing	12.1	51.6
废弃资源综合利用	Recycling and Disposal of Waste		
金属制品、机械和设备修理业	Metal Products,Machinery and Equipment Repair Industry	14.1	61.3
电力、热力生产和供应业	Production and Supply of Electric Power and Heat Power	5.9	88.8
燃气生产和供应业	Gas Mining and Supplying Industry	8.0	58.3
水的生产和供应业	Production and Supply of Water	5.2	42.9

continued 1

流动资产周转率（次）Rate of Annual Turnover Working Capitals (times)	成本费用利润率（%）Ratio of Profits to Cost (%)	工业产品销售率（%）Proportion of Industrial Products Sold (%)	产值利税率（%）Ratio of Output Value to Profits and Tax (%)	每百元固定资产实现利税（元）Profit and Tax per 100 yuan of Fixed Assets (yuan)	每百元销售收入实现利税（元）Profit and Tax per 100 yuan of Sales Revenue (yuan)
8.2	-2.4	98.4	4.3	36.6	4.7
1.4	5.9	97.7	8.8	9.2	9.5
1.9	9.8	94.6	17.5	60.0	19.9
3.0	19.0	92.8	18.3	26.7	19.9
1.3	7.0	92.2	9.3	28.1	10.6
2.8	11.8	97.5	14.5	43.8	16.0
3.7	5.7	96.3	8.2	32.2	7.9
1.7	5.7	96.6	7.0	20.2	8.6
1.1	4.9	96.1	6.5	11.0	7.2
0.7	9.6	96.8	12.0	40.2	13.4
1.0	8.0	90.0	10.6	24.6	12.2
2.0	3.4	97.6	5.3	17.3	6.7
0.9	4.8	96.7	7.3	11.6	6.5
1.0	3.0	96.1	6.3	16.1	7.5
1.1	4.5	93.1	6.3	10.3	6.1
1.1	5.7	96.9	8.7	14.9	9.1
2.4	4.3	97.4	7.7	28.3	8.2
1.6	4.6	99.2	11.7	137.7	10.3
2.9	-1.3	100.0	3.8	1.8	3.7
1.8	11.6	100.1	13.2	13.3	13.5
1.3	3.0	100.0	10.4	3.4	10.4

主要统计指标解释

工业 指从事自然资源的开采，对采掘品和农产品进行加工和再加工的物质生产部门。具体包括：（1）对自然资源的开采，如采矿、晒盐等（但不包括禽兽捕猎和水产捕捞）；（2）对农副产品的加工、再加工，如粮油加工、食品加工、缫丝、纺织、制革等；（3）对采掘品的加工、再加工，如炼铁、炼钢、化工生产、石油加工、机器制造、木材加工等，以及电力、自来水、煤气的生产和供应等；（4）对工业品的修理、翻新，如机器设备的修理、交通运输工具（如汽车）的修理等。

工业统计调查单位为独立核算法人工业企业。

独立核算法人工业企业指从事工业生产经营活动的单位。独立核算法人工业企业应同时具备以下条件：①依法成立，有自己的名称、组织机构和场所，能够承担民事责任；②独立拥有和使用资产，承担负债，有权与其他单位签订合同；③独立核算盈亏，并能够编制资产负债表。

国有及国有控股企业 指国有企业加上国有控股企业。国有企业（即原全民所有制工业或国营工业）指企业全部资产归国家所有，并按《中华人民共和国企业法人登记管理条例》规定登记注册的非公司制的经济组织。包括国有企业、国有独资公司和国有联营企业。1957年以前的公私合营和私营工业，后均改造为国营工业，1992年改为国有工业，这部分工业的资料不单独分列时，均包括在国有企业内。国有控股企业是对混合所有制经济的企业进行的“国有控股”分类。它是指这些企业的全部资产中国有资产（股份）相对其他所有者中的任何一个所有者占资（股）最多的企业。该分组反映了国有经济控股情况。

本篇涉及的其他企业登记注册类型的解释详见综合篇。

轻工业 指主要提供生活消费品和制作手工工具的工业。按其所使用的原料不同，可分为两大类：（1）以农产品为原料的轻工业，是指直接或间接以农产品为基本原料的轻工业。主要包括食品制造、饮料制造、烟草加工、纺织、缝纫、皮革和毛皮制作、造纸以及印刷等工业；（2）以非农产品为原料的轻工业，是指以工业品为原料的轻工业。主要包括文教体育用品、化学药品制造、合成纤维制造、日用化学制品、日用玻璃制品、日用金属制品、手工工具制造、医疗器械制造、文化和办公用机械制造等工业。

重工业 指为国民经济各部门提供物质技术基础的主要生产资料的工业。按其生产性质和产品用途，可以分为下列三类：（1）采掘（伐）工业，是指对自然资源的开采，包括石油开采、煤炭开采、金属矿开采、非金属矿开采等工业；（2）原材料工业，指向国民经济各部门提供基本材料、动力和燃料的工业。包括金属冶炼及加工、炼焦及焦炭、化学、化工：原料、水泥、人造板以及电力、石油和煤炭加工等工业；（3）加工工业，是指对工业原材料进行再加工制造的工业。包括装备国民经济各部门的机械设备制造工业、金属结构、水泥制品等工业，以及为农业提供的生产资料如化肥、农药等工业。

根据上述划分原则，修理业中以重工业产品为修理作业对象的划为重工业，反之划为轻工业。

工业总产值

（1）定义：

工业总产值是工业企业在一定时期内生产的以货币形式表现的工业最终产品和提供工业性劳务活动的总价值量。它反映一定时间内工业生产的总规模和总水平。

（2）计算原则：

工业生产的原则，即凡是企业在报告期生产的经检验合格的产品，不管是否在报告期销售，均包括在内。

最终产品的原则，即凡是计入工业总产值的产品，必须是本企业生产的经检验合格的，不需要再进行任何加工的最终产品。如果企业有中间产品（半成品）对外销售，则对外销售的中间产品应视为企业的最终产品。

工厂法原则，即工业总产值是以下业企业作为基本计算（核算）单位，即按企业的最终产品计算工业总产值。按这种方法计算的工业总产值，不允许同一产品价值在企业内部重复计算，不能把企业内部各个车间（分厂）生产的成果相加，但允许企业间的重复计算。

（3）内容及计算方法：

1995年全国工业普查对工业总产值（原规定）的内容及计算原则和方法做了某些修订，修订后的工业总产值（新规定）包括三项内容：即本期生产成品价值、对外加工费收入、在制品半成品期末期初差额价值三部分。

本期生产成品价值指企业本期生产，并在报告期内不再进行加工，经检验、包装入库的全部工业成品（半成品）价值合计，包括企业生产的自制设备及提供给本企业在建工程、其他非工业部门和福利部门等单位使用的成品价值。本期生产成品价值为按自备原材料生产的产品的数量乘以本期不含增值税（销项税额）的产品实际销售平均单价计算；会计核算中按成本价格转帐的自制设备和自产自用的成品，按成本价格计算生产成品价值。生产成品价值中不包括用定货者来料加工的成品（半成品）价值。

对外加工费收入指企业在报告期内完成的对外承接的工业品加工（包括用定货者来料加工产品）的加工费收入和对外工业修理作业所取得的加工费收入。对外加工费收入按不含增值税（销项税额）的价格计算，可根据会计“产品销售收入”科目的有关资料取得。

对于本企业对内非工业部门提供的加工修理、设备安装的劳务收入，如果企业会计核算基础较好，能取得这部分资料，而且这部分价值所占比重较大，应包括在对外加工费收入中。

自制半成品在制品期末期初差额价值指企业报告期在制品期末减期初的差额价值，本指标一般可以从会计核算资料中取得。如果会计产品成本核算中不计算半成品、在制品的成本，则总产值中也不包括这部分价值，反之则包括。

（4）工业总产值统计范围变化和计算方法修订情况：

1984年以前工业总产值不包括村办工业，村办工业总产值划归农业。1984年以后工业总产值包括村办正业。

1995年工业普查对工业总产值计算方法做了修订，即从1995年始按新修订（新规定）方法计算工业总产值。新规定与原规定的区别如下：

全价与加工费的计算原则不同：新规定为凡自备原材料，不论其生产繁简程度如何，一律按全价计算工业总产值；凡来料加工，允许按加工费计算工业总产值。原规定则视生产加工的繁简程度不同，规定哪些行业按全价，哪些行业按加工费计算工业总产值。

自制半成品、在产品期末期初差额价值的计算原则不同：新规定要求，凡会计产品成本核算时计算了成本的差额价值，总产值中就应包括，否则可不包括；原规定则按生产周期六个月的界限区分，凡生产周期六个月以上的企业，总产值计算中应包括这部分差额价值，否则可不包括。

计算价格不同：新规定按不含增值税（销项税额）的价格计算；原规定则按含增值税（销项税额）的价格计算。

工业增加值 指工业企业在报告期内以货币表现的工业生产活动的最终成果。

工业增加值有两种计算方法：一是生产法，即工业总产出减去工业中间投入加上应交增值税；二是收入法，即从收入的角度出发，根据生产要素在生产过程中应得到的收入份额计算，具体构成项目有固定资产折旧、劳动者报酬、生产税净额、营业盈余，这种方法也称要素分配法。本年鉴中的工业增加值是以收入法计算的。

生产法工业增加值的计算方法为：

工业增加值＝工业总产出-工业中间投入+应交增值税

（1）工业总产出：指工业企业在一定时期内工业生产活动的总成果。工业总产出包括：成品生产价值，对外加工费收入，自制半成品、在产品期末期初差额价值。1995年后用新规定计算的工业总产值代替。

（2）工业中间投入：指工业企业在工业生产活动中消耗的外购物质产品和对外支付的服务费用。服务费用包括支付给物质生产部门（工业、农业、批发零售贸易业、建筑业、运输邮电业）的服务费用和支付给非物质生产部门（如保险、金融、文化教育、科学研究、医疗卫生、行政管理等）的服务费用。工业中间投入的确定须遵循以下原则：必须从外部购入的，并已计入工业总产出的产品和服务价值；必须是本期投入生产，并一次性消耗掉（包括本期摊销的低值易耗品等）的产品和服务价值。

工业中间投入包括直接材料费用、制造费用中的工业中间投入、管理费用中的工业中间投入、销售费用中的工业中间投入和利息支出五部分。

资产总计 指企业拥有或控制的能以货币计量的经济资源，包括各种财产、债权和其他权利。资产按流动性分为流动资产、长期投资、固定资产、无形资产、递延资产和其他资产。该指标根据企业会计“资产负债表”中“资产总计”项目的期末数增列。

流动资产 指企业可以在一年内或者超过一年的一个生产周期内变现或者耗用的资产，包括现金及各种存款、短期投资，应收及预付款项、存货等。

固定资产原价 指企业在建造、购置、安装、改建、扩建、技术改造某项固定资产时所支出的全部货币总额。它一般包括买价、包装费、运杂费和安装费等。

固定资产净值 指固定资产原价减去历年已提折旧额后的净额。计算公式为：

固定资产净值=固定资产原价-累计折旧

负债合计 指企业所承担的能以货币计量，将以资产或劳务偿付的债务，偿还形式包括货币、资产或提供劳务。负债一般按偿还期长短分为流动负债和长期负债。根据会计“资产负债表”中“负债合计”的年末数填列。

所有者权益合计 指企业投资人对企业净资产的所有权。企业净资产为企业全部资产与企业全部负债的差额，包括实收资本、资本公积、盈余公积、未分配利润等。根据会计“资产负债表”中“所有者权益”项的期末数填列。

主营业务收入 指会计“利润表”中对应指标的本年累计数。未执行2001年《企业会计制度》的企业，用“产品销售收入”的本期累计数代替。

主营业务成本 指会计“利润表”中对应指标的本年累计数。未执行2001年《企业会计制度》的企业，用“产品销售成本”的本期累计数代替。

主营业务税金及附加 指会计“利润表”中对应指标的本年累计数。未执行2001年《企业会计制度》的企业，用“产品销售税金及附加”的本期累计数代替。

利润总额 指企业在生产经营过程中各种收入扣除各种耗费后的盈余，反映企业在报告期内实现的盈亏总额，包括营业利润、补贴收入、投资净收益和营业外收支净额。根据会计“利润表”中的对应指标的本期累计数填列。

本年应交增值税 指企业按税法规定，从事货物销售或提供加工、修理修配劳务等增加货物价值的活动本期应交纳的税金。指企业在报告期应交增值税额。计算公式为：

本年应交增值税=销项税额-（进项税额-进项税额转出）-出口抵减内销产品应纳税额-减免税款+出口退税

本年进项税额 指工业企业在报告期内购入货物或接受应税劳务而支付的、准予从销项税额中抵扣的增值税额。

本年销项税额 指工业企业在报告期内销售货物或提供应税劳务应收取的增值税额。

从业人员平均人数 是指报告期内每天拥有的从业人员人数。其计算公式为：

月平均人数=报告月内每天实有人数之和／报告月日历日数

季平均人数=季内各月平均人数之和／3

年平均人数=年内各月平均人数之和／12

总资产贡献率 反映企业全部资产的获利能力，是企业经营业绩和管理水平的集中体现，是评价和考核企业盈利能力的核心指标。计算公式为：

总资产贡献率（%）=（利润总额+税金总额+利息支出）／平均资金总额×100%

公式中：税金总额为产品销售税金及附加与应交增值税之和；平均资产总额为期初期末资产之和的算术平均值。

资产负债率 该指标既反映企业经营风险的大小，也反映企业利用债权人提供的资金从事经营活动的能力。计算公式为：

资产负债率（%）=负债总额／资产总额×100%

资产与负债均为报告期期末数。

流动资产周转次数 指一定时期内流动资产完成的周转次数，反映投入工业企业流动资金的周转速度。计算公式为：

流动资产周转次数：产品销售收入／全部流动资产平均余额

公式中：全部流动资产平均余额为期初和期末的流动资产之和的算术平均值。

成本费用利润率 反映企业投入的生产成本及费用的经济效益，同时也反映企业降低成本所取得的经济效益。计算公式为：

成本费用利润率（%）=利润总额／成本费用总额×100%

公式中：成本费用总额为产品销售成本、销售费用、管理费用、财务费用之和。

产品销售率 该指标反映工业产品已实现销售的程度，是分析工业产销衔接情况，研究工业产品满足社会需求的指标。计算公式为：

产品销售率（%）=工业销售产值／工业总产值（现价）×100%

Explanatory Notes on Main Statistical Indicators

Industry refers to the material production sector which is engaged in the extraction of natural resources and processing and reprocessing of minerals and agricultural products, including (1) extraction of natural resources, such as mining, salt production (but not including hunting and fishing); (2) processing and reprocessing of farm and sideline produces, such as rice husking, flour milling, wine making, oil pressing, silk reeling, spinning and weaving, and leather making; (3) manufacture of industrial products, such as steel making, iron smelting, chemicals manufacturing, petroleum processing, machine building, timber processing; water and gas production and electricity generation and supply; (4)repairing of industrial products such as the repairing of machinery and means of transport (including cars).

In industrial statistics surveys, the units of enquiry are corporate industrial enterprises with independent accounting systems.

Corporate industrial enterprises with independent accounting systems refer to enterprises engaging in industrial production activities, which meet the following requirements: (1) They are established legally, having their own names, organizations, location and able to take civil liability; (2) They possess and use their assets independently, assume liabilities and are entitled to sign contracts with other units; (3) They are financially independent and compile their own balance sheets.

State–owned and State–holding Enterprises refer to state-owned enterprises plus State-holding enterprises. State-owned enterprises (originally known as State-run enterprises with ownership by the whole society) are non-corporate economic entities registered in accordance with the Regulation of the People's Republic of China on the Management of Registration of Legal Enterprises, where all assets are owned by the State. Included in this category are State-owned enterprises, State-funded corporations and State-owned joint-operation enterprises. Joint State- private industries and private industries, which existed before 1957, were transformed into state-run industries since 1957, and into State-owned industries after 1992. Statistics on those enterprises are included in the State- owned industries instead of being grouped them separately. State-holding enterprises are a sub- classification of enterprises with mixed ownership, referring to enterprises where the percentage of State assets (or shares by the State) is larger than any other single share holder of the same enterprise. This sub- classification illustrates the control of the State over a particular industry.

For explanation of enterprises of other types of registration covered in this chapter, please refer to General Survey.

Light Industry refers to the industry that produces consumer goods and hand tools. It consists of two categories, depending on the materials used:

(1) Industries using farm products as raw materials. These are the branches of light industry which directly or indirectly use farm products as basic raw materials, including the manufacture of food and beverages, tobacco processing, textile, clothing, fur and leather manufacturing, paper making, printing, etc.

(2) Industries using non-farm products as raw materials. These are the branches of light industry which use manufactured goods as raw materials, including the manufacture of cultural, educational articles and sports goods, chemicals, synthetic fibre, chemical products for daily use, glass products for daily use, metal products for daily use, hand tools, medical apparatus and instruments, and the manufacture of cultural and office machinery.

Heavy Industry refers to the industry which produces capital goods, and provides various sectors of the national economy with necessary material and technical basis for production. It consists of the following three branches according to the purpose of production or the use of products:

(1) Mining, quarrying and logging industry, which refers to the industry that extracts natural resources, including extraction of petroleum, coal, metal and non-metal ores.

(2) Raw materials industry refers to the industry that provides various sectors of the national economy with raw materials, fuels and power. It includes smelting and processing of metals, coking and coke chemistry, chemical materials and building materials such as cement, plywood, and power, petroleum refining and coal dressing

(3) Manufacturing industry which refers to the industry that processes raw materials. It includes machine-building industries which equip sectors of the national economy; industries producing metal structure and cement products; and industries producing means of agricultural production, such as chemical fertilizers and pesticides.

In accordance with the above principles of classification, the repairing trades, which are engaged primarily in repairing products of heavy industry, are classified as heavy industry while those which are engaged in repairing products of light industry are classified as light industry.

Gross Industrial Output Value

(1) Definition: Gross industrial output value is the total volume of final industrial products produced and industrial services provided during a given period in monetary terms. It reflects the total achievements and overall scale of industrial production during a given period.

(2) Principles for calculation:

Statistics on industrial production follow the principle that all products produced by the enterprises and accepted through quality check during the reference period are to be included no matter whether they are sold or not during the reference period.

Determination of final products follows the principle that all products that are included in the calculation of gross industrial output value are the final products of the enterprise which have been accepted through quality check and require no further processing. If an enterprise has intermediate (semi-finished) products to sell, these intermediate products are considered as the final products of the enterprise.

Gross industrial output value is calculated following the principle of factory approach, i.e. industrial enterprise is used as the basic accounting unit in calculating the gross industrial output value. By this approach, value of the same product is not to be double-counted, and the output value of different workshops (branch factories) within the enterprise should not be added. However, this approach allows the possibility of double counting between enterprises.

(3) Content and method of calculation: The old definition of gross industrial output value was modified during the 1995 National Industrial Census. The revised (new) definition of gross industrial output value consists of 3 components: value of the finished products during the reference period, income from processing for external parties, and value of change in semi-finished products between the end and the beginning of the reference period.

Value of finished products during the reference period: refers to the value of all finished (semi-finished) industrial products that are produced during the reference period without the need for further processing, checked for acceptance, packed and put into the warehouse of the enterprise, including the value of own-produced equipment and the value of products provided to the projects under construction of the enterprise, and to other non-industrial or welfare units. Value of finished products during the reference period is calculated by the quantity of products produced using own materials multiplied by the average unit prices at which products are sold (excluding value-added tax). Own-produced equipment and products produced for own use are valued at cost prices as in the case of enterprise accounting. Value of finished products does not include the value of finished products (semi-finished products) that are produced using the materials from the clients who place the orders.

Income from external processing: refers to income from contracted external processing of industrial products (including processing of industrial products using materials from the clients), and the income from industrial repairing work provided to other parties. Income from external processing is calculated using information from the item "products sales income" in the enterprise accounting at the prices with value-added tax excluded.

For income from services such as processing, repairing and installation of equipment provided to non- industrial units within the enterprise, if the accounting work of the enterprise is good enough to separate it from other records, and the share of such services is significant, it should also be included in the income from external processing.

Value of change in semi-finished products between the end and the beginning of the reference period: refers to the value of change in semi-finished products between the end and the beginning of the reference period, which generally can be obtained from accounting records of enterprises. If the enterprise accounting excludes the cost of semi-finished products, then it should not be included in the gross industrial output value, and the reverse if otherwise.

(4) Changes in the scope and method of calculation of the gross industrial output value

Prior to 1984, the value of rural industry run by villages was classified into agriculture instead of industry Since 1984, it has been included in the gross industrial output value. Method of calculation for the gross industrial output value was modified in the industriaLcensus in 1995. The difference in the new method as compared with the old one is outlined below:

Principle in using full value vs. processing fee: The new method stipulates that all products produced using own materials are to be calculated with full value in reporting the gross industrial output value irrespective of the complexity of production, and for external processing, it allows calculation using processing fee. In the old method, however, the use of full value or processing fee was determined by the degree of complexity of production in different branches of industries.

Principle in determining the value of change in semi-finished products: The new method requires that value of change in semi-finished products should be included in the gross industrial output value if it is included in the accounting record of the enterprise, otherwise it should not be included. In the old method, it is determined by the type of enterprises in terms of production cycle. If the production cycle is over 6 months, the value of change in semi-finished products is included in the gross industrial output value, otherwise it is not.

Difference in prices: The new method uses prices excluding value-added tax in the calculation of gross industrial output value, while the old method used prices including value-added tax.

Value-added of Industry refers to the final results of industrial production of industrial enterprises in money terms during the reference period.

Industrial value-added can be calculated by two approaches: the production approach, i.e. gross industrial output value minus intermediate input plus value-added tax, and the income approach, i.e. income for various factors used in the course of production, including depreciation of fixed assets, remuneration of labourers, net of production tax, and operating surplus. Value-added of industry in the Yearbook is calculated by the income approach as follows:

Value-added of industry = gross industrial output - industrial intermediate input + value-added tax

(1) Gross industrial output: refers to the total achievements of industrial production activities during a given period. Gross industrial output includes value of finished products, income from external processing, and value of change in semi-finished products between the end and the beginning of the reference period. Since 1995, the gross industrial output value obtained by the new method is used in the calculation.

(2) Industrial intermediate input: refers to purchased goods and paid services consumed during the industrial production of enterprises. Fees paid for services include fees paid for the services provided by material production sectors (industry, agriculture, wholesale and retail trade, construction, transport, post and telecommunications) and by non-material production sectors (insurance, banking, culture, education, scientific research, health and medical care, public administration, etc.). The determination of industrial intermediate input follows the principle that the goods and services must be purchased from outside and included in the gross industrial output, and that the goods and services are inputted into production and consumed (include low-value consumables) during the reference period.

Industrial intermediate input includes 5 components, namely direct consumption of materials, industrial intermediate input in manufacturing cost, industrial intermediate input in management cost, industrial intermediate input in marketing cost and expenditure on interest.

Total Assets refer to all economic resources, in monetary term, these are owned or controlled by enterprises, including properties, creditor's equity and other economic rights of all forms. Classified by the degree of liquidity, total assets include working capitals, long-term investment, fixed assets, intangible assets, deferred assets and other assets. Data on this indicator can be obtained by the year-end figures of total assets in the Assets and Liability Table of accounting records of enterprises.

Working Capital refers to capital that an enterprise can cash or use during one year or one production cycle that may exceed one year, including cash and savings deposits of various forms, short-term investment, money receivable and prepaid money, inventories, etc.

Original Value of Fixed Assets refers to the total value, in monetary terms, that an enterprise spent on fixed assets, through construction, purchase, installation, transformation, expansion or technical upgrading. Generally, it covers cost of purchase, packing, transportation and installation, etc.

Net Value of Fixed Assets refers to the original value of fixed assets minus depreciation over the years, i.e.:

Net value of fixed assets = original value of fixed assets - cumulative depreciation

Total Liabilities refer to payable liabilities of enterprises that have to be repaid in terms of money, assets or labour services. In terms of payment, it can be divided into liquid liabilities and long-term liabilities. Data on this item is obtained from the ending figures on total liabilities from the Assets and Liability Table from the enterprises.

Total Equity refers to the ownership of net assets of enterprise by its investors. Net assets equal total assets minus total liabilities of the enterprise, including the paid-in capital, accumulation of capital and operating surplus and non-distributed profits. Data are obtained from the ending figures on "total equity" from the "balance sheets".

Revenue from Principal Business refers to the annual accumulation of the corresponding item in the "profit table" of the accountant. For enterprises that do not follow the 2001 Enterprise Accounting Standards, the year-end accumulation of revenue from the sales of products is used as a substitute.

Cost of Principal Business refers to the annual accumulation of the corresponding item in the "profit table" of the accountant. For enterprises that do not follow the 2001 Enterprise Accounting Standards, theyear-end accumulation of cost for the sales of products is used as a substitute.

Tax and Extra Charges from Principal Bosiness refer to the annual accumulation of the corresponding item in the "profit table" of the accountant. For enterprises that do not follow the 2001 Enterprise Accounting Standards, the year-end accumulation of tax and extra charges from the sales of products is used as a substitute.

Total Profits refers to the balance of various incomes minus various spendings in the course of operation, reflecting the total profits and losses of enterprises in reporting period. It includes: operating profits, income from subsidies, net investment income and net income from activities other than operation. Data are obtained from the annual accumulation of the corresponding item in the "profit table" of the accountant.

Value-added Tax Payable in the Current Year refers to the payable tax of enterprises which engaged in selling of goods or providing services that bring added value to the goods, such as processing, repairing, fitting and other activities should be paid according to Tax Law. It refers to the amount of the value-added tax which should be paid by the enterprises during the reference period. The formula is as tollows:

Value-added Tax Payable in the Current Year = tax on sales-(tax on purchase-transferred tax on purchase)- exports deduct tax payable on domestic sales-tax relief+the export tax rebate.

Tax on Purchase in Current Year refers to goods purchased by industrial enterprises or value added tax that should be paid but being granted the right to deduct from the tax on sales.

Tax on Sales in Current Year refers to value added tax on industrial enterprises from sales of goods or taxable services that should be charged value added tax.

Average number of employed persons refers to the number of employee everyday during the reference period, calculated with the following formula:

$$\text{Monthly average Number} = \frac{\text{sum of actual employees everyday in reference month}}{\text{number of calendar dates in reference month}}$$

$$\text{Quarterly average number} = \frac{\text{sum of monthly average number in reference quarter}}{3}$$

$$\text{Annual average number} = \frac{\text{sum of monthly average number in reference year}}{12}$$

Ratio of Profits, Taxes and Interests to Average Assets reflects the profit-making capability of all assets of the enterprise and is a key indicator manifesting the performance and management and evaluating the profit-making potential of the enterprise. It is calculated as

$$\text{Ratio of Profits, Taxes and Interests toAverageAssets(\%)} = \frac{\text{otal profits+ total taxes+ interest payment}}{\text{average assets}} \times 100\%$$

In the above formula, total taxes is the sum of tax and extra charges on the sales of products and value-added tax payable; and average assets is the arithmetic mean of the sum of beginning assets and ending assets.

Ratio of Debts to Assets reflects both the operation risk and the capability of the enterprise in making use of the capital from the creditors. It is calculated as follows:

$$\text{Ratio of Debts toAssets(\%)} = \frac{\text{total debts}}{\text{total assets}} \times 100\%$$

Both assets and debts are figures at the end of the reference period.

Turnover of Working Capital refers to the number of times of turnover of working capital in a given period of time, which reflects the speed of the turnover of working capital of industrial enterprises, and is calculated as follows:

$$\text{Turnover of Working Capital} = \frac{\text{sales revenue of products}}{\text{average balance of total working capital}}$$

In the above formula, average balance of total working capital refers to the arithmetic mean of the sum of working capital at the beginning and at the end of the reference period.

Ratio of Profits to Total Industrial Costs refers to the ratio of profits realized in a given period to the total costs in the same period, which reflects the economic efficiency of input cost and is calculated as follows:

$$\text{Ratio of Profits to Total Industrial Cost (\%)} = \frac{\text{total profits}}{\text{total costs}} \times 100\%$$

Total costs in the above formula are the sum of cost of products sold, marketing cost, management cost and financial cost.

Sales Ratio of Products is an indicator reflecting the actual sale of industrial products, analyzing the production-selling and supply-demand relations. It is calculated as:

$$\text{Sales Ratio of Products (\%)} = \frac{\text{value of industrial sales}}{\text{gross industrial output value (current prices)}} \times 100\%$$

13 能 源

ENERGY

资料整理：雷稳强
Data management:Lei Wen Qiang

第十三部分 能源

一、简要说明

本章资料包括规模以上工业能源购销存情况、全市单位GDP能耗、单位GDP电耗、规模以上工业单位增加值能耗、规模以上工业企业用水情况等，由西安市统计局能源处提供。

二、主要指标

规模以上工业综合能源消费量（吨标准煤）	5016252	比上年增长	1.1%
单位GDP能耗（吨标准煤/万元）	0.589	比上年下降	3.51%
单位GDP电耗（千瓦时/万元）	570.64	比上年下降	2.92%
规模以上工业单位增加值能耗（吨标准煤/万元）	0.449	比上年下降	10.52%

13 ENERGY

Ⅰ.Brief Introduction

Data in this chapter reflects energy purchases consumption and inventory of industrial enterprises above designated size,energy consumption per unit of GDP in whole city,electricity consumption per unit of GDP,energy consumption per unit of industrial value-added above designated size and statistics on water use of industrial enterprises above designated size. data in this chapter are provided and compiled by Energy Division ransportation Division of the Xi'an Bureau of Statistics.

Ⅱ.Major Indicators

		Increase over Preceding Year
Comprehensive Energy Consumption Above Designated Size(Tons of Standard Coal)	5016252	1.1%
Energy Consumption of GDP per Unit (Tons of Standard Coal /10 000 yuan)	0.589	-3.51%
Electricity Power Consumption of GDP per Unit (kilowatt-hour/10 000 yuan)	570.64	-2.92%
Energy Consumption of value added per Unit of Industrial Enterprises Above Designated Size (Tons of Standard Coal/10 000 yuan)	0.449	-10.52%

13-1 主要年份全市及各区县单位GDP能耗

Energy Consumption per Unit of GDP by City (District)

单位：吨标准煤 / 万元 (ton of SCE/10 000 yuan)

地区	Region	单位GDP能耗 Energy Consumption Per Unit of GDP								
		GDP按2005年价格计算 GDP are calculated at 2005 constant prices						GDP按2010年价格计算 GDP are calculated at 2010 constant prices		
		2005	2006	2007	2008	2009	2010	2010	2011	2012
西安市	**Xi'an**	**1.030**	**0.987**	**0.930**	**0.869**	**0.820**	**0.803**	**0.633**	**0.610**	**0.589**
新城区	Xincheng	0.828	0.794	0.749	0.705	0.664	0.656	0.524	0.506	0.488
碑林区	Beilin	0.801	0.768	0.726	0.685	0.644	0.639	0.454	0.437	0.421
莲湖区	Lianhu	0.942	0.904	0.862	0.794	0.749	0.722	0.543	0.522	0.503
灞桥区	Baqiao	1.803	1.757	1.648	1.545	1.456	1.394	0.819	0.788	0.759
未央区	Weiyang	1.026	0.985	0.932	0.870	0.817	0.806	0.678	0.654	0.634
雁塔区	Yanta	0.929	0.885	0.835	0.787	0.739	0.708	0.541	0.522	0.506
阎良区	Yanliang	0.831	0.783	0.745	0.700	0.661	0.644	0.516	0.499	0.481
临潼区	Lintong	1.035	1.004	0.946	0.869	0.829	0.789	0.597	0.576	0.556
长安区	Chang'an	1.339	1.257	1.187	1.125	1.063	1.041	0.634	0.611	0.589
蓝田县	Lantian	1.698	1.645	1.579	1.492	1.420	1.446	1.228	1.186	1.146
周至县	Zhouzhi	1.831	1.786	1.689	1.596	1.508	1.464	1.120	1.083	1.047
户　县	Huxian	2.532	2.454	2.311	2.133	2.015	1.978	1.307	1.257	1.211
高陵县	Gaoling	0.953	0.907	0.845	0.798	0.753	0.725	0.567	0.545	0.525

13-1 续表

Continued

地区	Region	比上年增长(%) Growth Rates over Preceding Year(%)						
		2006	2007	2008	2009	2010	2011	2012
西安市	**Xi'an**	**-4.15**	**-5.75**	**-6.65**	**-5.56**	**-2.06**	**-3.56**	**-3.51**
新城区	Xincheng	-4.15	-5.67	-5.79	-5.80	-1.15	-3.51	-3.50
碑林区	Beilin	-4.18	-5.44	-5.65	-5.95	-0.91	-3.89	-3.50
莲湖区	Lianhu	-4.07	-4.60	-7.93	-5.65	-3.58	-3.84	-3.60
灞桥区	Baqiao	-2.54	-6.20	-6.24	-5.80	-4.20	-3.81	-3.62
未央区	Weiyang	-3.97	-5.44	-6.63	-6.05	-1.31	-3.60	-3.60
雁塔区	Yanta	-4.71	-5.64	-5.80	-6.08	-4.18	-3.61	-3.61
阎良区	Yanliang	-5.77	-4.80	-6.08	-5.62	-0.61	-3.38	-3.50
临潼区	Lintong	-3.03	-5.73	-8.16	-4.58	-4.81	-3.52	-3.51
长安区	Chang'an	-6.15	-5.53	-5.22	-5.50	-2.08	-3.60	-3.63
蓝田县	Lantian	-3.13	-4.01	-5.50	-4.84	-2.06	-3.39	-3.40
周至县	Zhouzhi	-2.46	-5.43	-5.51	-5.50	-2.06	-3.30	-3.30
户　县	Huxian	-3.07	-5.85	-7.70	-5.50	-2.99	-3.85	-3.60
高陵县	Gaoling	-4.85	-6.85	-5.50	-5.70	-3.82	-3.93	-3.52

13-2 主要年份全市及各区县单位GDP电耗

Electricity Consumption per Unit of GDP by City and District

单位：千瓦时 / 万元 (kw. h/10 000 yuan)

地 区	Region	单位GDP电耗 Energy Consumption Per Unit of GDP								
		GDP按2005年价格计算 GDP are calculated at 2005 constant prices						GDP按2010年价格计算 GDP are calculated at 2010 constant prices		
		2005	2006	2007	2008	2009	2010	2010	2011	2012
西安市	**Xi'an**	**963.34**	**920.19**	**856.29**	**796.92**	**754.45**	**761.98**	**615.07**	**587.77**	**570.64**
新城区	Xincheng	740.68	714.54	624.76	590.40	544.38	529.86	450.10	417.16	385.27
碑林区	Beilin	578.78	557.34	536.48	520.04	477.09	469.01	376.07	337.21	318.44
莲湖区	Lianhu	735.51	697.56	677.92	635.02	590.14	567.40	489.95	451.03	423.38
灞桥区	Baqiao	1606.69	1534.34	1483.26	1367.56	1275.24	1309.49	968.39	895.00	822.64
未央区	Weiyang	1112.49	1055.75	1007.35	936.19	940.23	921.64	723.10	686.76	690.61
雁塔区	Yanta	1043.36	998.03	871.48	814.97	776.04	827.95	684.87	654.82	631.32
阎良区	Yanliang	632.75	620.65	574.19	535.33	517.29	497.13	398.54	398.71	377.18
临潼区	Lintong	1019.71	997.91	952.62	878.57	792.07	780.29	601.65	587.27	561.04
长安区	Chang'an	1055.34	996.57	910.94	844.84	774.85	797.92	590.44	621.09	609.14
蓝田县	Lantian	1135.17	1104.82	1087.11	1010.23	992.80	1031.64	754.15	684.77	604.04
周至县	Zhouzhi	815.19	788.52	756.79	714.80	709.39	688.20	537.35	607.54	684.76
户 县	Huxian	848.39	824.19	810.60	773.10	742.15	769.32	636.22	628.20	586.37
高陵县	Gaoling	1065.50	972.08	828.71	726.45	638.98	651.46	509.28	438.84	384.44

注：GDP为第二次经济普查调整后数据。

13-2 续表

Continued

地 区	Region	比上年增长(%) Growth Rates over Preceding Year(%)						
		2006	2007	2008	2009	2010	2011	2012
西安市	**Xi'an**	**-4.48**	**-6.94**	**-6.93**	**-5.33**	**1.00**	**-4.43**	**-2.92**
新城区	Xincheng	-3.53	-12.57	-5.50	-7.80	-2.67	-7.32	-7.65
碑林区	Beilin	-3.70	-3.74	-3.06	-8.26	-1.69	-10.33	-5.57
莲湖区	Lianhu	-5.16	-2.82	-6.33	-7.07	-3.85	-7.94	-6.13
灞桥区	Baqiao	-4.50	-3.33	-7.80	-6.75	2.69	-7.58	-8.08
未央区	Weiyang	-5.10	-4.59	-7.06	0.43	-1.98	-5.03	0.08
雁塔区	Yanta	-4.34	-12.68	-6.49	-4.78	6.69	-4.39	-4.16
阎良区	Yanliang	-1.91	-7.49	-6.77	-3.37	-3.90	0.04	-5.40
临潼区	Lintong	-2.14	-4.54	-7.77	-9.85	-1.49	-2.39	-4.47
长安区	Chang'an	-5.57	-8.59	-7.26	-8.28	2.98	5.19	-1.92
蓝田县	Lantian	-2.67	-1.60	-7.07	-1.73	3.91	-9.20	-11.79
周至县	Zhouzhi	-3.27	-4.02	-5.55	-0.76	-2.99	13.06	12.71
户 县	Huxian	-2.85	-1.65	-4.63	-4.00	3.66	-1.26	-6.66
高陵县	Gaoling	-8.77	-14.75	-12.34	-12.04	1.95	-13.83	-12.40

13-3 主要年份全市及各区县规模以上工业企业单位工业增加值能耗

Energy Consumption Per Unit of Industrial Value Added above Designated Size by City and District

单位：吨标准煤 / 万元 (ton of SCE/10 000 yuan)

地 区	Region	单位工业增加值能耗 Energy Consumption Per Unit of Industrial Value Added								
		工业增加值按2005年价格计算 VAI are calculated at 2005 constant prices						工业增加值按2010年价格计算 VAI are calculated at 2010 constant prices		
		2005	2006	2007	2008	2009	2010	2010	2011	2012
西安市	**Xi'an**	**1.220**	**1.100**	**1.092**	**0.915**	**0.800**	**0.703**	**0.593**	**0.502**	**0.449**
新城区	Xincheng	0.822	0.798	0.716	0.663	0.420	0.379	0.329	0.361	0.338
碑林区	Beilin	0.876	0.846	0.782	0.763	0.293	0.246	0.115	0.073	0.067
莲湖区	Lianhu	0.861	0.832	0.775	0.639	0.269	0.232	0.226	0.207	0.191
灞桥区	Baqiao	3.029	2.871	2.446	2.078	2.072	2.032	1.447	1.106	1.074
未央区	Weiyang	1.030	1.000	0.876	0.770	1.008	0.936	0.786	0.651	0.675
雁塔区	Yanta	1.358	1.308	1.123	1.000	0.578	0.414	0.359	0.341	0.242
阎良区	Yanliang	0.876	0.849	0.761	0.625	0.354	0.271	0.255	0.209	0.194
临潼区	Lintong	1.031	0.992	0.882	0.715	0.644	0.371	0.203	0.166	0.140
长安区	Chang'an	1.370	1.300	1.208	1.087	0.725	0.698	0.366	0.323	0.183
蓝田县	Lantian	2.579	2.515	2.133	2.084	3.670	3.487	2.534	2.087	1.484
周至县	Zhouzhi	1.946	1.900	1.891	1.842	0.364	0.336	0.257	0.237	0.202
户 县	Huxian	7.467	7.168	5.857	4.910	4.514	4.036	3.570	3.135	2.974
高陵县	Gaoling	0.966	0.905	0.719	0.693	0.239	0.221	0.223	0.189	0.169

注：本表2005—2010年(工业增加值按2005年价格)统计范围为主营业务收入500万元及以上的法人工业企业；2010—2011年(工业增加值按2010年价格)统计范围为主营业务收入2000万元及以上的法人工业企业。
能源消耗按当量值计算。

13-3 续表

Continued

地 区	Region	比上年增长(%) Growth Rates over Preceding Year(%)						
		2006	2007	2008	2009	2010	2011	2012
西安市	**Xi'an**	**-3.04**	**-12.56**	**-13.43**	**-10.48**	**-12.18**	**-15.44**	**-10.52**
新城区	Xincheng	-2.92	-10.26	-7.38	-2.68	-9.69	9.68	-6.44
碑林区	Beilin	-3.42	-7.59	-2.45	-0.44	-15.89	-36.63	-8.39
莲湖区	Lianhu	-3.47	-6.91	-17.61	0.89	-13.63	-8.19	-8.02
灞桥区	Baqiao	-5.22	-14.79	-15.04	0.29	-1.92	-23.61	-2.90
未央区	Weiyang	-2.91	-10.63	-12.15	-15.20	-7.18	-17.17	3.64
雁塔区	Yanta	-3.68	-14.14	-10.98	-13.98	-28.43	-4.88	-28.97
阎良区	Yanliang	-3.05	-10.42	-17.83	-18.36	-23.44	-18.11	-6.88
临潼区	Lintong	-3.82	-11.06	-18.99	3.05	-42.41	-18.32	-15.27
长安区	Chang'an	-5.11	-4.06	-10.05	-18.68	-3.67	-11.88	-43.40
蓝田县	Lantian	-2.48	-15.18	-2.29	-3.39	-5.00	-17.63	-28.90
周至县	Zhouzhi	-2.38	-0.48	-2.62	-12.27	-7.71	-7.56	-14.72
户 县	Huxian	-4.01	-18.29	-16.17	-18.48	-10.58	-12.19	-5.13
高陵县	Gaoling	-6.32	-20.52	-3.56	-18.90	-7.65	-15.26	-10.91

13-4 主要年份全社会用电量

Electricity Consumption of the Whole Society in Representative Years

单位：万千瓦时 (10 000 kw. h)

行业	Scetor	2000	2007	2008	2009	2010	2011	2012
总计	**Total**	**732373**	**1482896**	**1605089**	**1724067**	**1993751**	**2167453**	**2352571**
行业用电量合计	Total of Industry of Electricity	599855	1215799	1293574	1358483	1499903	1590486	1706859
按产业分	**Grouped by Sector**							
1. 第一产业	Primary Industry	77579	120134	127054	99083	108720	117984	109086
2. 第二产业	Secondary Industry	354245	700026	724852	766029	883259	910360	932622
3. 第三产业	Tertiary Industry	168031	395639	441668	493371	507924	562142	665151
按国民经济行业分	**Grouped by Industry**							
一、农、林、牧、渔、水利业	Agriculture ,Forestry,Animal Husbandry and Fishery	77579	120134	127054	99083	108720	117984	109086
二、工业	Industry	345175	674990	696291	724920	838317	859796	875018
1. 轻工业	Light Industry	152125	187323	182176	167144	177362	183766	175392
2. 重工业	Heavy Industry	193050	487667	514115	557776	660955	676030	699626
三、信息传输、计算机服务和软件业	Information Transmission,Computer Service and Software		21938	26680	29328	30760	33191	37444
四、建筑业	Construction	9070	25036	28561	41108	44942	50564	57605
五、交通运输、仓储及邮政业	Traffic,Transport, Storage and Post	22904	53825	56614	62031	58509	66684	69633
六、公共事业及管理组织	Public Utilities and Management Organization		144859	165024	177409	154074	164473	207271
七、商业、住宿和餐饮业	Commercial,Hotels and Catering Services		107343	111676	122203	148418	166558	199970
八、金融、房地产、商务及居民服务业	Finance,Real Estate,Business Affairs and Households Services		67674	81674	102400	116163	131236	150832
九、城乡居民生活用电	Electricity Consumption of Urban and Rural Residents	132518	267097	311515	365585	493848	576966	645713
1. 乡村	Rural	31281	38395	63072	99941	142059	169898	197937
2. 城市	City	101237	228702	248443	265644	351789	407068	447776

13-5 规模以上工业企业能源购进、消费及库存(2012年)

Energy Purchases Consumption and Inventory of Industrial Enterprises above Designated size (2012)

能源名称	Name(unit)	年初库存量 Stock (year-beginning)	购进量 Purchases 实物量 Quantity	金额(万元) Sum (10 000 yuan)
原煤(吨)	Raw Coal (ton)	559667	7489410	428301
洗精煤(吨)	Washed Coal(ton)	135	1348	81
其他洗煤(吨)	Other Washed Coals(ton)			
煤制品（吨）	Briquettes(ton)	411	7572	514
焦炭(吨)	Coke(ton)	891	9380	1867
其他焦化产品(吨)	Other Coking Products(ton)	2100	3000	550
焦炉煤气（万立方米）	Other Gases(10 000cu.m)			
天然气（气态）（万立方米）	Natural Gas(10 000cu.m)		16862	35656
液化天然气（液态）(吨)	Liquefied Natural Gas (Liquid)(ton)		12	8
原油(吨)	Crude Oil(ton)	66797	2150440	1214999
汽油(吨)	Gasoline(ton)	529	24103	20611
煤油(吨)	Kerosene(ton)	422	13757	10867
柴油(吨)	Diesel Oil(ton)	1323	54513	43684
燃料油(吨)	Fuel Oil(ton)	96	699	407
液化石油气(吨)	LPG(ton)		560	385
其它石油制品(吨)	Other Petroleum Products(ton)	48	3164	3553
热力(百万千焦)	Heat (1 million kilo-joule)		7476860	41526
电力(万千瓦时)	Electricity(10 000kwh)		595742	405470
其他燃料（吨标准煤）	Other Fuels(ton of SCE)	30	2160	873
能源合计(吨标准煤)	Total Energy(ton of SCE)			

13-5 续表 Continued

能源名称	Name(unit)	消费量 Consumption 合计 Total	工业生产消费 Industrial Production Consume	用于原材料 as Raw Material	非工业生产消费 Non-industrial Production Consume	年末库存 Stock (year-end)
原煤(吨)	Raw Coal (ton)	7512882	7412204	7512	100678	531786
洗精煤(吨)	Washed Coal(ton)	1336	1216		120	147
其他洗煤(吨)	Other Washed Coals(ton)					
煤制品（吨）	Briquettes(ton)	7289	6433		856	694
焦炭(吨)	Coke(ton)	9561	9561	750		710
其他焦化产品(吨)	Other Coking Products(ton)	4065	4065			1035
焦炉煤气（万立方米）	Other Gases(10 000cu.m)					
天然气（气态）（万立方米）	Natural Gas(10 000cu.m)	16883	16096		787	
液化天然气（液态）(吨)	Liquefied Natural Gas (Liquid)(ton)	12			12	
原油(吨)	Crude Oil(ton)	2174699	2174699			42538
汽油(吨)	Gasoline(ton)	24323	19883	289	4439	437
煤油(吨)	Kerosene(ton)	13218	13196		22	961
柴油(吨)	Diesel Oil(ton)	54390	52789	1076	1602	1424
燃料油(吨)	Fuel Oil(ton)	683	683			36
液化石油气(吨)	LPG(ton)	560	555		5	
其它石油制品(吨)	Other Petroleum Products(ton)	3168	3168			44
热力(百万千焦)	Heat (1 million kilo-joule)	11944800	10785851		1158949	
电力(万千瓦时)	Electricity(10 000kwh)	686064	668209		17855	
其他燃料（吨标准煤）	Other Fuels(ton of SCE)	2170	2170			20
能源合计(吨标准煤)	Total Energy(ton of SCE)	9913115	9758184		154931	

13-6 规模以上工业企业分行业主要能源品种消费量（2012年）

Major Energy Consumption above Designated Size by Sector (2012)

行业	Sector	原煤（吨）Raw Coal (ton)	天然气（万立方米）Natural Gas(10 000 cu.m)	原油（吨）Crude Oil (ton)
总计	**Total**	**7512882**	**16883**	**2174699**
煤炭开采和洗选业	Coal Mining and Dressing			
石油和天然气开采业	Petroleum and Natural Gas Extraction			
黑色金属矿采选业	Ferrous Metals Mining and Dressing			
有色金属矿采选业	Nonferrous Metals Mining and Dressing			
非金属矿采选业	Nonmetal Minerals Mining and Dressing			
开采辅助活动	Ancillary activities for mining	405	146	
其他采矿业	Other Mining Industry			
农副食品加工业	Agricultural Products and Non-stable Food Processing Industry	331011		
食品制造业	Food Production	79931	189	
酒、饮料和精制茶制造业	Wine, soft drinks and refined tea industry	124196	247	
烟草制品业	Tobacco Processing	8		
纺织业	Textile Industry	797		
纺织服装、服饰业	Textile, apparel industry		1	
皮革、毛皮、羽毛及其制品和制鞋业	Leather, Fur, Feather (eiderdown) and Their Products Industry			
木材加工和木、竹、藤、棕、草制品业	Timber Processing,Bamboo,Cane,Palm Fiber and Straw Products	5530		
家具制造业	Furniture Manufacturing	1		
造纸及纸制品业	Papermaking and Paper products	118388		
印刷和记录媒介复制业	Printing,Record Medium Reproduction	416	216	
文教、工美、体育和娱乐用品制造业	Culture, education, Craft art, sports and entertainment goods manufacturing industry			
石油加工、炼焦和核燃料加工业	Petroleum Refining, Ccoke Making and Nuclear Fuel Processing Industry	45548	95	2174699
化学原料和化学制品制造业	Raw Chemical Materials and Chemical Products	87181	470	
医药制造业	Medical and Pharmaceutical Products	54401	550	
化学纤维制造业	Chemical Fiber			
橡胶和塑料制品业	Rubber and plastic products industry	99336	4	
非金属矿物制品业	Nonmetal Mineral Products	290075	31	
黑色金属冶炼和压延加工业	Smelting and Pressing of Ferrous Metals	15307	4234	
有色金属冶炼和压延加工业	Smelting and Pressing of Nonferrou Metals	2524	754	
金属制品业	Metal Products	62278	470	
通用设备制造业	General Equipment Manufacturing Industry	8884	166	
专用设备制造业	Automotive Manufacturing	24658	498	
汽车制造业	Special Purpose Equipment	58242	4326	
铁路、船舶、航空航天和其他运输设备制造业	Railroad, marine, aerospace and other transportation equipment manufacturing	238448	1109	
电气机械和器材制造业	Electric Equipment and Machinery	19135	1985	
计算机、通信和其他电子设备制造业	Communication Equipment, Computer and Other Electronic Equipment Manufacturing Industry	2869	689	
仪器仪表制造业	Instrument manufacturing industry	536	192	
其他制造业	Other manufacturing	367		
废弃资源综合利用	Comprehensive utilization of waste resources			
金属制品、机械和设备修理业	Metal products, machinery and equipment repair industry			
电力、热力生产和供应业	Electric Power, Heating Power Generating and Supplying Industry	5842408	1	
燃气生产和供应业	Gas Mining and Supplying Industry		244	
水的生产和供应业	Water Processing and Supplying Industry		264	

13-6 续表 Continued

行 业	Sector	汽油（吨） Gasoline (ton)	柴油（吨） Diesel Oil (ton)	热能（百万千焦） Heat (million kilo joule)	电力（万千瓦时） Electricity (10 000 kwh)
总 计	**Total**	**24323**	**54390**	**11944800**	**686064**
煤炭开采和洗选业	Coal Mining and Dressing				
石油和天然气开采业	Petroleum and Natural Gas Extraction				
黑色金属矿采选业	Ferrous Metals Mining and Dressing				70
有色金属矿采选业	Nonferrous Metals Mining and Dressing				
非金属矿采选业	Nonmetal Minerals Mining and Dressing				
开采辅助活动	Ancillary activities for mining	134	1105		519
其他采矿业	Other Mining Industry				
农副食品加工业	Agricultural Products and Non-stable Food Processing Industry	1077	1161	2524770	29131
食品制造业	Food Production	1025	628	359958	15666
酒、饮料和精制茶制造业	Wine, soft drinks and refined tea industry	272	437	514282	20159
烟草制品业	Tobacco Processing	23		10512	192
纺织业	Textile Industry	49	11	391006	26589
纺织服装、服饰业	Textile, apparel industry	100	1		1239
皮革、毛皮、羽毛及其制品和制鞋业	Leather, Fur, Feather (eiderdown) and Their Products Industry	39		16010	198
木材加工和木、竹、藤、棕、草制品业	Timber Processing,Bamboo,Cane,Palm Fiber and Straw Products	84			5893
家具制造业	Furniture Manufacturing	161	145		1442
造纸及纸制品业	Papermaking and Paper products	213	71	885106	12527
印刷和记录媒介复制业	Printing,Record Medium Reproduction	528	79	86911	9248
文教、工美、体育和娱乐用品制造业	Culture, education, Craft art, sports and entertainment goods manufacturing industry	23	7		531
石油加工、炼焦和核燃料加工业	Petroleum Refining, Ccoke Making and Nuclear Fuel Processing Industry	150	59		35228
化学原料和化学制品制造业	Raw Chemical Materials and Chemical Products	559	503	832173	23179
医药制造业	Medical and Pharmaceutical Products	1324	98	177506	13833
化学纤维制造业	Chemical Fiber	18	10	734717	3199
橡胶和塑料制品业	Rubber and plastic products industry	278	2023	3356	19795
非金属矿物制品业	Nonmetal Mineral Products	1201	24266	67701	49545
黑色金属冶炼和压延加工业	Smelting and Pressing of Ferrous Metals	371	102	4119	24220
有色金属冶炼和压延加工业	Smelting and Pressing of Nonferrou Metals	435	243	207584	32266
金属制品业	Metal Products	1179	350	1038009	20716
通用设备制造业	General Equipment Manufacturing Industry	893	265	14420	9684
专用设备制造业	Automotive Manufacturing	3479	2152	91936	20083
汽车制造业	Special Purpose Equipment	3642	8447	672503	86621
铁路、船舶、航空航天和其他运输设备制造业	Railroad, marine, aerospace and other transportation equipment manufacturing	2401	3611	508431	50310
电气机械和器材制造业	Electric Equipment and Machinery	1615	878	1116311	40285
计算机、通信和其他电子设备制造业	Communication Equipment, Computer and Other Electronic Equipment Manufacturing Industry	579	139	647724	35165
仪器仪表制造业	Instrument manufacturing industry	1420	5242	183456	6199
其他制造业	Other manufacturing	26	191		397
废弃资源综合利用	Comprehensive utilization of waste resources				
金属制品、机械和设备修理业	Metal products, machinery and equipment repair industry	76			106
电力、热力生产和供应业	Electric Power, Heating Power Generating and Supplying Industry	117	2061	856300	80559
燃气生产和供应业	Gas Mining and Supplying Industry	585	87		3357
水的生产和供应业	Water Processing and Supplying Industry	247	17		7915

13-7 规模以上工业企业分行业综合能源消费量（2012年）

Comprehensive Energy Consumption by Sector above Designated Size (2012)

单位：吨标准煤 (ton of SCE)

行　业	Scetor	2012	比上年增长（%）Increase over Preceding Year (%)
总　计	**Total**	**5016252**	**1.1**
煤炭开采和洗选业	Coal Mining and Dressing		
石油和天然气开采业	Petroleum and Natural Gas Extraction		
黑色金属矿采选业	Ferrous Metals Mining and Dressing	86	-15.7
有色金属矿采选业	Nonferrous Metals Mining and Dressing		
非金属矿采选业	Nonmetal Minerals Mining and Dressing		
开采辅助活动	Ancillary activities for mining	86785	-5.1
其他采矿业	Other Mining Industry		
农副食品加工业	Agricultural Products and Non-stable Food Processing Industry	263259	23.7
食品制造业	Food Production	95262	21.9
酒、饮料和精制茶制造业	Wine, soft drinks and refined tea industry	134506	7.1
烟草制品业	Tobacco Processing	485	-10.4
纺织业	Textile Industry	42671	-16.7
纺织服装、服饰业	Textile, apparel industry	1597	0.9
皮革、毛皮、羽毛及其制品和制鞋业	Leather, Fur, Feather (eiderdown) and Their Products Industry	846	4.9
木材加工和木、竹、藤、棕、草制品业	Timber Processing,Bamboo,Cane,Palm Fiber and Straw Products	10955	-1.3
家具制造业	Furniture Manufacturing	2220	43.2
造纸及纸制品业	Papermaking and Paper products	97947	-55.4
印刷和记录媒介复制业	Printing,Record Medium Reproduction	18278	17.7
文教、工美、体育和娱乐用品制造业	Culture, education, Craft art, sports and entertainment goods manufacturing industry	775	-23.8
石油加工、炼焦和核燃料加工业	Petroleum Refining, Ccoke Making and Nuclear Fuel Processing Industry	399654	44.8
化学原料和化学制品制造业	Raw Chemical Materials and Chemical Products	115203	-34.7
医药制造业	Medical and Pharmaceutical Products	69538	-0.1
化学纤维制造业	Chemical Fiber	29027	9.2
橡胶和塑料制品业	Rubber and plastic products industry	56084	-12.9
非金属矿物制品业	Nonmetal Mineral Products	300941	-12.1
黑色金属冶炼和压延加工业	Smelting and Pressing of Ferrous Metals	107296	-4.8
有色金属冶炼和压延加工业	Smelting and Pressing of Nonferrou Metals	60815	2.7
金属制品业	Metal Products	97792	3.4
通用设备制造业	General Equipment Manufacturing Industry	18794	3.1
专用设备制造业	Automotive Manufacturing	57587	-6.7
汽车制造业	Special Purpose Equipment	206929	0.3
铁路、船舶、航空航天和其他运输设备制造业	Railroad, marine, aerospace and other transportation equipment manufacturing	218321	-1
电气机械和器材制造业	Electric Equipment and Machinery	131031	6.8
计算机、通信和其他电子设备制造业	Communication Equipment, Computer and Other Electronic Equipment Manufacturing Industry	56888	24.1
仪器仪表制造业	Instrument manufacturing industry	24691	16.3
其他制造业	Other manufacturing	1067	70.8
废弃资源综合利用	Comprehensive utilization of waste resources		
金属制品、机械和设备修理业	Metal products, machinery and equipment repair industry	224	203.3
电力、热力生产和供应业	Electric Power, Heating Power Generating and Supplying Industry	2288964	3.4
燃气生产和供应业	Gas Mining and Supplying Industry	8346	17.1
水的生产和供应业	Water Processing and Supplying Industry	11388	7.5

13-8 规模以上工业企业用水情况(2012年)

Statistics on Water Use of Industrial Enterprises above Designated Size (2012)

指　标	Item	取水量（万立方米）Water Use (10 000 cu. m)	支付费用的取水量（万立方米）Paid WaterUse (10 000 cu. m)	取水支付金额（万元）Money Paid for Water Use (10 000 yuan)	外供水量（万立方米）Outward Water Supply (10 000 cu. m)
合　计	**Total**	**63172**	**53041**	**78623**	**43076**
1. 陆地地表水	Surface Water	34687	34614	26518	33
其中：陆地湖咸水	Land lake Salt water	898	898	1167	
2. 地下水	Ground-water	16564	8606	22702	448
其中：地下咸水	Ground-Salt water	1250	1240	3038	
3. 自来水	Tap Water	10747	8684	28049	42595
4. 其他水	Other Water	1174	1137	1354	
其中：雨水收集利用	Rain Water Collected				
海水淡化水					
再生水(中水)	Reclaimed Water	1147	1111	1055	

13-9 规模以上工业企业分行业用水情况（2012年）

Volume of Water Use of Industrial Enterprises above Designated Size by Sector (2012)

行 业	Sector	取水量（万立方米）Water Use (10 000 cu. m)	支付费用的取水量 Paid Water Use
总 计	**Total**	**63172**	**53041**
煤炭开采和洗选业	Coal Mining and Dressing		
石油和天然气开采业	Petroleum and Natural Gas Extraction	7519	7519
黑色金属矿采选业	Ferrous Metals Mining and Dressing	13	
有色金属矿采选业	Nonferrous Metals Mining and Dressing		
非金属矿采选业	Nonmetal Minerals Mining and Dressing		
开采辅助活动	Ancillary activities for mining	1239	1239
其他采矿业	Other Mining Industry		
农副食品加工业	Agricultural Products and Non-stable Food Processing Industry	231	218
食品制造业	Food Production	458	341
酒、饮料和精制茶制造业	Wine, soft drinks and refined tea industry	986	708
烟草制品业	Tobacco Processing	95	88
纺织业	Textile Industry	137	137
纺织服装、服饰业	Textile, apparel industry	14	14
皮革、毛皮、羽毛及其制品和制鞋业	Leather, Fur, Feather (eiderdown) and Their Products Industry	1	1
木材加工和木、竹、藤、棕、草制品业	Timber Processing,Bamboo,Cane,Palm Fiber and Straw Products	1	1
家具制造业	Furniture Manufacturing	3	3
造纸及纸制品业	Papermaking and Paper products	611	548
印刷和记录媒介复制业	Printing,Record Medium Reproduction	65	65
文教、工美、体育和娱乐用品制造业	Culture, education, Craft art, sports and entertainment goods manufacturing industry	2	1
石油加工、炼焦和核燃料加工业	Petroleum Refining, Ccoke Making and Nuclear Fuel Processing Industry	198	178
化学原料和化学制品制造业	Raw Chemical Materials and Chemical Products	681	521
医药制造业	Medical and Pharmaceutical Products	491	490
化学纤维制造业	Chemical Fiber	34	34
橡胶和塑料制品业	Rubber and plastic products industry	139	138
非金属矿物制品业	Nonmetal Mineral Products	258	121
黑色金属冶炼和压延加工业	Smelting and Pressing of Ferrous Metals	38	32
有色金属冶炼和压延加工业	Smelting and Pressing of Nonferrou Metals	151	150
金属制品业	Metal Products	27	24
通用设备制造业	General Equipment Manufacturing Industry	82	70
专用设备制造业	Automotive Manufacturing	255	205
汽车制造业	Special Purpose Equipment	1025	974
铁路、船舶、航空航天和其他运输设备制造业	Railroad, marine, aerospace and other transportation equipment manufacturing	784	783
电气机械和器材制造业	Electric Equipment and Machinery	612	609
计算机、通信和其他电子设备制造业	Communication Equipment, Computer and Other Electronic Equipment Manufacturing Industry	271	271
仪器仪表制造业	Instrument manufacturing industry	187	186
其他制造业	Other manufacturing	42	41
废弃资源综合利用	Comprehensive utilization of waste resources		
金属制品、机械和设备修理业	Metal products, machinery and equipment repair industry	1	1
电力、热力生产和供应业	Electric Power, Heating Power Generating and Supplying Industry	3341	3336
燃气生产和供应业	Gas Mining and Supplying Industry	17	9
水的生产和供应业	Water Processing and Supplying Industry	43165	33986

13-9 续表 Continued

行 业	Sector	取水支付金额（万元）Maney Paid for Water Use (10 000 yuan)	外供水量（万立方米）Outward Water Supply (10 000 cu. m)
总 计	**Total**	**78623**	**43076**
煤炭开采和洗选业	Coal Mining and Dressing		
石油和天然气开采业	Petroleum and Natural Gas Extraction	23143	
黑色金属矿采选业	Ferrous Metals Mining and Dressing		
有色金属矿采选业	Nonferrous Metals Mining and Dressing		
非金属矿采选业	Nonmetal Minerals Mining and Dressing		
开采辅助活动	Ancillary activities for mining	3750	
其他采矿业	Other Mining Industry		
农副食品加工业	Agricultural Products and Non-stable Food Processing Industry	247	
食品制造业	Food Production	1045	
酒、饮料和精制茶制造业	Wine, soft drinks and refined tea industry	2335	
烟草制品业	Tobacco Processing	248	
纺织业	Textile Industry	460	1
纺织服装、服饰业	Textile, apparel industry	36	
皮革、毛皮、羽毛及其制品和制鞋业	Leather, Fur, Feather (eiderdown) and Their Products Industry	5	
木材加工和木、竹、藤、棕、草制品业	Timber Processing,Bamboo,Cane,Palm Fiber and Straw Products	4	
家具制造业	Furniture Manufacturing	8	
造纸及纸制品业	Papermaking and Paper products	982	
印刷和记录媒介复制业	Printing,Record Medium Reproduction	240	
文教、工美、体育和娱乐用品制造业	Culture, education, Craft art, sports and entertainment goods manufacturing industry	4	
石油加工、炼焦和核燃料加工业	Petroleum Refining, Ccoke Making and Nuclear Fuel Processing Industry	457	
化学原料和化学制品制造业	Raw Chemical Materials and Chemical Products	921	158
医药制造业	Medical and Pharmaceutical Products	1550	7
化学纤维制造业	Chemical Fiber	70	
橡胶和塑料制品业	Rubber and plastic products industry	418	1
非金属矿物制品业	Nonmetal Mineral Products	242	2
黑色金属冶炼和压延加工业	Smelting and Pressing of Ferrous Metals	74	
有色金属冶炼和压延加工业	Smelting and Pressing of Nonferrou Metals	375	2
金属制品业	Metal Products	76	
通用设备制造业	General Equipment Manufacturing Industry	281	
专用设备制造业	Automotive Manufacturing	710	2
汽车制造业	Special Purpose Equipment	3047	
铁路、船舶、航空航天和其他运输设备制造业	Railroad, marine, aerospace and other transportation equipment manufacturing	2495	3
电气机械和器材制造业	Electric Equipment and Machinery	1932	
计算机、通信和其他电子设备制造业	Communication Equipment, Computer and Other Electronic Equipment Manufacturing Industry	1106	
仪器仪表制造业	Instrument manufacturing industry	622	
其他制造业	Other manufacturing	158	5
废弃资源综合利用	Comprehensive utilization of waste resources		
金属制品、机械和设备修理业	Metal products, machinery and equipment repair industry	4	
电力、热力生产和供应业	Electric Power, Heating Power Generating and Supplying Industry	5512	
燃气生产和供应业	Gas Mining and Supplying Industry	39	
水的生产和供应业	Water Processing and Supplying Industry	26022	42895

13-10 规模以上工业企业分行业（GB/T4754-2002）综合能源消费量（2012年）

Comprehensive Energy Consumption by Sector(GB/T4754-2002) above Designated Size (2012)

单位：吨标准煤 (ton of SCE)

行 业	Sector	2012
总 计	**Total**	**5016252**
按工业行业大类分	Grouped by Sector	
煤炭开采和洗选业	Coal Mining and Dressing	
石油和天然气开采业	Petroleum and Natural Gas Extraction	86785
黑色金属矿采选业	Ferrous Metals Mining and Dressing	86
有色金属矿采选业	Nonferrous Metals Mining and Dressing	
非金属矿采选业	Nonmetal Minerals Mining and Dressing	
其他采矿业	Other Mining Industry	
农副食品加工业	Agricultural Products and Non-stable Food Processing Industry	263259
食品制造业	Food Production	95262
饮料制造业	Beverage Production	134506
烟草加工业	Tobacco Processing	485
纺织业	Textile Industry	42671
纺织服装、鞋、帽制造业	Textile Clothing, Footwear and Headgear Industry	1597
皮革、毛皮、羽毛（绒）及其制造业	Leather, Fur, Feather (eiderdown) and Their Products Industry	846
木材加工及竹、藤、棕、草制品业	Timber Processing,Bamboo,Cane,Palm Fiber and Straw Products	10955
家具制造业	Furniture Manufacturing	2220
造纸及纸制品业	Papermaking and Paper products	97947
印刷业、记录媒介的复制	Printing,Record Medium Reproduction	18278
文教体育用品制造业	Cultural,Educational and Sports Goods	775
石油加工、炼焦及核燃料加工业	Petroleum Refining, Ccoke Making and Nuclear Fuel Processing Industry	399654
化学原料及化学制品制造业	Raw Chemical Materials and Chemical Products	115203
医药制造业	Medical and Pharmaceutical Products	69538
化学纤维制造业	Chemical Fiber	29027
橡胶制品业	Rubber Products	3477
塑料制品业	Plastic Products	52607
非金属矿物制品业	Nonmetal Mineral Products	300941
黑色金属冶炼及压延加工业	Smelting and Pressing of Ferrous Metals	107296
有色金属冶炼及压延加工业	Smelting and Pressing of Nonferrou Metals	60815
金属制品业	Metal Products	97792
通用设备制造业	General Equipment Manufacturing Industry	18794
专用设备制造业	Special Purpose Equipment	206929
交通运输设备制造业	Transport Equipment	275908
电气机械及器材制造业	Electric Equipment and Machinery	131031
通信设备、计算机及其他电子设备制造业	Communication Equipment, Computer and Other Electronic Equipment Manufacturing Industry	56888
仪器仪表及文化、办公用机械制造业	Instruments,Meters,Cultural and Office	24691
工艺品及其他制造业	Handicraft and Other Stuff Manufacturing Industry	1291
废弃资源和废旧材料回收加工业	Discarded Resources and Waste Materials Salvaging and Processing Industry	
电力、热力的生产和供应业	Electric Power, Heating Power Generating and Supplying Industry	2288964
燃气生产和供应业	Gas Mining and Supplying Industry	8346
水的生产和供应业	Water Processing and Supplying Industry	11388

主要统计指标解释

能源消费总量 指一定时期内，地区各行业和居民生活消费的各种能源的总和。该指标是观察能源消费水平、构成和增长速度的总量指标。能源消费总量包括原煤和原油及其制品、天然气、电力等，不包括低热值燃料、生物质能和太阳能等的利用。能源消费总量分为终端能源消费量、能源加工转换损失量和能源损失量三部分。

（1）终端能源消费量：指一定时期内，全国生产和生活消费的各种能源在扣除了用于加工转换二次能源消费量和损失量以后的数量。

（2）能源加工转换损失量：指一定时期内，全国投入加工转换的各种能源数量之和与产出各种能源产品之和的差额。该指标是观察能源在加工转换过程中损失量变化的指标。

（3）能源损失量：指一定时期内，能源在输送、分配、储存过程中发生的损失和由客观原因造成的各种损失量，不包括各种气体能源放空、放散量。

工业生产能源消费 指工业企业为进行工业生产活动所消费的能源。

非工业生产能源消费 指在工业企业能源消费中，除“工业生产能源消费”以外的能源消费，即非工业生产用能和工业企业附属的不从事工业生产活动的非独立核算单位用能。

运输工具消费 指在厂区内、外进行交通运输活动的交通运输工具所消费的能源。

能源加工转换投入 能源的加工转换是指为了特定的用途，将一种能源（一般为一次能源），经过一定的下艺，加工或转换成另外一种能源（一般为二次能源）。能源加工转换的投入即能源加工、转换消费。

一次能源 是指自然界中以现成形式存在，不经任何改变或转换的天然能源资源，即从自然界直接取得并不改变其形态和品位的能源。如原煤、原油、天然气、核燃料、植物燃料、风能、水能、太阳能、地热能、海洋能、潮汐能等。

二次能源 是指为了满足生产工艺和生活的特定需要以合理利用能源，将一次能源直接或间接加工转换产生的其它种类和形式的人工能源。如原煤加工产出的洗煤；由煤炭加工转换产出的焦炭，煤气；由原油加工产出的汽油、煤油、柴油、燃料油、液化石油气、炼厂干气等；由煤炭、石油、天然气转换产出的电力。

综合能源消费量 报告期内工业企业在工业生产活动中实际消费的各种能源的总和净值。计算综合能源消费量时，需要先将使用的各种能源折算成标准燃料后再进行计算。

单位生产总值能耗 指一定时期内，一个国家或地区每生产一个单位的生产总值所消耗的能源。计算公式为：

单位生产总值能耗=能源消费总量／生产总值

单位生产总值电耗 指一定时期内，一个国家或地区每生产一个单位的生产总值所消耗的电力。计算公式为：

单位生产总值电耗=全社会用电量／生产总值

单位工业增加值能耗 指一定时期内，一个国家或地区每生产一个单位的工业增加值所消耗的能源。计算公式为：

单位工业增加值能耗=工业能源消费量／工业增加值

Explanatory Notes on Main Statistical Indicators

Total Energy Consumption refers to the total consumption of energy of various kinds by the production sectors and the households in the country in a given period of time. It is a comprehensive indicator to show the scale,composition and pace of increase of energy consumption. Total energy consumption includes that of coal,crude oil and their products,natural gas and electricity. However,it does not include the consumption of fuel of low calorific value, bio-energy and solar energy. Total energy consumption can be divided into three parts: end-use energy consumption; loss during the process of energy conversion; and energy loss.

(1) End-use Energy Consumption: It refers to the total energy consumption by the production sectors and the households in the country (region) in a given period of time. It does not include the consumption during the conversion of primary energy into secondary energy and the loss in the process of energy conversion.

(2) Loss During the Process of Energy Conversion: It refers to the total input of various kinds of energy for conversion, minus the total output of various kinds of energy in the country in a given period of time. It is an indicator to show the loss that occurs during the process of energy conversion.

(3) Energy Loss: It refers to the total of the loss of energy during the course of energy transport, distribution and storage and the loss caused by any objective reason in a given period of time. The loss of various kinds of gas due to gas discharges and stocktaking is not included.

Industry Consumption Energy refers to the volume of energy consumed by Industrial enterprises for industrial production activities.

Non-industry Consumption Energy refers to the energy consumed by industrial enterprises except for industrial production activities,means that energy consumed by non-industry production and not independent accounting units which was not engaged in industrial production activities affiliated to industrial enterprises.

Vehicle Energy refers to the energy consumed by vehicles which carried out transport activities in and out of factories.

Energy Processing Conversion Devoted energy processing conversion refers to for specialized application, a source of energy (normally primary energy) , after a certain technology , processed or converted to another kind of energy (normally secondary energy) . The input of energy conversion processing that is energy processing, and conversion consumption.

Primary Energy Source refers to natural energy resources as found naturally in the form of ready-made,without any change or conversion,as energy obtaineddirectly from natural and not change its shape and grade,such as raw coal, crude oil, natural gas, nuclear fuel, plantfuel, wind energy, water energy, solar energy,geothermalenergy, oceanic energy, tidal energy and so on.

Secondary Energy refers to other types and formsof artificial energy which was processed and conversed from primary energy sources directly or indirectly , in order to meet the specific needs in production process and life to use energy more effectively. Such as washing coalprocessed from raw coal; coke and coal gas processed andtransformed from raw coal; gasoline, kerosene, diesel oil, fuel oil, liquefied petroleum gas, dry gas refinery processed from crude oil; electric power conversed from coal, oil and natural gas.

Comprehensive energy consumption refers to the total and net energy actually consumed in industrial production activities by industrial enterprises in the reference period. When calculated the volume of consumption of comprehensive energy, should converted sorts of energy which was used into standards fuel firstly.

Energy Consumption per Unit of GDP refers to the energy consumption per unit of Gross Domestic Product in a country or the Gross Regional Product in a region in the same reference period. The formula is:

$$\text{Energy Consumption per Unit of GDP} = \frac{\text{Total Energy Consumption}}{\text{Gross Domestic Product}}$$

Electricity Consumption per Unit of GDP refers to the electricity consumption per unit of Gross Domestic Product in a country or the Gross Regional Product in a region in the same reference period. The formula is:

$$\text{Electricity Consumption per Unit of GDP} = \frac{\text{Total Electricity Consumption}}{\text{Gross Domestic Product}}$$

Energy Consumption per Unit of Industrial Value-added refers to the energy consumption per unit of industrial value-added in a country or region in the same reference period. The formula is:

$$\text{Energy Consumption per Unit of Industrial Value-added} = \frac{\text{Total Energy Consumption}}{\text{Industrial Value-added}}$$

14 建筑业

CONSTRUCTION

资料整理：陈海生
Data management:Chen Haisheng

第十四部分　建筑业

一、简要说明

本章资料主要包括建筑业基本情况、建筑业施工企业生产情况和财务状况，由西安市统计局固定资产投资处提供。

二、主要指标

企业个数（个）	396	比上年增加	60个
建筑业总产值（亿元）	1874.23	比上年增长	15.8%
#国有及国有控股企业	1364.7	比上年增长	6.8%
房屋建筑竣工面积（万平方米）	1985.31	比上年下降	17%
房屋建筑面积竣工率(%)	26.3	比上年下降	12.2个百分点

14 CONSTRUCTION

Ⅰ.Brief Introduction

This chapter consists of primarily the data basic situation of the construction industry, production situation and financial situation of the construction enterprises, provided by Fixed Asset Investment Division of the Xl'an Bureau of Statistics.

Ⅱ.Major Indicators

		Increase over Preceding Year
Number of Enterprises(item)	396	60
Total Output Value of Construction(100 mil. yuan)	1874.23	15.8%
State-owned Or State Holding Majority Shares	1364.7	6.8%
Floor Space of Buildings Completed(10 000 sq.m)	1985.31	-17%
Rate of Floor Space of Buildings Completed(%)	38.5	-12.2 percentage points

14-1 主要年份建筑业总产值

Total Output Value of Construction in Representative Year

单位：万元　　　　(10 000 yuan)

年份 Year	建筑业总产值 Total Output Value of Construction	国有及国有控股 State-owned Or State Holding Majority Shares	集体企业 Collective-owned Enterprises
2000	1059250	788704	148709
2001	1148091	918169	154749
2002	1334713	850278	153482
2003	1771126	1199911	134010
2004	2444242	2016792	165922
2005	3266535	2766785	196111
2006	4164782	3482016	236493
2007	6047524	4326279	326658
2008	9151199	6761190	4601423
2009	12965787	10672178	471533
2010	18203450	15203874	583928
2011	16190888	12783270	794189
2012	18742273	13647046	968291

注：1996年以后建筑业年报统计范围由往年的县及县以上（含县级建制镇）各种经济类型的建筑企业，改为具有建筑业资质等级四级及四级以上的各种经济类型的建筑施工企业；2002年改为具有建筑业资质等级的各种经济类型的建筑施工企业。
本表资料含劳务分包企业。

14-2 全市建筑施工总承包企业基本情况（2012年）

Basic situation of Construction General contracting business in whole city(2012)

指　　标	Item	合计 Total	国有及国有控股 State-owned Or State Holding Majority Shares
企业单位数（个）（施工总承包）	Number of Enterprises (unit) (Overall Contractor For Construction)	266	79
#二级以上企业	First and Second Class Enterprise	201	69
计算劳动生产率的平均人数（人）（施工总承包）	Average Number of Employed Persons in Calculation of Labor Productivity (person) (Overall Contractor For Construction)	364374	236957
#二级以上企业	First and Second Class Enterprise	349514	235791
建筑业总产值（亿元）（施工总承包）	Total Output Value of Construction(100 million yuan) (Overall Contractor For Construction)	1722.79	1296.15
#二级以上企业	First and Second Class Enterprise	1443.4	1291.1
全员劳动生产率 (元/人)（施工总承包）(按总产值计算)	Overall Labor Productivity (yuan/person) (Overall Contractor For Construction) (Calculated by Total Output Value)	479232	300114

14-3 施工总承包和专业承包建筑企业生产情况（2012年）

分 组	Classify	签订的合同额（万元）Contract Value (10 000 yuan)
总计	**Total**	**41418231**
#国有及国有控股	State-Owned and State Holding Majority Shares	33527355
一、按登记注册类型分	**Grouped by Registion Status**	
内资	Domestic Investment Enterprises	41407755
国有企业	State-owned Enterprises	15492792
集体企业	Collective-owned Enterprises	1632772
股份合作企业	Share-holding Corperative Enterprises	15033
联营企业	Joint Ownership Enterprises	1936
有限责任公司	Limited Liability Corporations	22242929
股份有限公司	Share-holding Corperation Ltd.	915767
私营企业	Private Enterprises	1099359
其他企业	Others	7167
港澳台商投资企业	Enterprises with Funds from Hong Kong,Macao and Taiwan	613
外商投资企业	Enterprises with Foreign Investment	9863
二、按国民经济行业分	**Grouped by Sector**	
房屋建筑业	Building Engineering Construction	13220719
土木工程建筑业	Civil Engineering Construction	25963224
建筑安装业	Installation of Construction	1581374
建筑装饰和其他建筑业	Architectural decoration and other construction	652914
三、按隶属关系分	**Grouped by Administrative Relationship**	
中央	Central	23198774
地方	Region	18219457
四、按企业资质等级分	**Grouped by Class of Enterprises**	
1. 施工总承包	Overall Contractor for Construction	39235288
#特级	Special Class	11594879
一级	First Class	23744618
二级	Second Class	3454187
2. 专业承包	Special Contractor	2182943
#一级以上	First Class	1275518

Main Indicators on Overall Constructing Contractors and Professional Contractors by Registration Status（2012）

建筑业总产值（万元）Total Output Value of Constrution (10 000 yuan)	建筑工程产值 Output Value of Constrution	安装工程产值 Output Value of Installation	其他产值 Others	计算劳动生产率的平均人数（人）Average Number of Employed Persons in Calculation of Labour Productivity(person)	期末从业人员数（人）Number of Employment at Year-end (person)	工程技术人员 Technical Personnel	企业总产值（万元）Total Output Value of Enterprises (10 000 yuan)
18742273	**16585579**	**1751769**	**404925**	**394977**	**391199**	**54090**	**20309734**
13647046	12329302	1030620	287124	247314	245390	32600	15144989
18731932	16585138	1741879	404915	394884	391108	54061	20299362
7879129	7226134	562359	90637	148008	166787	17486	8187596
968291	882274	70925	15091	39062	37900	5216	1001564
12252	12252			74	135	65	14652
1959	1959			120	120	35	1959
8732974	7537504	977190	218281	180757	156105	25891	9921037
473231	416131	12082	45018	10029	11914	2021	473645
659977	504766	119323	35889	16645	17839	3330	694790
4119	4119			189	308	17	4119
479	441	38		46	43	18	509
9863		9853	10	47	48	11	9863
8065398	7102181	740661	222555	202290	204606	25238	8162328
8915618	8444204	396520	74893	161739	159822	24089	10405466
1215849	598621	568606	48622	21687	17887	3157	1192873
545409	440573	45981	58854	9261	8884	1606	549066
7847996	7332334	443511	72152	130568	134868	20369	9069496
10894277	9253245	1308258	332774	264409	256331	33721	11240238
17227973	15631058	1264004	332911	370756	369968	50033	18573842
2236285	2213693	20000	2592	14994	25199	4154	3156935
12247677	11149219	946598	151860	280507	267542	34715	12627148
2345500	1978005	232126	135369	60611	62284	9366	2388011
1514300	954521	487765	72014	24221	21231	4057	1735892
831572	574403	195875	61295	14446	10677	2545	1089477

14-3 续表

分　组	Classify	房屋建筑施工面积（平方米）Number of Projects under Constrution (sq.m)	本年新开工 Beginning Projects in this year
总计	**Total**	**75310693**	**26010023**
#国有及国有控股	State-Owned and State Holding Majority Shares	50252121	13946362
一、按登记注册类型分	**Grouped by Registion Status**		
内资	Domestic Investment Enterprises	75310693	26010023
国有企业	State-owned Enterprises	33103148	7618804
集体企业	Collective-owned Enterprises	8406320	4641630
股份合作企业	Share-holding Corperative Enterprises		
联营企业	Joint Ownership Enterprises	22847	
有限责任公司	Limited Liability Corporations	29306788	12014958
股份有限公司	Share-holding Corperation Ltd.	628335	209156
私营企业	Private Enterprises	3843255	1525475
其他企业	Others		
港澳台商投资企业	Enterprises with Funds from Hong Kong,Macao and Taiwan		
外商投资企业	Enterprises with Foreign Investment		
二、按国民经济行业分	**Grouped by Sector**		
房屋建筑业	Building Engineering Construction	69136272	24075071
土木工程建筑业	Civil Engineering Construction	6096399	1915560
建筑安装业	Installation of Construction	78022	19392
建筑装饰和其他建筑业	Architectural decoration and other construction		
三、按隶属关系分	**Grouped by Administrative Relationship**		
中央	Central	14955152	3403973
地方	Region	60355541	22606050
四、按企业资质等级分	**Grouped by Class of Enterprises**		
1. 施工总承包	Overall Contractor for Construction	73669507	25467302
#特级	Special Class	5405185	2248305
一级	First Class	57419415	18278622
二级	Second Class	9724241	4304413
2. 专业承包	Special Contractor	1641186	542721
#一级以上	First Class	482300	361240

continued

房屋建筑 竣工面积 （平方米） Floor Space of Buildings Completed (sq.m)	自有机械设备 年末净值 （万元） Net Value of Mechanical Equipment owned by Constructions Enterprises at Year-end(10 000 yuan)	自有机械设备 年末总台数 （台） Number of Mechanical Equipment Owned By Construction Enterprises at Year-end(unit)	自有机械设备 年末总功率 （千瓦） Total Power of Mechanical Equipment Owned by Construction Enterprises at Year-end(kw)
19853086	**477885**	**104074**	**3013865**
11377410	347838	47664	2087803
19853086	477885	104073	3013864
7693974	161021	32384	1153592
3003339	21894	14754	199194
	408	47	1108
5833	413	36	302
8383045	261528	51613	1558916
89083	11271	1325	56562
677812	20706	3903	42800
	644	11	1390
		1	1
18961495	113304	66411	871614
813570	329966	29707	1911629
78021	13142	5063	94391
	21473	2893	136231
2823821	281328	25270	1430256
17029265	196557	78804	1583609
19557505	433733	98562	2583966
1306943	94844	10766	461508
14056241	277146	66904	1770910
3718644	52476	18049	323553
295581	44152	5512	429899
86713	38262	4238	250651

14-4 施工总承包和专业承包建筑业企业财务状况（2012年）

单位：万元

指 标	Item	总 计 Total
一. 年初存货	**Stocks at the end of year**	**2789582**
二. 期末资产负债	**Total Assets and Liabilities of the final**	
流动资产合计	Total Circulating Funds	15158761
#应收工程款	Receivable Project Money	4056471
#存货	Stock	3246494
固定资产合计	Fixed Assets	1293197
固定资产原价	Original Value of Fixed Assets	2140891
累计折旧	Accumulative Total Depreciation	1056254
#本年折旧	Depreciation Within the Year	214172
在建工程	Projects Under Construction	146937
资产总计	Total Assets	18553266
流动负债合计	Total Liquid Liabilities	13452766
#应付帐款	Accounts Payable	5548571
非流动负债合计	Total Non-Liquid Liabilities	620458
负债合计	Total Liabilities	14487472
所有者权益合计	Owner Rights and Interests	4058345
#实收资本	Actual Capital Hold	2953811
三. 损益及分配	**Profit or Loss and the Distribution**	
营业收入	Total Revenue	20890636
#主营业务收入	Revenue from Principal Business	20808506
营业成本	Total Cost	19016997
#主营业务成本	Cost of Principal Business	18874921
营业税金及附加	Taxs and Other Changes	626614
#主营业务税金及附加	Taxs and Other Changes on Principal Business	620741
其他业务利润	Profits from Other Operation	6652
销售费用	Sale Expenses	
管理费用	Management Expenses	699818
财务费用	Financial Expenses	90766
营业利润	Business Profits	515374
利润总额	Total Profits	517408
四. 人工成本	**Cost of Labor**	
应付职工薪酬	Salary Payable	1835791

Financial Status of Overall Constructing Contractors and Professional Contractors（2012）

(10 000 yuan)

国有及国有控股 State-Owned and State Holding Majority Shares Enterprises	中央企业 Enterprises Central	省属企业 Province Enterprises	市属企业 Municipal Enterprises
1983153	**1489979**	**395546**	**904057**
11636878	8500161	2464240	4194360
3223527	2075348	954679	1026444
2324098	1876381	397789	972323
793397	588850	222171	482176
1573462	1247378	303697	589816
833866	687902	134073	234278
172611	146486	26266	41421
31050	18886	39927	88124
14146733	10407366	3024061	5121839
11058027	8173659	2299332	2979775
4812454	3558882	983990	1005699
541279	491397	51746	77315
11616229	8670051	2360641	3456779
2530636	1737315	663419	1657610
1748572	1201930	500336	1251545
16104213	10963440	3932919	5994277
16034886	10916455	3922866	5969185
14830859	10082813	3659356	5274828
14729109	10049511	3606384	5219027
480763	317720	115791	193104
478909	316460	115439	188842
4261	5989	1519	-856
506772	372098	101774	225946
54788	35715	8249	46802
317654	239933	53328	222114
319106	241261	53468	222680
1341506	761427	428643	645721

14-5 劳务分包建筑业企业基本情况（2012年）

Basic Statistic on Enterprises of Work Subcontractors（2012）

单位：万元 (10 000 yuan)

指　标	Item	2012
一. 期末资产负债	**Total Assets and Liabilities of the final**	
固定资产原价	Original Value of Fixed Assets	1204
本年折旧	Depreciation In The Year	
资产总计	Total Assets	1580
负债合计	Total Liabilities	750
实收资本	Paid in Capital	714
二. 损益及分配	**Profit or Loss and the Distribution**	
营业收入	Total Revenue	1221
#主营业务收入	Revenue from Principal Business	1221
营业成本	Total Cost	1140
#主营业务成本	Cost of Principal Business	1140
营业税金及附加	Taxs and Other Changes	41
#主营业务税金及附加	Taxs and Other Changes on Principal Business	41
其他业务利润	Profits from Other Operation	
销售费用	Sale Expenses	
管理费用	Managenment Expenses	67
财务费用	Financial Expenses	1
营业利润	Business Profits	24
利润总额	**Total Profits**	**24**

14-6 各区县建筑业主要经济指标（2012年）

Main Indicators of Construction Enterprises by Region（2012）

区 县	Region	企业个数（个）Number of Enterprises (unit)	总产值（万元）Total Output Value (10 000 yuan)	计算劳动生产率的平均人数(人) Average Number of Employed Persons in Calculation of Labor Productivity(person)	全员劳动生产率（万元/人）Overall Labor Productivity (10 000 yuan/person)	利税总额（万元）Total Pre-tax Profits (1 0000 yuan)
新城区	Xincheng	31	2138000	24927	86	34142
碑林区	Beilin	41	5046267	81284	62	69712
莲湖区	Lianhu	35	2064152	31689	65	18229
灞桥区	Baqiao	32	202566	6914	29	4435
未央区	Weiyang	63	3139852	114309	27	122092
雁塔区	Yanta	115	4109126	57785	71	163050
阎良区	Yanliang	15	199517	9625	21	4329
临潼区	Lintong	13	121288	5509	22	12306
长安区	Chang'an	23	623185	15886	39	6883
蓝田县	Lantian	9	150420	5077	30	14753
周至县	Zhouzhi	7	59009	1114	53	2321
户 县	Huxian	6	119027	6103	20	650
高陵县	Gaoling	6	769864	30881	25	64507

14-7 各区县建筑业房屋施工及竣工面积（2012年）

Floor Space of Buildings under Construction & Completed by Region（2012）

区 县	Region	房屋建筑施工面积 (万平方米) Floor Space under Construction(10 000 sq.m)	本年新开工面积 Newly Started This Year	房屋建筑竣工面积 （万平方米） Floor Space of Buildings Completed(10 000 sq.m)	竣工房屋价值 （亿元） Value of Buildings Completed(100 million yuan)
新城区	Xincheng	1145.85	359.73	200.84	30.83
碑林区	Beilin	2542.69	837.78	717.10	136.65
莲湖区	Lianhu	1115.96	248.48	240.50	41.39
灞桥区	Baqiao	109.08	23.37	35.95	5.71
未央区	Weiyang	500.38	121.61	96.00	11.82
雁塔区	Yanta	1075.80	296.14	241.22	39.46
阎良区	Yanliang	81.58	41.21	31.01	4.85
临潼区	Lintong	120.85	43.43	80.78	8.29
长安区	Chang'an	168.47	96.62	47.41	6.30
蓝田县	Lantian	128.25	106.92	44.43	6.62
周至县	Zhouzhi	48.39	26.19	22.68	3.36
户 县	Huxian	114.11	43.82	29.61	3.54
高陵县	Gaoling	379.66	355.70	197.77	32.80

14-8 各区县建筑业企业主要经济效益指标（2012年）

Main Economic Benefit Indicators on Construction Enterprises by Region（2012）

区 县	Region	人均利润总额（元/人）Per Profit (yuan/person)	人均利税（元/人）Per Pre-tax Profits (yuan/person)	人均竣工产值（元/人）Per Output Value of Buildings Completed (yuan/person)	人均施工面积（平方米/人）Per Floor Space of Buildings Under Construcyion (sq.m/person)	人均竣工面积（平方米/人）Per Floor Space of Buildings Completed (sq.m/person)
新城区	Xincheng	13697	27372	414101	460	81
碑林区	Beilin	8576	21317	249860	313	88
莲湖区	Lianhu	5752	13589	191985	352	76
灞桥区	Baqiao	6414	9493	244156	158	52
未央区	Weiyang	10681	12537	68102	44	8
雁塔区	Yanta	28217	22258	271740	186	42
阎良区	Yanliang	4497	5312	91650	85	32
临潼区	Lintong	22339	12269	152986	219	147
长安区	Chang'an	4332	6215	75776	106	30
蓝田县	Lantian	29059	7420	200825	253	88
周至县	Zhouzhi	20833	16222	357130	434	204
户 县	Huxian	1066	6416	82250	187	49
高陵县	Gaoling	20889	8566	106210	123	64

14-8 续表 continued

区 县	Region	产值利润率（%）Ratio of Profits to Output Value (%)	产值利税率（%）Ratio of Pre-tax Profits to Output Value (%)	资本利润率（%）Ratio of Profits to Assets (%)	资本金利税率（%）Ratio of Pre-tax Profits to Assets（%）	资产负债率（%）Ratio of Debts to Assets（%）
新城区	Xincheng	1.4	2.8	18.4	36.8	86.7
碑林区	Beilin	1.5	3.8	12.8	31.8	80.6
莲湖区	Lianhu	1.2	2.8	10.6	25	79.3
灞桥区	Baqiao	2.2	3.2	8	11.8	70.1
未央区	Weiyang	3.4	3.9	19.4	22.8	81.2
雁塔区	Yanta	3.6	2.9	19.8	15.6	76.7
阎良区	Yanliang	2.2	2.6	7.7	9.1	62.3
临潼区	Lintong	10.1	5.6	76.6	42.1	46.1
长安区	Chang'an	1.8	2.5	13.8	19.8	59.7
蓝田县	Lantian	9.8	2.5	53.2	13.6	35.9
周至县	Zhouzhi	3.9	3.1	18.5	14.4	48.1
户 县	Huxian	0.5	3.3	3.1	18.8	53.2
高陵县	Gaoling	8.4	3.4	18	7.4	18.1

主要统计指标解释

建筑业统计单位 指从事房屋、构筑物建造和设备安装活动的法人企业。建筑业法人企业应具有建筑业资质并能够独立核算，同时其应具备以下条件：①依法成立，有自己的名称、组织机构和场所，能够承担民事责任；②独立拥有和使用资产，承担负债，有权与其他单位签订合同；③独立核算盈亏，能够编制资产负债表。

建筑业总产值 是以货币形式表现的建筑业企业在一定时期内生产的建筑业产品和提供的服务的总和。建筑业总产值包括：

（1）建筑工程产值：指列入建筑工程预算内的各种工程价值。

（2）安装工程产值：指设备安装工程价值，不包括被安装设备本身的价值。

（3）其他产值：建筑业总产值中除建筑工程、安装丁程以外的产值。包括房屋构筑物修理产值、非标准设备制造产值、总包企业向分包企业收取的管理费以及不能明确划分的施工活动所完成的产值。

a. 房屋构筑物修理产值：指房屋和构筑物修理所完成的产值，但不包括被修理房屋、构筑物本身价值和生产设备的修理价值。

b. 非标准设备制造产值：指加工制造没有定型的非标准生产设备的加了费和原材料价值（如化工厂、炼油厂用的各种罐、槽，矿井生产统一使用的各种漏斗、三角槽、阀门等）以及附属加工厂为本企业承建工程制作的非标准设备的价值。

建筑业增加值 指建筑业企业在报告期内以货币形式表现的建筑业生产经营活动的最终成果。

从2004年第一次全国经济普查开始，建筑业现价增加值按生产法和分配法（收入法）两种方法计算，以收入法的计算结果为准，即从收入的角度出发，根据生产要素在生产过程中应得的收入份额计算。具体计算方法：经济普查年度建筑业增加值按照《经济普查年度GDP核算方案》计算，非经济普查年度建筑业增加值按照们≥经济普查年度GDP核算方案》计算。

房屋建筑施工面积 指在报告期内施过工的全部房屋建筑面积，包括本期新开工的房屋面积、上期施工跨入本期继续施工的房屋面积、上期停　建在本期恢复施工的房屋面积、本期竣工的房屋面积及本期施丁后又停　建的房屋面积。

房屋建筑竣工面积 指在报告期内房屋建筑按照设计要求全部完工，达到了使用条件，经验收鉴定合格，正式移交使用单位的房屋建筑面积。

Explanatory Notes on Main Statistical Indicators

Statistical Unit in the Construction Industry refers to a corporate enterprise engaged in the construction of buildings and structures and in the installation of equipment. A corporate construction enterprise should have qualification certificates with independent accounting system, and should meet the following 3 requirements: a) being set up in line with relevant legal basis, having its full name, organization and location, and capable of taking civil liabilities; b) independently possessing and using its assets and assuming its liabilities, and entitled to sign contracts with other institutions; and c) making independent accounts of its profits and losses, and capable of compiling its own balance sheet.

Gross Output Value of Construction refers to total of construction products and services, expressed in money terms, produced or rendered by construction and installation enterprises during a given period of time. It includes:

(1)Output value of construction projects: the value of projects covered by the project budgets;

(2) Output value of installation projects: the value of the installation of equipment, (excluding the value of the equipment to be installed);

(3)Other output values: the output value of construction industry apart from that of construction projects and installation projects. It includes: output value of repair of buildings and structures; output value of non-standard equipment manufacturing; overhead expenses received by contracted enterprises from the sub-contracted enterprises and the completed output value of construction activities for which there is no clear definition.

a. Output value of repair of buildings and structures: the value created through the repairs of buildings or structures. It does not include the value of buildings or structures being repaired and the value of the repair of production equipment;

b. Output value of manufactured non-standard equipment: the value of non-standard production equipment, including raw materials and manufacturing cost, made for the construction project (i.e., chemical plant; kettles or tanks used by refineries; various fillers, triangle tanks, valves used by mines). It also includes the output value of equipment manufactured by subsidiary workshops.

Value-added of Construction refers to the final result of the activities of production and operation of enterprises of the construction industry in monetary terms during the reference period.

Starting from the 2004 economic census, value-added of construction is calculated by both production approach and income approach, with the figures from the income approach as the final figures. Under the income approach, calculation starts from the perspective of income and is based on the share of income derived from the production process by the relevant factors of production. Specifically, value-added of construction for the Census years is calculated in accordance with the Programme of Compilation of GDP and National Accounts for the Year of Economic Census, and value-added of construction for other years is calculated in accordance with the Programme of Compilation of GDP and National Accounts for the Non Economic Census Years.

Floor Space of Buildings Under Construction refers to floor space of buildings under construction during the reference period, including the floor space of buildings for which construction has newly started; buildings for which construction has started earlier and is continuing during the reference period; and buildings for which construction has been suspended earlier but has restarted during the reference period; buildings completed during the reference period; and buildings under construction but construction has subsequently been during the reference period.

Floor Space of Buildings Completed refers to the floor space of buildings that are completed in the reference period in accordance with the requirements of the design, up to the standard for being put into use, and having been checked and accepted by departments concerned as qualified ones.

15 运输和邮电

TRANSPORT,POSTAL AND TELECOMMUNICATION SERVICE

资料整理：曾文元

Data management:Zeng Wenyuan

第十五部分　运输和邮电

一、简要说明

本章资料包括交通运输业和邮电通信业的基本情况，主要是交通运输工具、货物和旅客运输量、邮电业务、邮政局所及服务点等基本情况。资料由西安市统计局社会科技处根据有关部门提供资料整理。

二、主要指标

旅客周转量（亿人公里）	338.74	比上年增长	5.1%
货物周转量（亿吨公里）	595.87	比上年增长	16.3%
邮电业务总量（亿元）	216.21		
全社会车辆数（万辆）	163.33	比上年增长	13.0%
#民用小轿车	75.21	比上年增长	21.5%

注：2012年邮电业务总量按2011不变价格计算，故与以往年份不可比。

15 TRANSPORT,POSTAL AND TELECOMMUNICATION SERVICES

Ⅰ.Brief Introduction

Data in this chapter consists of primarily basic data of communication, transportation and postal service industry, transportation facility, amount of goods and passenger transportation, basic data of postal service, post offices and service establishments of Xi'an City. Data in this chapter is compiled by Social & Science and Technology Division of the Xi'an Bureau of Statistics according to the data provided by department concerned of the municipal government.

Ⅱ.Major Indicators

		Increase over Preceding Year
Passenger-Km (100 mil. Person-km)	338.74	5.1%
Freight Ton-Km (100 mil. Ton-km)	595.87	16.3%
Amount of Postal and Telecommunication Service(100 mil. Yuan)	216.21	
Number of Vehides in the whole Sciety	163.33	13.0%
Civil Car	75.21	21.5%

Note: 2012 Postal and Telecommunication Services are calculated at 2011 constant prices,then can not be compared with previous years.

15-1 主要年份各种交通线路和桥梁

Transportation Routes and Number of Bridges in Representative Years

年 份 Year	铁路营业 里程（公里） Length of Railways in Operation (km)	公路里程 （公里） Length of Highways (km)	桥 梁 （座） Bridges (seat)
1978	555		
1979	555		
1980	555		
1981	569		
1982	569		
1983	569		
1984	569		
1985	697		
1986	697		
1987	1333		
1988	1339		
1989	1339	2563	
1990	1339	2586	
1991	1357	2785	
1992	1357	2786	
1993	1356	2801	
1994	1357	2830	
1995	1357	2852	
1996	1358	2877	
1997	1489	3026	
1998	1492	3047	
1999	1478	2789	
2000	1540	3010	
2001	1536	3298	
2002	1543	7862	629
2003	1522	8360	629
2004	1608	8360	629
2005	202	8500	634
2006	269	9530	634
2007	269	9672	1319
2008	269	11895	1710
2009	269	12378	1856
2010	269	12378	1856
2011	269	12599	1863
2012	269	13127	2190

注：2005年开始，铁路统计执行新的统计口径。

15-1 续表 continued

年　份 Year	桥梁长度 （米） Length of Bridge (m)	永久式桥梁 （座） Permanent Bridges (seat)	永久式桥梁 （米） Length of Permanent Bridges (m)	民航通航里程 （重复航线）（公里） Length of Total Civil Aviation Routes(km)
1978				
1979				
1980				
1981				
1982				
1983				
1984				
1985				
1986				
1987				
1988				
1989				
1990				
1991				
1992				65007
1993				83215
1994				100800
1995				119753
1996				126433
1997				173010
1998				180000
1999				141284
2000				139764
2001				154614
2002	29799	629	29799	211000
2003	29799	629	29799	381800
2004	29799	629	29799	386953
2005	46973	632	46915	485749
2006	46973	632	46915	418852
2007	91412	1275	90716	553355
2008	151996	1657	150980	515524
2009	154866	1803	153850	587904
2010	154866	1803	153850	742375
2011	149743	1811	148810	898628
2012	214978	2138	213985	981450

15-2 各种交通线路里程和桥梁数（2012年）

Length of Transportation Routes and Number of Bridges（2012）

指　　标	Item	2012
铁路营业里程（公里）	**Length of Railways in Operation (km)**	**269**
电气化营业里程	Length of Electrified Railways in Operation	
复线里程	Double-Tracking Length	
公路里程（公里）	**Length of Highways (km)**	**13127**
等级公路	Expressways and Class I to IV Highways	12587
高速	Expressway	465
一级	First Class	295
二级	Second Class	1496
三级	Third Class	1186
四级	Forth Class	8145
等外公路	Highways below Class IV	540
桥梁	**Bridges**	
永久式桥梁	Permanent	
座（座）	Seat (seat)	2138
长度（公里）	Length (km)	213985
民航通航里程(公里)(重复航线)	**Length of Total Civil Aviation Routes(km)**	**981450**
国际航线	**International routes**	
民航航线条数（条）	**Length of Civil Aviation routes(Article)**	**202**
国际航线（条）	International routes	11

15-3 主要年份全社会车辆数

Possession of Civil Vehicles in Representative Years

单位：辆、台 (unit)

年 份 Year	合计 Total	其中：汽车 Motor	#载客汽车 Passenget Vehicles	#载货汽车 Ordinary Trucks	其中：摩托车（辆） Motorcycles	拖拉机（台） Tractors
1999	279335	133192	63772	44348		38023
2000	310252	138318	89783	44974		37177
2001	369988	172436	110744	55453		31355
2002	454998	206653	134527	64623	176960	36083
2003	516719	242599	163872	70781	191834	34733
2004	512802	276012	195524	74557	156709	34755
2005	544586	377628	240923	82463	131440	34741
2006	608155	393778	296078	89772	131449	33236
2007	840376	522616	360081	97614	284594	32028
2008	875005	595735	430472	89093	247079	30176
2009	1012937	754803	567326	113430	224121	31347
2010	1253461	961283	739038	145740	259239	29151
2011	1445811	1174874	928669	171649	241132	25600
2012	1633257	1380125	1123105	186412	224279	24458

15-4 全社会车辆数（2012年）

Possession of Civil Vehicles（2012）

指 标	Item	2012
合计	**Total**	**1633257**
民用汽车（辆）	Motor(unit)	1380125
#私人汽车拥有量	Possession of Private Vehicles	1174425
载客汽车	Passenget Vehicles	1123105
#大 型	Large	14563
轿 车	Car	752084
普通载货汽车	Ordinary Trucks	186412
#重、中型	Heavy and Medium	61591
其他汽车	Others	70608
#三 轮	Three Wheelers	31102
拖拉机（台）	Tractors(unit)	24458
# 大中型	Large and Medium	12987
小 型	Small-sized	11471
摩托车（辆）	Motorcycle (unit)	224279
普通摩托车	Bicycle Motor	216873
挂车（辆）	Articulated Trailers (unit)	4342
其他类型车（辆）	Others (unit)	53

15-5 主要年份交通运输量及周转量

Passenger Traffic and Kilometers and Freight Traffic and Ton-kilometers in Representative Years

年 份 Year	客运量（万人次） Passenger Traffic (10 000 person-times)	旅客周转量（万人公里） Passenger-Km (10 000 person-Km)	货运量（万吨） Freight Traffic (10 000 tons)	货物周转量（万吨公里） Freight Ton-Km (10 000 ton-Km)
1978	1334		3723	
1979	1420		3919	
1980	1508		3655	
1981	1839		3379	
1982	2340		4067	
1983	3054		4225	
1984	2899		4966	
1985	2404		5681	
1986	2186		5409	
1987	3781		6294	
1988	5721		6968	
1989	6092		8742	
1990	5748		6980	
1991	4193		3389	
1992	4368		8233	
1993	8036		8406	
1994	8321		8754	
1995	9069		9590	
1996	9854		10577	
1997	8922		9358	
1998	9223		9429	
1999	10311	2130383	9766	3452383
2000	10756	2507896	10191	3691963
2001	9078	2658037	7728	4229430
2002	12527	2524444	9484	4544040
2003	11413	2596402	9392	5037684
2004	10832	3112374	14845	5850029
2005	10479	1607568	12051	1249525
2006	11245	1721217	11832	1354318
2007	12466	1753464	15124	1473182
2008	26501	2529007	27560	3490707
2009	28693	2582025	30606	3766806
2010	30294	2942957	34323	4301680
2011	33375	3223544	39231	5212010
2012	36154	3387448	44924	5958742

15-6 交通运输量及运输周转量（2012年）

Passenger Traffic and Kilometers and Freight Traffic and Ton-kilometers（2012）

指　标	Item	2012	2012比上年增长（%）Increase Rate in 2012 over 2011（%）
一、客运量合计（万人次）	**Passenger Traffic(10 000 person-times)**	**36154**	**5.3**
铁路	Railway	2919	1.8
公路	Highway	30893	5.2
民航	Civil Aviation	2342	10.7
二、旅客周转量合计（万人公里）	**Passenger-Km (10 000 person-Km)**	**3387448**	**4.8**
铁路	Railway	609287	0.8
公路	Highway	1708747	6.6
民航	Civil Aviation	1069415	4.2
三、货运量合计（万吨）	**Freight Traffic(l0 000 tons)**	**44924**	**14.5**
铁路	Railway	825	0.2
公路	Highway	44082	14.8
民航	Civil Aviation	17	1.3
四、货物周转量（万吨公里）	**Freight Ton-Kin (10 000 ton-Km)**	**5958742**	**14.3**
铁路	Railway	2219938	6.2
公路	Highway	3728976	19.9
民航	Civil Aviation	9828	-15.1

15-7 主要年份邮政电信情况

年份 Year	邮电业务总量（万元） Business Volume of Postal and Telecommunication Services(10 000 yuan)	#电信业务总量 Business Volume of Telecommunication Services	#邮政业务总量 Business Volume of Postal Services
1978	1420		
1979	1616		
1980	1640		
1981	1713		
1982	2154		
1983	2250		
1984	2484		
1985	2972		
1986	3244		
1987	3911		
1988	5327		
1989	5973		
1990	7843		
1991	5700		
1992	6610		
1993	36581		
1994	54034		
1995	76450		
1996	104566		
1997	124601		
1998	204927		
1999	306457		
2000	461628		
2001	367620		
2002	515259	470492	44767
2003	820943	770673	50270
2004	1027415	975045	52370
2005	1320447	1261033	59414
2006	1867560	1796533	71027
2007	2267633	2191250	76383
2008	2646662	2564524	82138
2009	2989246	2900836	88410
2010	3231059	3167750	63309
2011	2005025	1944329	60696
2012	2162035	2098273	63762

注：2002年及以后，邮政电信机构分离；2001—2010年邮电业务总量按2000年不变价格计算；2011年邮电业务总量按2010年不变价格计算，故与以往年份不可比。

Basic Statistic on Postal and Telecommunication Service in Representative Years

固定电话年末户数（户） Number of Immobile Telephone at Year-end (subscriber)	#农村电话用户数 Number of Telephone in Rural Areas at Year-end	移动电话用户年末数（户） Number of Mobile Phone at Year-end (subscriber)	互联网年末宽带用户（户） Number of Broad Band Net User (subscriber)
12828	1062		
13487	1052		
14024	1086		
14497	1125		
15357	1129		
16922	1156		
18611	1203		
21624	1239		
26373	1235		
30200	1290		
34265	1357		
39506	1498		
45267	1668		
49516	2479		
60727	2613		
101327	2671		
197398	5067		
299485	8386		
430270	13654		
573244	21202		
736998	37863		
874586	74761		
1242637	170199		
1711500	259374	1277400	17183
2095230	358803	1964200	35230
2538393	415593	2412392	160900
2934424	480276	3500900	243448
3214806	500847	4199570	339280
3159639	467526	5510720	508775
3145819	419446	6645863	586213
3068807	383869	7377575	813987
2891009	358238	11200566	1167916
2617691	335048	14230800	1461804
2703640	320189	16141463	1841027
3110176	335864	18035397	2023059

15-8 邮政业务及服务网点

Postal Service and Branch Post Office

指 标	Item	2010	2011	2012
一、邮政业务总量（万元）	**Business Volume of Postal Services(10 000 yuan)**	**63309**	**60696**	**63726**
二、邮政业务收入（万元）	**Gross Income of Post Services (10 000 yuan)**	**58831**	**65174**	**71778**
三、函件（万件）	**Number of Letters (10 000 pcs)**	**8176**	**3061**	**2769**
四、包件（万件）	**Parcels (10 000 pcs)**	**59**	**91**	**50**
五、汇票（万张）	**Money Order (10 000 pcs)**	**123**	**112**	**90**
六、报纸订销累计份数（万份）	**Accumulated Newspaper Prescribing and Sales Volume (10 000 pcs)**	**11724**	**12603**	**13052**
七、杂志订销累计份数（万份）	**Accumulated Magazine Prescribing and Sales Volume (10 000 pcs)**	**550**	**564**	**613**
八、特快专递类业务（万件）	**Express Mail Service Volume (10 000 pcs)**	**582**	**1901**	**129**
九、集邮业务量（万枚）	**Stamps For Collection (10 000 pcs)**	**860**	**1060**	**2312**
十、邮政营销网点（处）	**Number of Post Office Branch Establishments (unit)**	**305**	**277**	**279**
#设在农村的局所	In it: number of post offices in rural area	20	50	115
十一、邮政信筒信箱（个）	**Number of Mailboxes(unit)**	**1108**	**1108**	**1108**

注：2010年邮政储蓄业务归入金融业。

15-9 电信业务情况

Telecommunication Service

指 标	Item	2010	2011	2012
一、电信业务总量（万元）	**Business Volume of Telecommunication Services (10 000 yuan)**	**3167750**	**1944329**	**2098273**
二、电信业务总收入（万元）	**Gross Income of Telecommunication Services (10 000 yuan)**	**1038865**	**1029629**	**1162257**
三、固定电话年末户数（万户）	**Number of Immobile Telephone at Year-end (10 000 subscribers)**	**261.77**	**270.36**	**311.02**
#农村电话年末户数	Number of Telephone in Rural Areas at Year-end	33.5	32.02	33.59
四、长途电话通话总数（万次）	**Number of Long-distance Telephone Call (10 000 times)**	**101935**	**299828.81**	**173212.79**
五、电话交换机总容量（万门）	**Capacity (number) of Telephone Switchboard (10 000 lines)**	**449.05**	**441.49**	**878.27**
六、移动电话用户年末数（万户）	**Number of Mobile Phone at Year-end(10 000 subscribers)**	**1423.08**	**1614.15**	**1803.54**
#3G电话用户数	3G Mobile Phone Subscribers	33.4	177.37	394.97
七、互联网年末户数（万户）	**Number of Broad Band Net User (10 000 subscribers)**	**146.18**	**184.1**	**202.31**

主 要 统 计 指 标 解 释

铁路营业里程 又称营业长度（包括正式营业和临时营业里程），指办理客货运输业务的铁路正线总长度。凡是全线或部分建成双线及以上的线路，以第一线的实际长度计算；复线、站线、段管线、岔线和特殊用途线以及不计算运费的联络线都不计算营业里程。铁路营业里程是反映铁路运输业基础设施发展水平的重要指标，也是计算客货周转量、运输密度和机车车辆运用效率等指标的基础资料。

公路里程 指在一定时期内实际达到《公路工程技术标准JTJ01-88》规定的等级公路，并经公路主管部门正式验收交付使用的公路里程数。包括大中城市的郊区公路以及通过小城镇街道部分的公路里程和桥梁、隧道渡口的长度，不包括大中城市的街道、厂矿、林区生产用道和农业生产用道的里程。两条或多条公路共同经由同一路段，只计算一次，不得重复计算里程长度。它是反映公路建设发展规模的重要指标，也是计算运输网密度等指标的基础资料。

民用航空航线里程 指民航运输定期班机飞行的航线长度的总和。航线长度按机场之间的距离计算，通常有两种计算方法：一是将每条航线长度相加称为重复计算航线里程；一是将两线或两条以上航线经过同一区段里程，只计算一次航线长度称为不重复计算航线里程。一般常用的是后者，它能确切反映民航运输网的规模，是表明民航事业为国民经济服务和方便人民生活程度的主要指标。

货（客）运量 指在一定时期内，各种运输工具实际运送的货物（旅客）数量。它是反映运输业为国民经济和人民生活服务的数量指标，也是制定和检查运输生产计划、研究运输发展规模和速度的重要指标。货运按吨计算，客运按人计算。货物不论运输距离长短、货物类别，均按实际重量统计。旅客不论行程远近或票价多少，均按一人一次客运量统计；半价票、小孩票也按一人统计。

货物（旅客）周转量 指在一定时期内，由各种运输工具运送的货物（旅客）数量与其相应运输距离的乘积之总和。它是反映运输业生产总成果的重要指标，也是编制和检查运输生产计划，计算运输效率、劳动生产率以及核算运输单位成本的主要基础资料。计算货物周转量通常按发出站与到达站之间的最短距离，也就是计费距离计算。计算公式为：

货物（旅客）周转量=∑货物（旅客）运输量×运输距离

民用汽车拥有量 指报告期末，在公安交通管理部门按照《机动车注册登记工作规范》，已注册登记领有民用车辆牌照的全部汽车数量。汽车拥有量统计的主要分类：根据汽车结构分为载客汽车、载货汽车及其他汽车；根据汽车所有者不同分为个人（私人）汽车、单位汽车；根据汽车的使用性质分为营运汽车、非营运汽车；根据汽车大小规格不同载客汽车分为大型、中型、小型和微型，载货汽车分为重型、中型、轻型和微型。

邮电业务总量 指以价值量形式表现的邮电通信企业为社会提供各类邮电通信服务的总数量。邮电业务量按专业分类包括函件、包件、汇票、报刊发行、邮政快件、特快专递、邮政储蓄、集邮、公众电报、用户电报、传真、长途电话、出租电路、无线寻呼、移动电话、分组交换数据通信、出租代维等。计算方法为各类产品乘以相应的平均单价（不变价）之和，再加上出租电路和设备、代用户维护电话交换机和线路等的服务收入。它综合反映了一定时期邮电业务发展的总成果，是研究邮电业务量构成和发展趋势的重要指标。计算公式为：

邮电业务总量=∑（各类邮电业务量×不变单价）+出租代维及其他业务收入

移动电话用户 是指通过移动电话交换机进入移动电话网、占用移动电话号码的电话用户。用户数量以报告期末在移动电话营业部门实际办理登记手续进入移动电话网的户数进行计算，一部移动电话统计为一户。

电话用户 指接入国家公众固定电话网，并按固定电话业务进行经营管理的电话用户。1997年以前，电话用户分为市内电话用户和农村电话用户。“市内电话用户”是指接入县城及县以上城市的电话网上的电话用户；“农村电话用户”是指接入县邮电局农话台及县以下农村电话交换点，以县城为中心（除市活用户外）联通县、乡（镇）、行政村、村民小组的用户。从1997年起，电话用户数分组调整为以用户所在区域划分为“城市电话用户”和“乡村电话用户”，与过去的按市内电话和农村电话划分方法不同。而电话用户总数、电话机总部数统计范围不变。

农村电话用户 指县城关区以下的集镇和农村接入局用交换机的电话用户数。

局用交换机容量 是指安装在本地电信运营商内用于接续本地固定电话的电话交换机容量，有倍增设备按倍增后的数量计数。包括现用和备用的人工或自动交换机的全部容量。

互联网宽带接入端口 指用于接入互联网用户的各类实际安装运行的接入端口的数量，包括xDSL用户接入端口、LAN接入端口以及其他类型接入端口等，不包括窄带拨号接入端口。

Explanatory Notes on Main Statistical Indicators

Length of Railways in Operation refers to the total length of the trunk line under passenger and freight transportation(including both full operation and temporary operation). The calculation is based on the actual length of the first line even if this line has a full or partial double track or more tracks, excluding double tracks, station sidings, tracks under the charge of stations, branch lines, special-purpose lines and the non-payable connecting lines. The length of railways in operation is an important indicator to show the development of the infrastructure for the railway transport, and also the essential data to calculate volume of passenger freight transport,traffic density and utilization efficiency of the locomotives and carriages.

Length of Highways refers to the length of highways which are built in conformity with the grades specified by the highway engineering standard formulated by the Ministry of Communications, and have been formally checked and accepted by the departments of highways and put into use. The length of highways includes that of the suburb highways at large and medium- sized cities,highways passing through streets at small cities and towns,and also the length of bridges, tunnel and ferries. It does not include the length of streets in big and medium-sized cities and highways built for the production purpose at factories, mines, forest areas and agricultural areas. If two or more highways go the same section of the way, the length of the section is only calculated for once and no duplication is allowed. The length of highways is an important indicator to show the development of the highway construction and to provide essential information to calculate the transport network density.

Length of Civil Aviation Routes refers to the length of all routes for regular civil aviation flights. There are usually two ways to calculate the distance between airports connected by the route length: one is to put the length of all air routes together, called duplicated calculation of the length of the routes; the other is not to allow the duplication in calculation when two or more routes passing the same section of aviation routes. The latter is usually used, as it can precisely show the size of the civil aviation network and indicate the extent of civil aviation serving the national economy and the people.

Freight (Passenger) Traffic refers to the volume of freight (passenger) transported with various means. Freight transport is calculated in tons and passenger traffic is calculated in the number of persons. Despite the type of freight and travelling distance, the freight transport is calculated in the actual weight of the goods: and despite the travelling distance and ticket price, the passenger traffic is calculated by the principle that one person can be counted only once in one travel. The passenger who travel with a half price ticket or a child ticket is also calculated as one person. The freight (passenger) traffic provides a quantitative measure to show how the transport industry serves the national economy and people, and is also an important indicator for planning the transport industry and for studying the development scale and speed of the transport industry.

Freight Ton–kilometers(Passenger–kilometers) refer to the sum of the products of the volume of transported cargo (passengers) multiplying by the transport distance, usually using ton-kilometer and passenger-kilometer as units for measurement. Normally, the shortest distance between the departure station and the destination station (i.e., the payable distance) is the basis to calculate the freight ton-kilometers. This is an important indicator to show the total results of the transport industry, to prepare and examine the transport plan and to measure the efficiency, the labour productivity and the unit cost of transport.

The formula is as follows:

Freight Ton-kilometers(Passenger-kilometers)=Σ {Freight (Passenger) Traffic × Distance of Transportation }

Measuring unit: ton-kilometer (person-kilometer)

Possession of Civil Motor Vehicles refer to the total numbers of vehicles that are registered and received vehicles license tags according to the Work Standard for Motor Vehicles Registration formulated by the Transport Management Office under the department of public security at the end of the reference period. They are divided into categories. According to the structure of motor vehicles, they are divided into passenger vehicles, trucks and others; according to ownership into private vehicles and vehicles for the unit' s use; according to kind of usage into working vehicles and non-working vehicles; and according to size of vehicles into large passenger vehicles, medium-sized passenger vehicles, small passenger vehicles and mini passenger vehicles,heavytrucks, light-heavy trucks, light trucks and mini-trucks.

Business Volume of Post and Telecommunications refers to the total amount of post and telecommunications services, expressed in value terms, provided by the post and telecommunications departments for the society. Post and telecommunication services can be classified asletters, parcels, remittance, issue of newspapers and magazines, fast mail service, express mail service, savings deposits, stamps for collection, public and individual telegraph service, facsimiles, long-distance telephone service,leasing of telephone lines, urban paging service, mobile telephone service, data transfer and transmission, etc. The accounting approach is to multiply the service products of all types with their average unit price (constant price) to get sum of business value, plus income from other services such as leasing of telephone lines and equipment, maintenance of telephone switchboards and lines on behalf of customers. This indicator reflects the overall results of post and telecommunications service during a given period, and is important to study the composition of business service and the development of post and telecommunications service.

The formula is as follows:

Business Volume of Post and Telecommunications=Σ (Transaction of Post and Telecommunication Service x Constant Price) + Income from Leasing, Maintenance and other Services

Mobile Telephone Subscribers refer to the persons who own mobile telephone numbers and are connected with the mobile telephone communication network through the mobile telephone switchboards. The number of subscribers is calculated by the subscribers who have completed registration at mobile communication business centers and entered into the mobile telephone network. One mobile telephone is taken as a subscriber.

Telephone Subscribers refer to subscribers that are connected to the public line telephone network provided with telephone services. Before 1997, telephone subscribers were classified as city subscribers and village subscribers. City subscribers referred to those connected to city telephone networks in county towns and cities, while village subscribers referred to those connected to village telephone stations at and below counties. Since 1997, the classification of telephone subscribers was modified on the basis of physical location of the subscribers as Urban telephone subscribers and rural telephone subscribers , which is different from the previous classification of categorizing local telephones and rural telephones , while the definition of total subscribers and total number of telephones remain unchanged.

Rural Telephone Subscribers refer to telephone subscribers, located at towns under county town and country, that are connected to the public line telephone network.

Capacity of Office Telephone Exchanges refers to the capacity (measured in gate) of telephone exchanges installed in the offices of local telecommunication service providers for communication between fixed telephones. It includes the capacity of both manual and automatic exchanges in use and for stand-by purpose. Equipment with expansion function is to be counted by the expanded capacity.

Broadband Connection Terminals refer to the connection terminals to internet users actually installed and put into operation, including connection terminals for xDSL, connection terminals for LAN, and other connection terminals for xDSL. N-ISDN connection terminals are not included.

16 国内贸易

DOMESTIC TRADE

资料整理：马晓庆　杨　骏　左　宇　赵琳瑛　胡树建
Data management: Ma Xiaoqing　Yang Jun　Zuo Yu　Zhao linying　Hu Shujian

第十六部分　国内贸易

一、简要说明

本章资料主要包括社会消费品零售总额，批发零售贸易业商品购、销等情况，限额以上批发零售贸易业主要商品销售情况，限额以上批发零售贸易和住宿餐饮企业财务状况、经济效益，以及交易市场情况，由西安市统计局贸易外经处提供。

二、主要指标

批发零售贸易业网点（万个）	22.16	比上年增长	4.9%
餐饮业网点（万个）	4.57	比上年增长	4.6%
社会消费品零售总额（亿元）	2263.86	比上年增长	15.2%
#批发零售贸易业零售额	2004.90	比上年增长	16.2%

16 DOMESTIC TRADE

Ⅰ.Brief Introduction

Content of this chapter consists of total retail sales of consumer goods, sails data on commodity purchasing and sails of wholesale and retail trade, sales data on primary goods exceeds quotation, financial, economic performance and market data on wholesale and retail trade and food services industry exceeds quotation. Data in this chapter is compiled and provided by Trade and Foreign Economy Division of the Xi'an Bureau of Statistics.

Ⅱ.Maior Indicators

		Increase over Preceding Year
Establishments Engaged in Whole-sale and Retail Trade(10 000 unit)	22.16	4.9%
Establishments Engaged in Catering Zndustry(10 000 unit)	4.57	4.6%
Total Retail Sales of Consumer Goods (100 mil. yuan)	2263.86	15.2%
Retail Sales of Wholesale and Retail Enterprises	2004.90	16.2%

16-1 主要年份社会消费品零售额

Total Retail Sales of Consumer Goods in Representative Years

单位：亿元 (100 million yuan)

年 份 Year	社会消费品零售总额 Total Retail Sales of Consumer Goods	城镇 Urban	乡村 Village	批发和零售业 Wholesale Trades and Retail Trades	住宿餐饮业 Accommodation and Catering Trade	其他行业 Others
1978	12.70	8.82	3.88	11.01	0.53	0.21
1979	13.94	9.88	4.06	11.88	0.60	0.21
1980	15.88	11.53	4.35	13.05	0.80	0.20
1981	17.41	12.85	4.56	14.31	0.80	0.19
1982	18.54	13.79	4.75	15.25	0.88	0.27
1983	20.82	15.14	5.68	16.95	1.03	0.32
1984	24.87	19.13	5.74	19.47	1.29	0.46
1985	32.92	26.09	6.83	25.04	1.69	0.48
1986	37.50	29.25	8.25	28.88	1.97	0.64
1987	43.86	34.62	9.24	33.32	2.50	0.49
1988	59.65	47.74	11.91	44.84	2.97	0.78
1989	68.05	54.60	13.45	54.41	2.98	0.76
1990	72.77	59.42	13.35	57.46	3.79	0.90
1991	81.04	66.93	14.11	60.35	4.43	1.26
1992	100.84	89.17	11.67	71.86	6.13	2.30
1993	115.38	104.41	10.97	75.99	7.49	2.71
1994	144.64	131.56	13.08	89.79	9.12	3.43
1995	186.60	165.98	20.62	115.46	11.97	3.73
1996	222.94	198.19	24.75	145.05	15.83	4.02
1997	264.47	238.17	26.30	169.08	22.12	4.17
1998	291.45	257.39	34.06	183.43	30.97	4.27
1999	323.37	283.32	40.05	207.96	34.78	4.85
2000	360.42	317.12	43.30	232.89	41.42	5.43
2001	406.21	358.97	47.24	265.25	48.87	5.86
2002	459.76	409.86	49.90	309.36	51.42	6.45
2003	502.65	449.62	53.03	440.28	53.30	9.07
2004	578.60	520.94	57.66	509.60	56.87	12.13
2005	670.56	604.63	65.93	592.77	63.59	14.20
2006	784.95	708.31	76.64	694.03	74.77	16.15
2007	936.21	845.59	90.62	828.63	89.32	18.26
2008	1176.58	1063.93	112.65	1033.00	122.90	20.68
2009	1381.12	1249.79	131.33	1222.98	134.54	23.60
2010	1637.04	1570.16	66.88	1431.23	179.82	25.99
2011	1965.98	1908.65	57.33	1725.03	210.15	30.80
2012	2263.86	2195.18	68.68	2004.90	231.16	27.80

注：依据2008年第二次经济普查数据，对2005-2007年数据进行调整。
2009年以前按经营单位所在地分为市和县及县以下。
2002年以前按行业分组中不包括制造业零售额和农业对非农业居民零售额。

16-2 社会消费品零售总额（2012年）

Total Retail Sales of Consumer Goods（2012）

单位：亿元 (100 million yuan)

分 类	Classify	金 额 Sum
社会消费品零售总额	**Total Retail Sales of Consumer Goods**	**2263.86**
（一）按销售单位所在地分	Grouped by Region	
（1）城镇	Urban	2195. 18
#城区	District	1850.99
（2）乡村	Village	68.68
（二）按行业分：	Grouped by Sector	
（1）批发业	Wholesale Enterprises	340.40
限额以上单位	Enterprises Above Designated Size	317.68
限额以下单位	Enterprises Below Designated Size and Self-employed Laborers	22.72
（2）零售业	Retail Enterprises	1664.50
限额以上单位	Enterprises Above Designated Size	1312.62
限额以下单位	Enterprises Below Designated Size and Self-employed Laborers	351.88
（3）住宿和餐饮业	Accommodation and Catering Trade	231.16
限额以下单位	Enterprises Above Designated Size	108.61
限额以上单位	Enterprises Below Designated Size and Self-employed Laborers	122.55
（4）其他行业	Others	27.80

16-3 各区县社会消费品零售总额（2012年）

Total Retail Sales of Consumer Goods by Region（2012）

单位：亿元 (100 million yuan)

区县名称	Name of District and County	社会消费品零售总额 Total Retail Sales of Consumer Goods	批发零售贸易业零售额 Wholesale and Retail Trade of Retail Sales	住宿餐饮业零售额 Accommodation and Catering Trade of Retail Sales
新城区	Xincheng	392.96	366.65	21.21
碑林区	Beilin	392.32	344.03	45.79
莲湖区	Lianhu	323.21	291.15	31.56
灞桥区	Baqiao	55.01	47.55	7.26
未央区	Weiyang	318.57	299.56	18.91
雁塔区	Yanta	439.52	375.05	50.67
阎良区	Yanliang	26.78	22.03	4.55
临潼区	Lintong	55.93	48.52	6.41
长安区	Chang'an	127.86	98.00	27.86
蓝田县	Lantian	40.89	35.33	5.16
周至县	Zhouzhi	27.49	24.47	2.52
户 县	Huxian	44.67	38.03	6.34
高陵县	Gaoling	18.67	14.53	2.94

16-4 主要年份批发零售贸易业、餐饮业网点和人员

Wholesale and Retail Trade, Catering Outlets and Staff in Representative Years

单位：个、人 (unit, person)

年份 Year	批发业 Wholesale Trade		零售业 Retail Trade		餐饮业 Catering Services	
	网点 Branch Shop	人员 Personnel	网点 Branch Shop	人员 Personnel	网点 Branch Shop	人员 Personnel
1978	586	22136	5862	51462	442	9043
1979	462	14002	5387	49252	815	10349
1980	1505	28320	6312	51927	1893	16297
1981	597	17780	8800	74095	3397	25626
1982	881	25023	9811	68734	6422	25879
1983	1642	32597	17130	77863	6387	28054
1984	1875	34906	27043	136852	8484	25977
1985	1247	43311	35860	223076	11907	41025
1986	1706	42270	37503	241052	11977	48335
1987	3351	44475	42484	260450	13673	51361
1988	1829	40324	44330	282911	9576	47131
1989	1638	80078	46613	229705	10228	46420
1990	1558	37077	43244	219413	9800	34561
1991	1918	45583	48171	236235	10369	36813
1992	1864	36012	48422	258491	9916	38935
1993	5177	54255	43289	226572	11804	38318
1994	6338	58154	60292	318287	14296	56502
1995	6564	63337	69623	364430	15485	68782
1996	8008	67840	76828	437655	15668	78313
1997	8414	71178	80379	468811	20259	82917
1998	10780	85420	95056	515723	22500	100862
1999	10865	86630	96516	516163	24977	118442
2000	10393	81519	93928	492083	27531	124988
2001	10534	78285	95414	497448	28219	128738
2002	12220	107352	96815	465320	29219	140623
2003	13274	117740	99764	490169	32899	150883
2004	19696	102779	106477	281221	27905	132855
2005	20392	106138	112541	298285	30156	142176
2006	21243	110595	117168	312426	31694	148317
2007	21835	114497	122810	330583	34249	161517
2008	26813	148403	164642	470886	38134	201978
2009	26403	154777	165921	507706	39515	205364
2010	27887	166735	173218	544487	41289	219793
2011	30441	253618	180782	585680	43728	232552
2012	34165	280672	187466	611561	45667	241390

16-5 批发贸易业机构、网点、人员（2012年）

单位：个、人

分类	Classify	合计 Total 法人单位 Constitutional Unit	活动单位 Movemental Unit	网点 Branch Shop	人员 Personnel
总计	**Total**	**12698**	**13578**	**34165**	**280672**
一.按登记注册类型分组	**Grouped by Registered Kind**				
内资企业	Civil Funded Enterprises	12495	13238	14462	206389
国有企业	State-owned Enterprises	349	416	650	19166
集体企业	Collective-owned Enterprises	271	278	547	4053
股份合作企业	Cooperative Enterprises	235	259	260	9210
联营企业	Joint Ownership Enterprises	19	19	19	256
有限责任公司	Limited Liability Corporations	4089	4398	4587	80554
股份有限公司	Share-holding Corporations Ltd.	805	1042	1079	32991
私营企业	Private Enterprises	6315	6398	6676	55615
其他企业	Other Enterprises	412	428	644	4544
港澳台商投资企业	Enterprises with Funds from Hong Kong, Macao &Taiwan	135	260	260	7242
外商投资企业	Foreign Funded Enterprises	68	80	80	2618
个体经济	Individuals			19363	64423
二.按国民经济行业分组	**Grouped by Seetor**				
农、林、牧产品批发	Wholesale of Farm Produce and Livestock Products	271	299	1672	13363
食品、饮料及烟草制品批发	Wholesale of Food, Beverages and Tobaccos	774	802	6246	33340
纺织、服装及家庭用品批发	Wholesale of Textiles, Garments and Daily Articles	898	1131	3949	48167
文化、体育用品及器材批发	Wholesale of Culture, Sports Articles and Equipments	824	839	3131	38647
医药及医疗器材批发	Wholesale of Medicines and Medical Appliances	716	781	1333	18202
矿产品、建材及化工产品批发	Wholesale of Mineral Products, Building Materials and Chemical Products	3687	3731	7184	54576
机械设备、五金交电及电子产品批发	Wholesale of Machinery, Hardwares, Transport Means and Electronic Equipment	4143	4589	8283	49290
贸易经济与代理	Trade Broker and Agency	422	426	483	10057
其他批发	Other Wholesales	963	980	1884	15030

Organizations, Establishments and Staff Engaged in Whole-sale Trade（2012）

(unit, person)

城镇 Urban								乡村 Village			
				城区 County							
法人单位 Constitutional Unit	活动单位 Movemental Unit	网点 Branch Shop	人员 Personnel	法人单位 Constitutional Unit	活动单位 Movemental Unit	网点 Branch Shop	人员 Personnel	法人单位 Constitutional Unit	活动单位 Movemental Unit	网点 Branch Shop	人员 Personnel
12501	**13356**	**32300**	**273360**	**12310**	**13111**	**30355**	**265939**	**197**	**222**	**1865**	**7312**
12298	13016	14237	202439	12108	12772	13914	199031	197	222	225	3950
306	359	593	17079	271	297	488	15872	43	57	57	2087
225	230	499	3359	194	199	435	2864	46	48	48	694
234	258	258	9170	230	254	254	9120	1	1	2	40
19	19	19	256	19	19	19	256				
4083	4392	4581	80339	4068	4376	4564	80043	6	6	6	215
790	1027	1064	32901	785	1023	1060	32646	15	15	15	90
6232	6308	6584	54827	6136	6185	6460	53746	83	90	92	788
409	423	639	4508	405	419	634	4484	3	5	5	36
135	260	260	7242	134	259	259	7226				
68	80	80	2618	68	80	80	2598				
		17723	61061			16102	57084			1640	3362
227	249	1478	12563	190	203	1272	11777	44	50	194	800
741	762	6065	31166	713	729	5596	29276	33	40	181	2174
890	1120	3891	47795	872	1098	3394	46329	8	11	58	372
819	833	3045	38296	812	824	2928	37923	5	6	86	351
712	777	1293	17973	702	751	1237	17058	4	4	40	229
3641	3683	6662	53086	3594	3622	6350	51950	46	48	522	1490
4142	4587	8111	48971	4126	4570	7898	48385	1	2	172	319
419	423	460	10017	418	422	459	10011	3	3	23	40
910	922	1295	13493	883	892	1221	13230	53	58	589	1537

16-6 零售贸易业机构、网点、人员（2012年）

单位：个、人

分类	Classify	合计 Total 法人单位 Constitutional Unit	活动单位 Movemental Unit	网点 Branch Shop	人员 Personnel
总计	**Total**	**9470**	**10685**	**187466**	**611561**
一.按登记注册类型分组	**Grouped by Registered Kind**				
内资企业	Civil Funded Enterprises	9340	10511	11431	170877
国有企业	State-owned Enterprises	231	294	390	16040
集体企业	Collective-owned Enterprises	288	365	469	4742
股份合作企业	Cooperative Enterprises	110	130	148	7310
联营企业	Joint Ownership Enterprises	30	36	36	328
有限责任公司	Limited Liability Corporations	2854	3507	3730	70856
股份有限公司	Share-holding Corporations Ltd.	134	164	217	5649
私营企业	Private Enterprises	5465	5763	6180	63333
其他企业	Other Enterprises	228	252	261	2619
港澳台商投资企业	Enterprises with Funds from Hong Kong, Macao & Taiwan	41	65	65	6308
外商投资企业	Foreign Funded Enterprises	89	109	117	7855
个体经济	Individuals			175853	426521
二.按国民经济行业分组	**Grouped by Sector**				
综合零售	Intergrated Retail	1079	1206	29806	95934
食品、饮料及烟草制品专门零售	Retail of Food,Beverages and Tobaccos	666	799	39161	114127
纺织、服装及日用品专门零售	Special Retail of Textiles,Garments and Daily Consumer Articles	1186	1399	45159	154334
文化、体育用品及器材专门零售	Retail of Culture, Sports Appliances and Equipments	738	827	10301	38821
医药及医疗器材专门零售	Retail of Medicines and Medical Appliances	839	1062	8278	29717
汽车、摩托车、燃料及零售配件专门零售	Retail of Motor Vehicles, Motorcycles, Fuel and Parts	1005	1066	11424	55619
家用电器及电子产品专门零售	Special Retail of Household Electric Appliances and Electronic Products	1964	2232	14345	49550
五金、家具及室内装修材料专门零售	Special Retail of Hardware, Furniture and Decoration Materials	1443	1530	20121	50262
货摊、无店铺及其他零售业	Non-shop and Other Retail	550	564	8871	23197

Organizations, Establishments and Staff Engaged in Retail Trade （2012）

(unit, person)

城镇 Urban								乡村 Village			
				城区 County							
法人单位 Constitutional Unit	活动单位 Movemental Unit	网点 Branch Shop	人员 Personnel	法人单位 Constitutional Unit	活动单位 Movemental Unit	网点 Branch Shop	人员 Personnel	法人单位 Constitutional Unit	活动单位 Movemental Unit	网点 Branch Shop	人员 Personnel
9249	**10421**	**159888**	**554930**	**8811**	**9901**	**136689**	**502187**	**221**	**264**	**27578**	**56631**
9119	10247	10996	165782	8681	9727	10398	158625	221	264	435	5095
224	280	360	15587	200	238	271	15008	7	14	30	453
260	337	370	4233	232	261	276	3621	28	28	99	509
106	126	127	6980	94	114	114	6783	4	4	21	330
27	33	33	283	26	32	32	277	3	3	3	45
2839	3488	3707	70577	2800	3450	3668	70114	15	19	23	279
123	153	189	4946	120	137	173	4667	11	11	28	703
5322	5590	5964	60851	5000	5264	5629	55944	143	173	216	2482
218	240	246	2325	209	231	235	2211	10	12	15	294
41	65	65	6308	41	65	65	6308				
89	109	116	7839	89	109	116	7829			1	16
		148711	375001			126110	329425			27142	51520
993	1114	17140	70398	856	972	12326	58632	86	92	12666	25536
645	773	33692	104952	619	741	28315	90961	21	26	5469	9175
1163	1367	40453	146238	1098	1300	32625	130520	23	32	4706	8096
733	821	9421	36371	717	805	8722	34685	5	6	880	2450
820	1032	7421	26921	780	952	6552	24508	19	30	857	2796
975	1035	10847	54022	913	949	9077	52227	30	31	577	1597
1948	2207	13304	46086	1905	2164	12487	43397	16	25	1041	3464
1434	1520	19774	48411	1397	1478	18907	46176	9	10	347	1851
538	552	7836	21531	526	540	7678	21081	12	12	1035	1666

16-7 餐饮业机构、网点、人员（2012年）

单位：个、人

分 类	Classify	合计 法人单位 Constitutional Unit	Total 活动单位 Movemental Unit	网点 Branch Shop	人员 Personnel
总计	**Total**	**1790**	**2114**	**45667**	**241390**
一.按登记注册类型分组	**Grouped by Type of Registration**				
内资企业	Domestic Funded Enterprises	1748	1956	2084	77795
国有企业	State-owned Enterprises	35	42	43	3041
集体企业	Collective-owned Enterprises	17	20	20	761
股份合作企业	Share-holding Cooperative Enterprises	3	3	3	180
联营企业	Joint Ownership Enterprises	36	37	39	1089
有限责任公司	Limited Liability Corporations	438	509	550	28071
股份有限公司	Share-holding Corporations Ltd.	51	85	85	3972
私营企业	Private Enterprises	1118	1203	1264	39642
其他企业	Other Enterprises	50	57	80	1039
港澳台商投资企业	Enterprises with Funds from Hong Kong, Macao & Taiwan	17	120	120	6953
外商投资企业	Foreign Funded Enterprises	25	38	45	1902
个体经济	Individuals			43418	154740
二、按餐饮业行业分组	**Grouped by Sector of Catering Trade**				
正餐服务	Restaurant	1461	1590	25649	166916
快餐服务	Fast Food	116	212	4313	14756
饮料及冷饮服务	Beverages and Cold Drinks	108	157	1527	5194
其他餐饮服务	Others	105	155	14178	54524

Organizations ,Establishments and Staff Engaged in Catering Trade（2012）

(unit, person)

城镇 Urban								乡村 Village			
				城区 County							
法人单位 Constitutional Unit	活动单位 Movemental Unit	网点 Branch Shop	人员 Personnel	法人单位 Constitutional Unit	活动单位 Movemental Unit	网点 Branch Shop	人员 Personnel	法人单位 Constitutional Unit	活动单位 Movemental Unit	网点 Branch Shop	人员 Personnel
1698	**2016**	**40405**	**222518**	**1525**	**1838**	**35664**	**203658**	**92**	**98**	**5262**	**18872**
1657	1859	1987	76008	1484	1681	1809	72218	91	97	97	1787
34	41	42	3009	32	39	39	2830	1	1	1	32
17	20	20	761	16	17	17	501				
3	3	3	180	2	2	2	170				
26	27	29	768	23	24	26	650	10	10	10	321
435	506	547	28025	421	493	534	27504	3	3	3	46
48	81	81	3793	44	75	75	3690	3	4	4	179
1047	1127	1188	38488	902	980	1042	35922	71	76	76	1154
47	54	77	984	44	51	74	951	3	3	3	55
17	120	120	6953	17	120	120	6933				
24	37	44	1816	24	37	44	1816	1	1	1	86
		38254	137741			33691	122691			5164	16999
1374	1498	23978	156613	1222	1339	22570	149142	87	92	1671	10303
111	206	3618	13375	103	200	2770	11656	5	6	695	1381
108	157	1527	5194	106	155	1525	5181				
105	155	11282	47336	94	144	8799	37679			2896	7188

16-8 各区县批发、零售、餐饮业机构、网点、人员（2012年）

Organizations, Branch Shops and Staff of Wholesale,Retail and Catering Trade by Region（2012）

单位：个、人 (unit，person)

分　类	Classify	法人单位 Constitutional Unit	活动单位 Movemental Unit	网点 Branch Shop	人员 Personnel
一、批发业	**Wholesale Trade**	**12698**	**13578**	**34165**	**280672**
新城区	Xincheng	1385	1422	10812	52336
碑林区	Beilin	2230	2287	3690	36112
莲湖区	Lianhu	1549	1586	5209	25723
灞桥区	Baqiao	581	581	726	5589
未央区	Weiyang	4935	5575	6865	113684
雁塔区	Yanta	1514	1531	2307	27814
阎良区	Yanliang	55	57	392	1403
临潼区	Lintong	90	110	634	3942
长安区	Chang'an	122	134	867	5451
蓝田县	Lantian	61	68	936	2538
周至县	Zhouzhi	49	69	761	1816
户　县	Huxian	89	105	704	2752
高陵县	Gaoling	38	53	262	1512
二、零售业	**Retail Trade**	**9470**	**10685**	**187466**	**611561**
新城区	Xincheng	1315	1531	24043	113868
碑林区	Beilin	2121	2516	22972	75241
莲湖区	Lianhu	899	922	17173	52964
灞桥区	Baqiao	485	490	7220	21417
未央区	Weiyang	2156	2358	23944	84310

15-8 续表 continued

单位：个、人 (unit, person)

分 类	Classify	法人单位 Constitutional Unit	活动单位 Movemental Unit	网点 Branch Shop	人员 Personnel
雁塔区	Yanta	1559	1779	25953	112665
阎良区	Yanliang	87	92	5049	9088
临潼区	Lintong	100	126	7977	14128
长安区	Chang'an	319	348	22461	68996
蓝田县	Lantian	78	78	8636	15171
周至县	Zhouzhi	72	72	10239	13896
户 县	Huxian	201	280	8798	23232
高陵县	Gaoling	78	93	3001	6585
三、餐饮业	**Catering Trade**	**1790**	**2114**	**45667**	**241390**
新城区	Xincheng	127	147	2378	15341
碑林区	Beilin	346	534	5535	40587
莲湖区	Lianhu	215	236	4332	24943
灞桥区	Baqiao	67	71	2386	9431
未央区	Weiyang	150	160	5188	32089
雁塔区	Yanta	525	587	10560	61798
阎良区	Yanliang	29	31	1241	4964
临潼区	Lintong	30	36	1801	6139
长安区	Chang'an	106	110	6430	25482
蓝田县	Lantian	84	84	1896	5676
周至县	Zhouzhi	10	10	1486	3095
户 县	Huxian	56	58	1781	8915
高陵县	Gaoling	45	50	653	2930

16-9 限额以上批发零售贸易企业财务状况（2012年）

单位：万元

分 类	Classify	单位数（个）Number (unit)	资产总计 Total Assets	流动资产合计 Circulating Funds	固定资产合计 Total Fixed Assets
总计	**Totai**	**575**	**13299255.2**	**9780196.1**	**1372739.4**
一、批发企业	**Wholesale Enterprises**	**240**	**7444417.1**	**5717075.3**	**481136.6**
1. 按登记注册类型分组	Grouped by Category of Commodities				
内资企业	Domestic Funded Enterprises	234	6113144.4	4739542.1	472117.0
国有	State-owned Enterprises	3112	2136480.8	1541623.8	256381.4
集体	Collective-owned Enterprises	4	73485.2	33088.9	5404.0
股份合作	Corperative Enterprises				
联营	Joint Ownership Enterprises				
国有联营	State Joint Ownership Enterprises				
集体联营	Collective Joint Ownership Enterprises				
国有与集体联营	Joint State-collective Enterprises				
其他联营	Others Joint Ownership Enterprises				
有限责任公司	Limited Liability Corporrations	129	2570408.1	2298090.6	114351.4
国有独资公司	State Funded Corporations	1	19576.4	18748.7	324.3
其他有限责任公司	Other Limited Liability Corporrations	128	2550831.7	2279341.9	114027.1
股份有限公司	Other Limited Liability Corporrations	3	617729.2	234903.4	64016.7
私营	Other Limited Liability Corporrations	63	696724.2	615030.7	30552.4
私营独资	Private-funded Enterprises	4	7020.4	6770.5	96.8
私营合伙	Private Partnership Enterprises				
私营有限责任公司	Private Limited Liability Corporations	58	665975.0	585749.3	30237.7
私营股份有限公司	Private Share-holding Corporations Ltd.	1	23728.8	22510.9	217.9
其他	Other Enterprises	4	18316.9	16804.7	1411.1
港澳台商投资	Enterprises with Funds from Hong Kong, Macao &Taiwan	3	63858.6	61562.4	1885.0
外商投资	Foreign Funded Enterprises	3	1267414.1	915970.8	7134.6
2. 按国民经济行业分组	Grouped by Sector				

Financial Stares of Enterprises above Designated Size in Wholesale and Retail（2012）

(10 000 yuan)

固定资产原价 Original Value of Fixed Assets	累计折旧 Accumulated Depreciation	负债合计 Total Liabilities	流动负债合计 Circulating Liabilities	非流动负债 Non-Circulating Liabilities	所有者权益合计 Total Owners' Equities	实收资本 Paid in Capital	营业收入 Total Revenue	主营业务收入 Revenue from Principal Business
1926666.6	**576300.4**	**10044705.4**	**9683132.6**	**361974.3**	**3254549.8**	**1717506.7**	**32292266.4**	**31892066.6**
654844.1	**195899.7**	**5808677.3**	**5724423.6**	**86282.1**	**1635739.8**	**873251.6**	**20999062.2**	**20725580.5**
642946.3	193021.5	4672846.2	4588592.5	86282.1	1440298.2	726618.0	17811217.6	17537735.9
323448.9	68762.8	1447315.4	1437284.9	10030.6	689165.4	336510.5	5434308.3	5400415.1
8893.5	3489.5	67496.0	39761.9	27735.1	5989.2	4771.3	5503.6	5374.8
183946.6	70038.3	2224888.5	2193691.4	33224.7	345519.6	232529.2	8795502.4	8570647.5
658.9	334.6	14625.7	14625.7		4950.7	7844.3	90523.8	90521.6
183287.7	69703.7	2210262.8	2179065.7	33224.7	340568.9	224684.9	8704978.6	8480125.9
69320.4	25357.5	323081.8	319472.1	3609.7	294647.4	26973.3	1600566.2	1591151.7
55778.0	25225.6	590088.1	578615.8	11472.0	106636.1	124688.4	1925004.2	1919813.9
154.3	57.5	5131.8	5131.5		1888.6	1573.1	58318.9	58318.9
55333.4	25095.7	569116.6	557782.6	11334.0	96858.4	115248.3	1766811.9	1761621.6
290.3	72.4	15839.7	15701.7	138.0	7889.1	7867.0	99873.4	99873.4
1558.9	147.8	19976.4	19766.4	210.0	-1659.5	1145.3	50332.9	50332.9
3233.3	1348.3	52511.6	52511.6		11347.0	3073.6	361228.0	361228.0
8664.5	1529.9	1083319.5	1083319.5		184094.6	143560.0	2826616.6	2826616.6

16-9 续表1

单位：万元

分 类	Classify	营业成本 Total Cost	主营业务成本 Cost of Principal Business	营业税金及附加 Taxs and Other Changes	主营业务税金及附加 Taxs and Other Changes on Principal Business
总计	**Totai**	**29317206.9**	**29266866.9**	**209790.1**	**203004.6**
一、批发企业	**Wholesale Enterprises**	**19674461.1**	**19637793.7**	**90315.2**	**88910.3**
1. 按登记注册类型分组	Grouped by Category of Commodities				
内资企业	Domestic Funded Enterprises	16514031.5	16477364.1	89905.4	88572.7
国有	State-owned Enterprises	5032328.0	5008281.9	56898.9	56142.8
集体	Collective-owned Enterprises	4568.7	4383.4	29.5	29.5
股份合作	Corperative Enterprises				
联营	Joint Ownership Enterprises				
国有联营	State Joint Ownership Enterprises				
集体联营	Collective Joint Ownership Enterprises				
国有与集体联营	Joint State-collective Enterprises				
其他联营	Others Joint Ownership Enterprises				
有限责任公司	Limited Liability Corporrations	8097057.2	8095129.2	29353.0	29041.4
国有独资公司	State Funded Corporations	88866.1	88823.1	83.8	83.8
其他有限责任公司	Other Limited Liability Corporrations	8008191.1	8006306.1	29269.2	28957.6
股份有限公司	Other Limited Liability Corporrations	1497045.2	1488816.0	1502.5	1487.9
私营	Other Limited Liability Corporrations	1838263.6	1835984.8	2115.3	1864.9
私营独资	Private-funded Enterprises	36349.5	36349.5	293.2	293.2
私营合伙	Private Partnership Enterprises				
私营有限责任公司	Private Limited Liability Corporations	1709387.3	1707108.5	1605.7	1355.3
私营股份有限公司	Private Share-holding Corporations Ltd.	92526.8	92526.8	216.4	216.4
其他	Other Enterprises	44768.8	44768.8	6.2	6.2
港澳台商投资	Enterprises with Funds from Hong Kong, Macao &Taiwan	333464.6	333464.6	283.8	211.6
外商投资	Foreign Funded Enterprises	2826965.0	2826965.0	126.0	126.0
2. 按国民经济行业分组	Grouped by Sector				

continued 1

(10 000 yuan)

销售费用 Sale Expenses	管理费用 Managenment Expenses	财务费用 Financial Expenses	营业利润 Business Profits	利润总额 Total Profits	应付职工薪酬 Salary Payable	本年应交增值税 Value Added Tax Payable
987837.7	**517184.0**	**132204.6**	**1169287.2**	**909555.0**	**523739.6**	**476538.6**
394166.0	**199028.3**	**39748.2**	**601778.8**	**364545.8**	**269397.2**	**200199.8**
374485.0	191564.4	46145.9	589947.3	352391.2	259239.7	196358.3
104340.1	73378.6	12156.5	152531.2	159463.9	158931.5	63316.6
463.5	1198.2	-36.5	-144.4	117.3	494.6	6.1
180674.5	86969.5	18880.7	379642.5	153698.5	61422.3	108404.5
746.5	209.7	621.6	-3.9	102.0	190.9	32.6
179928.0	86759.8	18259.1	379646.4	153596.5	61231.4	108371.9
48497.1	7073.8	1989.1	44172.9	44021.9	18326.9	14883.2
34075.0	20373.5	12888.7	17460.2	-1141.5	19583.5	9214.4
392.7	677.3	355.2	20352.4	291.8	327.3	201.9
32570.4	19353.9	11896.0	-7930.7	-6471.8	11280.0	8834.9
1111.9	342.3	637.5	5038.5	5038.5	7976.2	177.6
6434.8	2570.8	267.4	-3715.1	-3768.9	480.9	533.5
16919.2	4159.8	-19.2	6419.8	6447.1	8845.3	2859.9
2761.8	3304.1	-6378.5	5411.7	5707.5	1312.2	981.6

16-9 续表2

单位：万元

分 类	Classify	单位数（个）Number (unit)	资产总计 Total Assets	流动资产合计 Circulating Funds	固定资产合计 Total Fixed Assets
农、林、牧产品批发	Wholesale of Farm produce and Livestock Products	4	89133.2	44555.0	9588.0
食品、饮料及烟草制品批发	Wholesale of Beverages and Tobaccos	19	477594.2	347790.5	82218.0
纺织、服装及家庭服务器批发	Wholesale of Beverages and Tobaccos Consumer Articles	20	391226.5	358185.9	23674.1
文化、体育用品及器材批发	Wholesale of Culture, Sports Applionces and Equipments	10	149649.6	82334.5	8455.7
医药及医疗器材批发	Wholesale of Medicines and Medical Appliances	34	489240.2	445704.1	8521.6
矿产品、建材及化工产品批发	Wholesale of Mineral Products, Building Materials and Chemical Products	100	5110386.0	3758310.0	325927.4
机械设备、五金产品及电子产品批发	Wholesale of Machinery, Hardware, and Electronic Equipment	49	718258.0	664366.2	20235.9
贸易经纪与代理	Trade Borker and Agency	2	11288.5	10585.5	360.3
其他批发	Other wholesale not Classified Elsewhere	2	7640.9	5243.6	2155.6
二、零售企业	**Retail Trade**	**335**	**5854838.1**	**4063120.8**	**891602.8**
1.按登记注册类型分组	Grouped by Category of Commodities				
内资	Domestic Funded Enterprises	305	4427092.0	3043446.5	755185.1
国有	State-owned Enterprises	15	194065.9	155553.1	33974.9
集体	Collective-owned Enterprises	20	15613.7	7840.7	6489.7
股份合作	Share-holding Cooperative Enterprises				
联营	Joint Ownership Enterprises	1	237.8	177.8	60.0
国有联营	State Joint Ownership Enterprises				
集体联营	Collective Joint Ownership Enterprises	1	237.8	177.8	60.0
国有与集体联营	Joint State-collective Enterprises				
其他联营	Others Joint Ownership Enterprises				
有限责任公司	Limited Liability Corporations	169	2266051.8	1617757.7	349944.7
国有独资	State Funded Corporations	2	42405.2	20530.2	13841.6

continued 2

(10 000 yuan)

固定资产原价 Original Value of Fixed Assets	累计折旧 Accumulated Depreciation	负债合计 Total Liabilities	流动负债合计 Circulating Liabilities	非流动负债 Non-Circulating Liabilities	所有者权益合计 Total Owners' Equities	实收资本 Paid in Capital	营业收入 Total Revenue	主营业务收入 Revenue from Principal Business
11596.8	3704.1	78798.1	50543.0	28256.1	10335.1	9448.2	11751.9	11751.9
115017.0	32799.0	126953.8	111355.4	15598.4	350640.4	33326.8	1228130.8	1226433.5
57308.7	33634.6	346200.3	345646.4	3009.5	45026.2	37899.1	1815541.6	1809340.1
13179.1	4723.4	78341.5	76091.5	2250.0	71308.1	42050.0	160798.7	160164.9
15069.4	6547.8	438572.5	434125.7	4446.7	50667.7	35398.8	1016652.6	1012992.1
406782.8	100909.2	4060541.4	4029082.5	31031.0	1049844.6	673538.0	14985315.9	14742577.1
32842.8	13050.0	664878.8	664298.6	580.0	53379.2	37139.6	1720305.7	1701837.0
431.1	70.8	10099.1	9778.7	320.4	1189.4	1251.1	34534.6	34453.5
2616.4	460.8	4291.8	3501.8	790.0	3349.1	3200.0	26030.4	26030.4
1271822.5	**380400.7**	**4236028.1**	**3958709.0**	**275692.2**	**1618810.0**	**844255.1**	**11293204.2**	**11166486.1**
1090791.3	335787.2	3273799.7	3024108.3	257456.7	1153292.3	581136.0	8583937.9	8478292.9
40499.8	6524.9	150398.6	94545.8	55852.8	43667.3	7427.8	320871.7	318950.6
9836.7	3347.0	14946.6	14333.5	620.1	667.1	2691.7	147182.8	147182.8
147.6	87.6	120.0	120.0		117.8	50.0	3470.7	3470.7
147.6	87.6	120.0	120.0		117.8	50.0	3470.7	3470.7
513995.8	164232.1	1661316.9	1505737.4	152434.4	604734.9	374764.6	4878582.6	4792846.6
21039.7	7198.1	31360.7	30612.7	748.0	11044.5	3065.4	47968.0	46941.4

16-9 续表3

单位：万元

分 类	Classify	营业成本 Total Cost	主营业务成本 Cost of Principal Business	营业税金及附加 Taxs and Other Changes	主营业务税金及附加 Taxs and Other Changes on Principal Business
农、林、牧产品批发	Wholesale of Farm produce and Livestock Products	10029.2	10029.2	161.5	161.5
食品、饮料及烟草制品批发	Wholesale of Beverages and Tobaccos	955497.9	954564.1	52130.4	51964.2
纺织、服装及家庭服务器批发	Wholesale of Beverages and Tobaccos Consumer Articles	1567294.6	1564910.7	23263.5	23263.5
文化、体育用品及器材批发	Wholesale of Culture, Sports Applionces and Equipments	145109.7	145035.8	217.1	197.6
医药及医疗器材批发	Wholesale of Medicines and Medical Appliances	960056.2	959988.7	949.5	706.7
矿产品、建材及化工产品批发	Wholesale of Mineral Products, Building Materials and Chemical Products	14377502.3	14362490.8	11631.1	11123.2
机械设备、五金产品及电子产品批发	Wholesale of Machinery, Hardware, and Electronic Equipment	1604836.6	1586665.5	1928.8	1460.3
贸易经纪与代理	Trade Borker and Agency	30373.9	30348.2	6.7	6.7
其他批发	Other wholesale not Classified Elsewhere	23760.7	23760.7	26.6	26.6
二、零售企业	**Retail Trade**	**9642745.8**	**9629073.2**	**119474.9**	**114094.3**
1.按登记注册类型分组	Grouped by Category of Commodities				
内资	Domestic Funded Enterprises	7266788.0	7257382.9	105690.9	100362.4
国有	State-owned Enterprises	269421.6	268977.4	1099.4	1084.3
集体	Collective-owned Enterprises	107602.0	107602.0	2486.4	2466.0
股份合作	Share-holding Cooperative Enterprises				
联营	Joint Ownership Enterprises	3189.9	3189.9	5.0	5.0
国有联营	State Joint Ownership Enterprises				
集体联营	Collective Joint Ownership Enterprises	3189.9	3189.9	5.0	5.0
国有与集体联营	Joint State-collective Enterprises				
其他联营	Others Joint Ownership Enterprises				
有限责任公司	Limited Liability Corporations	4164491.7	4156990.8	52218.2	47757.1
国有独资	State Funded Corporations	36614.8	36555.4	235.1	181.9

continued 3

(10 000 yuan)

销售费用 Sale Expenses	管理费用 Management Expenses	财务费用 Financial Expenses	营业利润 Business Profits	利润总额 Total Profits	应付职工薪酬 Salary Payable	本年应交增值税 Value Added Tax Payable
1073.2	1225.6	208.2	-529.1	441.3	768.4	118.5
44808.0	36693.5	2571.5	137046.1	140908.9	132766.7	40565.3
52006.4	28323.2	1848.3	142823.3	120487.5	28164.4	46166.7
7580.5	6086.7	-633.6	2502.1	1871.5	4256.0	1427.0
26099.1	14630.4	6510.9	7419.0	7818.0	12600.3	9471.8
194195.0	87393.2	28769.8	288608.7	85834.9	65388.8	93003.6
63588.0	23938.3	322.4	23215.5	6492.6	24563.2	9132.2
3089.8	600.1	24.9	439.2	439.0	490.9	13.3
1726.0	137.3	125.8	254.0	252.1	398.5	301.4
593671.7	**318155.7**	**92456.4**	**567508.4**	**545009.2**	**254342.4**	**276338.8**
427732.9	255418.8	71779.9	472229.5	440228.2	184855.5	249098.7
18776.6	25346.6	1185.8	4039.7	4299.4	14183.7	3396.0
719.2	2519.2	216.9	33706.7	33690.9	2488.8	3353.8
217.2	58.4	-0.8	1.0	-0.7	75.0	47.6
217.2	58.4	-0.8	1.0	-0.7	75.0	47.6
264227.5	134512.8	27659.6	249922.3	230951.0	111317.8	107404.8
7011.8	3835.7	-182.7	453.3	455.6	6635.9	1626.3

16-9 续表4

单位：万元

分 类	Classify	单位数（个） Number (unit)	资产总计 Total Assets	流动资产合计 Circulating Funds	固定资产合计 Total Fixed Assets
其他有限责任公司	Other Limited Liability Corporations	167	2223646.6	1597227.5	336103.1
股份有限公司	Share-holding Corporations Ltd.	7	1188020.7	751880.1	267877.7
私营	Private Enterprises	87	732200.9	489230.3	94929.8
私营独资	Private-funded Enterprises	5	5846.0	4236.5	714.1
私营合伙	Private Partnership Enterprises	3	1658.7	1088.4	286.2
私营有限责任公司	Private Limited Liability Corporations	73	694327.9	457681.0	90435.9
私营股份有限公司	Private Share-holding Corporations Ltd.	6	30368.3	26224.4	3493.6
其他	Other	6	30901.2	21006.8	1908.3
港澳台商投资	Enterprises with Funds from Hong Kong, Macao &Taiwan	15	947951.6	746902.5	66618.2
外商投资	Foreign Funded Enterprises	15	479794.5	272771.8	69799.5
2. 按国民经济行业分组	Grouped by Sector				
综合零售	Integrated Retail	77	2105868.6	1388041.1	343630.3
食品、饮料及烟草制品专门零售	Food, Beverages and Tobaccos Special Retail Trade	11	587480.3	376893.8	149358.3
纺织、服装及日用品专门零售	Special Retail of Textiles,Garments and Daily Consumer Articles	22	260702.7	107182.1	75765.3
文化、体育用品及器材专门零售	Retail of Culture,Sports Appliances and Equipments	18	201285.9	176174.0	14573.1
医药及医疗器材专门零售	Retail of Medicines and Medical Appliances	13	107309.2	99789.5	4522.2
汽车、摩托车、燃料及零配件专门零售	Retail of Motor Vehicles,Motorcycles, Fuel and Parts	138	1777921.4	1333985.0	158527.8
家用电器及电子产品专门零售	Special Retail of Household Electric Appliances and Electronic Products	29	478675.9	403581.9	58249.2
五金、家具及室内装饰材料专门零售	Special Retail of Hardware,Furniture and Decoration Materials	21	306731.3	153579.1	84115.4
货摊、无店铺及其他零售业	Non-shop and Other Retail	6	28862.8	23894.3	2861.2

continued 4

(10 000 yuan)

固定资产原价 Original Value of Fixed Assets	累计折旧 Accumulated Depreciation	负债合计 Total Liabilities	流动负债合计 Circulating Liabilities	非流动负债 Non-Circulating Liabilities	所有者权益合计 Total Owners' Equities	实收资本 Paid in Capital	营业收入 Total Revenue	主营业务收入 Revenue from Principal Business
492956.1	157034.0	1629956.2	1475124.7	151686.4	593690.4	371699.2	4830614.6	4745905.2
377144.3	109266.6	913533.3	905032.9	8500.4	274487.4	77542.0	1034464.7	1019889.8
145091.0	50161.2	510485.3	485322.4	36066.3	221715.6	113322.9	1786877.5	1783578.5
845.4	131.3	1900.9	1600.7	300.2	3945.1	2692.0	77544.9	77536.9
325.3	39.1	1078.3	1078.3	171.4	580.4	230.0	4609.7	4564.8
139170.3	48734.4	483436.2	458982.6	35185.6	210891.7	107790.9	1635012.2	1631766.1
4750.0	1256.4	24069.9	23660.8	409.1	6298.4	2610.0	69710.7	69710.7
4076.1	2167.8	22999.0	19016.3	3982.7	7902.2	5337.0	412487.9	412373.9
95642.9	29024.7	651700.1	624095.5	18212.4	296251.5	120071.0	1570501.1	1559565.2
85388.3	15588.8	310528.3	310505.2	23.1	169266.2	143048.1	1138765.2	1128628.0
492424.2	148974.9	1487339.0	1321751.6	165767.3	618529.6	260197.3	2687417.7	2594881.3
209211.1	59852.8	498862.7	497629.1	1233.6	88617.6	27522.7	264284.9	262983.3
123132.4	47367.1	139373.8	100824.0	49606.3	121328.9	103596.3	1248222.7	1246481.3
23242.2	8669.1	151155.1	144981.5	3390.6	50130.8	39657.6	213247.6	212202.0
7086.4	2564.2	99213.3	96691.2	2522.1	8095.9	17833.5	153628.1	153233.3
217675.0	59147.2	1403075.9	1383825.1	9496.5	374845.5	260700.9	4327446.4	4305921.5
77660.7	19411.5	224758.6	223518.7	1239.9	253917.3	81627.1	1275776.3	1267781.0
116554.9	32439.5	213517.6	171081.7	42435.9	93213.7	47484.0	1032289.8	1032289.8
4835.6	1974.4	18732.1	18406.1		10130.7	5635.7	90890.7	90712.6

16-9 续表5

单位：万元

分 类	Classify	营业成本 Total Cost	主营业务成本 Cost of Principal Business	营业税金及附加 Taxs and Other Changes	主营业务税金及附加 Taxs and Other Changes on Principal Business
其他有限责任公司	Other Limited Liability Corporations	4127876.9	4120435.4	51983.1	47575.2
股份有限公司	Share-holding Corporations Ltd.	868090.3	867202.8	10108.8	10108.8
私营	Private Enterprises	1521926.0	1521438.3	21121.2	20303.3
私营独资	Private-funded Enterprises	74177.9	74174.8	742.3	733.2
私营合伙	Private Partnership Enterprises	3821.4	3821.4	129.4	129.4
私营有限责任公司	Private Limited Liability Corporations	1378789.8	1378305.2	20126.5	19328.0
私营股份有限公司	Private Share-holding Corporations Ltd.	65136.9	65136.9	123.0	112.7
其他	Other	332066.5	331981.7	18651.9	18637.9
港澳台商投资	Enterprises with Funds from Hong Kong, Macao &Taiwan	1363298.2	1360116.3	9796.8	9744.7
外商投资	Foreign Funded Enterprises	1012659.6	1011574.0	3987.2	3987.2
2. 按国民经济行业分组	Grouped by Sector				
综合零售	Integrated Retail	2185585.7	2183273.7	26531.8	22214.4
食品、饮料及烟草制品专门零售	Food, Beverages and Tobaccos Special Retail Trade	222906.4	221227.6	786.6	784.9
纺织、服装及日用品专门零售	Special Retail of Textiles,Garments and Daily Consumer Articles	967031.6	965077.5	32649.2	32235.7
文化、体育用品及器材专门零售	Retail of Culture,Sports Appliances and Equipments	179170.4	179099.5	2615.1	2545.2
医药及医疗器材专门零售	Retail of Medicines and Medical Appliances	128089.0	128053.7	397.2	397.2
汽车、摩托车、燃料及零配件专门零售	Retail of Motor Vehicles,Motorcycles, Fuel and Parts	4012193.5	4005525.0	6186.6	6046.4
家用电器及电子产品专门零售	Special Retail of Household Electric Appliances and Electronic Products	1100055.5	1099102.5	22774.5	22372.5
五金、家具及室内装饰材料专门零售	Special Retail of Hardware,Furniture and Decoration Materials	769699.2	769699.2	27136.1	27100.2
货摊、无店铺及其他零售业	Non-shop and Other Retail	78014.5	78014.5	397.8	397.8

continued 5

(10 000 yuan)

销售费用 Sale Expenses	管理费用 Management Expenses	财务费用 Financial Expenses	营业利润 Business Profits	利润总额 Total Profits	应付职工薪酬 Salary Payable	本年应交增值税 Value Added Tax Payable
257215.7	130677.1	27842.3	249469.0	230495.4	104681.9	105778.5
42236.8	41752.8	28221.1	43706.1	34844.3	15196.5	48761.6
90366.4	42812.5	14138.9	99048.3	96502.0	39093.5	75827.3
803.1	691.3	123.5	1009.0	1043.4	526.1	12689.9
362.3	162.0	27.3	107.3	107.5	267.4	172.8
87314.3	40932.4	13662.2	96675.9	94100.5	37548.5	62505.2
1886.7	1026.8	325.9	1256.1	1250.6	751.5	459.4
11189.2	8416.5	358.4	41805.4	39941.3	2500.2	10307.6
103347.2	33330.0	10876.7	76026.4	78711.0	36790.2	11988.4
62591.6	29406.9	9799.8	19252.5	26070.0	32696.7	15251.7
251038.3	122502.5	19032.2	127132.6	139353.8	98575.9	51060.5
15943.9	10084.3	16221.2	-1639.4	-2821.6	6436.9	6414.7
66956.6	29670.2	4680.2	149742.1	132516.1	17148.2	35473.0
17832.9	12759.9	2798.3	-2556.3	-1328.9	12429.1	2565.0
15290.7	6036.4	-192.6	3470.9	4071.3	15109.0	2781.9
128786.8	78537.3	40982.5	62873.8	66373.6	79887.0	116656.6
74202.1	30707.6	1649.0	46975.2	47837.3	12796.8	27034.7
18080.8	22682.7	7229.7	180045.2	157359.9	9727.3	34177.4
5539.6	5174.8	55.9	1464.3	1647.7	2232.2	175.0

16-10 限额以上住宿和餐饮企业主要财务状况（2012年）

单位：万元

分　类	Classify	单位数（个）Number (unit)	资产总计 Total Assets	流动资产合计 Circulating Funds	固定资产合计 Total Fixed Assets
总计	**Total**	**505**	**2322134.8**	**702765.2**	**1071929.3**
一、住宿业	**Hotel Services**	**203**	**1676689.4**	**417757.3**	**913233.8**
1.按登记注册类型分组	Grouped by Type of Registration				
内资	Domestic Funded Enterprises	189	1426830.5	354393.4	769420.5
国有	State-owned Enterprises	43	256091.0	40418.9	152588.9
集体	Collective-owned Enterprises	4	4099.6	240.9	2458.3
股份合作	Cooperative Enterprises				
联营	Joint Ownership Enterprises				
国有联营	State Joint Ownership Enterprises				
集体联营	Collective Joint Ownership Enterprises				
国有与集体联营	Joint State-collective Enterprises				
其他联营	Others Joint Ownership Enterprises				
有限责任公司	Limited Liability Corporations	88	936507.4	229144.5	515887.0
国有独资公司	State Sole Funded Corporations				
其他有限责任公司	Other Limited Liability Corporations	88	936507.4	229144.5	515887.0
股份有限公司	Share-holding Corporations Ltd.	4	20866.5	2562.9	16311.1
私营	Private Enterprises	45	191914.4	79100.7	74725.4
私营独资	Private-funded Enterprises	6	10676.0	6158.5	1256.2
私营合伙	Private Partnership Enterprises				
私营有限责任公司	Private Limited Liability Corporations	37	176998.5	70320.0	73341.0
私营股份有限公司	Private Share-holding Corporations Ltd.	2	4239.9	2622.2	128.2
其他	Other Enterprises	5	17351.6	2925.5	7449.8
港澳台商投资	Enterprises with Funds from Hong Kong, Macao &Taiwan	5	117872.5	24251.4	62528.2
外商投资	Foreign Funded Enterprises	9	131986.4	39112.5	81285.1
2.按国民经济行业分组	Grouped by Sector				
旅游饭店	Tourist Hotel	165	1574326.8	377889.7	877216.2
一般旅馆	Normal Hotel	34	47475.8	19791.1	17706.4
其他住宿业	Others	4	54886.8	20076.5	18311.2

Finacial Status of Catering Eenterprises Above Designated Size（2012）

(10 000 yuan)

固定资产原价 Original Value of Fixed Assets	累计折旧 Accumulated Depreciation	负债合计 Total Liabilities	流动负债合计 Circulating Liabilities	非流动负债 Non-Circulating Liabilities	所有者权益合计 Total Owners' Equities	实收资本 Paid in Capital	营业收入 Total Revenue	主营业务收入 Revenue from Principal Business
1626991.1	**556667.8**	**1756151.4**	**1289496.9**	**438466.7**	**565983.4**	**845089.3**	**1301812.0**	**1286035.5**
1344677.8	**432779.6**	**1362873.2**	**933388.5**	**402834.0**	**313816.2**	**600078.9**	**537221.9**	**531178.9**
1064115	296030.1	1114133.4	856145.6	231337.1	312697.1	469112.5	432273.4	428188.2
274865.1	122310.0	214773.0	129223.7	58540.1	41318.0	120493.9	104518.4	103441.2
4047.2	2003.2	760.6	118.1	642.5	3339.0	395.2	5389.1	4790.1
636896.8	121600.3	735687.2	624664.5	110973.8	200820.2	261309.1	232757.8	230685.5
636896.8	121600.3	735687.2	624664.5	110973.8	200820.2	261309.1	232757.8	230685.5
24038.5	7727.4	18445.9	18445.9		2420.6	2597.9	9197.5	9197.5
113464.8	39036.4	132626.9	78688.6	54368.2	59287.5	80147.4	71994.0	71657.3
2282.3	1026.1	8854.4	6954.4	1900.0	1821.6	3498.7	9003.5	9001.9
111016.5	37972.5	121837.9	69799.6	52468.2	55160.6	74426.7	62531.4	62196.3
166.0	37.8	1934.6	1934.6		2305.3	2222.0	459.1	459.1
10802.6	3352.8	11839.8	5004.8	6812.5	5511.8	4169.0	8416.6	8416.6
121387.6	58859.4	68136.4	30906	37230.4	49736.1	69750.5	38883.8	38548.5
159175.2	77890.1	180603.4	46336.9	134266.5	-48617	61215.9	66064.7	64442.2
1288951.5	412612.7	1313017.0	891468.0	394946.3	261309.8	544038.4	477719.6	472157.0
31027.4	13779.2	34883.0	32947.3	1887.7	12592.8	27240.5	45353.1	44872.7
24698.9	6387.7	14973.2	8973.2	6000.0	39913.6	28800.0	14149.2	14149.2

16-10 续表1

单位：万元

分 类	Classify	营业成本 Total Cost	主营业务成本 Cost of Principal Business
总计	**Total**	**526592.2**	**516675.2**
一、住宿业	**Hotel Services**	**166190.8**	**159980.3**
1.按登记注册类型分组	Grouped by Type of Registration		
内资	Domestic Funded Enterprises	138655.2	133125.2
国有	State-owned Enterprises	32894.9	32746.8
集体	Collective-owned Enterprises	3452.7	3452.7
股份合作	Cooperative Enterprises		
联营	Joint Ownership Enterprises		
国有联营	State Joint Ownership Enterprises		
集体联营	Collective Joint Ownership Enterprises		
国有与集体联营	Joint State-collective Enterprises		
其他联营	Others Joint Ownership Enterprises		
有限责任公司	Limited Liability Corporations	75091.3	70220.0
国有独资公司	State Sole Funded Corporations		
其他有限责任公司	Other Limited Liability Corporations	75091.3	70220.0
股份有限公司	Share-holding Corporations Ltd.	2450.8	2450.8
私营	Private Enterprises	22844.1	22333.5
私营独资	Private-funded Enterprises	2868.0	2366.2
私营合伙	Private Partnership Enterprises		
私营有限责任公司	Private Limited Liability Corporations	19843.9	19835.1
私营股份有限公司	Private Share-holding Corporations Ltd.	132.2	132.2
其他	Other Enterprises	1921.4	1921.4
港澳台商投资	Enterprises with Funds from Hong Kong, Macao &Taiwan	9157.3	8994.0
外商投资	Foreign Funded Enterprises	18378.3	17861.1
2.按国民经济行业分组	Grouped by Sector		
旅游饭店	Tourist Hotel	145946	139786.7
一般旅馆	Normal Hotel	16550.6	16499.4
其他住宿业	Others	3694.2	3694.2

continued 1

(10 000 yuan)

营业税金及附加 Taxs and Other Changes	主营业务税金及附加 Taxs and Other Changes on Principal Business	销售费用 Sale Expenses	管理费用 Management Expenses	财务费用 Financial Expenses	营业利润 Business Profits	利润总额 Total Profits	应付职工薪酬 Salary Payable	本年应交增值税 Value Added Tax Payable
70346.6	**68187.2**	**422607.1**	**256098.2**	**29488.4**	**1193.0**	**3288.6**	**238865.4**	**11219.7**
28944.4	**27454.0**	**179151.4**	**170832.1**	**20382.0**	**–23695.5**	**–23139.5**	**108642.0**	**2810.0**
23353.8	21863.4	152068.7	136732.4	18158.1	-32113.9	-31081.8	90349.8	803.0
5544.0	5403.9	33230.4	35015.4	4805.3	-6978.2	-6226.6	24596.2	204.3
289.2	189.8	193.0	375.0	22.9	1056.3	890.3	493.8	33.6
12581.7	12010.1	85984.9	77202.7	9441.7	-22944.0	-22514.4	48361.1	520.1
12581.7	12010.1	85984.9	77202.7	9441.7	-22944.0	-22514.4	48361.1	520.1
512.2	512.2	4429.1	1899.4	35.9	-143.2	-142.3	2406.9	
3963.0	3283.7	23788.8	20842.3	3120.9	-2564.8	-2563.1	12309.6	25.5
504.3	504.3	2523.3	3123.2	277.4	-292.7	-348.5	2009.5	
3435.1	2755.8	21075.6	17565.3	2820.7	-2208.9	-2151.4	10165.7	10.4
23.6	23.6	189.9	153.8	22.8	-63.2	-63.2	134.4	15.1
463.7	463.7	4442.5	1397.6	731.4	-540.0	-525.7	2182.2	19.5
1994.9	1994.9	10574.6	14833.7	1168.1	1160.8	1134.5	5671.7	83.8
3595.7	3595.7	16508.1	19266.0	1055.8	7257.6	6807.8	12620.5	1923.2
25836.5	24353.3	162802.3	155067.4	19219.0	-26562.6	-25885.6	95938.7	2677.1
2441.8	2434.6	12273.5	11790.4	1074.7	1210.8	1045.8	9945.3	132.9
666.1	666.1	4075.6	3974.3	88.3	1656.3	1700.3	2758.0	

16-10 续表2

单位：万元

分类	Classify	单位数（个）Number (unit)	资产总计 Total Assets	流动资产合计 Circulating Funds	固定资产合计 Total Fixed Assets
二、餐饮业	**Catering Trade**	**302**	**645445.4**	**285007.9**	**158695.5**
1.按登记注册类型分组	Grouped by Type of Registration				
内资	Domestic Funded Enterprises	286	497943.0	236659.5	117708.6
国有	State-owned Enterprises	5	10143.0	3026.6	6612.9
集体	Collective-owned Enterprises	1	172.6	75.7	28.8
股份合作	Cooperative Enterprises	1	359.9	59.6	61.2
联营	Joint Ownership Enterprises				
国有联营	State Joint Ownership Enterprises				
集体联营	Collective Joint Ownership Enterprises				
国有与集体联营	Joint State-collective Enterprises				
其他联营	Others Joint Ownership Enterprises				
有限责任公司	Limited Liability Corporations	144	282088.5	159693.8	56291.6
国有独资公司	State Sole Funded Corporations	1	1494.0	948.0	546.0
其他有限责任公司	Other Limited Liability Corporations	143	280594.5	158745.8	55745.6
股份有限公司	Share-holding Corporations Ltd.	4	71702.4	15087.4	21730.0
私营	Private Enterprises	115	102509.7	50454.9	19890.2
私营独资	Private-funded Enterprises	15	3320.1	1298.2	1248.0
私营合伙	Private Partnership Enterprises	3	2882.7	1101.9	835.7
私营有限责任公司	Private Limited Liability Corporations	93	94522.7	47011.7	17306.5
私营股份有限公司	Private Share-holding Corporations Ltd.	4	1784.2	1043.1	500.0
其他	Other Enterprises	16	30966.9	8261.5	13093.9
港澳台商投资	Enterprises with Funds from Hong Kong, Macao &Taiwan	8	90072.9	31549.1	24221.0
外商投资	Foreign Funded Enterprises	8	57429.5	16799.3	16765.9
2.按国民经济行业分	Grouped by Sector				
正餐服务	Dinner	293	546920.9	244800.9	135679.2
快餐服务	Fast Food	9	98524.5	40207.0	23016.3
饮料及冷饮服务	Beverages and Cold Drinks				
其他餐饮业	Other Catering Services				

continued 2

(10 000 yuan)

固定资产原价 Original Value of Fixed Assets	累计折旧 Accumulated Depreciation	负债合计 Total Liabilities	流动负债合计 Circulating Liabilities	非流动负债 Non-Circulating Liabilities	所有者权益合计 Total Owners' Equities	实收资本 Paid in Capital	营业收入 Total Revenue	主营业务收入 Revenue from Principal Business
282313.3	**123888.2**	**393278.2**	**356108.4**	**35632.7**	**252167.2**	**245010.4**	**764590.1**	**754856.6**
207340.8	89900.5	319034.6	287468.6	29834.5	178908.4	195237.3	570745.8	568953.3
7812.4	1199.5	8407.5	5783.2	2624.3	1735.5	2090.0	8821.3	8821.3
35.8	7.0	167.6	167.6		5.0	5.0	480.9	480.9
101.0	39.8	309.9	309.9		50.0	50.0	845.4	845.4
101658.7	45777.0	185209.9	164172.5	18964.9	96878.6	128557.7	309962.0	308972.1
833.3	287.3	799.4	799.4		694.6	2000.0	917.7	917.0
100825.4	45489.7	184410.5	163373.1	18964.9	96184.0	126557.7	309044.3	308055.1
37145.5	14740.6	25211.9	23928.5	1283.6	46490.5	20190.8	57700.0	57515.9
44598.4	24904.2	84550.8	78429.9	6461.7	17958.9	32715.8	151846.9	151353.7
2070.8	872.8	1796.2	1417.5	734.9	1523.9	1355.0	8362.8	8362.8
963.8	128.1	1500.2	460.8	1039.4	1382.5	992.0	10550.1	10550.1
40678.0	23504.2	80263.8	75652.1	4687.4	14258.9	29468.8	128753.9	128260.7
885.8	399.1	990.6	899.5		793.6	900.0	4180.1	4180.1
15989.0	3232.4	15177.0	14677.0	500.0	15789.9	11628.0	41089.3	40964.0
47855.6	23636.7	48184.1	46335.8	2042.7	41888.8	29867.3	86759.9	86750.9
27116.9	10351.0	26059.5	22304.0	3755.5	31370.0	19905.8	107084.4	99152.4
242879.1	107470.3	346618.4	314551.6	30529.7	200302.5	220144.8	669691.2	667549.2
39434.2	16417.9	46659.8	41556.8	5103.0	51864.7	24865.6	94898.9	87307.4

16-10 续表3

单位：万元

分 类	Classify	营业成本 Total Cost	主营业务成本 Cost of Principal Business
二、餐饮业	**Catering Trade**	**360401.4**	**356694.9**
1.按登记注册类型分组	Grouped by Type of Registration		
内资	Domestic Funded Enterprises	276234.2	274528.7
国有	State-owned Enterprises	5503.9	5503.9
集体	Collective-owned Enterprises	322.4	322.4
股份合作	Cooperative Enterprises	373.8	373.8
联营	Joint Ownership Enterprises		
国有联营	State Joint Ownership Enterprises		
集体联营	Collective Joint Ownership Enterprises		
国有与集体联营	Joint State-collective Enterprises		
其他联营	Others Joint Ownership Enterprises		
有限责任公司	Limited Liability Corporations	142857.1	142269.0
国有独资公司	State Sole Funded Corporations	297.5	297.5
其他有限责任公司	Other Limited Liability Corporations	142559.6	141971.5
股份有限公司	Share-holding Corporations Ltd.	24176.0	24157.4
私营	Private Enterprises	79035.1	78747.6
私营独资	Private-funded Enterprises	4548.3	4548.3
私营合伙	Private Partnership Enterprises	9528.4	9528.4
私营有限责任公司	Private Limited Liability Corporations	63049.9	62762.4
私营股份有限公司	Private Share-holding Corporations Ltd.	1908.5	1908.5
其他	Other Enterprises	23965.9	23154.6
港澳台商投资	Enterprises with Funds from Hong Kong, Macao &Taiwan	37462.0	37462.0
外商投资	Foreign Funded Enterprises	46705.2	44704.2
2、按国民经济行业分	Grouped by Sector		
正餐服务	Dinner	319637.3	317775.8
快餐服务	Fast Food	40764.1	38919.1
饮料及冷饮服务	Beverages and Cold Drinks		
其他餐饮业	Other Catering Services		

continued 3

(10 000 yuan)

营业税金及附加 Taxs and Other Changes	主营业务税金及附加 Taxs and Other Changes on Principal Business	销售费用 Sale Expenses	管理费用 Managenment Expenses	财务费用 Financial Expenses	营业利润 Business Profits	利润总额 Total Profits	应付职工薪酬 Salary Payable	本年应交增值税 Value Added Tax Payable
41402.2	**40733.2**	**243455.7**	**85266.1**	**9106.4**	**24888.5**	**26428.1**	**130223.4**	**8409.7**
31085.1	30528.8	179845.1	66218.8	7837.7	9138.4	10204.4	106655.2	4070.8
460.5	460.5	2013.3	1096.3	19.4	-275.6	-283.9	1503.7	25.3
26.4			131.1	0.5	0.5	0.5	103.0	0.1
46.5	46.5	0.5	409.7	2.1	12.8	12.8	254.4	3.2
17097.1	16835.4	98736.2	40856.9	4769.3	4325.5	5490.3	59630.5	2420.8
56.1	56.1	561.1	584.7	-0.9	-580.8	-577.3	579.7	
17041.0	16779.3	98175.1	40272.2	4770.2	4906.3	6067.6	59050.8	2420.8
2928.2	2928.2	23369.7	2759.3	589.9	4081.5	4382.4	10923.7	768.8
8175.5	7907.4	46334.3	17046.9	1846.5	-591.3	-988.9	28648.5	732.9
537.4	537.4	2055.4	766.3	67.7	387.7	425.0	1813.4	79.3
216.4	216.4	850.7	207.6	319.9	-572.9	-573.3	481.6	3.0
7094.3	6977.2	41978.7	15733.4	1382.9	-485.2	-942.6	25564.9	568.7
327.4	176.4	1449.5	339.6	76.0	79.1	102.0	788.6	81.9
2350.9	2350.8	9391.1	3918.6	610.0	1585.0	1591.2	5591.4	119.7
4706.8	4610.8	36525.1	6670.5	1360.3	72.1	770.3	11951.5	799.2
5610.3	5593.6	27085.5	12376.8	-91.6	15678.0	15453.4	11616.7	3539.7
36552.8	35883.8	206945.1	78693.1	8427.5	19129.7	20423.4	118019.3	6731.5
4849.4	4849.4	36510.6	6573.0	678.9	5758.8	6004.7	12204.1	1678.2

16-11 限额以上批发零售贸易业商品购进、销售、库存总额（2012年）

单位：个、万元

分 类	Classify	单位数 Number of Enterprises	商品购进额 Total Purchases	进口 Exports
总计	**Total**	**673**	**34696780.2**	**380710.7**
一、批发企业	**Wholesale Enterprises**	**249**	**22614297.0**	**184892.3**
1.按登记注册类型分组	Grouped by Registration Status			
内资企业	Domestic Funded Enterprises	236	19254090.2	184892.3
国有	State-owned Enterprises	31	5451288.1	44959.9
集体	Collective-owned Enterprises	3	5393.0	
股份合作	Cooperative Enterprises			
联营	Joint Ownership Enterprises			
国有联营	State Joint Ownership Enterprises			
集体联营	Collective Joint Ownership Enterprises			
国有与集体联营	Joint State-collective Ownership Enterprises			
其他联营	Other Joint Ownership Enterprises			
有限责任公司	Limited Liability Corporations	130	9975218.0	113557.4
国有独资公司	State-funded Corporations	1	87899.3	
其他有限责任公司	Other Limited Liability Corporations	129	9887318.7	113557.4
股份有限公司	Stock Limited Corporation	5	1764551.5	
私营	Private Enterprises	63	2002954.9	26375.0
私营独资	Private-funded Enterprises	4	61200.7	
私营合伙	Private Limited Liability Corporations			
私营有限责任公司	Private Limited Liability Corporations	58	1859502.4	26375.0
私营股份有限公司	Private Share Holding Corporations	1	82251.8	
其他	Other	4	54684.7	
港澳台商投资	Enterprises Funded by Hong Kong, Macao and Taiwan	4	401266.7	
外商投资	Foreign Owned Enterprises	3	2904377.8	
2.按国民经济行业分组	Grouped by Economic Sector			
农、林、牧产品批发	Wholesale of Agricultural,Forestry and Animal Husbandry Products	4	12821.5	

Total Sales of Enterprises above Designated Size in Wholesale and Retail Trades Grouped by Category of Commodities（2012）

(unit，10 000 yuan)

商品销售额 Sales Value	批发额 Wholesale Trade	出口 Exports	零售额 Retail Trade	期末商品库存额 Value of Stock at Final goods
36866335.9	**20802114.1**	**754273.3**	**16064221.8**	**1722482.1**
23587350.7	**20430943.9**	**754273.3**	**3156406.8**	**743128.8**
20193292.1	17150592.3	754273.3	3042699.8	702964.5
5959933.3	5235619.5	690590.6	724313.8	214914.6
5880.6	5160.9		719.7	2126.5
10231619.1	8749080.9	53106.5	1482538.2	283845.8
89837.9	89837.9			4014.4
10141781.2	8659243	53106.5	1482538.2	279831.4
1886625.9	1162868.4		723757.5	17713.2
2055935.5	1945075.3	10576.2	110860.2	180014.9
62341.7	46569.2		15772.5	630.8
1892822.8	1820827.1	10576.2	71995.7	177514.1
100771.0	77679.0		23092.0	1870.0
53297.7	52787.3		510.4	4349.5
438554.0	324847.0		113707.0	23792.4
2901005.8	2901005.8			9284.4
12725.1	12725.1			9913.8

16-11 续表1

单位：个、万元

分类	Classify	单位数 Number of Enterprises	商品购进额 Total Purchases	进口 Exports
食品、饮料及烟草制品批发	Wholesale of Food, Beverages and Tobacco Products	20	1127825.3	
纺织、服装及家庭服务器批发	Wholesale of Textiles, Garments and Daily Articles	21	2087566.6	
文化、体育用品及器材批发	Wholesale of Culture, Sports Articles and Equipments	10	161104.4	
医药及医疗器材批发	Wholesale of Medicines and Medical Appliances	34	960894.8	
矿产品、建材及化工产品批发	Wholesale of Mineral Products, Building Materials and Chemical Products	99	16351403.3	150309.0
机械设备、五金产品及电子产品批发	Wholesale of Machinery, Hardwares, Transport Means and Electronic Products	51	1800373.2	33188.3
贸易经纪与代理	Trade Manage and Agent	7	82948.2	1395.0
其他批发	Other Wholesales	3	29359.7	
3.按经营形式分组	Grouped by Means of Operation			
独立门店	Independent Shop	185	18487818.3	161227.3
连锁总店	Headquarter of Chain Store	2	742435.4	
连锁门店	Chain Store			
其他	Other	62	3384043.3	23665.0
二.零售企业	**Retail Trade**	**424**	**12082483.2**	**195818.4**
1.按登记注册类型分组	Grouped by Registration Status			
内资	Domestic Funded Enterprises	308	8701148.3	114147.8
国有	State-owned Enterprises	18	410899.7	
集体	Collective-owned Enterprises	20	171634.3	
股份合作	Cooperative Enterprises			
联营	Joint Ownership Enterprises	1	3189.9	
国有联营	State Joint Ownership Enterprises			
集体联营	Collective Joint Ownership Enterprises	1	3189.9	
国有与集体联营	Joint State-collective Ownership Enterprises			

continued 1

(unit，10 000 yuan)

商品销售额 Sales Value	批发额 Wholesale Trade	出口 Exports	零售额 Retail Trade	期末商品库存额 Value of Stock at Final goods
1420387.1	1304783.7		115603.4	59265.6
2102744.9	1450499.5	3029.3	652245.4	78097.4
177416.3	176253.9	6420.3	1162.4	14298.1
1144885.2	1020136		124749.2	96547.0
16689744.1	14748163.6	188915.6	1941580.5	351638.2
1924755.7	1603689.8	534840.9	321065.9	120690.0
79440.9	79440.9	21067.2		3538.3
35251.4	35251.4			9140.4
18977372.7	16061470.2	277751.2	2915902.5	572732.8
990626.8	990626.8			30738.8
3619351.2	3378846.9	476522.1	240504.3	139657.2
13278985.2	**371170.2**		**12907815.0**	**979353.3**
9664021.2	329182.5		9334838.7	752268.4
357756.9	220.0		357536.9	78081.7
168082.2	1959.2		166123.0	5372.4
3470.7			3470.7	120.0
3470.7			3470.7	120.0

16-11 续表2

单位：个、万元

分　类	Classify	单位数 Number of Enterprises	商品购进额 Total Purchases	进口 Exports
其他联营	Other Joint Ownership Enterprises			
有限责任公司	Limited Liability Corporations	169	4793105.5	70923.0
国有独资	Stock Limited Corporation	2	56199.5	
其他有限责任公司	Other Limited Liability Corporations	167	4736906.0	70923.0
股份有限公司	Stock Limited Corporation	7	1007453.7	43224.8
私营	Private Enterprises	87	1836117.2	
私营独资	Private-funded Enterprises	5	16634.5	
私营合伙	Private Parmership Enterprises	3	5550.4	
私营有限责任公司	Private Limited Liability Corporations	73	1735685.4	
私营股份有限公司	Private Share Holding Corporations	6	78246.9	
其他	Others	6	478748	
港澳台商投资	Enterprises Funded by Hong Kong, Macao and Taiwan	15	1521874	27855.7
外商投资	Foreign Funded Enterprises	16	1245524.8	53814.9
2.按国民经济行业分组	Grouped by Registered Kind			
综合零售	General Retail Sales Trade	100	2712927.4	51052.8
食品、饮料及烟草制品专门零售	Retail of Food, Beverage and Tobaccos	25	324148.1	
纺织、服装及日用品专门零售	Retail of Textiles, Garments and Daily Articles	40	1419970.9	500.3
文化、体育用品及器材专门零售	Retail of Culture, Sports Articles and Equipments	27	269559.5	
医药及医疗器材专门零售	Retail of Medicines and Medical Appliances	13	172824.6	
汽车、摩托车、燃料及零配件专门零售	Retail of Motor Vehicles, Motorcycles, Feuls and Parts	144	4691837.3	144265.3
家用电器及电子产品专门零售	Retail of Household Electronic Equipments and Products	36	1228935.6	

continued 2

(unit, 10 000 yuan)

商品销售额 Sales Value	批发额 Wholesale Trade	出口 Exports	零售额 Retail Trade	期末商品库存额 Value of Stock at Final goods
5517738.6	234018.0		5283720.6	478434.8
56606.7			56606.7	16364.2
5461131.9	234018.0		5227113.9	462070.6
1094368.4	42493.8		1051874.6	72950.8
2042655.7	4779.0		2037876.7	115138.7
89593.5	3082.7		86510.8	732.6
5435.2			5435.2	597.5
1868261.4	1316.7		1866944.7	103598.7
79365.6	379.6		78986.0	10209.9
479948.7	45712.5		434236.2	2170.0
1676674.4	25512.9		1651161.5	142901.9
1322026.9	1900.5		1320126.4	58186.3
3187371.0	4205.0		3183166.0	206723.1
380396.7	19200.1		361196.6	49148.5
1484951.7	120272.5		1364679.2	67266.4
260343.8	23358.1		236985.7	79735.5
175389.3	6761.8		168627.5	31424.3
4790661.6	6038.4		4784623.2	451507.1
1534027.1	179923.9		1354103.2	66201.1

16-11 续表3

单位：个、万元

分类	Classify	单位数 Number of Enterprises	商品购进额 Total Purchases	进口 Exports
五金、家具及室内装饰材料专门零售	etail of Hardwares, Furniture and Room Decorative Building	29	1166165.7	
货摊、无店铺及其他零售业	No Fixed Stores and Other Retails	10	96114.1	
3.按经营形式分组	Grouped by Means of Operation			
独立门店	Independent Shop	371	9457580.9	144265.3
连锁总店	Headquarter of Chain Store	19	579844.6	51553.1
连锁门店	Chain Store	7	561687.5	
其他	Other	27	1483370.2	
4.按零售业态分组	Grouped by Retail Size			
有店铺	Retail of Shop	421	11998913.1	195818.4
食杂店	Grocery Store			
便利店	Convenience Store	3	29209.2	
折扣店	Dime Store			
超市	Supermarket	41	124723.3	
大型超市	Larget Supermarket	12	912518.2	51052.8
仓储会员店	Warehouse Club	2	7181.7	
百货店	Department Store	53	1764224	
专业店	Special Store	165	3157607.1	87212.6
专卖店	Monopoly Store	112	2998059.3	57553.0
家居建材商店	Home-building Material Store	14	906834.6	
购物中心	Shopping Center	10	1719895.4	
厂家直销中心	Factory Outlet Center	9	378660.3	
无店铺零售	Retail of No-shop	3	83570.1	
电视购物	TV Shopping	2	66049.2	
邮购	Mail Order			
网上商店	Online Stores	1	17520.9	
自动售货亭	Vending Machine			
电话购物	Tele Shopping			

continued 3

(unit, 10 000 yuan)

商品销售额 Sales Value	批发额 Wholesale Trade	出口 Exports	零售额 Retail Trade	期末商品库存额 Value of Stock at Final goods
1368550.9	11225.7		1357325.2	24025.0
97293.1	184.7		97108.4	3322.3
10168428.7	172701.4		9995727.3	687461.3
639758.8	12080.0		627678.8	57023.0
849596.8	48933.6		800663.2	83683.4
1621200.9	137455.2		1483745.7	151185.6
13194615.7	370985.5		12823630.2	976811.2
26335.4			26335.4	4642.2
113108.6	2620.5		110488.1	23121.4
1193947			1193947	101123.8
			8620.5	696.0
8620.5				
1958677.1	2119.2		1956557.9	91374.4
3534068.8	69985.3		3464083.5	311188.4
3052834.9	47903		3004931.9	356188.4
1107571.8	11225.7		1096346.1	12427.9
1804040.8	217034.4		1587006.4	40221.4
395410.8	20097.4		375313.4	35827.3
84369.5	184.7		84184.8	2542.1
65827.0	184.7		65642.3	869.5
18542.5			18542.5	1672.6

16–12 限额以上住宿和餐饮业经营情况（2012年）

Statistic on Hotel Services and Catering Services above Designed Size（2012）

单位：个、万元 (unit,10 000 yuan)

分类	Classify	单位数 Number of Enterprises	营业额 Business Revenue	客房收入 From Hotel Room	餐费收入 From Meals	商品销售收入 From Commodities
总计	**Total**	**644**	**1512272**	**314037**	**1044374**	**83320**
一、住宿业	**Lodging Services**	**216**	**598619**	**287095**	**250580**	**18962**
1、按登记注册类型分组	Grouped by Registration Status					
内资企业	Domestic Funded Enterprises	201	489363	232017	209794	15180
国有	State-owned Enterprises	49	120476	49837	51301	6476
集体	Collective-owned Enterprises	4	5389	1880	2947	160
股份合作	Cooperative Enterprises					
联营	Joint Ownership Enterprises					
国有联营	State Joint Ownership Enterprises					
集体联营	Collective Joint Ownership Enterprises					
国有与集体联营	Joint State-collective Ownership Enterprises					
其他联营	Other Joint Ownership Enterprises					
有限责任公司	Limited Liability Corporations	94	273055	137063	115651	5805
国有独资公司	State-funded Corporations					
其他有限责任公司	Other Limited Liability Corporations	94	273055	137063	115651	5805
股份有限公司	Stock Limited Corporation	4	9325	3920	2896	307
私营	Private Enterprises	45	71856	34804	33144	1969
私营独资	Private-funded Enterprises	6	9004	4015	4744	164
私营合伙	Private Partnership Enterprises					
私营有限责任公司	Private Limited Liability Corporations	37	62393	30496	28271	1767
私营股份有限公司	Private Share Holding Corporations	2	459	293	129	37
其他	Others	5	9263	4512	3856	464
港澳台商投资	Enterprises Funded by Hong Kong, Macao and Taiwan	6	42414	18227	13961	2640
外商投资	Foreign Funded Enterprises	9	66842	36852	26825	1143
2、按国民经济行业分组						
旅游饭店	Tour Restaurant	176	538158	260583	226405	14697
一般旅馆	Common Hotel	36	46312	22380	20391	1800
其他住宿业	Others	4	14149	4132	3784	2465

16-12 续表1 continued 1

单位：个、万元 (unit, 10 000 yuan)

分类	Classify	单位数 Number of Enterprises	营业额 Business Revenue	客房收入 From Hotel Room	餐费收入 From Meals	商品销售收入 From Commodities
二、餐饮业	**Catering Trade**	**428**	**913653**	**26941**	**793795**	**64358**
1、按登记注册类型分	Grouped by Registration Status					
内资	Domestic Funded Enterprises	296	601184	21977	507257	53232
国有	State-owned Enterprises	7	17644	1621	9446	4758
集体	Collective-owned Enterprises	1	481		481	
股份合作	Cooperative Enterprises	1	845	108	648	90
联营	Joint Ownership Enterprises					
国有联营	State Joint Ownership Enterprises					
集体联营	Collective Joint Ownership Enterprises					
国有与集体联营	Joint State-collective Ownership Enterprises					
其他联营	Other Joint Ownership Enterprises					
有限责任公司	Limited Liability Corporations	151	331460	16645	273427	33499
国有独资	State-funded Corporations	1	918		549	242
其他有限责任公司	Other Limited Liability Corporations	150	330543	16645	272878	33258
股份有限公司	Stock Limited Corporation	4	57696	1349	41542	6507
私营	Private Enterprises	115	151508	2060	143191	5557
私营独资	Private-funded Enterprises	15	8683		8107	576
私营合伙	Private Partnership Enterprises	3	10550		10499	44
私营有限责任公司	Private Limited Liability Corporations	93	128408	1973	121411	4858
私营股份有限公司	Private Share Holding Corporations	4	3867	88	3174	78
其他	Others	17	41550	194	38522	2821
港澳台商投资	Enterprises Funded by Hong Kong, Macao and Taiwan	8	86760	1072	83687	1299
外商投资	Foreign Funded Enterprises	8	107078	132	99318	26
2、按国民经济行业分						
正餐服务	Dinner Services	405	809571	26209	698192	64221
快餐服务	Fast Food Services	14	97986	715	89645	28
饮料及冷饮服务	Beverage and Cold Beverage Services					
其他餐饮业	Other Catering Services	9	6096	17	5958	109

16-13 限额以上批发和零售贸易业主要商品分类销售额（2012年）

Sale Values of Enterprises above Designated Size of Wholesale and Retail Trades by Category of Main Commodities（2012）

单位：万元 (10 000 yuan)

分 类	Classify	销售合计 Total Sales Value	批发 Wholesale Value	零售 Retail Value
总计	**Total**	**36740584**	**20462524**	**16278060**
粮油、食品饮料、烟酒类	Grain and Oil, Food and Beverages, Alcoholic Drinks and Tobacco	2687536	1345761	1341775
粮油、食品类	Cereals, Oils and Foodstuffs	1008891	204414	804477
# 粮油类	Grain and Oil	411889	45673	366216
肉禽蛋类	Meat, Poultry and Eggs	109856	20291	89565
水产品类	Aquatic Products	116956	4217	112739
蔬菜类	Vegetables	134271	87267	47004
干鲜瓜果类	Fresh and Dried Fruit Category	85083	28230	56853
饮料类	Beverages	486170	148542	337628
烟酒类	Tobacco and Liquor	1192476	992805	199671
服装、鞋帽、针、纺织品类	Clothing, Shoes, Hats and Textiles	4122977	978076	3144901
服装类	Clothing	3492968	885424	2607544
鞋帽类	Shoes and Hats	381656	46275	335381
针、纺织品类	Knitwear and Textiles	248353	46377	201976
化妆品类	Cosmetics	298635	55148	243487
金银珠宝类	Gold,Silver and Jewelry	427418	13592	413826
日用品类	Articles for Daily Use	641436	114191	527245
#洗涤用品类	Bathing and Washing	163165	74349	88816
儿童玩具类	Children's Toys	72236	13307	58929
五金、电料类	Hardwear and Electrical Materials	216625	73908	142717
体育、娱乐用品类	Sports and Recreation Articles	217153	33033	184120
书报杂志类	Newspapers and Magazines	167600	96743	70857
电子出版物及音像制品类	E-journal and Video Products	17864	2104	15760
家用电器和音像器材类	Household Appliances and Video Products	1337961	608138	729823
中西药品类	Traditional Chinese and Western Medicine	1316159	1033267	282892
#西药	Western Medicine	1084814	830081	254733
中草药及中成药	Chinese Herbal Medicine and Traditional Chinese Medicine	88971	73533	15438
文化办公用品类	Cultural and Official Goods	694610	377226	317384
家具类	Furniture	629192	2976	626216
通讯器材类	Communication Appliances	303113	48309	254804
煤炭及制品类	Coal and Related Products	1659611	1213763	445848
木材及制品类	Wood and Wooden Products			
石油及制品类	Petroleum and Related Products	9102068	7078973	2023095
化工材料及制品类	Raw Chemical Materials	68804	68804	
#化肥类	Chemical Fertilizers	58225	58225	
金属材料类	Metal Materials	5626750	5626750	
建筑及装潢材料类	Buildings and Decoration Materials	985631	251121	734510
机电产品及设备类	Mechanical and Electrical Products	518941	508705	10236
#农机类	Agricultural Machinery			
汽车类	Automobile	5593670	915010	4678660
种子饲料类	Seeds and Feedstuff	3196	3196	
棉麻类	Cotton,Hemp	1717	1717	
其他类	Others	101919	12015	89904

16-14 亿元以上商品交易市场成交情况(2012年)

Basic Statistics on Commodity Exchange Markets of Transaction Value over 100 Million Yuan（2012）

分　类	Classify	年末出租摊位数（个）Number of Rental Booths at Year-end (unit)	成交额（万元）Turnover (10 000 yuan)
粮油、食品饮料、烟酒类	Grain and Oil, Food and Beverages, Alcoholic Drinks and Tobacco	6247	727374
粮油、食品类	Cereals, Oils and Foodstuffs	4214	644506
# 粮油类	Grain and Oil	464	291893
肉禽蛋类	Meat, Poultry and Eggs	1058	82500
水产品类	Aquatic Products	716	23496
蔬菜类	Vegetables	1150	179255
干鲜瓜果类	Fresh and Dried Fruit Category	821	67282
饮料类	Beverages	1929	78729
烟酒类	Tobacco and Liquor	104	4139
服装、鞋帽、针、纺织品类	Clothing, Shoes, Hats and Textiles	6917	337674
服装类	Clothing	5690	206356
鞋帽类	Shoes and Hats	421	78657
针、纺织品类	Knitwear and Textiles	806	52661
化妆品类	Cosmetics	48	1530
金银珠宝类	Gold,Silver and Jewelry		
日用品类	Articles for Daily Use	730	22690
#洗涤用品类	Bathing and Washing	355	13900
儿童玩具类	Children's Toys	363	8440
五金、电料类	Hardwear and Electrical Materials	423	10250
体育、娱乐用品类	Sports and Recreation Articles	35	888
书报杂志类	Newspapers and Magazines	4	70
电子出版物及音像制品类	E-journal and Video Products	4	80
家用电器和音像器材类	Household Appliances and Video Products	201	29444
中西药品类	Traditional Chinese and Western Medicine	440	46376
#西药	Western Medicine		
中草药及中成药	Chinese Herbal Medicine and Traditional Chinese Medicine	440	46376
文化办公用品类	Cultural and Official Goods	1961	219305
家具类	Furniture		
通讯器材类	Communication Appliances	227	9640
煤炭及制品类	Coal and Related Products		
木材及制品类	Wood and Wooden Products		
石油及制品类	Petroleum and Related Products		
化工材料及制品类	Raw Chemical Materials	23	172154
#化肥类	Chemical Fertilizers		
金属材料类	Metal Materials	52	325302
建筑及装潢材料类	Buildings and Decoration Materials	503	17200
机电产品及设备类	Mechanical and Electrical Products	1410	174500
#农机类	Agricultural Machinery		
汽车类	Automobile	1380	544890
种子饲料类	Seeds and Feedstuff		
棉麻类	Cotton,Hemp		
其他类	Others	30	1211

16-15 批发和零售业连锁经营情况(2012年)

Basic Statistics on Chain Business of Wholesale and Retail Trades（2012）

指 标	Item	本年合计 Total	上年合计 Total Last Year	本年直营店 Ragular Chain
一、门店总数（个）	**Number of Stores(unit)**	**492**	**512**	**371**
二、年末从业人员数（人）	**Employees at Year-end(person)**	**14254**	**13671**	**12390**
三、年末零售营业面积（平方米）	**Operating Area of Retail at Year-end(sq.m)**	**590021**	**614756**	**422101**
四、连锁门店商品购进额（万元）	**Purchases Value of Chain Stores(1 0000 yuan)**	**1412021**	**1287208**	**1296102**
其中：统一配送商品购进额	Centralized Purchases and Delivery	830069	734883	816531
其中：自有配送中心配送商品购进额	Self Centralized Purchases and Delivery	816283	723380	802746
非自有配送中心配送商品购进额	Non-self Centralized Purchases and Delivery			
五、连锁门店商品销售额（万元）	**Sales Value of Chain Store(1 0000 yuan)**	**1834810**	**1655391**	**1660469**
其中：零售额	Retail Value	862122	796578	687780

16-15 续表 continued

指 标	Item	上年直营店 Ragular Chain Last Year	本年加盟店 Franchise	上年加盟店 Franchise Last Year
一、门店总数（个）	**Number of Stores(unit)**	**401**	**121**	**111**
二、年末从业人员数（人）	**Employees at Year-end(person)**	**11627**	**1864**	**2044**
三、年末零售营业面积（平方米）	**Operating Area of Retail at Year-end(sq.m)**	**447386**	**167920**	**167370**
四、连锁门店商品购进额（万元）	**Purchases Value of Chain Stores(1 0000 yuan)**	**1205011**	**115919**	**82196**
其中：统一配送商品购进额	Centralized Purchases and Delivery	722825	13538	12058
其中：自有配送中心配送商品购进额	Self Centralized Purchases and Delivery	711322	13538	12058
非自有配送中心配送商品购进额	Non-self Centralized Purchases and Delivery			
五、连锁门店商品销售额（万元）	**Sales Value of Chain Store(1 0000 yuan)**	**1533883**	**174341**	**121508**
其中：零售额	Retail Value	687602	174341	108976

16-16 住宿和餐饮业连锁经营情况(2012年)

Basic Statistics on Chain Business of Hotels and Catering Services（2012）

指 标	Item	本年合计 Total	上年合计 Total Last Year
一、门店总数（个）	**Number of Stores(unit)**	**152**	**127**
二、年末从业人员数（人）	**Employees at Year-end(person)**	**11002**	**10458**
三、年末餐饮营业面积（平方米）	**Operating Area of Retail at Year-end(sq.m)**	**66877**	**58985**
四、客房总数（间）	**Guest Rooms(room)**		
五、床位数（张）	**Guest Beds(bed)**		
六、餐位数（位）	**Dining Seats(set)**	**24562**	**20983**
七、连锁门店商品购进额（万元）	**Operating Area of Catering Services at Year end(room)(1 0000 yuan)**	**86311**	**75190**
其中：统一配送商品购进额	Centralized Purchases and Delivery	80808	69968
其中：自有配送中心配送商品购进额	Self Centralized Purchases and Delivery	78722	68249
非自有配送中心配送商品购进额	Non-self Centralized Purchases and Delivery		
八、连锁门店商品营业额（万元）	**Sales Value of Chain Store(1 0000 yuan)**	**126651**	**107471**
其中：餐费收入	Catering Revenues	126055	107050
商品销售额	Sales Value	596	421

16-16 续表 continued

指 标	Item	本年直营店 Ragular Chain	上年直营店 Ragular Chain Last Year
一、门店总数（个）	**Number of Stores(unit)**	**152**	**127**
二、年末从业人员数（人）	**Employees at Year-end(person)**	**11002**	**10458**
三、年末餐饮营业面积（平方米）	**Operating Area of Retail at Year-end(sq.m)**	**66877**	**58985**
四、客房总数（间）	**Guest Rooms(room)**		
五、床位数（张）	**Guest Beds(bed)**		
六、餐位数（位）	**Dining Seats(set)**	**24562**	**20983**
七、连锁门店商品购进额（万元）	**Operating Area of Catering Services at Year end(room)(1 0000 yuan)**	**86311**	**75190**
其中：统一配送商品购进额	Centralized Purchases and Delivery	80808	69968
其中：自有配送中心配送商品购进额	Self Centralized Purchases and Delivery	78722	68249
非自有配送中心配送商品购进额	Non-self Centralized Purchases and Delivery		
八、连锁门店商品营业额（万元）	**Sales Value of Chain Store(1 0000 yuan)**	**126651**	**107471**
其中：餐费收入	Catering Revenues	126055	107050
商品销售额	Sales Value	596	421

16-17 成品油批发企业（单位）能源购进、销售与库存(2012年)

Purchases,Sales and Stock of Refined Oil Wholesale Enterprises（2012）

（单位：吨） (ton)

指 标	Item	期初库存量 Stock at Beginning of the Year	本年购进量 Purchases This Year	其中：购自省(区、市)外 From Other Provinces (Regions,Cities)	本年销售量 Sales This Year	其中：销往省(区、市)外 For Other Provinces (Regions,Cities)	售予省内批发和零售企业 For Wholesale and Retail Trades	年末库存量 Stock at End of the Year
汽油	Gasoline	284837	4346559	146514	4310973	759332	3086730	303541
#93″	#93″	46622	3348427	105418	3211579	647207	2178658	52715
柴油	Diesel Oil	54064	7885345	2680081	7874689	2535509	4659368	93030
#0″	#0″	52268	5520046	751232	5523078	623642	4332896	47999
煤油	Kerosene	35119	747483	236787	754563	241112	29162	17562
燃料油	Fuel Oil		253890	253890	253890	253890		
润滑油	Lube	566	20439	17240	19441	6400	12611	651

16-18 成品油零售企业（单位）能源商品销售与库存(2012年)

Purchases,Sales and Stock of Refined Oil Retail Enterprises（2012）

（单位：吨） (ton)

指 标	Item	期初库存量 Stock at Beginning of the Year	本年销售量 Sales This Year	年末库存量 Stock at End of the Year
汽油	Gasoline	13207	722840	16719
#93″	#93″	6358	558455	14686
柴油	Diesel Oil	7947	771243	12220
#0″	#0″	7285	688607	10720
煤油	Kerosene		246	
燃料油	Fuel Oil			
润滑油	Lube	30	2306	28

主要统计指标解释

批发业 指批发商向批发、零售单位及其他企事业、机关单位批量销售生活用品和生产资料的活动，以及从事进出口贸易和贸易经纪与代理的活动。批发商可以对所批发的货物拥有所有权，并以本单位、公司的名义进行交易活动；也可以不拥有货物的所有权，而以中介身份做代理销售商。还包括各类商品批发市场中固定摊位的批发活动。

零售业 指百货商店、超级市场、专门零售商店、品牌专卖店、售货摊等主要面向最终消费者（如居民等）的销售活动。包括以互联网、邮政、电话、售货机等方式的销售活动，还包括在同地点，后面加工生产，前面销售的店铺（如前店后厂的面包房）。不包括：谷物、种子、饲料、牲畜、矿产品、生产用原料、化工原料、农用化工产品、机械设备（用车、计算机及通信设备等除外）等生产资料的销售（批发业）；非零售单位附带的零售活动（如汽车修理单位销售汽车零件）；商业零售单位所在商厦的物业管理（物业管理）；商业零售单位所在的商品市场、商业大厦的市场管理活动（市场管理）。

住宿业 指有偿为顾客提供临时住宿的服务活动，不包括提供长期住宿场所的活动（如出租房屋、公寓等）。

餐饮业 指在一定场所，对食物进行现场烹饪、调制，并出售给顾客主要供现场消费的服务活动。

社会消费品零售总额 指批发和零售业、餐饮业、新闻出版业、邮政业和其他服务业等，售予城乡居民用于生活消费的商品和社会集团用于公共消费的商品之总量。社会消费品零售总额包括：

一、批发和零售业企业（单位）售予城乡居民用于生活消费和社会集团用于公共消费的商品。包括：

1. 售予城乡居民的各种生活消费品；

2. 售予入境旅游的外国人、华侨、港澳台同胞的各类商品；

3. 售予行政事业单位、社会团体、军队和武警等机构的商品，以及以零售方式售予各类企业的商品。具体包括：用于非生产和社会交往的办公用品，如通讯设备、计算器具和设备、电讯网络设备、文印设备、音像 听器材和设备、纸张、本册、文具及装订文印材料、家具、日用电器、针纺织品、清洁卫生用品、文体用品、奖品、纪念品、礼品等；供内部人员乘坐的交通工具和燃料；用于办公设施修缮的各类配件、材料、工具等；用于取暖和防暑降温的设备、燃料、材料及食品等；专用于教学的用品和设备；非营利医疗机构的中、西药品、中药材和医疗设备器材；非专用的劳动保护用品；不对外营业的内部食堂用的餐具、炊具、设备、清洁卫生工具和食品、燃料等；军队、武警用于其人员生活的衣着品和个人用品；其他各类非生产性设备和用品。

二、餐饮业出售的主食、菜肴、烟酒饮料和其他商品。

三、新闻出版业、邮政业售予城乡居民、企事业单位、军队和武警等机构的书报杂志、音像制品、邮品等。

四、其他服务业出售的食品、烟酒饮料、服装鞋帽、日常生活用品、医药保健用品、艺术品、工艺美术品、玩具、殡葬用品以及其他消费品。

批发和零售业商品购进、销售、库存总额 指各种登记注册类型的批发和零售业企业（单位）以本企业（单位）为总体的，从国内、国外市场购进的商品总量，销售和出口的商品总量、库存的商品总量等情况。该指标可以反映商品流转过程中商品的购进、销售、库存之间的比例关系和存在的问题。

购进总额 指从本企业（单位）以外的单位和个人购进（包括从境外直接进口）作为转卖或加工后转卖的商品总额。它反映批发和零售业从国内、国外市场上购进商品的总量。商品购进包括：（1）从工农业生产者购进的商品；（2）从出版社、报社的出版发行部门购进的图书、杂志和报纸；（3）从各种登记注册类型的批发和零售业企业（单位）购进的商品；（4）从其他单位购进的商品，如从机关、团体、企业等单位购进的剩余物资，从住宿和餐饮业、其他服务业购进的商品，从海关、市场管理部门购进的缉私和没收的商品，从居民手中收购的废旧商品等； （5）从国（境）外直接进口的商品。不包括企业（单位）为自身经营用和未通过买卖行为而收入的商品以及销售退回、商品升溢等。

销售总额 指对本企业（单位）以外的单位和个人出售（包括对境外直接出口）的商品总额。它反映批发和零售业在国内市场上销售商品以及出口商品的总量。商品销售包括：（1）售给城乡居民和社会集团消费用的商品；（2）售给工业、农业、建筑业、运输邮电业、批发和零售业、住宿和餐饮业、其他服务业等作为生产、经营使用的商品；（3）售给批发和零售业作为转卖或加工后转卖的商品；（4）对国（境）外直接出口的商品。不包括出售本企业（单位）自用的废旧包装用品，未通过买卖行为付出的商品，经本单位介绍、由买卖双方直接结算、本单位只收取手续费的业务，购货退出的商品以及商品损耗和损失等。

库存总额 指报告期末各种登记注册类型的批发和零售业企业（单位）已取得所有权的商品。它反映批发和零售业企业（单位）的商品库存情况和对市场商品供应的保证程度。商品库存包括：（1）存放在批发和零售业经营单位（如门市部、批发站、经营处）仓库、货场、货柜和货架中的商品；（2）挑选、整理、包装中的商品；（3）已记入购进而尚未运到本单位的商品，即发货单或银行承兑凭证已到而货未到的商品；（4）寄放他处的商品，如因购货方拒绝承付而暂时存放在购货方的商品和已办完加工成品收回手续而未提回的商品；（5）委托其他单位代销（未作销售或调出）尚未售出的商品；（6）代其他单位购进尚未交付的商品。不包括所有权不属于本单位的商品、委托外单位加工生产尚未收回成品的商品、外贸企业代理其他单位从国外进口尚未付给订货单位的商品、代国家物资储备部门保管的商品等。

住宿和餐饮业营业额 指住宿和餐饮业法人企业（单位）在经营活动中因提供服务或销售商品等取得的收入。包括：客房收入、餐费收入、商品销售额和其他收入。客房收入指住宿和餐饮业法人企业（单位）在经营活动中因提供住宿服务取得的收入。餐费收入指住宿和餐饮业法人企业、（单位）因为顾客提供就餐服务取得的收入，包括经烹饪、调制加工后出售的各种食品，如主食、炒菜、凉拌菜等的收入。商品销售额指住宿和餐饮业法人企业（单位）伴随服务而出售商品所取得的收入（含增值税）。其他收入指营业收入中除客房收入、餐费收入、商品销售额以外的其他收入，包括娱乐、健身和商务服务等。

连锁企业（或称连锁店、连锁公司） 指在核心企业或总店的领导下，由分散的、经营同类商品或服务的企业或活动单位，采取共同方针，实行集中采购和分散销售的有机结合，通过规范化经营，实现规模效益的经济联合组织形式。一般连锁店应由若干个分店组成。其经营特征：（1）经营同类商品；（2）使用统一商号；（3）统一采购配送，采购与销售相分离（部分商品可根据物流合理和保质保鲜原则，由供应商直接送货到门店，其余均由总部统一配送）。

连锁门店的形式分为直营连锁和加盟连锁。

直营连锁也叫正规连锁。指连锁门店均由总部独资或控　设，在总部的直接领导下统一经营。总部采取纵深似的管理方式，直接下令掌管所有的零售门店，零售门店也必须完全接受总部指挥。这是大型垄断商业资本通过吞并、兼并或独资、控　等途径，发展壮大自身实力和规模的一种形式。

加盟连锁包括特许连锁和自由连锁两种形式，

特许连锁指各连锁门店（被特许人）通过合同形式，取得使用总部（特许人）商标、商号、经营技术和销售总部　发的商品的特许权，各加盟连锁门店为独立法人，在总部指导下统一经营。

自由连锁也称自愿连锁。指连锁公司的门店均为独立法人，各自的资产所有权关系不变，在公司总部的指导下共同经营。各成员店使用共同的店名，与总部订阅有关购、销、宣传等方面的合同，并按合同　展经营活动。在合同规定的范围之外，各成员店可以自由活动。根据自愿原则，各成员店可自由加入连锁体系，也可自由退出。

Explanatory Notes on Main Statistical Indicators

Wholesale Trade refers to the activities of wholesaler selling at wholesale commodities for daily use and capital goods to enterprises of wholesale and retail trades and other enterprises, institutions and government offices, including the activities of wholesaler engaged in import and export and acting as a trade agent. The wholesaler may have the right of ownership over the commodities of wholesale and trade in the name of its own or a company, the wholesaler may not have the right of ownership, only acts an agent. The wholesale trade also include the activities of wholesaler at the fixed stalls of the wholesale market of different commodities.

Retail Trade refers to the activities of department store,supermarket, franchised store, brand store, retail stall and on-the-spot-making-selling store selling commodities to the final consumers (citizens) by any means including internet, post, telephone, sales machine. Retail trade excludes the activities of sales of capital goods such a grain, seed, feed, livestock, mineral products, raw material for production, industrial chemicals, chemical products for farm, machine and equipment (vehicle, computer and communication equipment), and the activities of supplementary sales of non-retailer such as the sales of spare parts of car repair business

Hotel Services refer to the activities of enterprises providing paid services of lodging to the customer, excluding the activities of providing long period of services of lodging (such as leased house and apartments).

Catering Services refer to the activities of enterprises providing on-the-spot services of selling food cooked and prepared to the customer in certain sites

Total Retail Sales of Consumer Goods refer to the sum of retail sales of commodities sold by wholesale and retail trades, catering services, publishing, post and telecommunications and other service industries to urban and rural households for household consumption and to social institutions for public consumption. Retail sales of consumer goods include:

1) Sales sold by wholesale and retail trades to urban~thA and rural households for household consumption and to social institutions for public consumption.

a) of commodities to urban and rural households;

b) of commodities to foreigners, overseas Chinese and Chinese compatriots from Hong Kong, Macao and Taiwan visiting China;

c) of commodities to government agencies, institutions, social organizations, military and armed police units, and commodities to enterprises in the form of retail sales. More specifically, they include: office facilities and articles for non-production purposes such as communications equipment, computing equipment and instruments, TV and network equipment, printing and copying equipment, audio-visual equipment and instruments, paper, notebooks, stationeries, furniture, electric appliances, knitwear, sanitation and cleaning articles, cultural and sport articles, articles for prizes, souvenirs, etc.; transport vehicles and fuels for employees; materials, spare parts and tools for the maintenance of office facilities; equipment, fuels, materials and food for winter heating or summer cooling purposes; articles and equipment for teaching purpose; Chinese and western medicines and medical equipment and facilities purchased by non profit-making medical institutes; non- specialized work safety articles; cooking utensils, tableware, equipment, cleaning articles, food and fuels purchased by in-house cafeterias; clothes and personal articles purchased by military or armed police units for their officials and soldiers; and other equipment and articles for non-production purposes.

2) Sales of stable food, cooked dishes, beverages, tobaccos and other articles by catering units.

3) Sales of books, newspapers, magazines, audio-visual products and post products by publishing, post and telecommunications departments to urban and rural households and to enterprises, institutions, military and armed police units.

4) Sales of food, beverages, tobaccos, clothing, hats, footwear, articles for daily use, medicines, medical and health articles, work of art, handicrafts, toys, funeral articles and other articles by other service industries.

Purchase, Sales and Stock of Commodities by Wholesale and Retail Trades refer to the total volume of commodities purchased, total volume of sales and exports, and the stock of commodities by wholesale and retail enterprises (establishments) of different status of registration from domestic and overseas markets. This indicator reflects the relationship among purchase, sales and stock of commodities in the circulation of goods and reveals the existing problems.

Total Purchases of Commodities refer to the total value of purchases of commodities by enterprises (establishments)from other establishments or individuals (including direct import from abroad) for the purpose of re-selling, either with or without further processing of the commodities purchased. The commodities include: (1) commodities purchased from agricultural and industrial producer, wholesaler, retailer, publishing house and other service business; (2) commodities purchased from institutions and government departments; (3) confiscated goods purchased from the customs authorities or market management agencies; (4) second-hand goods and wastes purchased from residents; The commodities exclude 1 commodities purchased by enterprises (establishments) for use in their own business operation, commodities obtained without buying or selling procedures such as materials, consumable goods of low value, office appliances, etc. 2 received goods without trading, such as goods handed over from others, borrowed goods, preserved goods for others, donated goods from others, processed and retrieved goods, etc. 3. goods of direct settlement between buyer and seller with handling fees introduced by others, 4. goods returned or refused to pay by the buyer, 5. excessive goods.

Total Sales of Commodities refer to value of commodities sold by the establishments to other establishments and individuals (including goods sold for self consumption, including the value-added tax). The commodities include: (1) commodities sold to urban and rural residents and social groups for their consumption; (2) commodities sold to establishments in all industries for their production and operation, including agriculture, industry, construction, transportation, post and telecommunications, catering services, and public utility including commodities sold to wholesale and retail establishments for re-selling, with or without further processing; and (3) commodities for direct export to abroad.Excluded are (1) extended commodities without trading, such as goods handed over to other enterprises and institutions because of the change of organizations, lent goods, returned goods preserved for others, extended processing materials and samples donated to others, (2) goods of direct settlement between buyer and seller with handling fees introduced by others, (3)goods returned after purchase, (4) damaged and spoiled goods, (5) waste and used goods of selfuse,

Total Stock of Commodities refers to total commodities possessed by wholesaler and retailer of various types of registration status at the end of the reference period, reflecting the commodity stock level of various wholesaler and retailer and the potential for market supply. It includes: (1) commodities located in storage, garages, counters, and shelves of operating places (such as sale stores, wholesale centres, and operating offices) ; (2) commodities in the process of being selected, sorted, and packed; (3) commodities not arrived but recorded as purchase in the account, i.e. commodities not arrived but payment receipts for the commodities from the sellers or the banks arrived; (4) commodities deposited in other places rather than places mentioned above, for instance: commodities in the hold of purchasers temporarily due to the refusal of payment and commodities not taken back after going through the formalities; (5) commodities entrusted to other units to sell but not sold yet; (6) commodities purchased for other units but not delivered yet. Commodities not included as stock are those not owned by the enterprises (units), commodities on commission for processing but not yet delivered, imported commodities of agency of foreign trade enterprise but not yet delivered to ordering units and finally those put in stock on behalf of the state material reserves units.

Business Revenue of Hotels and Catering Services refers to revenue received from providing services or selling commodities by corporate enterprises and establishments engaged in hotels and catering services, including income from hotels, from catering services, from selling of commodities and from other services. Income from hotels refers to income of corporate enterprises and establishments engaged in hotels and catering services by providing lodging services. Income from catering services refers to income of corporate enterprises and establishments engaged in hotels and catering services by providing catering services, including selling of cooked or prepared foods such as staple food, cooked dishes or cold dishes. Income from selling of commodities refers to income of corporate enterprises and establishments engaged in hotels and catering services by selling commodities (including value-added tax) that accompany the services they provide. Income from other activities refers to income received other than income from hotels, catering services or selling of commodities, such as income from providing recreation, fitness or business services.

Chain Head Stores (headquarter) refer to the core leading stores responsible for development, allocation, administration and utilization of resources (name of stores, brand of stores, operation model, service standard, management way, ect.) of chain stores. Chain stores refers to the stores engaged in providing homogeneous commodities or services, with the central leadership of head store and guided by common policies, conduct centralized purchase and distributed selling of commodities, in order to gain better efficiency through standardized operation. The chain stores include regular chain stores, franchise chain stores and voluntary chain stores.

Regular Chain store refers to chain stores that are invested or controlled by the headquarters. They operate under direct and unified management from the headquarters.

Franchise chain store refers to the chain stores (franchisees) which are franchised with operation resources such as trade marks, names, patent and operation know-how by the franchisors in form of contract and pay the operation fees to the franchisors

Voluntary chain store refers the stores operate jointly on the voluntary bases while maintaining their status of independent legal entities with full ownership of their assets. They sell goods of same brand from same channel of resource to the consumers.

17 对外经济贸易和旅游

FOREIGN TRADE AND ECONOMIC COOPERATION TOURISM

资料整理：马晓庆　赵琳瑛

Data management:Ma Xiaoqing Zhao linying

第十七部分　对外经济贸易和旅游

一、简要说明

本章资料包括对外经济贸易、利用外资和旅游等方面资料，由西安市统计局贸易外经处根据西安市商务局、海关和旅游局提供资料整理。

二、主要指标

进出口总额（亿美元）	130.14	比上年增长	3.3%
#出　口	72.99	比上年增长	25.3%
实际利用外商直接投资额（亿美元）	24.78	比上年增长	23.6%
国际旅游人数（万人次）	115.35	比上年增长	15.1%
国际旅游收入（亿美元）	7.49	比上年增长	16.8%

16　FOREIGN TRADE AND ECONOMIC COOPERATION,TOURISM

Ⅰ.Brief Introduction

Data in this chapter consists of data on foreign trade, using of foreign capital and fund and tourism. Data on foreign economy and trade and tourism are compiled and provided by Foreign Economy Division of the Xi'an Bureau of Statistics according to the data from Xi'an Bureau of Commerce, Xi'an Custom Office and Xi'an Bureau of Tourism.

Ⅱ.Major Indicators

		Increase over Preceding Year
Total Imports and Exports (USD 100 mil.)	130.14	3.3%
#Toal Exports	72.99	25.3%
Total Amount of Foreign Direst zwestment (USD 100 mil.)	24.78	23.6%
Total Number of International Tourists (10 000 persons)	115.35	15.1%
Total Foreign Exchange Earnings (USD 100 mil.)	7.49	16.8%

17-1 主要年份外资、外贸和国际旅游基本情况

Main Indicators on Foreign Investments,International Trading and International Tourism In Representative Years

指 标	Item	1990	1995	2000	2005	2006
一、利用外资签定协议项目（个）	**Number of Projects of Foreign Capital Used through the Signed Agreements and Contracts (unit)**	**11**	**184**	**135**	**157**	**190**
利用外资签定协议金额(万美元)	Value of Foreign Capital Used through the Signed Agreements and Contracts(USD 10 000)	415	28956	54123	21499	182525
外商实际直接投资额(万美元)	Value of Foreign Direct Investment (USD 10 000)	1154	18653	15633	57113	82463
二、进出口总额（万美元）	**Total Imports and Exports (USD 10 000)**	**38229**	**137510**	**173696**	**90146**	**415403**
#进口总额	Total Imports	9939	27347	67634	26705	142541
出口总额	Total Exports	28290	110163	106062	63441	272862
进出口差额(出口-进口)	Balance of Imports and Exports	18351	82816	38428	36736	130321
三、国际旅游者人数总计(万人次)	**Total Number of International Tourists (10 000 person-times)**	**25.88**	**41.35**	**65.03**	**77.56**	**86.73**
#外国人	Foreigners	15.40	37.11	54.65	65.86	73.40
港、澳、台同胞	Chinese Compatriot From Hong Kong, Macao and Taiwan	10.07	4.16	10.38	11.70	13.33
四、国际旅游者人天数总计（万人天）	**Total Number of Days of International Tourists (10 000 person/day)**	**55.03**	**84.44**	**162.69**	**24.93**	**253.17**
#外国人	Foreigners	33.48	75.71	131.44	90.99	214.10
港、澳、台同胞	Chinese Compatriot From Hong Kong, Macao and Taiwan	21.55	8.56	31.15	33.94	39.07
五、国际旅游收入（亿元）	**Earning of International Tourism (100 millon yuan)**	**1.96**	**10.38**	**22.41**	**33.54**	**37.83**
#商品收入	Income from Mercantile	0.44	2.57	7.71	11.25	15.93
劳务收入	Income from Labour Service	1.52	7.81	14.70	22.29	21.90
六、旅游者在西安人均停留天数(天)	Number of Days of Average Tourists Staying in Xi'an (day)	**2.1**	**2.0**	**2.5**	**2.9**	**2.9**

注：1990年和1995年国际旅游者中含华侨。
本表数据来源于市商务局、西安海关、市旅游局。

17-1 续表 continued

指　标	Item	2007	2008	2009	2010	2011	2012
一、利用外资签定协议项目（个）	**Number of Projects of Foreign Capital Used through the Signed Agreements and Contracts (unit)**	**135**	**100**	**65**	**82**	**99**	**87**
利用外资签定协议金额(万美元)	Value of Foreign Capital Used through the Signed Agreements and Contracts(USD 10 000)	143978	118230	60027	119689	120083	360264
外商实际直接投资额(万美元)	Value of Foreign Direct Investment (USD 10 000)	111567	114738	121872	156653	200522	247800
二、进出口总额（万美元）	**Total Imports and Exports (USD 10 000)**	**536162**	**704029**	**724618**	**1039273**	**1260179**	**1301446**
#进口总额	Total Imports	189029	256916	391504	507544	677517	571568
出口总额	Total Exports	347133	447113	333114	531729	582662	729878
进出口差额(出口-进口)	Balance of Imports and Exports	158104	190197	-58390	24185	-94855	158310
三、国际旅游者人数总计(万人次)	**Total Number of International Tourists (10 000 person-times)**	**100.01**	**63.20**	**67.29**	**84.18**	**100.23**	**115.34**
#外国人	Foreigners	85.09	53.58	59.09	73.21	88.63	101.40
港、澳、台同胞	Chinese Compatriot From Hong Kong, Macao and Taiwan	14.92	9.62	8.20	10.97	11.60	13.94
四、国际旅游者人天数总计（万人天）	**Total Number of Days of International Tourists (10 000 person/day)**	**290.02**	**162.93**	**195.14**	**241.67**	**287.09**	**334.44**
#外国人	Foreigners	246.76	138.72	171.36	211.48	254.78	294.90
港、澳、台同胞	Chinese Compatriot From Hong Kong, Macao and Taiwan	43.26	24.21	23.78	30.19	32.31	39.54
五、国际旅游收入（亿元）	**Earning of International Tourism (100 millon yuan)**	**42.43**	**28.72**	**31.05**	**42.40**	**51.28**	**59.89**
#商品收入	Income from Mercantile	15.19	9.74	8.94	11.87	11.38	14.19
劳务收入	Income from Labour Service	27.24	18.98	22.11	30.53	39.90	45.70
六、旅游者在西安人均停留天数(天)	**Number of Days of Average Tourists Staying in Xi'an (day)**	**2.9**	**2.6**	**2.9**	**2.9**	**2.9**	**2.9**

17-2 主要年份利用外资情况

Utilization of Foreign Capital In Representative Years

单位：万美元 (USD 10 000)

年 份 Year	利用外资签订协议金额 Value of Foreign Capital Used through the Signed Agreements and Contracts	外商实际直接投资额 Direct Foreign Investment
1983	3500	800
1984	8	
1985	8361	1106
1986	19919	4010
1987	3218	5552
1988	2423	6758
1989	1645	11632
1990	415	1154
1991	591	1094
1992	24165	5200
1993	57289	8996
1994	20321	15240
1995	28956	18653
1996	35978	20510
1997	27214	22057
1998	40034	22286
1999	40390	13801
2000	54123	15633
2001	60736	17687
2002	70692	20281
2003	96380	25557
2004	78312	27595
2005	121499	57113
2006	182525	82463
2007	143978	111567
2008	118230	114738
2009	60027	121872
2010	119689	156653
2011	120083	200522
2012	360264	247800

注：本表数据来源于市商务局

17-3　外国和港澳台地区在西安直接投资（2012年）

Direct Investments from Foreign Countries and Hong Kong, Macao and Taiwan in Xi'an（2012）

分　类	Classity	新签协议情况 New-signed Agreement Circumstances		外商实际直接投资额（万美元） Value of Foreign Direct Investment (USD 10 000)
		合同数（个） Number of Constracts (unit)	利用外资签定协议金额（万美元） Value of Foreign Captial Used through the Signed (USD10 000)	
合　计	**Total**	**87**	**360264**	**247800**
一、按投资方式分	**Grouped by Investment Mode**			
1.中外合资经营企业	Joint-venture Enterprises	34	51227	95132
2.中外合作经营企业	Cooperation Enterprises		6770	847
3.外资企业	Wholly Foreign-owned Enterprises	53	302267	151821
4.外资企业再投资	Re-investment from Foreign-funded Enterprises			
二、按国民经济行业分组	**Grouped by Sector**			
1.农、林、牧、渔业	Agriculture,Forestry,Animal,Husbandy and Fishery	1	9	133
2.采矿业	Mining	1		6250
3.制造业	Manufacturing	41	305998	144144
4.电力、燃气及水的生产供应业	Production and Distribution of Electricity,Gas and Water			300
5.建筑业	Construction			
6.批发和零售业	Retail Trads and Catering ServicesReal Estate	8	9586	20321
7.交通运输、仓储和邮政业	Transporation,Storage,Postal and Telecommunications	2	2604	2624
8.住宿和餐饮业	Hotels and Catering Services	3	272	292
9.信息传输、软件和信息技术服务业	Information Transmission,Software and Information Technology Services	12	3917	3450
10.金融业	Financial Intermediation			1021
11.房地产	Real Estate	5	32505	62384
12.租赁和商务服务业	Leasing and Business Services	12	5361	2478
13.科学研究和技术服务业	Scientific Research and Technical Services	1	141	
14.水利、环境和公共设施管理业	Management of Water Conservancy, Environment and Public Facilities			
15.居民服务、修理和其他服务业	Services to Households, Repairs and Other Services	1	10	
16.教育	Education			
17.卫生和社会工作	Health and Social Work		-140	4363
18.文化、体育和娱乐业	Culture, Sports and Entertainment			40
19.公共管理社会保障和社会组织	Public Administration, Social Security and Social Organizations			
20.国际组织	International Organizations			
三、按投资国别、地区分组	**Grouped by Different Countries and Regions**			
香港	Hong Kong	33	66679	130264
澳门	Macao	1		
台湾省	Taiwan	2	856	3768
日本	Japan	5	-1036	2536
泰国	Tailand			
马来西亚	Malaysia	1	1325	
新加坡	Singapore	6	13047	13984
韩国	Korea	13	240659	36660
德意志联邦国	Germany	1	211	520
意大利	Italy			184
法国	France			198
英国	England	2	87	4606
捷克共和国	Czechoslovakia			
加拿大	Canada	3	37	15
美国	America	7	5684	2089
澳大利亚	Australia			70
维尔京群岛	Virgin Islands	9	17082	21688
其它	Others	4	15633	31218

注：本表数据来源于市商务局。

17-4 各区县、开发区外商实际直接投资（2012年）

Direct Investment by Foreign Entrepreneurs by Region and Development Zone （2012）

单位：万美元 (USD 10 000)

区县及开发区	Region and Economic Zone	2009	2010	2011	2012
区、县合计	**Sum of Region**	**29766**	**38855**	**49726**	**58119**
新城区	Xincheng	3740	4900	6765	7800
碑林区	Beilin	4780	5150	6273	7800
莲湖区	Lianhu	3953	5471	7405	7800
灞桥区	Baqiao	4300	5215	6001	7397
未央区	Weiyang	3902	5023	6202	7800
雁塔区	Yanta	4087	5488	6912	8190
阎良区	Yanliang	675	1208	2070	2200
临潼区	Lintong	970	1200	2000	2400
长安区	Chang'an	1219	1680	2300	2768
蓝田县	Lantian	605	950	1089	1100
周至县	Zhouzhi	315	550	600	650
户　县	Huxian	560	970	1050	1100
高陵县	Gaoling	660	1050	1060	1115
开发区合计	**Sum of Development Zones**	**92107**	**117798**	**150797**	**189681**
高新区	GaoXin	40613	51130	64935	81776
经开区	JingKai	33661	42608	54201	68202
曲江新区	Qujiang	12589	17187	21002	26433
浐灞生态区	Chanba Eco-District	2400	3070	3856	4837
航空基地	Aviation Industry Base	1016	1239	1701	2072
航天基地	Aerospace Base	1208	1554	2030	2403
国际港务区	International Trade&Logistic Park	620	1010	1571	2082
沣东新城	FengDongXinCheng			1500	1876

注：本表数据来源于市商务局。

17–5 主要年份进出口总额

Total Imports and Exports In Representative Years

单位：万美元 (USD 10 000)

年份 Year	进出口总额 Total Imports and Exports	出口总额 Total Exports	进口总额 Total Imports
1987	13596	7540	6056
1988	36750	24632	12118
1989	32715	21564	11151
1990	38229	28290	9939
1991	55356	41511	13845
1992	70467	53060	17407
1993	93330	62393	30937
1994	104752	76897	27855
1995	137510	110163	27347
1996	143187	91745	51442
1997	150668	107753	42915
1998	180589	100492	80097
1999	172919	94495	78424
2000	173696	106062	67634
2001	169914	87948	81966
2002	186966	112479	74487
2003	230932	140327	90605
2004	309295	203539	105756
2005	390146	263441	126705
2006	415403	272862	142541
2007	536162	347133	189029
2008	704029	447113	256916
2009	724618	333114	391504
2010	1039273	531729	507544
2011	1260179	582662	677517
2012	1301446	729878	571568

注：本表数据来源于西安海关。

17-6 外贸商品进出口总额分国别和地区（2012年）

Total Value of Imports and Exports by Country and Region（2012）

单位：万美元 (USD 10 000)

国别和地区	Country and Region	进出口总额 Total Imports and Exports	出口 Exports
亚洲	**Asia**	**540911**	**336299**
#香港	Hong kong	88613	87488
台湾省	Taiwan	91301	26003
日本	Japan	79979	39370
菲律宾	Phiilippines	7052	3616
马来西亚	Malaysia	18861	15879
韩国	Korea	48282	26508
非洲	**Africa**	**66321**	**61413**
#埃及	Egypt	6566	6563
突尼斯	Tunisia	591	588
埃塞俄比亚	Ethiopia	567	552
博茨瓦纳	Botswana	18	18
南非	South Africa	9361	9258
欧洲	**Europe**	**289816**	**149486**
#德意志联邦国	Germany	86630	36442
法国	France	22534	12445
意大利	Italy	16548	7190
荷兰	Netherland	18635	13872
英国	England	31826	22744
瑞士	Switzerland	10141	429
西班牙	Spain	4181	3410
俄罗斯联邦	Russia	22736	20569
拉丁美洲	**Latin America**	**50231**	**28423**
#哥伦比亚	Colombia	1241	1239
巴西	Brazil	22152	8597
阿根廷	Argentina	1537	1483
北美洲	**North America**	**322900**	**144541**
加拿大	Canada	15319	9340
美国	America	307581	135200
大洋洲及太平洋岛屿	**Oceanic and Pacific Islands**	**31267**	**9716**
#澳大利亚	Australia	28936	7699
新西兰	New Zealand	1063	748

注：本表数据来源于西安海关。

17-7　主要商品分大类出口金额

单位：万美元

商品分类	HS Section and Division	2000	2001
食用蔬菜、根及块茎	Edible Vegetables, Certain,Roots amd Tubers	1095	1957
蔬菜、水果、坚果或植物其他部分的制品	Vegetables, Fruits, Nuts, or Products Made of Other Parts of Plants	2076	2684
矿砂、矿渣及矿灰	Ores,Slags and Ash	4083	4649
无机化学品；贵金属、稀土金属、放射性元素及其同位素的有机及无机化合物	Inorganic Chemicals,Organic or Inorganic Compounds of Precious Metals,of Rare Earth Metals,of Radioactive Elements or of Isotopes	3714	4141
有机化学品	Organic Chemicals	2367	3279
羊毛、动物细毛或粗毛、马毛纱线及其机织物	Wool ,Fine or Coarse Animal Hair; Horsehair Yarn and Woven Fabric	810	829
棉花	Cotton	3197	2734
化学纤维短纤	Short Staple Chemical' Fibers	5061	3612
针织或钩编的服装及衣着附件	Articles of Apparel and Clothing Accessories, Knitted or Crocheted	6753	1632
非针织或非钩编的服装及衣着附件	Articles of Apparel and Clothing Accessories, not Knitted or Crocheted	7269	3319
其它纺织制成品；成套物品；旧衣着及旧纺织品	Other Made Up Textile Articles;Sets;Worn Clothing and Worn Textile Articles;Rags Articles	1649	1002
鞋靴、护膝和类似品及其零件	Footwear,Gaiters and The Like;Parts of Such Articles Headgear and Parts Thereof	1347	279
玻璃及其制品	Glass and Glassware	3376	3838
钢铁	Iron and Steel	3534	1197
钢铁制品	Articles of Iron or Steel	5535	6401
铅及制品	Lead Areticles Thereof	1371	1363
锌及制品	Zinc Areticles Thereof	4031	1945
其他贱金属、金属陶瓷及其制品	Other Base Metals,Germets;Areticles Thereof	1066	1704
贱金属工具、器具、利口器、餐匙、餐叉及其零件	Tools,Implements,Cutlery,Spons and Forks, of Base Metal;Parts Thereof of Base Metal	2933	2669
核反应堆、锅炉、机器、机械器具及其零件	Nuclear Reactors ,Boilers, Machinery and Mechanical Appliances; and Parts Thereof	10915	11979
电机、电气设备及其零件；录音机及放声机、电视图象、声音的录制和重放设备及其零件、附件	Electrical Machinery and Equipment and Parts Thereof;Sound Recorders and Repreducers, Television Image and Sound Recordes and Repreducers,and Parts and Accessories of Such Articles	8339	8696
光学、照相、电影、计量、检验、医疗或外科仪器及设备、精密仪器及设备；上述物品的零配件、附件	Optical,Photographic,Cinematographic,Measuring, Checking,Precision Medical or Surgical Instruments and Apparatus;Parts and Accessories Thereof	2020	2818
家具、寝具、褥垫、弹簧床垫、软床垫及类似的填充制品；未列名灯具及照明装置；发光标志、发光名牌及类似品；活动房屋	Mattresses,Mattress Supports,Cushions and Similar Stuffed Furnishings;Lamps and Lighting Fittings, not Elsewhere Spcified or Included;Illumihated Signs,Illuminated	2587	2150

Export Value of Major Merchandise by Type

(USD 10 000)

2002	2003	2004	2005	2006	2007	2008	2009	2010	2011	2012
1275	1379	1386	1190	1136	1232	1374	803	4740	2016	1961
3470	4490	7786	10531	15374	37426	29270	21920	41289	36763	2576
8714	11224	30590	63247	52046	47378	40502	6141	325	4709	1679
4141	5814	5806	10997	10916	16508	15882	9774	24875	11735	8911
4883	4757	4837	8569	11923	11182	13954	16294	982	20067	17890
1313	1600	1640	903	1400	1065	720	460	10133	796	562
3826	3984	3133	3240	3808	3255	3213	2346	98	2628	2185
2512	2120	1987	1471	1556	1767	1181	2217	479	2586	2375
2660	341	7465	5736	5332	5345	4371	3617	3209	3366	12316
3629	4981	5543	5068	4078	3875	3623	2919	3394	3262	7050
1432	2203	2667	3000	3342	3090	3187	2813	544	2838	4412
296	585	2687	1368	216	348	380	367	150	1003	5252
5542	6667	8083	8576	8272	6246	6538	5574	928	8073	10995
2167	2779	5244	5314	4900	11366	11966	4254	18549	16681	8407
7414	8474	10398	13959	16903	17329	26568	11943	5998	25319	24259
444	232	43	12	158	1650	2	1	10	2	4913
1895	2200	522	135	4119	2470	46	78	28545	10	11
1546	3150	6419	11233	17695	23414	27576	11276	3556	28092	21397
2613	3232	3406	3052	3607	3917	4083	2777	2893	3641	5176
16140	21281	24696	30832	36174	47381	75911	52372	130296	99631	127795
8962	15106	19812	23605	22801	33393	56758	53355	136	137105	183536
5395	3339	1847	2341	3521	4230	6348	5255	196	11066	14908
2715	3994	4955	4773	5086	8301	8296	4769	5328	3860	25644

17-8 主要商品分大类进口金额

Import Value of Major Merchandise by Type

单位：万美元 (USD 10 000)

商品分类	HS Section and Division	2000	2004	2005	2006	2007
无机化学品；贵金属、稀土金属、放射性元素及其同位素的有机及无机化合物	Inorganic Chemicals,Organic or Inorganic Compounds of Precious Metals,of Rare Earth Metals,of Radioactive Elements or of Isotopes	1467	89	317	709	1039
有机化学品	Organic Chemicals	7257	14829	15237	13521	14536
塑料及其制品	Plastic and Articles Thereof	2559	2560	4317	2889	5149
钢铁	Iron and Steel	2467	1205	752	1014	1270
铜及制品	Copper and Articles Thereof	2367	842	689	8035	22683
铝及制品	Aluminium and Articles Thereof	2652	1634	3627	3172	3223
核反应堆、锅炉、机器、机械器具及其零件	Nuclear Reactors ,Boilers, Machinery and Mechanical Appliances; and Parts Thereof	12990	37185	38050	33065	55243
电机、电气设备及其零件；录音机及放声机、电视图象、声音的录制和重放设备及其零件、附件	Electrical Machinery and Equipment and Parts Thereof;Sound Recorders and Repreducers, Television Image and Sound Recordes and Repreducers,and Parts and Accessories of Such Articles	5911	16102	23337	2 1279	25164
车辆及其零件、附件、铁道及电车道车辆除外	Vehicles Other Than Railway or Tramway Rolling-Stock, and Rarts and Accessories Thereof	1530	3291	1387	1228	1529
航空器、航天器及其零配件	Aircraft, Spacecraft and Parts Thereof	10443	814	8800	17879	2463
光学、照相、电影、计量、检验、医疗或外科仪器及设备、精密仪器及设备；上述物品的零配件、附件	Optical,Photographic,Cinematographic,Measuring, Checking,Precision Medical or Surgical	3673	10358	10424	12152	17026

17-8 续表 continued

单位：万美元 (USD 10 000)

商品分类	HS Section and Division	2008	2009	2010	2011	2012
无机化学品；贵金属、稀土金属、放射性元素及其同位素的有机及无机化合物	Inorganic Chemicals,Organic or Inorganic Compounds of Precious Metals,of Rare Earth Metals,of Radioactive Elements or of Isotopes	6001	5040	7513	19766	13329
有机化学品	Organic Chemicals	15692	14186	13949	18100	12331
塑料及其制品	Plastic and Articles Thereof	2553	3134	4091	3250	3107
钢铁	Iron and Steel	3888	2537	10949	10643	5928
铜及制品	Copper and Articles Thereof	11097	41195	43343	78482	11857
铝及制品	Aluminium and Articles Thereof	4767	6505	3116	5913	8649
核反应堆、锅炉、机器、机械器具及其零件	Nuclear Reactors ,Boilers, Machinery and Mechanical Appliances; and Parts Thereof	68504	87493	134753	135240	98802
电机、电气设备及其零件；录音机及放声机、电视图象、声音的录制和重放设备及其零件、附件	Electrical Machinery and Equipment and Parts Thereof;Sound Recorders and Repreducers, Television Image and Sound Recordes and Repreducers,and Parts and Accessories of Such Articles	48008	113034	207937	230957	257444
车辆及其零件、附件、铁道及电车道车辆除外	Vehicles Other Than Railway or Tramway Rolling-Stock, and Rarts and Accessories Thereof	3789	1798	3109	1527	2222
航空器、航天器及其零配件	Aircraft, Spacecraft and Parts Thereof	26148	13057	3620	4654	8516
光学、照相、电影、计量、检验、医疗或外科仪器及设备、精密仪器及设备；上述物品的零配件、附件	Optical,Photographic,Cinematographic,Measuring, Checking,Precision Medical or Surgical	17737	24210	37414	39317	48206

注：本表数据来源于西安海关。

17-9 主要年份旅游人数及收入

Number of Tourists and Tourism Earnings In Representative Years

年 份 Year	接待旅游者人数（万人次） Number of Tourists (10 000 person-times)	国际旅游人数（万人次） Number of International Tourists	旅游总收入（万元） Total Tourism Earnings (10 000 yuan)	国际旅游收入（万元） Earning of International Tourists	国际旅游者在西安人均停留天数（天） Number of Days of Average International Tourists Staying in Xi'an(day)
1980	4.00	4.00	1757	1757	3.8
1981	6.71	6.71	2314	2314	3.4
1982	9.09	9.09	3172	3172	2.8
1983	12.38	12.38	3720	3720	2.5
1984	15.13	15.13	4579	4579	2.3
1985	21.15	21.15	7029	7029	2.2
1986	25.78	25.78	10886	10886	2.2
1987	30.15	30.15	16588	16588	2.1
1988	36.58	36.58	21152	21152	2.0
1989	21.20	21.20	14125	14125	1.9
1990	25.88	25.88	19628	19628	2.1
1991	31.00	31.00	29051	29051	2.3
1992	40.16	40.16	40966	40966	2.2
1993	43.50	43.50	48951	48951	1.9
1994	41.49	41.49	82000	82000	2.2
1995	791.35	41.35	440000	103818	2.0
1996	925.39	45.39	470000	149400	2.6
1997	1010.53	48.53	510000	166359	2.6
1998	1105.80	47.98	560000	160244	2.6
1999	1260.40	55.41	830000	186282	2.5
2000	1567.00	65.03	1050000	224100	2.5
2001	1752.20	67.20	1130000	240700	2.4
2002	1984.13	74.13	1310000	260000	2.2
2003	1647.67	33.66	1064200	121200	2.5
2004	2149.03	65.03	1544000	273900	2.9
2005	2423.60	77.56	1785000	335380	2.9
2006	2738.70	86.73	2043000	378270	2.9
2007	3118.01	100.01	2372000	424263	2.9
2008	3232.20	63.20	2435200	287200	2.6
2009	3929.29	67.29	2974000	310500	2.9
2010	5285.18	84.18	4051800	424000	2.9
2011	6653.23	100.23	5301500	512800	2.9
2012	7978.35	115.35	6543900	598900	2.9

注：本表数据来源于市旅游局。

17-10 主要年份国际旅游收入

Earning of International Tourism In Representative Years

单位：万美元 (USD 10 000)

项 目	Item	2000	2002	2003	2004	2005	2006	2007	2008	2009	2010	2011	2012
合 计	**Total**	**27000**	**32000**	**14600**	**33000**	**40900**	**46700**	**54323**	**35900**	**9000**	**53000**	**64100**	**74862**
一、长途交通费	**Long Distance Transportation**	**7047**	**6816**	**3109**	**8415**	**12311**	**11442**	**14286**	**10016**	**2597**	**19292**	**26153**	**26876**
1. 飞机	Airplane	6011	5536	2526	7524	9407	9527	10918	7467	9438	15264	19807	20887
2. 火车	Train	273	288	131	264	858	561	2009	1436	2262	2968	2692	3369
3. 汽车	Highway	763	992	452	627	2046	1354	1359	1113	897	1060	3654	2620
二、游览	**Sightseeing**	**1296**	**1120**	**511**	**1155**	**2045**	**2335**	**2335**	**1831**	**2262**	**3445**	**3846**	**4641**
三、住宿	**Accommodation**	**3051**	**4480**	**2044**	**4752**	**4621**	**5977**	**6573**	**4523**	**5343**	**6572**	**6859**	**9358**
四、餐饮	**Food and Beverage**	**2673**	**3264**	**1489**	**2673**	**3823**	**2195**	**3804**	**2908**	**3471**	**4929**	**2436**	**3444**
五、娱乐	**Entertainment**	**1512**	**896**	**409**	**990**	**1779**	**747**	**1847**	**2046**	**1833**	**2120**	**3525**	**5240**
六、购物	**Shopping**	**6615**	**9600**	**4380**	**9900**	**9897**	**17466**	**15645**	**9262**	**7761**	**9911**	**11794**	**14298**
七、邮电通讯	**Post and Communication Services**	**1350**	**1120**	**512**	**957**	**2454**	**1261**	**1794**	**1652**	**1131**	**1272**	**1474**	**1572**
八、市内交通	**Local Transportation**	**1566**	**768**	**350**	**726**	**858**	**841**	**1249**	**1041**	**975**	**2120**	**2564**	**2770**
九、其它	**Others**	**1890**	**3936**	**1796**	**3432**	**3112**	**4436**	**6790**	**2621**	**3627**	**3339**	**5449**	**6663**

注：本表数据来源于市旅游局。

17-11 主要涉外星级宾馆接待海外旅游者情况

Mainly Concerning Oversea Tourists Reception in Star Hotels in Representative Years

单位：人次 (person-time)

项 目	Item	2005	2006	2007	2008	2009	2010	2011	2012
海外旅游者人数	**International Tourists**	**775620**	**867273**	**1000063**	**632036**	**672909**	**841819**	**1002326**	**1153469**
外国人	Foreigners	658578	733963	850905	535837	590870	732065	886276	1014036
#日本	Japan	75639	85708	93135	43017	60192	70368	61844	62238
菲律宾	Philippines	2165	1910	2162	1466	1708	2213	2587	2311
新加坡	Singapore	6148	6395	7309	6335	7570	10158	12759	12028
美国	America	116913	121788	146089	104742	100445	106042	117485	124490
加拿大	Canada	16807	20075	29193	19047	21901	28409	37511	36494
英国	England	45956	50046	56560	40299	43068	41023	44386	43145
法国	France	49414	49113	58216	37415	39350	42337	42114	46870
德意志联邦国	Germany	37527	41446	50882	32892	36371	40166	40777	45860
意大利	Italy	16909	16493	21444	9445	15316	15868	19737	20770
瑞士	Switzerland	3748	4080	5047	3763	4479	5528	5933	7006
澳大利亚	Australia	28645	30146	36581	24784	26349	30507	34411	38180
新西兰	New Zealand	4522	3296	4978	4027	4238	5005	5248	5399
港、澳、台同胞	Chinese Compatriots from Hong Kong, Macao and Taiwan	117042	133310	149158	96199	82039	109754	116050	139433
#台湾同胞	Taiwan	57958	66601	74962	44552	37464	54119	58197	70051

注：本表数据来源于市旅游局。

17-12 主要年份旅行社及A级景点

Statistics of Travel Agencies and Level-A Scenic Spots in Representative Years

项 目	Item	2005	2006	2007	2008	2009	2010	2011	2012
旅行社数（个）	Number of Travel Agencies (unit)	221	240	262	271	303	334	365	395
旅行社营业收入（亿元）	Revenue of Travel Agencies (100 millon yuan)	17.82	19.98	26.48	17.85	21.34	31.22	44.31	49.49
旅游A级景点数（个）	Number of Level-A Scenic Spots(unit)	18	23	23	23	24	34	43	55
旅游A级景点年接待游客人次（万人次）	Number of Tourists Received at Level-A Scenic Spots (10 000 person times)	930	1314	1410	1420	1504	2726.2	4295	5306

注：本表数据来源于市旅游局。

主要统计指标解释

进出口总额 指实际进出我国国境的货物总金额。包括对外贸易实际进出口货物，来料加工装配进出口货物，国家间、联合国及国际组织无偿援助物资和赠送品，华侨、港澳台同胞和外籍华人捐赠品，租赁期满归承租人所有的租赁货物，进料加工进出口货物，边境地方贸易及边境地区小额贸易进出口货物（边民互市贸易除外），中外合资企业、中外合作经营企业、外商独资经营企业进出口货物和公用物品，到、离岸价格在规定限额以上的进出口货样和广告品（无商业价值、无使用价值和免费提供出口的除外），从保税仓库提取在中国境内销售的进口货物，以及其他进出口货物。该指标可以观察一个国家在对外贸易方面的总规模。我国规定出口货物按离岸价格统计，进口货物按到岸价格统计。

商品经营单位所在地进、出口额 指在所在地海关注册登记的有进出口经营权的企业实际进、出口额。

商品目的地进口额和商品货源地出口额 目的地进口额指进口货物的消费、使用或最终抵运地的实际进口额；货源地出口额指出口货物的产地或原始发货地的实际出口额。

利用外资 指我国各级政府、部门、企业和其他经济组织通过对外借款、吸收外商直接投资以及用其他方式筹措的境外现汇、设备、技术等。

外商直接投资 指外国企业和经济组织或个人（包括华侨、港澳台胞以及我国在境外注册的企业）按我国有关政策、法规，用现汇、实物、技术等在我国境内开办外商独资企业、与我国境内的企业或经济组织共同举办中外合资经营企业、合作经营企业或合作开发资源的投资（包括外商投资收益的再投资），以及经政府有关部门批准的项目投资总额内企业从境外借入的资金。

旅游人数：

（1）入境旅游人数：指报告期内来我国观光、度假、探亲访友、就医疗养、购物、参加会议或从事经济、文化、体育、宗教活动的外国人、港澳台同胞等入境游客。统计时，外国人、港澳台同胞每入境一次统计1人次。

（2）出境人数：指中国（大陆）居民因公或因私出境前往其他国家、中国香港特别行政区、澳门特别行政区和台湾省观光、度假、探亲访友、就医疗养、购物、参加会议或从事经济、文化、体育、宗教活动的人数，即出境游客。统计时，按每出境一次统计1人次。

（3）国内旅游人数：指在报告期内在中国（大陆）观光游览、度假、探亲访友、就医疗养、购物、参加会议或从事经济、文化、体育、宗教活动的中国（大陆）居民人数，其出游的目的不是通过所从事的活动谋取报酬。统计时，国内游客按每出游一次统计1人次。

国际旅游（外汇）收入 指入境游客在中国（大陆）境内旅行、游览过程中用于交通、参观游览、住宿、餐饮、购物、娱乐等全部花费。

国内旅游收入 又称旅游总花费指国内游客在国内旅行、游览过程中用于交通、参观游览、住宿、餐饮、购物、娱乐等全部花费。

国际旅行社 指经营业务范围包括入境旅游业务、出境旅游业务和国内旅游业务的旅行社。

国内旅行社 指经营范围仅限于国内旅游业务的旅行社。

星级饭店 指设备、设施、服务符合《旅游饭店星级的划分与评定》（CB／T14308—2003），通过相关旅游管理部门评定，并取得星级饭店称号的饭店（含预备星级饭店）。

Explanatory Notes on Main Statistical Indicators

Total Imports and Exports at Customs refer to the real value of commodities imported and exported across the border of China. They include the actual imports and exports through foreign trade, imported and exported goods under the processing and assembling trades and materials, supplies and gifts as aid given gratis between governments and by the United Nations and other international organizations, and contributions donated by overseas Chinese, compatriots in Hong Kong and Macao and Chinese with foreign citizenship, leasing commodities owned by tenant at the expiration of leasing period, the imported and exported commodities processed with imported materials, commodities trading in border areas (excluding mutual exchange goods), the imported and exported commodities and articles for public use of the Sino-foreign joint ventures, cooperative enterprises and ventures with sole foreign investment. Also included is import or export of samples and advertising goods for which CIF or FOB value are beyond the permitted ceiling (excluding goods of no trading or use value and free commodities for export), imported goods sold in China from bonded warehouses and other imported or exported goods. The indicator of the total imports and exports at customs can be used to observe the total size of external trade in a country. In accordance with the stipulation of the Chinese government, imports are calculated at CIF, while exports are calculated at FOB.

Import Export Value by Location of China's Foreign Trade Managing Units refers to actual value of imports and exports carried out by corporations which have been registered by the local Customs house and are vested with right to run import export business.

Import Value of Commodities by Place of Destination and Export Value of Commodities by Place of Origin in China The former indicator refers to the value of import commodities of the places of their consumption, utilization or the places of their final destination. The latter indicator refers to the value of export commodities of the places of their origin or the places of the commodities dispatched.

Utilization of Foreign Capitals refers to remittance, equipment and technology financed from abroad, by loans, foreign direct investment and other forms undertaken by the Chinese governments at all levels, by various departments, enterprises and other economic units.

Foreign Borrowings refer to funds borrowed from abroad through formal signing of borrowing agreements with foreign institutions, including loans of foreign governments, loans of international financial institutions, commercial loans of foreign banks, export credit, and funds raised by Chinese bonds (and shares before 1996) issued abroad. It is an important part of China's utilization of foreign capitals.

Foreign Direct Investment refers to the investments inside China by foreign enterprises and economic organizations or individuals (including overseas Chinese, compatriots from Hong Kong, Macao and Taiwan, and Chinese enterprises registered abroad), following the relevant policies and laws of China, for the establishment of ventures exclusively with foreign own investment, Sino-foreign joint ventures and cooperative enterprises or for co-operative exploration of resources with enterprises or economic organizations in China.

Number of Tourists

(1) Visitor arrivals refer to the number of foreigners,Chinese compatriots from Hong Kong, Macao and Taiwan Chinese (mainland) who come to China (mainland) for sight-seeing,vacation,visiting relatives, medical treatment, shopping, attending conference, or to engage in economic, cultural, sports and religious activities. In compiling statistics, each time of entering China is counted as one person-time.

(2) Number of Chinese residents going abroad refer to the number of Chinese (mainland) residents going to other countries, Hong Kong Special Administrative region, Macao Special Administrative region and Taiwan for on official or private purposes, for sight-seeing, vacation, visiting relatives, medical treatment, shopping, attending conference, or to engage in economic, cultural, sports and religious

activities. In compiling statistics, each time of leaving is counted as one person-time.

(3) Number of domestic tourists refers to the number of Chinese (mainland) residents who travel within China (mainland) for sight-seeing, vacation, visiting relatives, medical treatment, shopping, attending conference, or to engage in economic, cultural, sports and religious activities. In compiling statistics, each time of travelling is counted as one person-time.

Foreign Exchange Earnings from International Tourism refer to the total expenditure of foreigners, overseas Chinese,Chinese compatriots from Hong Kong,Macao and Taiwan during their stay in the mainland of China on transportation,sighting,accommodation, food,shopping and entertainment.

Income from Domestic Tourism refer to expenditure of domestic tourists on transportation,sighting, accommodation, food, shopping and entertainment while they travel.

International Travel Agencies refer to travel agencies engaged in tourism entering China, Chinese residents going abroad and domestic tourism.

Domestic Travel Agencies refer to travel agencies only engaged in domestic tourism.

Star–rated Hotels refer to hotels rated with stars as assessed by the relevant tourism authorities according to GB/T14308-2003 standard with reference to their infrastructure, facilities and service levels.

18 金融业

FINANCIAL INTERMEDIATION

资料整理：刘　婷
Data management:Chen Haisheng

第十八部分　金融业

一、简要说明

本章资料包括金融、证券和保险业情况，由西安市统计局综合处根据人民银行西安分行营业管理部和市金融办提供资料整理。

二、主要指标

金融机构人民币（含外资）存款余额（亿元）	12125.53	比年初增加	1698.27亿元
金融机构人民币（含外资）贷款余额（亿元）	8635.22	比年初增加	1070.29亿元
保费收入（亿元）	173.21	比上年增长	6.5%

18　FINANCIAL INTERMEDIATION

Ⅰ.Brief Introduction

This chapter includes information of the financial, securities and insurance, compiled by Integration Division of the Xi'an Bureau of Statistics, according to data from Xi'an Branch Management Department of the People's Bank of China, Provincial Banking Bureau and Xi'an Financial Office.

Ⅱ.Major Indicators

		Increase over Preceding Year
Deposit in Financial Institution(100 mil. Yuan)	12125.53	1698.27
Loans in Financial Institutions(100 mil. Yuan)	8635.22	1070.29
Premiums(100 mil. Yuan)	173.21	6.5%

18-1 西安银行系统机构、人员数

Number of Institution and Employed Person in Finance System in Xi'an

机构名称	Name of Institution	2011 机构数（个）Number of Institution (unit)	2011 年末人数（人）Number of Staff and Workers (person)	2012 机构数（个）Number of Institution (unit)	2012 年末人数（人）Number of Staff and Workers (person)
合　计	**Total**	**1763**	**31450**	**1803**	**33430**
1.人民银行西安分行营业管理部	Management Department of the People's Bank of China Xi'an Branch	1	403	1	396
2.中国工商银行西安分行	Industrial and Commercial Bank of China Shaanxi Branch	193	4946	193	4959
3.中国农业银行西安分行	Agricultural Bank of China Shaanxi Branch	165	3038	165	3160
4.中国银行西安分行	Bank of China Xi'an Branch	122	3266	122	3309
5.中国建设银行西安分行	Construction Bank of China Shaanxi Branch	177	3851	179	4059
6.国家开发银行西安分行	National Development Bank Xi'an Branch	1	171	1	179
7.中国农业发展银行西安分行	Agricultural Development Bank of China Xi'an Branch	10	258	10	253
8.中国进出口银行	Export Import Bank of Xi'an Branch	1	66	1	80
9.交通银行西安分行	Bank of Communication Xi'an Branch	49	1062	50	1197
10.中信实业银行西安分行	CITIC Industrial Bank Xi'an Branch	19	659	20	774
11.中国光大银行西安分行	China Everbright Bank Xi'an Branch	17	573	20	711
12.华夏银行西安分行	China Huaxia Bank Xi'an Branch	10	321	11	347
13.招商银行西安分行	China Merchants Bank Xi'an Branch	24	1053	25	1102
14.上海浦东发银行西安分行	Pufa Bank Xi'an Branch	12	567	13	612
15.兴业银行西安分行	Fujian Industrial Bank Xi'an Branch	13	755	15	876
16.民生银行西安分行	China Minsheng Banking Corp., Ltd Xi'an Branch	15	781	17	863
17.浙商银行西安分行	China Zheshang Bank Xi'an Branch	2	161	3	191
18.恒丰银行西安分行	Evergrowing Bank Xi'an Branch	1	80	2	84
19.中国邮政储蓄银行西安分行	The postal savings bank branch in Xi'an	274	734	280	762
20.西安银行	Bank of Xi'an	114	2283	115	2249
21.重庆银行西安分行	Bank of Chongqing, Xi'an Branch	1	72	2	132
22.北京银行西安分行	Bank of Beijing, Xi'an Branch	4	286	7	367
23.长安银行	Bank of Changan	3	108	6	213
24.昆仑银行西安分行	Kunlun Xi'an Branch Bank	1	147	3	243
25.齐商银行西安分行	Qi Commercial Bank Xi'an Branch	2	63	3	83
26.成都银行西安分行	Bank of Chengdu, Xi'an Branch	1	78	2	114
27.宁夏银行西安分行	Bank of Ningxia Xi'an Branch			3	134
28.农村信用社联合社	Rural Credit Cooperatives Association	520	5237	522	5623
29.东亚银行西安分行	Dongya Bank Xi'an Branch	6	303	7	290
30.汇丰银行西安分行	Huifeng Bank Xi'an Branch	3	60	3	51
31.渣打银行西安分行	British Standard Chartered bank Xi'an Branch	1	42	1	40
32.西安高陵阳光村镇银行	Xi'an Gaoling sunshine village bank	1	26	1	25

18-2 金融机构（含外资）本外币存贷款年末余额（2012年）

Financial institution Including Foreign-funded Balance of Bisic Currency and Foreign Currency at Year-end（2012）

单位：亿元 (100 million yuan)

指　标	Item	2012	比年初增减额 Increase or decrease compared with the beginning of the Year
存款余额合计（汇率：6.2855）	**Total Deposit (Exchange Rate: 6.2855)**	**12285.96**	**1762.65**
一、单位存款	**Company Deposit**	**7043.22**	**989.03**
#活期存款	Demand Deposits	3652.2	490.58
定期存款	Time Deposits	1696.23	209.26
二、个人存款	**Personal Deposits**	**4961.13**	**729.31**
#储蓄存款	Savings Deposits	4826.67	636.53
三、财政性存款	**Fiscal Deposits**	**50.55**	**-8.65**
四、临时性存款	**Temporary Deposit**	**29.39**	**14.89**
五.委托存款	**Consignment Deposits**	**18.59**	**-18.84**
六.其他存款	**Other Deposits**	**183.08**	**56.91**
贷款余额合计（汇率：6.2855）	**Total Loans (Exchange Rate: 6.2855)**	**8808.04**	**1107.84**
一、境内贷款	**Domestic Loans**	**8789.85**	**1107.9**
短期贷款	Short-term Loans	1995.29	521.17
中长期贷款	Medium-term and Long-term loans	6452.08	604.44
融资租赁	Financial Leasing	1.08	-0.77
票据融资	Bill Financing	336.79	-18.05
各项垫款	Various Advance Funds	4.61	1.11
二、境外贷款	**Foreign Loans**	**18.19**	**-0.06**

18-3 金融机构（不含外资）本外币存贷款年末余额（2012年）

Domestic Funded Financial institution balance of Bisic Currency and Foreign Currency at Year-end (2012)

单位：亿元　　(100 million yuan)

指　标	Item	2012	比年初增加额 Increase or decrease compared with the beginning of the Year
存款余额合计	**Total Deposit**	**12198.56**	**1758.42**
一、单位存款	**Company Deposit**	**6978.59**	**983.58**
#活期存款	Demand Deposits	3623.14	488.75
定期存款	Time Deposits	1660.67	205.64
二、个人存款	**Personal Deposits**	**4938.35**	**730.53**
#储蓄存款	Savings Deposits	4803.89	636.76
三、财政性存款	**Fiscal Deposits**	**50.55**	**-8.65**
四、临时性存款	**Temporary Deposit**	**29.40**	**14.89**
五、委托存款	**Consignment Deposits**	**18.59**	**-18.84**
六、其他存款	**Other Deposits**	**183.08**	**56.91**
贷款余额合计	**Total Loans**	**8728.83**	**1102.21**
一、境内贷款	**Domestic Loans**	**8710.68**	**1102.27**
短期贷款	Short-term Loans	1977.98	522.51
中长期贷款	Medium-term and Long-term loans	6396.05	603.11
融资租赁	Financial Leasing	1.08	-0.77
票据融资	Bill Financing	330.96	-23.69
各项垫款	Various Advance Funds	4.61	1.11
二、境外贷款	**Foreign Loans**	**18.15**	**-0.06**

18-4 主要年份金融机构（含外资）人民币存款年末余额

Year-end Balance of Deposit in Financial Institutions Including Foreign-funded in Representative Years

单位：亿元 (100 million yuan)

年份 Year	合计 Total	其中：Among	
		单位存款 Company Deposit	储蓄存款 Savings Deposits
1978	12.82		3.72
1980	20.99		5.48
1985	40.68		16.70
1990	112.37	31.10	62.23
1995	359.51	114.54	230.63
1996	619.98	199.85	394.02
1997	602.50	227.61	358.78
1998	799.54	245.44	499.68
1999	1014.27	347.49	586.40
2000	1335.63	540.19	675.83
2001	1629.72	674.49	800.86
2002	2191.47	884.69	988.04
2003	2665.87	1041.43	1210.56
2004	3061.66	1159.98	1432.86
2005	3599.70	1237.37	1716.76
2006	4066.16	1374.91	1950.53
2007	4582.71	1702.12	2002.38
2008	5749.35	2213.67	2513.70
2009	7522.08	3077.99	3084.20
2010	8933.23	3556.78	3641.09
2011	10430.27	5997.60	4155.65
2012	12125.53	6927.84	4787.03

18-5 主要年份金融机构（含外资）人民币贷款年末余额

Year-end Balance of Loans in Financial Institutions Including Foreign-funded in Representative Years

单位：亿元 (100 million yuan)

年 份 Year	合计 Total	其 中：Among 短期贷款 Short-term Loans	中长期贷款 Medium-term&Long-term Loans
1978	23.56		
1980	26.40		
1985	48.60		
1990	131.67	101.13	23.78
1995	334.50	252.30	73.32
1996	477.97	333.88	90.12
1997	443.76	342.79	87.27
1998	597.34	448.74	118.42
1999	786.20	589.52	150.64
2000	972.51	652.00	241.27
2001	1185.97	666.41	387.82
2002	1598.42	780.69	502.03
2003	1954.18	946.64	743.72
2004	2052.33	950.50	850.01
2005	2158.10	830.68	1013.32
2006	2344.77	812.33	1310.57
2007	2683.77	883.32	1593.37
2008	3275.12	1031.62	1905.08
2009	4482.63	1155.83	2908.75
2010	6482.28	1097.60	5075.98
2011	7564.93	1431.29	5776.48
2012	8635.22	1917.51	6378.88

18-6 金融机构（含外资）人民币存贷款年末余额（2012年）

Year-end Balance of Deposit and Loans in Financial Institutionst Including Foreign-funded（2012）

单位：亿元 (100 million yuan)

指 标	Item	2012	比年初增减额 Increase or decrease compared with the beginning of the Year
存款余额合计	**Total Deposit**	**12125.53**	**1698.27**
一、单位存款	**Company Deposit**	**6927.84**	**930.24**
#活期存款	Demand Deposits	3558.43	434.67
定期存款	Time Deposits	1691.47	208.76
二、个人存款	**Personal Deposits**	**4919.99**	**725.29**
#储蓄存款	Savings Deposits	4787.03	631.39
三、财政性存款	**Fiscal Deposits**	**50.54**	**-8.65**
四、临时性存款	**Temporary Deposit**	**25.50**	**13.25**
五. 委托存款	**Trusted Deposits**	**18.58**	**-18.78**
六. 其他存款	**Other Deposits**	**183.08**	**56.92**
贷款余额合计	**Total Loans**	**8635.22**	**1070.29**
一、境内贷款	**Domestic Loans**	**8634.77**	**1070.32**
（一）短期贷款	Short-term Loans	1917.51	486.21
1. 个人贷款及透支	Individual Loans and Overdrafts	194.21	82.29
2. 单位贷款及透支	Unit Loans and Overdrafts	1609.97	362.57
3. 普通并购贷款	Ordinary Merging Loans		-0.80
4. 银团贷款	Syndicated Loans	7.41	3.20
5. 贸易融资	Trade Finance	105.92	38.95
（二）中长期贷款	Medium-term&Long-term Loans	6378.88	602.47
1. 个人贷款	Individual Loans and Overdrafts	1592.96	275.89
2. 单位贷款	Unit Loans and Overdrafts	3991.09	176.72
3. 普通并购贷款	Ordinary Merging Loans	31.93	24.68
4. 贸易融资	Syndicated Loans	0.23	0.23
5. 银团贷款	Trade Finance	762.67	124.95
（三）融资租赁	Financial Leasing	1.08	-0.76
（四）票据融资	Bill Financing	336.79	-17.92
（五）各项垫款	Various Advance Funds	0.51	0.32
二、境外贷款	**Foreign Loans**	**0.45**	**-0.03**

18-7 金融机构（不含外资）人民币存贷款年末余额（2012年）

Year-end Balance of Deposit and Loans in Financial Institutions Not Including Foreign-funded (2012)

单位：亿元 (100 million yuan)

指 标	Item	2012	比年初增减额 Increase or decrease compared with the beginning of the Year
存款余额合计	**Total Deposit**	**12044.68**	**1696.89**
一、单位存款	**Company Deposit**	**6868.14**	**927.62**
#活期存款	Demand Deposits	3532.90	434.36
定期存款	Time Deposits	1657.30	206.44
二、个人存款	**Personal Deposits**	**4898.84**	**726.53**
#储蓄存款	Savings Deposits	4765.88	632.63
三、财政性存款	**Fiscal Deposits**	**50.55**	**-8.65**
四、临时性存款	**Temporary Deposit**	**25.49**	**13.25**
五. 委托存款	**Trusted Deposits**	**18.58**	**-18.78**
六. 其他存款	**Other Deposits**	**183.08**	**56.92**
贷款余额合计	**Total Loans**	**8559.27**	**1063.02**
一、境内贷款	**Domestic Loans**	**8558.85**	**1063.04**
（一）短期贷款	Short-term Loans	1901.33	486.69
1. 个人贷款及透支	Individual Loans and Overdrafts	192.93	81.03
2. 单位贷款及透支	Unit Loans and Overdrafts	1595.07	364.31
3. 普通并购贷款	Ordinary Merging Loans		-0.80
4. 银团贷款	Syndicated Loans	7.41	3.20
5. 贸易融资	Trade Finance	105.92	38.95
（二）中长期贷款	Medium-term&Long-term Loans	6324.97	600.37
1. 个人贷款	Individual Loans and Overdrafts	1579.27	271.62
2. 单位贷款	Unit Loans and Overdrafts	3950.87	178.89
3. 普通并购贷款	Ordinary Merging Loans	31.93	24.68
4. 贸易融资	Trade Finance	0.23	0.23
5. 银团贷款	Syndicated Loans	762.67	124.95
（三）融资租赁	Financial Leasing	1.08	-0.77
（四）票据融资	Bill Financing	330.96	-23.57
（五）各项垫款	Various Advance Funds	0.51	0.32
二、境外贷款	**Foreign Loans**	**0.42**	**-0.02**

18-8 保险业务情况

Indicators of Insurance Business

指 标	Item	2011	2012
保险金额（亿元）	**Amount Insured(100 million yuan)**	**44511.2**	**35199.1**
保费收入（万元）	**Premiums(10 000 yuan)**	**1625666.2**	**1732088.5**
一、财产险	**Property Insurance**	**449625.3**	**521619.4**
（一）财产保险	Property Insurance	422738.7	484475.7
1. 机动车辆及第三者责任	Motor Vehicle and Outside Person Liability	364584.6	431459.5
2. 企业财产险	Enterprise Property Insurance	37452.1	41398.3
3. 货物运输险	Freight Transport Insurance	4208.2	4312.2
4. 家庭财产险	Family Property Insurance	365.5	323.1
5. 建工及安工保险及其责任险	Construction and Installation Projects Insurance and Related Libility Insurance	15004.0	5937.9
6. 其他	Others	1124.3	1044.7
（二）责任保险	Liability Insurance	8987.7	10719.1
（三）信用保险	Export Credit Insurance	8187.5	8257.0
（四）保证保险	Guarantee Insurance	8798.3	15420.7
（五）农业保险	Agriculture Insurance	913.1	2746.9
二、人身险	**Personnel Insurance**	**1176040.9**	**1210469.0**
（一）人寿保险	Life Insurance	1072364.2	1077710.2
1. 非分红保险	Non Dividend Insurance	95292.4	99072.8
2. 分红保险	Dividend Insurance	966023.7	967751.1
3. 投资连接保险	Insurance Connection Insurance	361.5	345.7
4. 万能保险	Universal Insurance	10686.6	10540.6
（二）意外伤害险	Unforeseen Injury Insurance	37064.2	40432.9
（三）健康保险	Health Insurance	66612.6	92326.0
赔款支出和各项给付（万元）	**Indemnity and Other Expenditure(10 000 yuan)**	**371420.9**	**475482.9**
一、财产险	**Property Insurance**	**199915.5**	**274284.6**
（一）财产保险	Property Insurance	192899.6	263916.9
1. 机动车辆及第三者责任	Motor Vehicle and Outside Person Liability	163878.3	235665.3
2. 企业财产险	Enterprise Property Insurance	15150.8	18804.8
3. 家庭财产保险	Freight Transport Insurance	130.1	66.2
4. 货物运输保险	Family Property Insurance	1341.7	1147.7
5. 建工及安工保险及其责任险	Construction and Installation Projects Insurance and Related Libility Insurance	11345.1	7893.0
6. 其他	Others	1053.7	339.9
（二）责任保险	Liability Insurance	3114.1	4713.3
（三）信用保险	Export Credit Insurance	2324.1	5357.3
（四）保证保险	Guarantee Insurance	578.5	-581.0
（五）农业保险	Agriculture Insurance	999.2	878.1
二、人身险	**Personnel Insurance**	**171505.4**	**201198.3**
（一）人寿保险	Life Insurance	140239.9	167146.1
1. 非分红保险	Non Dividend Insurance	40016.8	50928.6
2. 分红保险	Dividend Insurance	98168.6	113556.5
3. 投资连接保险	Insurance Connection Insurance	595.1	327.2
4. 万能保险	Universal Insurance	1459.4	2333.8
（二）意外伤害险	Unforeseen Injury Insurance Health Insurance	7571.9	9013.3
（三）健康保险	Health Insurance	23693.5	25038.9
退保金（万元）	**Withdrawal(10 000 yuan)**	**90545.9**	**107664.8**
#人寿保险	Life Insurance	89150.4	105908.8
1. 非分红保险	Ordinary Life Insurance	4302.5	5514.2
2. 分红保险	Dividend Insurance	84803.5	100373.3
3. 投资连接保险	Insurance Connection Insurance	1.6	0.1
4. 万能保险	Universal Insurance	42.8	21.3

18-9 西安地区证券期货系统机构、人员数

Number of Institution and Employed Person in Securities and Futures System in Xi'an

机构名称	Name of Institution	2011		2012	
		机构数（个）Number of Institution (unit)	年末人数（人）Number of Staff and Workers (person)	机构数（个）Number of Institution (unit)	年末人数（人）Number of Staff and Workers (person)
证券经营机构	**Securities Company and the Sales Department**				
一、证券公司	**Securities Company**				
西部证券股份有限公司	Western Securities Company Ltd.	60	2344	64	2130
陕西开源证券经纪有限责任公司	KaiYuan Securities Company Ltd.	8	224	16	413
西安华弘证券经纪有限责任公司	Xi'an Huahong Securities Brokerage Co., Ltd.	6	238	9	291
二、证券营业部（含外地公司在西安营业部）	**Sales Department (include Xi'an departments of nonlocal companies.)**	**66**	**2989**	**69**	**5946**
期货经纪公司	**Futures Company**	**3**	**345**	**3**	**377**
迈科期货经纪有限公司	Maike Futures Company Ltd.	1	177	1	184
陕西长安期货经纪有限公司	Shaanxi ChangAn Futures Company Ltd.	1	77	1	89
西部期货经纪有限公司	Western Futures Brokerage Co., Ltd.	1	91	1	104

注：证券公司包括三家证券公司在西安和外地的营业部。

18-10 证券期货市场基本情况（2012年）

Basic Facts on Securities and Futures Markets（2012）

指标名称	Item	2012
一、上市证券公司情况	**Listed Securities Companies**	
拥有上市股份公司（个）	Number of Listed Share-holding Companies(unit)	29
占全国比重（%）	Percentage to National Total(%)	1.2
上市股份公司总股本（亿股）	Total Capital of Listed Share-holding Companies (100 millon shares)	219.02
#流通股(亿股)	Negotiable Shares(100 million shares)	150.58
总市值（亿元）	Total Market Capitalization(100 million yuan)	1778.04
累计证券市场筹措资金（亿元）	Accumulated Capital Raised by Securities Markets(100 millon yuan)	567.22
二、证券经营机构情况	**Securities Trading Organizations**	
拥有证券公司（个）	Number of Securities Companies(unit)	3
证券营业部（个）（含外地公司在西安营业部）	Number of Securities Business Departments(unit)	69
投资者开户数（万户）	Number of Investors Who have Opened an Account(10 000 accounts)	171
证券交易总额（亿元）	Total Turnover(100 million yuan)	8752
三、期货市场情况	**Futures Market**	
拥有期货经纪公司（个）	Number of Futures Business Management Companies(unit)	3
期货营业部（个）	Number of Futures Business,Departments(unit)	24
期货代理交易额（亿元）	Total Transaction Value in Futures Commissioning (100 million yuan)	32000
每个经纪公司平均拥有注册资金（万元）	Average Registered Capital of Each Business Management Company(10 000 yuan)	13333

主 要 统 计 指 标 解 释

信贷资金 指金融机构以信用方式积聚和分配的货币资金。金融机构信贷资金的来源有各项存款、金融债券、对国际金融机构负债、流通中现金、其他项目等；信贷资金的运用有各项贷款、有价证券及投资、金银占款、外汇占款、财政借款及在国际金融机构中的资产等。

存款 指企业、机关、团体或居民根据资金必须收回的原则，把货币资金存入银行或其他信贷机构保管并取得一定利息的一种信用活动形式。根据存款对象或性质的不同可划分为企业存款、财政存款、机关团体存款、城乡储蓄存款、农业存款、信托及委托类存款、其他存款等科目。它是银行信贷资金的主要来源。

贷款 指银行或其他信贷机构根据资金必须归还的原则，按一定利率，为企业、个人等提供资金的一种信用活动形式。我国银行贷款分为短期贷款、委托及信托类贷款、其他类贷款等。

保险公司 在中国境内的、经过保险监督管理部门批准设立，并依法登记注册的各类商业保险公司。

保险金额 指保险人承担赔偿或者给付保险金责任的最高限额。

保费 指投保人为取得保险人在约定范围内所承担赔偿责任而支付给保险人的费用。

赔款指保险人根据保险合同的规定，向被保险人支付的赔偿保险责任损失的金额。

给付 包括死伤医疗给付和满期给付。死伤医疗给付是指保险人根据人寿保险及长期健康保险合同的规定，因被保险人在保险期内发生保险责任范围内的保险事故支付给被保险人（或受益人）的金额。满期给付是指被保险人生存期满，保险人按人寿保险合同规定支付给被保险人的满期保险金额。

Explanatory Notes on Main Statistical Indicators

Credit Funds refer to the monetary funds accumulated and distributed in the means of credit by the financial institutions. The sources of credit funds include various deposits, financial bonds, liabilities to international financial institutions, currency in circulation, other items. The uses of credit funds include loans, securities and investment, position for bullion and silver purchase, position for foreign exchange purchase, advances to treasury, and assets with international financial institutions..

Deposit is a form of credit by which enterprises, institutions, organizations or households can put money into banks and other credit institutions for safekeeping and interest earning under the principle of free withdrawal. According to different depositors, deposits are divided into enterprise deposits, fiscal deposits, deposits of government agencies and organizations, savings deposits of rural and urban households, agricultural savings deposits, entrusted deposits and other deposits. Deposits are major sources of the credit funds of banks.

Loan is a form of credit by which banks and other credit institutions provide funds at certain interest rate to enterprises and individuals in the light of the principle of unconditional repayment. Loans from Chinese banks include short-term loan, medium- term and long-term loans, entrusted loans, and other loans.

Insurance Companies refer to commercial insurance companies of various forms registered by law and established in China with the approval of insurance regulatory agencies.

Amount Insured refers to the maximum that the insurant will get for the claim of the case insured.

Premium is the fee paid by the insurant to the insurer to obtain the obligation of compensation from the insurance within the agreed terms.

Settled Claim is the compensation paid by the insurer to the insurant in accordance with the insurance contract.

Payment includes payment for death, injury or medical treatment and payment at maturity. Payment for death, injury or medical treatment refers to the money paid to the insurant (or the beneficiary) in accordance with the life or health insurance contract when the insurant encounters accidents within the insured period covered in the contract. Payment at maturity refers to the payment to the insurant in accordance with the life insurance contract at the end of the insured period.

19 教育和科技

EDUCATION,SCIENCE AND TDCHNOLOGY

资料整理：郝　静　齐昆峰

Data management:Hao Jing Qi Kunfeng

第十九部分　教育和科技

一、简要说明

本章资料包括教育事业、科技事业基本情况，由西安市统计局社会科技处根据西安市教委等有关部门提供资料整理。

二、主要指标

普通高等学校数（所）	62	比上年增加	1所
普通高等学校（本专科）在校学生（万人）	72.40	比上年增长	5.7%
研究生在校人数（万人）	8.33	比上年增长	3.7%

19　EDUCATION,SCIENCE AND TECHNOLOGY

Ⅰ.Brief Introduction

Data in this chapter consists of primarily data of educational undertakings, science and technology Activities of Xi'an city, compiled by Social & Science and Technology Division of the Xi'an Bureau of Statistics according to data from Xi'an Municipal Government Departments concerned.

Ⅱ Major Indicators

		Increase over Preceding Year
Number of Schools Regular Institutions of Higher Education(unit)	62	1
Student Enrollment of Regular Institutions of Higher Education(10 000 persons)	72.40	5.7%
Postgraduates(10 000 persons)	8.33	3.7%

19-1 主要年份各类普通教育基本情况

Basic Statistics on Regular Eduction in Representative Years

指 标	Item	2000	2005	2006	2007	2008	2009	2010	2011	2012
学校数（所）	**Number of Schools (units)**									
普通高等学校	Regular Institutions of Higher Educatior	25	44	47	48	48	49	50	61	62
普通中等专业学校	Regular Specialized Secondary Schools	47	32	31	30	29	28	28	24	24
普通中学	Regular Secondary School	466	460	457	453	442	439	436	423	419
小学	Primary Schools	2323	1980	1929	1872	1781	1666	1531	1424	1322
幼儿园	Kindergarten	367	737	863	830	905	896	1004	1122	1239
毕业生人数（万人）	**Graduates (10 000 persons)**									
普通高等学校	Regular Institutions of Higher Educatior	3.0	11.1	13.0	15.8	17.6	16.9	18.3	19.7	20.9
普通中等专业学校	Regular Specialized Secondary Schools	1.6	1.4	1.8	2.0	2.6	2.7	2.5	2.3	2.1
普通中学	Regular Secondary School	12.0	18.8	18.0	18.4	18.0	17.8	17.0	16.4	15.6
小学	Primary Schools	13.8	11.9	11.5	11.4	10.6	10.0	9.6	8.9	8.9
幼儿园	Kindergarten								6.4	7.6
招生数（万人）	**New Enrollment (10 000 persons)**									
普通高等学校	Regular Institutions of Higher Educatior	7.5	16.5	17.1	19.0	21.5	21.3	21.7	23.1	25.2
普通中等专业学校	Regular Specialized Secondary Schools	1.9	2.3	2.6	2.9	2.6	2.2	2.1	2.0	1.7
普通中学	Regular Secondary School	17.9	18.5	18.6	18.0	17.2	16.6	16.2	15.4	15.0
小学	Primary Schools	11.5	8.5	9.2	8.7	8.3	7.8	8.6	8.8	8.9
幼儿园	Kindergarten	8.7	6.6	6.9	6.7	7.7	7.2	8.4	10.0	11.6
在校学生数（万人）	**Total Enrollment (10 000 persons)**									
普通高等学校	Regular Institutions of Higher Educatior	19.4	53.1	57.1	62.3	66.7	70.3	73.3	76.6	80.7
普通中等专业学校	Regular Specialized Secondary Schools	6.0	6.2	7.3	8.0	8.1	7.4	6.8	6.1	5.4
普通中学	Regular Secondary School	48.3	55.7	56.1	54.7	52.8	50.6	48.9	47.2	45.3
小学	Primary Schools	77.8	60.5	59.3	56.8	54.7	52.5	51.6	51.4	50.9
幼儿园	Kindergarten	12.9	12.8	13.4	14.1	15.5	16.3	18.4	24.0	27.1
教职工数（人）	**Staff and Teachers (persons)**									
普通高等学校	Regular Institutions of Higher Educatior	38067	57285	61414	65624	69048	70818	72247	72739	74041
普通中等专业学校	Regular Specialized Secondary Schools	6964	3924	3621	3548	3417	2965	3249	2868	2733
普通中学	Regular Secondary School	34385	39456	39341	39171	39088	39002	39207	41135	41197
小学	Primary Schools	35336	33907	34460	34901	34653	34389	34118	32457	32208
幼儿园	Kindergarten	6346	10528	12335	13468	14932	15928	18710	23680	27735
专任教师（人）	**Number of Full-time Teachers (persons)**									
普通高等学校	Regular Institutions of Higher Educatior	15679	29498	32891	36717	38926	40605	42098	42734	44487
普通中等专业学校	Regular Specialized Secondary Schools	3172	2130	2014	2011	1904	1720	1845	1723	1595
普通中学	Regular Secondary School	26230	31094	31203	31373	31425	31415	31506	33122	31526
小学	Primary Schools	30215	29674	30018	30533	30382	30334	29944	28453	29651
幼儿园	Kindergarten	2995	5959	7106	7951	8704	9240	10638	12577	14293

注：本表数据来源于市教育局。

本表中普通高等学校毕业生、招生、在校生含研究生及普通高等学校中普通本、专科学生数。

19–2 各级各类学校校数、教职工、专任教师数(2012年)

Basic Facts on Regular Education Teacher by School Type (2012)

指　标	Item	学校数（所）Number of Schools (units)	教职工数(人) Number of Staff and Teachers (persons)	专任教师（人）Full-time Teachers (persons)
一、高等教育	**Higher education**	**77**	**76661**	**46012**
(一)研究生培养机构	Postgraduates	(46)		
1、高等学校	Institutions of Higher Schools	(22)		
2、科研机构	Scientific Research Institution	(24)		
(二)普通高等学校	Regular Institutions of Higher Schools	62	74041	44487
1、本科院校	Universities and Colleges of Undergraduate Course	41	63617	38551
其中：独立学院	Non-university Tertiary	11	6984	4530
2、专科院校	Higher Vocational Colleges	21	10424	5936
其中：高等职业学校	Higher Vocational College	19	8996	5357
(三)成人高等学校	Adult Higher Schools	15	2620	1525
二、中等职业教育	**Secondary Occupation Education**	**220**	**18690**	**13212**
1、普通中等专业学校	Regular Specialized Secondary Schools	24	2733	1595
2、成人中等专业学校	Adult Secondary Specialized Schools	6	1357	736
3、职业高中学校	Vocational Hight Schools	78	5190	3443
4、技工学校	Technical Schools	112	9410	7438
其中：市属	Municipal schools	43	2265	1865
三、基础教育	**Elementary Education**	**2989**	**101535**	**75756**
(一) 普通中等教育	Regular Institutions Education	419	41197	31526
1､高中	Senior High Schools	170		11894
完全中学	Complete Secondary Schools	104	13164	5319
高级中学	Senior Secondary Schools	51	7683	6157
十二年一贯制学校	Twelve-year Consistency Schools	15	2289	418
2､初中	Junior Middle Schools	249		19632
初级中学	Junior Middle Schools	221	16063	13166
九年一贯制学校	Nine-year Consistency Schools	28	1998	771
完全中学	Complete Secondary Schools	(104)		5079
十二年一贯制学校	Twelve-year Consistency Schools	(15)		616
附设普通初中班的学校	Senior Secondary Schools with Regular Junior Secondary Classes	(3)		(28)
(二)普通初等教育	Regular Primary Education	1322	32208	29651
独立小学	Independent Primary Schools	1322		28146
教学点	Teaching Points	(130)		
九年一贯制学校	Nine-year Consistency Schools	(28)		852
十二年一贯制学校	Twelve-year Consistency Schools	(15)		653
附设小学班的学校	Schools with Primary Classes	(5)		(38)
(三)特殊教育	Special Education Schools	8	352	248
特殊教育学校	Special Education Schools	8	352	248
附设特教班的学校	Schools with Special Edution Classes	(1)		(1)
(四)工读学校	Reformatory Schools	1	43	38
(五)学前教育	Preschool Education	1239	27735	14293
幼儿园	Kindergarten	1239	27735	14293
附设幼儿班的学校	Schools with Nursery Classes	(328)		(442)
另有：成人中小学	Adult Junior Secondary schools and Adult Primary Schools	86	106	48
另有：技术培训机构	Technique Training Institution	2048	9867	5591

注：本表数据来源于市教育局。
本表为西安市行政区划内各级各类学校全口径数据（不含军事院校、党校）。
技工学校数据由西安市人力资源和社会保障局提供。
按照事业统计主体校原则，完全中学、十二年一贯学校数计入普通高中，九年一贯制学校的校数记入普通初中。
教职工数按照办学类型划分,为使用方便,专任教师同时按照办学层次列出。
( ) 内数据不计入总计。

19-3 各级各类教育学生情况（2012年）

Basic Facts on Education Student by School Type (2012)

单位：人 (persons)

指 标	Item	毕业生数 Number of Graduates	招生数 New Enrollment	在校学生数 Total Enrollment	女生 Female Students
一、高等教育	**Higher education**	**301820**	**359522**	**1090079**	**499758**
(一)研究生	Postgraduates	22963	28065	84712	35606
1、高等学校	Institutions of Higher Schools	22578	27618	83306	35246
2、科研机构	Scientific Research Institution	385	447	1406	360
(二)普通高等教育	Regular Institutions of Higher Schools	186388	224606	723961	341688
1、本科	Universities Course Schools	103015	143186	494750	
2、专科	Junior Colleges	83373	81420	229211	
(三)成人高等教育	Higher Vocational Colleges	50517	50772	159821	66961
其中：成人高等学校	Contains:Adult Higher Education	6447	6218	20067	
(四)网络本专科生	Network Undergraduate and clooege students	41952	56079	121585	55503
1、本科	Universities Course Schools	21099	23693	50552	
2、专科	Junior Colleges	20853	32386	71033	
二、中等职业教育	**Secondary Occupation Education**	**104698**	**76892**	**281779**	**74899**
1、普通中等专业学校	Regular Specialized Secondary Schools	21489	16702	54306	30475
2、成人中等专业学校	Adult Secondary Specialized Schools	1802	2423	13315	5199
3、职业高中学校	Vocational high Schools	25171	25439	70974	39225
其中：市属	Municipal schools	24048	24995	67969	37285
4、技工学校	Technical Schools	56236	32328	143184	
其中：市属	Municipal schools	18004	9468	29821	
三、基础教育	**Elementary Education**	**321602**	**355131**	**1234116**	**579822**
(一)普通中等教育	Regular Institutions Education	156429	149816	453312	212603
1、高中	Senior High Schools	60243	60048	180468	88013
完全中学	Complete Secondary Schools	26290	25970	77984	38763
高级中学	Senior Secondary Schools	32020	32238	97168	46695
十二年一贯制学校	Twelve-year Consistency Schools	1933	1840	5316	2555
2、初中	Junior Middle Schools	96186	89768	272844	124590
初级中学	Junior Middle Schools	59792	49784	156952	71322
九年一贯制学校	Nine-year Consistency Schools	2964	3398	9961	4417
十二年一贯制学校	Twelve-year Consistency Schools	2921	3506	10495	4688
完全中学	Complete Secondary Schools	30509	33080	95436	44163
(二)普通初等教育	Regular Primary Education	88822	88786	508534	232187
小学	Pricmary Schools	83039	82716	473601	216392
九年一贯制学校	Nine-year Consistency Schools	3402	3473	19884	9057
十二年一贯制学校	Twelve-year Consistency Schools	2381	2597	15049	6738
(三)特殊教育	Special Education Schools	197	220	1392	525
1．特殊教育学校	Special Education Schools	124	152	802	329
2．小学附设特教班	Primary Schools with Special Education Classes			7	
3．小学随班就读	Elementary Inclusive	58	49	499	172
4．初中随班就读就读	Junior Mainstreaming	15	19	84	24
(四)工读学校	Reformatory Schools	12	35	68	
(五)学前教育	Preschool Education	76142	116274	270810	126928
1．独立幼儿园	Independent Kindergartens	68026	104847	255954	119955
2．附设幼儿园	Attached Kindergartens	8116	11427	14856	6973
另有：成人中小学	Adult Junior Secondary schools and Adult Primary Schools	(598)		(762)	(376)
另有：职业技术培训机构	Vocational and Technical Institutions	(321235)		(389703)	(200492)

注：本表数据来源于市教育局。
（ ）内数据不计入总计。

19-4 主要年份普通高等学校和科研机构研究生情况

Basic Statistics on Regular Institutions Schools and Post-graduates of Scientific Research Institution in Representative Years

单位：人 (person)

年 份 Year	毕业生人数 Number of Graduates	高等学校 Higher Schools	招收数 New Enrollment	高等学校 Higher Schools	在校学生数 Total Enrollment	高等学校 Higher Schools
1978					232	232
1980					651	651
1985					4799	4799
1990	2051	2051	1662	1662	5275	5275
1995	1769	1769	2712	2712	7974	7974
1998	2316	2316	3888	3888	10833	10833
1999	2903	2903	5020	5020	12986	12986
2000	3236	3236	6924	6924	16620	16620
2001	3881	3770	9274	8966	22564	21855
2002	4103	3952	11282	10882	28446	27471
2003	5971	5765	14322	13882	36936	35790
2004	8384	8127	17310	16871	45402	44169
2005	10416	10127	18583	18106	52699	51310
2006	12914	12552	19581	19105	58433	56951
2007	15506	15124	20570	20167	64137	62801
2008	17234	16788	21892	21443	67296	65834
2009	19025	18574	24879	24400	72366	70908
2010	19526	19129	25971	25477	76993	75483
2011	20965	20605	26686	26256	81696	80332
2012	22963	22578	28065	27618	84712	83306

注：本表数据来源于市教育局。

19-5 主要年份普通高等学校基本情况

Baisc Statistics on Regular Higher Education in Representative Years

单位：万人 (10 000 persons)

年份 Year	学校数（所） Number of Schools (units)	毕业生数 Number of Graduates	招生数 New Enrollment	在校学生数 Total Enrollment	教职工数 Number of Staff and Teachers	专任教师 Full-time Teachers
1978	21	0.60	1.31	2.88	2.24	0.87
1980	24	0.21	1.08	4.17	2.55	0.97
1985	28	1.17	2.28	6.49	3.40	1.28
1990	31	2.11	2.00	7.50	4.15	1.56
1995	32	2.87	3.13	10.07	4.21	1.59
1998	29	2.61	3.30	11.58	3.91	1.50
1999	29	2.84	5.12	13.79	3.95	1.52
2000	25	2.71	6.79	17.75	3.81	1.57
2001	32	3.31	8.31	23.24	4.30	1.75
2002	35	3.82	10.75	30.15	4.67	2.06
2003	37	5.89	12.21	36.42	4.92	2.21
2004	41	7.66	13.17	40.29	5.45	2.69
2005	44	10.08	14.68	47.79	5.73	2.95
2006	47	11.75	15.15	51.40	6.14	3.29
2007	48	14.33	16.96	56.03	6.56	3.67
2008	48	15.82	19.31	60.10	6.90	3.89
2009	49	15.04	18.84	63.22	7.08	4.06
2010	50	16.33	19.16	65.74	7.22	4.21
2011	61	17.68	20.52	68.52	7.27	4.27
2012	62	18.64	22.46	72.40	7.40	4.45

注：本表数据来源于市教育局。
此表仅包括本专科。
本表对往年个别数据有调整。

19-6 主要年份普通中等专业学校基本情况

Baisc Statistics on Regular Specialized Secondary Schools in Representative Years

单位：万人 (10 000 persons)

年 份 Year	学校数（所） Number of Schools (units)	毕业生数 Number of Graduates	招生数 New Enrollment	在校学生数 Total Enrollment	教职工数(人) Number of Staff and Teachers (person)	专任教师 Full-time Teachers
1978	19	0.19	0.45	0.82	3937	1110
1980	31	0.18	0.42	1.50	3895	1474
1985	37	0.43	0.76	1.70	6071	2363
1990	44	0.56	0.68	2.09	7136	2891
1995	46	0.97	1.37	3.74	5903	2533
1996	47	1.15	1.61	4.18	5940	2573
1997	47	1.20	1.65	4.63	6124	2731
1998	47	1.26	1.62	5.08	6181	2840
1999	46	1.42	2.11	5.75	6385	2865
2000	47	1.63	1.90	6.02	6964	3172
2001	47	1.70	1.58	5.63	5252	2467
2002	46	1.60	1.69	5.57	5170	2508
2003	34	1.62	1.80	5.28	4562	2302
2004	35	1.40	2.09	5.71	4676	2388
2005	32	1.44	2.26	6.16	3924	2130
2006	31	1.84	2.61	7.30	3621	2014
2007	30	2.03	2.91	7.97	3548	2011
2008	29	2.58	2.55	8.06	3278	1814
2009	28	2.70	2.15	7.44	2965	1720
2010	28	2.45	2.08	6.75	3249	1845
2011	24	2.34	1.96	6.11	2868	1723
2012	24	2.15	1.67	5.43	2733	1595

注：本表数据来源于市教育局。
本表对往年个别数据做了调整。

19–7 主要年份普通中学基本情况

Baisc Statistics on Regular Secondary Schools in Representative Years

单位：万人 (10 000 persons)

年 份 Year	学校数（所）Number of Schools (units)	毕业生数 Number of Graduates	招生数 New Enrollment	在校学生数 Total Enrollment	教职工数(人) Number of Staff and Teachers (person)	专任教师 Full-time Teachers
1978	962			44.16	27380	20660
1980	1002	12.33	14.03	44.08	29867	22530
1985	563	10.72	13.05	38.24	30063	22050
1990	518	9.11	10.49	30.03	30739	22386
1995	485	8.13	12.40	32.32	30423	21984
1996	462	8.67	13.03	35.25	30902	22478
1997	466	9.96	13.83	37.16	31682	23129
1998	467	10.64	15.00	39.79	32371	23884
1999	469	11.21	16.58	43.49	33387	25114
2000	466	12.01	17.88	48.31	34385	26230
2001	470	13.85	18.98	52.50	35442	27190
2002	467	15.76	19.68	55.36	36706	28335
2003	467	16.76	18.78	56.44	38252	29887
2004	461	18.01	18.85	56.54	39121	30600
2005	460	18.82	18.83	55.74	39456	31094
2006	457	18.04	18.61	56.11	39341	31203
2007	453	18.37	17.96	54.68	39171	31373
2008	442	17.99	17.16	52.83	39088	31425
2009	439	17.80	16.57	50.63	39002	31415
2010	436	17.01	16.15	48.89	39207	31506
2011	423	16.44	15.42	47.20	41135	31675
2012	419	15.64	14.98	45.33	41197	31526

注：本表数据来源于市教育局。

19-8 各区县普通中学基本情况（2012年）

Baisc Statistics on Regular Secondary Schools by Region (2012)

单位：所、人 (unit, person)

区县	Region	学校数 Number of Schools	毕业生数 Number of Graduates	高中 Senior	招生数 New Enrollment	高中 Senior	在校学生数 Total Enrollment	女生 Female Students	高中 Senior	教职工数 Number of Staff and Teachers	专任教师 Full-time Teachers
合计	**Total**	**419**	**156429**	**60243**	**149816**	**60048**	**453312**	**212603**	**180468**	**41197**	**31526**
新城区	Xincheng	25	11772	4242	12377	4111	36771	17861	12589	2670	1980
碑林区	Beilin	36	16898	6966	16800	7056	50065	23407	21559	4077	3025
莲湖区	Lianhu	21	11272	4073	12070	4045	35213	16995	12387	2988	2117
灞桥区	Baqiao	27	7670	2853	7389	2521	22266	10764	7714	2227	1658
未央区	Weiyang	26	8200	3602	10292	4284	28799	14264	12370	3042	1926
雁塔区	Yanta	44	15742	5987	16406	5737	48623	22950	16826	4649	3193
阎良区	Yanliang	12	4832	2125	3994	1618	12824	6243	5295	1229	921
临潼区	Lintong	32	13870	4753	12242	5016	37962	18503	14803	3458	2899
长安区	Chang'an	48	16717	6997	14409	6558	44936	20961	20227	4297	3575
蓝田县	Lantian	46	12909	4270	12115	5061	37088	17794	14518	3417	2626
周至县	Zhouzhi	34	15588	5845	13102	6353	40449	16603	18291	3625	2915
户县	Huxian	39	12870	5655	11250	5087	35574	15383	15670	3220	2805
高陵县	Gaoling	15	4508	1873	3860	1566	12439	6149	5286	1194	1026
沣东新城	Fengdongxincheng	14	3581	1002	3510	1035	10303	4726	2933	1104	860

注：本表数据来源于市教育局。
本表中教职工数按照办学类型划分，专任教师按办学层次划分，请使用中注意。

19-9 主要年份职业高中基本情况

Baisc Statistics on Vocational Secondary Schools in Representatove Years

单位：(所、人) (unit, person)

年 份 Year	学校数 Number of Schools	毕业生数 Number of Graduates	招生数 New Enrollment	在校学生数 Total Enrollment	教职工数 Number of Staff and Teachers	专任教师 Full-time Teachers
1985	40	1661	8346	17621	1375	868
1990	58	5936	8095	20151	2674	1574
1995	71	8976	12490	32673	2394	1877
1996	67	9235	10563	25955	3098	1735
1997	73	8756	13390	29068	2993	1709
1998	89	7753	13949	31264	3152	1823
1999	91	8480	13062	31973	3217	1908
2000	95	9949	13903	32188	3311	1997
2001	85	10300	15591	34336	3517	2113
2002	78	8659	17231	39428	3461	2192
2003	87	10755	17310	44033	4036	2458
2004	83	12177	17865	46358	4101	2515
2005	91	15092	20603	51766	4750	2892
2006	96	14887	21158	53828	5193	3126
2007	86	14881	24434	56012	4899	3064
2008	84	15813	30201	62963	4878	3008
2009	84	14691	31042	72388	5129	3179
2010	84	18100	30042	78244	5222	3178
2011	78	22493	27641	75108	4849	3173
2012	77	24048	24995	67969	4775	3148

注：本表数据来源于市教育局。
本表仅包括市属部分。

19-10 各区县职业高中基本情况（2012年）

Basic Statistics on Vocational Secondary Schools by Region (2012)

单位：所、人 (unit, person)

区 县	Region	学校数 Number of Schools	毕业生数 Number of Graduates	招生数 New Enrollment	在校学生数 Total Enrollment	女生 Female Students	教职工数 Number of Staff and Teachers	专任教师 Full-time Teachers
合 计	**Total**	**77**	**24048**	**24995**	**67969**	**37285**	**4775**	**3148**
新城区	Xincheng	10	3861	3453	10142	6034	758	480
碑林区	Beilin	7	1430	3192	6704	2402	500	317
莲湖区	Lianhu	6	2339	3030	7866	4513	492	278
灞桥区	Baqiao	10	1512	1587	4280	2999	426	222
未央区	Weiyang	5	2167	1073	4656	3850	341	224
雁塔区	Yanta	11	3486	2555	7243	3452	608	350
阎良区	Yanliang	1	273	1105	2081	854	110	89
临潼区	Lintong	5	2483	2208	3872	2005	284	220
长安区	Chang'an	7	2108	2350	6643	3924	607	433
蓝田县	Lantian	1	404	674	1703	888	17	13
周至县	Zhouzhi	5	911	1855	5852	2704	295	248
户 县	Huxian	5	1457	977	3576	2058	198	168
高陵县	Gaoling	1	1006	745	2519	1073	66	62
沣东新城	Fengdongxincheng	3	611	191	832	529	73	44

注：本表数据来源于市教育局。
此表仅包括市属部分。

19-11 主要年份小学基本情况

Basic Statistics on Primary Schools in Representative Years

单位：万人 (10 000 persons)

年 份 Year	学校数（所） Number of Schools (units)	毕业生数 Number of Graduates	招生数 New Enrollment	在校学生数 Total Enrollment	教职工数(人) Number of Staff and Teachers (person)	专任教师(人) Full-time Teachers (person)
1978	2667	13.07	14.10	74.03	29744	26428
1980	2337	11.91	12.57	73.36	31770	28360
1985	2337	11.21	9.57	62.16	31075	26430
1990	2343	8.67	10.85	61.87	37788	29090
1995	2360	9.93	14.09	79.36	35568	30270
1996	2362	10.48	13.63	81.81	35821	30267
1997	2368	10.98	12.48	82.67	35767	30117
1998	2361	12.18	11.88	82.03	35576	30089
1999	2354	13.65	11.61	79.81	35639	30196
2000	2323	13.83	11.51	77.81	35336	30215
2001	2277	14.2	11.07	74.51	34257	29281
2002	2137	13.89	10.13	70.78	34143	29428
2003	2084	12.97	9.28	66.78	34080	29531
2004	2016	12.37	9.12	63.75	33794	29367
2005	1980	11.92	8.47	60.47	33907	29674
2006	1929	11.53	9.16	59.33	34460	30018
2007	1872	11.38	8.67	56.83	34901	30533
2008	1781	10.58	8.33	54.66	34653	30382
2009	1666	9.96	7.84	52.52	34389	30334
2010	1531	9.61	8.64	51.56	34118	29944
2011	1424	8.92	8.77	51.39	32457	29900
2012	1322	8.88	8.88	50.85	32208	29651

注：本表数据来源于市教育局。

19-12 各区县小学基本情况（2012年）

Basic Statistics on Primary Schools by Region (2012)

单位：所、人 (unit, person)

区 县	Region	学校数 Number of Schools	毕业生数 Number of Graduates	招生数 New Enrollment	在校学生数 Total Enrollment	女 生 Female Students	教职工数 Number of Staff and Teachers	专任教师 Full-time Teachers
合　计	**Total**	**1322**	**88822**	**88786**	**508534**	**232187**	**32208**	**29651**
新城区	Xincheng	34	7175	5816	37322	16995	1863	1739
碑林区	Beilin	43	6978	6656	39027	18160	2232	1861
莲湖区	Lianhu	50	7575	8010	45315	21118	2406	2201
灞桥区	Baqiao	75	5531	6265	34553	15922	1997	1665
未央区	Weiyang	48	6866	8886	46106	21272	1647	1918
雁塔区	Yanta	69	11226	12842	70405	32118	3263	3287
阎良区	Yanliang	22	2681	2333	13442	6427	1089	822
临潼区	Lintong	156	7861	6239	37899	17627	3268	3013
长安区	Chang'an	168	7372	8803	46924	21971	3747	3119
蓝田县	Lantian	244	7436	5580	35010	16286	2969	2836
周至县	Zhouzhi	145	6749	5561	36191	14877	2782	2661
户　县	Huxian	132	6067	5266	32326	13795	2205	2145
高陵县	Gaoling	86	2327	2728	13958	6620	1548	1352
沣东新城	Fengdongxincheng	50	2978	3801	20056	8999	1192	1032

注：本表数据来源于市教育局。
本表中教职工数按照办学类型划分，专任教师数按办学层次划分，请使用中注意。

19-13 主要年份幼儿园基本情况

Basic Statistics on Kindergartens in Representative Years

年 份 Year	幼儿园(所) Number of Kindergartens (unit)	班数(个) Number of Class (unit)	在园幼儿数(万人) Student Enrollment (10000 persons)	教职工数(人) Number of Staff and Teachers (person)	专任教师(人) Full-time Teachers(persons)
1978	363		4	3568	1315
1980	186		10	5525	2657
1985	310	3135	10	6887	2770
1990	256	3816	14	6123	2058
1995	257	4464	16	6173	2659
1996	244	4313	15	5918	2661
1997	228	4243	15	6065	2748
1998	235	4195	13	6272	2910
1999	234	4222	13	6329	2982
2000	367	4142	13	6346	2995
2001	366	4306	12	6224	3069
2002	378	4186	12	6541	3397
2003	610	4470	12	8959	4853
2004	660	4507	12	9870	5577
2005	737	4712	13	10528	5959
2006	863	5037	13	12335	7106
2007	830	5081	14	13468	7951
2008	905	5506	15	14932	8704
2009	896	5710	16	15928	9240
2010	1004	6420	18	18710	10638
2011	1122	8010	24	23680	12577
2012	1239	8729	27.1	27735	14293

注：本表数据来源于市教育局。
幼儿园在园人数中包括学前班。

19-14 主要年份特殊教育学校基本情况

Basic Statistics on Special Education Schools in Representative Years

单位：所、人 (unit, person)

年 份 Year	学校数 Number of Schools	毕业生数 Number of Graduates	招生数 New Enrollment	在校学生数 Total Enrollment	教职工数 Number of Staff and Teachers	专任教师 Full-time Teachers
1978						
1980	1	48	64	315	66	43
1985	2	14	36	318	94	59
1990	5	35	111	451	142	96
1995	5	27	147	1363	204	141
1996	5	60	164	1520	210	150
1997	5	153	164	1655	210	148
1998	5	266	140	2145	232	157
1999	5	349	115	1912	235	160
2000	5	269	145	1880	230	156
2001	5	237	209	1915	238	162
2002	5	216	148	1661	232	157
2003	5	156	161	1380	237	166
2004	5	137	142	1290	236	167
2005	5	184	182	1445	240	169
2006	6	171	143	1425	254	178
2007	6	169	114	1342	259	190
2008	6	83	96	1286	259	190
2009	7	311	202	1523	335	234
2010	8	214	402	1529	340	235
2011	8	280	222	1393	343	231
2012	8	197	220	1392	352	248

注：本表数据来源于市教育局。
包括盲、聋、哑、弱智儿童教育在内。

19-15 基础教育监测评价情况(2012年)

Monitoring and Evaluation of Basic Education(2012)

指 标	Item	2012
入学率(%)	Enrollment Rate(%)	
小学	Primary Schools	99. 97
初中	Junior Middle Schools	99. 67
重读率(%)	Restduy-Rate(%)	
小学	Primary schools	0.12
初中	Junior Middle Schools	0.02
巩固率(%)	The Consolidation Rate (%)	
小学(六年)	Primary Schools (six years)	96.97
初中(三年)	Junior Middle Schools (three years)	94.86
毕业班学生毕业率(%)	The Graduate Rate(%)	
小学	Primary school	100.17
初中	Junior middle school	98.74
专任教师学历合格率(%)	Qualified Rate Of Full-time Teacher Education (%)	
小学	Primary Schools	99.95
初中	Junior Middle Schools	99.35
高中	Senior Middle Schools	97.25
幼儿园	Kindergartens	98.10
小学教师专科以上学历达到率(%)	Rate of Primary School Teachers with College degree or Above (%)	91.14
初中教师本科以上学历达到率(%)	Rate of Junior Middle SchoolTeachers with Bachelor degree or Above (%)	83.55
高中教师研究生以上学历达到率(%)	Rate of Senior Middle School Teachers with Postgraduate degree or Above (%)	11.12

注：本表数据来源于市教育局。

19-16 主要年份平均每万人口在校学生数及构成

单位：人、%

年 份 Year	平均每万人 高等学校在校学生数 Per 10000 people on average Hight Education Students in the school	平均每万人 高中阶段在校学生 Per 10000 people on average Number of Senior high School Students in the school	平均每万人 初中在校学生 Per 10000 people on average Number of Junior Secondary School Students in the school
1978	58		
1980	84		
1985	117		
1990	123		
1995	168		
1996	177		
1997	180		
1998	189		
1999	224		
2000	282		
2001	366		
2002	470		
2003	560		
2004	618	463	517
2005	715	492	489
2006	760	534	484
2007	817	543	466
2008	863	571	444
2009	901	619	413
2010	939	635	361
2011	1090	576	337
2012	1132	541	319

注：本表数据来源于市教育局。

The Number of Students in the School in Major Years Per 10000 Pepole on Average

(persons,%)

平均每万人 小学在校学生数 Per 10000 people on average Number of Primary School Students in the school	普通高等学校在校学生 占学生总数比重 Senior high School Students in the school in accounting for the proportion of the total number of students	中等学校在校学生 占学生总数比重 Junior Secondary School students in the school in accounting for the proportion of the total number of students	小学在校学生 占学生总数比重 Primary School students in the school in accounting for the proportion of the total number of students
1486	2.3	34.9	58.6
1434	3.1	33.2	55.3
1124	5.3	31.3	50.9
1016	6.7	25.1	51.7
1224	7.3	28.0	53.6
1249	7.6	28.8	53.5
1249	7.6	29.8	53.1
1228	8.0	31.3	52.0
1183	9.3	33.2	49.2
1131	11.5	34.8	46.0
1072	14.6	35.9	42.6
1007	18.2	36.4	39.0
932	20.1	33.8	33.5
879	22.2	35.2	31.6
815	26.4	36.2	30.1
788	27.7	37.1	28.7
744	29.3	36.3	26.7
708	30.8	36.1	25.2
672	31.8	36.5	23.7
660	33.0	35.0	23.2
604	29.8	30.1	19.9
595	31.0	28.2	19.5

19-17 民办教育情况(2012年)

Private Education Situation (2012)

单位：所、人 (unit, person)

指　标	Item	学校数 Number of Schools	毕业生数 Number of Graduates	招生数 New Enrollment
一、民办高等教育(民办高校)	**Private higher Education (Institutions)**	**16**	**71204**	**87921**
二、民办中等教育	**Private Secondary Education**	**95**	**41269**	**36585**
1. 民办普通高中	Ordinary High School	31	6628	6524
2. 民办中等专业学校	Specialized Secondary School	1	3834	538
3. 民办职业高中	Vocational hight school	44	12863	9954
4. 民办普通初中	Ordinary Junior middle school	19	17944	19569
三、民办普通小学	**Private Primary School**	**36**	**7033**	**8639**
四、民办幼儿园	**Private kindergarten**	**990**	**48875**	**80142**
另有：民办培训机构（不计校数）	Private Training Institutions (Not included in the totals number of schools)	470	134024	

19-17 续表 continued

单位：所、人 (unit, person)

指　标	Item	在校学生数 Total Enrollment	教职工数 Number of Teachers and Staff	专任教师 Full-time Teachers	聘请外校教师 Teachers hired from Outside Schools
一、民办高等教育(民办高校)	**Private higher Education (Institutions)**	**267961**	**20597**	**12438**	
二、民办中等教育	**Private Secondary Education**	**109366**	**2673**	**1547**	**476**
1. 民办普通高中	Ordinary High School	18637			
2. 民办中等专业学校	Specialized Secondary Schools	4999	210	106	
3. 民办职业高中	Vocational hight school	28819	2463	1441	476
4. 民办普通初中	Ordinary Junior middle school	56911			
三、民办普通小学	**Private Primary School**	**46446**	**2301**	**1704**	**2**
四、民办幼儿园	**Private kindergarten**	**189904**	**20888**	**10588**	**111**
另有：民办培训机构（不计校数）	Private Training Institutions (Not included in the totals number of schools)	201632	6299	4137	3818

注：本表数据来源于市教育局。
毕业生数中，幼儿园为离园人数。
民办高等教育在校生为民办高校普通、成人本专科学生数。
聘请校外教师中，小学、中学、幼儿园为代课教师和兼任教师之和。
民办普通高中中含完全中学19所、12年一贯制7所；民办普通初中中含9年一贯制7所。

19-18 研究与试验发展（R&D）情况

Research and Experiment Development Facts

指　标	Item	2011	2012
一、单位数（个）	**Number of Units(unit)**	**1546**	**1631**
#科研单位	Units of Scientific Research	77	81
高等院校	Institutions of Higher Education	47	48
大中型工业企业	Large-scale and Medium-scale Industrial Enterprises	216	231
#有R&D活动单位数	Number of Units with R&D Activities	341	387
科研单位	Units of Scientific Research	46	49
高等院校	Institutions of Higher Education	47	48
大中型工业企业	Large-scale and Medium-scale Industrial Enterprises	92	109
二、科技活动人员（人）	**Personnel Eagaged in Scientific and Technical Activities (person)**	**147814**	**162232**
科研单位	Units of Scientific Research	35407	36430
高等院校	Institutions of Higher Education	40821	42652
大中型工业企业	Large-scale and Medium-scale Industrial Enterprises	48110	57458
三、R&D经费内部支出（万元）	**Interier Expenditures for R&D(10 000 yuan)**	**2025288**	**2294743**
科研单位	Units of Scientific Research	1039723	1117292
高等院校	Institutions of Higher Education	282926	289010
大中型工业企业	Large-scale and Medium-scale Industrial Enterprises	574223	724620
四、R&D项目（课题）（个）	**Number of Projects of R&D(item)**	**26433**	**30155**
科研单位	Units of Scientific Research	1463	1797
高等院校	Institutions of Higher Education	21708	24042
大中型工业企业	Large-scale and Medium-scale Industrial Enterprises	2086	2987

注：本表单位数含规模以上工业企业、非工业企业和事业单位。

19–19 科研院所研究与试验发展（R&D）情况

Research and Experiment Development Facts in Scientific Research Institutions

指　标	Item	2011	2012
一、基本情况	**Basic Facts**		
单位数（个）	Number of Unit(unit)	77	81
#有R&D活动的单位数	Number of Units with Scientific and Technical Activities	46	49
科技活动人员（人）	Number of Personnel Engaged in Scientific Research (person)	35407	36430
# R&D人员	R&D Personnel	25869	26201
其中：女性	Femalc	8025	8155
其中：博士毕业	Doctor	887	978
硕士毕业	Master	6375	6542
本科毕业	Undergraduate	10943	10650
二、R&D人员折合全时当量（人/年）	**Full Time Equivalent of R&D Personnel (person/year)**	**24251**	**24400**
其中：研究人员	Personnel Engaged in Research	14744	14831
其中：基础研究	Basic Research	2081	1665
应用研究生	Applied Research	7159	6941
试验发展	Experiment Development	15010	15794
三、R&D经费内部支出（万元）	**Raising and Use of Funds for Scientific and(10 000 yuan) Technical Activities**	**1039723**	**1117292**
在支出中：1、基础研究	Expenditure on: Basic Research	34884	47905
2、应用研究生	Applied Research	209314	205908
3、试验发展	Experiment Development	795526	863479
在支出中：1、日常支出	Expenditure on: Daily Expenditure	784907	852894
#人员劳务费	Service Fees of Personnel	186747	181420
2、资产性支出	Assets Expenditure	254816	264399
#仪器和设备	Instruments and Equipment	168340	114090
在支出中：1、政府资金	Expenditure on: Government Funds	955814	1017985
2、企业资金	Enterpreises Funds	19389	24233
3、境外资金	Overseas Funds	1814	
4、其他资金	Others	62706	75076
四、R&D产出	**Achievements of R&D**		
专利申请数（个）	Number of Patent Applications (item)	1275	1608
#发明专利	Number of Invention Patents	891	1149
专利授权数（个）	Number of Patents Awarded (item)	656	738
#发明专利	Number of Invention Patents	413	431
有效发明专利数（件）	Number of Effective Invention Patents	903	1397
发表科技论文（篇）	Scientific and Technical Thesis (piece)	5031	5406
出版科技著作（种）	Scientific and Technical Works Published (book)	69	77

19-20 大专院校研究与试验发展（R&D）情况

Research and Experiment Development Facts in Universities

指 标	Item	2011	2012
一、基本情况	**Basic Facts**		
单位数（个）	Number of Unit(unit)	47	48
#有R&D活动的单位数	Number of Units with Scientific and Technical Activities	47	48
从事科技活动人员（人）	Number of Personnel Engaged in Scientific Research (person)	40821	42652
# R&D人员	R&D Personnel	17074	17979
其中：女性	Female	5415	5720
其中：博士毕业	Doctor	4828	5426
硕士毕业	Master	5893	6078
本科毕业	Undergraduate	4887	5086
二、R&D人员折合全时当量（人/年）	**Full Time Equivalent of R&D Personnel (person/year)**	**11110**	**8968**
其中：研究人员	Personnel Engaged in Research	7257	7868
其中：基础研究	Basic Research	3707	3935
应用研究生	Applied Research	3736	3939
试验发展	Experiment Development	969	1093
三、R&D经费内部支出（万元）	**Raising and Use of Funds for Scientific and(10 000 yuan) Technical Activities**	**282926**	**289010**
在支出中：1、基础研究	Expenditure on: Basic Research	84050	88080
2、应用研究生	Applied Research	130622	128323
3、试验发展	Experiment Development	68252	72608
在支出中：1、日常支出	Expenditure on: Daily Expenditure	229332	252036
#人员劳务费	Service Fees of Personnel	35910	35901
2、资产性支出	Assets Expenditure	53592	36975
#仪器和设备	Instruments and Equipment	34660	24640
在支出中：1、政府资金	Expenditure on: Government Funds	168748	180089
2、企业资金	Enterpreises Funds	100161	99693
3、境外资金	Overseas Funds	1002	885
4、其他资金	Others	13015	8343
四、R&D产出	**Achievements of R&D**		
专利申请数（个）	Number of Patent Applications (item)	4976	5390
#发明专利	Number of Invention Patents	3189	3453
专利授权数（个）	Number of Patents Awarded (item)	2765	3748
#发明专利	Number of Invention Patents	1508	2075
有效发明专利数（件）	Number of Effective Invention Patents	8358	6060
发表科技论文（篇）	Scientific and Technical Thesis (piece)	43260	41498
出版科技著作（种）	Scientific and Technical Works Published (book)	986	991

19-21　大中型工业企业研究与试验发展（R&D）情况

Research and Experiment Development Facts in Large-size and Medium-size Industrial Enterprises

指　标	Item	2011	2012
一、基本情况	**Basic Facts**		
单位数（个）	Number of Unit(unit)	216	231
有（R&D）活动的单位数	Number of Units with Scientific and Technical Activities	92	109
从事科技活动人员（人）	Number of Personnel Engaged in Scientific Research (person)	48110	57458
#（R&D）人员	R&D Personnel	23635	35400
其中：女性	Female	7152	10323
二、R&D人员折合全时当量（人/年）	**Full Time Equivalent of R&D Personnel (person/year)**	**17622**	**22276**
其中：研究人员	Personnel Engaged in Research	8586	11046
其中：基础研究	Basic Research		21
应用研究生	Applied Research	539	1163
试验发展	Experiment Development	17083	21092
三、R&D经费内部支出（万元）	**Raising and Use of Funds for Scientific and Technical Activities(10 000 yuan)**	**574223**	**724620**
在支出中：1、基础研究	Expenditure on: Basic Research		183
2、应用研究	Applied Research	53936	49253
3、试验发展	Experiment Development	520287	675184
在支出中：1、日常支出	Expenditure on: Daily Expenditure	480859	651634
#人员劳务费	Service Fees of Personnel	87728	121173
2、资产性支出	Assets Expenditure	93364	72986
#仪器和设备	Instruments and Equipment	5113	69883
在支出中：1、政府资金	Expenditure on: Government Funds	91593	163880
2、企业资金	Enterpreises Funds	473774	551583
3、境外资金	Overseas Funds	363	
4、其他资金	Others	8493	9158
四、R&D产出	**Achievements of R&D**		
专利申请数（个）	Number of Patent Applications (item)	2057	2795
#发明专利	Number of Invention Patents	878	1123
专利授权数（个）	Number of Patents Awarded (item)		
#发明专利	Number of Invention Patents		
有效发明专利数（件）	Number of Effective Invention Patents	1103	2962
发表科技论文（篇）	Scientific and Technical Thesis (piece)	1693	2576
出版科技著作（种）	Scientific and Technical Works Published (book)		

注：2012年大中型工业企业科技年报为省统计局反馈数据，包括5家省直报单位。

19-22 主要年份企事业单位知识产权情况

Intellectual Property Right of Enterprises and Institutions in Representative Years

指 标	Item	2005	2006	2007	2008	2009	2010	2011	2012
一、科技活动情况	**Science and technology activities**								
科技活动人员（人）	People involved into activities(person)	82789	86978	87095	91994	137934	128559	147814	162232
科技活动机构数（个）	units involved into activities(unit)	358	365	380	411	569	490	625	616
二、知识产权拥有量情况	**Number of IPR**								
1. 专利情况（件）	Patents(item)								
（1）累计申请专利	Accumulated patent applications	21912	26084	32852	42436	55208	74694	102411	139290
当年申请专利	Patent applictions in this year	2950	4172	6768	9584	12772	19486	27717	36983
#发明专利	Invention patents	1268	1325	1886	3049	5014	7176	11689	15029
（2）累计授权专利	Accumulated patents awarded	11670	13442	15971	19256	23962	31999	41273	53118
当年授权专利	Patents awarded in this year	1280	1772	2529	3285	4706	8037	9274	11862
#发明专利	Invention patents	331	461	595	749	1121	1651	2738	3475
2. 商标情况（件）	Trade marks(item)								
（1）当年注册商标申请	Trade mark registration claimed in this year	3682	7132	5559	7613	8972	21562	15620	18230
（2）累计注册商标	Accumulated trade mark registrations	18461	20808	22860	26386	23078	52387	39381	65733
#当年注册商标	Trade mark registrations in this year	2330	2347	2052	3526	5278	18107	12278	12120
三、民事知识产权维权情况（件）	**IPR controversy(item)**	**106**	**108**	**131**	**212**	**427**	**241**	**512**	**631**
1. 专利纠纷	Patent controversies	27	30	44	47	37	69	104	107
2. 商标纠纷	Trade mark controversies	19	24	32	51	42	29	49	107
3. 著作权纠纷	Copyright controversies	53	49	36	91	319	110	315	365
4. 技术合同纠纷	Technological contract controversies	1	1	3	3	9	6	15	9
5. 发现权与发明权纠纷	Discover and invention controversies	1							
6. 其他知识产权纠纷	Others IPR controvers	5	4	16	20	20	27	29	43

注：本表数据由市科技局、陕西省工商局、陕西省新闻出版局、西安市中级人民法院等提供。

19-23 主要年份高新技术产业开发区情况

Basic Statistics of Hi-Tech Development Zone in Representative Years

指 标	Item	2005	2006	2007	2008	2009	2010	2011	2012
1. 高新技术企业数（个）	Number of High-tech Enterprises(unit)	1029	1062	1311	1324	592	672	774	690
2. 年末从业人员（人）	Number of Persons Employed at year-end (person)	296401	346000	368757	388644	275141	287140	296723	320259
从事技术开发人数	Number of Persons Engaged in Technology Development	28792	34600	39248	48355	64212	67708	78636	81787
3. 技术开发经费支出总额（万元）	Expenditures on Technology Development(10 000 yuan)	254161	565166	705066	777516	756767	1031223	1322923	1768282
研究与发展支出	Expenditures on Research and Development	115026	414537	533924	581716	585449	669083	831822	1273311
4. 利润总额（万元）	Total Profits (10 000 yuan)	388404	654258	1087311	1231146	1308432	1707925	2224850	2905877
5. 上缴税费总额（万元）	Sum of tax (10 000 yuan)	356599	464700	1394194	1576472	1486556	1964820	2586712	3383678
6. 出口创汇总额（千美元）	Foreign Exchange Earnings of Exports(USD 1 000)	527014	1460251	1927114	2188721	1177000	4951265	6447050	6591977

19-24 高新技术产业开发区发展规模（2012年）

Development Status of Hi-Tech Development Zone (2012)

指 标	Item	合计 Total	新建区 Newly constructed Zone
累计已开发面积（平方公里）	Accumulated Areas Developed (sq.km)	40	40
高新区工商注册（个）	Registered Enterprises in Hi-tech Zones (unit)	17427	17427
#工业型技术开发技术服务型企业数	Number of industrial technology developing enterprises	8783	8783
#三资企业数	Enterprises of Joiut Venture,Cooperation and Foreign-funded	1086	1086
已认定的高新技术企业数	Hi-tech Enterprises Designated	690	690

注：本表数据来源于西安市高新技术开发区。

19-25 主要年份高新技术产业开发区建设与集资情况

Capital Construction and Funds-Raising of Hi-Tech Development Zone in Representative Years

指 标	Item	2005	2006	2007	2008	2009	2010	2011	2012
一、基建投资（亿元）	**Investment on Capital Construction (100 million yuan)**								
本年基建投资	Investment on Capital Construction of this year	91.26	114.59	132.17	159.78	196.90	255.57	266.51	350.88
1. 生产业务用房	Building for Production	31.81	50.76	59.69	60.53	69.23	94.74	105.35	
2. 住宅	Residential Buildings	41.35	40.61	47.75	77.05	79.00	97.30	86.32	
3. 公用设施	Public Installations	6.36	10.15	11.94	6.72	4.91	7.35	5.99	
4. 基础设施	Fundamental Facilities	8.63	8.53	7.50	9.60	24.66	32.98	32.41	
5. 征地拆迁	Resettlement	3.11	4.54	5.29	5.88	17.00	13.59	36.44	
二、开发面积	**Area Developed**								
新建区累计开发土地面积（平方公里）	Accumulated Area Developed in Newly Constructed Zone (sq.km)	22.35	35.00	35.00	35.00	35.00	35.00	35.00	40.00
#当年新开发土地面积	Area Developed in this year		1.27						5.00
累计竣工建筑面积（万平方米）	Accumulated Floor Space Completed (10 000 sq.m)	1104.72	1325.98	1558.70	1782.43	2085.66	419.87	2748.09	3095.09
#当年竣工建筑面积	Floor Space Completed in this year	188.60	221.30	232.70	223.76	303.23	334.20	328.22	347.00
三、当年内资金筹集情况（亿元）	**Funds Raised in this year (100 million yuan)**								
当年内资金筹集总额	Total Funds Raised in this year	160.20	155.58	152.85	179.57	202.58	300.30	291.82	
#政府拨款	Allocations from the Government	5.50	6.50	11.66	21.41	25.98	33.07	45.35	
贷款	Loans	108.20	108.34	100.00	106.18	125.47	165.68	154.01	
四、吸引外资（亿美元）	**Foreign Investment(100 million USD)**								
年末累计境外客商协议投资额	Contracted Foreign Investment Accumulated at Year-end	21.92	28.14	32.35	36.26	43.76	52.76	56.71	74.11
年末累计境外客商实际投资额	Actual Foreign Investment Accumulated at Year-end	9.26	12.18	16.08	20.29	24.63	29.75	36.24	45.02
#当年实际投资额	Actual Investmen in this year	1.98	2.92	3.90	4.21	4.34	5.11	6.49	8.18

注：本表数据来源于西安市高新技术开发区。

主要统计指标解释

普通高等学校 指按国家规定的设置标准和审批程序批准举办的，通过全国普通高等学校统一招生考试，招收高中毕业生为主要培养对象，实施高等学历教育的全日制大学、独立设置的学院和高等专科学校、高等职业学校及其他机构（独立学院和分校、大专班）。

大学、独立设置的学院主要实施本科层次以上教育。高等专科学校、高等职业学校实施专科层次教育。其他机构是承担国家普通招生计划任务不计校数的机构，包括独立学院、普通高等学校分校、大专班和批准筹建的普通高等学校等。独立学院指由普通本科高校按新机制、新模式举办的本科层次的二级学院，一些普通本科高校按公办机制和模式建立的二级学院，“分校”或其他类似的二级办学机构不属此范畴。

成人高等学校 指按照国家规定的设置标准和审批程序批准举办的，通过全国成人高等教育统一招生考试，招收具有高中毕业或同等学历的人员为主要培养对象，利用函授、业余、脱产等多种形式对其实施高等学历教育的学校。包括职工高等学校、农民高等学校、管理干部学院、教育学院、独立函授学院、广播电视大学、其他机构等。其他机构是承担国家成人招生计划任务不计校数的机构。

小学学龄儿童净入学率 指调查范围内已入小学学习的学龄儿童占校内外学龄儿童总数（包括弱智儿童，不包括盲聋哑儿童）的比重。计算公式为：

小学学龄儿童净入学率（%）=已入学的小学学龄儿童数／校内外小学学龄儿童总数×100%

研究与试验发展（R&D） 指在科学技术领域，为增加知识总量，以及运用这些知识去创造新的应用进行的系统的创造性的活动，包括基础研究、应用研究、试验发展三类活动。国际上通常采用R&D活动的规模和强度指标反映一国的科技实力和核心竞争力。

基础研究 指为了获得关于现象和可观察事实的基本原理的新知识（揭示客观事物的本质、运动规律，获得新发现、新学说）而进行的实验性或理论性研究，它不以任何专门或特定的应用或使用为目的。其成果以科学论文和科学著作为主要形式。用来反映知识的原始创新能力。

应用研究 指为获得新知识而进行的创造性研究，主要针对某一特定的目的或目标。应用研究是为了确定基础研究成果可能的用途，或是为达到预定的目标探索应采取的新方法（原理性）或新途径。其成果形式以科学论文、专著、原理性模型或发明专利为主。用来反映对基础研究成果应用途径的探索。

试验发展 指利用从基础研究、应用研究和实际经验所获得的现有知识，为产生新的产品、材料和装置，建立新的工艺、系统和服务，以及对已产生和建立的上述各项作实质性的改进而进行的系统性丁作。其成果形式主要是专利、专有技术、具有新产品基本特征的产品原型或具有新装置基本特征的原始样机等。在社会科学领域，试验发展是指把通过基础研究、应用研究获得的知识转变成可以实施的计划（包括为进行检验和评估实施示范项目）的过程。人文科学领域没有对应的试验发展活动。主要反映将科研成果转化为技术和产品的能力，是科技推动经济社会发展的物化成果。

R&D人员 指参与研究与试验发展项目研究、管理和辅助工作的人员，包括项目（课题）组人员，企业科技行政管理人员和直接为项目（课题）活动提供服务的辅助人员。反映投入从事拥有自主知识产权的研究开发活动的人力规模。

R&D人员全时当量 指全时人员数加非全时人员按工作量折算为全时人员数的总和。例如：有两个全时人员和三个非全时人员（工作时间分别为20%、30%和70%），则全时当量为2+0.2+0.3+0.7=3.2人年。为国际上比较科技人力投入而制定的可比指标。

R&D经费内部支出 合计指调查单位用于内部开展R&D活动（基础研究、应用研究和试验发展）的实际支出。包括用于R&D项目（课题）活动的直接支出，以及间接用TR&D活动的管理费、服务费、与R&D有关的基本建设支出以及外协加工费等。不包括生产性活动支出、归还贷款支出以及与外单位合作或委托外单位进行R&D活动而转拨给对方的经费支出。

R&D经费内部支出中政府资金 指R&D经费内部支出中来自各级政府部门的各类资金，包括财政科学技术拨款、科学基金、教育等部门事业费以及政府部门预算外资金的实际支出。

R&D经费内部支出中企业资金 指R&D经费内部支出中来自本企业的自有资金和接受其他企业委托而获得的经费，以及科研院所、高校等事业单位从企业获得的资金的实际支出。

R&D项目（课题）数 指在当年立项并开展研究工作、以前年份立项仍继续进行研究的研发项目（课题）数，包括当年完成和年内研究：工作已告失败的研发项目（课题），但不包括委托外单位进行的研发项目（课题）数。

R&D项目（课题）人员全时当量 指实际参加研发项目（课题）活动人员折合的全时当量。

R&D项目（课题）经费内部支出 指调查单位内部在报告年度进行研发项目（课题）研究和试制等的实际支出。包括劳务费、其他日常支出、固定资产购建费、外协加工费等，不包括委托或与外单位合作进行项目（课题）研究而拨付给对方使用的经费。

新产品产值 指报告期企业生产的新产品的产值。新产品是指采用新技术原理、新设计构思研制、生产的全新产品，或在结构、材质、工艺等某一方面比原有产品有明显改进，从而显著提高了产品性能或扩大了使用功能的产品。新产品产值、新产品销售收入既包括经政府有关部门认定并在有效期内的新产品，也包括企业自行研制开发，未经政府有关部门认定，从投产之日起一年之内的新产品。

新产品销售收入 指报告期企业销售新产品实现的销售收入。

专利 是专利权的简称，是对发明人的发明创造经审查合格后，由专利局依据专利法授予发明人和设计人对该项发明创造享有的专有权。包括发明、实用新型和外观设计。反映拥有自主知识产权的科技和设计成果情况。

发明（专利） 指对产品、方法或者其改进所提出的新的技术方案。是国际通行的反映拥有自主知识产权技术的核心指标。

实用新型（专利） 指对产品的形状、构造或者其结合所提出的适于实用的新的技术方案。反映具有一定技术含量的技术成果情况。

外观设计（专利） 指对产品的形状、图案、色彩或者其结合所作出的富有美感并适于工业上应用的新设计。反映拥有自主知识产权的外观设计成果情况。

工业企业R&D投入强度 指研究与试验发展经费内部支出与主营业务收入的比值。

Explanatory Notes on Main Statistical Indicators

Regular Institutions of Higher Education refer to educational establishments set up according to the government evaluation and approval procedures, recruiting graduates from senior secondary schools as the main target by National Matriculation TEST. They include full-time universities, colleges, institutions of higher professional education, institutions of higher vocational education, institutions of higher vocational education and others (non-university tertiary, branch schools and undergraduate classes) .

Universities and colleges primarily provide undergraduate courses; institutions of higher professional education and institutions of higher vocational education primarily provide professional trainings; and others refer to educational establishments, which are responsible for enrolling higher education students under the State Plan but not enumerated in the total number of schools, including: branch schools of universities and colleges, and universities and colleges that have been approved and under plan for construction. Non-university tertiary refers to the regular undergraduate branch college which is running in new mechanism and mode, excluding the branch schools and other similar branches of educational institutions.

Institutions of Higher Education for Adults refer to educational establishments, set up in line with relevant rules approved by the government, enrolling staff and workers with senior secondary school or equivalent education, and providing higher education courses in many forms of correspondence, spare time, or full time for adults. Professionals thus trained receive a qualification equivalent to graduates studying regular courses at regular universities, colleges and professional colleges. Institutions of higher learning for adults include schools of higher education for staff and workers, schools of higher education for peasants, colleges for management cadres, pedagogical colleges, independent correspondence colleges, Radio and TV universities and other educational establishments. Other educational establishments have undertakings to enrol adult students but not enumerated in the schools under the State Plan.

Net Enrolment Ratio of Primary Schools refers to the proportion of school age children enrolled at schools to the total number of school age children both in and outside schools (including retarded children, but excluding blind, deaf and mute children) . The formula is:

$$\text{Net Enrolment Ratio Of Primary Schools} = \frac{\text{Total Primary School-age Children at Schools}}{\text{Total Primary School-age WnerdlihChether or Not Attending School}} \times 100\%$$

Research and Development (R&D) refers to systematic and creative activities in the field of science and technology aiming at increasing the knowledge and using the knowledge for new application. R&D includes 3 categories of activities: basic research, applied research and experimentation for development. The scale and intensity of R&D are widely used internationally to reflect the strength of S&T and the core competitiveness of a country in the world.

Basic Research refers to empirical or theoretical research aiming at obtaining new knowledge on the fundamental principles regarding phenomena or observable facts to reveal the intrinsic nature and underlying laws and to acquire new discoveries or new theories. Basic research takes no specific or designated application as the aim of the research. Results of basic research are mainly released or disseminated in the form of scientific papers or monographs. This indicator reflects the innovation capacity for original knowledge.

Applied Research refers to creative research aiming at obtaining new knowledge on a specific objective or target. Purpose of the applied research is to identify the possible uses of results from basic research, or to explore new (fundamental) methods or new approaches. Results of applied research are expressed in the form of scientific papers, monographs, fundamental models or invention patents. This indicator reflects the exploration of ways to apply the results of basic research.

Experiments and Development refer to systematic activities aiming at using the knowledge from basic and applied researches or from practical experience to develop new products, materials and equipment, to establish new production process, systems and services, or to make substantial improvement on the existing products, process or services. Results of experiment and development activities are embodied in patents, exclusive technology, and monotype of new products or equipment. In social sciences, experiment and development activities refer to the process of converting the knowledge from basic or applied researches into feasible programmes (including conduct of demonstration projects for assessment and evaluation) . There are no experiment and development activities in the science of humanities. This indicator reflects the capability of transferring the results of S&T into technique and products, and measures the realization of S&T in spearheading the economic and social development.

R&D Personnel refer to persons engaged in research, management and supporting activities ofR & D, including persons in the project teams, persons engaged in the management of S&T activities of enterprises and supporting staff providing direct service to the research projects. This indicator reflects the size of personnel engaged in R&D activities with independent intellectual property.

Full-time Equivalent of R&D Personnel refers to the sum of the full-time persons and the full-time equivalent of part-time persons converted by workload. For instance, if there are 2 full-time persons and 3 part-time workers (20%, 30% and 70% of working hours respectively on R&D activities) , the full-time equivalent are 2+0.2+0.3+0.7=3.2 person-years. This is an internationally comparable indicator of S&T manpower input.

Total Internal Expenditure of Funds on R&D refers to the real expenditure of surveyed units on their own R&D activities (basic research, application study, test and development) including direct expenditure on R&D activities, indirect expenditure of management and services on R&D activities, expenditure on capital construction and material processing by others. Excluding the expenditure on production activities, return of loan, and fees transferred to cooperated and entrusted agencies on R&D activities.

Internal Expenditure of Government Funds refersto the expenditure of funds on R&D activities from government agencies at different levels, including appropriate funds on science and technology from financial departments, scientific funds, operating expenses from education departments and the real expenditure of extra budgetary funds from government agencies.

Internal Expenditure of Funds of Enterprises refers to the expenditure of funds on R&D activities from self-raised funds of enterprises and funds from other enterprises through entrustment, and the expenditure of funds of institutions, such as institution of scientific research and universities, from enterprises.

Number of R&D Projects (subjects) refers to the number of R&D projects (subjects) set up and implemented at the reference year, and the number of R&D projects (subjects) set up in former years and under implementation, including the projects (subjects) finished and failed at the reference year, excluding the projects (subjects) implemented by others through entrustment.

Full-time Equivalent of R&D Personnel refers to the full-time equivalent of persons actually engaged in R&D projects. (subjects)

Internal Expenditure of Funds on R&D Projects (subjects) refers to the real expenditure of internal funds of the surveyed units on research and test of R&D projects (subjects) at the reference year, including service fee, other daily expenditure, cost for capital goods, cost of external process; excluding expenditure of funds transferred to other cooperated and entrusted units of the projects.

Output Value of New Products refers to the output value of new products during the reporting period. The new products refer to brand new products produced with new technology and new design, or product that represent noticeable improvement in terms of structure, material, or production process for improving significantly the character of function of the older versions. The output value and sales income of the new products include those of new products certified by relevant government agencies within the period of certification, as well as new products designed and produced by enterprises within a year without certification by government agencies.

Sales Income of New Products refers to the real sales income of new products of the enterprises at the reporting period.

Patent is an abbreviation for the patent right and refers to the exclusive right of ownership by the inventors or designers for the creation or inventions, given from the patent offices after due process of assessment and approval in accordance with the Patent Law. Patents are granted for inventions, utility models and designs. This indicator reflects the achievements of S&T and design with independent intellectual property.

Patented Inventions refer to new technical proposals to the products or methods or their modifications. This is universal core indicator reflecting the technologies with independent intellectual property.

Patented Utility Models refer to the practical and new technical proposals on the shape and structure of the product or the combination of both. This indicator reflects the condition of technological results with certain technical content.

Designs refer to the aesthetics and industrially applicable new designs for the shape, pattern and colour of the product, or their combinations. This indicator reflects the appearance design achievements with independent intellectual property.

Intensity of Input into R&D of Industrial Enterprises refers to the percentage of main operation income spent on R&D activities by industrial enterprises.

20 文化、体育、卫生、社会福利和其他

CULTURE,SPORTS,PUBLIC HEALTH,SOCIAL WELFARE INSTITUTIONS AND OTHER SOCIAL ACTIVITIES

资料整理：郝　静

Data management:Hao jing

第二十部分　文化、体育、卫生、社会福利和其他

一、简要说明

本章资料主要包括文化、卫生、民政、体育、计划生育、共青团、妇联以及公检法等方面的内容，由西安市统计局社会科技处根据西安市文广新局、卫生局、民政局、体育局、妇联、共青团市委、计划生育委员会以及公安局、检察院、法院等部门提供资料整理。

二、主要指标

图书馆总藏量（千册件）	6123	比上年增加	1216千册件
医院数（所）	276	比上年增加	8所
医院床位数（万张）	3.92	比上年增加	3237张

20 CULTURE,SPORTS,SANITATION,SOCIAL WELFARE INSTITUTIONS AND OTHER SOCIAL ACTIVITIES

Ⅰ.Brief Introduction

Data in this chapter primarily consists of data of culture, sanitation, civil administration, physical education, family planning, Communist Youth League, the Women's Federation, public security organs, procuratorial organs and people's court, compiled by Social Science & Technology Division of Xi'an Bureau of Statistics according to data from Xi'an Bureau of Cuture, Bureau of Sanitation, Bureau of Civial Adnimistration, Bureau of PE, the Women's Federation, Municipal Committee of Communist Youth League, Committee of Family Planning, Bureau of Public Security, Procuratorate, People's Court and other department concerned.

Ⅱ.Major Indicators

		Increase over Preceding Year
Number of Collections in Libraries(1 000 vol.)	6123	1216
Number of Hospitals(unit)	276	8
Number of Beds(10 000 units)	3.92	3237 units

20-1 文化事业机构和人数（2012年）

Number of Institutions and Personnel in Culture and Art（2012）

项　　目	Item	机构数（个）Number of Institutions (unit)	人员数（人）Number of Personnel (person)
一、电影事业	**Career of Film**		
制片厂	Studio	1	
发行放映管理机构	Number of Film Projection and Publication Administrating Institutions	2	8
电影放映单位	Unit of Film shows	157	1340
#电影院	Cinema	26	1113
影剧院	Theaters	5	80
放映队	Film Projection Team	126	147
二、艺术事业	**Art**		
艺术表演团体	Art Performance Troupes	19	2706
艺术表演场所	Art Centers	17	391
三、艺术科研机构	**Art Scientific Research Institution**	**2**	**65**
四、图书馆事业	**Libraries**	**15**	**525**
五、群众文化事业	**Mass Culture**		
群众艺术馆	Activities of Mass Art Centres	2	128
文化馆	Cultural Centers	14	241
文化站	Culture Stations	181	673
农村文化室	Rural Cultural Center	2652	
六、文化部门教育机构	**Education Institution of Culture Department**	**2**	**125**

注：本表数据来源于市文广新局。
　　2011年艺术表演团体有20个，人员有2439个。

20-2 文化事业发展情况（2012年）

Basic Statistics on Culture Development（2012）

指　　标	Item	2012
电影放映场数（千场）	Number of Film Shows (1 000 shows)	273
电影观众人数（千人次）	Number of Spectators (1 000 person-times)	8973
电影票房收入（万元）	Box-office Receipts(10 000 yuan)	34600
艺术表演团体演出场次（场）	Number of Art Performance Troupes Performers(shows)	6564
#国内演出场次	Number of domestic Performance	6335
艺术表演观众人次（千人次）	Number of Spectators(1000 person-times)	8460
图书馆藏书数（千册件）	Number of Collections in Libraries (1000 volumes)	6123
书刊文献外借人次（千人次）	Books, Journals and Documents Borrowing (1 000 person-times)	907
书刊文献外借册次（千册次）	Books, Journals and Documents Borrowing (1 000 Volume-times)	2356
县以上公共图书馆购书经费（万元）	Book-purchase Fund of Public Library above the County Level(Ten thousand yuan	1399

注：本表数据来源于市文广新局。

20-3 主要年份群众艺术馆、文化馆（站）活动情况

Basic Statistics on Activities of Mass Art Centers and Cultural Centers in Representative Years

指　　标	Item	2005	2006	2007	2008	2009	2010	2011	2012
机构数（个）	Number of Insititutions (units)	192	193	197	197	197	197	196	197
举办展览个数（个）	Number of Exhibitions (units)	458	667	511	520	716	705	592	652
举办展览参观人次（千人次）	Number of Exhibition Visitors(1000 person-times)							375	416
组织文艺活动次数（次）	Art Performances and Story-telling Sessions (times)	1439	2251	2884	2378	3158	3729	4544	3273
组织文艺活动参加人次（千人次）	Number of Culture Activities attendees (1000 person-times)							1778	1377
举办训练班班次（个）	Number of Training Courses (units)	1137	1327	1625	1109	1467	3018	2224	1798
举办训练班结业人次（千人次）	Number of Certificate Trained Persons (1000 person-times)	37	43	67	87	96	133	115	143
组织各类理论研讨和讲座次数（个）	Number of Theoretical Discussion and Seminars(1000 person-times)							106	78
组织各类理论研讨和讲座参加人次（千人次）	Number of Persons in Theoretical Discussion and Seminars(1000 person-times)							15	14
本年收入（千元）	Income of this year (1 000 yuan)	11257	12981	21111	22571	40891	42937	55367	88475
本年支出（千元）	Expenditure of this year (1 000 yuan)	10924	12706	21007	22458	42826	45160	62368	84522

注：本表数据来源于市文广新局。

20-4 文物保护业基本情况（2012年）

Basic Statistics on Cultural Relics Protection（2012）

指 标	Item	机 构（个）Insititution (unit)	人 员（人）Personnel (person)	文物藏品 实际数量（件）Factual Number of Collections(piece)	一级品 Grade One	举办陈列展览次数(次)	参观人次（千人次）Number of Visitors (1000 person-times)
总 计	**Total**	**140**	**3788**	**864030**	**5407**	**394**	**14420**
文物行政管理机关	Protection and Management Agencies	16	189				
文物保护管理机构	Cultural Relics administrative Departments						
其他文物机构	Other Agencies	7	287	42736			
博物馆	Museums	85	2568	759511	5166	376	12350
文物商店	Cultural Relics Agencies						
文物科研机构	Scientific Research of Historical Relics Preservation	3	233	32766	209		

注：本表数据来源于市文物局。
2010年前为省市直属文物单位数据，2011年为全口径数据(含民营、院校等)。

20-5 主要年份广播电台及节目制作情况

Basic Statistics of Broadcasting Stations and Program Production in Representative Years

指 标	Item	2004	2005	2006	2007	2008	2009	2010	2011	2012
省、地广播电台（座）	Broadcasting Stations at the Province and District Level(set)	2	2	2	2	2	2	2	1	1
省、地广播电视台（座）	Broadcasting Station at Province and District Level(set)								1	1
县级广播电视台（座）	Number of Wire Broadcasting Stations and TV Relaying Stations(set)	6	6	6	6	6	6	6	6	6
中短波、调频发射台及转播台（座）	Medium/Short Ware and FM Broadcast Transmission Stations and Relaying Stations(set)	280	280	290	40	46	51	55	54	59
节目套数（套）	Number of Programs(set)	14	14	15	17	17	18	18	19	20
全年播出时间(时)	Broadcasting Hours annually(hour)			90520	108405	113880	123005	124100	121723	129856
广播人口覆盖率（%）	Listener Rating(%)	98.85	99.35	99.36	99.37	99.37	99.37	99.4	99.42	99.45
制作广播节目(时)	Productions of Broadcasting(hour)	74696	81840	84083	97013	103328	110455	110639	83368	104300
#新闻资讯类	News Programs							13786	13821	14025
专题服务类	Special Subject Programs							24451	16318	21891
综艺类	Variety Programs							37720	28679	28096
广播剧类	Literature Programs							2406	2014	1720
广告类	Advertisements							28339	14202	19547
其他类	Service Programs							3937	8334	19021

注：本表数据来源于市文物局。
2010年制作广播节目时间分类发生变化，故2009年及以前无数据。

20-6 主要年份电视台及节目制作情况

Basic Statistics of TV Stations and Production of TV Program in Representative Years

指标	Item	2004	2005	2006	2007	2008	2009	2010	2011	2012
电视台（座）	Number of Television Stations (set)	2	2	2	2	2	2	2	1	1
发射台及转播台（座）	Number of Television Transmission Stations and Relaying Stations (set)	297	297	297	8	8	10	10	10	11
无线电视节目（套）	Program Productions of Non-cable television Stations (set)	5	6	5	5	5	7	6	6	6
有线电视节目（套）	Program Productions of cable television Stations (set)	10	9	10	16	17	15	16	16	16
全年播出时间（时）	Broadcasting Hours annually(hour)			119028	130260	140608	138372	141856	147003	137936
电视人口覆盖率（%）	Viewer Rating (%)	97.07	97.67	97.85	98.33	98.35	98.41	98.57	98.6	98.83
制作电视节目（时）	Earth Stations of Satellite TV (hour)	18643	27377	36337	25883	26097	27131	29626	43925	30091
#新闻资讯类	News and Information Programs							8930	10656	11169
专题服务类	Special Subject Programs							7762	19191	7689
综艺类	Variety Programs							3942	5202	5458
广播剧类	Literature Programs							1729	3781	113
广告类	Advertisement							3313	3200	3663
其他类	Service Programs							3950	1894	1997
有线电视用户（万户）	Users of Cable television Stations (10 000 households)	91.4	102.21	115.16	125.28	138.79	146.84	164.64	179.29	188.71
有线广播电视干线网总长度(公里)	The total length of cable broadcasting and television arteries of communication(km)								62494	62494
有线电视入户率(%)	The Rate of Cable Television(%)								79.08	80.53

注：本表数据来源于市文广新局。
2010年制作电视节目时间分类发生变化，故2009年及以前无数据。

20-7 体育事业基本情况（市属）（2012年）

The Basic Situations of Sport（Under Municipality）（2012）

单位：人、枚 (person, unit)

指标	Item	2012
一、体育部门职工人数	**Number of Staffs and Workers in Physical Education System**	**1300**
#运动员	Athletes	860
教练员	Coaches	131
二、等级裁判员发展人数	**Number of the Development of Grade Referees**	**216**
三、等级运动员发展人数	**Number of the Development of Grade Athletes**	**195**
四、全年获得奖牌数	**Number of Full-year Medals**	**343**
#国家级金牌	National Gold	12
国家级银牌	National Silver	11
省级金牌	Provincial Gold	182
省级银牌	Provincial Silver	138

注：本表数据来源于市体育局。

20-8 少年儿童分项业余体校情况（市属）（2012年）

Basic Statistics of Youth Part-time Physical Training School（2012）

单位：人 (person)

指　标	Item	2012
一、在读学生数	**Total Enrollment**	**7505**
田径	Track and Field	3000
游泳	Swimming	2000
体操	Gymnastics	70
举重	Weightlifting	200
国际式摔跤	Wrestling	75
柔道	Judo	60
射击	Shooting	200
射箭	Archery	100
足球	Football	350
篮球	Basketball	400
排球	Volleyball	150
乒乓球	Table Tennis	300
拳击	Boxing	50
武术	Wu Shu	160
跆拳道	Kickboxing	250
跳水	Diving	80
棒球	Baseball	60
二、职工数	**Number of Staff and Workers**	**1300**

注：本表数据来源于市体育局。

20-9 群众体育事业（2012年）

Mass Sports（2012）

指　标	Item	2011	2012
全民健身广场（个）	Number of National fitness square(unit)	594	620
社会体育指导员（人）	Social Sports Instructor(person)	7376	8600
晨晚健身站点（个）	Morning and Evening Fitness sites(unit)	1600	1600
社区建有体育组织比重（%）	The community has a sports organization proportion (%)	88	100
全国、全省体育先进社区（个）	National, provincial advanced sports community (unit)	21	25
全国农村体育先进示范站（个）	Advanced model of the National Rural Sports Station (unit)	15	15
体育人口(万人)	Sports population(10 000 persons)	380	420

注：本表数据来源于市体育局。

20-10 主要年份卫生机构、床位、人员情况

Number of Health Care Institutions, Beds and Employed Persons in Health Care Institutions in Representative Years

年份 Year	卫生机构数（个） Number of Health Care Institutions (units)	医院数（个） Number of Health Care Hospital (units)	卫生机构床位数（张） Number of Health Care Bed (units)	医院床位数（张） Number of Hospital Bed (units)	卫生技术人员数（人） Number of Medical Technical Personnel (persons)
2008	2239	276	34618	30582	47433
2009	2162	261	36849	32371	51641
2010	2385	258	39407	34274	56579
2011	5554	268	41010	35976	61281
2012	5576	276	44239	39213	66899

注：本表数据来源于市卫生局。
　　2008年及以后为新的统计口径、分类。

20-11 卫生机构、床位及人员情况（2012年）

卫生机构	Health Care Institutions	机构数（个）Number of Institutions (unit)	床位数（张）Number of Beds (unit)
总 计	**Total**	**5576**	**44239**
一、医院	**Hospitals**	**276**	**39213**
综合医院	General Hospitals	207	30830
中医医院	Hospitals Specialized in Traditional Chinese Medicine	33	3127
中西医结合医院	Hospitals Integrating Traditional Chinese Medicine with Western Therapeutics in Practice	2	415
民族医院	Nationalities Hospitals		
专科医院	Specialized Hospitals	34	4841
口腔医院	Dental Hospitals	3	91
眼科医院	Eye Hospitals	5	255
耳鼻喉科医院	ENT Hospitals		
肿瘤医院	Cancer Hospitals	1	656
心血管病医院	Cardiovascular Hospitals	1	100
胸科医院	Chest Hospitals		
血液病医院	Blood Disease Hospitals		
妇产（科）医院	Obstetrics and Gynecologist Hospitals	3	128
儿童医院	Children's Hospitals	1	888
精神病医院	Psychiatric Hospitals	5	1040
传染病医院	Hospitals for Infectious Diseases	1	300
皮肤病医院	Skin Hospitals		
结核病医院	Tuberculosis Hospitals	1	680
麻风病医院	Leprosy Hospitals		
职业病医院	Occupational Diseases Hospitals		
骨科医院	Orthopedic Hospitals	3	191
康复医院	Rehabilitation Hospitals	3	20
整形外科医院	Plastic Surgery Hospitals		
美容医院	Beauty Hospitals		
其他专科医院	Other Specialized Hospitals	7	492
护理院	Nursing Centets		
二、基层医疗卫生机构	**Commuting health care service centre**	**5228**	**3292**
社区卫生服务中心(站)	Community Health Care Center(Station)	201	1799
社区卫生服务中心	Community Health Care Center	128	1799
社区卫生服务站	Community Health Care Station	73	

注：本表数据来源于市卫生局。

Number of Health Care Institutions, Beds and Employed Persons in Health Care Institutions（2012）

人员合计（人）Total Number of Employed Persons (person)	卫生技术人员 Medical Technical Personnel	执业(助理)医师数 Licensed (Assistant) Doctors	#执业医师 Chartered Doctors
86096	**66899**	**23051**	**20414**
60311	**48457**	**15167**	**14263**
48327	39207	12389	11719
4541	3637	1210	1091
745	585	149	146
6698	5028	1419	1307
433	343	140	134
306	240	69	61
947	665	186	185
116	97	28	28
274	250	65	51
1870	1486	393	383
795	513	130	123
464	280	64	63
476	356	92	90
196	158	62	45
78	57	28	20
743	583	162	124
20806	**14809**	**6839**	**5199**
5067	4137	1445	1063
4497	3649	1255	905
570	488	190	158

20-11 续表1

卫生机构	Health Care Institutions	人员合计（人） 卫生技术人员中 注册护士 Registered Nurses	药师（士） Junior Paramedics
总 计	**Total**	**27837**	**3380**
一、医院	**Hospitals**	**22338**	**2435**
综合医院	General Hospitals	18118	1834
中医医院	Hospitals Specialized in Traditional Chinese Medicine	1424	330
中西医结合医院	Hospitals Integrating Traditional Chinese Medicine with Western Therapeutics in Practice	267	37
民族医院	Nationalities Hospitals		
专科医院	Specialized Hospitals	2529	234
口腔医院	Dental Hospitals	118	6
眼科医院	Eye Hospitals	113	8
耳鼻喉科医院	ENT Hospitals		
肿瘤医院	Cancer Hospitals	370	25
心血管病医院	Cardiovascular Hospitals	52	3
胸科医院	Chest Hospitals		
血液病医院	Blood Disease Hospitals		
妇产（科）医院	Obstetrics and Gynecologist Hospitals	140	12
儿童医院	Children s Hospitals	835	73
精神病医院	Psychiatric Hospitals	273	26
传染病医院	Hospitals for Infectious Diseases	146	15
皮肤病医院	Skin Hospitals		
结核病医院	Tuberculosis Hospitals	174	22
麻风病医院	Leprosy Hospitals		
职业病医院	Occupational Diseases Hospitals		
骨科医院	Orthopedic Hospitals	50	9
康复医院	Rehabilitation Hospitals	13	
整形外科医院	Plastic Surgery Hospitals		
美容医院	Beauty Hospitals		
其他专科医院	Other Specialized Hospitals	245	35
护理院	Nursing Centets		
二、基层医疗卫生机构	**Commuting health care service centre**	**4560**	**834**
社区卫生服务中心(站)	Community Health Care Center(Station)	1305	289
社区卫生服务中心	Community Health Care Center	1105	249
社区卫生服务站	Community Health Care Station	200	40

continued 1

Total Number of Employed Persons (persons)				
Among:Medical Technical Personnel		其他技术人员	管理人员	工勤技能人员
技师（士）				
Technicians	#检验师 Laboratory Technicians	Other Technical Personnel	Administrative Personnel	Logistics Technical Workers
3953	**2830**	**633**	**6939**	**7555**
2903	**2028**	**500**	**5527**	**5827**
2273	1618	403	4171	4546
265	146	69	444	391
47	32	5	112	43
318	232	23	800	847
12	7		65	25
3	3	1	29	36
44	25	9	111	162
10	6		13	6
18	10		16	8
94	78	2	161	221
25	15	6	148	128
22	22	1	90	93
33	23	2	85	33
10	5		16	22
11	11		10	11
36	27	2	56	102
628	**422**	**1**	**732**	**1194**
260	183	1	425	504
236	160		371	477
24	23	1	54	27

20-11 续表2

卫生机构	Health Care Institutions	机构数（个）Number of Institutions (unit)	床位数（张）Number of Beds (unit)
卫生院	Health Center	100	1372
街道卫生院	Urban Health-center		
乡镇卫生院	Rural Health-center	100	1372
中心卫生院	Center Health-center	23	710
乡卫生院	Country Health-center	77	662
村卫生室	Village clinics	3085	
门诊部	Outpatient department	160	121
综合门诊部	Comprehensive out-patient department	119	83
中医门诊部	Chinese medicine out-patient department	19	6
中西医结合门诊部	Integrative Medicine outpatient department	2	6
民族医门诊部	The national medicine out-patient department		
专科门诊部	Specialist out-patient department	20	26
诊所、卫生所、医务室	Clinic, health center, Infirmary	1682	
诊所	Clinic	1353	
卫生所、医务室	Clinic, Infirmary	329	
护理站	Nurses' station		
三、专科公共卫生机构	**College of public health institutions**	**53**	**1612**
疾病预防控制中心	Center for Disease Control and Prevention	17	
专科疾病防治院（所、站）	Specialized disease prevention and cure center (place, station)	1	700
1. 专科疾病防治院（所）	Specialist for Disease Control and Prevention center (place)	1	700
2. 专科疾病防治所（站、中心）	Specialized disease prevention (station, center)		
健康教育所（站、中心）	Health Education Institute (station, center)	2	
妇幼保健院（所、站）	Maternal and Child Health Hospital (Station)	15	912
1. 妇幼保健院	Maternal and Child Health Hospital	9	912
2. 妇幼保健所	Maternal and Child Health	2	
3. 妇幼保健站	Maternal and Child Health Station	4	
4. 生殖保健中心	Center for Reproductive Health		
急救中心（站）	Emergency Center	1	
采供血机构	Blood Collection Agencies	1	
卫生监督所（中心）	Health Supervision Agencies (Center)	15	
计划生育技术服务机构	Familiy Planning Technical Serverice Institution	1	
四、其他卫生机构	**Other Health Institution**	**19**	**122**
疗养院	Nursing Centres	1	122
卫生监督检验（监测、检测）所站	Health Supervision and inspection Agencies		
医学科学研究机构	Medical scientific research institutions	3	
医学在职培训机构	Medical training institutions	5	
临床检验中心（所、站）	Clinical testing center (place, station)	1	
其他	other	9	

continued 2

人员合计（人）Total Number of Employed Persons (person)	卫生技术人员 Medical Technical Personnel	卫生技术人员中执业(助理)医师数 Licensed (Assistant) Doctors	#执业医师 Chartered Doctors
2619	2041	591	365
2619	2041	591	365
1114	881	254	169
1505	1160	337	196
5079	1009	822	310
2312	2029	919	784
1827	1630	704	606
220	190	109	100
17	13	10	8
248	196	96	70
5729	5593	3062	2677
4291	4239	2382	2083
1438	1354	680	594
4413	**3354**	**941**	**852**
1029	776	270	247
292	200	75	73
292	200	75	73
67	28	6	6
2146	1691	533	471
2001	1583	485	429
38	31	15	13
107	77	33	29
128	51	38	38
148	95	16	15
571	497		
32	16	3	2
566	**279**	**104**	**100**
74	40	14	14
155	87	51	50
204	86	11	10
45	39	16	16
88	27	12	10

20-11 续表3

卫生机构	Health Care Institutions	人员合计（人） 卫生技术人员中注册护士 注册护士 Registered Nurses	药师 Junior Paramedics
卫生院	Health Center	457	121
街道卫生院	Urban Health-center		
乡镇卫生院	Rural Health-center	457	121
中心卫生院	Center Health-center	228	48
乡卫生院	Country Health-center	229	73
村卫生室	Village clinics	187	
门诊部	Outpatient department	667	183
综合门诊部	Comprehensive out-patient department	558	146
中医门诊部	Chinese medicine out-patient department	38	30
中西医结合门诊部	Integrative Medicine outpatient department	2	
民族医门诊部	The national medicine out-patient department		
专科门诊部	Specialist out-patient department	69	7
诊所、卫生所、医务室	Clinic, health center, Infirmary	1944	241
诊所	Clinic	1416	173
卫生所、医务室	Clinic, Infirmary	528	68
护理站	Nurses' station		
三、专科公共卫生机构	**College of public health institutions**	**883**	**101**
疾病预防控制中心	Center for Disease Control and Prevention	39	15
专科疾病防治院（所、站）	Specialized disease prevention and cure center (place, station)	71	11
1. 专科疾病防治院（所）	Specialist for Disease Control and Prevention center (place)	71	11
2. 专科疾病防治所（站、中心）	Specialized disease prevention (station, center)		
健康教育所（站、中心）	Health Education Institute (station, center)	1	
妇幼保健院（所、站）	Maternal and Child Health Hospital (Station)	728	67
1. 妇幼保健院	Maternal and Child Health Hospital	693	61
2. 妇幼保健所	Maternal and Child Health	7	3
3. 妇幼保健站	Maternal and Child Health Station	28	3
4. 生殖保健中心	Center for Reproductive Health		
急救中心（站）	Emergency Center	11	1
采供血机构	Blood Collection Agencies	27	7
卫生监督所（中心）	Health Supervision Agencies (Center)		
计划生育技术服务机构	Familiy Planning Technical Serverice Institution	6	
四、其他卫生机构	**Other Health Institution**	**56**	**10**
疗养院	Nursing Centres	19	2
卫生监督检验(监测、检测)所站	Health Supervision and inspection Agencies		
医学科学研究机构	Medical scientific research institutions	15	4
医学在职培训机构	Medical training institutions		1
临床检验中心（所、站）	Clinical testing center (place, station)	13	
其他	other	9	3

continued 3

Total Number of Employed Persons (person)				
Among:Medical Technical Personnel		其他技术人员	管理人员	工勤技能人员
技师（士）				
	#检验师			
Technicians	Laboratory Technicians	Other Technical Personnel	Administrative Personnel	Logistics Technical Workers
183	103		307	271
183	103		307	271
101	53		121	112
82	50		186	159
139	101			283
121	88			197
7	6			30
1	1			4
10	6			52
46	35			136
14	9			52
32	26			84
392	**356**	**70**	**532**	**457**
211	200	3	129	121
17	14	2	57	33
17	14	2	57	33
		19	17	3
130	108	4	242	209
122	101	4	222	192
2	2		3	4
6	5		17	13
		11	29	37
34	34	4	38	11
		27	12	35
			8	8
30	**24**	**62**	**148**	**77**
2	2		16	18
17	12	13	30	25
2	2	49	52	17
6	5		1	5
3	3		49	12

20-12 各区县卫生机构、床位及人员情况（2012年）

Number of Health Care Institutions, Beds and Employed Persons in Health Care Institutions By Region（2012）

区 县	Region	机构（个） Number of Health Care Institutions (unit)	床位（张） Number of Beds (unit)	人员合计（人） Total Number of Employed Persons (person)	#卫生技术人员 Total Number of Medical Technical Personnel
全 市	**Total**	**5576**	**44239**	**86096**	**66899**
新城区	Xincheng	307	6637	13625	10725
碑林区	Beilin	328	6325	12991	10580
莲湖区	Lianhu	346	5444	10724	8854
灞桥区	Baqiao	537	2094	4860	3962
未央区	Weiyang	265	3148	5479	4435
雁塔区	Yanta	477	8171	15129	12123
阎良区	Yanliang	158	1402	2388	1864
临潼区	Lintong	469	1911	3445	2287
长安区	Chang'an	785	3226	5650	4038
蓝田县	Lantian	631	1005	2317	1494
周至县	Zhouzhi	476	1235	3384	2130
户 县	Huxian	585	2414	4008	2794
高陵县	Gaoling	212	1227	2096	1613

注：本表数据来源于市卫生局。

20-13 主要年份卫生机构各类人员情况

Number of Employed Persons in Health Care Institutions in Representative Years

单位：人　　　　(person)

指　标	Item	2000	2005	2006	2007	2008	2009	2010	2011	2012
人员合计	**Total**	**53111**	**52821**	**54912**	**55551**	**59934**	**65003**	**71230**	**79999**	**86096**
#卫生技术人员	Medical Technical Personnel	41836	42255	43862	43707	47433	51641	56579	61281	66899
执业（助理）医师	Licensed (Assistant) Doctors	18750	17730	18007	17266	18066	19284	18763	21551	23051
执业医师	Chartered Doctors	16146	15533	15778	15142	15975	17286	16613	18904	20414
注册护士	Registered Nurses	14344	14004	15538	15337	17186	20167	22640	25043	27837
药师(士)	Junior Paramedics	3475	3084	2987	2707	2721	2814	3030	3127	3380
技师（士）	Technicians	2179	2252	2242	3046	3168	3350	4589	3622	3953
#检验师	Laboratory Technicians	2179	2252	2242	2150	2204	2290	2439	2622	2830
其他	Other	3088	5185	5088	5351	6292	6026	7557	7938	8678
其他技术人员	Other Technical Personnel	855	1425	1601	1399	1051	1325	1156	895	633
管理人员	Administrative Personnel	5647	5199	5309	5532	6007	6067	6416	6769	6939
工勤技能人员	Logistics Technical Workers	4773	3942	4140	4913	5443	5970	7079	6789	7555

注：本表数据来源于市卫生局。
本表2011年人员合计中包括乡村医生3856人和卫生员409人；本表2012年人员合计中包括乡村医生3611人和卫生员459人。

20-14 医疗卫生机构门诊、住院及病床使用情况（2012年）

指 标	Item	总诊疗人次数 总计 Total
总 计	**Total**	**47744605**
一、医院	**Hospitals**	**24460993**
综合医院	General Hospitals	19774848
中医医院	Hospitals Specialized in Traditional Chinese Medicine	1947479
中西医结合医院	Hospitals Integrating Traditional Chinese Medicine with Western Therapeutics in Practice	184522
民族医院	Nationalities Hospitals	
专科医院	Specialized Hospitals	2554144
口腔医院	Dental Hospitals	287826
眼科医院	Eye Hospitals	105115
耳鼻喉科医院	ENT Hospitals	
肿瘤医院	Cancer Hospitals	53437
心血管病医院	Cardiovascular Hospitals	30593
胸科医院	Chest Hospitals	
血液病医院	Blood Disease Hospitals	
妇产（科）医院	Obstetrics and Gynecologist Hospitals	114530
儿童医院	Children's Hospitals	1463341
精神病医院	Psychiatric Hospitals	103719
传染病医院	Hospitals for Infectious Diseases	43830
皮肤病医院	Skin Hospitals	
结核病医院	Tuberculosis Hospitals	79741
麻风病医院	Leprosy Hospitals	
职业病医院	Occupational Diseases Hospitals	
骨科医院	Orthopedic Hospitals	94411
康复医院	Rehabilitation Hospitals	45043
整形外科医院	Plastic Surgery Hospitals	

注：本表数据来源于市卫生局。

Medical and Health Institutions Outpatient, Inpatient and Utilization of Beds(2012)

Total Number of Clinics				观察室 Observation Room		急诊死亡率 (%)
门、急诊人次数				留观病例数 (人次)	死亡人数 (人)	
	门诊人次数	急诊人次数				
Number of Outpatient and Emergency	Number of Outpatients	Number of Emergency	死亡人数 (人) Number of Deaths	Number of Patients Receiving (person time)	Number of Deaths (persons)	Emergency Mortality (%)
46685902	**44184514**	**2501388**	**2515**	**20185**	**85**	0.1
24330210	**22118169**	**2212041**	**2500**	**18825**	**85**	0.11
19667080	17821394	1845686	2392	17576	81	0.13
1941949	1881439	60510	34	409	4	0.06
184522	174790	9732	37	74		0.38
2536659	2240546	296113	37	766		0.01
279840	276964	2876				
105115	103480	1635				
53437	53430	7				
22493	19381	3112		28		
114530	101320	13210		67		
1463341	1211933	251408	33			0.01
103559	103203	356		3		
42591	36408	6183	1	91		0.02
79741	79328	413	1			0.24
94411	85480	8931				
45043	45043					

20-14 续表1

指 标	Item	入院人数合计（人）Total Number of Admission Patients (person)	出院人数合计（人）Total Number of Discharge Patients (person)
总计	**Total**	**1310186**	**1308457**
一、医院	**Hospitals**	**1192851**	**1191838**
综合医院	General Hospitals	992058	992409
中医医院	Hospitals Specialized in Traditional Chinese Medicine	80503	79969
中西医结合医院	Hospitals Integrating Traditional Chinese Medicine with Western Therapeutics in Practice	8007	7908
民族医院	Nationalities Hospitals		
专科医院	Specialized Hospitals	112283	111552
口腔医院	Dental Hospitals	1818	1827
眼科医院	Eye Hospitals	8879	8845
耳鼻喉科医院	ENT Hospitals		
肿瘤医院	Cancer Hospitals	18404	18411
心血管病医院	Cardiovascular Hospitals	2500	2465
胸科医院	Chest Hospitals		
血液病医院	Blood Disease Hospitals		
妇产（科）医院	Obstetrics and Gynecologist Hospitals	3331	3260
儿童医院	Childrens Hospitals	41452	41364
精神病医院	Psychiatric Hospitals	7133	7018
传染病医院	Hospitals for Infectious Diseases	6705	6594
皮肤病医院	Skin Hospitals		
结核病医院	Tuberculosis Hospitals	9571	9530
麻风病医院	Leprosy Hospitals		
职业病医院	Occupational Diseases Hospitals		
骨科医院	Orthopedic Hospitals	3243	3141
康复医院	Rehabilitation Hospitals	180	180
整形外科医院	Plastic Surgery Hospitals		

continued 1

出院人数中的死亡人数（人） Number of Hospital Csualty (person)	病床周转次数（次） Nnumber of Bed Rumover (time)	病床使用率（%） Bed occupancy rate (%)	出院者平均住院日（天） Average Stay Days in Hospital (day)
7629	**30.36**	**87.35**	**10.43**
7588	**31.07**	**90.14**	**10.52**
6887	32.82	89.03	9.84
290	26.83	93.97	12.77
69	19.06	97.62	18.34
342	23.57	94.17	14.36
1	20.08	61.18	11.3
	36.08	58.17	5.87
176	29.43	120.5	14.91
	24.65	81	10.5
	25.47	38.12	5.41
119	46.55	107.96	8.47
1	7.06	90.24	43.56
45	23.77	136.87	21.38
	14.01	105.72	27.38
	16.45	61.23	13.76
	9.00	98.36	40.00

20-14 续表2

指 标	Item	总诊疗人次数 总计 Total
美容医院	Beauty Hospitals	
其他医院	Other Hospitals	132558
护理院	Nursing Centets	
二、基层医疗卫生机构	**Commuting health care service centre**	**21789137**
社区卫生服务中心（站）	Community Health Care Center(Station)	3389142
社区卫生服务中心	Community Health Care Center	2779406
社区卫生服务站	Community Health Care Station	609736
卫生院	Health Center	1040753
街道卫生院	Urban Health-center	
乡镇卫生院	Rural Health-center	1040753
中心卫生院	Center Health-center	443158
乡卫生院	Country Health-center	597595
村卫生室	Village clinics	10581629
门诊部	Outpatient department	1497484
诊所、卫生所、医务室	Clinic, health center, Infirmary	5280129
诊所	Clinic	4158540
卫生所、医务室	Clinic, Infirmary	1121589
护理站	Nurses' station	
三、专业公共卫生机构	**College of public health institutions**	1492731
专科疾病防治院（所、站）	Specialized disease prevention and cure center (place, station)	28280
妇幼保健院（所、站）	Maternal and Child Health Hospital (Station)	1355194
（内）妇幼保健院	Maternal and Child Health Hospital	1257659
急救中心（站）	Emergency Center	109257
四、其他卫生机构	**Other Health Institution**	1744
疗养院	Sanatorium	1744
临床检验中心	Clinical testing center	

continued 2

门、急诊人次数 Total Number of Clinics				观察室 Observation Room		急诊死亡率（%）
Number of Outpatient and Emergency	门诊人次数 Number of Outpatients	急诊人次数 Number of Emergency	死亡人数（人） Number of Deaths	留观病例数（人次） Number of Patients Receiving (person)	死亡人数（人） Number of Deaths (person)	Emergency Mortality (%)
132558	124576	7982	2	577		0.03
20861217	**20738337**	**122880**	**15**	**1310**		**0.01**
3274943	3181594	93349	12	264		0.01
2685962	2605290	80672	12	264		0.01
588981	576304	12677				
1034226	1004695	29531	3	1046		0.01
1034226	1004695	29531	3	1046		0.01
440463	426292	14171	3	10		0.02
593763	578403	15360		1036		
9884947	9884947					
1476460	1476460					
5190641	5190641					
4088595	4088595					
1102046	1102046					
1492731	1326264	166467		50		
28280	28168	112				
1355194	1298096	57098		50		
1257659	1200561	57098		50		
109257		109257				
1744	1744					
1744	1744					

20-14 续表3

指　标	Item	入院人数合计（人）Total Number of Admissions (person)	出院人数合计（人）Total Number of Discharge Patients (person)
美容医院	Beauty Hospitals		
其他医院	Other Hospitals	9067	8917
护理院	Nursing Centets		
二、基层医疗卫生机构	**Commuting health care service centre**	**62136**	**61662**
社区卫生服务中心（站）	Community Health Care Center(Station)	37682	37614
社区卫生服务中心	Community Health Care Center	37682	37614
社区卫生服务站	Community Health Care Station		
卫生院	Health Center	23562	23156
街道卫生院	Urban Health-center		
乡镇卫生院	Rural Health-center	23562	23156
中心卫生院	Center Health-center	14094	13834
乡卫生院	Country Health-center	9468	9322
村卫生室	Village clinics		
门诊部	Outpatient department	892	892
诊所、卫生所、医务室	Clinic, health center, Infirmary		
诊所	Clinic		
卫生所、医务室	Clinic, Infirmary		
护理站	Nurses' station		
三、专业公共卫生机构	**College of public health institutions**	54010	53778
专科疾病防治院（所、站）	Specialized disease prevention and cure center (place, station)	5274	5173
妇幼保健院（所、站）	Maternal and Child Health Hospital (Station)	48736	48605
（内）妇幼保健院	Maternal and Child Health Hospital	48736	48605
急救中心（站）	Emergency Center		
四、其他卫生机构	**Other Health Institution**	1189	1179
疗养院	Sanatorium	1189	1179
临床检验中心	Clinical testing center		

continued 3

出院人数中的死亡人数（人） Number of Hospital Csualty (person)	病床周转次数（次） Nnumber of Bed Rumover (time)	病床使用率（%） Bed occupancy rate (%)	出院者平均住院日（天） Average Stay Days in Hospital (day)
	18.12	57.64	11.5
20	**19.62**	**48.56**	**8.95**
17	21.24	53.15	9.05
17	21.24	53.15	9.05
3	16.88	42.64	9.12
3	16.88	42.64	9.12
3	19.48	48.3	8.95
	14.08	36.57	9.37
21	36.66	101.03	9.95
18	9.32	121.86	46.92
3	53.29	88.36	6.02
3	53.29	88.36	6.02
	9.66	46.8	17.41
	9.66	46.8	17.41

20-15 社会福利事业单位基本情况（2012年）

Basic Statistics on Social Welfare Insititutions (2012)

单位：个、人 (unit, person)

指 标	Item	机构数 Number of Institutions	年末职工人数 Number of Staff at the Year End	床位数 Number of Beds	年末在院人数 Number of Persons Housed at the Year-end
一、社会福利院情况	**Statistics on Social Welfare**				
1. 社会福利院	Social Welfare Homes	4	89	1285	941
2. 儿童福利院	Baby Welfare Homes	1	77	800	767
3. 社会福利医院	Social Welfare Hospitals	1	149	500	425
4. 收养性老年福利机构	Welfare Units Adopting the Elderly	57	1221	8069	5107
城镇	Urban	45	1082	5940	3964
农村	Rural	12	139	2129	1143

注：本表数据来源于市民政局。

20-16 主要年份社会福利事业单位机构、人员情况

Number of Social Welfare Institutions and Employed Persons

单位：个、人 (unit, person)

指 标	Item	2000	2005	2006	2007	2008	2009	2010	2011	2012
一、机构(个)	**Insititutions**									
烈士纪念建筑物管理单位	Institutions Managing Memorial Buildings of Martyrs	2	2	2	2	2	2	2	2	2
救助类单位	Units Providing Assistance	8	8	8	8	8	8	8	8	8
殡仪服务单位	Funeral Service Units	18	20	22	21	20	20	22	21	22
殡仪馆	Funeral Homes	4	4	4	5	4	4	4	5	5
公墓	Cemeteries	12	13	14	13	12	12	14	12	12
殡葬管理单位	Funeral Management Units	2	3	4	3	4	4	4	4	6
二、人员(人)	**Staff**									
烈士纪念建筑物管理单位	Institutions Managing Memorial Buildings of Martyrs	43	43	40	37	39	39	37	38	40
救助类单位	Units Providing Assistance	99	112	116	113	110	118	116	119	130
殡仪服务单位	Funeral Service Units	613	756	765	902	1015	1046	1371	1313	1400
殡仪馆	Funeral Homes	164	204	177	239	220	218	375	408	442
公墓	Cemeteries	425	516	533	624	745	776	939	838	869
殡葬管理单位	Funeral Management Units	24	36	55	39	50	52	57	67	89

注：本表数据来源于市民政局。

20-17 全市及各区县福利企业单位基本情况（2012年）

Basic Statistics on Social Welfare Insititutions (2012)

单位：个、人 (unit, person)

区 县	Region	单位数 Number of Enterprise	年末职工人数 Number of Staff and Workers at the end of year	年末残疾职工人数 Number of Disabled Staff and Workers at the end of year	残疾职工中女性 Number of Female Disabled Staff and Workers
合 计	**Total**	**99**	**6331**	**2437**	**968**
市本级	City Level	13	833	351	94
新城区	Xincheng	10	386	182	68
碑林区	Beilin				
莲湖区	Lianhu	13	988	383	136
灞桥区	Baqiao	20	1257	471	248
未央区	Weiyang	9	939	337	162
雁塔区	Yanta	2	114	39	25
阎良区	Yanliang	3	141	68	16
临潼区	Lintong	2	199	62	40
长安区	Chang'an	10	568	213	58
蓝田县	Lantian	2	156	64	18
周至县	Zhouzhi	2	105	34	9
户 县	Huxian	13	645	233	94
高陵县	Gaoling				
沣东新城	Fengdongxincheng				

注：本表数据来源于市民政局。

20-18 社会保险基本情况

Basic Sitiation of Social Insurance

单位：万人 (10 000 persons)

指 标	Item	2011	2012
基本养老保险参保人数	Number of Basic Old-age Insurance(10 000 person)	467.67	515.97
1. 城镇企业职工养老保险参保人数	Number of Town Enterprise Worker Old-age Insurance	215.81	241.63
2. 机关事业单位养老保险参保人数	Number of Institution Old-age Insurance	26.41	27.41
3. 城乡居民养老保险参保人数	Number of Rural Residents Old-age Insurance	225.45	246.93
城镇基本医疗保险参保人数	Number of urban basic medical insurance	404.27	413.15
失业保险参保人数	Number of unemployed insurance	134.82	139.84
生育保险参保人数	Number of Maternity insurance	95.45	97.19
工伤保险参保人数	Number of industrial injury insurance	123.07	133.47

注：本表数据来源于市人社局。

20-19 全市及各区县新型农村合作医疗情况(2012年)

Situation of the New Rural Cooperative Medical Care of the Whole City and Area County（2012）

区 县	Region	参加农村新型合作医疗人数（万人） Participate in the new rural cooperative medical Population (10 000 persons)	农村新型合作医疗参合率(%) Participate in the new rural cooperative medical care ration (%)
合 计	**Total**	**397.53**	**97.7**
新城区	Xincheng		
碑林区	Beilin		
莲湖区	Lianhu		
灞桥区	Baqiao	28. 57	99.6
未央区	Weiyang	18.86	100
雁塔区	Yanta	17.24	100
阎良区	Yanliang	16.33	99.7
临潼区	Lintong	55.2	99.9
长安区	Chang'an	79.76	95.6
蓝田县	Lantian	55.38	95.6
周至县	Zhouzhi	56.79	98.9
户 县	Huxian	46.93	95.7
高陵县	Gaoling	22.46	100

注：本表数据来源于市卫生局。

20-20 全市及各区县优抚对象人员情况（2012年）

Statistics on Persons Enjoying Favoured Treatment by Region (2012)

单位：人 (person)

区 县	Region	革命伤残人员 Number of Disabled Veterans	烈军属人员 Number of Family Members of Martyrs and Soldiers	在乡红军老战士 Old Red Army Men in Hometown	在乡复员军人 Demobilized Soldiers in Hometown	在乡退伍军人 Veterans in Hometown
全 市	**Total**	**5017**	**477**	**3**	**6759**	**3998**
市本级	City Level	71				
新城区	Xincheng	670	27		16	
碑林区	Beilin	608	16	1	13	6
莲湖区	Lianhu	705	42	1	35	5
灞桥区	Baqiao	265	33		590	254
未央区	Weiyang	201	9		138	5
雁塔区	Yanta	699	15		140	584
阎良区	Yanliang	94	27		285	55
临潼区	Lintong	277	48		1033	279
长安区	Chang'an	376	36		991	154
蓝田县	Lantian	225	47		795	1701
周至县	Zhouzhi	334	129		1028	216
户 县	Huxian	288	19		896	133
高陵县	Gaoling	125	23	1	568	156
沣东新城	Fengdongxincheng	79	6		231	450

注：本表数据来源于市民政局。

20-21 全市及各区县计划生育和婚姻登记情况（2012年）

Conditions of Birth Control and Marriage Registration by Region (2012)

区 县	Region	晚婚率（%） Late Marriage Rate(%)	计划生育率（%） Family Planning Rate(%)	综合节育率（%） Contraceptive Rate(%)
合 计	**Total**	**70.3**	**99.4**	**92.3**
新城区	Xincheng	98.9	100.0	86.0
碑林区	Beilin	99.4	99.9	89.8
莲湖区	Lianhu	99.3	99.9	90.3
灞桥区	Baqiao	74.7	99.7	96.3
未央区	Weiyang	75.1	99.8	91.7
雁塔区	Yanta	56.8	99.8	90.4
阎良区	Yanliang	75.2	99.2	92.3
临潼区	Lintong	74.0	99.1	93.5
长安区	Chang'an	73.2	99.3	94.0
蓝田县	Lantian	65.2	98.8	91.6
周至县	Zhouzhi	50.5	98.9	94.2
户 县	Huxian	63.1	98.7	93.4
高陵县	Gaoling	59.6	99.7	90.2
沣东新城	Fengdongxincheng	74. 3	99. 9	92. 9

注：本表数据来源于市计生委、市民政局、市法院。

20-21 续表1 continued 1

区 县	Region	独生子女领证率（%） Only-child Certificate Rate	结婚对数（对） Marriages (couple)	再婚人数（人） Remarriages(person)	离婚对数（对） Divorced Couple (couple)
合 计	**Total**	**47.5**	**89877**	**24130**	**18579**
新城区	Xincheng	49.8	5715	2032	1685
碑林区	Beilin	59.3	11186	2562	2153
莲湖区	Lianhu	65.8	7224	2459	2007
灞桥区	Baqiao	49.1	5564	1641	1030
未央区	Weiyang	66.1	5715	1715	1366
雁塔区	Yanta	58.3	9612	3074	2589
阎良区	Yanliang	64.9	3141	1054	756
临潼区	Lintong	27.8	7266	1528	1302
长安区	Chang'an	37.1	11957	3174	2149
蓝田县	Lantian	24.2	5832	1165	950
周至县	Zhouzhi	14.2	6473	1160	795
户 县	Huxian	30.6	6003	1329	959
高陵县	Gaoling	39.0	4142	1229	820
沣东新城	Fengdongxincheng	49.8	47	8	18

20-22 全市及各区县妇幼卫生保健情况

Care Health Conditions of Women and Child by Region

区 县	Region	5岁以下儿童死亡率（‰）Mortality rate of Children under 5-year-old(‰)		新生儿死亡率（‰）Infant Mortality Ratio in 2012(‰)		婴儿死亡率（‰）Neonatal Mortality Ratio (‰)	
		2011	2012	2011	2012	2011	2012
合 计	**Total**	**5.46**	**4.07**	**3.22**	**2.29**	**4.63**	**3.24**
新城区	Xincheng	1.14	1.50	1.14	1.00	1.14	1.50
碑林区	Beilin	9.09	3.57	6.06	2.14	8.58	3.21
莲湖区	Lianhu	6.60	2.69	5.05	2.01	5.82	2.69
灞桥区	Baqiao	3.67	1.39	2.44	0.46	2.69	1.16
未央区	Weiyang	3.53	2.70	1.60	1.62	2.73	2.30
雁塔区	Yanta	3.89	4.05	2.05	2.27	3.28	2.91
阎良区	Yanliang	9.26	6.72	5.89	3.78	8.00	5.88
临潼区	Lintong	4.60	4.85	2.47	2.35	3.62	3.44
长安区	Chang'an	5.94	3.80	3.69	2.25	5.31	3.34
蓝田县	Lantian	6.04	5.76	2.92	3.05	4.48	3.73
周至县	Zhouzhi	6.14	6.45	3.59	3.67	5.84	4.69
户 县	Huxian	5.96	3.24	3.62	1.44	5.11	2.88
高陵县	Gaoling	7.02	4.91	3.93	3.46	5.34	4.33

注：本表数据来源于市卫生局。

20-22 续表1 continued 1

区 县	Region	孕产妇死亡率（1/10万）Maternal Mortality Ratio (one in hundred thousandth)		产妇住院分娩比例（%）Proportion of maternal Hospital Births (%)	
		2011	2012	2011	2012
合 计	**Total**	**17.99**	**11.58**	**99.57**	**100.00**
新城区	Xincheng			100.00	100.00
碑林区	Beilin			100.00	100.00
莲湖区	Lianhu		33.58	100.00	100.00
灞桥区	Baqiao	48.90		100.00	100.00
未央区	Weiyang	16.04		100.00	100.00
雁塔区	Yanta	40.95		100.00	100.00
阎良区	Yanliang			100.00	99.96
临潼区	Lintong		15.64	100.00	100.00
长安区	Chang'an	17.99	15.52	100.00	100.00
蓝田县	Lantian	38.99	33.89	99.71	99.78
周至县	Zhouzhi	29.94	14.66	96.27	99.77
户 县	Huxian			99.98	100.00
高陵县	Gaoling		28.87	100.00	100.00

20–23 主要年份律师、公证及调解情况

Basic Statistics on Lawyer, Notaries and Mediation in Representative Years

指 标	Item	2000	2005	2006	2007	2008	2009	2010	2011	2012
一、律师工作	**Lawyers**									
律师事务所（个）	Number of Law Offices (unit)	46	65	70	71	73	79	95	97	105
律师（人）	Lawyers(person)	534	866	902	864	940	1058	1202	1347	1522
#专职	Full-time	469	825	851	808	865	1001	1139	1275	1439
兼职	Part-time	65	41	51	56	66	55	63	68	73
二、公证工作	**Notarization**									
公证处（个）	Number of Notary Offices (unit)	14	14	14	14	14	14	14	14	14
公证人员（人）	Notarial Personnel (person)	158	192	205	243	189	194	202	233	235
#公证员	Notaries	96	93	102	156	100	102	112	118	116
办理公证件数（件）	Number of Notarized Documents Issued (case)	79199	68110	70777	70863	74440	88637	106491	108120	119605
国内	Domestic	62060	46427	45717	42996	43640	57190	72670	68239	79167
民事	Civil	24576	11737	13258	15466	15782	22337	24813	24356	32442
经济	Economics	37484	34690	32459	27530	27858	34853	47857	43883	46725
涉外	Foreign-related	16990	21451	24857	27616	30481	31082	33410	39545	39888
港澳台	Hong Kong. Macao and Taiwan related	149	232	203	251	319	365	411	336	550
三、人民调解工作	**Number of People Mediations**									
已建调委会数(个)	Number of Mediation Committees (unit)	4379	3904	3952	3952	3961	3961	3911	4031	4053
调节人员数（人）	Number of Mediators (person)	13059	16156	15930	15525	15424	17198	15717	12848	15080
调解纠纷数（件）	Number of Civil Disputes Mediated (case)	34212	17770	17608	14986	12223	23185	22247	33851	39230
#调节成功数	Number of Cases Successfully Mediated	31574	14084	14597	13756	11201	21373	22164	32109	37510

注：本表数据来源于市司法局。

20-24 主要年份共青团组织情况

Basic Facts on Communist Youth League in Representative Years

单位：个、人 (unit, person)

指标	Item	2000	2005	2006	2007	2008	2009	2010	2011	2012
一、基层团组织	**Grass-root Youth League Organisations**	**10323**	**7726**	**9560**	**9329**	**10985**	**9054**	**7006**	**11248**	**9097**
二、共青团员	**Youth League Members**	**278165**	**344035**	**329669**	**327332**	**348141**	**324785**	**308141**	**345682**	**336156**
#女团员	Female Youth League Members	134289	153493	142431	141271	145777	144027	142379	159725	157924
三、专职团干部	**Full-time Youth League Cadre**	**845**	**537**	**524**	**576**	**601**	**387**	**311**	**270**	**680**

注：本表数据来源于共青团西安市委员会。

20-25 妇联组织情况（2012年）

Women's Organizations Status (2012)

单位：个 (unit)

指标	Item	2012
一、妇联组织	**Women's Organizations**	
市级妇联	Municipal Women's Federation	1
街道妇联	Street Women's Federation	104
社区妇联	Community Women's Federation	656
县（区）妇联	County (district) Women's Federation	13
乡（镇）妇联	Township (town) Women's Federation	70
村妇代会	Village Women's Representative Conference	2887
二、非公有制经济组织中妇女组织	**Women's Organizations in Non-public Economic Organizations**	
个体劳动者协会中的妇女组织	Women's Organizations in Association of Individual Workers	13
专业市场中的妇女组织	Women's Organizations in the Professional Market	
私营企业中的妇女组织	Women's Organizations in the Private Sector	69
三资企业中的妇女组织	Foreign-funded Enterprises in the Women's Organizations	
三、机关事业单位妇女组织	**Women's Organizations in Government Departments and Institutions**	
直属机关妇委会（妇工委）	Women's Committee of Direct-affiliated Departments	
部门机关妇委会（妇工委）	Women's Committee of Affiliated Departments	91
事业单位妇委会（妇工委）	Women's Committee of Government Institutions	
四、民主党派妇女组织	**Women's Organizations of Democratic Parties**	
民主党派妇委会	Women's Committee of Democratic Parties	7
五、团体会员	**Members of Organisation**	
工会女职工委员会	Women Staff Committee of Labor Unions	3358
民政部门登记注册的妇女社团	Women's Communities Registered at Civil Administration Departments	6

注：本表数据来源于市妇联。

20-26 妇联工作情况（2012年）

Basic Facts on Women's Federation (2012)

单位：个、人 (unit, person)

指　标	Item	2012
一、双学双比活动	Double Learning and Double Competition Activities	
（一）科技培训	Scientific and Technical Training	
接受技术培训人数	Number of People Receiving Technical Training	18330
获得绿色证书人数	Number of People Gaining Green Certificates	85
女农民技术员人数		397
妇代会主任中农民技术员数	Number of Farmer in Women's Head Technicians	133
（二）巾帼扶贫	Women Aid-the-poor Project	
脱贫户数	Households out of Poverty	652
扶贫项目数	Number of Poverty Alleviation Projects	8
二、巾帼建功活动	**Women Make Achievements**	
（一）巾帼建功	Women Make Achievements	
评选巾帼建功标兵数	Number of Pacemakes	100
巾帼建功先进工作者数	Number of Advanced Workers	79
巾帼建功先进协调单位数	Number of Advanced Supporting Units	
巾帼文明示范岗数	Number of Model Workers	116
（二）下岗失业妇女再就业	Re-employment of Laid-off and Unemployed Women	
妇女就业服务机构数	Number of Institutions for Women's Employment Services	
妇联主办的劳务市场	Labor Markets Sponsored by Women's Federation	11
三、三八红旗手	**Models of Women**	**110**
四、三八红旗集体	**Models of Women Group**	**21**
五、实施春雷计划	**Carrying out of CHUNLEI Project**	
资助女童入学或返校数	Helping Women Children Enter School or Back School	98
社会捐资总额（万元）	Amount of Money That Social Attributes (10 000yuan)	38
六、来信来访情况(件)	**Conditions of Letters and Visits(case)**	
女职工劳动保护信访案件	Cases about Labor Protection of Employed Women through Letters and Visits	29
侵犯妇女财产权利信访案件	Cases about Encroachment of Women's Property through Letters and Visits	223

注：本表数据来源于市妇联。

20-27 主要年份安全生产情况

Dato on Sasfety in Production in Representative Years

指 标	Item	2006	2007	2008	2009	2010	2011	2012
全市合计	**Sum of Entire City**							
事故数(起)	Number of Cases (case)	6065	5685	4138	4225	4173	4199	5029
死亡人数（人）	Number of Deaths (person)	676	648	591	586	568	566	553
受伤人数（人）	Number of Injuries (person)	3090	3013	2472	2264	2529	2271	2492
损失（万元）	Economic Loss (10 000 yuan)	3004.1	2308.4	2802	3128.9	3666.8	2780.5	4524.8
道路交通事故	**Road Accidents**							
事故数(起)	Number of Traffic Accident (case)	3709	3643	2576	2702	2323	2264	2446
死亡人数（人）	Number of Deaths (person)	617	597	551	531	531	531	516
受伤人数（人）	Number of Injuries (person)	3075	3002	2464	2247	2520	2260	2486
损失（万元）	Economic Loss (10 000 yuan)	1328.3	1038	522.8	851.7	736.6	611.9	1011.1
火灾事故	**Fire Accidents**							
事故数(起)	Number of Cases (case)	2310	2009	1537	1485	1825	1920	2568
死亡人数（人）	Number of Deaths (person)	9	13	11	17	13	8	16
受伤人数（人）	Number of Injuries (person)	9	11	4	3	7	3	4
损失（万元）	Economic Loss (10 000 yuan)	1376	773.9	1907.7	1850.6	2224.2	1587.2	1206.5
农机事故	**Farm Machinery Accidents**							
事故数(起)	Number of Cases (case)	2	3	2	11	5		2
死亡人数（人）	Number of Deaths (person)	1	3	1				2
受伤人数（人）	Number of Injuries (person)	1		1	2	2		0
损失（万元）	Economic Loss (10 000 yuan)				1.1	3.1		12.4
工矿商贸事故	**Accidents in Industry,Mine,Business and Trade**							
事故数(起)	Number of Cases (case)	42	30	22	27	20	15	13
死亡人数（人）	Number of Deaths (person)	47	35	27	38	24	27	19
受伤人数（人）	Number of Injuries (person)	5		3	12		8	2
损失（万元）	Economic Loss (10 000 yuan)	293	496.5	366.5	425.5	703	581.5	707.7
特种设备	**Special Accidents**							
事故数(起)	Number of Cases (case)	2		1				
死亡人数(人)	Number of Deaths (person)	2		1				
受伤人数(人)	Number of Injuries (person)							
损失（万元）	Economic Loss (10 000 yuan)	6.8		5				

注：本表数据来源于市安监局。
2006年及以前道路交通数据不含高速公路数据。
2009年及以后工矿商贸事故数据含特种设备数据。

20-28 主要年份刑事案件情况

Data on Criminal Cases in Representative Years

指 标	Item	2006	2007	2008	2009	2010	2011	2012
一、案件数情况	**Data on Number of Cases**							
立案数（起）	Number of Registered Cases(case)	43856	43583	41811	42321	48566	71499	61071
破案数（起）	Number of Cleared up Cases(case)	13952	17241	19284	21921	18906	17585	20788
破案率（%）	Percent of Cleared up Cases(%)	31.8	39.6	46.1	51.8	38.9	24.6	34
抓获作案成员(人)	Number of Criminals Caught(person)	11068	12717	12364	11870	13104	14672	16980
二、查获犯罪集团情况	**Data on Hunted down and Seized Criminal Gangs**							
查获犯罪集团个数（个）	Number of Hunted down and Seized Criminal Gangs (person)	203	230	211	154	186	209	853
查获犯罪集团人数（人）	Number of Members of Hunted down and Seized Criminal Gangs (person)	938	1061	916	663	939	970	3332
涉及案件（起）	Number of Cases Involved(case)	847	1225	1328	622	1172	485	2039
三、涉枪案件情况	**Data on Cases with Guns Involved**							
立案数（起）	Number of Registered Cases(case)	37	10	11	25	16	13	30
破案数（起）	Number of Cleared up Cases(case)	35	8	9	24	11	10	25
破案率（%）	Percent of Cleared up Cases(%)	94.6	80	81.8	96	68.8	76.9	83.3

注：本表数据来源于市公安局。

20-29 主要年份治安案件情况

Data on Public Order Cases in Representative Years

指 标	Item	2006	2007	2008	2009	2010	2011	2012
受理数（起）	Number of Accepted Cases(case)	40550	41213	45226	45925	58968	63289	60747
查处数（起）	Number of Investigated and Prosecuted Cases(case)	35598	38737	44202	45871	57151	62647	59949
查处率（%）	Percent of Investigated and Prosecuted Cases(%)	87.8	94	97.7	99.9	96.9	99	98.7
查处违法人数（人）	Number of Investigated and Prosecuted Law-breakers and Crime Committer(person)	37109	36739	38606	39214	45856	44199	34346

注：本表数据来源于市公安局。

20–30 各区县刑事、治安案件情况（2012年）

Data on Criminal Cases and Public Order Cases Grouped by Region (2012)

单位：件 (case)

区 县	Region	刑事案件 Criminal cases			治安案件 Public order cases		
		立案数 Number of Registered Cases	破案数 Number of Cleared up Cases	破案率（%）Percent of Ceared up Cases (%)	受理数 Number of Accepted Cases	查处数 Number of Investigated and Prosecuted Cases	查处率（%）Percent of Investigated and Prosecuted Cases(%)
新城区	Xincheng	5065	1465	28.9	5240	5240	100
碑林区	Beilin	5326	2495	46.8	10120	10116	99.96
莲湖区	Lianhu	7025	3367	47.9	5157	5126	99.4
灞桥区	Baqiao	3832	1047	27.3	7038	7038	100
未央区	Weiyang	5224	1501	28.7	5163	4987	96.6
雁塔区	Yanta	11829	2677	22.6	6922	6772	97.8
阎良区	Yanliang	858	640	74.6	1038	969	93.4
临潼区	Lintong	2293	1080	47.1	2122	2055	96.8
长安区	Chang'an	3821	818	21.4	1766	1755	99.4
蓝田县	Lantian	1108	365	32.9	903	854	94.6
周至县	Zhouzhi	1216	414	34	664	664	100
户 县	Huxian	1492	766	51.3	3049	2871	94.2
高陵县	Gaoling	1124	563	50.1	809	809	100

注：本表数据来源于市公安局。

20-31 主要年份西安市人民检察院案件办理情况

Data on Acceptance of Cases of Xi'an People's Procuratorate

指　标	Item	2006	2007	2008	2009	2010	2011	2012
总　计	**Toatl**							
一、贪污贿赂案件立案人数（人）	**Number of Persons Invovled in Case about Corporation and Bribery(person)**	**185**	**166**	**177**	**176**	**184**	**166**	**175**
二、渎职侵权案件立案人数（人）	**Number of Persons Invovled in Case about Misprison and Toetious(person)**	**35**	**35**	**40**	**32**	**40**	**33**	**38**
三、审查逮捕案件受理件数（件）	**Examination and Arresting(case)**	**3175**	**3497**	**3835**	**3656**	**4229**	**5741**	**5024**
四、逮捕各类案件人数（人）	**Arresting of Criminals of each kind(person)**	**4597**	**5012**	**5817**	**5429**	**6183**	**8787**	**7168**
决定逮捕贪污贿赂犯罪嫌疑人（人）	Suspects of Corporation and Bribery to be Arrested (person)	101	73	104	97	51	34	43
决定逮捕渎职、侵权犯罪嫌疑人（人）	Suspects of Misprision and Tortious to be Arrested (person)	16	4	11	11	2		6
批准逮捕刑事犯罪嫌疑人（人）	Suspects of Criminal to be Arrested (person)	4480	4935	5702	5321	6130	8753	7119
五、刑事立案监督、侦察活动监督（件）	**Supervision of Acceptance of Criminal Cases and Investigation (case)**	**185**	**204**	**222**	**173**	**623**	**89**	**263**
六、审查起诉案件受理件数（件）	**Examination and Prosecution (case)**	**3492**	**3805**	**4325**	**4242**	**4662**	**6298**	**6747**
七、起诉各类案件人数（人）	**Prosecution of Criminals of each kind(person)**	**4709**	**5096**	**5608**	**5614**	**5946**	**8276**	**7307**
起诉贪污贿赂犯罪被告人（人）	Prosecution of Criminals of Corruption and Bribery to be Defendants(person)	169	126	158	159	163	129	157
起诉渎职、侵权犯罪被告人（人）	Prosecution of Misprision and Tortious to be Defendants (person)	16	23	15	11	22	13	29
起诉刑事犯罪被告人（人）	Prosecution of Criminal to be Defendants (person)	4524	4947	5435	5444	5761	8134	7121

注：本表数据来源于市检察院。
本表对往年个别数据做了调整。

20-32 西安市中级人民法院案件基本情况（2012年）

Xi'an Intermediate People's Court Basic Data of the Law Cases (2012)

单位：件、万元 (case,10 000 yuan)

指 标	Item	合计结案 Number of Total Case	诉讼标的总金额 Subject Matter of Litigation the Total Amount	中级人民法院结案 Number of the Intermediate People's Court Case	中级人民法院诉讼标底总金额 The Intermediate People's Court Litigation Total Amount
合 计	**Total**	**75293**	**993103.65**	**8997**	**529759.46**
一、刑事	**Criminal**	**5785**	**9792.91**	**909**	**2463.62**
二、民事	**Civil and Commercial Matters**	**49048**	**599142.53**	**6840**	**339353.41**
三、行政	**Administration**	**941**		**178**	
四、申诉、申请再审	**Appeals, Apply for Retrial**	**3100**		**280**	
五、司法赔偿	**Judicial Indemnification**	**13**	**112.07**	**13**	**112.07**
六、执行	**Execution**	**16406**	**384056.14**	**777**	**187830.36**

20-32 续表 continued

单位：件、万元 (case,10 000 yuan)

指 标	Item	基层人民法院结案 Number of the Basic People's Court Case	基层人民法院诉讼标的总金额 The Basic People's Court Litigation Total Amount	其中人民法院结案 Number of the People's Tribunal Case	其中人民法庭标的总金额 Total Number of the People's Tribunal Litigation
合 计	**Total**	**66296**	**463344.19**	**14420**	**64101.33**
一、刑事	**Criminal**	**4876**	**7329.29**		
二、民事	**Civil and Commercial Matters**	**42208**	**259789.12**	**14420**	**64101.33**
三、行政	**Administration**	**763**			
四、申诉、申请再审	**Appeals, Apply for Retrial**	**2820**			
五、司法赔偿	**Judicial Indemnification**				
六、执行	**Execution**	**15629**	**196225.78**		

注：本表数据来源于市中级人民法院。

主要统计指标解释

艺术表演团体 指由文化部门主办或实行行业管理（经文化市场行政部门审批或已申报登记并领取相关许可证），专门从事表演艺术等活动的各类专业艺术表演团体，含民间职业剧团。如话剧团、方言话剧团、滑稽剧团、儿童剧团、歌剧团、木偶团、皮影团等以及由若干剧种组成的综合性专业艺术表演团体。不包括群众业余文艺表演团体。

艺术表演场馆 指由文化部门主办或实行行业管理（经文化市场行政部门审批或已申报登记并领取相关许可证），有观众席、舞台、灯光设备，公开售票、专供文艺团体演出的文化活动场所。附属于文化部门机构内非独立核算的剧场、排演场，公开营业的也应单独统计。

电影放映单位 指具有放映机器设备、固定或不固定的放映场所与专职或兼职的放映技术人员，经有关部门登记批准，经常为一定的观众对象放映电影的机构。包括经批准对外开放进行营业，并与电影发行放映管理机构分帐的专用放映单位和军委系统租片单位。

广播节目综合人口覆盖率 指根据国家广电总局制定的《广播电视人口覆盖率统计技术标准和方法》进行统计调查的，在对象区内采用无线、有线、卫星等技术手段能够收听到包括中央、省、地市、县广播节目其中任意一套的人口数占全国总人口数的百分比。

电视节目综合人口覆盖率 指根据国家广电总局制定的《广播电视人口覆盖率统计技术标准和方法》进行统计调查的，在对象区内采用无线、有线、卫星等技术手段能够收看到包括中央、省、地市、县级电视节目中任意一套的人口数占全国总人口数的百分比。

有线电视入户率 通过广播电视有线传输网收看电视节目的用户数占全国总户数的百分比。

等级运动员人数 指经考核正式批准授予等级运动员称号的人数。运动员等级分为国际级运动健将、运动健将、一级运动员、二级运动员、二级运动员、少年级运动员。

等级裁判员人数 指经考核正式批准授予等级裁判员称号的人数。裁判员等级分为国际裁判、国家级裁判、一级裁判、二级裁判、三级裁判。

体育场 指有400米跑道（中心含足球场），有固定道牙，跑道6条以上，并有固定看台的室外田径场地。体育场按看台容纳观众人数分为：甲级25000人以上，乙级15000-25000人，丙级5000-15000人，丁级5000，以下。

体育馆 指有固定看台，可供篮球、排球、羽毛球、乒乓球、体操等项目训练比赛活动用的室内运动场地。体育馆按看台容纳观众人数分为：甲级6000人以上，乙级4000-6000人，丙级2000-4000人，丁级2000人以下。

卫生机构 指从卫生行政部门取得《医疗机构执业许可证》，或从民政、工商行政、机构编制管理部门取得法人单位登记证书，为社会提供医疗保健、疾病控制、卫生监督服务或从事医学科研和教育等工作的单位。卫生机构包括医院、疗养院、社区卫生服务中心（站）、卫生院、门诊部、诊所（卫生所、医务室）、急救中心（站）、采供血机构、妇幼保健院（所、站）、专科疾病防治院（所、站）、疾病预防控制中心（防疫站）、卫生监督所、卫生监督监测机构、医学科研机构、医学在职培训机构、健康教育所（站）等其他卫生机构。

医疗机构 指从卫生行政部门取得《医疗机构执业许可证》的机构，包括医院、疗养院、社区卫生服务中心（站）、卫生院、门诊部、诊所（卫生所、医务室）、妇幼保健院（所、站）、专科疾病防治院（所、站）、急救中心（站）和临床检验中心。

社区卫生服务中心（站） 指为本社区居民提供预防、医疗、保健、康复、健康教育、计划生育技术服务等的基层卫生机构。包括社区卫生服务中心和社区卫生服务站。

卫生人员 指在医疗、预防保健、医学科研和在职教育等卫生机构工作的职工，包括卫生技术人员、其他技术人员、管理人员和工勤人员。

卫生技术人员 包括执业（助理）医师、注册护士、药师（士）、检验和影像人员等卫生专业人员。不包括从事管理工作的卫生技术人员。

执业医师 指《医师执业证》“级别”为“执业医师”且实际从事医疗、预防保健工作的人员，不包括实际从事管理工作的执业医师。执业医师类别分为临床、中医、口腔和公共卫生四类。

执业助理医师 指《医师执业证》“级别”为“执业助理医师”且实际从事医疗、预防保健工作的人员，不包括实际从事管理工作的执业助理医师。执业助理医师类别同样分为临床、中医、口腔和公共卫生四类。

死亡率（疾病） 指在一定时期内，在一定人群中，死于某病的频率。

死亡率=某期间内（因某病）死亡总数/同期平均人口数×100%

社会福利企业 指以集中安置有一定劳动能力的残疾人员就业为目的（残疾职工占生产人员10%以上）、带有社会福利性质的企业总称。主要包括福利工厂、假肢厂和其他福利企业。

公证人员 指在国家公证机关依法办理公证事务的司法人员，包括公证员、助理公证员和在公证处工作的其他人员。

办理公证文书 指公证处在一定时期内办结的公证文书件数。公证文书按司法部规定或批准的格式制作，包括国内公证和涉外公证两部分。国内公证分为经济合同公证和民事法律关系公证两大类。

调解人员 指在人民调解委员会担负调解民间一般民事纠纷和轻微违法行为引起纠纷的工作人员，包括调解委员会的委员和调解小组的调解员。

调解民间纠纷 指调解委员会依照法律规定，根据自愿原则，用说服教育的方法调解民间发生的有关民事权利和义务的争执，促成当事双方达到协议和谅解，解决纠纷。包括婚姻家庭纠纷，财产权益纠纷等，不包括法院受理调解的民事案件数。

受理劳动争议案件数 指劳动争议仲裁委员会根据国家有关规定，对劳动争议当事人的申请予以审查，符合受理条件而正式立案、准备处理的劳动争议案件数。

立案 指检察机关对犯罪线索进行初步调查后，认为存在职务犯罪事实并需要追究刑事责任时，依法决定作为刑事案件进行侦查的诉讼活动，是追究犯罪的开始。

Explanatory Notes on Main Statistical Indicators

Arts Performance Troupes refer to the various professional performing arts groups, which sponsored by the cultural sectors or guided by the cultural society (approved by the cultural market administration, or registered and permitted with the relative certificat e) ,including non-governmental troupes, such as drama troupes, dialect troupes, comedy troupes, children troupes, Opera troupes, puppetry troupes, Shadowgraph troupes, etc., comprehensive professional arts performance troupes. The mass sparetime arts performance troupes are not included.

Arts Performance Places refer to the various sites for cultural activities, which sponsored by the cultural sectors or guided by the cultural society (approved by the cultural market administration, or registered and permitted with the relative certificate) , with the facility of auditorium, stage, and lighting, and selling tickets in public, including the opera halls and rehearse sites, etc. which are affiliated to the culture sectors without independent financial accounts and open to the public.

Film Projection Units refer to units with film projection equipment, full or part time projectionists, permanent or non permanent places, approved by related administrative departments to show films regularly for certain groups of audience, including those film projection units which have been approved to give commercial shows and run business with independent accounting system as well as those film-renting units of the military system.

Radio Coverage of Population refers to the percentage of population, which can listen to one of central, provincial, city, prefecture, and county radio programs by wireless, cable, satellite and other technical means, in the surveying area, to total population, according to Statistical Standard and Method on Television and Radio Coverage of Population established by the State Administration of Broadcasting, Film and Television.

Television Coverage of Population refers to the percentage of population, which can watch one of central, provincial, city, prefecture, and county television programs by wireless, cable, satellite and other technical means, in the surveying area, to total population, according to Statistical Standard and Method on Television and Radio Coverage of Population established by the State Administration of Broadcasting, Film and Television.

Cable Television Coverage of Household refers to the percentage of household, which can watch television by cable of radio and television network, to total household.

Number of Athletes in Grades refers to the number of athletes who have been given titles through examination. The titles of athletes include international masters of sports, masters of sports, first-grade, second-grade and third-grade sportsmen and young athletes.

Number of Referees in Grades refers to the number of referees who have been given titles after examination. They are classified as international referees, national referees and referees of the first, second and third grades.

Stadiums refer to stadiums for track and field events with six lane 400-meter tracks around soccer fields, permanent track marks and permanent bleachers. Stadiums are classified according to seating capacity. they include: class a stadiums seating 25000 people each. class b stadiums seating 15000 to 25000 people each. Class C stadiums seating 5000 to 15000 people each, and Class D stadiums seating fewer than 5000 people.

Gymnasiums refer to indoor sports grounds with permanent seats in which basketball, volleyball. badminton, table tennis and gymnastics competitions can be held. Gymnasiums are classified according to seating capacity. They include Class A gymnasiums seating over 6000 people. Class B gymnasiums seating 4000 to 6000 people. Class C gymnasiums seating 2000 to 4000 people, and Class D gymnasiums seating fewer than 2000 people.

Health Care Institutions refer to the units which have been qualified the Certification of Health Care Institution by the administration of public health, or qualified the Certification of Corporate Unit by the civil affairs, administration for industry and commerce, commission office for public sector reform, and engaging in medical care, disease prevention and control, health supervision and inspection, medicine research and health education, etc., including: hospitals, sanatoriums, community health service centers (stations) , health centers, clinics (health stations and infirmaries) , first-aid centres (stations) , blood gathering and supplying institutions, women and children care agencies (centres and stations) , special disease prevention and curing agencies (centres and stations) , disease prevention and control centres (epidemic prevention stations) , health supervision and inspection agencies, sanitary inspection institutions, medicinal scientific research and on-job training institutions, health education centres and so on.

Medical Organizations refer to the institutions which have been qualified the Certification of Health Care Institution by the administration of public health, including: hospitals, sanatoriums, community health service centers (stations) , health centers, clinics (health stations and infirmaries) , women and children care agencies (centres and stations) , special disease prevention and curing agencies (centres and stations) , first-aid centres (stations) and clinic inspection centers.

Community Health Service Centres (stations) refer to the primary units that provide the health care for community residents, such as disease prevention and control, medical treatment, health care, rehabilitation, health education, family planning technical services, including community health service centres and community health service stations.

Health Care Employee refer to all employee engaged in the health care institutions, such as medical organizations, disease prevention and control centres, health care agencies, medicinal scientific research and on-job training institutions, including medical technical personnel, other technical personnel, manager and labour.

Medical Technical Personnel refer to the professional staff engaged in health care, including licensed (assistant) doctors, registered nurse, pharmacists, laboratory technician, and imaging staff, excluding the medical technical personnel engaged in management job.

Licensed Doctors refer to the medical workers who have obtained the licenses of qualified doctors and are employed in medical treatment, disease prevention or healthcare institutions, excluding the licensed doctors engaged in management job. The licensed doctors are divided into 4 categories: clinician, Chinese medicine physicians, dentist and public health physicians.

Licensed Assistant Doctors refer to the medical workers who have obtained the licenses of qualified assistant doctors and are employed in medical treatment, disease prevention or healthcare institutions, excluding the licensed assistant doctors engaged in management job. The classification of licensed assistant doctors is cliniciam Chinese medicine, dentist and public health.

Mortality Rate refers to the ratio of deaths caused by diseases at reference period to the certain group of population.

Mortality Rate = total deaths (caused by diseases) at reference period/average population at same period x 100%.

Social Welfare Enterprises refers to those welfare-oriented enterprises employing a significant number of handicapped people with certain labour ability (handicapped employees shall exceed 10% of the production staff) , including welfare factories, artificial limb plants as well as other welfare enterprises.

Notary Personnel refers to judicial workers of the state notary offices handling notarization work according to law. They include notaries, assistant notaries, and other people working for notary offices.

Notarized Documents refer to the documents settled by notary offices in a year. The notary documents are drawn up in accordance with the regulations of the Ministry of Justice, including domestic documents and foreign-related documents. Domestic documents are divided into two major categories, documents on economic contracts and documents on civil legal relations.

Mediators refer to workers on peoples mediation committees responsible for mediating in civil disputes and cases of slight infraction of the law. They include members of the mediation committees and mediators of mediation groups.

Mediation of Civil Disputes refers to mediation committees work in mediating in civil disputes concerning civil rights and duties through persuasion and education in accordance with the provisions of law on a voluntary basis, so as to solve disputes by helping the parties involved come to an agreement and understanding. these disputes include divorce cases and disputes over property ownership, but exclude the civil cases to be handled by the court.

Number of Labour Dispute Cases Accepted refers to the number of cases of labour dispute submitted that, after being reviewed by the labour dispute arbitration committees in line with the relevant state regulations, are accepted and registered for treatment.

Acceptance of Case refers to the decision made by the procurators office to confirm the act of crime after initial investigation and to start legal proceedings of the case as criminal case.

21 企业调查

ENTERPRISES INVESTIGATION

资料整理：薛　燕

Data management:Xue Yan

第二十一部分　企业调查

一、简要说明

本章资料主要包括各行业企业景气调查指数和企业家信心指数等，由西安市统计局社会经济调查中心提供。

二、主要指标

企业景气指数	121.7
企业家信心指数	116.7

21 ENTERPRISES INVESTIGATION

Ⅰ.Brief Introduction

Data in this chapter consists prosperity survey indices of various industries and Entrepreneur Expectation Indicator, provided by Xi'an Municipal Bureau of Statics .

Ⅱ.Major Indicators

Business Climate Index	121.7
Entrepreneur Expectation Indicator	116.7

21-1 企业景气指数（2012年）

Business Climate Index（2012）

指　标	Item	一季度 First Quarter	二季度 Second Quarter	三季度 Third Quarter	四季度 Fonh Quarter
企业景气指数	**Business Climate Index**	**127.8**	**127.4**	**121.6**	**121.7**
按行业门类分	Grouped by Sector				
工业	Industry	119.4	122.6	124.2	121.4
建筑业	Construction	125.8	132.0	113.3	129.3
交通运输、仓储及邮政业	Transport, Storage and Post	136.8	137.9	138.9	143.2
批发和零售业	Wholesale and Retail Sales	119.1	113.1	114.8	106.1
房地产业	Real Estate	111.7	111.6	116.6	111.7
社会服务业	Social Services	138.7	133.3	121.3	117.3
信息传输、计算机服务和软件业	Information Transmission, Computer Service and Safeware Service	162.0	157.8	133.3	162.3
住宿和餐饮业	Hotels and Catering Services	135.5	131.1	125.6	111.1
按企业(单位)登记注册类型分组	Grouped by Registration				
国有企业	State-owned Enterprises	134.3	129.2	124.1	127.9
集体企业	Collective-owned Enterprises	89.7	101.1	107.0	87.1
股份合作企业	Share-holding Cooperative Enterprises	131.8	100.0	100.0	135.8
联营企业	Joint Ownership Enterprises	100.0	100.0	100.0	100.0
有限责任公司	Limited Liability Corporations	126.2	121.5	118.0	108.3
股份有限公司	Share-holding Corporations Ltd.	127.5	134.6	130.6	127.9
私营企业	Privately Owned Enterprises	103.8	99.7	102.5	103.1
港澳台商投资企业	Enterprises Invested by Foreigners or Investors from Hongkong,Macro and Taiwan	128.6	132.9	99.7	123.4
外商投资企业	Foreign Funded Enterprises	111.9	110.6	110.1	112.3
按企业规模分	Grouped by Size of Enterprises				
大型企业	Large-size	130.1	129.7	129.4	138.3
中型企业	Medium-size	130.3	125.4	122.5	109.5
小型企业	Small-size	125.8	121.9	108.7	107.1

21-2 企业家信心指数（2012年）

Entrepreneur Expectation Indicator（2012）

指　　标	Item	一季度 First Season	二季度 Second Season	三季度 Third Season	四季度 Fourth Season
企业景气指数	**Entrepreneur Expectation Indicator**	**127.3**	**127.5**	**110.9**	**116.7**
按行业门类分	Grouped by Sector				
工业	Industry	118.8	123.1	108.5	112.4
建筑业	Construction	111.5	125.3	93.3	122.6
交通运输、仓储及邮政业	Transport, Storage and Post	123.1	116.8	111.6	129.5
批发和零售业	Wholesale and Retail Sales	115.5	105.2	107.9	119.1
房地产业	Real Estate	68.3	88.3	80.0	90.0
社会服务业	Social Services	160.0	150.7	124.0	116.0
信息传输、计算机服务和软件业	Information Transmission, Computer Service and Safeware Service	164.0	157.8	137.7	140.0
住宿和餐饮业	Hotels and Catering Services	138.9	130.0	134.4	123.3
按企业(单位)登记注册类型分组	Grouped by Registration				
国有企业	State-owned Enterprises	120.8	131.5	119.0	115.6
集体企业	Collective-owned Enterprises	86.9	102.5	87.9	90.1
股份合作企业	Share-holding Cooperative Enterprises	135.8	100.0	104.0	135.8
联营企业	Joint Ownership Enterprises	100.0	100.0	100.0	100.0
有限责任公司	Limited Liability Corporations	129.2	123.7	106.5	112.1
股份有限公司	Share-holding Corporations Ltd.	127.8	134.1	129.0	130.5
私营企业	Privately Owned Enterprises	113.7	102.9	87.0	100.5
港澳台商投资企业	Enterprises Invested by Foreigners or Investors from Hongkong,Macro and Taiwan	106.9	101.9	108.9	116.3
外商投资企业	Foreign Funded Enterprises	111.1	100.3	99.1	111.1
按企业规模分	Grouped by Size of Enterprises				
大型企业	Large-size	123.1	136.7	136.4	130.8
中型企业	Medium-size	129.3	129.8	111.1	116.9
小型企业	Small-size	125.2	120.9	105.4	106.4

主 要 统 计 指 标 解 释

企业景气指数：是根据企业家对本企业综合生产经营情况所作的判断与预期（通常是对“良好”、“一般”、“不佳”的选择）而编制的指数，用以综合反映企业的生产经营状况。企业景气指数也称“企业综合生产经营景气指数”。

企业家信心指数：是根据企业家对企业外部市场经济环境与宏观政策的认识、看法判断和预期（通常是对“乐观”、“一般”、“不乐观”的选择）而编制的指数，用以综合反映企业家对宏观经济环境的感受与信心。企业家信心指数也称“宏观经济景气指数”。

景气指数的表示方式：景气指数的表示范围在0~200之间，其含义：100为景气指数的临界值，表明景气状况变化不大；100~200为景气区间，表明景气状况趋于上升或改善，越接近于200，状况越景气；0~100为不景气区间，表明经济状况趋于下降或恶化，越接近于0，状况越不景气。

Explanatory Notes on Main Statistical Indicators

Business Climate Index it is an index worked out according to the judgment and anticipation (normally a choice from good, ordinary, not good) of entrepreneurs made based on synthetic productive and operational situation of the enterprise. It is used to reflect synthetically the productive and operational situation of the enterprise. It is also referred to as synthetic and productiveoperational prosperity index of enterprise.

Confidence index of entrepreneur it is an index worked out according to the judgment and anticipation (normally a choice from optimistic , ordinary , not optimistic) of entrepreneurs made based on their understandings and views of the market and economic environment outside the enterprise and the macro policies. It is used to reflect synthetically the confidence and feelings of the entrepreneurs to the macro economic environment. It is also referred to as macro-economy prosperity index.

The way to express prosperity index the range of prosperity index is from 0 to 200; 100 is the critical value, and means economic situation didn't change largely; from 100 to 200 is the interval of prosperity; and from 0 to 100 is the interval of not prosperity, meaning economic situation is going down or worse, the closer to 0, the worse the economic situation.

中国统计出版社最新图书简目

（仅供参考，以最后出书为准）

统计资料

中国统计年鉴-2013
2013中国发展报告
中国劳动统计年鉴-2013
中国建筑业统计年鉴-2013
中国商品交易市场统计年鉴-2013
中国民政统计年鉴-2013
中国科技统计年鉴-2013
中国高技术产业统计年鉴-2013
全国农产品成本收益资料汇编-2013
大中型批发零售和住宿餐饮企业统计年鉴-2013
第二次全国R&D资源清查资料汇编—工业企业卷
第二次全国R&D资源清查资料汇编—综合卷
中国统计摘要-2013
中国第三产业统计年鉴-2013
中国社会统计年鉴-2013
中国人口和就业统计年鉴-2013
中国房地产统计年鉴-2013
中国贸易外经统计年鉴-2013
中国农村统计年鉴-2013
中国教育经费统计年鉴-2013
中国科学技术协会统计年鉴-2013
中国住户调查年鉴-2013
中国县域统计年鉴-2013
中国人才资源统计报告-2011
中国民族统计年鉴-2013
国际统计年鉴-2013
中国区域经济统计年鉴-2013
中国城市统计年鉴-2013
中国工业经济统计年鉴-2013
中国能源统计年鉴-2013
2013中国地区经济监测报告
中国农产品价格调查年鉴-2013
中国农村贫困监测报告-2013
工业企业科技活动资料-2013
中国价格统计年鉴-2013
中国农村全面建设小康监测报告-2013
中国零售和餐饮连锁企业统计年鉴-2013
2010年中国第六次人口普查公报

2013年省级综合统计年鉴系列

北京天津河北山西内蒙古
河南湖北湖南广东广西
辽宁吉林黑龙江上海江苏
海南重庆四川贵州云南
浙江安徽福建江西山东
西藏陕西甘肃青海宁夏
新疆新疆生产建设兵团

2013年市(县)级综合统计年鉴系列

天津滨海新区
运城忻州临汾呼和浩特包头
上海浦东新区南京苏州无锡
杭州宁波绍兴台州温州
厦门经济特区宁德南昌上饶
十堰荆州荆门咸宁长沙广州
石家庄唐山邯郸太原大同
通辽沈阳大连长春吉林市
常州徐州南通盐城镇江淮安
金华嘉兴衢州舟山
济南青岛潍坊郑州洛阳南阳
东莞惠州深圳桂林南宁柳州
贵阳昆明西安兰州庆阳
长治阳泉晋城朔州晋中
四平哈尔滨黑龙江垦区
宿迁泰州连云港江阴丹阳
福州福州经济技术开发区
三门峡商丘平顶山武汉宜昌
来宾河池海口三亚成都绵阳
银川乌鲁木齐

2010年人口普查资料系列

中国2010年人口普查资料
浙江安徽福建江西山东
西藏陕西甘肃青海宁夏
中国分县2010年人口普查资料
北京天津河北山西内蒙古
河南湖北湖南广东广西
新疆新疆生产建设兵团
中国分乡镇、街道2010年人口普查资料
辽宁吉林黑龙江上海江苏
海南重庆四川贵州云南
河南省各市2010年人口普查资料丛书
中国分民族2010年人口普查资料

“十一五”规划教材

统计学（“十二五”规划，黄良文）
抽样调查理论与实践（“十二五”规划，冯士雍）
统计学（“十二五”规划，单微）
试验设计（“十二五”规划，茆诗松）
贝叶斯统计（“十二五”规划，茆诗松）
统计学：从数据到结论（十二五规划，吴喜之）
非参数统计（吴喜之）
多元统计分析（任雪松）
经济计量学教程（贺铿）
社会统计学（蒋萍）
国民经济核算教程(杨灿)
概率论与数理统计（茆诗松）
应用时间序列分析（王振龙）
质量管理统计方法（茆诗松）
市场调查与预测（蒋志华）
概率论与数理统计(经济、管理类专业使用，朱胜）
医学统计学（陆守曾）
现代金融投资统计分析（李腊生）
统计指数理论及应用（徐国祥）
统计实验系列教材（许涤龙）
统计学原理（非统计专业用，朱胜）

重点图书

挑大学选专业2013—高考志愿填报指南
挑大学选专业2013—考研择校指南